AF251688

# Livelihoods and Landscapes

# Afrika-Studiecentrum Series

*In collaboration with SAVUSA*
*(South Africa – Vrije Universiteit – Strategic Alliances)*

*Series Editor*

## Dr. Harry Wels

Vrije Universiteit , The Netherlands

*Editorial Board*

Prof. Bill Freund (University of KwaZulu-Natal, South Africa)
Dr. Lungisile Ntsebeza (University of Cape Town, South Africa)
Prof. John Sender (School for Oriental and African Studies, United Kingdom)
Prof. Bram van de Beek (Vrije Universiteit, the Netherlands)
Dr. Marja Spierenburg (Vrije Universiteit, the Netherlands)

VOLUME 9

# Livelihoods and Landscapes

## The People of Guquka and Koloni and their Resources

*Edited by*

Paul Hebinck

Peter C. Lent

BRILL

LEIDEN · BOSTON
2007

Photo Cover by Paul Hebinck

This book is printed on acid-free paper.

A C.I.P. record for this book is available from the Library of Congress.

ISSN   1570-9310
ISBN   978 90 04 16169 6

Copyright 2007 by Koninklijke Brill NV, Leiden, The Netherlands.
Koninklijke Brill NV incorporates the imprints Brill, Hotei Publishing,
IDC Publishers, Martinus Nijhoff Publishers and VSP.

All rights reserved. No part of this publication may be reproduced, translated, stored in
a retrieval system, or transmitted in any form or by any means, electronic, mechanical,
photocopying, recording or otherwise, without prior written permission from the publisher.

Authorization to photocopy items for internal or personal use is granted by Koninklijke Brill NV
provided that the appropriate fees are paid directly to The Copyright Clearance Center,
222 Rosewood Drive, Suite 910, Danvers, MA 01923, USA.
Fees are subject to change.

PRINTED IN THE NETHERLANDS

# Contents

# List of tables

# List of figures



# List of maps

# List of photos

# Acknowledgements

This book could not have been written without a range of researchers and funding agencies who together enabled the efforts of many. Without these actors and supporters the research and the book would not have been possible.

Key among them are The University of Fort Hare and the Department of Agriculture, Eastern Cape Province through its funding of the Agricultural and Rural Development Research Institute (ARDRI). ARDRI began the 'core' project that set out 'to investigate land use systems in the rural areas of the central Eastern Cape and their potential for improvement'. All ARDRI staff was engaged in this research, including Wim van Averbeke, acting director at the time, Peter Scogings, Mthozami Goqwana, Joyce Mafu, Patrick Masika, Thembakazi Nqodi, Msigisi Mbuti, Jon Yoganathan. Phumla Mei, Nomokhaya Monde, Xholiswa Nqwadla. Greg Holbrook and Anthony Bediako joined ARDRI subsequently. The 'Agrarian Research Development Programme' with funding from the Dutch Embassy in Pretoria financed a Master thesis project that later evolved into a PhD thesis and facilitated the organisation of seminars and fieldwork.

From the beginning ARDRI sought international partners to add skills and perspectives to its core project. Relationships with Coventry University (with funds from the British Council) and the University of Ghent (funded by the Flemish Government) opened up possibilities for British and Belgium students to engage in Honours and Master thesis work and PhD research. Responsible for this kind of collaboration with the University of Fort Hare was Prof. Phil Harris from Coventry University and Prof. Eric van Ranst and Prof. Hubert Verplancke. Carmela Lo Presti and James Bennett, both from Coventry University, joined the project to do their B.Sc. Honours and PhD research, respec tively. Ann Verdoodt. Jo Bonroy, and Stephan Buys from the University of Ghent and Anniek Thys from the Hogeschool Ghent were engaged in various M.Sc. thesis research work. Peter Lent joined ARDRI during 1998. Funded by USAID, Lent acted first in the capacity of science editor and instructor and later became more and more involved in this and other areas of research.

In 1997, ARDRI, together with Wageningen University, the Netherlands, submitted a proposal to the newly established South African Netherlands Programme on Alternatives in Development (SANPAD). Funding was granted and this brought Paul Hebinck as co-Investigator to ARDRI for field research. The Wageningen link also provided space for Deanne Nederveen and Lothar Smith in 2000 to ARDRI for post graduate research work. SANPAD also funded the B.A Honours research by Saul Rosenberg from Rhodes University and the M.Sc. research project by Guilty Mupakati from the University of Fort

Hare. In 1999 Peter Lent succeeded Wim van Averbeke as Project Leader (University of Fort Hare) for the SANPAD project.

A major input to the formation of the book was the seminar held at the Geological Institute, University of Ghent. The seminar *Rural livelihoods in the central Eastern Cape, South Africa* was held from 20-22 June, 2000 and was sponsored by the Science Policy Programming Administration of the Ministry of the Flemish Community. This workshop brought most of the researchers together to discuss a possible synthesis of their work.

Throughout the research and the book-writing stages we felt enormously encouraged by our colleagues at the University of Fort Hare. In their many capacities Prof. Jan Raats and Prof. Gavin Frazer showed a sound combination of curiosity and academic rigour which provided us with new ideas and sources of information. Prof. Charlie Shackleton and Prof. Chris de Wet, Rhodes University, and Dr. Edward Lahiff from PLAAS, University of the West Cape, encouraged us to document in detail the results of our empirical investigations. We thank the two anonymous reviewers of the first draft of the book. Their comments were extremely useful for preparing the final manuscript. We also extend our gratitude to SAVUSA (South Africa - Vrije Universiteit - Strategic Alliances) for allowing us to present a detailed analysis.

We also express great appreciation to Deanne van Nederveen and to Sue Abraham (Rhodes University) for their skills in drafting the maps and figures appearing in this book and their patience with us.

It goes without saying that this book would have been possible without the openness and participation of a lot of people in Guquka and Koloni.

# Editor's note

Throughout the book certain terms are used that require explanation as some of them originate from previous political conjunctures. Notions like 'tribe' and 'natives or 'native reserves' clearly emerged from colonial and racial discourses, to which interpretation we do not adhere. Rather than 'tribe, for instance, we would prefer socio-ethnic group. Native reserves were those areas identified by the Land Act of 1913 and the Land and Trust Act of 1936 that were set aside for black people. Later acts, such as the Group Areas acts served to implement the further racial segregation. In most cases, the 'Native Reserves' were turned into Homelands or Bantustans.

Use of the terms 'Ciskei' and 'Transkei' requires explanation. According to Switzer (1993) these names emerged during the times when whites were expanding eastward from the original place of settlement in the Cape. At about the same time the Xhosa were expanding westward and had crossed the Great Kei River. Thus from a colonial administration's point of view Ciskei denoted 'this side' (the Cape Town side) of the Great Kei River and Transkei referred to the area across the Great Kei River. To an extent, the Xhosa that lived in the Ciskei (Rharhabe) and those that lived in the Transkei (Gcaleka), belonged to separate polities, but when successive governments implemented racial segregation policies, the importance of the notions of Ciskei and Transkei was highly exaggerated and loaded with political meanings. Important to this book is that Ciskei and Transkei have a clear geographical or regional meaning and these are still in popular use. Likewise, 'black' is used to refer to African, coloured and Indian people collectively.

References to older currencies such as English pounds, shillings and so on were avoided as much as possible. South Africa used Pounds until 1960. The currency most frequently used in this book is the Rand. For the reader's convenience, Table 0.1 below contains the average conversion rate for the Rand per US Dollar and Euro for the year 1996-2006. The Euro was introduced in 2000; various European currencies before that were converted into the Euro.

Regarding area measurements, the *'morgen'* (originally the area a Dutch farmer during Medieval times could plough in a morning) is taken as 1 *morgen* = 0.85 ha. Acres are converted to hectares at 2.5 acres = 1 ha.

Wherever Maps, Figures and Tables are the result of fieldwork by the authors, no source will be mentioned.

*Table 0.1*
Conversion rates for the Rand per US Dollar and
Euro: 1996-2006; mean values

| Year | 1 USD | 1 Euro |
| --- | --- | --- |
| 1996 | 4.30 | 5.38 |
| 1997 | 4.61 | 5.21 |
| 1998 | 5.54 | 6.21 |
| 1999 | 6.11 | 6.52 |
| 2000 | 6.94 | 6.39 |
| 2001 | 8.58 | 7.72 |
| 2002 | 10.52 | 9.91 |
| 2003 | 7.57 | 8.54 |
| 2004 | 6.45 | 8.01 |
| 2005 | 6.37 | 7.92 |
| 2006* | 6.68 | 8.34 |

* until October 17, 2006

1

# Investigating rural livelihoods and landscapes in Guquka and Koloni: An introduction

Paul Hebinck[*]

## Setting the scene

From under a tree on an April morning in 2004 I watch the arrival of a taxi in Guquka. People return from a trip to nearby Alice. The reason for the taxi ride becomes clear as people disembark. The taxi not only unloads Mrs. Tibani and others but also her groceries including two big bags of maize meal and sugar, cooking oil and other smaller items. The children that are waiting alongside the road with the wheelbarrow are there for a purpose, helping mother to carry the groceries home. I in turn assist the children to carry the heavy bags of maize and sugar. Her husband earns a living in Knysna as a petrol attendant. The remittances he sends home pay for the groceries she has just bought.

At the other side of the road a radio plays *Kwaito* music – the music of the townships. It is so loud that the whole village must hear it. Outside the house, next to the huge speaker from which the music blasts forth, sits John. He is a young man. He tells me after a while that he returned to the village two months

---

[*]   I wish to acknowledge the comments by the co-authors of this volume. Gustavo Blanco, Han van Dijk, Ignace Heitkönig, Nick Parrott, Jan Douwe Van der Ploeg, Charlie Shackleton, Derk Jan Stobbelaar and Gerard Verschoor all also read drafts and provided valuable comments.

ago after having unsuccessfully sought employment in Port Elizabeth. He had to return to the village when he had run out of money. Here, he depends on the pensions of his grandparents with whom he shares the house. Asked whether he will try to gain some kind of local income he shakes his head wearily; "Some time soon I will go back to Port Elizabeth again to try to find a job, so I can't start something here". Despite previous failures in securing urban employment, seeking an uncertain living in such an urban area seems preferable to initiating a local activity, especially when the activity is agriculture.

A few days earlier, an armoured truck had parked in the centre of the village, close to the school. It was a busy day as many older people were queuing to collect their social grants, pensions and other welfare payments. The officials looked on with some suspicion as I intended to park a car close by. I did not blame them as 'pension cars' have been robbed.

In Koloni – some 60 km further to the East as the crow flies – I met Mr. Kama on a windy day in April 2004. He is in his late thirties and used to work in a hotel in Cape Town as a waiter. Some time ago he had to come home to bury his father. He told me he wanted to go back but did not have the money to travel to Cape Town where his previous job is still waiting for him. I asked him how he manages to make ends meet and was told that he takes care of other people's homes while they are away for periods of time. Sometimes, he said, we do not see them for years. He also herds cattle for a family member in return for some food and does odd jobs here and there. A year later, he was still in the village.

These are not isolated events but rather recurrent and, above all, interlocking phenomena. Almost every day, a taxi arrives to bring people back to their homes after a trip to town to visit friends or buy groceries. The same taxi also brings a labour migrant home during his or her annual visit 'home'. Some of them, like John, would not be returning to work because of retrenchments or their failing to secure a job. Social grants, pensions and remittances continue to play a key role in the way rural people make a living. The dual spatial realities linking the urban and the rural and the related forms of mobility are important characteristics of contemporary rural life.

Plenty of similar situations and stories have been told to us over the years, since 1996 when we started to study people's livelihoods in Guquka and Koloni and how their relationships with their immediate natural environment have evolved over time. Over the years these stories became backed up by interviews during which questions were raised about almost everything related to the history of settlement; production and consumption patterns; spatial mobility and social relations. These were combined with numerous observations of ongoing activities; counting cattle and small stock; digging in archives and interpreting aerial photographs. Taken together the data collected illuminate the background to the situations sketched out here.

If we were to generalise from the events described earlier, we could, for example, conclude that the villagers buy their food rather than produce it themselves. This would seem to be the case, as the arable fields that they have access to are hardly used for growing crops. Land lying fallow is a quite common phenomenon in the Eastern Cape, which bearing in mind the many discussions held with academics and students at the University of Fort Hare, demands detailed explanations. Is it really, as a well known economist from the University of KwaZulu-Natal once stated, an expression of inefficiency in the use of land and labour by Africans? Can it, as is often suggested, be explained by the pensions and social grants that the welfare state, South Africa, maintains? Why carry out land reform when land is not being used 'properly' and productively? Or is it more complex? Are there socio-historical factors and processes that help explain what is happening? Did not colonialism and Apartheid push rural men off their land to work as labour migrants while leaving their wives and kids behind? What did past government interventions such as betterment planning accomplish, and why was this resisted and appreciated at the same time? What explains the variation of cultivation of arable lands from year to year? Are these fields not, as Shackleton has shown in his many publications, used for other purposes, and do we not need to look at all these uses of the rangelands? We may also make a mistake by simply assuming that villagers are or should be producing their own food.

These and other intriguing and challenging questions are raised in this book, which aims to unravel the complexities and dynamics of rural life in Guquka and Koloni. The book is, as it were, the intellectual outcome of a research journey through livelihoods and landscapes, one in which a variety of disciplines have been called upon to answer fundamental questions of rural development in contemporary South Africa, and specifically in the central Eastern Cape.

Before explaining some of the key concepts that have played a central role in making sense of all the data that were collected and which analytical perspectives and debates helped to order and interpret the data, a more general account of the two villages is provided to help contextualise the analytical and methodological choices that were made.

## Guquka and Koloni: A first descriptive account

Guquka and Koloni are situated in the central Eastern Cape, in the former Ciskei homeland (Map 1.1). Administratively, they fall within the boundaries of the Amatola District Municipality, one of the five district municipalities that now make up the Eastern Cape Province.

Guquka is a small 'rural' village that lies about 25 km from the R63 road that links Alice to King William's Town. The village is reached by turning off the R63 in the direction Hogsback and Cathcart (R345). At a distance of 23 km from that junction and just after passing the entrance to Phandulwazi Agricultural High School, Guquka appears on the right side of the road tucked away in the rolling foothills of the Amatola Mountain Range. Historically, the settlement forms part of the Makhuzeni Tribal Area (Map 4.2).

Socially, Guquka is organised around 125 homesteads. Most homesteads are kin related. The homesteads occur on residential plots which are separated by barbed wire fences. In 2004, occupancy of homesteads varied widely. The residential plots often contain one or more dwellings, livestock *kraals* and home gardens. Arable fields are located below the village and the communal range-land is on all other sides (Map 4.1). A limited portion of the arable land is planted with crops. There are forests on the mountain tops above the village.

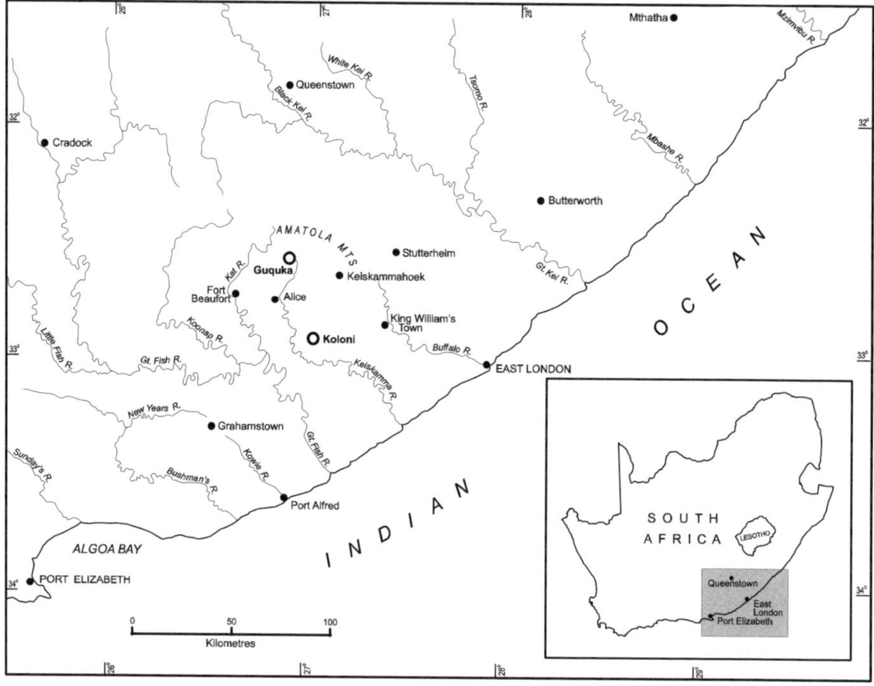


*Map 1.1*     Location of the villages in the Eastern Cape Province

Koloni can be reached from the Alice-King William's Town road (R63). From the Madubele turnoff to Koloni is about 8 km via a gravel road. The village is about 40 km from Kings William's Town and 25 km from Alice. The social and spatial arrangements at Koloni are rather similar to those of Guquka (Map 4.3). Compared to Guquka where the arrangement of the residential plots appears quite irregular, most of the 133 homesteads align parallel roads. Quite a few homes are vacant and some are abandoned or even demolished; the owners live elsewhere in Cape Town, East London and other big cities. Most villagers that own cattle have their *kraals* in front of their residential plots.

As in Guquka, a limited portion of arable land is cultivated. Grazing is carefully monitored and organised in fenced camps. Despite this cattle also graze on open spaces in the residential area.

Pinning down exactly how many people live in the villages is rather difficult because of the extreme social and spatial mobility. People come and go, are present or absent for varying periods of time. The extent of vacancy may indicate that for now, at least, their livelihoods have become (partly) disconnected from the villages. Yet, some of the houses are brand new and built according to the latest architecture of the major cities, indicating that some people return home and can invest locally. Then there are the migrants who return frequently, and while in the cities send home money for their families in the villages. All this points to a form of social mobility and spatial separation in which people and their livelihoods maintain at least a partial connection with the landscape. Part and parcel of this landscape is the quite common phenomena of beer parties and ritual slaughtering of animals (usually a goat) to celebrate the return of a migrant or a visit of a family member.

This kind of mobility is facilitated by taxis that have stands at the main tarred road. Taxis link people to nearby towns like Alice, Middledrift and King William's Town where they go to shop, to work or return home after a visit to their family. Usually people walk from the village to the main road to get a taxi. Taxi drivers charge an extra fee (usually 1 Rand) for every parcel people carry home. Now and then taxis drive into the villages.

A series of gravel roads run through the villages. Occasionally, along these roads one finds local village markets where some residents sell products from their home gardens. A few villagers run a business from home (*spaza* shops) selling consumer items. In some houses (*shebeens*) beer, either home brewed or purchased from wholesalers, is sold and drunk. The local shops and markets are overshadowed in importance by nearby urban markets, particularly when it comes to purchasing food.

Villagers from Guquka fetch most of their water from the river. Once there was a big water tank filled by a pump but by 2000 this was no longer operational. By contrast, in Koloni there are communal water taps and some water troughs for cattle. Water is available for free, provided by the state. Electricity was introduced in Koloni in 1992, and in 1998 in Guquka. The use of electric equipment has since gradually expanded. Most of the houses have electric lights and in some one finds refrigerators and cookers. Mobile phones are quite common these days.

Guquka has a primary school combined with a crèche and a day-care centre. After hours the school building is used for community meetings. There is no high school in the village, and most children attend high school at Gilton, about 2 km west of Guquka. Some children attend high school in Khayalethu across the Tyume River. Koloni has both a primary and a secondary school. The secondary school serves Koloni and several nearby villages. The number of children attending school in Koloni and Guquka is decreasing rapidly due to whole families leaving the villages to live and work elsewhere.

Neighbouring Gilton has a small clinic and Guquka residents use this for their primary health care needs. For higher level services they rely on private medical doctors or the Victoria Hospital in Alice. Koloni has a clinic near the school. It is open between Monday and Friday and staffed by three or four nurses. They run a demonstration garden to encourage people to improve their diets.

Economically, Koloni and Guquka resemble the contemporary realities one encounters across the former *Bantustans* (Homelands) of South Africa (Francis 2000, Lahiff 2000, Bernstein 1998, Lipton *et al.* 1996a, 1996b). These can be summarised as declining agriculture, seemingly overgrazed rangelands with livestock and varying degrees of soil erosion. Vegetable gardens at residential sites often provide a major source of food security. At the same time, when one takes a closer look at the resources used for making a living, one comes across a diversity of other resources that are often overlooked in the analysis of agricultural and rural development in contemporary South Africa. *Kraal* manure, *veld* and forest products and a wide variety of small stock are resources upon which people build their livelihoods, albeit to varying degrees and intensity. Unemployment is rife, particularly among the youth. The local village labour market is limited to house construction, repairs, fencing, toilet building, some carpentry, domestic work, and labour for ploughing and weeding of arable fields and gardens of others. The economy does not provide sufficient local employment opportunities to villagers, and people look for employment in Gauteng, Cape Town, Knysna, King William's Town, East London and the nearby industrial zone, Dimbaza. Migrancy is an important dimension of village life but migration patterns have changed considerably since the abolishment of Apartheid and other restrictions on the movement of labour. One of the outcomes of this is that homes are increasingly vacant for longer periods of time. The villages are predominantly inhabited by elderly people and young children. Residents rely heavily on welfare payments and social grants.

## Positioning the book: Debates and readership

This book attempts to draw a holistic picture of contemporary processes of agriculture and rural development in the Eastern Cape. In so doing, it engages with current academic debates about the dynamics of agricultural and rural development processes in southern Africa. Drawing on unique, empirical material and acknowledging the differentiated nature of local peoples' responses to externally induced developments the book seeks to give proper recognition to the interplay between internal factors and processes. In so doing it questions a common feature of the theses of deagrarianisation (Bryceson 2002a, 2002b, Manona 1999), diversification (Ellis 2000) and modernisation (Hayami and Ruttan 1985), which all appear to assume that the shift from agricultural and land-based livelihoods to more diversified livelihoods is an inevitable and a structural process. This book aims to provide a counterpoint to these positions which, unfortunately, have drawn attention away from analyses of the processes of production and the productive use of the landscape. Studies on agriculture and rural land-based activities have become increasingly overshadowed by socio-cultural and economic studies of urban and industrial life (Sapire and Beall 1995, Bank 2001, 2002, Ngwane 2003), while rural studies have shifted to studying consumption and poverty (du Toit 2004) and analysing the meaning of the shift of consumption from one's own fields to supermarkets (Weatherspoon and Reardon 2003). Few recent studies, however, address the issues of agricultural production, power relations and processes of agrarian transformation (Bernstein 1998, 2004, Cousins 2007, Shackleton *et al.* 2001, 2002).

This book presents a detailed image of how contemporary agrarian society in two villages is constituted. The book also relates to the Keiskammahoek series of studies conducted by academics from Rhodes University. The first sets of studies were done between 1947 and 1951 and entailed a multi-disciplinary research project (involving botany, geology, soil sciences, sociology and anthropology). They were published in 1952 (Mountain 1952, Houghton and Walton 1952, Wilson *et al.* 1952, Mills and Wilson 1952). These studies are unique in being the first of their kind of detailed empirical studies in the so-called 'Reserves'. A follow-up social study was conducted in the 1990s (De Wet and Whisson 1997). Individual PhD studies were done in the same area during the late 1970s. These studies provide a kind of benchmark for this research project in Guquka and Koloni: in terms of content and orientation, and also geographically. Keiskammahoek is about 50 km away from Guquka and Koloni. Both sets of studies presented interesting generalisations about social, economic and natural conditions in the region but they also offer specific information about villages and individuals. Mills and Wilson (1952: 128) concluded at the time that "none of the families ... [made] a living out of farming". Leibrand and Sperber (1999) drew similar conclusions. This book about Guquka and Koloni draws on their data and conclusions, which gives a useful perspective on the historical and institutional dimensions of development in the two villages. In their introduction De Wet and Whisson (1997: xiii) caution that

> (the) dominant paradigm(s) of the 1950s were (was) evolutionist and structural functional – the former favoured by the economists and natural scientists who perceived progress in terms of the ' natives' being trained to accept superior ways and methods, the latter by anthropologists who perceived change largely in terms of external forces impinging on what would otherwise be communities in stable equilibrium.

De Wet and Whisson argued that a simple replication was, however, not possible, if only because theoretical perspectives have shifted. "The overarching realities in natural, economic and social science, as interpreted by scholars in the field, were no longer unquestioned". Ranger (1978) and Long (1977) were among the early academics that propagated a social theory that questions received wisdom. Such a 'paradigm shift' as Long (2001) refers to it, also entailed that analytical categories such as 'class', 'household', 'community' and 'communal' became analytically less accurate.

Taking this lesson seriously, the analyses in this book have moved away from the preoccupation with structural and functionalist interpretations that characterised most social science work on social and ecological transformation in the region in the 1970s and 1980s (Palmer and Parsons 1977). Thus by examining the empirical evidence presented in this book we point at two but contrasting patterns. The first validates a deagrarianisation hypothesis and supports what the Keiskammahoek studies already showed in the 1950s. A second pattern, however, suggests that against all odds perhaps, the remnants of a peasantry exists in both villages. In this sense the book follows the footsteps of Bundy (1977, 1988) who examined the rise and fall of the peasantry in South Africa. We take the questions formulated by Bundy seriously but explore the dynamics of social transformation in a non-structuralist mode. The persistence of a peasantry does not only raise the question of why peasants have not totally disappeared but also of what the prospects are for a process of *peasantisation*, which can be defined as the process by which rural people continue to make a living from utilising land-based resources.

*Repeasantisation* then is the process of taking this up again, even after a long period of absence due to labour migration. Peasantisation is also a process by which the agricultural labour process becomes regrounded on primarily non-commodity circuits; i.e. labour and inputs are progressively drawn from the local economy and ecology (Van der Ploeg 2003, Altieri 2002b, Toledo 1990). In many cases this entails a continuous repositioning *vis-à-vis* the predominant markets and technology.

This book also reflects these shifting paradigms, for instance in rangeland ecology and the study of management of collectively held rangelands (Vetter 2004, Scoones 1999). Are these rangelands threatened by overgrazing, and is this due to overstocking and mismanagement? Can this be explained by the collective nature of rangeland management (as opposed to private tenure in the large farm sector) or does livestock have multiple meanings which need to be taken into account? (Cousins 1996, 1998, Shackleton *et al.* 2005, Moll 2005). Are things even more complex? For example, does the evidence gathered support non-equilibrium thinking, which argues that rangeland ecologies are driven primarily by abiotic factors such as variable rainfall which result in highly variable and unpredictable primary production. Under this view rangeland degradation is less due to overgrazing, as vegetation cover and productivity respond to primary rainfall. However, this may be an oversimplification, as livestock holders try to minimise animal mortality through bringing in extra feed and fodder from elsewhere. This artificially maintains higher numbers of livestock on the rangeland at times of highest vulnerability, i.e. during a drought. This in turn does not allow a sufficient period of recovery for the *veld* when the rains do return. Degradation then is quite possible, and, even quite likely (Shackleton, C.M. pers. comm. 2006).

The book also specifically engages with the policy debate in South Africa about development prospects in the former homelands. The entry point is a debate on policy alternatives from a rural livelihoods perspective. The current crop of policy makers, advisors and experts emphasise the need for creating conditions conducive to modern production, just as their forebears did with betterment planning in the 1930s. They have put policies in place to revive agricultural production that are designed to reverse the province's dependence on food grown elsewhere. Whether these or other polices are realistic and will realise their objectives remains to be seen. In contrast to programmes like *Siyakhula*, that are largely based on experts' prescriptions about what rural people *should* be doing, a policy based on a livelihood perspective would begin with by focusing on the skills and resources that rural people possess and would be embedded in and build on their existing activities. Recognising the substantial variations that exist among villages and among years, and that rural livelihoods are intrinsically connected with urban-based livelihoods and *vice versa*, the strategy proposed here is supports *repeasantisation* in rural villages, through full or partial commercialisation of smallholder agriculture. The concluding chapter discusses what such a strategy would look like.

To reflect on these broader and relevant policy questions, the book sets out to examine how and why the people of Guquka and Koloni have, over the years, (re)constructed their livelihoods so that nowadays these increasingly revolve around non-land-based activities in which labour migration and claims against the state for pensions and social grants and against kin for remittances predominate. Despite this, land or natural resource based activities remain important and, as will be explored, form a crucial dimension of peoples' lives, even if they have been working and living outside the village for many years. Politically, socially, and culturally the villagers retain an attachment to the land and derive social identities from that bond, although to varying degrees. The analyses also point out that growing of crops has reduced substantially over the years and that the gathering of *veld* products plays an important role in rural livelihoods. Natural resources are frequently undervalued and underestimated by people from outside the communities. Hence a considerable part of the book is devoted to an analysis of the land and natural resource-based activities that are variously combined with activities carried out elsewhere. What the book does not disclose is the nature and dynamics of those parts of people's lives and livelihoods that take place elsewhere, for instance in cities removed from our two villages. Other studies provide a vivid picture of that part of social life and we will rely on and refer the reader to insights provided by academics like Bank (2001, 2002), Mears (2004) and Ngwane (2001, 2003).

## The history of the research:
## From farming systems to rural livelihood – landscape interactions

The research that eventually evolved into this book started as the 'core-project' of the Agricultural and Rural Development Research Institute (ARDRI) at the University of Fort Hare. This project was launched in 1995 and was initially framed as "an in-depth investigation of the land use systems in the communal areas of the central Eastern Cape and their potential for improvement" (ARDRI 1996). The project began in a farming systems mode and sought answers to what farming systems were being practiced; why people continued to be involved with agriculture; what benefits they derived from farming; what aspirations they had, what major constraints prevented them from achieving their goals, and how to address these constraints. Since farming potentials were the main criteria for site selection, the physical environment became the entry point. Three zones were identified: a sub-humid zone, a semi-arid zone with marginal potential for summer crops, and a very dry semi-arid zone where dryland crop production was thought to be extremely risky. Livestock production, the other important type of farming in the area, was also considered when selecting the sites. Whereas the productivity of the rangeland was considered to be closely associated to climatic conditions and agro-ecological zoning, the range management system was also identified as a critical issue. Previous research had indicated that range management practices differed considerably and were associated with earlier government interventions, like betterment planning. Initially three villages were selected: Guquka, Koloni and Hlosini. At an early stage of the project Hlosini was dropped for logistical and financial reasons.

From the start ARDRI sought international partners to accomplish this research, and these brought in additional skills and techniques but also newer perspectives and research experiences. Relationships with Coventry University (UK) and the University of Ghent (Belgium) brought, respectively, an agronomy and soil science perspective. The link with Wageningen University (the Netherlands) added GIS skills plus a focus on understanding resources, and provided sociological and anthropological perspectives to the farming systems research framework.

The farming systems approach did not appear to fully capture the processes of social and environmental transformation. With an initial overemphasis on the primary role of agricultural production in people's lives, the research barely took into account other uses that rural people make of the environment, for example, gathering forest and non-timber forest products. Struggling conceptually with explaining why arable fields were being left uncultivated, the emphasis was refocused to include a detailed analysis of the role of other sources of income, the dynamics of labour migration, its impact on natural resource management and particularly on the organisation of common property resources. How could changes over time and the variations and fluctuations between years and fields be explained? As the research progressed, the interpretations of the process of social and environmental change became increasingly influenced by the more recent research paradigm of multiple rural livelihoods. Surprisingly, none of these shortcomings of farming systems research and critical issues are mentioned in a recent book that captures the history and experiences of farming systems research (Collinson 2000).

A workshop organised in 2000 at the University of Ghent, Belgium, rather successfully brought the different disciplines and insights together by exploring the data from a livelihood perspective and exploring whether this concept could play the role of an integrating theoretical concept. Processes resulting in soil erosion and degradation, and the use of the rangelands also demanded a critical examination from the point of view of an ongoing process of environmental transformation. Research questions were rephrased to allow for a critical analysis of human-nature interactions, how people utilise their natural environment and through this construct the landscape that can be observed today. The focus on institutions became more prominent. The transformation of the landscape, vegetational change, livestock foraging and use of rangelands for a range of purposes also began to receive much more attention. At the same time, the research adopted a much firmer historical grounding so as to reconstruct livelihood and landscape transformations as unique, locally specific processes. The concepts of livelihoods and landscapes proved useful in that they helped to provide a common focus for the research that combined the disciplines of ecology, agronomy, sociology, anthropology, economics, geography and history. Thus, these two concepts came to play a key role in this book. The following sub-sections discuss their relevance and how they were interlinked.

*Livelihood focus*
The notion 'livelihood' has proven to be a useful concept since it helps to draw a picture of the many ways in which people construct a living. The concept has most often been applied to rural areas and, as such livelihood analysis often includes farming but emphasises that this is not the only way in which rural people make a living (Bagchi *et al.* 1998, Carney 1998, Scoones 1998, Francis 2000, 2002, Ellis 1998, 2000, Hebinck and Bourdillon 2001, Long 2001, Slater 2002, Murray 2001, 2002, Whitehead 2002, Brocklesby and Fisher 2003, De Haan and Zoomers 2005). In their attempts to make a living, people use a variety of resources, such as social networks, labour, land, capital, knowledge, employment, technology and markets to produce food, harvest natural resources and to generate their incomes. Wide-ranging interpersonal networks link rural and urban areas, on-farm and off-farm work, dry-land and irrigated farming. Livelihood transcends sectoral economic boundaries (e.g. agriculture and industry, formal employment and informal activities) as well as geographical boundaries, particularly those between urban and rural environments. In constructing their livelihoods people's behaviour is not simply determined by cultural and social structures; instead they are actively engaged as social actors,

constantly manoeuvring to improve their lives (Long 2001). Through these endeavours they engage with others over a range of issues, such as the use of natural resources, rights to land and property, prices for their commodities and even how to understand the world around them.

The treatment of livelihood in this book builds on a number of methodological cornerstones.

1. Livelihoods are treated as revolving around the utilisation of *resources*, which can be tangible and non-tangible, social and natural. People draw upon a range of resources and combine them into a coherent whole in order to make a living. Resources are also the foundations of power and wealth (Peach and Constatin 1972). In taking resources as the departure point this analysis differs from the so-called Sustainable Livelihood Framework (Carney 1998, Scoones 1998) and the Livelihood Platform developed by Ellis (2000). Both these frameworks centre on the notion of 'capital' (subdivided into human, financial, social, physical, and natural capital). Several commentators have drawn attention to the problematic use of the term 'capital' (Arce 2003, Murray 2002, Whitehead 2002 and Hebinck and Bourdillon 2001). One criticism is that the notion of 'capital' appears to rule out resources being drawn from outside commodity circuits (e.g. networks based on kinship or neighbourhood) and thereby ignores the importance of non-commoditised resources. 'Capital' is an economic metaphor that does not fully do justice to the nature of people's activities, which are not entirely oriented towards material gain. Whereas others (Ellis, Carney) use the notion 'capital' I prefer the notion of resources as theoretically more adequate for examining livelihoods, how these are utilised and what meanings are attributed to them by social actors. Central to this is the notion that resources do not reflect bio-physical qualities but also social relations and that these should not be concealed. Marx (1975) drew attention to this in his analysis of how commodities conceal social relations ('commodity fetishism'). Resources and their utilisation are connected to power relations that govern and shape the bundle of rights to these resources such as access and use, and whether actors can derive wealth and other benefits from their utilisation (Leach *et al.* 1999, Bebbington 1999). Resources are not to be viewed as one-dimensional as having multiple meanings for different categories of people (Long 2001, Cousins 1996, Peach and Constatin 1972). The same is true of resource utilisation: resources are not static and are to be interpreted rigidly, but rather they are continuously unfolding and being reconfigured in many different ways and directions.

    The chapters in the book examine and probe whether and how livelihoods hinge on local and actor-specific configurations of resources and how such configurations are subject to changing actor strategies and social networks. It also examines how such configurations are shaped by agro-ecological and macro-political processes.

2. Livelihoods can only properly be understood when seen as embedded in the *institutions* that social actors create through their daily lives. North (1990) described institutions as the rules of the game in a society, or, more formally, the humanly devised protocols that shape human interaction. They encompass norms, social values, rules, and regulations which shape – but not necessarily determine – opportunities for people to access and utilise resources. Institutions mediate people-environment relations (Leach *et al.* 1999, Agrawal and Gibson 2001). In this context governance has come to be the guiding concept for the study of the management of natural resources. Central questions here include understanding how such institutions developed, how rules and laws are designed and, more importantly, how these are understood in the localities.

   It is of key importance to combine the analysis of rules and rights with patterns of resource utilisation and agency. Leach *et al.* (1999) draw on the work of Sen (1984) and use his concepts of 'endowments' and 'entitlements' to distinguish between the rights and resources that social actors *can* have (endowments) and what people derive from these: what social actors take and receive in practice (entitlements). Entitlements reflect relationships of power to take command over endowments (by effectuating rights) which in turn enhance the capabilities of social actors to utilise resources (Leach *et al.* 1999). Control over food derives from rights over land and/or employment, which provide social security and so contributes to well-being. Peoples' identities are often derived from what they do with their entitlements. In this way the concept of livelihood is enriched with human agency and power as well as with knowledge and social identity.

3. Livelihood is too often equated solely with having a job or with working, and is portrayed as consisting of portfolios of resources and income gene-rating activities (Brons 2005). The work of the Liptons' (Lipton *et al.* 1996a, 1996b) and of May (1996, 2000) exemplifies this narrow focused on economic aspects of peoples activities. I argue that livelihoods encompass more and that people's cultural repertoires should not be ignored. Elements of life style and value choices, status, sense of identity *vis-à-vis* other actors, and local forms of organisation are too important to be ignored in any at-tempt to come to grips with livelihoods.

   In some situations and chapters, it initially seemed rather difficult to escape from narrow interpretations of livelihood. The nature of the data collected and available for analysis and the quantitative analytical techniques employed often appear to preclude broader analysis. This study recognises the importance of labelling or categorising livelihoods. Often this has been done by identifying broad strategies which usefully convey the idea of social heterogeneity and different responses to change. Scoones (1998) and Ellis (2000) contributed constructively to this by categorising various strategies of rural people: (1) agricultural intensification or extensification, (2) diversification, and (3) migration. This typology offers useful insights into the broader and diverse rhythms of social change and provides relevant categories for describing and analysing livelihoods. This book reflects on this categorisation and attempts to arrive at a locally specific and relevant set of categories. To counteract the tendency of limiting analysis of livelihoods to employment and cash income, life histories were collected and are used to illustrate how actors value resources and interpret their world.

4. Studies have shown that livelihoods are rather *heterogeneous* in at least two respects. First, there is not one 'ideal' livelihood that can be constructed, either in practice or in theory. The Sustainable Livelihood Framework (Carney 1998) and the Livelihood Platform framework (Ellis 2000) seem to set out from some kind of normative framework that places the knowledge of experts at the forefront. While interpreting and analysing data, we should be wary of allowing our findings to, even inadvertently, acquire the status of norms that people should follow (Hebinck and Bourdillon 2001). Equally an analysis of how rural livelihoods evolve and the ways in which natural resources are utilised should be subject to sharp and critical interpretation by observers. To paraphrase Chambers (1997) we need to ask what knowledge is and whose knowledge.

   Second, heterogeneity also encompasses aspects of social and economic differentiation. A range of studies (Francis 2002, Murray 2002, O'Laughlin 2002, Bagchi *et al.* 1998) and the case material presented in the various chapters in the book, show that it is necessary to take such differentiation into account. These aspects of development are usually described under the heading of socio-economic inequalities, which largely revolve around access and control of the key factors of production (e.g. land, capital and labour) as well as incomes from wages and salaries. Such inequalities perpetuate themselves in that most rural livelihoods involve insecurity and risks, such as drought, exposure to disease (among cattle and humans), loss of income and retrenchment. Many rural people are constantly having to respond to these risks. Some rural people however have managed to construct more secure livelihoods, with guaranteed access to land, jobs and social networks. The case studies presented in this book underline the relevance of concept-ualising livelihoods as evolving in arenas where negotiations and bargaining take place within homesteads, between members of communities or villages and between social actors with unequal power. Poor people often find it more difficult to deal with those risks and vulnerabilities.

5. This book investigates livelihoods in their *historical* contexts. The analysis of life histories underlines that livelihoods are not static and that they change within the lifecycle of individuals. Methodologically, the analysis builds upon the notion of the livelihood trajectory which refers to a pathway through time and to "the consequences of the changing ways individuals construct a livelihood over time" (Bagchi *et al.* 1998, Murray 2002). The life history account of the Kas Maine by Van Onselen (1996) is a seminal con-

tribution to the study of social change which focused on social actors, their careers, networks and strategies. As Van Onselen's and other life history accounts have shown these strategies may change over time, due to altering conditions, which sometimes bring about rapid and sometimes slow changes. Sometimes they involve ruptures with the past whereas other changes are more gradual in nature. Sometimes they are induced by global developments and at other times by events and influences closer to home. Life history studies prompt us to take into account that social actors (individuals and/or groups) respond to different changes in many different ways (Long 2001). Examining livelihoods over a longer period of time enables us to observe these changes in how livelihoods are constructed and how they take different directions. This allows us to better understand why such changes occur. An analysis of trajectories also has the analytical advantage of "bridging the micro-macro divide by a process of aggregation 'upwards' from the lives of individuals" (Bagchi *et al.* 1998). History then becomes a manifold process of interaction between micro and macro events; between external events and internal actions.

*Landscape*

Alongside livelihoods, landscape became a guiding notion for ordering and interpreting data. One challenge of this book was to find a way to marry social science perspectives of landscape (and place) with those of the natural sciences, notably ecology, agronomy and biology. Since the Enlightenment, science has conceptualised natural and social phenomena as *a priori* separate. The organisation of science in various faculties (e.g. Social Sciences, Agriculture, Sciences) is a consequence of such processes, resulting in nature being very often investigated as if it were disconnected from society (Fairhead and Leach 1996). The challenge is to merge these seemingly contradictory perspectives. The challenges lie in the different paradigms and cognitive frames of interpretation, as each approach makes use of distinct methodologies and scientific traditions of analysis and presentation.

There is a social science perspective that aims to prevent predetermined interpretations of the direction and dynamics of development (linearity versus non-linearity; homogeneity versus heterogeneity) and one that attributes agency to social actors, for instance, in the way they understand and construct livelihoods and read landscapes (Long 2001). From these perspectives landscapes are seen as constructed and transformed by social actors who actively shape them (Cosgrove 1998). Social actors attribute certain meanings to the landscape and the resources it contains (Fairhead and Leach 1996, Scoones 1999, Leach and Mearns 1996, Ingold 2000, Mendras 1970). Landscapes have clear historical dimensions (McGregor 2005), are partly the materialisation of culture (Escobar 2001, Cosgrove 1998) as well as the product of institutional arrangements, such as property rights (Batterburry and Bebbington 1999). Particular environmental features have been and continue to be created through human action. Whether these are patches of land with higher soil fertility (as in the Friesian Woodlands of the Netherlands – Sonneveld *et al.* 2004), patches of savannah forest in West Africa (Fairhead and Leach 1996, Nyerges 1996, Bassett and Zuéli 2003) or the seemingly overgrazed and degraded range lands and underutilised arable fields in South Africa's former homelands (this book), an understanding of land-use histories and the interplay between social, institutional, political and economic processes over time is essential.

The social science perspective contrasts with that of the natural sciences that views landscapes as a natural environment, consisting of non-biological resources such as soils, nutrients, air, and water, and biological resources, plants and animals etc. Landscapes are physical, non-distinct entities within ecosystems, where all resources are linked by interactive, dynamic processes. The natural environment is dynamic, complex, and spatially heterogeneous at both small and large scales. Biological processes related to the landscape are generally considered to be responsive to gradients in climate and soils, again at a range of scales (Townsend *et al.* 2000). While maps of landscapes or forests suggest that there are distinct boundaries between units, this is not a true representation of reality; hence boundaries are usually drawn as fuzzy shades. The analyses of the natural environment encompass units as small as individual fields, or even patches within fields, or individual homesteads, upward to the community, its environment and beyond, and include the interactions among these scales. Landscape sets the scene and provides the natural resources for people to construct their livelihoods. Natural scientists today seek a broader understanding of landscape dynamics by given more prominence to the human dimensions of ecosystem processes (Wu and Hobbs 2002, Carpenter 2005, Berkes *et al.* 1998). Spatial relationships among natural phenomena have are thus seen as modified by human land use and settlement patterns. The notion of landscape is gradually being redefined to include social or anthropogenic elements.

*Linking livelihoods and landscapes: Coproduction*
By linking the notions of livelihood and landscape the analytical capacity of each approach can be enriched. This can be achieved by adopting a cognitive frame that is referred to as a co-evolution (Winder *et al.* 2005, Norgaard 1994) or coproduction (Jasanoff 2004) that provide a means to study the processes of social *and* natural and ecological change. The interesting and challenging aspect here is that nature is a living, dynamic and evolving entity. Coproduction or co-evolution refers to the ongoing interactions between the 'natural' and the 'social' which mutually transform each other (Van der Ploeg 2003, Zimmerer and Bassett 2003, Gerritsen 2002, Roep 2001, Scoones 1999). In this book the two terms are used interchangeably here. The subtle differentiation between the two lies in viewing coproduction as the process by which social and natural

resources are reconfigured through conscious human action and agency and co-evolution as less consciously managed human-environmental relationships.

Research in this tradition stresses that development processes (and thus resource utilisation and the production of wealth derived from these) should not be treated *per se* as one dimensional and linear. Rather the rhythms of social and ecological change are characterised by heterogeneity and non-linearity (Scoones 1999, Baker 2000, Van der Ploeg 2003, Mango and Hebinck 2004). Thus many different patterns of coproduction emerge and may coexist. These patterns may be range from sustainable, and socially and ecologically desirable forms to unsustainable, socially and ecologically undesirable forms of coproduction.

Taking the co-evolution/coproduction stance also implies that livelihoods should be understood as coproduction; that is, an outcome of a continuous encounter and interaction between the natural and the political, the social and the cultural. The interrelationships and interdependences in the landscape are not there because of coincidences or because of predetermined natural laws, but are the result of historical processes of coproduction. At the same time it represents the attempts of social actors to create institutions that fit with the natural environment. Resource utilisation *per se* can be studied by investigating livelihoods.

Linking livelihoods and landscapes in this way opens up the possibility to conceptualise livelihoods as a script through which people read, understand, order and utilise the landscape and give meaning to it. Jasanoff (2004) refers to coproduction as occurring "along well documented development pathways" (livelihoods in the terminology of this book). These pathways are constituted by institutions, peoples' practices and resource configurations which take place in historical contexts and find their expression in livelihood identities and narratives. Coproduction conveys the idea that landscapes are created by people and that they are the outcome of coproduction. The landscape combines and brings together the working of rules and laws with practices of people that command political power. This occurs in a context in which state agencies and markets are increasingly powerful and yet curiously often rather distant. The landscape is the outcome of the way local people understand and order their natural environment. Thus, for example, the phenomenon of fallow arable fields referred to earlier is a specific pattern of coproduction or rather the outcome of locally specific livelihood-landscape interactions. However, such understanding and ordering also occurs within the constraints and opportunities posed by the prevailing physio-climatic conditions. It makes a difference if an arable field is situated at the south or north side of a mountain range. Thus, the features of a landscape are not only moulded by human agency.

Agriculture and the growing of crops is coproduction. Using land does not simply mean applying a series of technical operations and instruments. Rather it is an emergent property of the interactions between the land and the society that lives from it. Natural limitations produced by geological and geomorphological conditions may restrict land use, but they can be removed and altered by social actors applying their skills and experiences. Soils can be improved as can maize seeds, and given the many phenoforms that can be found in rural areas or ecosystems; this can be done in many ways (Sonneveld *et al.* 2004, Mango and Hebinck 2004). Farmers in an irrigation scheme in Zimbabwe remarked that improving your field is not easy, as it takes a long time and requires a lot of manure *and* magic. This expressed their clear feeling of attachment to their land (Magadlela and Hebinck 1995).

Key to an analysis of the processes that underlay livelihood-landscape interactions is a firm grounding in the *locality* that places emphasis how local people and other relevant actors such as policy makers and scientists (including ourselves) read the landscape *and* the changes that occur around them. Thus, focusing on the practices of everyday life allows one to see locally specific modes of exploitation of resources and the social form(s) of organisation that these are embedded in. It allows one to document visible, but also unexpected, practices. Some social scientists (Long 2001, Moore 2005) are beginning to link this with issues of agency, fragmentation and power differentials They point at the many ways in which people skilfully manage to get around laws and regulations and to resist political interventions to defend their own interests. This imply that coproduction should not be uncritically regarded. As argued earlier, there is not just one form of coproduction and some forms are embedded in practices that lead to unsustainable social and natural resource use practices.

Landscapes in Guquka and Koloni are thus constituted by people, their institutions and artefacts, soils and fauna and flora. The latter are formed by natural processes and influenced by natural phenomena (e.g. climate) and transformed by human actors irregularly cultivating crops, gathering fuel wood and other natural resource products, herding cattle, fixing fences, claiming pensions, negotiating legal structures, adapting rules and regulations, attempting to access information, making use of roads; engaging in labour migrancy, and using supermarkets and other local food markets. Managing such landscapes involves 'building a homestead' and involves intricate urban-rural relationships (McAllister 2001). Such management, needless to say, revolves around livelihoods, which are socially and spatially heterogeneous as well as temporally.

## Methodological and interpretative considerations

Linking 'livelihood' and 'landscape' together entails interdisciplinary modes of analyses. This section discusses some of the methodological dimensions and research steps involved in analysing livelihoods and landscapes. These cannot be separated from an account of some contentious issues from which interdisciplinary work apparently cannot escape. The two broad categories of scientists, social scientists and natural scientists do not always share the same interpretations of social and ecological change and place a different emphasis on the social. It goes without saying that these contentious issues also play a key role in processes of rural transformation that, arguably, increasingly revolve around contestations.

*Contentious issues 1: 'Household' – 'homestead'; 'community' – 'institutions'*
A first area of difference between social and natural scientists concerns the use of the terms 'household' and 'community'. Whereas a natural scientist aims to reduce social complexity by using notions like household and community, social scientists increase complexity. This book does not necessarily take the household or community as an entry point, although the notion is used in some chapters but released from its classical conceptualisation. I prefer to take social actors and what they do, their relationships with other actors and the natural environment as the entry point and unit of analysis. Similarly, I prefer institutions as an expression of process rather than community *per se*.

*Household-homestead.* Many commentators, including social scientists, have argued that the household is the most appropriate unit of analysis (Ellis 2000) and many authors used this (Leibrand and Sperber 1997, Van Averbeke 1998a). Many authors have also argued against it such usage. They feel that the household is an elusive concept and that there is a need to more clearly problematise the use of the 'household' model within livelihoods analysis. They argue that the household should not be treated as a 'black box' for which some combined utility function is assumed (Seekings and Natrass 2005, Bagchi *et al.* 1998, Hart 1992, Guyer and Peters 1987, Wilk and Netting 1984, Guyer 1981). Earlier case material (Hebinck and Smith 2001) has highlighted an, at least partial, ongoing erosion of kinship relations, as have many other studies on social change in Africa. To deal with such changes I argue for a redefinition of the household and social relationships, which implies that the unit of analysis needs to be reconsidered. In the household has served as the main unit of analysis past and indeed, many surveys and analyses continue this practice. Murray (1998) commented that in most household surveys anonymous individual 'household heads' are interviewed in one place, at one time. This subverts "the realistic possibility both of return visits to the same households [or members of the 'household'] and also of comprehending adequately the related activities of other household members" (Murray 1998: 5, 6, see also Murray 2001). Wilk and Netting (1984) in their turn argued that the analysis should shift from examining structures to paying attention to activities, and the roles that social actors play therein. One should not make the mistake of assuming that wages, rewards and transfers are pooled and decisions are harmoniously arrived at about how to spend this pool. One strategy for circumventing this difficulty is to interview those that 'matter' among the members of the homestead; that is those who are involved in making decisions and those involved in activities that directly and indirectly sustain the homestead. This does not only include the

men (including the so-called head of the household) and women (often referred
to as housewives when married or as female heads of households often engaged
independently from their absent husbands in income earning activities) and
where appropriate older children. In many cases these children have children of
their own. It is not uncommon in South Africa to encounter social units that are
three-generational. Such broader analysis will provide a better picture of what
actually happens in the homestead and how the resources at its disposal are or
have been utilised. Thus it is preferable to look at the social actors and their
practices. The term social actors designates both individuals as well as groups
sharing certain characteristics (age, ethnicity, gender class) and institutions like
the church or political parties (Long 2001). Such a focus prevents a mistaken
reification of the household. The perspective that takes into account the whereabouts and activities of individuals or groups that jointly constitute the homestead, which is the place that draws social actors together.

In my view homestead is a better term and unit than households for such
analysis as it better captures social and spatial mobility. Barber (1998, cited in
Ellis 2000: 20) underlines that the homestead is the broadest social grouping as
a unit that includes all those individuals who belong to a particular (rural)
homestead in the sense that they have the right to be based there and to participate as full members of the grouping. In this sense, homestead denotes residency, co-residency and locality, as well as shelter and social security, for its
members. Homestead also captures that some activities that take place are
spatially removed from the homestead in the physical sense. Homestead contains a social expression of place (and space), a sense of belonging and identity
which contains elements of the past and present (Escobar 2001, Cosgrove 1998)
as well as of the future (McAllister 2001). Being a member of a homestead
often, but not always, implies hereditary rights to key resources, such as land
and cattle, which represent the resources accumulated in the (recent) past by
previous generations. A homestead is associated with family and kinship. Very
often a homestead accommodates more than one generation of the same family.
The composition of many homesteads varies over time as individuals move
about (Seekings and Nattrass 2005). Categories such as Single Homestead
Household and Multiple Homestead Household (De Wet and Holbrook 1997)
express the fact that homesteads may be separated spatially but not socially.
Alderson-Smith (1984) made a similar analysis in Peru by emphasising the
existence of confederations of 'households'.

*Community-institutions.* A similar critique should be made of uncritical acceptance of the notion of 'community'. Leach *et al.* (1997) complained that "it is
striking the degree to which simplistic notions of community are being rein-
vented in the context of practical efforts towards community based sustainable
development". The use of community is often misleading as it assumes homogeneity and harmony while often the opposite is the case. Communities are not
static either. They are composed of people who actively monitor, interpret and

shape the world around them and struggle for resources. This echoes the perspective that revolves around social actors, agency and action. Structure, or rules and norms are the product of people's practices, interactions and actions. Some of these actions may be intended; others may have unintended outcomes (Long 2001, Long and Van der Ploeg 1994). The embedding in a wider economic, political and cultural institutional framework, or the structural location within society, constrains social behaviour. The decisions and actions of actors may well be affected by what happens elsewhere, but it does not follow that these decisions and actions are determined. As a result they are not simply reducible to the expression of the actor's position within a system of social relations. The actions of people are shaped, but not necessarily structured or determined, by outside forces.

For these reasons Agrawal and Gibson (2001) stress the importance of unpacking the concept of community. Gender, age, social and economic inequalities, unequal access to resources, and power differences all paint a picture of communities that are social and spatially differentiated, rather then equal and consensus driven (Arce and Fisher 2003). The analysis of case material presented in the various chapters in this book underlines this argument and contrasts with the often held views of solidarity. Not that solidarity is completely absent, on the contrary, but negotiations between villagers to utilise and share key resources often fail pitifully. Another critical attribute to community is viewing it as a natural entity, based on common kinship, language, customs and authority. In contrast, this book underlines that community boundaries may be delineated and strengthened by relationships between members of different communities. Agrawal and Gibson (2001) argue for a focus on the multiple interests of actors within communities, on the basis of how these actors shape decision making processes. The recent literature shows a relative consensus that one way to escape from the simplistic notion and interpretation of community is to focus instead on institutions (Ostrom 1987, 1990, 2004, Poteete and Ostrom 2004, Leach *et al.* 1999), as a more fruitful approach to understanding what constitutes a community.

There is, however, disagreement in the literature on how the governance of institutions and their dynamics should be understood. The major contention is between, one the one hand, perspectives that emphasise the normative and structural aspects of organisations and their influence on social behaviour and on the relationship patterns between people and resources (Uphoff 1986, North 1990) and, on the other, those which present institutions as rules and regulations that provide individuals with room for manoeuvre (Ostrom 1990, Scott 1985, Long 2001). An institution may thus simultaneously be used to denote a process, an object and a subject. A key question is whether (and to what extent) we attribute power to those social actors that create institutions, and who formulate and maintain the rules to which others feel bound, or whether agency should also be attributed to those with less power.

The distinction between 'formal' and 'informal', which is often made in the analysis of governance and institutions, denotes differences between what exists on paper, the idealised, and what actually happens in practice, which is not always visible and thus is harder to grasp. Focusing on the practice, on what people do in their daily lives, allows one to see locally specific forms of organisation. Various authors referred to 'unruly' social practices that challenge legal rules that govern entitlement to resources. Yet, typically, informal practices and forms of organisation provide people with room for manoeuvre to pursue their individual interests. Cousins (1996, 2000) highlighted the importance of the processes of negotiation between the actors involved over common property resources. Several social scientists link informal practices with agency and power differences, pointing at the many ways in which people manage to get around the law and resist forms of oppression to defend their own interests.

The perspective outlined above does not necessarily reject the notion of community, but, as Leach *et al.* (1999: 230) phrased it "rather contextualise it by describing a more or less temporary unity of situation, interest or purpose." Where relevant and applicable the choice is made in this book to use more neutral terms to denote community, like village and villagers or settlement. Similarly, the use of homestead is preferred to household to denote a family and people living under one roof and eating from the same pot. Whether they share resources and, for instance, pool income can only be understood in their particular context.

*Contentious issues 2: Environmental degradation and the understanding of resources*

A second area of differences between social scientists and natural scientists also requires some attention before we begin our empirical investigations. This concerns different understandings of environmental degradation and different conceptualisations of resources. These issues of contention cannot be disconnected from their context and aspects of knowledge, intervention and governance; as these are, as we will see, inextricably intertwined.

Environmental degradation has for a long time been assumed to reflect a growing lack of synchrony between the 'community' and its natural environment. The seemingly still dominant Malthusian perspective views population growth as triggering resource degradation e.g. environmental problems emerging as an outcome of population increase, overgrazing and uncontrolled intensification of land use (Hardin 1968) or an absence of a sound scientific background to land use (Trollope 1985). Scoones (1999), Baker (2000) and Vetter (2004) have all reviewed the rangeland ecology literature, and pointed out that the scientific core of the Malthusian view of ecological change is linear and centred around equilibrium thinking, both features of the paradigms that dominated until the mid 1970s. Interventions to combat degradation were often based on simple population-growth models, describing the supposedly stable features of the intrinsic growth rate and carrying capacity. Population models identified carrying capacities and maximum sustained yield levels for use in managing animal populations. These insights have formed the background for many intervention programmes to prevent resource degradation.

Two new aspects have now emerged to inform the analysis of resource utilisation and environmental problems. The first is the need for proper contextualisation. The second is recognition of the need for a closer and more critical look at the knowledge of the 'experts' and of local people, including an understanding of how these forms of knowledge are intertwined with resource management.

Warren (2002) and Battebury and Bebbington (1999) argue that we need to contextualise resource degradation. Similarly, Leach *et al.* (1999) advocated an approach that moves away from framing environmental problems in terms of population pressure on a limited natural-resource base, to a disaggregated approach that considers the role of the institutions that mediate the relationship between different social actors and their environment. Kepe and Scoones (1999) have shown the usefulness of such an institutional focus by revealing how the making of particular grasslands is associated with specific institutional arrangements. Like Leach *et al.* (1999) I do not dispute the population growth narrative and framing of environmental problems but prefer to properly contextualise environmental problems.

Variants of the Malthusian view have formed the scientific background and starting point for a range of interventions – like betterment planning in South Africa – aimed at preventing environmental degradation. The analysis of Trollope (1985), Lakcr *et al.* (1975) and the Tomlinson Commission Report (1955) resonates with these views, as do many contemporary agrarian science curricula. Yet this book shows how population dynamics (rather then population growth *per se*) contextualise environmental problems and how state interventions intended to mitigate these problems often work in unexpected and less than optimal ways. Labour migration and land tenure have pushed rural people off their land and turned them into workers and pensioners, rather than facilitating their presence on the land. Such a presence might lead to more caring for the land and responses to degradation.

An essential element of such contextualisation involves reconsidering what constitutes a resource. In our interpretation of resource degradation it matters whether one adheres to static, linear views or whether one adopts a dynamic, non-linear view that centres on the idea that resources unfold. Natural scientists for a long time have tended to describe and value resources in terms of their intrinsic values, considering all natural resources as resources, irrespective of whether people utilise them or not. While most (but not all) natural scientists ignored social praxis, this is the point from which social scientists start. They argue that natural resources are only resources when they are accessed and utilised in one way or another and thereby appropriated and transformed. A natural scientist identifies with the potential use of such resources and hence engages, for instance, with experimental work to show what natural and social conditions are required or need to be created to fully exploit their potential. Nowadays, they often do this in a participatory way and the experiments may identify how a natural resource should be utilised and improved. In many cases this is followed by prescriptions designed by experts on how to best use or exploit the resource.

Work by Carpenter (2005), Berkes *et al.* (1998) and Wu and Hobb (1998) attempted rather well to bridge natural and social sciences, both in practice and in discourse and terminology. Notwithstanding these experiences and advances, expert views on what constitutes resources or a 'good' or 'sustainable' livelihood have become extremely important as these are often used to underpin and legitimatise policies that regulate the use of resources. Manure policies in the Netherlands to reduce groundwater and air pollution because of ammonia evaporation, could not be designed without scientific analyses that defined manure and what constitutes good manure. Experts may attempt to direct and prescribe the course of events, but they certainly do not have the power to structure (or determine) the behaviour of a range of social actors. The potential for action lies in many social locations and is not simply embedded in the expert system. A range of studies have demonstrated that social actors contest and rework such intervention programmes that are mostly based on views of experts (i.e. consultants, academics, policy makers). Long (2001) explored these processes, identifying the continuous adaptation, struggle and meshing of cultural elements and social practices that occur. Technology development and transfer necessarily involves an interface between the world of designers and experts and that of the users (Hebinck 2001). A focus on how farmers and other social actors redesign external prescriptions and how adaptations take place, may enable us to explain why certain modes of utilisation proposed by experts are often contested by local people (Arce 2003, Van der Ploeg 2003, Mango and Hebinck 2004). Baker (2000) critically examined the ecological knowledge of experts and highlighted the importance of whether experts employ equilibrium or non-equilibrium thinking when designing interventions. She argued that the methods of West African farmers reflect a close adaptation to a fluctuating, non-equilibrial physical environment, while most intervention programmes have long been based on equilibrial ecology (see also Vetter 2004). Baker (2000) calls for an autecological approach that emphasises the locally specific nature of development processes. Altieri (2002a, 2002b) and Toledo (1990) in turn prefer agroecology to denote a similar perspective that links and embeds the understanding of agriculture and ecosystem dynamics in a social analysis and *vice versa*.

Ticktin (2004) examined the ecological implications of natural resource harvesting by local people in Asia, and argued that researchers and forest managers need to work with resource harvesters in designing and evaluating management practices if they want to prevent or mitigate against the negative effects of harvesting. However, in such partnerships it is crucial to reflect on whose point of view prevails. While the locally specific context plays an enormously important role, the relationships of power between experts and local people, the history of resource use, competing claims, and the locals' perceptions of their social and natural environment all play influential roles. Joshi *et al.* (2004) reflect upon this by critically exploring local knowledge and asking how local knowledge can be captured and be used to complement and inspire 'science'. Beinart (2003) has made an extremely useful and important contribution to the debate on conservation by exploring the history of thought and ideas behind conservation policies. Through a bibliographical approach, Beinart opened up the networks of individuals and groups, and how they link with the institutions of science and power. Travel abroad and inviting peers to South Africa have also both played a major role in separating expert knowledge from local environments, allowing the decontextualised importing of concepts and notions of farming and conservation that have been developed in very different conditions. Draper *et al.* (2004) and Singh and Houtum (2002) follow a similar approach by pointing at the global networks that shape the developmental discourse. Scott (1998) made the argument that expert knowledge underpins a technocratic discourse that often ignores the way rural people read and utilise their landscape in their attempt to construct their livelihoods. "Seeing like a state" often involves imposing its ways of seeing on people's lives.

Natural scientists and notably ecologists' perceptions and understanding of resources and their effects on eco-system dynamics have changed dramatically. More recently, and notably since the mid-1970s, some agronomists, and ecologists in particular, have adopted non-equilibrium thinking (Scoones 1999). Variability, complexity and non-linearity are the core of the 'new ecology' theory and static notions of carrying capacity and climax vegetation are now being challenged. Scoones (1999), Baker (2000) and Vetter (2004) point out that one of the implications of this is that uncertainty and surprise have become central to the understanding of ecological dynamics. The nature and direction of social development and ecological change begins to be viewed as less certain (Leach *et al.* 2002, Winder *et al.* 2005). Simple intervention models become increasingly untenable. Theoretically one may link the idea that we are no longer certain of the outcomes of social and ecological change with understanding change as a continuous process of co-evolution or coproduction. Perceiving resources as unfolding and being reconfigured is an almost logical consequence of such a view.

Zimmerman (as elaborated by Peach and Constatin 1972), in his well known and much cited work on the world's resources, expounded the view that resources are not static. Resources are dynamic and their nature and qualities change. Resources, poetically speaking, unfold through their utilisation by social actors (Van der Ploeg 2003, Wiskerke and Van der Ploeg 2004). Social actors create and transform natural and social resources and mould them to make them useful and bring them together in an internally coherent way. This view, which is consistent with the coproduction perspective, also implies that social resources are formed by a historical process of coproduction. The locally, actor specific, resource configurations achieved in this way form the basis for making a living. It follows from this that a particular resource can be used in many different ways. There is not simply one ideal way of resource utilisation. What was once seen as an irrelevant resource might become very vital (or *vice versa*). This makes resources and their utilisation time, space and scale specific. Resources are valorised, that is they are converted to realise value. The prevailing social, economic, institutional and historical context in which these resources appear influence what value is and how it is represented. The views among the social actors on this matter are not always shared and often are contested.

*Multidisciplinary methods*
This book is the result of insights gained through different disciplinary perspectives and it attempts to draw a holistic picture. It builds on the work of many authors and their respective disciplinary knowledge and skills. The collaboration has yielded unique results. The origins of the attempts to construct an interdisciplinary understanding of landscape and livelihood interactions are partly explained by the nature of the beginning of the research in 1996 (the 'core project' of ARDRI), which aimed to build a holistic perspective. This allowed for different disciplines to explore the dynamics of agriculture from their perspectives and seek ways to integrate the findings.

The research began in 1996 with the organisation of a number of village meetings, particular with members of the residents' associations to seek permission for the research. Data collection commenced with the design of a questionnaire to capture the elements of the farming systems in the two villages. The questions included were intended to develop an understanding of the crop and livestock production systems. Other sources of income (remittances, pensions and wages) were included as they were seen as instrumental for removing constraints in arable and livestock production. The survey was held from July 1996 to June 1997 and subsequently entered in a data base during July and October 1997 (ARDRI Survey 1997). This survey targeted every homestead in the two villages that was present at that time. The survey was updated between August and October 1999 by Nomakhaya Monde (Monde 2003) who used similar questions but a smaller sample size. Data were also collected through group discussions covering a range of topics such as erosion, grazing management and service provision. At a later stage more detailed case studies and life histories were recorded, based on cases selected from preliminary analyses of the data base. The life histories were continuously updated as much as possible until early 2006. A rapid re-appraisal of the villagers' livelihood activities was conducted in April 2004. In this re-appraisal key informants were interviewed during transect walks which provided information on livelihood activities, livestock holdings and the composition of each of the homesteads. In many cases this information was supplemented by short interviews with the residents of the homesteads.

Aerial photographs taken in different years were collected for interpretation of social and land use changes over a longer period of time. The specifics of the photographs are provided in chapter 7. In addition to these sources of information, traveller accounts, often documented by others (Mostert 1992, Coleman 1999, Crampton 2004) and other more archival sources such as the Deeds Registry at King William's Town were consulted, not only to corroborate findings of field-work but to provide other detailed information oral history did not or could not reveal.

These diverse methods of data collection provided by detailed histories and ethnographic accounts of past and present processes of social and ecological transformations, and the surveys offered quantitative data for descriptive and statistical analyses. Soil sampling, measurements of crop yields, GIS analyses and aerial photograph interpretation were applied in various components as part of the overall effort. Finally, extensive literature reviews were used to support comparative analyses and interpretation.

*Interdisciplinary research steps and questions*
The origins of these attempts to construct an interdisciplinary understanding of landscape and livelihood interactions are multiple. This is only partly explained by the nature of the beginning of the research in 1996 (the 'core project' of ARDRI) that aimed to build a holistic perspective. Such a project setting allowed for different disciplines to explore the dynamics of agriculture from their perspectives and seek ways to integrate the findings.

Given the emphasis on the interconnection between landscapes and livelihoods, which are a joint outcome of coproduction, the analysis firmly grounds the interactions between the institutions, practices and resource configurations of people as taking place in historical and locally specific contexts and finding expression in livelihood identities and narratives. A large part of the book is devoted to an interdisciplinary treatment of natural and social resources and how these interact. Methodologically, the research can be divided into three steps and areas of investigation:

1. Examining how contemporary livelihoods, institutions and social relations relate to those of the past. What transformations have occurred in livelihoods and the landscape?
2. Examining how present cropping patterns, livestock production and foraging and the environmental impacts of these relate to past patterns. What kind of land use patterns have emerged over time in the two villages? What has been the role of interventions and what did they achieve?
3. Asking about other past and present uses of land. Are the three land categories (arable, residential and grazing or rangelands) introduced by the colonial administration at the end of the 19$^{th}$ century still referred to? Is this method

of categorising land relevant and useful? Are these categories fixed or have changes and shifts occurred over time?

Livelihoods are examined by looking at the key resources and how access to these resources is arranged by social actors. How and in what ways do (and did) actors attempt to coherently combine the resources, and convert them into new resources and/or relevant commodities? Special attention is paid to the question of how the resources are combined into a coherent whole, particularly when this concerns shifts in crop and livestock production. People's ideas and their explanations were sought and recorded during interviews so as to (re)construct their views on the past, present and the future. The issues and processes surrounding the negotiations to access and use key resources and their subsequent management is achieved through an institutional analysis which attempts to go beyond normal methods of analysis. Observing and debating practices, whether formally sanctioned or informally condoned, played a key role.

The landscape and its parts were examined in many ways. Aerial photograph interpretations, GIS analyses and consulting historical records and accounts were only one aspect of the analysis of the historical changes that have occurred in the landscape. The use of land in the three land use categories was monitored through observation, counting livestock and monitoring their moves, quantifying what people and cattle gather from these lands and measuring crop yields. This work took place between 1996 and 2004. Soil samples of the arable fields gave insights into soil quality and the potential capacity of the land. Attempts were made to understand the vegetation and ecology of the region in terms of its history of continual transition and the unique outcomes of the particular histories. These histories of land use were documented in detail and are linked to the livelihood trajectories of the people in the village. This takes us beyond the narrow identification of land categories as created by planners and raises questions over the fixing of rights to each category and over what people do with their entitlements to these and other interlinked resources.

The units of analyses vary among chapters. The very nature of a combined analysis of livelihoods and landscapes, constituted by multiple realities and fragmentation, dictates that a wide of spatial units such as field, patches within fields, the rangeland or *veld* play important roles in social relations, urban-rural linkages and the cultural repertoires of people. The homestead, family, individuals and their social relations as well as the urban-rural spaces in which these actors are embedded all constitute important arenas. Livelihoods, as this book shows, span a wide range of social and spatial domains and this needs to be taken into account.

Such a treatment goes beyond a single disciplinary point of view that often identifies and categorises resources as natural, physical, financial, human and social. Central to the book's perspective is that these resources have multiple usages and it is though this multiplicity of meaning that various kinds of livelihoods and landscapes are constructed. An understanding of how these agrarian micro practices are used and combined with others, what social, cultural and economic values are attributed to these resources, and what role these play in the struggle of rural people to make a living is essential for understanding life in contemporary rural South Africa.

This book attempts to incorporate critical views, particularly those regarding soil fertility, rangeland and the management of other resources, and bring these together with interpretations of history, land use, agricultural policy changes and social change. The book brings together interpretations constructed from a mixture of accounts derived from a range of sources, including villagers (men, women and children) and academics (such as historians, economists, sociologists, ecologists and other experts) whose accounts are documented in the form of published articles and books, research reports and archives.

All these accounts need to be treated carefully and contextualised properly. Some of the villagers' accounts may provide a romantic view of the past, especially those of elderly people. Other accounts point at emerging new life styles echoing some kind of modernity. These accounts point at a mixture of the constraints felt by the younger generations and how elderly people use their patriarchal authority.

## The organisation of the book

The book consists of 14 chapters. The book is structured on the assumption that livelihood transformations can be read from the transformations that occur at the level of landscape and also *vice versa*, that the landscape tells us something about the nature and dynamics of rural livelihoods. The book describes the characteristics of landscape and livelihoods, analyses how these interact through time and evaluates the outcomes of these interactions. The chapters do this from different angles. If the landscape is a way of seeing, as Cosgrove (1998) argued, this book shows how the various authors see the landscape and the livelihoods making use of the landscape.

The second and third chapters deal with the broader perspective of the central Eastern Cape Province and depict the regional and historical context of the two villages. In so doing they provide a general background for the rest of the book. This broader perspective is important as peoples' lives and development opportunities are not contained in, nor demarcated by, the boundaries of the two villages; neither are their livelihoods limited to the natural, economic and social resources that lie within the boundaries of the villages. Chapter 2 depicts the history and major political and economic trends and changes in the region. It covers the processes of transformation from the pre-colonial times until the end of the 20th century. The third chapter describes the agro-ecological landscape in broad terms placing an emphasis on the quality and quantity of the key natural resources of the region around the two villages.

Chapters 4 through to 13 focus on more specific aspects of livelihoods and landscapes in the two villages. Chapter 4 recounts the history of the villages from the early days of settlement in a period of lull in the many frontier or Cape wars. A timeline of critical events identifies major developments and livelihood issues. Aspects of the immediate landscape are described in chapter 5. This chapter partly reconstructs the transformation of the landscape and examines the consequences of such transformation for the quantity and quality of natural resources in the immediate environment of the two villages. Like chapter 4, chapter 5 is a stepping stone for the further analyses of changes in livelihoods and landscapes and the opportunities that these provide.

Chapter 6 in turn examines the instruments of coproduction: institutions and the practices of governance. Depicting the formal changes, how these are interpreted and reflecting on what these changes mean for everyday life in the two settlements, this chapter provides a vivid picture of the processes of management and negotiations around issues of rights to land and the areas that are collectively held and managed. Chapter 7 elaborates on the changes that have taken place over time in the use of the landscape. Spatial and historical analyses are presented based on a unique time series of aerial photographs. This treatment aims to link the changes occurring in livelihoods of the people of Guquka and Koloni (chapter 2) with the changes in the use of the landscape. The chapter also explores the impact of betterment planning on land use patterns. Chapters 8, 9 and 10 examine in detail the various ways in which the landscape provides a source for livelihoods. These chapters all deal with land use and the changes that have occurred. Chapter 8 deals with the growing of crops both on the arable fields and in home gardens and addresses the issue of why 'under-cultivation' or underutilisation of these fields is so persistent. Chapter 9 provides a detailed analysis of the history of livestock production, of the role that rangelands as well as arable fields and residential areas play as a forage source for livestock. Chapter 10 focuses on what people gather from the land: fuel wood, plants and herbs and timber. The *veld* caters for many needs and this in turn raises the issue of the sustainable management of these resources.

Chapters 11, 12 and 13 scrutinise the broader issues of livelihood and social change. Migration of whole families has had an impact on the demographics of the villages as well as the nature of social relationships. Recent census data show that these villages are largely inhabited by elderly people as younger generations and their families leave; some for good. Chapter 12 examines the relevance of categorising livelihoods into broad categories ('grantholders', 'remitters', 'wage earners', 'farmers', 'petty entrepreneurs' and 'diversifiers'). The chapter shows that livelihoods actually interlock around various domains of the use of land-based resources. Chapter 13 brings the life histories or trajectories to the fore. This chapter documents the everyday lives of people, how these have changed and when and how poverty emerges. In its own way this case material shows the heterogeneity of livelihoods.

In conclusion, chapter 14 aims to bring together the major issues that have been debated extensively in the book, formulates a set of conclusions and provides some suggestions as to what kind of agrarian polices would enhance land-based livelihoods in the Eastern Cape Province. By drawing on detailed insights into the past and present uses of the landscape and the kind of livelihoods that have emerged over time it is hoped that the book can also say something useful about current policies and the future. It challenges the current thrust of agrarian policies by arguing for state support for (re)peasantisation. The dynamics and impact of state interventions in the past and their effects on rural livelihoods give grounds for questioning the theoretical grounding and likely efficacy of contemporary rural development policies.

# 2

# Rural transformation in the Eastern Cape

Paul Hebinck and Wim van Averbeke[*]

## Introduction

The nature of land-based activities in the Eastern Cape has changed significantly during the past two centuries. In stark contrast to pre-colonial times, when agriculture and other activities based on the utilisation of natural resources were at the centre of people's livelihoods, agriculture has lost its overall importance for the majority of rural African people. Nowadays, their livelihoods revolve largely around migratory labour, remittances and social pensions. This development is not restricted to the Eastern Cape but also has occurred in other parts of South Africa (Lahiff 2000, Lipton *et al.* 1996a, 1996b, Francis 2000).

This chapter presents a history of important changes in the livelihoods in the Eastern Cape with an emphasis on African people. It focuses on the processes and events that have shaped the overall development trajectories of these people and how these have affected their land-based activities. Empirically, the chapter draws on many sources of information. Historians, economists, agronomists, anthropologists and sociologists alike have extensively documented the history of the Eastern Cape.

---

[*]   The authors thank Frans Huyzendveldt for his comments on the last draft.

Our analysis in this chapter is wide in scope and does not focus specifically on the villages of Guquka and Koloni. The broader picture that is presented allows for the incorporation of valuable analytical insights generated by other scholars. Spatially, the area of interest is the former Ciskei, and the focus of the analysis is that of rural transformation. Where relevant, information on the former Transkei is also included.

By and large, this chapter is structured chronologically, depicting the process of rural transformation in the Eastern Cape region. The first section shortly describes the origins of the Xhosa people. The second part explores pre-colonial society and its patterns of settlement and livelihood. The third deals in general terms with colonisation and analyzes processes of commoditisation and rural resistance to colonialism. No attempt is made to depict agricultural development by distinguishing various periods. Bundy (1988), Lewis (1984), Switzer (1993), Wilson (1975), Simkins (1981) and Knight and Lenta (1980) all agree that the hay day of African agriculture occurred around the start of the 20$^{th}$ century. There is also agreement on the main trend of decline, with some important variations, as elaborated in chapter 8. Disagreement prevails on when this decline started. Was it at the end of the 19$^{th}$ century in Ciskei and during the early 1930s in Transkei, as Wilson (1975) argued, or can it be dated back to the mid 1940s, as Simkins 1981 attempted to show? There is no a consensus in the literature as to why African agriculture declined, and we do not attempt to reach such a consensus but rather make use of the insights generated. The decline was most likely set in motion by a combination of factors involving population dynamics, labour migration, market formation, mounting pressure on the land, declining fertility, and adverse agro-ecological conditions. Policy and the ways in which the state attempted to intervene in black agrarian society were also important (Simkins 1981, Knight and Lenta 1980).

The overview and analysis in the literature are biased towards arable production and focus less on livestock and other goods and services people obtain from the landscape. Recent studies have clearly identified the important role and function of natural resource harvesting for rural livelihoods (see chapter 10).

## African people in the Eastern Cape

For a long time Southern Africa was inhabited by the Khoi and San (previously called Bushmen). The Bantu-speaking tribes arrived later. The term 'Bantu' refers to a group of more than 450 languages that can be traced back to proto-Bantu speech in which the word *ntu* meant person. Southern Nigeria and Cameroon are regarded as the cradle of proto-Bantu speech (Lamphear and Falola 1995). From about the second millennium BC, the proto-Bantu people gradually moved into the equatorial forest of west central Africa. In the forest their livelihood was based on the cultivation of root crops and fishing. They were still Stone Age people and livestock rearing was of little importance. During the first millennium BC, the first groups had started to penetrate the savannah. Here, they made contact with other civilisations, including iron workers, whose skills they acquired. By the 5th century AD Early Iron Age Bantu-speakers had spread through much of Africa south of the equator, but they kept to the well-watered parts, along forest margins and river valleys. Their spread was helped along by the introduction of new food crops, including bananas and yams, from southeast Asia during the 2nd century AD (Lamphear and Falola 1995). The Bantu-speakers moved into the drier parts of the subcontinent when they were introduced to pastoralism and the production of drought resistant grain crops, such as sorghum and millet. Pastoral traditions were adopted from Nilotic-speaking people from the Sudan, who migrated south along the Upper Nile, whilst Cushitic-speaking people from the southern part of Ethiopia are believed to be responsible for transferring cereal production to the Bantu-speakers. By the start of the second millennium AD Bantu-speaking communities had moved into most of the dry areas of Africa south of the equator (Lamphear and Falola 1995).

The first wave of Bantu-speakers reached southern Africa about 400 AD and by 700 AD they were living as far south as the present Transkei (Bergh 1984). During a second wave of migration, the ancestors of the Nguni, Sotho and Tsonga arrived in southern Africa around 1200 AD (Hammond-Tooke 1993). Adaptation to the diverse ecology of South Africa was again necessary, producing different agricultural and social traditions. These differences became most pronounced between groups that settled on the *highveld* (the Sotho), for whom crop production remained important, and groups that settled between the escarpment and the Indian Ocean (the Nguni), who developed a cattle tradition (Warmelo 1937, Hammond-Tooke 1993).

The Nguni took over land occupied by the San who survived on gathering and hunting, and particularly the Khoi (previously called Hottentots), who were a pastoral people. The Khoi occupied the coastal zone of South Africa between the Mzimvubu River in KwaZulu-Natal and the Cape. By 1736 the Nguni had cleared all land northeast of the Keiskamma River of independent Khoi tribes (Mostert 1992, Bergh 1984).

Contemporary Nguni people are subdivided into North- and South-Nguni. The Zulu-, Swazi- and Ndebele-speaking people make up the North-Nguni. The amalgamation of Xhosa-speaking people, including the Mpondo, Mpondomise, Thembu, and Xhosa, and several immigrant North-Nguni tribes constitute the South-Nguni. They inhabit the area currently known as the Eastern Cape, but large numbers of them are also found in the Western Cape, particularly the Cape Town area, as a result of rural to urban migration. In terms of settlement history, the Xhosa were the southernmost Nguni tribe. They were most influenced by interaction with the Khoi. For example, the abundance of clicks in the Xhosa language has been linked to Khoi influence (Bergh 1984). The Xhosa people are the focus of the rest of this chapter.

# Pre-colonial Nguni society in the 18<sup>th</sup> century

Topographically and ecologically, the coastal zone, in which the Xhosa settled, was extremely varied. Numerous small rivers dissected the terrain, resulting in a series of wooded valleys and grassy hill slopes and crests. Each of these units contained the natural resources that provided for subsistence, such as pasture, rich alluvial soils for cultivation, clay, thatching grass, wood, water and game.

The Xhosa settlement pattern was adapted to this coastal landscape, and consisted of dispersed single homesteads (*imizi*) separated from each other by distances varying from a few hundred metres to several kilometres. The homestead (*umzi*), rather then the family *per se*, constituted the productive unit (Lewis 1984, Hoernlé 1937). The *umzi* consisted of a group of kin-related households who lived together and who recognised the leadership of the head of one of the constituent households. Each male head of household had one or more wives. The *umzi* constituted a cooperative work unit (Mostert 1992, McAllister 2001, Kuckertz 1985). Physically, the *umzi* consisted of a small number of huts (*indlu*) made of wood and grass mats arranged around the cattle *kraal* or byre, creating a sort of small village. Mostert (1992) and Lewis (1984) explain that these villages ranged in size from two to about 50 huts. Each village had its gardens and a substantial territory, representing the hunting grounds and pastures that were common to households of the village. Each settlement was essentially self-sufficient (Hoernlé 1937, Schapera and Goodwin 1937, Peires 1981, Bundy 1988, Switzer 1993). There was little domestic production for exchange, except perhaps for pots, baskets, iron goods and utensils. A certain amount of irregular trade nevertheless took place, principally through barter. Some commodities were also exchanged for labour (Schapera and Goodwin 1937).

The political organisation of the Xhosa is important because it had a bearing on processes of homestead expansion and patterns of wealth accumulation. Politically, the Xhosa nation was hierarchical and patriarchal. The head of a homestead was subordinate to a chief. Xhosa chiefs answered to the head of the royal clan 'Tshawe', who was referred to as the Paramount Chief or King. Chiefs accumulated wealth by receiving tribute in the form of cattle and fines (Hoernlé 1937). They, in turn, redistributed parts of their wealth to their supporters, who in most cases were those who had managed to obtain influence and prestige among dependents or adherents of the chief. It was, as Lewis (1984: 4) pointed out, "the economic and social goal of most married men to establish their own homestead". Lewis adds that "it was far from certain that everybody succeeded in doing so".

Key to the dynamics in Xhosa society was

> ... the tendency of the homestead to expand and acquire indebted adherents. These adherents were from amongst the poor who lacked sufficient cattle, or access to suitable land, to be able to start a homestead of their own. They gained access to

cattle by serving the head of the homestead. The acquisition of such clients was crucial to the expansion of the homestead and the organisation of the dominant class around the Chief (Lewis 1984: 4).

In this way the head of the homestead occupied a position of power. He owned most of the cattle, acquired a second wife and enjoyed access to political power through the Chief.

Xhosa chiefs were not despots. They could not, as a rule, impose an unduly heavy burden on the people. Hammond-Tooke (1993) spoke of *'tribal democracy'*, since there was a prevailing ethos of consensus (Mayer 1980). The driving force leading to indebtedness was the need to acquire cattle (*lobola*) to conclude a marriage that cemented relations between families. This was the major avenue for adult men to establish their own homestead as alluded to before. This practice in turn shaped the division of labour within each household based on gender.

Lewis (1984) established the link between cattle ownership, particularly the unequal distribution of cattle, and the expansion of the Xhosa society. When a homestead reached a certain size further expansion became impossible, mainly because of lack of adequate pastures. Similarly, when the chiefdom neared its limits of expansion, groups of people sought political leadership, usually in the form of a brother to the chief, and hived off to establish themselves on new territory. Historical evidence exists for this process of expansion and occupation of new territory from the 17th century onwards, proceeding westward across the Kei River, as noted earlier, and then across the Great Fish River. This expansion also resulted in the separation of the Xhosa into two major chiefdoms, the Gcaleka, who lived east of the Kei, and the Rharhabe to the west of the Kei (Soga 1937, Mostert 1992, Hammond-Tooke 1993). The influx of cattle farmers of Dutch descent (the *trekboers*), who migrated eastwards during the 18th century to escape the control of the Cape Colony, and the arrival of English settlers in the area around Grahamstown, starting in 1820, effectively blocked further westward expansion of the Xhosa. This intensified struggles among Xhosa chiefdoms and between chiefdoms and the Colony. Initially, conflict between the Xhosa, particularly the Dlambe chiefdom of the Rharhabe, and the Colony centred on the Xhosa occupation of the *Zuurveld*. The Xhosa were forcefully expelled from this land, situated between the Bushmans River and the Great Fish River, through a military campaign in 1811 (Mostert 1992, Peires, 1981, Lewis 1984).

The livelihood of the Xhosa people in both the material and non-material sense was based on agriculture combined with gathering and hunting. Xhosa agriculture had two main components: the production of livestock, consisting mainly of cattle but also including small stock such as goats and later sheep (Brown 1969), and the production of crops and vegetables in small fields along the rivers and in homestead gardens (Schapera and Goodwin 1937, Bundy 1988, Thompson 1990, Mostert 1992). Domestic production was divided into a male domain, which controlled all aspects of cattle herding, and a female sphere, which performed work with crops. Within each homestead, the male and female spheres together constituted a unity with the means of production: cattle, pasturage, and arable land. Male control over all aspects of cattle management made women dependent on men because even for sustenance cattle occupied a more important place than did crops (Lewis 1984).

The primary component of the farming system, apart from its political, social and cultural meanings, was the rearing of cattle for milk. The milk was usually kept in pots or sacks until it had curdled (Schapera and Goodwin 1937, Peires 1981). Other products from cattle were the skins, used for clothing, bags and other useful artefacts. Oxen also served as a means of transport. The slaughter of cattle was – and largely still is – restricted to ceremonies, such as weddings and funerals, and rituals such as male initiation and those for seeking the approval of the ancestors. Cattle management relied heavily on the quality of the pastures, which were held under a common property regime. No fodder was grown, but after crops were harvested cattle were allowed to graze the stover and weeds left in the fields. The Nguni people's knowledge of cattle and pastures was considerable (Wilson 1974, Soga 1931). Peires (1981) points out that Xhosa people practised burning to allow early spring grazing and combined this with high density grazing in order to improve the palatability of *sourveld* pastures.

The second component of Nguni agriculture revolved around cultivating grains, roots and vegetables in small fields and gardens. This was predominantly a female domain, but men participated in the clearing of new land. A change in gender roles took place in the Eastern Cape from about the middle of the 19th century, when men became involved in ploughing fields using oxen (Bundy 1988). For a long time sorghum was the principal grain crop, but once maize was introduced in the 17th century, it rapidly rose to prominence and by the beginning of the 19th century it featured widely in Xhosa gardens (Maclennan 1986). Beer made from sorghum was an important food; besides offering nutrition it also represented a critical social resource. This drink played a vital role in festivities and was also a means of exchange for labour, a tribute to chiefs and an offering to the spirits.

Fields were usually allocated to each of the wives in a household. These fields were subdivided into sections, and each section was planted to a particular crop. A field in the late 18th century typically consisted of a maize plot, a second for sorghum, and a third plot for the rest of the crops and vegetables. To prepare the land women made use of a digging stick, which consisted of a flattened piece of hardwood (Schapera and Goodwin 1937, Stuart and Malcolm 1986, Brown 1969). Although the Xhosa were an Iron Age people, who manufactured axes and spears, the use of iron hoes in crop production only became common after Europeans arrived. The planting of crops began by broadcasting seed saved from the previous harvest, followed by land preparation, which consisted of uprooting weeds and grasses with a digging stick and simultaneously working the crop seed into the soil. This labourious task was done by the women working on their knees. The uprooted weeds were left as a mulch to protect the emerging crops against desiccation and birds, and this was removed when the crop was ready for weeding (Stuart and Malcolm 1986, Brown 1969).

The Xhosa did not use manure to fertilise their fields, despite its abundant availability in the *kraals* where cattle was kept during the night, perhaps because of the sacred role of the cattle *kraal* in the lives of Xhosa society (Hammond-Tooke 1993). Fallowing fields every fifth year (Peires 1981) and shifting cultivation (Schapera and Goodwin 1937: 134, Brown 1969) were the two main methods in which Xhosa farmers addressed declining soil fertility and crop yields. The Xhosa also attempted to ensure good crops through 'doctoring' or magic. This often involved the passing of smoke, generated by burning specific animal skins or wild plants over the field, or the planting of particular shrubs on the edge of plots to act as charms (Soga 1931). Such doctoring was done primarily to protect crops against a wide range of threats including pests and diseases.

Birds and wild pigs were probably the main causes of crop damage, and fields were guarded, largely by women, to deter them (Schapera and Goodwin 1937, Stuart and Malcolm 1986, Brown 1969). After planting, the men built a simple shelter for the female guard and a rudimentary fence of brushwood around the field to discourage entry by livestock and wild animals in search of food. After the harvest the fence was used as firewood.

Grains were harvested and carried to the homestead where they were allowed to dry (Schapera and Goodwin 1937, Stuart and Malcolm 1986, Brown 1969). Storage of grains occurred in two ways, either in baskets woven from reeds or, if for later use, in underground grain pits (Stuart and Malcolm 1986, Brown 1969, Soga 1931). Males dug the grain pits in the cattle *kraals*. These pits had the shape of cones or bottles, narrow at the top, and widening towards the bottom. The soil was scooped out, and the inner walls were waterproofed with cattle dung plastering (Stuart and Malcolm 1986, Brown 1969). The grain was poured in these small cellars, and then the opening was sealed first with flat stones and then with a layer of cattle dung (Schapera and Goodwin 1937, Brown 1969). Inside these pits the grain was subject to a degree of fermentation, giving it a sour taste. Reportedly, grain could be stored for two to three years in such pits, but once a pit was opened the grain remained edible only for a short period. When a homestead opened a pit, neighbouring homesteads were invited to share in the consumption of the grain, knowing that this favour would be reciprocated (Peires 1981).

For their food requirements the Xhosa also relied on the surrounding natural environment. The gathering of wild fruits and other edible plant parts, the collecting of honey, and the hunting of wildlife all contributed to the diet (Schapera and Goodwin 1937, Stuart and Malcolm 1986). The importance of hunting and

gathering in sustaining human life relative to agriculture varied, depending on
the status and size of the cattle herd and the abundance of crop harvests.

There is little evidence of any great improvement in the techniques or productivity of Xhosa agriculture during the 17th and 18th century. There is also
little evidence of famine and widespread impoverishment during the pre-colonial era, despite significant differences of wealth among the Xhosa. Xhosa well-
being revolved around cattle, hunting, cropping and gathering, and in case any
of these activities failed the others could be relied upon even under extreme
conditions.

## Colonisation: 1820s and onwards

Starting around 1770 the *trekboers* and the Xhosa met and were soon in competition for the same resources, because both groups relied heavily on cattle
farming for their livelihood (Mostert 1992, Giliomee 2003, Beinart 2003,
Crampton 2004). Initially their co-existence was relative peaceful but inherently
unstable. The first armed conflicts over land between Xhosa and *trekboers*
occurred towards the end of the 18th century and concerned control over the
*Zuurveld* (Mayer 1980, Thompson 1993, Mostert 1992, Giliomee 2003). The
military arm of the British colonial power, that had taken control of the Cape in
1801, joined the conflict and expelled the Xhosa tribes from the *Zuurveld* in
1811 (Giliomee 2003, Mostert 1992, MacLennan 1986). This area was made
available for the 1820 settlers.

Until 1878, wars between the Xhosa and the Colony occurred frequently.
These nine wars, referred to as the Frontier Wars or Xhosa-Cape Wars all
tended to follow a similar pattern. Xhosa tribes, aggrieved by loss of land
needed for subsistence, attacked the Colony in a bid to regain lost territory. In
each case, the Colony, in possession of superior weaponry and logistics, was
able to reverse initial successes of the Xhosa and force them to surrender. In
nearly all cases, the peace imposed on the Xhosa required them to give up more
land, planting the seed for the next military conflict.

In the meantime the balance of power in southern Africa was also upset by
the rise of the Zulu nation during the 1820s (Thompson 1993, Stuart and
Malcolm 1986). The unprecedented violence and bloodshed that accompanied
the Zulu military campaigns brought about a chain reaction of conflict and
displacement. Among the Zulu this episode is known as the *Mfecane* or 'great
crushing'. Some of the displaced groups adopted a lifestyle of roving robbers to
survive, attacking other tribes and stealing their livestock (Bergh 1984, Stuart
and Malcolm 1986). One particular group of refugees, the *Mfengu*, was to play
an important role in the subsequent history of the central Eastern Cape. There is
still controversy about the tribal coherence of the *Mfengu*, with some historians
arguing that it was a creation of the British (Stapleton 1996). Nevertheless, the
*Mfengu* who had settled among the Gcaleka Xhosa under Hintsa in the
Transkei, were offered protection by the British, and about 16,000 were moved

to Peddie in 1835 (Mayer 1980, Bundy 1988). When the British annexed the land between the Great Fish and Kei rivers in 1847 and made it into a separate colony, called *British Kaffraria*, the Peddie *Mfengu* were to reap important benefits. Politically, the main function of the new colony was to protect the Cape Colony from the Xhosa by acting as a buffer zone (Mostert 1992, Thompson 1993). After having been cleared of Xhosa people, *British Kaffraria* was settled by people loyal to the Colony. Two groups of people benefited from this opportunity, namely European immigrants, mainly of German descent (Schwär and Pape 1958, Mostert 1992), and pro-colonial Africans, amongst whom the *Mfengu* were the most important (Mayer 1980, Stuart and Malcolm 1986, Lewis 1984). In return for joining the colonial forces against the Xhosa, in the so-called *Mlanjeni*'s War from 1850 to 1853, the *Mfengu* were rewarded with land in the districts of Victoria East and King William's Town (Bundy 1988). Also, in 1866 30,000 Mfengu were settled on land cleared of Xhosa people east of the Kei River, in the districts of Butterworth, Nqamakwe, and Tsomo, an area that became known as 'Fingoland' (Mayer 1980, Bundy 1988, De Wet and Whisson 1997).

Loss of land increasingly strained the traditional way of life of the Xhosa people. According to Peires (1981), from about 1835 onwards, part of the Xhosa nation was forced to adopt new life styles to survive, mainly as workers in the rural economy of the Eastern Cape. Soon after *Mlanjeni*'s War, lung sickness, a lethal cattle disease originating in Europe, affected the Xhosa herds, and some chiefdoms lost more than 80% of their animals (Peires 1981, Mostert 1992). Four years later, the Xhosa nation was subjected to another shock in the form of the 'great cattle killing' of 1857. This event, described in detail by Peires (1989) and Crampton (2004), was triggered by the prophecy of Nongqawuse, a young African woman who called for a national cleansing ritual to rid the land of the white intruders and bring back the days of yore. Her prophecy demanded the killing of cattle and the destruction of homesteads and granaries. About 400,000 cattle, nearly a third of the entire Xhosa herd, were destroyed within a few months, and a massive famine followed. Within a year an estimated 40,000 Xhosa people had died of starvation, and another 33,000 had left their land and moved into the Cape Colony to become labourers on farms and villages (Thompson 1993, Crampton 2004, Switzer 1993, Peires 1989). The loss of land and cattle, the two pillars of the Xhosa farming system, fundamentally upset the traditional subsistence system and forced them to modify their way of life in order to survive. The drastic reduction in the resident population that ensued from this was used by the colonial state to confiscate land in the Ciskeian region.

Beinart (2003: 335) sums up the situation after the completion of colonial conquest at the end of the 19th century as follows:

> Black people in the Eastern Cape had only access to land in three areas. The Transkei, heart of the pre-colonial Xhosa chiefdoms, was governed by the Transkeian

Territories General Council. A second area, the Ciskei, where conquest had deprived the Xhosa chiefdoms of their land, consisted of smaller reserves, mission stations and African-owned farms, scattered with white-owned land. The Ciskei included two large districts occupied by Africans, namely Herschel and Glen Grey. A Chief Native Commissioner administered the Ciskei. A third area where Africans were living was on white owned farms in the Eastern Cape where they had limited access to land and livestock as tenants.

## Transformation of African agriculture, 1860-1925: Commodity production and social differentiation

The influx of white settlers, missionaries and the presence of traders brought new technology to southern Africa. The metal hoe and the animal-drawn plough constituted important technical innovations for African agriculture in the Eastern Cape (Bundy 1988, Soga 1931). Compared to cultivating land using digging sticks, women equipped with metal hoes went about the task much more quickly, enabling larger areas of land to be cultivated. The capacity to increase cultivation was further enhanced by the introduction of the ox-drawn plough. Sheep for the production of wool were brought in as were new crops including wheat, oats, barley and potatoes (Mayer 1980, Bundy 1988). Production of these new commodities was mainly market-oriented and not for home consumption, in contrast to the indigenous crops and cattle, and their exchange involved money, not barter goods.

Up to the mid-1850s, investments in arable production or sheep farming were not yet significant in many Mfengu and Xhosa communities (Lewis 1984). Drawing on census data obtained in 1854 for Peddie, Victoria East, Tyumie and Fort Beaufort Lewis (1984) pointed out that ownership and use of ploughs, wagons and sheep was not widespread. At that time, the majority was still engaged in digging stick or hoe cultivation, and any expansion of agricultural production was mainly the result of the cultivation of larger areas and new land. The only areas where cultivation had overtaken pastoralism in relative importance were found around mission stations. Besides introducing Christianity, the missionaries preached of progress to be achieved through investment in agriculture. Monica Wilson (1975) associated the emergence of African peasant communities in the region with the establishment of missionary stations and missionary education. The Mfengu, and a Khoi settlement in the Kat River Valley were the two groups of African producers in the Eastern Cape that most readily adopted new technology and the marketing of farm produce (Bundy 1988). Indeed, the influence of the missionaries on the Mfengu and the Khoi in the Kat River may explain why these two groups were the earliest innovators (Ranger 1978, M. Wilson 1975). However, Lewis (1984) pointed out that the mission settlements were not entirely composed of Mfengu, but rather had mixed populations with many Xhosa absorbed into them.

Trade between Africans and the Colony was not new. Hesitant at first, markets where Africans exchanged ivory and hides for European products, such as beads and metal implements, had evolved into regular events by the 1830s, but this primarily involved barter trade (Hammond-Tooke 1993).

Lewis (1984) argued that the Mfengu in particular began to respond to colonial policies to create conditions under which they and the Xhosa who did not participate in the cleansing could meet the needs of the starving Xhosa after the 'Great Cattle Killing'. The colonial government employed this strategy to avoid having to pay for relief food. Either food would be purchased or families would be forced onto the colonial labour market. Thus, the cattle killing created a unique market for food, and the starving Xhosa were prepared to pay extraordinary prices for grain. Lewis (1984: 10-12) argued that most of the 4,462 households in the key Mfengu areas participated in commodity production. He noted that

> ... the small number of producers capable of producing on a large scale, and the large amount of grain delivered in small quantities of between 10 and 180 lbs reinforces the conclusion that many producers were in fact involved in creating the overall result depicted in the market returns.

The cattle killing triggered commodity production among the so-called non-believers. After the 1850s commodity production began to expand gradually.

Following the establishment of a colonial administration, African homesteads became subject to taxation. The Mfengu were the first to start paying a 'hut tax' in 1848 (Switzer 1993). Paying the taxes represented an important incentive to commoditise production, although the income derived from the marketable surplus was often just enough to pay the 'hut tax'. By selling part of the grain they needed for subsistence African homesteads were left with only two options – engage in wage labour to earn money to repurchase grain or accept declining levels of home consumption. Indebtedness to traders and extractions by headmen and chiefs for providing access to land and other services also may explain why commodity sales gradually expanded. The sale of wool became a popular way to generate cash for taxes and eventually for purchasing goods such as clothing, implements and furniture.

Many sources confirm that the transformation of black farming occurred during the 1860s in the Ciskei but took place much later in other parts of the Eastern Cape (Lewis 1984, Bundy 1988, Beinart 1980, 1982, Switzer 1993). As part of these transformations black farmers made considerable adaptations to their farming systems to benefit from the new opportunities the markets provided and in fact managed to compete with white farmers.

Socially, the gradual expansion of commodity production was an unequal process. Some households were able to expand total production by way of ownership of ploughs and oxen, large families to provide sufficient labour and political power to ensure access to land of good quality. The majority who lacked these advantages were not able to do so. Thus, as Lewis (1984) pointed out, the dominance of a few households. Using census data he established that the 25% best resourced households controlled almost 57% of the cultivated land, while the poorest 25% accounted for only 5.5%. The social differentiation already present in pre-colonial Xhosa society contributed to these differences in the ability of individual households to participate in commodity production. Yet, by the 1860s, most households in the Ciskei region were dependent on agricultural production for the generation of cash, which had become an indispensable element in the economy of the homestead. The majority of Africans were caught in a downward spiral of impoverishment because participation in the market economy often meant giving up what was necessary for subsistence. They had no other alternative than to supplement their meagre incomes from farming by rendering services to wealthier Africans and whites. Shepherding, shearing, and wagon-driving offered opportunities for temporary off-farm employment. Furthermore, the ability of large numbers of poor African homesteads to subsist as farmers on limited areas of land was possible because they had limited wants, food security being their main concern, and they continued the old traditions of sharing and collaboration among members of homesteads, particularly among the Xhosa (Bundy 1988). However, Lewis (1984) pointed out that as commodity production expanded and the importance of cultivation increased, households became increasingly individualised. This was particularly so in the Mfengu settlements where the homestead structure was not as strong as among the Xhosa. Cultivation also increased the importance of private ownership of ploughs and oxen.

The second half of the 19th century also saw the emergence of a group of landless Africans who survived by selling their labour to white farmers, or seeking urban employment, and consequently settled around towns such as East London and Grahamstown in what were to become African 'locations' (Mayer 1980, Peires 1981). Bundy (1988) referred to this process as a sequence of *'peasantisation'* succeeded by *'de-peasantisation'* and *'proletarianisation'* in the Ciskei and Transkei – but not, as Ranger (1978: 106) pointed out, "a relentless overall movement from peasant to proletarian". Comaroff and Comaroff (1990) characterised this process as *'peasantrisation'*, aptly expressing that the process of labour migration not necessarily implied the complete cutting of ties with the rural communities. This book advances rather similar conclusions.

During the19th century social differentiation increased in the Eastern Cape. Even among the Xhosa relatively wealthy peasants constituted a small minority. Economic differentiation was strongly associated with the ownership of ploughs, the ability to mobilise labour and the ownership of sheep and cattle. The pattern of differentiation based on ploughs and cattle gradually had shifted to revolving on wages, as we will see later in the chapter.

The nature of farming had also begun to change with the digging stick replaced by the hoe and later oxen-drawn plough, and the expansion of markets. Moreover, territorial expansion allowed the opening of new lands for cultivation which increased productivity substantially. These new fields had higher organic matter and were more fertile and resistant to erosion.

## Rural resistance

When the chiefdoms at the frontier were faced with a novel and critical threat, two contrasting responses, of accommodation and resistance emerged, the 'Red' and the 'School'. Mayer (1961, 1980) pointed out that among the Xhosa social identity and ideology of resistance emerged as two contrasting responses to the increasingly intensified contacts with whites, modern colonial society and above all, Christianity.

'Red' expressed an identity and an ideology of resistance to colonialism and life styles associated with whites and modernity. The 'School' identity, in contrast, is an ideology of accommodating and embracing modern life styles which came about from incorporation into and association with colonial society dominated by whites and continuous attempts of the colonial state to co-opt and Christianise black people. The 'Red' way of life (*ubuqaba*) is a folk culture that dwells on unhappy experiences with the white men (*abelungu*) and the black Christians (*amagqoboka*). It was, as Mayer (1980: 5) put it,

> ... the acts of deception, cruelty and greed by the Whites, and treachery by the converts who allied themselves with the Whites, that made them adhere to the moral teaching of their own religion. The ancestor religion which had supported patterns of relations internal to Nguni society came to play a part in a self-conscious ideology of resistance.

Essential to Red folk culture is that it is embedded in the various stages of socialisation and growing up. Childhood and early adolescence is generally spent by herding stock. Ancestral religion and respect for parental authority is firmly rooted as is a keen interest in livestock, fighting and beer drinking (O'Connel 1980).

At the time the Nguni people made contact with Europeans, their society generally favoured a disposition of resistance. The Xhosa who fought the white invaders resisted Christianity, which was to them a subversive ideology. However, other Nguni groups, like the Mfengu, with a history of displacement showed a much greater aptitude for and readiness to assimilate western cultural elements (Mayer 1980, Hammond-Tooke 1993). It was the Mfengu who were settled on land in the Amatola Mountains (chapter 4). However, at the time not all Mfengu accepted the new religion, nor did all Xhosa resist it. Mayer (1980) estimated that in 1912 half of the Mfengu were professing Christians.

The state-sponsored settlement of the Mfengu and the 'cattle killing' of the Xhosa are considered to be turning points in the process of the incorporation of the two peoples in the colonial economy and in their exposure to white ideologies. An ideological offensive by the colonial state coincided with the period of disaster for the Xhosa. Loss of territory and later, the 'cattle killing' occurred during a period of a close alliance between the state and the missionaries (Switzer 1993). The state pressed ahead with a policy of disintegrating the pre-colonial structures in the name of assimilation. Substantial efforts were made to concentrate people in villages, some of them, such as Koloni, were near to or on mission stations. Widening opportunities for black education, particularly for the Xhosa in *British Kaffraria,* created conditions in which the School culture began to develop into a distinct lifestyle. In contrast, in most of the Transkei the power of the chiefs was not undermined to the same degree, and educational opportunities were not as widespread. Such conditions allowed the Red ideology to prosper.

An ideological split in the attitude of missionaries towards assimilation occurred at the time when large numbers of Xhosa were forced into economic dependence on whites. The cleavage revolved around assimilation through education and adoption of western values ('creating a black elite') and the fear of a policy of assimilation confining blacks, Christians and 'pagans' alike, to their role as humble cultivators, farm workers and migrant labourers. Racist notions slowly overtook these rather humanistic views. After black peasants were no longer restrained in their attempt to engage in market production few homesteads in any one location could hope to rise above poverty. Mayer (1980) pointed out that a state of equilibrium ensued between the School and the Red people so that each was able to develop and maintain its own folk culture, even in the Ciskei where white towns were never far away. The migrant labour system, so characteristic for southern Africa, did not dramatically change this equilibrium. In the many phases of labour migrancy, the Red and School distinction was reproduced over time, as is reflected in the different ways the Red and School Xhosa perceived the nature of their ties with their rural communities as migrant labourers. Mayer (1961) predicted a decline of the Red folk culture, but Bank (1999) argued that Mayer greatly underestimated the resilience of this culture in towns. He showed that the Red cultural form initially declined during the 1980s but was later actively reconstructed as an urban resistance ideology.

## Agricultural development in the reserves

During the last decade of the 19th century a complex set of factors worked together to fundamentally reshape rural livelihoods of African people and particularly the role of agriculture (Bundy 1988, Mayer 1980). Effectively, the so-called native areas to which black people became confined over the years because of racial segregation policies of successive governments were gradually reshaped into labour reserves. Native reserves were those areas identified by the Land Act of 1913 and the Land and Trust Act of 1936 that were set aside for black people. Land ownership by black people was largely restricted to these areas. This has contributed to the situation in most parts of the Ciskei and western Transkei that by the late 1950s African farming with its limited prosperity had declined substantially. Instead, a vicious circle of overpopulation, deterioration of natural resources, migration and impoverishment was increasingly manifesting itself. Switzer (1993) characterised this as the 'underdevelopment' of the African reserves.

The discovery of diamonds (1867) and gold (1880) in South Africa marked the emergence of the mining sector in the country. This had a profound impact on the agricultural sector (Wilson 1975). State revenue from the mines was spent to develop the commercialisation of white farming, creating economic conditions that encouraged white farmers to abandon the practice of keeping peasant squatters on their farms in favour of the development of their farms for crop production. For this, they sought access and control over a permanent work force and the removal from their farms of African families who occupied plots or had land use rights obtained by payment of rent, sharecropping arrangements, or labour tenancy (Bundy 1988).

The mining and white agricultural sectors held considerable political power in South Africa, and together they encouraged the promulgation of legislation, which served their respective purposes for the control over African labour (Seekings and Nattrass 2006). One set of legislation aimed at denying Africans access to white-owned land by prohibiting different forms of tenancy with farm owners. Various anti-squatting laws culminated in the Natives Land Act No. 27 of 1913, which was the initial legislative enactment embodying the principles of territorial segregation and separation of land rights between natives (Africans) and non-natives. A second set of legislation aimed at limiting the amount of land Africans could hold. An early example of such a legislative enactment was the Glen Grey Act (Cape Act No. 25 of 1894), which introduced the "one man one plot" principle and was extended to include the Ciskei and Transkei areas. Limiting the size of plots ensured that landholders had to seek additional income off-farm and making the plots indivisible destined all but the eldest son of the landowner to find off-farm livelihoods (Yawitch 1981, Switzer 1993, Maree and de Vos 1975). Raising taxes also served to increase the need for cash among rural Africans, augmenting the pressure on them to sell their labour to meet tax obligations (Lewis 1984, Bundy 1988, Switzer 1993).

Until the early 20th century, the state had only actively intervened to address access to land and labour. After the establishment of the Union of South Africa in 1910, the state started to support white-dominated agriculture more aggressively. Mbongwa *et al.* (1996) pointed out that between 1910 and 1935, 87 acts were passed to legitimise the provision of state support to white farmers. These policies intervened in the pricing of agricultural commodities to raise them well above competition level, assisted poorer whites in their attempt to rationalise their enterprises economically, and provided agricultural credit. Cooperatives were formed and railway extensions, which largely bypassed black farming areas, were constructed. The state introduced an agricultural expert system through the establishment of a National Department of Agriculture in 1924 and agricultural colleges and research stations (F Wilson 1975, Beinart 2003).

The Commission for the Socio-Economic Development of the Bantu Areas within the Union of South Africa (also known as the Tomlinson Report published in 1955) commented that various commissions had reported on "destructive agricultural methods and their recommendations to teach the native to use their land efficiently". The Report narrated that the "first Bantu agricultural school was only founded in 1905 (in the Transkei) and a special technical agricultural service in the Native Affairs Department – the Native Agricultural and Lands Branch – was only brought into being in 1929". Experimental farms and training colleges were established at Elsenburg in 1917 in the Western Cape, Cedara in Natal, Fort Cox Agricultural College (early 1930s) in the Ciskei and Tsolo Agricultural College in the Transkei.

*Economic change in the reserves*
During the early years of the 20th century the Transkei and Ciskei received a multitude of economic refugees who had left white farms when their existing tenancy arrangements ended. This influx increased the population of these territories, raising pressure on the available natural resources. Marginal land was taken into cultivation and pressure on the available rangelands increased (Bundy 1988, Switzer 1993). This overcrowding reduced the capacity of the natural resources to buffer the effects of adverse conditions. As a result, the vulnerability of farmers to droughts and other disasters increased, forcing them into debt, and limiting their ability to cope and continue their rural existence. This rather gloomy picture is acknowledged and made evident by the Lansdown Commission based on a series of official investigations in the mid-1940s. The Commission painted a far from idyllic picture of living conditions in the reserve. The Commission found evidence of overpopulation relative to production in the reserves, resulting in widespread malnutrition and dependence on migrant remittances (Seekings and Nattrass 2006). These and other reports pointed at the myth of subsistence in the reserves.

One of the reasons was the role that wages and salaries had begun to play in rural homesteads' ability to earn a living. The possibilities to access these sources of income was primarily based on education and skills (in the case of salaries) and/or provided only access to low-paid and low-skilled employment on white farms and mines. Thus the pattern of social differentiation in previous conjunctures primarily based on land, labour and cattle ownership nevertheless set out to revolve on wages and salaries which also sharpened social inequalities in the reserves. Houghton and Walton (1952) reported based on an income and expenditure survey held in Keiskammahoek in the late 1940s not only on the state of poverty so characteristic of the reserves. Their findings also showed a high degree of social differentiation of inequality. The average family had four head of cattle, seven sheep and a few goats. But one in three had no cattle; fewer than one in three had six or more head of cattle. The typical well-to-do homestead was headed by a teacher who received a salary that was six times more than the average household income. The homestead head employed a

herdboy to take care of the cattle. The average homestead relied for their livelihood on remittances from two to three family members in town. The typical
poor homestead was headed by a widow and had almost no income. The older
children who had migrated to town remitted to their rural homes, but significantly less money than on average. These poor homesteads were heavily indebted and relied on neighbours to supplement the meagre old age pensions.

Macro-economically, importation of cheap maize and wheat from America
deflated the prices of these commodities. Moreover, the commercialisation of
white agriculture was accompanied by a shift from livestock to crop production,
adding to the overall supply of grains. Contrary to their white counterparts
whose access to markets improved by the development of South Africa's railway system, African producers continued to rely on wagons and sledges to
transport their goods from farm to trader, and from trader to market. These
unfavourable economic conditions discouraged the marketing of small amounts
of grain by a multitude of peasants, and consequently the importance of African
farmers as suppliers of grains declined (Bundy 1988). In many rural areas
inhabited by African people, the local trader was the only practical outlet to
dispose of agricultural produce and to purchase inputs and household utensils
(Bundy 1988, Switzer 1993). Remoteness, reliance on a single marketing chan-
nel and lack of bargaining power disadvantaged African farmers in two ways:
they received low prices for their commodities, and paid dearly for their purchases.

Thus, during the last two decades of the 19th century the majority of rural
African homesteads lost their ability to maintain a rural life style based essentially on agriculture. From that time onwards, they had to increasingly supplement their declining agricultural production with income from wages. The
decline of African agriculture, the increasing levels of poverty among rural
Africans, and the changes in their livelihood strategies that characterised this
period are illustrated in Tables 2.1, 2.2 and 2.3, and Figure 2.1.

Table 2.1 shows that income derived by African farmers in Victoria East
from sales of agricultural products in 1925 was just about half of the income
earned in 1875, mainly because of a decline in the sales of wool and grain. One
explanation for the reduction in wool sales by African farmers between 1875
and 1925 may be that part of the available grazing land was converted to crop-
land. The reduction in income from grain sales suggests a re-orientation of crop
production from market-oriented to home consumption.

From 1875 to 1925, the African population of Victoria East increased from
6,900 to 15,800. This increase of 129% over a period of 50 years must have
been partly due to migration of African people into the district. During this
same period annual *per capita* cash-income declined considerably, from £3.05
to £1.27.

*Table 2.1*     Sales of agricultural produce by African producers in the Magisterial District of Victoria East in 1875 and 1925

| Sales of agricultural produce | 1875 | 1925 | Change (%) |
|---|---|---|---|
| Wool (£) | 12,541 | 6,471 | - 48.4 |
| Hides, skins and horns (£) | 2,457 | 1,728 | - 29.7 |
| Grains (£) | 4,275 | 2,177 | - 49.1 |
| Total (£) | 19,273 | 10,376 | - 46.2 |

*Source*: Adapted from Bundy (1988: 223) and Switzer (1993: 239)

*Table 2.2*     Income per capita in the Magisterial District of Victoria East in 1875 and 1925

| Income category | Annual income per capita in 1875 | | Annual income per capita in 1925 | |
|---|---|---|---|---|
| | Value (£) | % | Value (£) | % |
| Agriculture | 2.79 | 91.5 | 0.66 | 52.0 |
| Other | 0.26 | 8.5 | 0.61 | 48.0 |
| Total | 3.05 | 100.0 | 1.27 | 100.0 |

*Source*: Adapted from Bundy (1988: 223)

Further, the importance of agriculture as a source of income declined from more than 90% of cash income in 1875 to only about 50% by 1925, indicating that other sources of income were becoming increasingly important.

Table 2.2 shows that in 1875 rural Africans in Victoria East paid for 91.5% of income was from agriculture. At that time, only 20.4% of the value of these purchases consisted of food and groceries, whilst 56.9% were spent on clothing and blankets, and 22.7% on farm implements, furniture and other durable goods (Table 2.3).

In 1925, the proportion of expenditure spent on food and groceries had increased to 63.6%. On the other hand, expenditure on clothing and durable goods, both indicators of wealth, had declined to 23.9% and 12.5% respectively. In 1925, per capita expenditure on clothing and blankets had dropped to 17% of its 1875 level, and that on durable goods to 23% of what it was in 1875. Per capita expenditure on food was the only expenditure category that showed an increase in absolute terms. This does not suggest that in 1925 Africans were eating more or better than in 1875. Rather it indicates that, as a group, Africans in Victoria East had lost part of the capacity they had in 1875 to provide for their own food requirements. The data also clearly show an ongoing process of impoverishment of African people in the District between 1875 and 1925.

*Table 2.3*    Expenditure patterns of African people in the Magisterial District of Victoria East in 1875 and 1925: Total value and *per capita* expenditure

| Expenditure category | Annual expenditure (£) | | | | | |
| --- | --- | --- | --- | --- | --- | --- |
| | 1875 | | | 1925 | | |
| | Per capita | Total value | (%) | Per capita | Total value | (%) |
| Clothing (mainly blankets) | 1.74 | 12,000 | 56.9 | 0.30 | 4,792 | 23.9 |
| Durable goods | 0.69 | 15,784 | 22.7 | 0.16 | 2,508 | 12.5 |
| Food | 0.62 | 4,289 | 20.4 | 0.81 | 12,748 | 63.6 |
| Total | 3.05 | 34,073 | 100.0 | 1.27 | 20,048 | 100.0 |

*Source*: Adapted from Bundy (1988: 223)

The decline in African homestead production is partly explained by the increase in landlessness, which stood at approx. 20% in 1875, and about 25% in 1925 (Bundy 1988) and partly by the 53.3% reduction in the area of land per person, brought about by the increase in number of people with access to land from 5,600 in 1875 to 12,000 in 1925. The third cause, not necessarily substantiated by facts and figures, was the exhaustion and degradation of the natural resource, brought about by the change in land use during the second half of the 19th century (Beinart 2003, F. Wilson 1975). Switzer (1993) pointed out that only about 20% of the Ciskei was deemed arable. Already early in 20th century inhabitants of the reserves were no longer able to feed themselves from their own agricultural production. Simkins (1981) argued that this situation was prevalent as early as 1918 in the Ciskei. He reported that in 1927 Africans there produced only 25-50% of their own food requirements and in the Transkei between 50% and 75%. In 1960 this had declined further to less than 25% in the Ciskei and to less than 50% in most districts of the Transkei.

Engagement in the emerging male migrant labour system was one of the main avenues by which rural African households found new sources of income, and such labour increased in importance steadily. Figure 2.1 illustrates this trend from 1893 to 1916 for the Transkei. Unfortunately, data for the Ciskei are not available, but it may be assumed that labour migration followed a similar pattern.

Bundy (1988) showed that annual fluctuations in labour migration from the African areas were linked to agricultural crop production which fluctuated from year to year. Besides, most such production was consumed before it reached the market. Bad years brought about by drought or epidemics affecting the health of livestock and caused labour migration to peak. The opposite occurred during good years. As was indicated earlier, rural African society in the Eastern Cape consisted of a small number of relatively wealthy peasants, a larger number of poor peasants, and a group of landless people. Next to the landless, the poor peasants were economically most vulnerable and the first to be forced into migrant labour.

Interestingly, the wealthier among the peasantry, who during the period 1840 to 1880 had invested in agriculture, by buying land, implements, livestock, and wagons for transport. They also began to re-orient their investments to the education of their children, confirming that at the dawn of the 20th century, farming had lost much of its attractiveness as a livelihood option for African people.

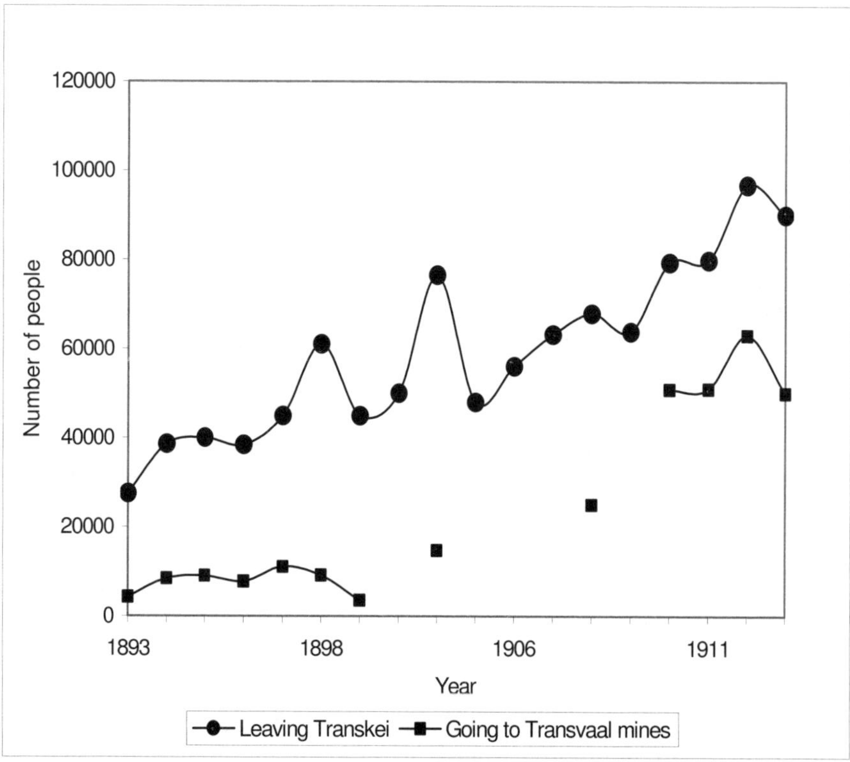


*Figure 2.1*    Trends in labour migration from Transkei, 1893-1916

*Source*: Adapted from Bundy (1988: 223)

### Agricultural change in the reserves

The migrant labour system encouraged the recruitment of male Africans in their prime, and housed them in compounds, also called hostels. The families of miners and urban workers remained in the African territories, and when these workers were too old or sick for the hard work in the mines they returned to their rural homes. Initially, the objective of the system was to avoid upward pressure on wages, as was the case in many western industrialising nations, where an urban proletariat was established. When women started to join the labour migration from the 1930s onwards (Switzer 1993), encouraging the development of urbanised Africans, the objective changed. The new aim was to expel all non-whites, especially Africans who were not gainfully employed, from declared whites-only parts of South Africa, and place them into one of the native reserves, later referred to as homelands. Labour passes were issued to Africans employed in white areas, and a massive control system was established to enforce the pass laws. During the mid-1970s, at the height of the government's labour and influx control effort, the maintenance of this system consumed 14% of the national budget (Switzer 1993). On white-owned farms conditions also changed. Mechanisation reduced the need for labour, causing a surplus of people on farms (Marcus 1989).

On the question of when exactly agricultural declined in the homelands, Simkins (1981) argued that total agricultural production (valued at constant prices) in South Africa's reserves did not fall over the period 1918-1965. However, output *per capita* dropped from 111 in the mid-1920s to 99 in the late 1920s to 100 in 1946 (indexed as 100) and further to 67 towards the end of the mid-1960s. One must locate in contrast to what Wilson (1975) had argued, Simkins continued, that "the really dramatic decline in production *per capita* occurred in the period after 1948 rather than before that date" (Simkins 1981: 263). Knight and Lenta (1981) calculated that production *per capita* fell steadily during the 1920-1970 period. This happened despite an increase in capital equipment, and this fits with the argument that labour was substituted rather than land. Rising taxes and land rents and increasing competition from white farmers contributed to the decline.

The migrant labour system and the restriction of movements to urban areas led to increased population pressure on the natural resources in the African areas. For example, the population of the Transkei increased from 640,000 in 1891 to 870,000 in 1911 (Stuart and Malcolm 1986) 1,202,200 in 1951 (Tomlinson Commission 1955), 1,961,300 in 1970, 2,621,000 in 1980 (Switzer 1993) and 3,527,700 in 1991 (Transkei Land Reform Research Group 1995). Chapter 10 provides demographic data for the Ciskei demonstrating a similar trend. Such an increase occurred without a substantial enlargement of the total area in the reserves, thus substantially increasing the human density and pressure on the land. Knight and Lenta (1981) underscored this trend with data indicating that in 1913 the density in the reserves averaged 5 ha per person. This density had further increased to 2.1 ha per person in 1970. Table 2.4 sheds another light on the density figures by pointing out the distribution of arable land for the years 1968 and 1970 for the Transkei and Ciskei, respectively. Homesteads with access to less than 5.2 ha comprised 98% of the total. At the time, agricultural experts calculated that homesteads in King William's Town district required between 5 and 7.5 ha to make a living from agriculture (Maree and de Vos 1975). Beinart (2003) commented that through the second half of the 20th century an increasing rural population eked out a living with more intensive techniques, especially the use of ploughs, on declining areas of land. It should come as no surprise that during the 20th century the livelihoods of rural African households became increasingly dependent on sources of income other than agriculture, with remittances from migrant workers and later on social pension schemes being the most important.

As the duration of mine contracts increased from the initial 3 to 6 months to 12 and 14 months, those who remained behind, namely women, children and the elderly did the farming. Earlier it was shown that gender roles in African agriculture changed in response to colonisation, the adoption of the plough, and the transformation of agriculture from subsistence to partially commercial. These processes had encouraged the entry of males in crop production. The migrant labour system shifted the bulk of the workload in agriculture back to women.

*Table 2.4*    Arable land per homestead in selected districts of the Ciskei and Transkei, 1970 and 1968

| Land size categories (ha) | Ciskei (1970) | | | Transkei (1968) | | |
|---|---|---|---|---|---|---|
| | Victoria East (%) | Middle-drift (%) | Total (ha) | Bizana (%) | Kentani (%) | Total (%) |
| No land | 47.38 | 18.23 | 32.95 | 18.02 | 8.97 | 13.91 |
| 0.4-0.8 | 3.04 | 4.56 | 3.79 | 7.71 | 2.02 | 5.13 |
| 1.2-1.6 | 7.32 | 19.2 | 13.21 | 27.91 | 17.44 | 23.51 |
| 2.0-2.4 | 10.37 | 35.20 | 22.67 | 22.63 | 29.54 | 26.76 |
| 2.8-3.2 | 26.74 | 18.62 | 22.72 | 10.48 | 19.96 | 14.78 |
| 3.6-4.0 | 1.43 | 1.65 | 1.53 | 10.73 | 14.11 | 12.27 |
| 4.4-4.8 | 1.14 | 0.87 | 1.01 | 1.01 | 3.73 | 2.24 |
| 5.2-5.6 | 0.29 | 0.29 | 0.29 | 0.42 | 0.70 | 0.55 |
| 6.0-6.4 | 1.62 | 0.77 | 1.20 | 0.59 | 1.61 | 1.06 |
| 6.8-8.0 | 0.00 | 0.39 | 0.19 | 0.08 | 1.40 | 0.68 |
| 8.4-10.0 | 0.67 | 0.10 | 0.38 | 0.17 | 0.20 | 0.18 |
| 10.4-12.0 | 0.00 | 0.10 | 0.05 | 0.00 | 0.10 | 0.05 |
| 12.4-14.0 | 0.00 | 0.00 | 0.00 | 0.00 | 0.20 | 0.09 |
| 14.4-18.0 | 0.00 | 0.00 | 0.00 | 0.25 | 0.00 | 0.14 |
| total | 100.0 | 100.0 | 100.0 | 100.0 | 100.0 | 100.0 |

*Source*: Maree and de Vos (1975: 27)

A reduction in availability of male labour led to a reduction in labour-intensive crops (such as sorghum, that requires scaring off birds) in favour of crops such as maize that also required labour but at more widely spaced intervals (Beinart 1980).

A pattern of extensive mixed cropping had emerged since the early years of the 20th century whereby maize was intercropped with pumpkins, beans and sweet potatoes. A larger area could be ploughed, for there was no need for the daily presence of labour in the field, except during planting, weeding and harvesting. Communal working parties were frequently organised to do the work (McAllister 2001, Kuckertz 1985). Ploughs and draught oxen were critical to sustain the system of work, and ownership became widespread. Beinart (1980: 88) suggested that in Pondoland the total and *per capita* output of crops increased during the decades when mass migrancy became institutionalised. Livestock production showed similar patterns. This trend may have been due to migrants investing part of their wages into agriculture. The oral histories collected in Guquka and Koloni suggest a similar pattern in the rural Ciskei (chapter 4).

Today, in contrast, land use can be described as under-cultivation. Arable production is limited in both the former Ciskei and Transkei (McAllister 2001, Andrew and Fox 2003, 2004). The extent to which land degradation in the form of nutrient depletion, physical deterioration and erosion of soils contributed to the decline of African agriculture during the last decades of the 19th century and the beginning of the 20th century will probably never be determined. Reports on Victoria East, Herschel, Fingoland and Keiskammahoek, all once examples of successful African farming, not only remarked on the general decline in farming, but also on the desiccated and degraded appearance of the landscape (Start and Malcolm 1986, Switzer 1993). According to Bundy (1988), the Native Economic Commission of 1932 described the desolation as a descent of the reserves at a rapid pace towards desert conditions, and said that the process of ruination threatened to produce an appalling problem of native poverty. There is growing evidence that much of the hill-slope erosion occurring in the African areas of the Eastern Cape is associated with cultivation (Scogings *et al.* 2000), and that a lot of the more severe forms of erosion already scarred many local landscapes by the 1930s (Beinart 1984, 2003, Coleman n.d.).

## Migrancy and social transformation

Labour migration brought about a complex set of interlocking processes of social and economic change. In the first place, rural life increasingly depended on the wages of migrants. Secondly, migration reshaped the existing power relations within the homestead. Thirdly, labour migration also affected and transformed agriculture. Finally, migration patterns changed dramatically over the years.

*Rural ties*

The system of labour migration created conditions whereby generally, the men in the productive age group 15-45, migrated to towns. Furthermore, it was expected of this generation that they would make themselves available for such migrant labour. Most homesteads in the Ciskei and Transkei had at least one male migrant. The labour migrant system did not end the ties between migrants and their rural communities nor cause a clear-cut separation from the land. On the contrary, migrants transferred part of their wages to their rural villages in the form of remittances to sustain homestead consumption and production. Various sources underscore that rural and agricultural production was not enough to meet daily food needs. Migrants' remittances were spent on purchasing supplementary foodstuffs on the nearby rural and urban markets (McAllister 1980, 2001, Beinart 1980, 1982). Migrants also set money aside to purchase cattle or to invest in crop production (Sharp and Spiegel 1990, chapter 4).

Moreover, initially wage labour in town was for the migrant an attempt, as one migrant expressed it, to

> ... get enough to get back to what is important for me ... I grew up on the land and then I worked here at different places to earn money to plant and to build up my farm. Later that all changed and I had to work here to earn a living and I lost sight of the land (quoted in Minkley 1992: 752).

This quotation signifies the changes in labour migration but also that remittances were mainly initially invested into rural and agricultural production at the homestead. This is in contrast to the present-day patterns.

Research in East-London by Mayer (1961) and Bank (1999) demonstrated on that the 'Red' and 'School' ideologies are relevant metaphors for investigating the heterogeneous nature of urban-rural ties. The 'Red' migrant was generally inclined to save as much as possible from his wages to send to his homestead with a view to sustain his homestead or to build his own. The 'School' migrant, in contrast, was less oriented to transfer money to the rural homestead and more induced to use his earnings in order to make life in town bearable. Bank (1999) reported, for instance, on conflicts between 'Red' and 'School' migrants in the migrant hostels about the quality of food and the frequency of eating meat. 'Red' and 'School' people in this way signify the differentiated nature in the way migrants maintained ties with their rural roots. A 'School' migrant opted for an urban-based livelihood. A 'Red' migrant sought ways to retain his rural ties, visiting the rural home as often as possible to protect his interests.

McAllister (1980, 2001) showed that the returning migrant is culturally embedded and actively participates in various rituals to celebrate his visit or return home. Beer parties represent 'rituals of labour migration' to be understood as *rites de passage*. 'Building the homestead' is an activity that relies primarily on migrant earnings, and this activity is clearly associated with the ancestor belief system. The ritualisation of labour migration and the perceived interest of the ancestral shades in their descendents' migratory ventures are partly traced to the role of such earnings in building the homestead. A visiting or returning migrant would pay respect to the ancestors and bring gifts for people.

*Social change in the homestead*
Migration also reshaped power relations within the homestead as tensions emerged over the control of resources. The balance of power and decision-making gradually shifted from the homestead head to the sons. By accessing and controlling cash through migrant work younger men became increasingly responsible for replacing stock and for earning their own *lobola*. The continued importance of *lobola* helped to ensure that wages were brought home and circulated in the villages. Beinart (1980) and others maintained that both fathers and sons had an interest in keeping the wages at home, but who would control this? The tensions frequently took the form of sons and brothers leaving their homestead and building their own at a stage earlier than was formerly the case. Sons were no longer dependent as before on their fathers, for they could obtain what they needed by purchase. A decline in the incidence of polygamous home-steads underlined the decline in the size of the homestead (Beinart 1980). This change was not a sudden process and did not occur in one generation. New technology, combined with wages, gradually enabled a smaller family unit to survive. Such changes radically transformed the position of the migrant in the family. As a migrant established his own homestead – and he would often have to continue migrating once he had done so – he would become both homestead head and migrant. His son(s) in turn may have gone out to work while he stayed at home, but they would move off, perhaps before his death (Beinart 1980).

The absence of so many men working in town and the mines also affected the gender division of labour within the homestead and gave women more room for manoeuvre. Minkley (1992) argued that the frequent return of labourers back to the rural areas and subsequent re-entry in urban jobs were attempts to control 'the women', on whom their power and access to the rural areas rested to a significant degree. Women were resented and bemoaned as "they made life more difficult", and increasingly "they refused to listen". An answer seemingly lay in the assertion of patriarchal control through wage labour (in order to re-assert production and control in the rural areas) and ironically, its avoidance, on a regular and systematic basis in order to retain 'manliness' and not become 'urbanised'. Sharp and Spiegel (1990) expand in detail on the phrase that "women refused to listen". Married men bitterly opposed their wives engaging in most kinds of local income-generating activity such as running '*shebeens*' (selling liquor), an attractive source of income, easily accessible and convenient as it can simply be combined with domestic work. Women also argued that they had more discretion over income from *shebeens* than from remittances. The condemnation by men of this business did not extend to all such activities. A 'good wife' was the woman who diligently invested a portion of her husband's remittances, along with her own labour, in crop production for domestic use and sale. Wives were meant to contribute to building the homestead as a rural resource base for retirement. Recognition gained ground on the men's part that their wives would use some of the returns from cultivation to generate a cash income in a variety of ways. For example, brewing beer from a small portion of grain was allowed and the cash generated would be their discretionary income.

Interestingly, the fortunes of fathers and elderly people generally changed to their advantage at a later stage when the old age pension schemes widened to include black people as well. The pension system, perhaps unintended, restored the family power structure again in favour of the elderly (Sagner 2000). Independently of their sons, fathers at pension age again gained control of cash resources and might accumulate wealth.

*Changing patterns of migration*
The institutionalisation of Apartheid and the labour pass system and its subsequent abolishment fundamentally altered patterns of migration. The early labour migrant system predominantly entailed the temporary migration of men. Labour controls and the pass system, combined with racial segregation policies at a later stage, institutionalised a system of migrants returning home on an occasional basis and settling back home after retirement. Red and School identities alike were not allowed to emerge in town on a permanent basis, preventing the establishment of an urban identity other than one based on hostel life (Mayer 1961, Bank 1999, 2001, 2002). Similarly, and as important, was that social life in town was generally not based on establishing a family with wives and children in town.

The establishment of the homeland industries as an outcome of state policy to create independent homelands or *Bantustans* also had a clear impact on the nature of migration. The Ciskei was constituted as a homeland which became 'independent' in 1981. Whereas before, employment opportunities were basically situated in white areas (East London, Grahamstown, Cape Town, the Rand mining region), the homeland governments and civil services established industries providing for jobs much closer to the rural villages. In the Ciskei the establishment of the 'capital city' of Bhisho and employment opportunities at the University of Fort Hare in Alice were also significant (Morrow 2006). While the patterns of labour migration to more distant towns and mines continued, and thus men were away for a long period from their homes, migration also took the form of workers commuting on a daily or weekly basis from their rural home to work.

Political changes, notably the abolishment of the labour pass system, the relaxation of many other Apartheid policies, and finally the political defeat of the Apartheid state in 1994, again influenced migration patterns. With the relaxation and finally the abolishment of Apartheid, imposed restrictions on migrations disappeared. This changed the institutionalised pattern of male migration to broaden opportunities for the migration of entire families to the major cities and townships. As we will see in chapter 11, this had a profound impact on the population composition and age and sex distribution in many rural villages in the Ciskei and Transkei including Koloni and Guquka.

## State intervention in the African rural areas

Land degradation in the native areas in the form of soil erosion, land denudation, and the drying-up of springs caught the attention of the South African Government. The 1932 Native Economic Commission called for a development programme to teach Africans how to use their land more economically and to halt resource degradation (Yawitch 1981). The 1936 Native Trust and Land Act No 18 provided the legal framework for government services to begin the reclamation and rehabilitation of the so-called native areas. The Act had two important objectives, namely to address the problem of over-crowding in the native areas by allocating additional land, and to halt or prevent degradation on both old and new land allocations by means of land use (betterment) planning. The South African Native Trust handled the allocation of additional lands and the land concerned became known as Trust land. The key concern of early (1936 to 1950) betterment planning was to protect and rehabilitate the natural resources. Government introduced policies aimed at limiting livestock numbers to address perceived denudation of the rangeland, and engaged in the construction of contour banks in an attempt to prevent soil erosion. Implementation of the planning started in the late 1930s, but was subject to much resistance, thus proceeding rather slowly (Switzer 1993, Mager 1992, 1999, McAllister 1989, De Wet 1987, 1989, Beinart 2003, Hendricks 1989). The African population especially resisted the restrictions on livestock numbers. Chapter 4 describes how betterment was received differently in Guquka and Koloni.

The contestation of the restrictions placed on livestock numbers can be explained by the existing but contrasting views about carrying capacity and on what cattle represents. The limiting of stock numbers and subsequent measures to cull were instigated by scientists and agricultural experts who held that overstocking led to ruining the land and weakening of cattle. The widely used system of *kraaling* among both white and black farmers was seen as a prime example of ignorant farming that led to overgrazing as well as selective grazing. These views emerged during the great drought at the beginning of the 20th century, which brought environmental concerns to the fore within state circles and among the general public (Wilson 1975, Beinart 2003). Such views were also sustained by the idea that communal farming (that is, African farming in contrast to private white farming) entailed an inefficient exploitation of cattle as an economic resource. In the eyes of government officials and experts, the very nature of peasant agriculture seemed destined to trigger environmental or ecological collapse. These views persisted for a long time and fed betterment planning approaches some 20 to 30 years later. The culling of stock was contrary to the 'peasant' logic that sought to accumulate and retain stock as much as possible. For black farmers sheep and wool represented a means for paying their taxes. Recently, researchers have shown that the 'peasant' principle of cattle rearing is embedded in the multiple meanings of cattle. Cattle represents both a consumption (*lobola*, milk, meat, status) and productive (draught power, manure, savings) meaning (Cousins 1996, Lahiff 2000, Shackleton *et al.* 2005). The multiple meaning of cattle is often referred to as the so-called 'cattle complex' (Commaroff and Commaroff 1990, Kuper 1982).

Notwithstanding all this, one cannot ignore degradation and overgrazing. Bundy (1988) for instance talks about gullies because of overgrazing and ploughing. Chapters 7, 8 and 9 will expand on this for Guquka and Koloni.

In 1955, *The Commission for the Socio-Economic Development of the Bantu Areas within the Union of South Africa* headed by Tomlinson (Tomlinson Commission 1955) released its report on the most comprehensive investigation of socio-economic conditions in the native reserves ever. One of its key recommendations was that the rural population needed to be subdivided into a landless group and a group of 'progressive farmers'. The Tomlinson Commission rejected the 'one-man-one-plot' principle of land allocation. Instead, it called for the allocation of land holdings sufficiently large to form an economic farming unit. It also recommended the abolition of communal tenure, to be replaced by a system of private tenure but subject to restrictions to avoid accumulation of land. An economic farming unit was to be sufficiently large to enable a family to make a decent living from full-time farming. Initially, the ability to generate an annual farm income of £120 was proposed as the criterion on which to base the size of a holding. This was later reduced to £57, mainly because the higher income would have required the removal of 80% of the African population from the reserves, whereas an income of £57 limited the required removals to about 50% of the population (Yawitch 1981). In order to accommodate the landless that already existed, and the future landless that would emerge as the plan was implemented, the Commission recommended the development of urban centres and industries in the native areas. The Commission realised that these recommendations represented a fundamental restructuring of society in these areas, and called for a massive investment by the state to make this change possible. The South African Government rejected two of the Commission's key recommendations, namely the abolition of communal tenure, and the establishment of white-owned industries in the native areas. Financially, implementation of the plan was considered far too costly. Politically, the recommendations were not acceptable, because removal of 50% of the population in the native areas would lead to massive resistance. However, government did realise that provisions had to be made for the expected future influx of vast numbers of people into these areas. This influx was implied by the implementation of the grand Apartheid plan that envisaged all non-white South Africans to be citizens of an appropriate ethnic homeland. According to Yawitch (1989), betterment planning after 1955 became one of a complex set of policies developed in response to the government's desire to maintain control over the population in the 'Native Areas'. Two key elements of betterment planning after 1950 contributed to improving control over the 'surplus people' residing in the homelands. Firstly, people were moved from their small and dispersed clusters of homesteads to a single village. This broke the relationship of kin and replaced it by one of neighbours. Often, total strangers would become neighbours, creating a general atmosphere of distrust. Secondly, the government interfered with traditional leadership. Chiefs and headmen became government employees, who were expected to support government policy in order to maintain their status and benefits. Those who opposed government were replaced (Westaway 1997).

Betterment planning applied to Trust lands and land held under communal tenure. Land held under quitrent tenure was also affected. In the Eastern Cape, most land held by Africans was by means of communal tenure, especially in the Transkei where it applied to 85% of the land (Transkei Land Reform Research Group 1995). Several studies have demonstrated that the implementation of betterment planning had an adverse effect on agricultural production (McAllister 1988, De Wet 1989, Hendricks 1989, Steyn 1988, Lahiff 2000), emphasized separation of natural resources from homesteads, and disrupted co-operative work arrangements based on kinship relations. In accordance with the Apartheid objectives, native areas or homelands were encouraged to adopt self-governance. The Transkei became independent in 1975 and the Ciskei in 1981 (chapter 6). The general policy goal of controlling the African population in these areas was maintained by the governments of these new states, but there was also an effort to provide local livelihood opportunities for the resident people. One of the policy avenues used was to support African farming. Government support came in the form of subsidised tractor services, an increase in public extension services, and services supporting production, marketing and access to finance. Parastatals such as Ulimocor and the Ciskei Agricultural Bank in Ciskei, and Tracor and the Agricultural Bank of Transkei were established to supply these services. There were also large capital investments in agriculture, especially in the form of irrigation schemes in the valleys of major rivers. In Ciskei, these included the Keiskammahoek and Zanyokwe schemes along the Keiskamma River, the Tyefu Scheme in the valley of the Great Fish River, and the Shiloh Irrigation Scheme along the Klipplaat (Van Averbeke *et al.* 1998c, Green and Hirsch 1982). Many of these interventions had limited success or were financially not sustainable. The tractor services ended because they were too costly for the state to support. The irrigation schemes were not financially sound either (Katling 1996), and nearly all collapsed when the para-statals managing these projects were closed down by the homeland govern-ments, and farmers were left to manage the schemes themselves. Agricultural banks were instructed to restructure and reduce their reliance on subsidies by the state, making access to finance by small-scale farmers more difficult than before. The public agricultural extension service was criticised for its lack of impact (Bembridge 1985, Steyn 1988), and its budget was reduced progress-ively (Van Averbeke *et al.* 1997).

In the Ciskei, the main impact of the homeland administrations on local livelihoods was through employment in its civil service. Leibrand and Sperber (1997) showed that household income in Keiskammahoek District increased threefold in real terms during the period 1950 to 1985. They demonstrated that this increase was mainly due to income derived from employment in the home-land civil service. During the 1980s, salaries and wages earned in public service employment and in the industrial centre of Dimbaza created in 1968 took over the role of mining remittances as the main source of income for rural house-holds in the Ciskei as employment levels in the South African mining sector dropped steadily. The repealing of legislation restricting the movement of Afri-cans also made it possible for entire households to migrate to urban areas, instead of the male-only migration of the past (chapter 11).

## State social policies: Old age pensions and social grants

The implementation of old-age pensions and the extension of these benefits to Africans since 1944 provided a key resource for contemporary livelihoods (Francis 2000). To date old age pensions and a range of social grants constitute the core of the South African state's social policy. The establishment and insti-tutionalisation of the old-age pension is the result of workers struggle for secu-rity. Originating from white miners' struggles and strikes as early as 1911 (Bhorat 1995) to get compensation in case of disability because of the heavy and dangerous work in the mines, the scheme slowly evolved and was broad-ened to include Africans. From the mid-1940s onwards various grants for blindness, invalidism and child support were paid to eligible people (Switzer 1993). To qualify for an old-age pension, South African males had to be 65 years old and females 60 years old. These requirements have not been changed. However, until 1993, the monetary value of old-age pensions was determined by race. In the past, black people received only about half the amount that was being paid to whites and practically this was implemented by paying black people an old-age pension only every second month. A recent entry in the social grants system is a child support grant and a grant for people affected by HIV/AIDS is considered. When a person has contributed towards a pension scheme through his or her employer, and the monetary value of the work-related pension exceeds that of the old-age pension, that person is not allowed to claim an-old-age pension. Work-related pensions can be combined with an old-age pension when the monetary value of the work-related pension is less than that of the old-age pension, but in such cases the value of the old-age pension claim against the state is limited to the deficit.

The contemporary old-age pension scheme entails a transfer of cash to all South Africans based on age and is annually adjusted for inflation. During 2006 the grant provided a monthly payment of R820 for men above the age of 65 and women older than 60. In 2003, that same pension was R450. Case and Deaton (1998) have shown that in 1993 this scheme involved the transfer of cash sums of about twice the median per capita income of African households. Their analysis underlined the redistributive effects of these pensions. These old-age pensions were not only of direct economic value (allowing people to purchase food, clothes, and other essentials of life) but were also of eminent social and symbolic significance. The pension scheme ended the monopolised access of the younger generation to cash. Census data from 1951 showed that nationwide about 52% of all qualifying Africans received an old-age pension; a similar proportion occurred in the Ciskei and Transkei (Sagner 2000). Chapter 10 provides more recent data, which suggest that in villages like Guquka and Koloni the contribution of pensions and other grants nowadays constitutes the largest component of total cash income. The predominance of pensioners in the rural areas invoked Beinart (2001) to coin the term 'pensionariat'.

The old-age pension scheme is particularly significant and socially important in that it provided security to widows and their dependents. As the size of the grant increased over the years, these recipients progressively achieved the status of 'earners'. In some areas, widows accounted for 80% or more of the beneficiaries. Consequently, old-age pensions are often referred to as widow's pensions (Sagner 2000: 547).

During the 1990s, the South African economy was restructured in order to become globally competitive. Unemployment rates increased because the economy failed to absorb new entrants into the labour market, whilst existing jobs were lost due to retrenchments in the private and public sector. In 1993, the government increased the value of welfare grants paid to African people, by removing the disparities that existed along racial lines. As a result, state transfers in the form of welfare grants and old-age pensions became a major source of income, which in some households supported three generations (chapters 10 and 11).

## Livelihood trends

The general theme of this chapter and this book deals with the patterns and trends in African livelihoods and how those resonate with the utilisation of natural resources. Any attempt to show historical trends and changes over time depends on the available data. Narrowing livelihoods to cash income ignores the other contributions. Nevertheless, a selection of income data collected in different parts of the Ciskei were combined to construct Figure 2.2.

Since local factors influence the relative importance of different sources of income, the data are intended to show general trends only. Several of these are evident. Firstly, the graph clearly demonstrates the declining role of agriculture in the livelihoods of rural Africans residing in the Ciskei region.

This decline was persistent from the late 19th century until about 1990 but appears to have ended during the last decade of the 20th century. Secondly, the importance of remittances as a source of income of rural households declined during the second half of the 20th century, whilst earnings from local employment increased, especially during the period 1950 to 1990, which coincides with Apartheid and the homeland era. Thirdly, the importance of welfare grants, mainly in the form of old-age pensions and increasingly also HIV/AIDS and child support grants, increased dramatically during the final decades of the 20th century, because of an increase in the value of these grants, and because of the ageing of the rural African population. The recent decline in the importance of remittances and the ageing of the rural population was due, at least in part, to the permanent and semi-permanent migration of young, economically active families from rural to urban areas (chapter 11).

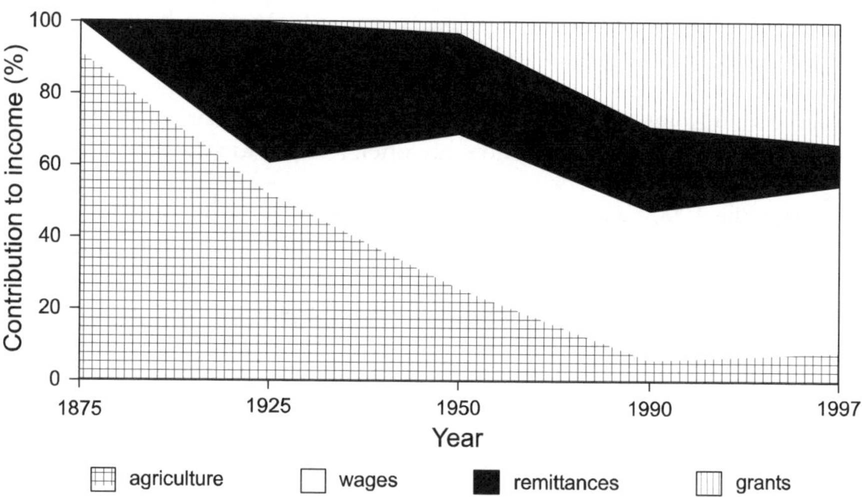


*Figure 2.2*     Trends in the income of rural households in the Ciskei region during the period 1875 to 1997

*Sources*:
The 1875 and 1925 data cover Victoria East (Bundy 1988)
The 1950 and 1990 data cover villages in Keiskammahoek District (Houghton and Walton 1952, Sperber 1993)
The 1997 data are for Koloni and Guquka only (ARDRI-Survey 1997)

N.B.: In-kind income did not feature in the 1875 and 1925 data, but some is included from 1950 onwards. Welfare grants include the transfer of money in the form of old-age pensions and other grants. The 1990 data on income remitted to the rural homestead by short-term migrants, who return home monthly or more frequently, are included in the category 'wages' to improve the basis for comparison with the 1997 data. Thus, for the years 1990 and 1997, the category 'remittances' refers to income remitted to the rural homestead by migrants who returned home less frequently than once a month.

Where does this leave African agriculture in the Eastern Cape today? Rural households in the Eastern Cape are characterised by considerable physical, human, economic and material differentiation, and do not constitute a homogeneous group (Williams *et al.* 1989, Sperber 1993). Although there are considerable local differences, it is appropriate to refer to the majority of rural African people in the Eastern Cape as rural dwellers or villagers, and not as peasants or farmer's *sensu strictu*, because agriculture plays a marginal role in their livelihoods. A study in four tribal authorities in the Ciskei conducted during the mid-1980s showed that farming was important to only one in five rural households (Williams *et al.* 1989, see also chapter 10). Landlessness on its own, which may affect 50% or more of households in a particular rural community (chapter 6), does not fully explain the high levels of non-participation in agriculture. Recent studies in both the Ciskei and Transkei regions of the Eastern Cape show that the proportion of available arable land being cultivated does not usually exceed 35%, and may be as low as 10 to 15%, irrespective of the cropping potential of that land (chapters 7 and 8). Other constraints that have been identified include institutional inefficiencies preventing the emergence of a land rental market (chapters 6 and 8), infrastructural decline notably of roads and fences (Van Averbeke 1999, Perret and L'Hopitallier 2000), the absence of appropriate storage, processing and retail systems for grains and other agricultural produce at village level (ISER 2001) and a decline in farming knowledge (Van Averbeke 1999, see also chapter 8).

## Conclusions

The chapter describes how a transformation of people's livelihoods has occurred in the region. The focus is on general trends with an attempt to look at the many ways by which people have responded to externally and internally induced changes. In the past, their lives revolved around a clear relationship with their natural environment for the provision of goods and services such as land, crops, meat, cattle, water, pastures. Today, the role of agriculture has diminished dramatically; rural people's livelihoods now revolve largely around migratory labour, remittances and social grants and pensions. This is not only restricted to the Eastern Cape.

The African people in the Eastern Cape region were confronted with rapidly changing conditions from the late 1700s onwards. They responded to these changes in many ways. To some changes like the loss of land and territory and diminishing political power, they had to accommodate themselves, but only after years of fierce resistance in various wars. Changes in life styles have occurred due to encroaching western and Christian norms and values since their first contacts with elements of white society in the mid-17th century.

Colonialism and the formation of the colonial state brought radically new material conditions to bear on peoples like the Xhosa. Military conquests and wars, the influx of white settlers and violent conflicts over land, imposition of taxes, and continuous polices of racial segregation implied a general loss of land for the Xhosa forcing to seek for alternative resources for making a living. The emergence of South Africa's mineral revolution in the late 19th century ushered the country as a whole into the age of industrial capitalism and propelled a general demand for cheap migratory labour. The changing nature of regional and global agricultural commodity markets also affected the ability of African commodity producers to derive a livelihood based on land. By the end of the 20th century, rural households responded to poverty and unemployment by migrating to urban areas, and there were few if any indications of a revival of the rural economy based on more intensive exploitation of local natural and human resources.

Changes also originate from transformation at the level of Xhosa society. Some of theses took the form of shocks (e.g. the 'great cattle killing' in the 1860s) forcing the Xhosa in order to survive to dramatically modify their livelihood strategies. The changing gender division of labour partly because of the migration of predominantly male labour affected the livelihoods of African people and their use of natural resources in more subtle ways. Moreover, processes of 'internal' social differentiation, as the dynamic outcome of a combination of demographic factors, the patterns of ownership of land and cattle, and the opportunities for some to occupy vacant land also needs to be taken into account. The noted expansion and intensification of commodity production during the bloom of African agriculture was thus not a uniform process.

The remainders of the book illuminate in much more detail the currents and undercurrents of contemporary processes of change. The focus will be on diversity while not losing sight of main trends like poverty and wealth; landed and landless; institutional constraints; migrants and pensioners, as these continue to reflect ongoing processes of rural and environmental transformation as well as shape.

3

# Agro-ecology, land use and smallholder farming in the Central Eastern Cape

Wim van Averbeke and James Bennett

## Introduction

At a local level, farming and land-based livelihoods are linked to the particular natural resources that are available. The description and characterisation of these resources and their limitations provide the bio-physical context in which farming and land-based livelihoods need to be understood. This chapter starts with a description and characterisation of the agro-ecology of the central Eastern Cape, and proceeds with a generalised description of how these natural resources are used, with special emphasis on farming. This description follows the historical subdivision of the central Eastern Cape into the former Border and Ciskei regions, because important historical differences in terms of farm size and land use persist. The last part of the chapter presents a detailed description of natural resources, land use and farming in the historical Ciskei region, because both Guquka and Koloni form part of it.

## Agro-ecological regions

The central Eastern Cape covers an area of about 18,024 km$^2$, and incorporates two historical regions, namely the Border region immediately west of the Great Kei river covering 9924 km$^2$ and the former Ciskei 8100 km$^2$. Roughly, it has the Kat and lower Fish River as its western boundary and the Great Kei and Black Kei rivers as its eastern and northern boundary. In the south it borders the Indian Ocean (see Map 1.1).

The central Eastern Cape can be subdivided into five major land units. Four of these are encountered when travelling from the coast in a northern direction, namely the Coastal Belt, the Coastal Plateau, the Amatola and Winterberg Mountains, and the Midland Plateau. The valleys of the major river systems that cut through these four units make up the fifth unit.

*The Coastal Belt*
Stretching about 30 to 40 km inland, the Coastal Belt rises rapidly from sea level to an altitude of about 100 m, and thereafter gradually to an altitude of about 300 m at the boundary with the Coastal Plateau. Numerous steeply incised river valleys dissect it, causing intense relief at local level. Mean annual rainfall increases from 624 mm at Fish River Point in the southwest to about 850 mm in the northeast. The Coastal Belt receives most of its rain during summer, but the influence of cold fronts sweeping the southern edge of the continent, predominantly a winter phenomenon, causes approximately 40% of the rain to fall in winter. Moderated by the Indian Ocean, the climate is frost-free. Mean daily minimum temperature is between 17 and 18°C in January and about 10°C in July, but extreme minimum temperatures as low as 3°C have been recorded (Marais 1975). Land and sea breezes commonly occur, but they may be superseded by westerly winds, which are described as persistent, strong and disagreeable (Marais 1975). The climate is suitable for year-round production of a range of crops, including selected sub-tropical fruits, of which pineapples are the most common.

Soils are generally shallow and often prone to water logging, especially those situated on level crests and valley bottoms. Cultivation occurs mainly on the valley slopes. Soils on valley slopes usually show evidence of leaching, and have an acid reaction. They appear to resist erosion, enabling their cultivation on gradients exceeding 20% without excessive loss of soil, at least during the initial years. The natural vegetation is dominated by Coastal Mixed *Grassveld* and Acacia Savanna, and the numerous steeply sloping river valleys are covered with Valley *Bushveld*. The use of natural vegetation mainly involves beef production. Around East London dairy farming on planted pastures is common.

*The Coastal Plateau*
Geomorphologically, the Coastal Plateau is a continuation of the Coastal Belt, rising gradually from an altitude of 300 m in the south, and reaching altitudes between 700 m and 900 m at the edge of the Amatola and Winterberg mountain ranges. Climatically, the plateau differs from the Coastal Belt. The influence of the Indian Ocean is less pronounced, making it hotter in summer and colder in winter. The proportion of rain falling in winter is typically between 20 and 30%. The rainfall pattern can be described as bimodal, because a mid-summer dry

period separates the spring and the autumn peaks. Generally, the climate is dry in the west, with a mean annual rainfall of about 500 mm, and gets wetter towards the east, where the mean annual rainfall may reach about 750 mm. According to Marais (1975), mean annual rainfall on the coastal plateau may vary considerably over short distances. This appears largely due to differences in altitude and position in the local landscape. For this reason, local relief features need to be considered carefully when assessing rainfall of a particular site. Marais (1975) cites the example of King William's Town to demonstrate local variability in mean annual rainfall. The town, which is nestled in the valley of the Buffalo River, has a mean annual rainfall of 536 mm. At the country club, which is on the plateau overlooking the town and only 7 km from the centre, the mean annual rainfall is 618 mm.

On the Coastal Plateau, the mean daily maximum temperature is about 29°C in January and 21°C in July. Extreme maximum temperatures of 44°C in January and 32 °C in July have been observed. These high temperatures are usually associated with the occurrence of "bergwinds". These strong, hot and desiccating winds can cause considerable damage to crops, both mechanically and by scorching the leaves (Marais 1975). Frost occurs throughout, although the mean daily minimum temperature in July is about 5°C. The frost period increases from about 30 days in the south to 60 days in the north. As a result, the plateau has two distinct growing seasons, namely a summer season during which crops sensitive to frost can be grown, and a winter season for frost-resistant crops. When grown under rainfed conditions both summer and winter crops rely on stored soil water during some part of their growing cycles. As a result, successful cropping depends heavily on the adequacy of the water holding capacity of the soils (Van Averbeke and Marais 1991). In the drier parts the pH of the soils is close to neutral but in the wetter parts slightly or moderately acid. The low phosphorus content of soils is an important limitation to plant growth (Hensley and Laker 1975). The general absence of deep and adequately drained soils causes the area of land suited to crop production to be limited to about 10% of the total. Red soils of the Shortlands and Hutton form (Soil Classification Working Group 1991) are the most productive (Van Averbeke and Marais 1991). Derived from dolerite, these soils are usually deep, resistant to erosion (D'Huyvetter 1985), and chemically fertile (Hensley and Laker 1975). The natural vegetation is dominated by Acacia Savanna in the dry parts and Dohne *Sourveld* in wetter areas. Most of the land is best suited to extensive livestock production, involving a combination of goats and cattle on Acacia Savanna, and cattle or sheep on Dohne *Sourveld*.

*The Amatola and Winterberg mountains*
he Amatola and Winterberg mountain ranges run east to west, at a distance of about 70 km from the coast in the eastern part of the central Eastern Cape and about 120 km in the western. Rising sharply from the Coastal Plateau to an

altitude varying between 1500 and 2000 m, the southern slopes of the mountain range appear as a dark-green forested belt. The sudden increase in altitude, causing orographic rain, explains why the southern slopes and mountain peaks enjoy a mean annual rainfall that is much higher than on the Coastal Plateau. As on the coastal plateau, mean annual rainfall varies considerably, depending on altitude and exposure. The high altitude causes the frequency of frost to be higher than on the Coastal Plateau and the growing season to be shorter. Overall, the climate in the mountains is cooler than on the Coastal Plateau, and misty conditions prevail during much of the year. Snow falls regularly during the winter, especially on the high peaks, but it hardly ever lasts longer than a few days. A large portion of the mountain range, which has a width of only about 10 to 15 km, is under mature Afromontane forest, pine plantation, or wattle. The rest supports Dohne *Sourveld*, fynbos or scrub. Rock outcrop and stony soils are found on the steep slopes, but pockets of deep Clovelly and Hutton type soils occur on slopes that are gentler. Due to the high rainfall, leaching conditions prevail, explaining why most soils test acid throughout the profile. Soils on the southern foot slopes of the mountains are usually deep, lateritic, and often susceptible to erosion. The mountain range is the source and main catchment area of three important river systems, namely the Kat River, the Keiskamma and Tyume rivers, and the Buffalo River. In terms of land use, the mountain ranges are suited for forestry and the production of cattle, goats and sheep. Cultivation is very limited, although climatically the area lends itself well for a range of high-value niche crops, such as seed-potatoes, cherries and proteas. This potential remains largely untapped.

*The Midland Plateau*
The Midland Plateau is found in the rain shadow to the north of the Amatola and Winterberg mountain ranges. Situated at an elevation ranging between 900 and 1,200 m, about 300 to 400 m higher than the northern parts of the Coastal Plateau, the Midland Plateau is characterised by many residual table-topped hills (inselbergs). Often these hills are capped by dolerite. Dolerite has a composition similar to basalt. About 100 million years ago, magma was injected into the existing sedimentary mother rock, giving rise to dolerite sills and dykes. Being more resistant to erosion than sedimentary rocks, dolerite dykes and sills protect underlying sedimentary rocks against being worn away, explaining the occurrence of the residual table-topped hills. The plateau forms part of the summer rainfall region, receiving about 600 mm annually. The climate is little influenced by the ocean and can best be described as continental (Marais 1975). Thus, it is hotter in summer and colder in winter compared to the Coastal Belt and Coastal Plateau. The mean daily maximum temperature is about 30°C in January and the mean daily minimum just under 3°C in July. Absolute maximum temperature in summer may go up to 40°C, while minimum temperatures of –6°C have been recorded during winter. On the plateau crests the dominant vegetation is Karroid Danthonia Mountain *veld*, whilst valleys are covered with

Cymbopogon-Themeda *veld*, but this has been invaded by *Acacia karoo* and Karoo shrubs, a change apparently encouraged by soil erosion. The Midland Plateau was once renowned for its wool and wheat production, but this potential has been reduced by land degradation. The area is characterised by duplex soils. These soils show an abrupt increase in clay content at the transition between top and subsoil, and they are usually very susceptible to erosion when mismanaged.

*The river valleys*
The valleys of the Kat, Fish, Tyume, Keiskamma and Kei rivers form the fifth agro-ecological unit. They are drier than the surrounding landscape, and support an unique vegetation, referred to as the Valley *Bushveld*, consisting of scrub forest dominated by tree-Euphorbia. Soils on the valley slopes are usually shallow and rocky, but at the foot of the slopes and in the valley bottoms deep soils occur. Often, soils at the foot of the slopes show signs of water logging (pale grey), but those in the valley bottoms tend to be better drained. In most cases it is these valley-bottom soils that have been exploited for the development of irrigation schemes. These include Tyefu along the Fish River, Keiskamma and Zanyokwe in the valley of the Keiskamma River, Horseshoe along the Buffalo river north of King William's Town, Shiloh near Whitlesea on the Klipplaat River, Hertzog and Kat River citrus farms in the Kat River Valley, as well as several small projects along the Tyume River north of Alice.

## Vegetation types

The five agro-ecological regions that make up the central Eastern Cape contain four of the major vegetation biomes of Low and Rebelo (1998). These, in turn, can be subdivided further into nine *veld* types according to Acocks' (1988) *veld* classification system (Beckerling *et al.* 1995). In Table 3.1 relationships among these three categorisations are summarised.

The vegetation biomes found in the region differ in their potential for livestock production because of their varying composition in terms of the proportion of grasses, bushes and trees they contain and the relative productivity of the various plant species for livestock production purposes. Particularly for grasses species composition is important and it forms the basis for a broad classification of grassland into *sweetveld* and *sourveld*.

There are several important characteristics associated with these two categories of *veld*, but in simple terms *sweetveld* is *veld* which remains palatable and nutritious when mature, whereas *sourveld* provides palatable material only during the growing season (Tainton 1999). Some broad indications of the composition and productive potential of each vegetation biome are provided below.

*Table 3.1*      Summary of agro-ecological regions, vegetation biomes and rangeland
                 types in the central Eastern Cape Region

| Agro-ecological zone | Vegetation Biome | Rangeland Type |
|---|---|---|
| Coastal Belt | Forest Biome | Coastal Forest and *Thornveld* |
| | | Alexandria Forest |
| Coastal Plateau | Savanna Biome | Eastern Province *Thornveld* |
| | | False *Thornveld* of the Eastern Cape |
| Valleys | Thicket Biome | Valley *Bushveld* |
| Mountains | | Highland *Sourveld* and Dohne *Sourveld* |
| | Grassland Biome | Karroid *Merxmullera* Mountain *Veld* |
| Midland Plateau | | Invasion of Grassveld by *Acacia karroo* |
| | | Dry *Cymbopogon-Themeda Veld* |

### The Forest Biome

Of the two rangeland types that compose the Forest Biome, the Coastal Forest
and *Thornveld* offers the greater potential for livestock production. Whereas the
Alexandria Forest consists mainly of dense forest, the Coastal Forest and
*Thornveld* is a mixture of forest interspersed with patches of open *thornveld*,
which afford some limited opportunity for the grazing of livestock (Beckerling
*et al.* 1995). The *veld* of both rangeland types can be described as sour to mixed
depending on the rainfall aspect and soil type, which further limits the productivity of the available rangeland outside the growing season. Agriculture is predominantly crop-oriented although extensive livestock production is practised
on those areas where *thornveld* and bush intrusion is less problematic or where
this is actively controlled (Van Averbeke 2000). Thus, the potential of the
biome for livestock production is limited both spatially and temporally and can
be described as fairly poor overall in comparison to some of the other biomes in
the region.

### The Savanna Biome

The vegetation of the Savanna Biome in the central Eastern Cape consists of
*thornveld*, dominated by *Acacia karroo*, with a dense *grassveld* layer of variable
nature. In some areas this is *grassveld* is sourish to mixed but it is predominantly sweet in classification. This, combined with the generally flat topography
makes it well-suited to livestock production for both grazers and browsers
throughout the year in most areas of its occurrence and the sing this productivity
is largely dependent on the utilisation of appropriate management strategies.

  *Sweetveld* in summer rainfall areas such as the central Eastern Cape is prone
to damage by heavy grazing (i.e. has fairly low resistance to grazing-induced
change) but has the capacity to recover rapidly in terms of both composition and
density (i.e. has a fairly high level of inherent resilience) (Tainton 1999). This
has important implications for management. Strategies should generally focus

on allowing livestock numbers to track climatic variability but ensuring that they are appropriately distributed in space and time to allow for range recovery. In areas of very extensive animal production on communal rangeland this can effectively be achieved through active herding to different areas. However, in a communal area such as the former Ciskei where range area is comparatively limited this is not possible. Rather, rotational grazing of livestock to facilitate optimal range recovery is only possible through some system of paddocking as introduced to the former Ciskei under betterment. However, given the enormous demands on grazing resources in communal areas, few communities are able to perpetuate previous rotational grazing practices. Where management systems have disintegrated rangeland productivity will inevitably be compromised although the implications of this for communal livestock production are debateable (see below).

### The Thicket Biome

In the former Ciskei the Thicket Biome is constituted entirely by the valley *bushveld* associated with the valleys of the Keiskamma, Tyume, Bira, Kat and Great Fish rivers and is the most extensive *veld* type in the region. The vegetation tends to be scrubby and consists of a combination of thicket and *Acacia karroo thornveld* or *Euphorbia* forest with limited *grassveld*. The *veld* type is very sweet and therefore very sensitive to both overgrazing and overbrowsing (Beckerling *et al.* 1995). Such sensitivity severely limits the livestock production potential of the biome as the vegetation can only support limited numbers of animals under very extensive stocking strategies. Despite its extent this biome is probably the least suited in the region to the demands of communal livestock production and considerable areas of it are now under management for wildlife conservation.

### The Grassland Biome

Locally, the four *veld* types that constitute the Grassland Biome differ considerably in their productivity and therefore in the way in which they can be used for livestock production. The Highland *Sourveld* and Dohne *Sourveld* is associated with mountainous regions and, as its name implies, is dominated by dense and inherently sour *grassveld*. In contrast to the *sweetveld* described above, this type of rangeland is characterised by being resistant and is capable of tolerating quite high levels of grazing pressure without producing any noticeable shift in species composition although high pressure does lower productivity (Tainton 1999). It is productive during the spring and early summer, although this rapidly declines during the autumn and remains low throughout the winter. This means that without supplementary feeding livestock productivity drops off markedly at this time and animals may even die. Thus, even in communal areas some livestock owners producing on this *sourveld* have to be prepared to grow forage crops or buy in supplementary feed to maintain their animals.

The other three *veld* types in this biome are essentially mixed or sweet in nature and tend to be quite sensitive to degradation. Livestock production, whilst possible for a larger proportion of the year than in the sour, mountainous areas cannot be undertaken under the same high stocking rates and necessitates a more conservative approach.

Overall, the potential of the biome for livestock production can be considered as reasonable, being better than that of the forest and thicket biomes although not as high as the savanna biome.

## General land use

Land in the central Eastern Cape is used mainly for livestock production. In 1989, 98% of the region's land area was used for agriculture. Of the agricultural land 86% was covered by natural pasture (Antrobus *et al.* 1994). Other important land uses were planted or natural forest and cultivated land. In 1995, the region's natural pasture supported approximately 341,000 cattle, 667,000 sheep, and 306,000 goats (Department of Agriculture 1995). On average, the stocking rate was 3.25 ha per large stock unit (LSU) in the Border region and 2.90 ha per LSU in the Ciskei region. The rule of thumb in pasture management is that six small stock units (sheep and goats) are equivalent to one LSU. Using this rule to convert the populations of the three livestock species to LSU, in 1995 the overall LSU ratio of goats: sheep: cattle in the central Eastern Cape was approximately 1:2:7. The ratio clearly demonstrates the dominance of cattle in the region's livestock production system. The Border and Ciskei regions differed mainly in terms of the importance of goats in the livestock mix. In the Border region, where the ratio was 1:6:15, goats were fairly rare, but they were a lot more prominent in the Ciskei where the ratio was 1:1:4. The main reason for this regional difference is that goats formed an integral part of the contemporary farming system of black smallholders in the Ciskei region, who use goats for milk and ritual slaughter, whereas in the Border region, where white farmers continue to dominate, the incorporation of goats in the farming system was relatively rare. Since 1994, when foreign tourists started to return to South Africa, several white-owned cattle farms in the Border region have been converted wholly of partly into game farms.

Overall, the agro-ecology of the central Eastern Cape favours mixed farming dominated by livestock production in which most of the animal nutrition is supplied by natural range. This was also how the land was used during precolonial times as discussed in chapter 2.

Land use in the Border and Ciskei regions differs. In the Border region much of the arable land supports livestock production, being planted to fodder crops, such as silage maize and lucerne, or to cultivated pasture grasses. Along the coast, climatic conditions encourage use of arable land for pineapple production. Vegetable production in open fields, and increasingly in tunnels, is important around East London, especially northeast of the city. Due to its political history (see chapter 2), farming in Ciskei developed differently from that in the Border region. One of the most striking differences is that farm units in Ciskei tend to be small compared to those in the Border region. A typical smallholding in Ciskei covers about 12 ha, but a farm unit in the Border region is about 500 ha in size. Another difference is that much of the land in Ciskei is held by means of communal tenure, whilst farms in the Border region are in private hands. As in the Border region, most land in the Ciskei region is under natural *veld*. The natural range is also primarily used for livestock production, but also provides homesteads with wood and herbs for various uses. On their fields, which typically range from one to three ha in size, smallholders in the Ciskei region produce mainly food crops, particularly maize. Homestead gardens are planted to a wide range of crops and vegetables. Since both Guquka and Koloni lie in what was once the Ciskei, the rest of this chapter deals specifically with agriculture as practised in this region.

## Livestock production on smallholdings

*Livestock numbers*
It is difficult to find recent data on livestock numbers in the communal areas of the central Eastern Cape Province. Since 1994, data tend to be dealt with at a provincial level. An overview of cattle numbers in the former Ciskei is presented in Table 3.2.

An overview of small stock numbers in the former Ciskei is presented in Table 3.3. It is clear from Table 3.2 that there was a crash in animal numbers during the early 1980s. In 1984, the number of cattle had been reduced to half of what it was in 1978. This decline was precipitated by droughts, particularly that of 1982-83. By 1985 there was evidence of a recovery in cattle numbers, and continued through to 1990, remaining virtually unchanged in 1995.

*Table 3.2*      Cattle numbers in the former Ciskei

| Year | 1977-78[1] | 1981-82[1] | 1983-84[1] | 1984-85[1] | 1990[2] | 1995[3] |
|---|---|---|---|---|---|---|
| No. of animals | 190,000 | 150,000 | 75,000 | 83,180 | 162,000 | 161,929 |

*Sources*:
[1] Hundleby *et al.* (1986)      [3] Van Averbeke *et al.* (2000)
[2] Fraser (1992)

Similar cycles of large declines in cattle numbers and subsequent recovery of the herds to their original levels were described by Beinart (1992) for the former Transkei Homeland. This lends support to the theory that in spite of short-term fluctuations, cattle numbers have remained relatively constant over the long term in the communal areas of South Africa (Tapson 1993). It also suggests that in spite of changing times the desire to own cattle remains largely undiminished among people living in these areas.

As with cattle, sheep numbers in the former Ciskei declined sharply between the early 1970s and the mid 1980s to less than half their former numbers. It is likely that this can again be attributed to the severe drought episode of the early 1980s. However, numbers showed little or no recovery in the decade after 1985, suggesting that the decline was part of a long-term trend. The reasons for this decline are investigated in more detail later on, and also in Chapter 9. Goat numbers in the Ciskei apparently remained fairly constant throughout the 1970s, 80s and 90s. This is consistent with their general hardiness.

*Table 3.3*     Sheep and goat numbers in the former Ciskei

| Year | 1972[1] | 1979-80[2] | 1984-85[3] | 1990[2] | 1995[4] |
|---|---|---|---|---|---|
| Sheep | 478,000 | 249,719 | 224,920 | 289,454 | 239,972 |
| Goats | 220,000 | 226,509 | 274,490 | 281,135 | 249,991 |

*Sources*:
[1] Brown *et al.* (1975)          [3] Hundleby *et al.* (1986)
[2] Fraser (1992)                  [4] Van Averbeke *et al.* (2000)

*Distribution of livestock ownership*
There is an overwhelming body of evidence to suggest that while many people in communal areas continue to own stock, the average number of animals held by individuals is small and the majority of animals are owned by a relatively small number of people (Ainslie 2002, Kepe 2002, Vetter 2003). Bembridge (1979) provided an indication of herd size in the former Ciskei (Table 3.4).

*Table 3.4*     Distribution of cattle herd size in the Ciskei, 1970s

| Number of animals | 1-4 | 5-8 | 9-12 | 13-16 | 16+ |
|---|---|---|---|---|---|
| % of owners | 47.5 | 28.5 | 13 | 6 | 5 |

*Source*: Adapted from Bembridge 1979

Table 3.4 shows that three decades ago nearly half of all owners had very small cattle herds consisting of four or fewer animals. This skewed distribution of livestock ownership was confirmed in recent work by Ainslie (2002), in the Peddie Magisterial District of the former Ciskei. He found that 53% of cattle owners held 16 animals or less, and only one in five held 13 or more cattle. Bembridge (1979) judged that a homestead needed a herd of at least 9 cattle to meet its various subsistence needs. By this measure only 24% of owners in the Ciskei had a cattle herd that was large enough. Tapson and Rose (1984), work-ing in KwaZulu, argued that a considerably larger minimum herd size of 18 animals was required by Zulu households to effectively fulfil all the livelihood functions required of cattle (milk, draught, sale, slaughter) and allow the herd to perpetuate itself. Only about 5% of Ciskeian cattle owners were able to meet this requirement in 1979, and judging from the herd size information of Ainslie (2002), this proportion is unlikely to have changed greatly. Consequently, regardless of the benchmark of minimum effective herd size the implication is that cattle production alone is capable of providing an effective livelihood strategy for only a handful of owners in the region.

Comparable data for small stock are more difficult to find. Steyn (1982) recorded a mean flock size of 18 animals for sheep and 10 for goats, among owners in the Amatola basin in the Ciskei. However, means do not convey the spread of the size of small stock holdings that exists among individual owners. Vetter (2003) showed that while the vast majority of owners in Herschel held relatively few sheep, one individual had nearly 1000 animals, and three more held more than 100 animals each. Not only did these large holdings dramatically skew the mean flock size in the area (mean =129, median =36), but they also underlined the very uneven nature of livestock holdings, particularly of small stock. Just over 20% of the owners interviewed held 80% of sheep, and the data for goats were even more extreme, with 60% of goats being held by just 10% of owners. For cattle, distribution was far more even, with some 80% of animals being held by about 50% of owners. However, the apparently egalitarian distribution of cattle among livestock owners disguised a serious gender bias, which also applied to small stock. Across all livestock types, females consistently had far smaller holdings than men. Male livestock owners had median holdings of 9 cattle, 45 sheep and 27 goats, while for females the medians were 5.5, 9 and 8, respectively. Moreover, the bias in cattle ownership is probably greater in reality than such figures suggest. Ainslie (2002) has pointed out that even where females are nominally identified as the 'owners' of cattle, they are often widows who are only holding the animals to allow them be passed on to the oldest son. Responsibility for the maintenance of these animals and decisions over sales and marketing will invariably rest with male kin. This is consistent with local tradition, which views on ownership and husbandry of sheep, goats and especially cattle as a male domain (Coertze 1986). Thus, few if any females can be said to 'own' cattle. The implications of this are debateable. While, responsibility for livestock primarily rests with males, there is much to suggest that the benefits from them (livestock products, money from sales) accrue to the household rather than to the male owner. In this respect 'ownership' may be more a reflection of traditional gender roles than a claim over the resultant benefits.

Theft has increasingly come to impact on livestock ownership in communal areas of Eastern Cape. Although, the scale of the problem varies regionally, where it is severe it is a disincentive to livestock ownership. Little published information is available for the former Ciskei, but case material presented in chapter 9 for sheep theft illustrates the problem. In the former Transkei stealing of livestock appears to be a severe problem. For example, in part of the Maluti District, theft was largely responsible for a drop in cattle numbers from 1,300 animals in 1997 to just 500 animals in 1999 (Ntshona and Turner 2002). Similarly, Kepe (2002) reported widespread cattle theft in Lusikisiki district. This is particularly associated with the winter months, when cattle are often allowed to roam unsupervised on the arable fields. The authorities are finding it difficult to deal with the problem due lack of resources and the involvement of well-organised gangs. This has prompted the establishment of vigilante groups, who are often indiscriminate in how and from whom they 'reclaim' cattle, a response that has accentuated the problem (Kepe 2002).

*Livestock breeds*

Cattle currently held in communal areas of central Eastern Cape Province are a mixture of African, European and prototype Afrikaner breeds (Hundleby *et al.* 1986). The main African breed is the Nguni, which is descended from the original Sanga cattle brought from central and Eastern Africa by the ancestors of the Nguni people (Coertze 1986). Several European cattle breeds are present with dairy breeds, such as Jersey, Gurnsey and Ayrshire, and Brown Swiss being particularly common. Cross-breeding between European and Nguni stocks has taken place since the first contact between the settlers and the Xhosa in the early 19th century. The result is that most of the animals in communal areas are of mixed breed (Hundleby *et al.* 1986). Much of the interbreeding that has taken place can also be attributed to cattle improvement schemes, which were a feature of the agricultural policy of the former Ciskei. Here the emphasis was on introduction of improved breeds of European origin, such as the Brown Swiss. This inevitably resulted in cross-breeding with indigenous breeds in the communal environment. In the case of the Brown Swiss this also had the unfortunate outcome of crossbred offspring being treated with disfavour by their owners, as they tend to be grey in colour, which in Xhosa custom associates them with the much feared river spirits (Hundleby *et al.* 1986). More recent cattle improvement programmes have been more sympathetic to such considerations and have tended to work with indigenous Nguni breeds, particularly the related Nkone breed (Masika and Magadlela 2001).

Similarly, the lack of control over mating has resulted in the majority of small stock being of mixed breed. Sheep tend to be a mixture of merino and local Döhne merino breeds (Vetter 2003). Goats tend to be mostly of boer stock with some also mixed with indigenous breeds from other parts of Africa (Mafu and Masika 2002).

*Livestock productivity and its important constraints*

The productivity of livestock in communal areas of the central Eastern Cape is relatively low when assessed from a commercial perspective. One measure of this is the level of offtake of animals for slaughter and sale as a percentage of the total herd size. Brown *et al.* (1975) estimated an annual offtake of 7% of the cattle herd held by farmers in the communal areas of Ciskei, whereas herd off-take on local commercial farms was about 20%. Data for small stock, and more recent figures for cattle, are difficult to find, but Vetter (2003) reported mean offtake levels of 6.4% for cattle 18.1% for sheep and 8.8% for goats in the Herschel district of the former Transkei. These data refer only to 'useful' off-take from the herd in form of sales or slaughter, and do not take into account changes in herd size due to mortality or theft (see below). Cattle offtake in Herschel was remarkably similar to the estimate arrived at by Brown *et al.* (1975) for the Ciskei, suggesting that offtake has remained consistently low. It is difficult to assess how representative the Herschel data for sheep and goat turnover is for the current situation in the central Eastern Cape region. Certainly, the figure for sheep appears high, and Vetter (2003) explicitly points out that the mean offtake value was affected by a few owners with very large flocks producing at a commercial level. Unfortunately, comparative data for median values were not available. Nevertheless, the general picture in the communal livestock production systems of the region is one of relatively low levels of animal performance.

Cultural factors aside, from a production perspective two main factors appear to mitigate against levels of animal performance being improved in communal systems, i.e. low reproductive rate and high levels of mortality. Successful production of offspring among livestock in communal herds is low when compared to commercial animals, although most information in support of this contention is old. Using the results of several studies, Bembridge (1979) concluded that the weaning rates among communal livestock during the 1970s were very low compared to commercial animals (Table 3.5).

*Table 3.5*     Weaning rates (%) among livestock in communal areas during 1970s compared with commercial systems

| Production system | Livestock type | | |
|---|---|---|---|
| | Cattle | Sheep | Goats |
| Communal system | 32-40 | 45-60 | 70 |
| Commercial system | 78 | 90 | - |

*Source*: Bembridge (1979)

Brown *et al.* (1975) attributed the low rate of reproductive success to several factors. The main reason they cited was the poor quality of the available forage on the communal rangelands, which he attributed to overgrazing. Too many animals for the forage that is available results in low levels of animal performance, with females experiencing difficulties in conception and embryo development as well as poor levels of milk production once offspring are born. Milk production may also be affected by milking of lactating females (particularly cows) for home consumption. This reduces the amount of milk available for the calves, reducing their rate of growth (Brown 1975). However, the low reproductive success of livestock in communal areas can only be perceived as a generalised picture. Spatially and temporally, forage quality and quantity vary enormously and animal performance, and reproduction tends to track this variability. Thus, in a good year animal numbers can increase rapidly, particularly following a period of drought when competition for forage resources has been diminished (Behnke and Scoones 1993).

Another characteristic of communal livestock production that contributes to low breeding success is the lack of control over mating. Since communal rangelands contain animals belonging to a multitude of owners, females in season will mate with whichever male is available at the time. This may result not only in less productive offspring, but also in inbreeding. For many livestock species, problems of lack of conception and inbreeding are often exacerbated by the low number of male animals available to service females in oestrus. For example, with cattle it is not uncommon that in a village there may be only one or two bulls available to mate with all the cows (Vetter 2003), but this appears less problematic for other species. For example for goats Mafu and Masika (2002) reported that buck to doe ratios fell within the recommended 1: 30-40 ratio at the villages of Sheshegu and Ncera.

There is little doubt that high rate of offspring mortality is one of the major obstacles to reproductive success in communal areas. Many offspring die during birth due to the general lack of veterinary support, particularly the birth is difficult. The magnitude and severity of the problem is apparent from both historical and contemporary data. Bembridge (1979) estimated the mean calf mortality in the Ciskei of 20%. Vetter (2003) reported similarly high levels of offspring mortality among lambs (18.1%) and goat kids (27.9%).

One of the causes of the high mortality rates among livestock is the incidence of diseases amongst both offspring and adult animals. Among cattle, the most important diseases are gall sickness (anaplasmosis) and redwater (both tick-borne), foot rot and brucellosis (spontaneous abortion of offspring). Infections are also problematic, and among cattle they often are the result of poor veterinary practices by unqualified people. One of the most common causes of infection among young male cattle is unhygienic castration, which often involves blunt knives and misguided treatment of the resulting wound using soil, ash or dung (Kepe 2002).

Sheep are particularly vulnerable to disease when young if not properly cared for. Diseases include diarrhoea (particularly among lambs), sheep scab, blue tongue, and pulp kidney (Ntshona and Turner 2002). For many sheep owners in communal areas disease takes a heavy toll on their flocks leading to the common perception that sheep are difficult animals to maintain. This, combined with difficulties in marketing wool, may to some extent explain the downturn in sheep numbers in the Ciskei during the past few decades (Table 2.3). Goats, in comparison, have a reputation for being more hardy and self-reliant. Research conducted by ARDRI in the villages of Ncera and Sheshegu in the central Eastern Cape region, suggests that the most commonly reported diseases among goats are gall sickness and heartwater (cowdriosis), which are tick-borne diseases; lameness due to foot rot and tick bites between the hooves, and scab caused by itch mites (Mafu and Masika 2002). Owners in these villages treated their goats using both conventional and traditional methods, in different combinations. The combination of herbal and conventional remedies was based on the belief that mixing the two types of remedies gave better results than sole use of either (Mafu and Masika 2002).

Among African livestock farmers in central Eastern Cape the use of herbal remedies in the treatment of livestock ailments remains common and such remedies are locally perceived to be particularly effective against gall sickness, babesiosis and heartwater (Mululuma and Masika 2000). Reliance on such traditional techniques is prompted to a large extent by the lack of extension services and veterinary support in many communal areas and by the prohibitive cost of conventional livestock medicines. Nevertheless, this ethno-veterinary knowledge is only retained by a few older individuals and is not being embraced by the younger generation (Mululuma and Masika 2000). Among households who do not employ herbal remedies, outlay on medicines and vaccines can be very significant, running into thousands of Rand per annum (Ntshona and Turner 2002, Vetter 2003).

Any attempt to explain the relatively poor levels of productivity of communal livestock herds from a commercial perspective must give adequate recognition to the objectives of the communal farmer. Certainly, the offtake values presented above for cattle, sheep and goats corroborate to a large extent the different uses these livestock have. The relatively low turnover rates among cattle and goats reflect their primary importance for investment and ceremony respectively. In contrast the high turnover of sheep seems to reflect their widespread use as animals of slaughter and sale for short-term economic gain, although some individuals do tend to continue to maintain large flocks primarily for wool (Vetter 2003). Thus, despite unfavourable levels of performance in comparison with commercial systems, from a livelihood perspective the value of livestock to owners in communal areas cannot be underestimated.

*Rangeland management*
Grazing of rangeland for livestock production in communal areas of Eastern Cape is currently subject to varying levels of management control. This is largely dependent on the original history of management imposition by the state and subsequent social, and to some extent ecological, change (Bennett 2002).

The imposition of state control over grazing management was achieved through the widespread application of betterment planning (see chapter 1). The betterment system was widely implemented in the former Ciskei, such that by 1973/74, some 79% of the region had been planned and of this almost 87% was under some form of rangeland (*veld*) management (Trollope and Coetzee 1975). An important feature of rangeland management, introduced with betterment, was the rotational grazing of range camps. This generally took the form of the one-herd-four-camp system, whereby one grazing camp was rested for the entire year and the remaining three were grazed on a rotational basis (Trollope and Coetzee 1975). This resting system was perpetuated under state control in the Ciskei until the mid-1970s, when the South African Bantu Trust, responsible for its enforcement, was dissolved and control devolved to individual communities (Forbes and Trollope 1991).

It appears that very few communities in communal areas of Eastern Cape now perpetuate any of the rotational grazing practices associated with betterment. Vetter (2003) relates that in Herschel district, efforts to maintain the system slowly collapsed, such that by the mid-1990s even the most rudimentary attempts at grazing management had disappeared. Nevertheless, in some administrative areas of Herschel, such as Bensonvale and Tugela, local committees were still adhering to a limited form of control over grazing through rotational resting of the old grazing camps to ensure adequate winter forage, but their efforts were severely compromised by inadequate fencing, shortage of grazing elsewhere and lack of political authority. The situation is similar in the former Ciskei. Cousins (1996), has documented conflicts over grazing rights among several of the villages in Sheshegu and Tyefu locations. On this basis he suggests these areas have little if any control over grazing management. Furthermore, it would appear that this scenario is not restricted only to rural villages but is also typical of the informal settlements associated with many of the towns in the region. Higginbottom (1995) documented the degeneration of previously regulated grazing systems associated with municipal commonage into open-access in the town of Peddie in the former Ciskei. Thus, the general situation with regard to management of rangeland grazing in the region seems to be one in which previously enforced common property systems have disintegrated into 'open-access' systems of the type associated with the 'tragedy of the commons' scenario described by Hardin (1968).

One fodder-control strategy, which does seem to have been perpetuated with slightly more success, concerns the use of the arable land allocations as an additional forage reserve during the dry season. Once crops have been harvested at the end of the growing season, the crop stubble is left on the fields to function as a forage reserve, and this is augmented by grass that has been conserved on uncultivated fields (ARDRI 1996, Vetter 2003). These reserves seem to be particularly important for cattle and in some cases individual farmers will actually remove the crop residues from their fields and feed them to their own cattle separately, to ensure they get maximum benefit from them (Vetter 2003). Indeed, the high value attached to cattle is also expressed in the willingness of owners to buy supplementary feed for them when natural forage is scarce (Vetter 2003). This also extends to sheep, where there appears to be a general recognition among smallholders of the need for additional feed inputs, particularly when they are lambs. Vetter (2003) found that in addition to buying supplementary feed, nearly 40% of sheep owners planted feed crops (wheat or oats) for their animals. Thus, for cattle and sheep at least, farmers in communal areas appear acutely aware of the benefits of supplementary feeding. However, the extent to which this is practised appears to be determined primarily by household income (Ntshona and Turner 2002).

*Rangeland quality in communal areas*
Given that many of the communal grazing systems in the central Eastern Cape appear to have degenerated into 'open-access', with little effort to control grazing management, it is important to consider the possible effects of this on rangeland quality. Historically, there were repeated claims from state officials and pasture scientists that rangeland in the Ciskei region was degraded and incapable of supporting the high levels of grazing to which it was subjected. However, such claims tended to be largely speculative and highly subjective, involving little or no empirical support. Trollope and Coetzee (1975) contended that "... malpractices such as overstocking and poor pasture management have led to the destruction of the vegetative cover in large areas of the Ciskei". They go on to argue that the implementation of betterment grazing management systems "... has caused a significant improvement in the condition of the *veld* in the Ciskei, particularly in the mixed and *sourveld* areas". However, the few data that are included seem to support the opposite conclusion. Data are presented from a botanical survey of a severely overstocked area of *sweetveld*, at Cildara location in Middledrift district, from which the authors conclude that desirable grass species such as *Themeda triandra*, *Digitaria eriantha* and *Sporobolus fimbriatus* had survived in significant quantities. These findings could not easily be reconciled with the general consensus of opinion at the time that overstocking by commercial standards resulted in range degradation.

More recently, attempts have been made to conduct objective measurements of rangeland condition in communal areas. Goqwana (1998) conducted an assessment of *veld* condition at four villages in Middledrift district in the former Ciskei. He employed the key species approach for *veld* condition assessment developed by researchers at Fort Hare University (Scogings *et al.* 1994, Beckerling *et al.* 1995). *Veld* condition scores were in the region of 60-80% for all villages, and on this basis he concluded that the overall condition of the grass sward could be described as good to excellent in all cases, even by commercial farming standards. Furthermore, the botanical composition of the sward was also good, being quite varied and dominated by desirable species such as *Themeda triandra*, *Digitaria eriantha* and *Heteropogon contortus*. This was despite the fact that stocking rates at all the villages were at least three times higher than recommended for the area, and two of the villages practised no form of grazing management and were grazed at an 'open-access' level.

In contrast Vetter (2003), working in communal villages in Herschel District found that the level of range degradation was considerably higher than in comparable commercial farms and that the proportion of valuable grazing species such as *Themeda triandra* in the sward was considerably reduced. This area is largely *sourveld* and high grazing pressure seemed to have overcome the inherent ability of the sward to resist change and resulted in a fundamental change in species composition and greatly lowered associated productivity that is largely irreversible.

The available evidence indicates that the relationship between animal numbers and rangeland condition is not as clear as pasture scientists previously believed. Rather, it appears that whilst some communal areas of rangeland in the Eastern Cape have undergone considerable and irreversible degradation in response to intensive grazing pressure there are also others that have supported high livestock populations over long periods without experiencing irreversible degradation.

## Smallholder crop production

In chapter two it was pointed out that the pre-colonial South-Nguni farming system had two principal components. The primary activity conducted by men was cattle farming, with milk as the main product. Grain crops (sorghum and later maize) and vegetables (cucurbits mainly) were grown by women in gardens. While home gardening maintained its importance in the local farming system, crop production on a field scale came to the fore after the introduction of labour-saving technology, first the metal hoe and later animal-drawn equipment.

In the former Ciskei region production of crops is subject to several limitations. The most important are water deficits in all areas except the Amatola and Winterberg mountain ranges (Marais 1975), and limited availability of land capable of supporting cultivation (Hensley and Laker 1975). In 1989, 8.2% of the Ciskei region was cultivated (Antrobus *et al.* 1994), but a considerable proportion of that land was of poor quality. Good arable land is restricted by slope and soil depth, and usually occurs in isolated pockets of limited extent. Low soil fertility and soil acidity in areas where mean annual rainfall exceeds 600 mm are also factors limiting crop growth and yield.

*Water deficits*
During the 1980s the potential for rainfed cropping of important soil-slope-climate combinations, called ecotopes, found on the Coastal Plateau was evaluated empirically (Van Averbeke and Marais 1991). This evaluation was conducted along similar lines as the Benchmark Soils Project (Beinroth *et al.* 1980). It was apparent from the evaluation of the water regimes of the major land types in Ciskei by Marais (1975) that the degree of water sufficiency was the key factor limiting rainfed crop production. An evaluation of 113 field

experiments conducted over a period of five years on 16 ecotopes showed rainfall and effective rooting depth of soils to be important determinants of crop
yield. Under similar climatic conditions, deep soils produced higher yields than
shallow soils, because they stored more water than shallow soils, enabling the
crop to subsist for longer on stored water when there was no rain.

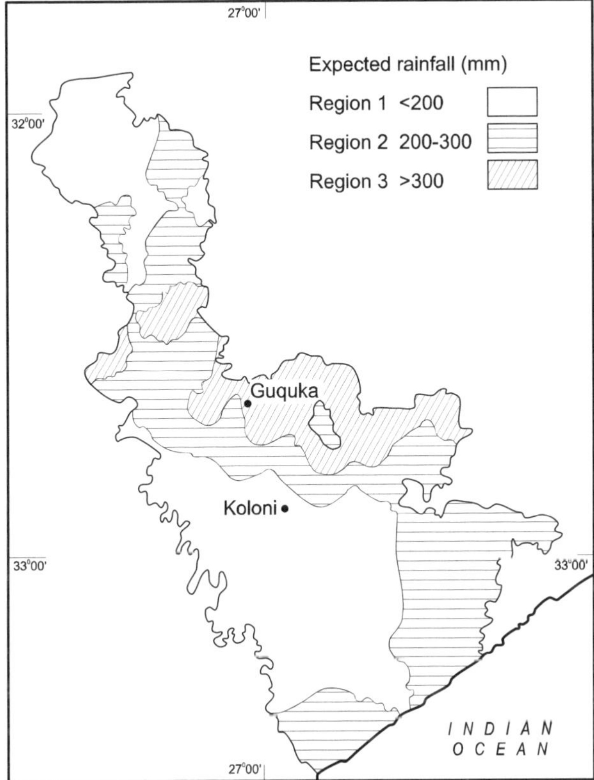


*Map 3.1*        Rainfall expected at the 75% level of probability for the period October to
                February inclusive in the former Ciskei

*Source*: Van Averbeke (1989)


Based on their experimental results Van Averbeke and Marais (1991) concluded that relatively risk-free maize production on the Coastal Plateau required
three conditions to be met: (1) land with a slope not exceeding 6%, (2) a soil
with an effective rooting depth of at least 900 mm, and (3) an expected rainfall
of at least 290 mm during the growing period of the crop. In Map 3.1, the Ciskei
region has been subdivided into three zones based on the rainfall expected at the
75% level of probability for the period October to February inclusive (Austin
1989a, Van Averbeke 1989). This period represents the growing period of a

long-season maize cultivar that was planted early. The high rainfall zone, where at least 300 mm of rain can be expected during this period, is limited to the Amatola and Winterberg mountain ranges and the adjacent fringe of the Coastal Plateau. Here, maize production is largely free of risk as long as the crop is planted in soils with a rooting depth of 900 mm or more. A moderately dry zone with an expected rainfall ranging between 200 and 300 mm is found along the coast, and on parts of the Coastal and Midland Plateaus that neighbour the mountains. In this zone selecting soils with adequate storage capacity and effective conservation of water during the fallow period are critical factors for success in dryland maize production. The dry zone, where the expected rainfall during the growing season is less than 200 mm, is extremely marginal for dryland maize. This zone covers large parts of the Coastal and Midland plateaus. To harvest at least one ton of maize grain per ha in seven to eight seasons out of every ten, selection of suitable soils and effective soil water conservation during the fallow season are even more critical than in the moderately dry zone. In addition, planting density should be reduced from about 20,000 to 30,000 plants per ha to 10,000 plants per ha to increase the amount of stored soil water per plant (Van Averbeke 1989).

*Low soil fertility*
Low soil fertility is the other important factor limiting crop production in Ciskei (Hensley and Laker 1975). Generally, cultivated soils are low in organic matter and plant available phosphorus, and many test acid (Mandirigana *et al.* 2001). Garden soils tend to have higher fertility than field soils. Similar differences in fertility between garden and field soils were reported for the Transkei (Mkile 2001) and KwaZulu-Natal (Roberts *et al.* 2003). Evidence from Transkei suggests that differences in soil fertility between field and garden soils are mainly due to differences in nutrient supply, primarily in the form of *kraal* manure, with gardens receiving larger and more regular applications than fields (Mkile *et al.* 2001).

When water and nutrients are in short supply, controlling weeds is critical in crop production. In dryland maize a strong linear relationship between biomass of weeds and reduction in grain yield has been demonstrated (Marais 1985). In a maize crop weeds need to be controlled effectively during the interval of 30 to 60 days after planting to avoid a major reduction in grain yield. Up to 2% per day of the grain yield may be lost as a result of not controlling weeds during this interval of the growing season. On most smallholdings weeds are controlled by hand hoeing. Often only one or two people take care of the weeding of a field and it may take them several weeks to complete the task. Marais (1985) identified two important limitations associated with the control of weeds in smallholder maize production: delayed commencement of weeding, usually 40 days after planting, and the protracted period over which weeding occurred. He estimated that the combination of these limitations was responsible for an average reduction in grain yield of 44%.

*Field cropping*

In smallholder farming in the Eastern Cape, including the Ciskei region, the main field crop-is maize, but often maize is intercropped with other food crops (Steyn 1988, Silwana 2000). In the Eastern Cape maize is usually intercropped with varying combinations of dry beans, pumpkins and bitter watermelons. In humid areas, such as the coastal zone of Transkei, dry beans and pumpkins feature prominently in the mix (Silwana 2000, Mkile 2001). In the dry areas of the Ciskei region bitter watermelons are common. Intercropping maize with cucurbits, such as pumpkins and bitter watermelons, helps to control weeds (Wahua 1985, Silwana 2001). The prominence of cucurbits in such arrangements suggests an attempt by farmers to reduce the drudgery of controlling weeds by hand, but they do not necessarily select a particular intercrop mixture with that specific purpose in mind. In personal contacts they usually refer to homestead traditions that evolved over time as the main explanation for their specific intercropping practices.

*Home gardening*

Earlier it was indicated that cropping on a field scale has declined to very low levels in the former Ciskei. At present, most rural households in the region limit production of crops to home gardens. These may range in size from 100 $m^2$ to 10,000 $m^2$. In settlements where betterment was implemented, which applies to at least 79% of Ciskei (Coetzee and Trollope 1975), home gardens are situated within the confines of the residential sites. Since residential sites in Ciskei tend to be relatively small, home gardens rarely exceed 1,000 $m^2$. In the Transkei region withdrawal from crop production on a field scale has also been reported (Mc Allister 2001 and Andrew and Fox 2003), but here home gardens tend to be larger than in the Ciskei region (Mkile 2001).

In both regions home garden production has been subject to intensification. In the Transkei this has taken various forms including scale enlargement, intercropping and higher levels of nutrient additions in the form of animal manures (Andrew and Fox 2003, Mkile 2001). In the Ciskei, where water is usually the limiting factor, smallholders often improve soil water availability in their gardens. Where water for irrigation is available, crops are occasionally irrigated, especially at planting or when a lack of rain threatens survival of the growing plants (Monde 2000). Where water is not available, a few innovative gardeners have adopted and modified water harvesting and conservation technologies. One technology involves the diversion of water running off roads using cement-lined micro-dams. Water in these micro-dams is used to irrigate garden crops using hose pipes. Another is the use of organic mulches to reduce surface evaporation. Expansion of home gardens has been achieved in part by bringing vacant residential plots into production or by excising small parcels of land from the rangeland neighbouring the homestead.

## Conclusions

Agro-ecologically, the central Eastern Cape is diverse. Mean annual rainfall varies from 450 to 1700 mm, and altitude ranges from sea level to about 2200 m. Temperature regimes also differ, from moderate subtropical near the coast to *highveld* conditions with cold winters and hot summers in the north. The diversity in physical attributes of the land is reflected in the vegetation cover. Yet, in spite of the considerable agro-ecological variety of the region, land use is fairly uniform throughout, consisting of mixed farming with emphasis on livestock (beef) production. Generally, land available for cultivation is limited in extent for reasons of water deficit, steep relief and poor soil quality. On many commercial farms arable land is used to grow fodder crops in support of the livestock enterprise. On smallholdings it is used to produce grain crops for human consumption, primarily maize. Land use around East London, the main urban centre in the region, differs from that in the other parts. Here arable land is used for the production of dairy, vegetables and pine apples. The valleys of major rivers, where cultivated land is often used for citrus, are the other important exception.

Smallholder farming in the region occurs primarily in the communal areas of the former Ciskei. Smallholder livestock production generally involves mixed holdings of cattle, sheep and goats in varying proportions dependent largely on the local vegetation biome. Livestock numbers are constrained only by the productivity of the natural rangeland rather than by adherence to recommended stocking rates. Overall numbers are high and ownership continues to be widespread. However, individual holdings are generally limited and certainly too small to allow most owners a livelihood based purely on their stock. Rather, livestock are farmed at a subsistence level and fulfil a number of important livelihood functions. Consequently, levels of animal offtake tend to be low compared to commercial herds. The management activities of smallholder livestock farmers also tend to be more limited, despite facing the same agro-ecological constraints as commercial farmers. Seasonal herding is practised where appropriate, but management practices such as rotational grazing, introduced under betterment planning, have largely been abandoned. Fodder supplementation tends to be limited to the use of the arable land allocations as a winter forage reserve and the purchase of supplementary feed when this can be afforded. Given these low levels of fodder flow management, the productivity of smallholder livestock farming in the central Eastern Cape remains closely tied to local levels of rangeland productivity, which is subject to considerable spatial and temporal variability.

Crop production is subject to several environmental limitations. Water deficit is the key limiting factor, followed by low soil fertility. Sustainable production of maize, the principal crop in the region, depends on local conditions of soil and rainfall and on the application of management practices that reduce the effect of the prevailing limiting factors. These practices include soil water conservation, the application of fertilizers and effective control of weeds. For various reasons, many contemporary rural homesteads do not produce crops on a field scale. Instead they focus on crop production in home gardens. Compared to fields, home gardens are used more intensively, receiving more nutrients and water. These interventions address the key limitations experienced in local plant production, enabling higher productivity than is generally being achieved on a field scale. However, considering the limited size of the home gardens in the region, which are typically smaller than 1000 m$^2$, home gardening on its own, however intensive it may be, rarely addresses limitations in homestead food production.

4

# A social history of Guquka and Koloni: Settlement and resources

Paul Hebinck and Lothar Smith[*]

## Introduction

This chapter elucidates the history of the two villages and should be read against the historical background provided in chapter 2. Here we focus primarily on the dynamics of settlement and the social processes that, over time, have shaped these villages. Although there are some discrepancies in accounts, formal and informal, of when Koloni was first established it is thought that both villages have their origins around 1850, in the aftermath of the Frontier Wars between the colonising English and the Xhosa.

During and following the Frontier Wars the colonial state enabled and allowed settlement on conquered land by the fore fathers of the current villagers. Settlement and, more specifically, the allocation and arrangement of access to natural resources, was based on a neat, explicit and sometimes exclusionary distinction of land categories for settlement, arable purposes and livestock grazing. The colonial state saw this as a means of facilitating crop cultivation and livestock keeping as central elements of rural livelihoods. Yet, this settle-

---

[*] The authors thank Frans Huyzendveldt and Nick Parrott for comments on the last draft of this chapter.

ment pattern contrasted starkly with previously existing settlement patterns and use of the landscape. This chapter deals with the specifics of settlement, the introduction of various categories of land use and land tenure, the allocation of land, the dynamics of betterment planning as a government response to resource degradation, and related aspects of natural resource management.

Guquka and Koloni had rather contrasting experiences of betterment planning which is conventionally viewed in the literature (see chapter 2) as an attempt to socially and physically restructure and reorganise the so-called native reserves. Labour migration later shaped the patterns of resource utilisation and the expansion of the two settlements over the years. The pension and social grant systems played a crucial role in shifting the source of people's livelihoods towards the use of resources located beyond the boundaries of the villages. Since the origin and social history of Guquka and Koloni differ, we start by describing these separately. Despite these differences, there are clear similarities, particularly in more recent times.

The data for this chapter are based primarily on oral accounts of villagers collected during the period 1997 to 2004. Some of the data and analysis have been written up in ARDRI Research Reports (Van Averbeke *et al.* 1998). Other data have been used in conferences and seminar papers (Hebinck and Smith 2001, Hebinck 2004), while some are only recorded and stored as field notes (Smith, 2000, field notes; Hebinck 2004, field notes).

The researchers, together with their assistants, purposefully selected informants who could provide historical accounts of the two villages. This was considered necessary, as written recordings of the history of the two villages are scant. The historical literature and travellers' accounts only contain general references and descriptions relating to the larger area surrounding the two villages (e.g. the Tyume River Valley, Amatola Mountains and the Hogsback Plateau). The informants in the two villages, all elderly males, were interviewed in group sessions. In addition, Chief Mqalo, the traditional leader of Guquka, who resided in the neighbouring village of Gilton, and Mr. Ngxowa and Mr. Kama, respectively the former and present chairmen of the Residents' Committee at Koloni, were interviewed on different occasions about the history of their villages. Unfortunately, the Chief of Koloni, *Nkosi* Zwelimjongile Siseko, who was residing in Qhibira, south of Koloni, was not available for an interview, due to illness.

The role of chiefs in South Africa has been changing over the years (chapter 6). In Guquka and Koloni their influence has substantially diminished in the past century, in comparison to other parts of South Africa. As the process of devolution of tribal authority is discussed extensively in chapter 6, our comments here are limited to a few observations that relate directly to the role of the chiefs in the historical changes that have taken place in the two villages. In the past the role of the chief was especially important for the (re)allocation of land for residential and arable purposes. This chapter elaborates on this and describes how this worked shortly after settlement. In the later half of the 20th Century their responsibilities were taken over by appointed or elected civic organisations such as Residents Associations and Range Management Committees and the chiefs' positions as tribal leaders are now primarily ceremonial. However, their traditional status as keepers of village history is still respected (Soga 1931, Mtuze 2004). It is also in this context that we refer to the views of chiefs and other traditional leaders.

## History of Guquka

The social history of Guquka is one of motion: people have been on the move for a long time, albeit for different reasons. Its past involves autonomous settlement and male labour migration. In the second half of the $20^{th}$ century, its history was further shaped by an influx of people who had endured forced removals from areas declared 'white'. In the late 1980s to early 1990s, when the Apartheid system began to dissolve, whole families began to migrate from the village. Most recently, from the late 1990s onwards, migrants, retrenched workers and pensioners from other, usually urban, parts of South Africa have begun to return to the village.

*Origin*
The people of Guquka derive from a migration movement that dates back to the mid $19^{th}$ century. Part of the Makhuzeni clan migrated to the fertile Tyume River basin that forms part of the Amatola Mountain range. This migration followed the defeat of the Ngika under Paramount Chief Sandile, and occurred after the end of the 1850-1853 Frontier War (see chapter 2) and as a result of their expulsion from the river valley. After the British cleared the Tyume valley of these Xhosa, other clans and tribes moved in and occupied the valley. In contrast to other British controlled areas of the Eastern Cape, (including Koloni), settlement in Guquka was largely autonomous. According to local accounts, some of the settlers belonged to the Mfengu or adopted Mfengu traditions (see chapter 2).

Mrs. Warsdale, an amateur historian who is well-versed with the history of white settlement in the Tyume Valley, claims that white farmers, including British soldiers who wanted to farm, began to occupy parts of the Tyume valley by 1847. The well-known missionary, Brown, also settled in the Tyume valley and farmed on the Pleasant View Estate (pers. comm. Warsdale, April 2004). Over time an active relationship between these white settlers and the people of Guquka emerged, as described later in the chapter.

Chief Mqalo, chief over what was later designated as the Makhuzeni Tribal Area, in 2004 at an age of 87 years, explained the settlement of his people in Makhuzeni as an autonomous process. In a series of interviews between 2000 and 2004, he told how his people originated from Zululand. Around 1820 a group of people under the leadership of a man named Jama decided to move from Zululand to escape the turmoil caused by the 'Mfecane' (see chapter 2).

They migrated through the territory east of the Great Kei River controlled by the Xhosa Chief Hintsa. Here the group split in two. Jama decided to stay and align with Hintsa, while Mqalo, the current Chief's great-grandfather, migrated further with his followers across the Great Kei River, to an area west of the Great Fish River (close to where Port Elisabeth is today) and then to Ndabathemba where they stayed for a while. During this migration, migrants from other clans and tribes joined them. They moved with their cattle, surviving on their milk, continuously looking for good grazing land. From the Port Elizabeth area they moved to Fort Beaufort, on to Ndabexirhe and later to the Amatola region. Around 1830 they arrived in the Tyume valley, which at that time was still controlled by the Ngqika Xhosa. According to the current Chief, Mqalo and his group were given permission to settle in the valley by Chief Tyali, son of Ngqika and brother of Maqoma. The area became their tribal area called Makhuzeni and Mqalo subsequently became their chief (chapter 6).

Prior to the arrival of Mqalo and his people, the Makhuzeni region must have looked different, as chapter 5 shows. Mqalo, the father of the current chief, subdivided and allocated the Makhuzeni area to different groups, and a number of settlements, located close to each other, were established. This subdivision was overseen by the colonial administration. In addition to Guquka, these settlements included the present-day villages of Gilton, Msompondo and Mpundu. To this day, the people of these villages share the same communal rangelands. Mqalo originally established more settlements, including Kwezana, whose residents were later relocated by betterment planners to one of the other villages between 1930 and 1950.

Upon arrival in the Tyume valley, some of the land was cleared of shrubs and trees to open it up for cultivation. The method by which this was done is not well documented, although it is known that that the Southern Nguni made use of digging sticks and hoes and that fire also played an important management role (see chapter 2).

The cleared land was used mostly for cultivating grains that were mainly meant for consumption by women during their menstruation period, as custom dictated that they should not consume dairy products at such times. In addition, various kinds of vegetables were cultivated in gardens adjacent to residential compounds. The rangelands supported the livestock, allowed for hunting and provided various other resources to the villagers. Mostert (1993) describes the Tyume Valley as being an excellent cattle grazing area at that time. For Mqalo's people cattle also provided a social means for survival that could be bartered for other resources, used at ceremonies and as 'lobola' (Schapera 1937, Soga 1931, Mtuze 2004).

Thus the land was well endowed with resources that enabled the villagers to combine hunting and gathering with crop cultivation and animal husbandry (particularly cattle). Together these resources usually provided sufficient means to meet people's needs for consumption, shelter and social-cultural reproduction. During this early period, people kept cattle so they could directly use their produce, such as sour milk. Water was taken from the river, and game played an important role in their diet. The villagers lived in huts (*'amanukwalo'*), consisting of wooden poles interwoven with reed or grass with a fireplace in the middle. The floor was dug out and plastered with manure. According to Chief Mqalo, each village had access to the surrounding rangelands, including mountain and valley-bottom pastures. This ensured that adequate grazing was available for livestock throughout the seasons. Accounts of travellers (Mostert 1993) and local people confirm this.

*Demarcation of land and land tenure*
As their settlement was overseen by the colonial administration, the allocation and partitioning of land to communities and individual homesteads reflected the ideas and views of the then administrators. Land tenure in the central Eastern Cape has been largely shaped by colonial interventions. A survey held in 1899 by colonial government surveyors demarcated and fixed the boundaries of each tribal area in the Tyume valley. The colonial administration made a further distinction between land allocated for crops (then termed a garden lot, but referred to in this book as an arable allotment), which ere between three to four *morgen* (2.5 to 3.4 ha) in size, and land intended for residential purposes (building lots). The remaining land was designated as 'commonage'.

Table 4.1 shows the current proportions of these land categories. Chapter 7 describes the changes in these over time in more detail. Map 4.1 shows the distribution of these three land use categories across the landscape.

*Table 4.1*      Size (ha) of major land categories as of 1997

|  | Guquka | Koloni |
|---|---|---|
| Residential land | 34 | 33 |
| Arable allotments | 160 | 405 |
| Communal rangelands | 578* | 661 |
| Woodlot | -- | 17 |
| Total | 772 | 1114 |

* The boundaries are poorly defined

*Source*: ARDRI Survey 1997

The chief allocated rights to these three categories of land to the heads of families. The original title deed made out to Nolesi, the widow of the late Skepe Mqalo, grandfather of the current Chief is shown in Photo 4.1.

This deed has been passed down through the generations to the present Chief Mqalo who showed it to us at his residence in Gilton in 2004. A copy can also be found in the Deeds Registry at King William's Town.

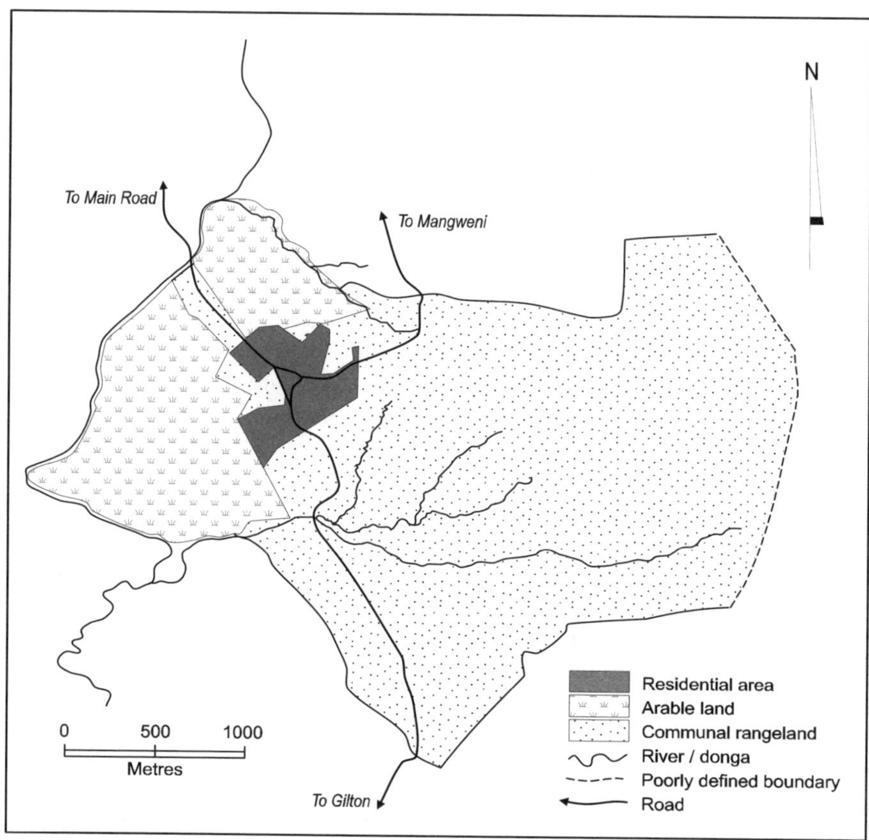


*Map 4.1*    Location of residential areas, communal rangeland and arable land in
             Guquka

This quitrent deed granted access to and use of building lot 172 and garden lot
177 on payment of a perpetual quitrent (annual payment) of two shillings and
six pence (sterling), which was first paid on the first of January 1902. The Glen
Grey Act (1894) later designated ownership of the rangelands as 'communal'.
Chief Mqalo confirmed that the rangeland was 'open to everybody'. Residency
in the village grants people access to the 'commonage' to this day.

The first families to settle in Guquka, who are still referred to as the 'old'
families (Holbrook 1998), were given similar deeds granting them rights to
arable, residential and grazing lands. Residential sites and fields (referred to as
garden lots or arable allotments) were registered under quitrent, with the title
deeds being issued to the male heads of the families.

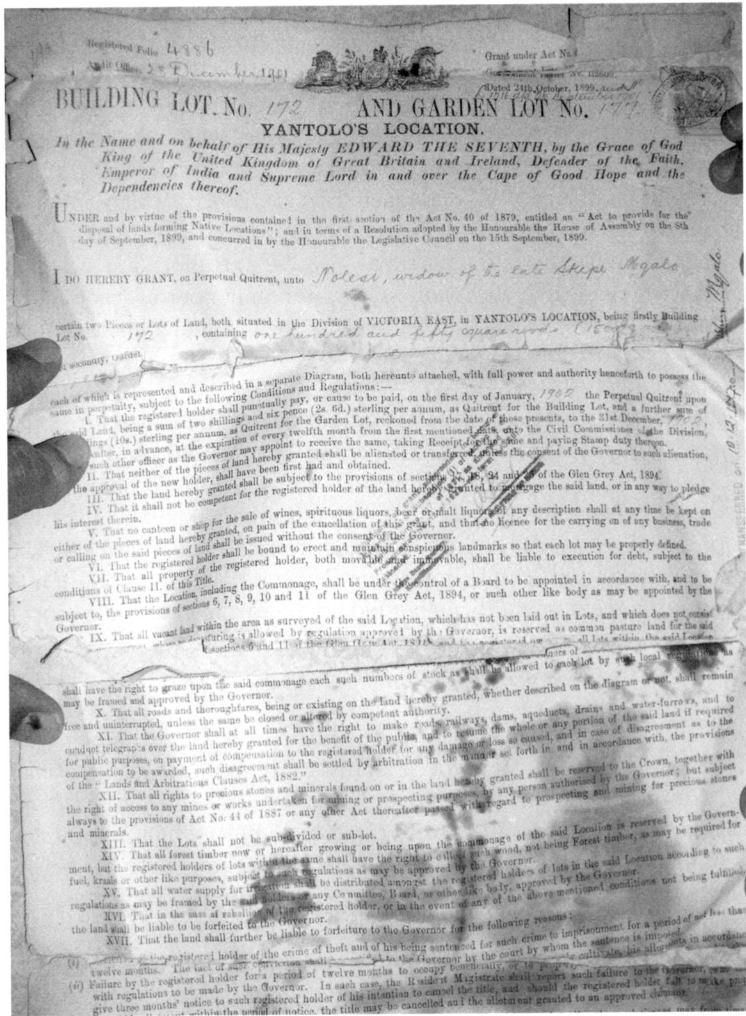

*Photo 4.1*   Chief Mqalo's original title deed issued in 1899 to his late grandmother.
(Photo by Hebinck)

Quitrent is a form of individual tenure, but unlike freehold tenure, it requires the deed holders to pay an annual rent for their land. Each deed specifies the location of the arable allotment and the residential plot, and the annual rent payable for each. Upon the death of the male titleholder the oldest son inherits the deeds, but this usually only occurs after the widow has passed away. Historians record that quitrent title deeds were issued in the former Ciskei and in parts of the Transkei from 1849 to 1879 (Mills and Wilson 1952, Cokwana

1988) but apparently as the land allocation history of Guquka demonstrated also much later.

The Deeds Registry of Yantalo Location, Victoria East District located at King William's Town shows that most land was allocated and registered during the late 1890s. Quitrent tenure has not yet been not converted to freehold tenure and the status and future of quitrent is uncertain at the moment (chapter 6).

In 1910 a second land survey was conducted, at the end of which "a lot of land" was taken away and provided to white farmers. Chief Mqalo explained that the colonial administration thought that "the Mqalo allocation was too large". The area was renamed as the Yantolo Location in honour of Yantolo the regent before Mqalo, for the concessions he made to the colonial administration.


*Interactions with white farmers*

All the white farmers who settled in the Valley were given land under a freehold tenure arrangement. Up to the 1950s, interaction between black and white farmers in the Tyume valley was limited; while there was little co-operation or exchange they seldom came into conflict. The white farmers bought cattle from the black people, while the latter bought firewood from the white farmers. The main interaction was through employment, particularly domestic work. Chief Mqalo: "Kitchen girls were paid 70 cents a month and a sheep cost 80 cents". Today Chief Mqalo would pay 2,500 Rand for 6 sheep and pays his domestic servant 400 Rand a month, so the relative value of labour has not changed dramatically since then.

Some local villagers that we interviewed said that their interactions with white farmers went beyond exchanges of labour and farm products. They sometimes borrowed thrashers from white farmers, possibly in exchange for their own labour. There were white trading stores close to Guquka which bought and sold grain from black farmers. The farmers bought coffee, tea, sugar but generally not staples, which they mostly produced at home. The trading store was a two-way mechanism and did quite well as their trade was boosted by the relatively large sums of money that flowed into the villages from remittances from migrant labour.

The 1950s and 1960s were a period when the Apartheid laws following the 1936 Land and Trust Act, were enforced and when white people (both traders and farmers) were removed from the valley. One of the effects of this was to reduce local employment opportunities, especially for women. Pleasant View Estate, on the road to Hogsback, was vacated in 1968 (Warsdale, pers. comm. 2004). Records for rainfall data also stopped being collected in the same year (Bennett, pers. comm.).


*Betterment planning*

The Tomlinson Commission Report published in 1955 (chapter 2) reflected and formally acknowledged the view that emerged during the 1940s and 1950s, that improving the natural environment in areas designated as 'native reserves' was an urgent priority. These interventions, which became known as betterment planning, were also introduced and implemented in the Makhuzeni area. Betterment planners brought all the high-lying homesteads of settlements, such as Kwezana, down to the valleys or plains and incorporated them in the current settlements. Elderly informants remember clearly how clusters of homesteads were destroyed and converted into grazing land. This land was divided up and fenced off into grazing camps. The arable land was also fenced off. The neighbouring village of Gilton was assigned its own section of grazing land, while Guquka had to share its grazing camps with Msopondo and Kayalethu (see Map 4.2).

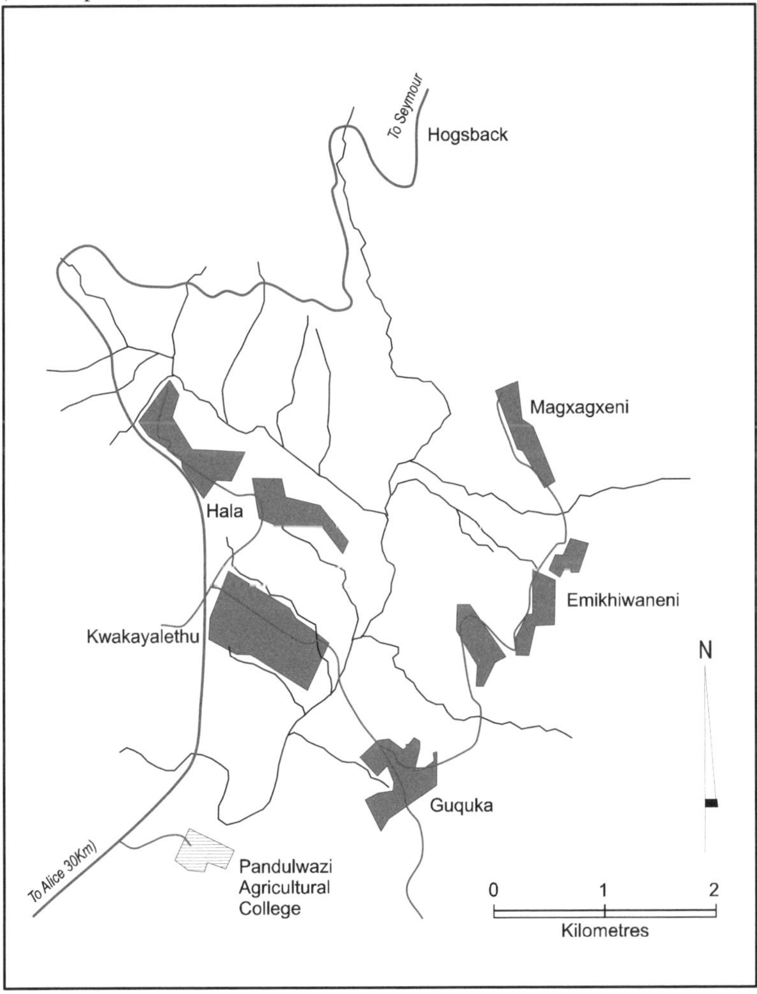


*Map 4.2*    Location of Guquka and surrounding villages

The enforcement of the grazing camp management system was accompanied by the imposition of a rotational grazing system, to be implemented by livestock owners. The villagers of Guquka disliked the fences that separated the commons that they had shared with neighbouring villages. One fence ran right down from the mountains to the valley and prevented them from grazing their cattle as they had done before. Over time, this system broke down, as local people stole fencing materials to use to fence off their own homesteads. This, in turn, led to cattle starting to graze on the arable lands.

During the betterment government officials controlled livestock numbers and enforced culling. Mr. Tabana asserts that today he can count the number of people with livestock 'on one hand', and that the number of livestock owners has substantially reduced over the years (chapter 8). In his view, the reduction in the size of villagers' herds can be traced to the combined effect of serious spells of drought, e.g. in the early 1980s, and the culling and land reallocation practises introduced under betterment planning. He remembers how government surveyors who came to Guquka in 1965 to implement betterment planning ordered the people to cull their cattle:

> I was working with some old men in the fields in the late 1960s when we got a message from the Paramount Chief that there were too many stock and that the government was going to cut the numbers ... He did not discuss this with the people of the villages. He just had the order to obey. There was nothing to discuss with the people, as he could not say anything to the surveyor.
> He just had to agree to each and everything the surveyor said and pass it on to the headmen who then had to chase the people.A gentleman with six oxen could keep four only, and one cow. If the cow calved the owner was obliged to sell one of his oxen. If the gentleman would not sell some of his animals he was taken to jail, or the police would come and take away his cattle and sell them at a low price to punish him for not obeying the rules. Before, we had been lucky, as the government had never made us sell our sheep and cattle. We only sold them when we needed money. Those times ended from then on.

Betterment in villages like Guquka was contested because it had adverse effects on villagers' ability to manage their herds in a time of social and climatic changes. Generally, betterment planning and other government-instituted changes such as the enforcement of the Hut Tax and labour controls (the pass laws also locally known as 'Dom' passes) had a negative affect on their economic and social security. In addition to the culling programme, betterment planning placed other constraints on the use of land based resources. Betterment planning was intended to halt the ecological deterioration of communal grazing lands. Yet, according to local informants, the programme's main effect was to trigger the permanent decline of animal husbandry. This, in turn, negatively affected crop production which depended on animal draught power at crucial phases during the growing season. From a local perspective the ecological improvements that the betterment planners intended to create had an overall negative impact on their activities.

Other sources suggest that the natural resource base was already deteriorating and that this legitimised the interventions introduced under betterment planning. Bundy (1988) points out that the changes to the grazing regime caused by betterment planning, which had already started to change from a seasonal to continuous grazing of valley pastures had resulted in gully and sheet erosion. He argues that the introduction of mechanised ploughing for crop cultivation also resulted in widespread gully erosion. Chapter 7 explores the degree to which this also occurred Guquka.

Chief Mqalo remembers that white farmers first brought tractors into the valley in the 1920s. People in the Makhuzeni region started to use them from about 1939 although on a very limited basis, due to the financial constraints of villagers. Most villagers continued to use draught power to pull wooden ploughs. Only later, in the 1950s, did tractor ploughing became more popular, particularly during the Homeland period (1981-1990) when "there were four tractors stationed here allocated by the Agricultural Department. These were called 'Trust Tractors' and were available for use by the villagers at a nominal fee".

*Influx of people*
Between 1950 and 1960, Apartheid laws were enforced, firmly establishing the segregation of races by allocating them to certain areas (chapter 2). These led to the forced removal of black people from white designated areas (and *vice versa*). Guquka faced an influx of black people, especially in the early 1960s, from areas declared 'white', such as nearby Cathcart and Hogsback. This influx was due to not only Apartheid laws but also the result of white farmers actively removing 'surplus' people from their lands. Many farm workers and members of their families lost their employment or their place to stay on white farms and had to find a place in the designated 'black areas'. These new immigrants to Guquka had various ethnic identities. Some had kinship ties with residents of Guquka and the neighbouring villages; others did not. Village authorities allocated each newcomer a residential plot and they were subsequently given a Permission to Occupy (PTO) (chapter 6). However, newcomers had different rights from the older families, as Mengezelei Mbangi explained. When he came to Guquka in the 1960s he enquired about keeping livestock and was told that only 'size 20 homesteads' could keep livestock. In Guquka, the term 'size 20 homestead' refers to a homestead with quitrent title to land in the village. Conversely, a 'size 10 homestead' is a one that occupies a residential site, taken from the 'commonage' and only held by PTO. Mengezelei explained that the authority kept a 'cattle book' in which the names of livestock owners and their holdings were recorded. The tribal authority ruled that 'size 10 homesteads' wishing to invest in cattle had to register their animals in the name of a 'size 20

household'. Mengezelei was not comfortable with that arrangement and decided to keep only livestock that could "stay around the house" (Van Averbeke 2005).

Newcomers were also denied access to arable allotments because these had all been already allocated to existing residents. As a result, the newcomers could hardly make a living from local resources and had to gain their livelihood elsewhere.

It is important to point out the social and political implications of the distinction between 'old families' and 'newcomers'. Most of the 'newcomers' were labour tenants at white farms, while the members of the 'old' families see themselves as descendants of the original settlers. Holbrook (1998) has shown that the old families, whose heads had served in the tribal authority, still hold most of the land, most of the livestock, and through their assets, they represent the moral authority in the village. This will be discussed further in chapters 8 and 9.

*Social identity*

The residents of Guquka clearly have a mixed socio-ethnic background. Some are Xhosa, others are Mfengu (see chapter 2). Despite their mixed origin, there is consensus over their identity as 'School' rather than 'Red', which implies that they respect and follow the traditions and allegiances largely derived from the Mfengu. One of the associations of the labels of 'School' or 'Red' is of being 'modern' as opposed to 'traditional'; and being 'educated' as opposed to 'pagan'. By adopting the 'School' identity, the people of Guquka present themselves as being educated, modern, progressive minded and forward looking. While notions of 'School' and 'Red' are interesting, they suggest a homogeneity within the village, especially in terms of how people seek to organize their lives, which is not supported by the available evidence. Yet the people, including the chief, immediately and often strongly identify themselves as 'School', showing that these designations are still relevant and important to them. These identities, however, do not directly explain the historical or contemporary patterns of resource use (see for example Mayer 1961, Hunt Davis 1979, and Bank 2002). The approach that we take in this book is to examine the relationship between patterns of resource use and various social categories of livelihoods.

*Settlement expansion*

Chapter 7 provides a general picture of the expansion of the settlement over the years (see Figure 7.5), which has been fuelled by both natural population growth as well as influxes of people from other areas. In response to this population increase, a clear priority has been given to meeting demand for residential land as opposed to maintaining land for communal grazing land. At Guquka, the reduction of pasturage in favour of residential land continues; although the increase in the size and population of the village seems to have slowed from

1985 onwards, due to changing migration patterns and related livelihood strategies. Chapter 11 provides details on such contemporary developments.

*Loss of grazing land*
One critical event, still regarded of much importance especially by the older
generations, is the loss of a section of their rangeland located high in the
Amatola Mountains to the 'white' Hogsback region during the seventies. In
1978 Chief Mqalo and a plantation company in Hogsback reached an agreement
to plant trees on the mountaintop belonging to Makhuzeni, which specified that
once the pine trees were harvested, the Makhuzeni people would share the benefits. According to chief Mqalo, "the land was not used much except for the
collection of wild fruits".

Other informants from Guquka, interviewed in 2000, provided different and
contrasting accounts of this critical event. They explained that Makhuzeni livestock owners used large parts of the Hogsback plateau as rangeland for their
cattle and goats, especially during the summer periods (Van Averbeke *et al.*
1998: 12, Coleman 1999: 35). They adamantly argued that, in addition to
grazing, the mountain was also used for hunting and collecting fruits and
medicinal plants. Frustrated about the loss of one of their key resources, the
residents of Guquka and Msompondo decided to fight the pine tree encroachment by burning down the trees. Operationally the action was successful, but
the authorities retaliated. Some local youths were arrested and thrown in jail,
charged with arson. Fearing more arrests, the Makhuzeni community suspended
the burning of plantations. The foresters exploited this lull in resistance to ban
cattle from young plantations, blaming the animals for damage to trees. Cattle
found roaming in pine plantations were impounded and taken to Seymour or
Cathcart, from where owners found it extremely difficult to retrieve them. Many
livestock farmers lost animals in this way (Van Averbeke *et al.* 1988a).

The villagers sabotaged the agreement, not only because it meant a reduction
in the size of their grazing lands but, more importantly, also the loss of suitable
grazing land. The loss of mountain pastures limited the number of cattle that
could be reared on the rangeland around Guquka. This reduced cattle numbers,
and wealth within the communities (*ibid.*) and status.

This loss not only reduced stock numbers, but also negatively influenced
crop production, as this had always relied to some degree on animal traction.
Only a few people could afford to hire tractors. The oxen were weaker at the
end of the winter and barely able to plough the fields. One informant described
the situation:

> Our cattle used to be on top there on the mountain in the summer season. When you
> see those cattle, you could compare them to those [commercial] farm cattle, fit and
> tough. Since the government took away those lands in 1960 we have become used to
> the cattle eating the grass around us here ... this grass is bitter compared to the sweet
> grass of the hills.

The Makhuzeni community's resistance to the loss of their mountain pastures continued for a long time but eventually faded when it became clear that the newly installed Ciskei Homeland Government would not support their claim to the land. Soon after the last remaining area of pasture above Guquka village was planted with pine trees. Today, the mountain plateau is virtually completely covered with pine, leaving little space for forage for cattle. The practice of driving cattle up the mountain is much less common than in the past. Recently, the villagers have reached an agreement on shared use of the plateau (chapters 7 and 9) under which they can again graze their cattle there.

## History of Koloni

In contrast to Guquka, whose history revolves around a relatively autonomous process of settlement, Koloni's history is far more associated with planned settlement by the British during the troubled period of the Frontier Wars in the 1850s (chapter 2). Koloni has had similar experiences with labour migration, but compared with Guquka, it has not needed to accommodate a sudden influx of people from elsewhere in the region. Expansions of the village were largely planned and foreseen and seemingly uncontested. Map 4.3 shows the current layout of Koloni. The amount of land within each land use category is shown in Table 4.1 below.

*Origin*
Koloni is situated in an area that was allocated to the AmaGqunukhwebe under Chief Kama by George Cathcart. After the end of *Mlanjeni*'s War in 1852, Cathcart moved this group of AmaGqunukhwebe as part of his overall military strategy of settling loyal clans in the Ciskei region to act as a buffer between the Ngqika and Galeca Xhosa and the Colony. The AmaGqunukhwebe originally lived in the area near Bedford (Bruintjieshoogte) across the Fish River, about 80 km west of Koloni. They were one of the Xhosa clans that settled farthest to the west of the Kei River (Peires 1981). The British resettled them in the Middledrift District (where Koloni is situated) as a reward for their support in the later Frontier Wars. Parsons (1982), Mostert (1993) and Bundy (1988) all assert that this occurred after the British annexation of the Ciskei area once Sandile, Paramount chief of the Ngqika-Xhosa, had been defeated and replaced with Sarili of the Gcaleka-Xhosa in 1850. The Middledrift area was more suitable for livestock farming than the area around Bedford, making the move attractive.

It is generally agreed that the village was established somewhere between 1853 and 1890, near to the Perksdale Mission. This mission was part of a grant made to Chief Kama by Sir George Grey in 1853. Holden (1877), a Methodist missionary stationed at Annshaw, provided detailed accounts of these times. Kama, chief of the Amaqgunukwebe was born in 1798, and was mentioned as key figure who remained loyal to the colonial government during *Mlanjeni*'s

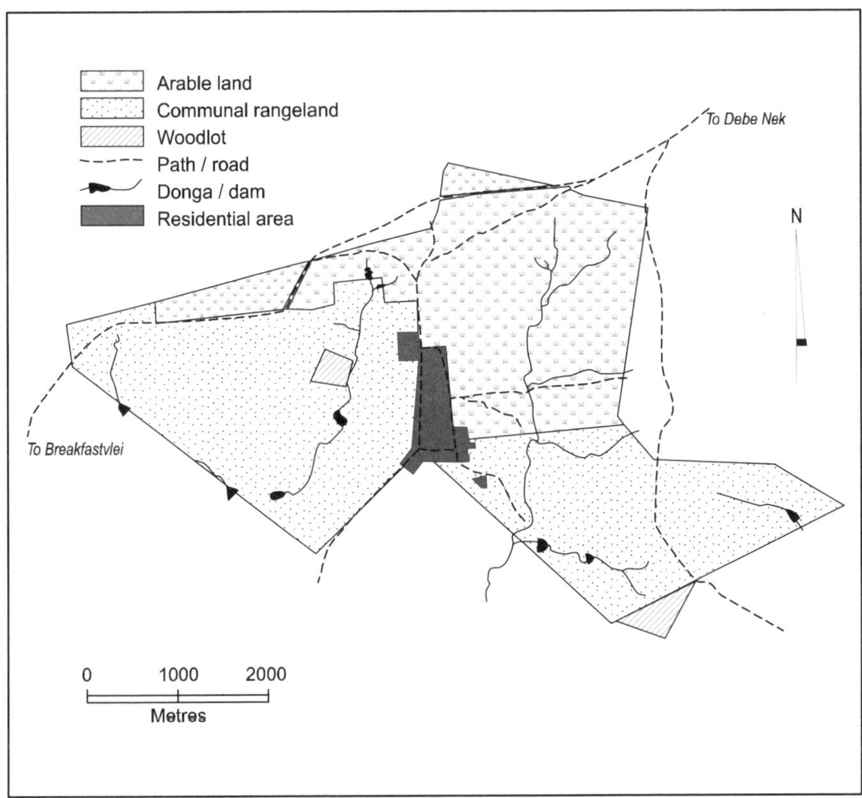


*Map 4.3*      Location of residential areas, communal rangeland and arable land in Koloni

War (1850-1853). He and his people were rewarded with land along the Keiskamma River, running southwards from Middledrift; bounded by the Keiskamma and Ncera rivers on the south-west and west, respectively, and by the road between Alice and King William's Town on the north. They moved to this land in 1853 and shortly afterwards the Annshaw Mission Station was founded. Kama allocated land to those that settled at Koloni and facilitated the spread of Christianity by allowing mission stations to be built. He had earlier been baptized on August 19th 1825. Holden took charge of Annshaw Mission in 1871 and wrote that he arranged to have the locations of Annshaw and Peceleni (Perksdale) surveyed. This survey revealed existing village and garden allotments for individuals or families and a large commonage for public grazing land allotment holders. So Perksdale, later renamed Peuleni, must have been formed before 1871, and certainly before Chief Kama died in 1875.

There is agreement about the ethnic background of those who came to settle
and as to whose land it was. The presence of the nearby Perksdale Mission
would have attracted dispersed Xhosa and small groups of Mfengu, who could
then be found in every frontier town and on small holdings on mission stations
and elsewhere (Holden 1877). Parsons (1982) and Switzer (1993) linked this
dispersal pattern to the policies of George Grey, who succeeded Harry Smith as
the Cape Colony governor. Grey envisaged and implemented a set of policies
through which he hoped to 'civilize the blacks' and create a Colony that would
be divided by class rather than race. His government encouraged Europeans and
'loyal natives' (including the Mfengu and other ethnic groups who had joined
the colonial forces in *Mlanjeni*'s War) to settle close to each other. Grey pursued a 'checkerboard' strategy where white farms and small black reserves were
intermingled, with the hope of creating interactions between the two groups
which would ultimately result in the reserves evolving into small holdings
(Parsons 1982: 114-16). Holden (1877) confirms that the land was given to
Kama to "form a breakwater against any future incursion of barbarous tribes".
The story goes that Koloni was founded by seven families from different ethnic
backgrounds, who had been previously staying on white farms before moving to
Koloni. Oral history confirms that Koloni was originally called Farm A and that
the neighbouring villages had been white commercial farms before they were
bought up by the state in the early 1920s.

*Social identity*
The residents of Koloni, like those of Guquka, lay claim to a 'School' denomi-
nation and orientation. The implications of this become clearer by discussing
betterment planning. Records of people who settled in the British controlled
areas (Peddie, Grahamstown) indicate that 'School' people were apt agricultu-
ralists who traded and engaged with the British. Many of them obtained education and converting to Christianity.

   Whatever their original affiliation, the villagers of Koloni currently regard
themselves as Xhosa of the AmaGqunukwebe clan, the same clan to which residents of nearby villages belong. A Bantu Affairs Betterment Report backs this
up, also specifying that they were 'Fingos' (i.e. 'Mfengu') (Bantu Affairs Commission 1962).

*Land tenure*
There is some confusion over the original ownership of the land on which
Koloni was established. The land was originally allocated to the Peuleni Mission Station. Elderly residents of the village, like Mr. Nyathi, claim that the
Koloni's residential and garden lots were allotted to families by government
sale. He says that this land was adjacent to the lands of the mission and sold by
the state under 'freehold tenure'. The first buyers were from different origins,
some from nearby local villages (especially from around Middledrift and
Keiskammahoek), others from farther away (such as Peddie). To settle in

Koloni, one had to apply to Chief Kama to buy a residential and arable plot. The freehold title also provided access to the communal range lands of the village.

Chief Kama initially stayed in Middledrift before moving to GaGqumukwebe/Qibira with his tribe in the 1920s. This was because, in the words of one respondent, "although Middledrift gets plenty of rain, the land there is like gravel, there is no grass there like you can find here". Mr. Nyathi explained that Koloni and the neighbouring villages had originally been white commercial farms. The government bought these up in the early 1920s and planned them according to a pattern of separate residential, arable and grazing land areas. Although most respondents do not know the exact date their ancestors arrived in the village, they claim that it was around the time the government put the land up for sale. One respondent indicated that the first headman of the village died in 1912. He was followed by Dazadaza Rebe, indicating that Koloni was established somewhat earlier. As indicated before, the first families to settle in the village had diverse origins, although Chief Kama gave priority to the interests of those who had come from Middledrift. Mr. Nyathi remembers:

If you came from another area not under his rule, such as Peddie, you had to get a permit from your chief there to come and settle here in Koloni. Chief Kama would ask: 'What is wrong at Peddie? What did the chief there tell you?'

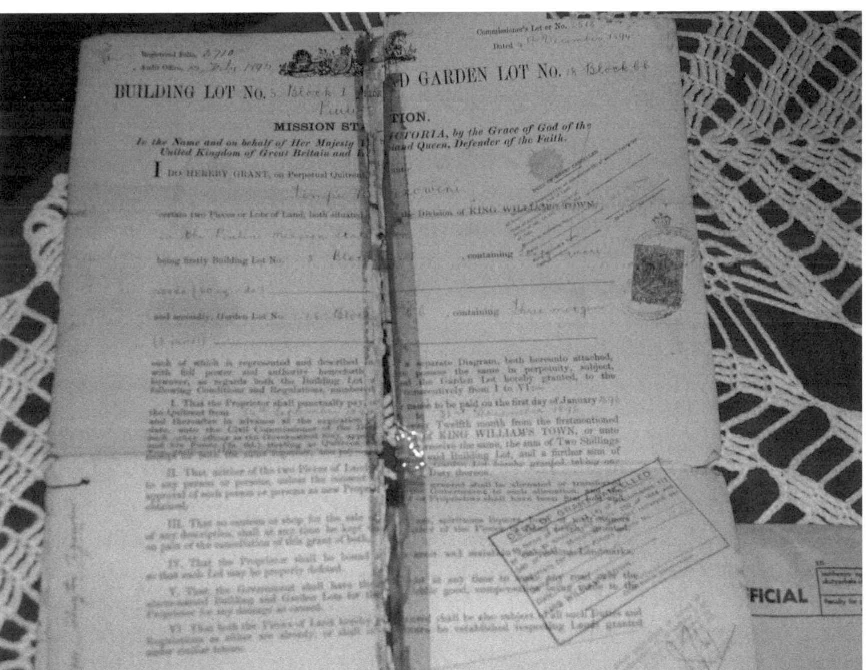

*Photo 4.2*     Quitrent title deed of Mr. Ngxowa. (Photo by Hebinck)

According to some informants, the Nyathi, Rebe and Ngxowa families were among the first to settle in the village. When they 'bought' their plots in the 1920s the village was still relatively open and many plots had not yet been sold. Some elder respondents were boys at that time and still remember this well. They assert that their fathers arrived before 1920.

Evidence from the Deeds Registry in King Williams' Town and the title deeds shown to us by some of the people, clearly indicated that the land was surveyed in 1874 by a surveyor named Thos van Renen on instruction of the Minister of Native Affairs. On the basis of this survey land was allocated to individuals through Quitrent title deeds.

As in Guquka, the land was classified into residential and arable plots and rangelands with plot sizes being fixed (Table 4.1). The Chief or headman allocated the plots to individuals. The title deed of Mr. Ngxowa was issued to his grandfather in 1889.

Quitrent implied the payment of an annual sum to the government. The obligation to make such a perpetual payment may explain why people now say that they bought the land. Years later, i.e. in the mid-1980s, this land was changing hands. Mrs. Mlilwana, a widow in her late eighties, talked about how she and her husband bought their residential plot and arable field in 1985. It took them some two years to locate the owner. They finally found out that he lived in Queenstown and managed to convince him to sell the land.

This and other accounts enable us to establish the most probable course of events: settlement in Koloni was a gradual process whereby families settled when they could negotiate access to land. This gradual nature also has a specific spatial reflection. There is proof that some owners (see chapter 6) did not use some of the residential and arable sites, which could only be obtained as a pair. By the end of the 1920s, many residential sites were still unoccupied. Indeed to this day, the various plots in Koloni that are clearly demarcated for residential and/or agricultural purposes are still not in use. Mr. Ngxowa, the former chairperson of the Koloni Residents Association once remarked that "a lot of land is wasted". Younger residents complain about residential sites being derelict and that they cannot use them. On other occasions informants clearly showed resentment about land being left unused for long periods. Nevertheless, because of the nature of the title arrangements these sites could not easily be re-allocated to another family by the chief or headman, as would have been the case under a communal tenure system, as the land had a title, held by the owner.

The statement in Photo 4.3 was written by Mrs. Ngxowa, who gave it to us in April 2004. It underlines that the settlement of Koloni was gradual. It also tells about clashes between chiefs and missionaries, who both considered themselves as the 'owners' of the land, with the right to dispose of it as they saw fit.

Her statement that few families had settled at the time of betterment, also suggests that Koloni's settlement was a gradual process that extended beyond 1938, when betterment was introduced to the village.

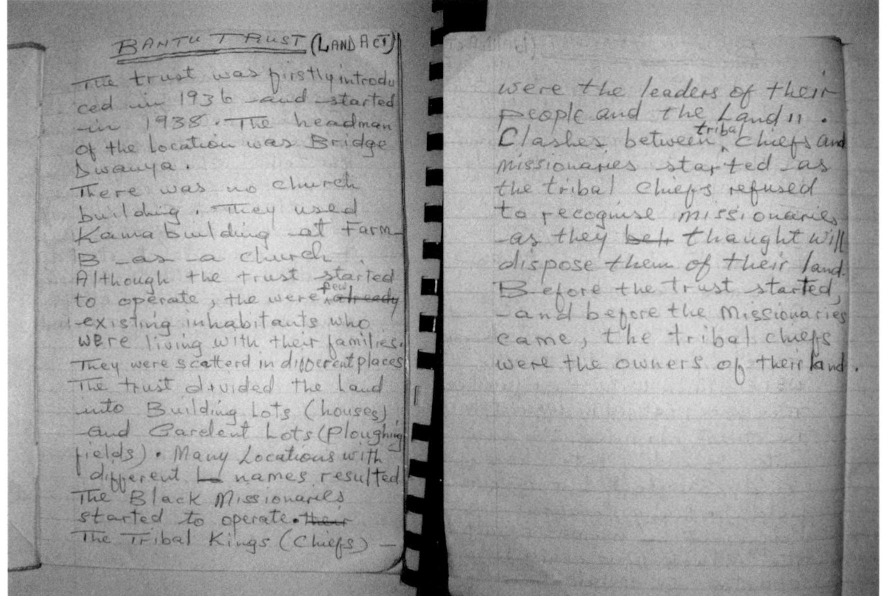

*Photo 4.3*     Written statement by Mrs. Ngxowa about history of Koloni.
                (Photo by Hebinck)

*Betterment planning*

Oral evidence underlines that agriculture was the primary source of livelihood for most homesteads in the village until the mid 1950s/1960s. During this time there was generally no need to seek work elsewhere, as crop and livestock production provided more income than could be obtained from migrant labour. Following developments that they had noted elsewhere, the villagers began, on their own accord and expense, to fence off their arable fields (Ndlovu 1991: 22-23). They expanded their livestock holdings by establishing bull camps. They also constructed two water dams. The commons were not fenced off at this time because they were shared with neighbouring villages and, being large, were expensive to fence.

This interest in agricultural improvements drew the attention of government officials. In 1936, the Principal of Fort Cox College of Agriculture suggested to the Chief Native Commissioner that Koloni could be a suitable test case for betterment planning (Ndlovu 1991). The villagers fully co-operated with, and were interested in, this government initiative. At this time most other villages were opposed to betterment, so Koloni was favoured by the state whenever it was allocating resources, whether for infrastructure and services, but especially for agriculture. Koloni was one of two villages in the Ciskei region selected as a 'pilot' betterment village. The Ciskei Bantu Affairs Report mentions that Koloni as a "location was planned in May 1937" and that "the location was declared a Betterment Area" (Bantu Affairs Commission 1962). This meant that Koloni's "… stock numbers have been determined and the carrying capacity fixed, and stock culling has already been applied". The report also categorises Koloni residents as "co-operative and … prepared to assist in fulfilling plans put forward for the betterment of themselves and their location". This is quite a contrast to the situation in Guquka. The report makes it clear that conservation of soil terraces was necessary, and was augmented by erecting fences to protect crops from cattle. It also mentions the presence of two woodlots, each 5 *morgen* in size.

The Trust, as betterment was locally referred to, institutionalised separate bull camps in Koloni (chapter 9), established fodder plots and further expanded the dams to ensure year-round water supplies for the cattle. These interventions sought to ensure more constant cattle numbers and to balance stock herding with soil and water preservation measures. Betterment officials also introduced good-quality rams into the Koloni sheep flock to improve wool production. When tractor services became available, Koloni farmers were first in line for access. Agricultural technicians trained farmers in sheep shearing and wool classing and assisted in marketing the village clip. Crop production was diversified beyond the traditional cultivation of monocultures of maize and 'kaffircorn' (sorghum) and herd quality was improved by introducing the Shorthorn and Afrikaner cattle breeds. Attention was given to marketing produce.

Bundy (1988: 36) discussed whether the missionaries at the Perksdale Mission turned Koloni residents into farmers, or whether Africans chose to enter farming in the following way:

> … 'missionary successes' might justifiably be described in retrospect as 'African successes', in that the initial decision to invite the missionary and the subsequent cultural adaptations were conscious and deliberate choices by chiefs, clans or individuals.

Initially agriculture in Koloni, both crop farming and animal production, showed much promise. Ndlovu (1991: 53) cites an elder informant who recalls the period before 1940: "There was no need to go to work, even if you worked during the ploughing season you came home because crop growing was more beneficial than the cent you got from migrating".

Ndlovu (*ibid.*: 29) also explains the importance of the quitrent form of land tenure in Koloni at this time:

> The landowners are the wealthier and relatively more educated and therefore are looked upon as a superior group by people living in communal and Trust lands. Much of this superior attitude of the landowners, it is argued, derives not only from the sense of freedom from authority, engendered by the security of tenure, but also from their rather better standards of living.

This would suggest that agriculture was indeed of much importance in Koloni until at least the 1940s. Key informant interviews suggest that crop production peaked during the 1960s. Aerial photographs of the village taken in 1963, show that the ploughed and terraced arable land, most probably done by heavy equipment (chapter 7).

This underlines the eagerness and interest in agricultural development shown by the village. Respondents explain that this was at least partly the result of the interest and encouragement of the village headmen, Ngxowa and DazaDaza Rebe. Ngxowa initiated a number of new approaches on his fields that he learned about through agricultural education. He motivated all the villagers to start cultivating their fields. One key informant, Mr. Moyoma, remembers how under the leadership of Ngxowa and Rebe he and his father had been seriously involved with agriculture, producing fields of pumpkins, 'bedseed' (akin to wheat) and maize during the summer months, and peas in the winter time.

Betterment, however, was *not* the first time that the village had interacted with and picked up 'white farming techniques'. Some of the elder respondents told how Koloni had previously received some assistance from a few white farmers who, under a government contract, provided technical assistance in agricultural production to the village. They had introduced various new breeds and breeding techniques, introduced animal traction (for the arable fields), and initiated other measures to improve crop production. White farmers also taught the villagers to plant peas and to add these to the cycle of crops to rejuvenate the soils. They introduced sheep breeding and taught villagers how to shear the sheep and set up a shearing shed. After a few years, they left the village, leaving behind the shearing shed, ploughs and other tools for the villagers to use.

According to elder respondents, the village enthusiastically followed the involvement of white farmers and, later, the Trust officials. Ndlovu (1991: 2) explains the willing participation of the villagers in betterment planning: "... there were people who, after realising the wholesale deterioration of their land and stock, a sign to them of a diminishing livelihood, decided to collaborate with the government". Through this kind of cooperation, they expected to reverse the deterioration of their natural resources and increase agricultural production, thereby improving their, locally derived, standard of living.

According to informants, the collaboration of Koloni with government officials did not go down well with neighbouring communities who were jealous of the number of projects that headman Rebe had been able to introduce to his village. Neighbouring communities, especially those also belonging to the AmaGqunukhwebe clan, were highly critical of the advantages that Koloni had gained. Their own situations contrasted greatly with that of Koloni. They were subject to the restrictions imposed by betterment planning (especially over the number of stock) without receiving any of the opportunities enjoyed by Koloni. Thus, after a few years of quarrelling, the Paramount Chief of the AmaQunukwebe, under the pressure of protests ('*toyi-toyi*') from the other villages, fired

Koloni's headman Daza Daza Rebe in 1935. His brother Sipho took over the headmanship. However, this change of headman had little effect on the assistance Koloni continued to receive through betterment planning, especially during the 1950s and 1960s.

These various betterment programmes brought improvements and boosted the agriculture of Koloni. This contrasts sharply with the impact of government interventions in other parts of the Ciskei region (De Wet 1987, 1989), especially those measures that resulted in a large-scale resettlement in the Ciskei region of 'surplus people' from areas designated for white South Africans. Only the Middledrift district, where Koloni is located, was exempt from this resettlement process. This is one fundamental difference in the settlement history of the two villages of Guquka and Koloni.

*Settlement expansion*
In the early 1980s a 'squatter settlement' as it is called to this day by villagers was established. Under the auspices of the village authorities, this settlement was created on one of the grazing camps to accommodate the offspring of the villagers. In Koloni, this move is still perceived as a one-off action to accommodate 'our children', the younger generation who needed space to build new compounds as extensions, or satellites, of existing homesteads in the village. The construction of this settlement was announced and approved in an amendment of Soil Conservation scheme No. (60)N.2/11/3/12 dated February 1962 (Bantu Affairs Commission 1962), but was not enacted until September 1985 when it was signed by the Ciskei Minister of Agriculture. It specified that a "total area of 35 hectares of land situated in camp No. 4 is hereby withdrawn from grazing and set aside for residential purposes to accommodate the natural increase of the population". The residential sites of the squatter camp were allocated under 'permission to occupy' (PTO) right of tenure. Thus these 'squatters' were not provided with arable fields, as there were none available. Therefore it was possible for the younger generations to live in the village, though they needed to derive their incomes elsewhere, or participate in agriculture through sharecropping or other access arrangements that would allow them to employ local resources.

The 'squatter settlement' also provided the opportunity for people from other places to come and build a house in Koloni. Yet many of these new immigrants did not finish the construction of their houses. Mr. Kama, Chairman of the Koloni Residents Association claimed many of those who came later migrated on to East London and other major cities. Those who did come to occupy houses in the squatter camp were mostly young, unmarried women, often with young children.

Map 7.7 illustrates the expansion of the Koloni settlement over the years. From this map and the aerial photo sequence (Figure 7.3), the expansion of the residential area of the village into the communal rangelands can also be noted.

## General trends in the history of Guquka and Koloni

It is clear that, since the early days of settlement, there has been a considerable transformation in rural livelihoods in both villages. The Xhosa, who now inhabit the area that includes Guquka and Koloni, used to live from what the land provided. The role and relative importance of land-based activities in the two villages began to change around the end of the 19th century, roughly some 30 years after settlement. The role of agriculture, or rather cultivation, began to change dramatically from the mid 1960s onwards (chapter 7). In both villages, the pension and social grant system play an important role in livelihoods. Although this influence cannot be precisely dated it is likely that this started to be significant in the early 1940s (see chapter 2). Its importance is explored in more detail in chapters 12 and 13.

Labour migration has played a central role in the lives of the inhabitants of both villages and its character has changing dramatically over time. Another feature common to both villages has been the effect of recent retrenchments (which have seen a return of villagers) and the lack of opportunities to earn a living locally. The effect that these influences have had on population dynamics will be examined in more detail in chapter 11.

*Labour migration*
At the turn of the 19th century, the expansion of South African industry (most notably the gold mines) triggered the migration of male labour from Guquka and other villages. Commoners, headmen and chiefs alike went to the mines and factories to work on 6- to 9-month contracts. Their motivations to migrate were similar, although their status was taken into account in their new jobs and they occupied different positions in the mines and factories. The father of Chief Mqalo worked in the mines in Johannesburg as a police officer (*'mashlugnane'*) earning 5 pounds per year. He went to the mines, as he could not survive on the 2 pounds a year he received from government for his formal village function and had to find money elsewhere. Chief Mqalo also worked in the mines as a clerk from 1946 until 1966. This time span is a good indication of how long commoners also spent in the mines.

Labour migration was characterised by rather well-defined cycles of working in the urban areas and returning to the rural homesteads. Their time in the mines coincided with the winter period, which enabled the men to remain actively engaged in cultivation when home. Young women from Guquka sometimes accepted jobs as domestic workers on neighbouring white-owned farms. When later, from about 1930 onwards, the duration of mining contracts was extended, visits to the rural homesteads were shortened and increasingly occurred during the Christmas holiday season. The Christmas period is not the best time to plant crops, because of little rainfall (chapters 3).

The Glen Grey Act of 1894 induced the need for such labour migration in two main ways. Firstly, it set a limit of (up to) four *morgen* (3.4 ha) on the amount of arable land that could be held by each 'African family' (as this was labelled by the then Government). Secondly, it imposed a labour tax on every 'African family' that could not prove that at least one of their members was involved in wage employment for a minimum of three months per year.

Migrant wages emerged as a new and important source of cash for the villagers, most especially the men. At the same time women were finding short-term employment on white farms in the nearby Tyume valley. The men brought their wages back to the homesteads to invest in cattle (for '*lobola*'), to buy clothing and feed their family. One of the key informants from Guquka expressed clearly that migration secured the resources to acquire the *lobola* and to 'build a homestead':

> When I became a grown up, I still stayed with my brothers and sisters at my parents' place. My brothers were older than me, and had to get their wives. For that, they went to find jobs to raise the money so they could pay the *lobola*. ... I also had to get myself a job for that reason. I also saw that my friends, with whom I had grown up, were coming back from work wearing new clothes and shoes, and having some money. I could not expect them to give me some of their money, so I also decided to leave my job of looking after the cattle of my family to go and find a job.

Initially migration was mainly temporary and, according to informants, its main purpose was to strengthen village-based livelihoods. Very few homesteads were able to derive an income from local resources and activities alone and the income from wages formed a necessary addition to incomes produced from locally land-based resources.

Migration contributed to relatively large sums of money flowing to the villages and helped the expansion of a commodity economy. The institutionalisation of pension and other social grant schemes added a further flow of money to the rural homelands. The significance of pensions, grants and remittances is discussed in general terms in chapter 2 and in more detail in chapters 12 and 13. By the time that the stringent Apartheid legislation was implemented rural livelihoods had already begun to include incomes and resources derived from outside the locality. Initially, part of these external income sources was used to invest in sustaining local agricultural production, but their role changed over the following decades.

The significance and heavy dependence on outside incomes for local agricultural production had dire consequences as, over the next 40-50 years, the continuity of arable production was jeopardised as migrant wages were increasingly invested in meeting other needs, such as education, health and buying food. In the end, there was not enough money remaining to secure the inputs needed for arable production, such as renting a tractor to plough the land (chapter 8).

Migration increasingly became a long-term phenomenon, with migrants returning home only once or twice a year. Migrants only had a few weeks of annual leave to return home and in many cases this leave had to taken from about the middle of December to the middle of January. Increasingly the short time spent at home was used to relax and socialise and no longer to work in the fields. The Christmas return of urban migrants, carrying with them their annual bonus, developed into a period of festivities. This period was also used to attend to important rituals, such as the initiation of young males, in which men play a central role. Social activities competed for time with agrarian activities, particularly cultivation. Ngwane (2003) provides a vivid account of Christmas time visits.

This migration pattern was shaped by a steady increase of urban employment opportunities in the secondary and tertiary sectors during and after the Second World War (Seekings and Nattrass 2005). The institutionalisation of the Ciskei Homeland Government in the late 1950s and early 1960s and through various acts, including the Promotion of Bantu Self-Government Act (Mears 2004: 10) generated employment. Homeland formation enabled an expansion of a black bureaucracy that was able to govern the Ciskei Homeland separately from the Republic of South Africa and led to the creation in 1968 of the Dimbaza Industrial Zone near King William's Town. This created employment opportunities that were closer to home, opening up the opportunity of commuting rather than migrating.

Migration institutionalised co-residence of people in their place of birth and their place of work and mobility between these places. In the beginning, migration predominantly involved males and was, above all, temporal. Pass laws, the levying of a hut tax and (later) Apartheid regulations, all restricted the scope for permanent migration. As a result, migration from the villages to urban and industrial areas became cyclical. While migration in the past was more short term (spanning a few months of absence), more recent migration patterns have a much more long term and often more permanent character (chapter 11).

*Local employment and retrenchments*
By the 1960s changes began to take place that brought the local economy more under the influence of the national one. These included: declining agricultural productivity in the village (despite government interventions) as mounting pressure on available arable lands affected soil fertility, changing perspectives on the way that *lobola* should be paid, i.e. in 'cash' rather than in 'kind' and, a general decline in interest in agriculture among younger generations as they saw more promise in urban derived incomes *and* an urban life style. Hence, by the 1960s, a growing number of homesteads had come to rely substantially on incomes derived from non-local resources. Spells of drought in the 1970s and early 1980s further hastened this trend.

The implementation of the homeland policy of the South African state during the 1960s and 1970s led to the formation of 'independent' homeland states. This coincided with the expansion of employment opportunities within the Ciskei homeland. Those who were able to secure such employment found that they could commute to work, a big change from working in distant locations and being absent for long periods.

During the early 1980s, the Government of Ciskei pursued a policy of poverty alleviation. One of its strategies was to urge large organisations, such as the University of Fort Hare, to provide employment to as many local people as possible. Van Averbeke (2005) captured the dynamics of this as follows. Fort Hare was a small university with between five and six thousand students. At that time, the rector and the management of the university was entirely white and supported the Apartheid policy of separate development. Since Fort Hare was located within the boundaries of the (then) independent homeland of Ciskei, there was a certain obligation to support the homeland government. The university management adopted a maximum employment policy and dramatically increased the number of service workers. By the end of the 1980s, their number exceeded 1,200 – about one for every five students. The employment conditions of the service workers, who did cleaning, cooking, gardening, farm work and security work followed the policy of maximum employment. The large majority were casual workers, who could be summarily dismissed. Besides a monthly wage, an annual bonus, and membership of the Unemployment Insurance Fund, they had none of the benefits enjoyed by permanent staff, such as subsidised medical insurance and a pension scheme, travel and housing allowances, and free education at Fort Hare for family members. Wages of services workers were very low, but generally, allowed employees and their families to subsist.

During the 1980s, workers' unions in South Africa increasingly grew in strength. As a large employer, Fort Hare was a centre of organised labour activity. The union at Fort Hare actively engaged with management to improve conditions of service workers, and was not afraid to use strike action in pursuit of its demands. Wages tripled by the end of 1989. A new management was appointed in 1990, consisting of African academics with credentials from the liberation struggle. With the upcoming 1994 political changes in mind, the decision over whether to reduce worker numbers at Fort Hare was extremely contentious, even though the budget of the University required this action. Rather than doing this, the University management chose instead to broaden the benefits available to service workers to include membership of a pension fund, housing subsidies and free education for their children. This had a positive impact on the local economy. For example, several new shops opened in Alice and existing retailers saw an increase in trade. Benefits also flowed to neighbouring rural settlements, such as Gqumahashe, Tyali, Mavuso, Lower Ncera, Ngcele and Kwezana, where the workers and their families lived. Higher wages stimulated the construction of new houses or the extension of existing dwellings and the erection of fences around residential sites or fields. Mostly local people were employed in these tasks.

However, the pro-worker policy of the University drained its financial reserves. In 1995, the budget showed a deficit for the first time, and the situation worsened in 1996. In 1997, the financial status of Fort Hare was so precarious that drastic action was required, which came in the form of the wholesale retrenchment of service workers. All the functions of the service departments were outsourced. The University encouraged workers to establish their own companies and submit tenders, but in the end, the majority of the retrenched workers became unemployed (Van Averbeke 2005).

In the 1990s an economic decline, regionally and nationally, led to further large-scale retrenchments and reduced opportunities for new entrants (the younger rural generations) into commuter-based migrant labour. The retrenchments at the University of Fort Hare were especially significant for Guquka. The same period also saw a constitutional change in the government, and the subsequent demolition of the homeland government apparatus, which further reduced employment opportunities in government. Urban wage employment opportunities also diminished rapidly. On a macro-economic level, South Africa's economy continues to go through some drastic changes, with employment opportunities in the industrial and service sectors falling, while the profitability of these sectors increases . Structural reorganisations within these sectors designed to enhance their efficiency appears to accelerate this process (*Mail & Guardian* 14-20 October 2005).

The onset of a national economic recession and a shrinking labour market has further reinforced the difficulties, noted earlier, in maintaining or expanding agricultural and livestock production beyond their current levels. This has become an increasingly difficult task as money from remittances and pensions is increasingly being used to meet other needs, such as securing nutritional, health and education needs.

## Time line for Guquka and Koloni

By way of summary, the following Tables (4.2 and 4.3) present a time line showing the main trends and events in the history of Guquka and Koloni.

## Conclusion

This chapter has provided a historical overview of the settlement of the villages of Guquka and Koloni, and the ensuing changes in terms of resource management and livelihoods. This historical overview also provides a background for the chapters that follow, which describe natural resource management, the agricultural practises and livelihood patterns of villagers, in more detail.

In terms of *settlement patterns*, the two villages have quite different histories, despite their origins tracing back to the same period, the mid-19th century. The settlement of Guquka is closely linked with those of its neighbouring villages. Its origin, like these neighbouring villages, stemmed from the settlement of the Makhuzeni tribe in the Tyume valley. The establishment of Koloni, on the other hand, seems much less coherent. This is reflected in the disparate origins of those who came to settle in the village (although villagers now claim in unison to be AmaGqunukhwebe), in terms of how its access to surrounding land has always been contested by neighbouring villages, and even in the somewhat varying accounts of the village's origins.

In contrast to nearly all other parts of the Ciskei homeland, Koloni welcomed betterment planning as a way to increase its agricultural output. Initial ventures with state officials gave rise to various improvements to agricultural practises in the village. Nonetheless, these improvements turned out to only have a temporary effect and did not prevent a later decline in agricultural production (see chapter 8), although as this chapter shows, this decline began much later in Koloni than it did in Guquka. This may be explained by Koloni's

*Table 4.2*      Time line and events for Guquka

| Time/period | Critical events |
| --- | --- |
| 1853 | Expulsion of Xhosa from Tyume Valley following the 1850-1853 frontier war |
| 1870 | Settlement of Makhuzeni. Guquka village established under Chief Mqalo |
| 1899 | Land is surveyed and the tribal area is demarcated |
| 1910 | Second land survey held. Land reallocated to white farmers |
| Late 1900s | Labour migration to the mines takes momentum |
| 1939 – 1960s | Fencing of rangelands due to betterment planning. Hut and poll taxes push rural people to seek waged incomes |
| 1960s | Influx of immigrants following forced removals elsewhere<br>Formation of Ciskei Homeland State creating nearby employment opportunities and facilitating commuting<br>Agriculture begins to decline; increased dependency on 'external' sources of income<br>Allocation of rangelands for residential purposes |
| 1978 | Loss of grazing land to the Hogsback Pine Forest Company |
| 1980s | Drought reduces livestock numbers |
| 1990s – present | Retrenchments and rise in unemployment due to collapse of homeland government after 1994 and budget cuts at University of Fort Hare (mid 1997)<br>Migration begins to take on a more permanent character<br>Withdrawal of government support to agriculture; later reinstated and reconsidered, albeit primarily with a policy interest in land reforms and/or commercial agricultural activities. |

*Table 4.3*      Time line and events for Koloni

| Time/period | Critical Events |
| --- | --- |
| 1850-1900 | Establishment of Koloni on the Perksdale Mission following settlement by the British |
| 1874 | Land surveyed and residential and arable allotments demarcated and allocated |
| 1850s-1930s | Agriculture forms the prime source of livelihoods of villagers<br>Male migration to the mines and industrial areas of South Africa is limited compared to other rural parts of the Eastern Cape Region |
| Mid 1930s | Involvement of white farmers with village agriculture improves production, introduces new crops and stock management techniques<br>Villagers instigate betterment-like initiatives for improved natural resource management which are noted by government officials<br>Koloni is made one of two pilot villages in the Eastern Cape Region by government officials. Their scheme is met with full commitment and support of villagers |
| 1960-1970s | Formation of Ciskei Homeland State, creating relatively nearby (<50km) employment opportunities and facilitating commuting<br>Agricultural productivity declines due to droughts and a declining interest in agriculture<br>Labour migration increases, furthering reliance on 'external' incomes<br>Limited influx of immigrants |
| 1980 | A 'squatter camp' is constructed on one of the grazing camps to give residential lots to younger generations of the village |
| 1990s present | General retrenchments due to the collapse of the homeland government leads to a rise in unemployment<br>The demise of the homeland government also means a withdrawal of government support to agriculture<br>The 'squatter camp' continues to expand, partly due to the sale of residential plots to 'outsiders'<br>Migration begins to take on a more permanent character. |

relative success in accessing state resources during and after the époque of betterment planning. Male labour migration to earn cash incomes appeared later in Koloni than it did in Guquka.

For some time now, people in both settlements have sought to secure their livelihoods through external non-local resources rather than from local and natural ones. In this process the meaning of 'local' and 'rural' becomes the subject of continual negotiation and contestation, and this is addressed in various chapters of this book. Chapters 11, 12 and 13 explore how this has affected livelihoods and led to shifts in homestead and family arrangements, while chapters 8, 9 and 10 examine the continuities and discontinuities in the use of various natural resources in the villages.

5

# Natural resource base and agricultural potentials

Peter C. Lent

## Introduction

The intent of this chapter is to set the stage by providing a description of the physical environment and the quality of natural resources that are available to the people of Guquka and Koloni. I describe climate and rainfall patterns, topography, vegetation, soils of the *veld* and arable fields, water bodies and streams. Further, models and yield gap analyses are referenced in order to examine the agricultural potential of the two study areas. Thus, the chapter serves to compare and contrast the two villages with regard to opportunities, constraints and options for land-based livelihoods. The actual nature of such livelihoods are dealt with in chapters 8 through 13.

This chapter is based largely on literature and secondary sources, including soil surveys and related data collection carried out in both villages in 1998 (Bonroy 1999, Bonroy and Verdoodt 1999, Bonroy *et al.* 2000, Verdoodt 1999, Verdoodt *et al.* 2000 and Verdoodt *et al.* 2003). These studies involved surveys of the soils on the arable allotments on a scale of 1: 5000. The results of this survey and topographic information about the area were captured in a GIS (Geographic Information System). An analysis of the local climate was also conducted, including rainfall, temperature, radiation, and potential evapotranspiration. A detailed account of the methodology employed in the soils inventory and mapping and the modelling exercises appears in Verdoodt (1999) for

Guquka and Bonroy (1999) for Koloni. In addition Mupukati (2005) carried out fieldwork in Guquka in 2000, focusing on soil erosion.

Rainfall data were extracted from the CIRADA database (Austin 1989a), and further details appear in Bonroy and Verdoodt (1999). This digital database covers the former Ciskei portion of the Central Eastern Cape and interpolates rainfall observations between neighbouring meteorological stations. Specifically, for Guquka, data were extrapolated from the 20-year database of observations at the University of Fort Hare Farm, a meteorological station situated about 25 km downstream of Guquka. For Koloni, Bonroy (1999) also used data from the weather station on the Fort Hare Research Farm, situated about 20 km west of Koloni. Since both Koloni and the Research Farm are situated on the Coastal Plateau it was assumed that climatic conditions at Koloni were generally similar to that at the weather station.

## Guquka

Guquka lies in a cluster of villages in the upper reaches of the Tyume River catchment at an elevation of approximately 900 m (Map 4.1) at the foot of the 400 m high Hogsback Escarpment. Above the escarpment lies an extensive plateau and above that, the dolerite-capped Amatola Mountains reach almost to 2000 m in places, including the Hogsback Peaks at 1824 and 1937 m and Gaika's Kop at 1963 m.

The sedimentary rocks are of the Beaufort Group, laid down 230 million years ago and consisting of the Katberg formation of pinkish grey sandstones, and the Balfour formation, which consists of 70% grey mudstones, 25% fine sandstones and 5% grey shales. Between 150 and 190 million years ago igneous intrusions formed dolerite sheets, dykes and sills. Alluvial terraces were laid down in the river basins about 2 million years ago. The most recent formation consists of unconsolidated and highly erodible colluvium found on valley side-slopes around the community (Hill, Kaplan, Scott & Partners 1977).

Because of its elevation on the upper reaches of the Tyume River Guquka is at the very upper limits of the Coastal Plateau agro-ecological zone described in chapter 3; only a few hundred m farther up the river lie the lowest reaches of Afro-montane forests.

The true River-valley Unit or zone, described in chapter 3, begins downstream from the village. The arable allotments of Guquka extend down to the Tyume River, the main tributary of the Keiskamma River. The Keiskamma in turn enters the Indian Ocean near the town of Hamburg. Flow from the Tyume River feeds Binfield Park Dam located about 5 km downstream from Guquka. This Dam has a capacity of 19 million $m^3$ but as of 2004 was under-utilised, having a surplus capacity of about 9 million $m^3$ (Amatola Water Board 2005). Despite the proximity of this abundant water resource Guquka does not benefit; the limited irrigation developments (chapter 3) and all provisions for domestic consumption are directed downstream.

*Rainfall*
Rain is primarily of cyclonic origin from cold fronts that sweep over the country or from high-pressure systems situated on the coast that bring moist air from the sea. Since the rainfall is primarily cyclonic and orographic in nature, due to relief, the amount of rain received at a particular location depends mostly on its height above sea level, distance from the sea and aspect (Austin 1989a). In the Guquka area, altitude is clearly the major determinant of the spatial distribution of rainfall. At lower elevations rainfall can be as low as 500 mm per annum rising to about 1400 mm in the Amatola Mountains at 1200 to 1500 m above sea level (Austin 1989a).

In general, the upper catchment has a sub-humid, summer rainfall climate with an annual rainfall ranging from 700mm to 800 mm with frequent frost during winter. The two main rainfall stations in the study area are Hogsback and Wolfridge. Hogsback rainfall station is S $32^0$ 35'; E $26^0$ 56' while Wolfridge is S $32^0$ 39' and E $27^0$ 00', but both are at higher elevation than Guquka. Because of the steep slopes rainfall patterns vary greatly over short distances here. Austin (1989a) plotted the mean monthly rainfall for Wolfridge (Map 5.1). The only recent rainfall data for Guquka itself, from Bennett (2002), is short term but is shown here to illustrate the monthly rainfall distribution (Map 5.1, see also Map 3.1). Guquka is said to be characterised by a bimodal distribution (De Wet and Van Averbeke 1995, Els 1971), as is seen in Figure 5.1. However, this pattern is not evident from the longer term data for nearby Wolfridge. In both areas the period of maximum rainfall occurs during summer, although a small

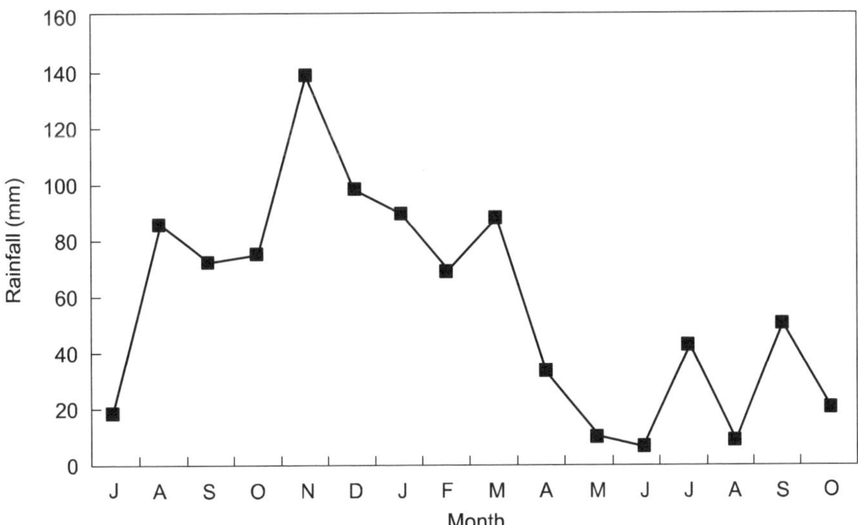


*Figure 5.1*    Rainfall Guquka during 1998
*Source*: Bennett (2002)

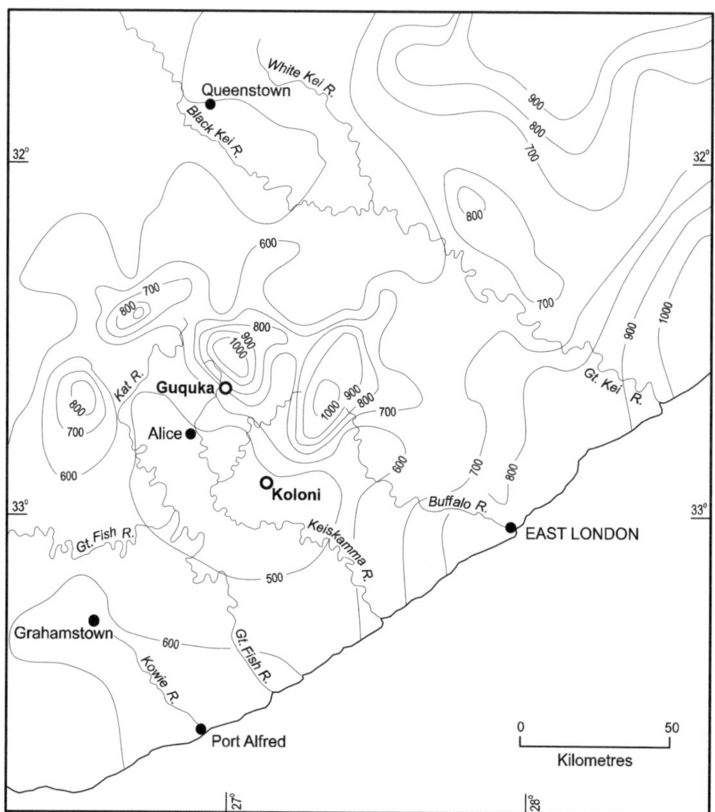



*Map 5.1*      Rainfall isohyets Eastern Cape

*Source*: Austin (1989b)


decline in rainfall during March may be responsible for considerable crop water stress (Verdoodt *et al.* 2003). Winter (typically June and July) corresponds with the dry period. At the residential area (Map 4.1) long-term mean annual rainfall is approximately 650 mm, making it generally suitable for rain-fed cropping, although the year to year variability is high (chapter 3). Table 5.1 provides a summary of climatic data for the Guquka area.


*Geology and soils*

The study area is predominantly underlain by sandstone, shale and mudstones of the Beaufort and Ecca groups of the Karoo Supergroup deposited in the Triassic and Permian periods. The greater part of the catchment is underlain by sandstone and mudstone of the lower Beaufort Series (Magagula 1999) Sandstone of the Middle Beaufort Series is found in the north and north-eastern part of the Tyume catchment. Most of the high lying grounds are dolerites (Hill, Kaplan, Scott & Partners 1977). Soils derived from the Beaufort group are nutrient poor whereas those from the dolerite are generally nutrient rich. Due to the high rainfall experienced above 800 m, however, these latter soils are very acid and leached.

The area has a rather complex topography with steep slopes and undulating terrain. Slopes with gradients between 15% and 30% are predominant, constituting 42% of the basin, while 16% are between 30% and 55%, and 4% are above 55%. Those below 15% constitute 38% of the landscape (Hill, Kaplan, Scott & Partners 1977). These proportions emphasize the general scarcity of land suitable for large scale crop production in the area surrounding Guquka.

*Table 5.1*    Some biophysical characteristics of Guquka and Koloni

| Characteristic | Guquka | Koloni |
| --- | --- | --- |
| Lat./Long. | S32°39', E26°57' | S32°54', E27°05' |
| Elevation | 770 m | 590 m |
| Geomorphology | Mountain basin | Coastal plateau |
| Climate | Subhumid, summer rainfall | Semi-arid, summer rainfall |
| Winter frost | Hard frosts likely | Frost occurs rarely |
| Annual rainfall (expected) | 700-800 mm | 400-550 mm |
| Recorded annual rainfall * | 657mm (12 mos. 1998-99) | 661 mm (1999) |
| Erosion potential | High | Moderate |
| Vegetation | Highland/Dohne *Sourveld* & mixed *veld* | False *Thornveld* (mixed *sweetveld*) |
| Soils (Depth, texture, degree of leaching) | Variable depth, loams to sandy loams with some clay patches, moderate leaching | Generally shallow, loam to sandy loam, not leached |
| Irrigation potential | Good but water-logging potential high | Not recommended |

* Bennett (2002)

*Source*: Lent (2000)

The broad area around Guquka is dominated by three major soil types and a variety of less extensive categories, as mapped by Hill, Kaplan, Scott & Partners 1977. However, a detailed soil map is available only for the arable land allotments in Guquka. The topographic units with variable slopes and the different parent materials present in Guquka introduce a great variability in the soilscape. Soils of the Rietvlei Series are alluvial and colluvial materials, which form level terraces and slopes with a rather uneven micro-relief. The resulting soil is a dark brown fine sandy clay loam.

Second are soils drived from Beaufort sediments and consisting of a dark greyish brown, apedal, fine sandy loam layers that overlie loamy gravel at a depth of 60 cm and 90 cm. The deeper subsoil is frequently a yellowish brown clay or sandy clay of relatively slow permeability. These soils have moderately high rainfall efficiency, and the nature of the subsoil suggests that these soils have a wetter than normal moisture regime. This is favourable for dry land crop production. However, some lower lying soils may be too wet for short periods after heavy rains because somewhat impermeable subsoil layers occur at shallow depths.

Third are soils predominantly of brown fine sandy clay loam overlying gravel, which in turn overlies weathering rock within 60 cm of the surface. Soil depth is shallow over the greater part of the area making these soils droughty in periods of low rainfall. In contrast, lower and mid-slope soils often stay too wet for considerable time after heavy rains. The erosion history of these areas is dealt with in chapter 7.

*Vegetation*
The flora and vegetation of the Amatola Mountains is predominantly Afromontane in affinity but has elements of the Cape flora and Southeast African endemics. It is part of a series of 'isolated' 'islands' of related composition occurring only on the higher mountain range. This Afromontane flora is generally distinct from that of the surrounding lowlands and contains approximately 4000 vascular plant species, of which 75% are endemic to it (Marais 1994).

Although now much modified (Coleman 1999), the original natural vegetation in the Hogsback area and the headwaters of the Tyume was of two broad types. First is the indigenous forest found on the southern facing cliffs and escarpment kloofs (canyons) typically dominated by yellowwoods, trees of the genus *Podocarpus*. (Cowling and Hilton-Taylor 1998). These forests receive high rainfall and occur on younger and nutrient richer soils. The aspect is cooler and therefore, moister. The Amatola mountain range has one of the richest forest communities in southern Africa and the central region around Hogsback probably has the greatest diversity of Afromontane species within the range. A number of species in the different vegetation types are endemic to the Amatolas or reach their southernmost or northernmost distribution in this area. Phillipson (1987) recorded 1215 indigenous species of plants found in the Amatolas which represents 30% of the total number of Afromontane species and 5% of the southern Africa flora. Of the 1215 plant species recorded in the Amatola Mountains some are no longer common in the area (Kirkman and Wilson 1999). This is because of the impact of alien invasive vegetation species on the grasslands, including the establishment of pine plantations in the area. Nevertheless, these remain rich and diverse forest communities, historically accessible to the people of Guquka (Che and Lent 2004).

The second major type is sour *grassveld* (Döhne *Sourveld*), occurring on the plateaus and spurs. These grasslands are generally situated on older, nutrient poor soils. Rooi grass (*Themeda triandra*), wire grass (*Aristida junciformis*), sickle grass (*Pogonarthria squarrosa*) and thatchgrass (*Hyparrhenia hirta*) are common species. Other forbs and herbs include those of the genus *Watsonia* and wand flower (*Dierama pulcherrimum*). The term 'sourveld' refers to the low level of nutrients in key forage species at the end of the rainy season.

The original *veld* above the escarpment was described in glowing terms by one of the first travellers in the region. In 1836, Captain William Cornwallis Harris visited the Bontebok Flats, which comprised the plateau from Hogsback to the Windvogelberg near Cathcart. His narrative described vegetation of great beauty spreading across the vast plateau area. He spoke of

> ... a boundless billowy succession of surge-like sward undulations ... illuminated by a dwarf flora, endless in variety as in profusion ... and the whole acres positively derive their complexion from the beds of blossoming bulbs by which they are completely covered. Alternate patches of green, yellow, purple or crimson ... impart to the country the appearance of being spread with a carpet of gigantic pattern; but over the whole tract not a solitary tree, no not even a bush of so much as a foot in height, is anywhere to be seen ... (Cornwallis Harris 1986: 92; cited by Coleman 1999).

On the plateau also are sponge wetlands that feed numerous streams and there are a number of peat '*vleis*' (bogs or meadows) near Hogsback. The main plant species found in the wetland areas are Restio spp. with ground orchids commonly occurring. The mountain summits are islands of Afromontane vegetation. They are characterised by sugarbush (*Protca simplex*) and ground orchids (Coleman 1999).

Sclerophyllous Shrublands, also referred to as *macchia* or *fynbos*, also occur on the plateau (Hill Kaplan Scott & Partners 1977, Coleman 1999). Macchia is a successional phase that tends to occur in response to overgrazing and protection from fire. There is a dynamic relationship between grassland, fynbos and forest, depending on the soils and *veld* management, and especially the fire burning regime (Cowling *et al.* 1997, Trollope 1973). Rock outcrop vegetation is found scattered along the cliffs and rocky outcrops on the mountain sides and here nana-berry (*Rhus dentata*) and ouhout (*Leucosidea sericea*) are conspicuous diagnostic species.

Due to the changes in land use over the past two hundred years as the original limited distribution of Afromontane vegetation in the area a large number of plants now have reduced distribution and populations. Bulbous plants have been particularly affected and their present populations give rise to concern. There are 66 species listed. Only about 20,000 ha of Döhne *Sourveld* are formally protected in South Africa, most of which is in and on the edges of indigenous forest and very little of it is still grassland (Coleman 1999).

Below the escarpment in the immediate vicinity of Guquka the dominant vegetation type was referred to as mixed *veld* by Hill, Kaplan, Scott & Partners (1977), based upon its transition status between sour *veld* and sweet. More recently this is referred to as Eragrotis–Sporobolus Grassland in the South African land cover classification system. Forbs form a significant portion of the plant cover. Species found include smut grass (*Sporobolus capensis*), grasses of the genus *Eragrostis*, and pincushion grass (*Microchloa caffra*). *Themeda* and *Hyparrhenia* (thatch grass) are also characteristic of mixed *veld*. Lovegrass (*Eragrostis plana*) is common in the vicinity of *kraals*. *Richardia humistrata* is an abundant forb, its rosette habit helping to protect the soil from erosion.

In the land cover classification a cultivation variant is identified consisting of cultivated areas, associated with fallow lands that are characterised by pioneer and seral species. Abandoned and other fallow lands in the mixed *veld* areas are generally dominated by hatchgrass or, where heavily grazed, by couch grass (*Cynodon dactylon*). Particularly at lower elevations nearer the river the fallow lands will be less 'sour'. These cultivated and fallow lands are dealt with in greater detail in chapters 7, 8 and 9.

In and around the residential area there are heavily grazed grasslands where *C. dactylon* is the dominant species with associated species that include weeping lovegrass (*Eragrostis curvula*), *E. plana* and *S. capensis*.

Invasive alien species are important elements of the landscape both above and below the escarpment and include black wattle (*Acacia mearnsii*), blackwood (*Acacia melanoxylon*), cluster pine (*Pinus pinaster*), radiata pine (*Pinus radiata*), patula pine (*Pinus patula*), and gums of the genus *Eucalyptus* (Kirkman & Wilson 1999, Marais 1994). As noted earlier, much of the land above the escarpment has been converted to plantations for the cultivation of pine trees (Coleman 1999), following the recommendations made in Hill, Kaplan, Scott & Partners (1977).

The parastatal, SA Forestry Company, (SAFCOL) has leased 7500 ha of state land from the Department of Water Affairs and Forestry, mostly in pine plantations. An environmental management plan for the Hogsback Plantation was drawn up in 1994 in consultation with the Hogsback community (Coleman 1999). The Department of Water Affairs and Forestry (DWAF) owns and manages state land to the east of the Tyume River, including the three Hogsback Peaks, and the 218 ha Auckland Nature Reserve. The main responsibility of the agency here is the conservation of the indigenous forests.

DWAF intends to privatise the plantations that belonged both to the former Ciskei Department of Agriculture and Forestry and to the South African government. These lands formed part of Chief Mqalo's grazing which was expropriated by the government (chapter 4). It is at present part of a land dispute and there are land claims lodged with the regional Land Claims Commission. Nevertheless, these extensive plantations of exotics continue to play important roles influencing the ecology and hydrology of Guquka and supporting the economy of the area (Coleman 1999).

Overall, it is clear from the above that residents of Guquka potentially have access to an extremely wide variety of vegetation types and plant species existing over a range of elevations and climatic conditions but all located within a few kilometres of the village. In more recent times this has included not only indigenous vegetation but also an array of introduced plants.

## Description of the arable allotment soils

The position of the arable allotments was described in chapter 4 and shown in Map 4.1. The detailed soil mapping and description done on these allotments (Verdoodt 1999, Verdoodt *et al.* 2003) was based not only on the presence of typical soil forms but also on the threats of active erosion that restrict the possibilities for agricultural use. Orthophotos were used in the field and as a base for the final maps of soil units and soil depth. Three topographic units can be distinguished: the flat river valley, the sloping plateau and, at some places, steep slopes, separating the first two units (Verdoodt *et al.* 2003). The external soil-forming factors, together with the active erosion, results in soils of varying suitability for crop production.

In order to give an overview of the importance of the different soil types present in the Arable Allotments of Guquka, Table 5.2 shows the area covered by each unit and its contribution to overall allotment area.

The following material is taken largely from Bonroy and Verdoodt (1999), Verdoodt *et al.* (2000) and Verdoodt *et al.* (2003). The river valley is characterised by deep alluvial and colluvial soils. The banks along the river are mainly classified as Lowland Valsrivier (Soil Classification Working Group 1991). This deep, well-drained, dark coloured, colluvial soil has a strongly developed structure. The soil has a relatively high agricultural value.

The well-drained Lowland Oakleaf soil form is a deep, young soil, characterised by a moderate to strong structural development and a small increase in clay in the B horizon. On the riverbanks, deposits of coarse material result in sandy-loam soils. Further away from the banks, the soils show finer texture. The agricultural value is generally high, but some imperfectly drained Lowland Oakleaf exists bordering poorly drained soils in the depressions of the valley.

In the lowest parts of the river valley, the run-off from the neighbouring steep slopes above accumulates and gives rise to poorly drained soils, such as the Katspruit, which is saturated for a long time every year. Katspruit, Kroonstad and imperfectly drained Oakleaf are present as a complex in the north of Guquka. Due to the poor drainage (water-logging) and low chemical fertility, the agricultural potential of these soils is strongly limited.

In the southwest portion, an upland Valsrivier soil form occurs on a dolerite substrate. A brown to reddish-coloured matrix with high clay percentage and good drainage is typical for this unit. Some intrusions of dolerite are also present on the ridge, resulting in a complex of upland Valsrivier and the related soil type, Swartland. These soils have high clay content and strong structural development. The high organic matter content and chemical fertility are favourable for crop growth. The reddish colour of the matrix is visible from the soil surface.

*Table 5.2*     Proportions of soil mapping units on Guquka arable allotments with an evaluation of soils

| Soil unit | Area in arable allotments | | Evaluation of soil resource for crops |
|---|---|---|---|
| | Ha | % | |
| Well drained Oakleaf | 61.28 | 38.4 | OK, Sunflowers best |
| Imperfectly drained Oakleaf | 24.05 | 15.1 | Generally poor |
| Katspruit, Kroonstad & imperfectly drained Oakleaf Complex | 13.49 | 8.5 | Generally poor |
| Katspruit | 8.92 | 5.6 | Not suitable |
| Lowland Valsrivier | 8.66 | 5.4 | Good for maize |
| Westleigh-Longlands Complex | 7.87 | 4.9 | Degraded, not suitable |
| Glenrosa | 7.30 | 4.6 | Sunflowers best |
| Mispah | 7.27 | 4.6 | Not suitable |
| Assoc. Upland Valsrivier, Swartland | 5.90 | 3.7 | Good for crops |
| Sheet and gully erosion | 4.08 | 2.6 | Not suitable |
| Sheet erosion | 3.58 | 2.2 | Not suitable |
| Donga (gullies) | 3.12 | 2.0 | Not suitable |
| Gully erosion | 2.60 | 1.6 | Not suitable |
| Westleigh-Glenrosa Complex | 1.35 | 0.9 | Not suitable |
| Waterlogged | 0.08 | 0.1 | Not suitable |
| Total | 159.55 | 100 | |

*Source*: Adapted from Verdoodt (1999)

The well-drained upland Oakleaf has been developed through weathering in situ or from drifted material. The parent material is mudstone, sandstone or unconsolidated colluvium of mudstone and dolerite. On the ridges, drainage is good, but in the depressions, water accumulates and drainage becomes imperfect.

The highest parts of the area are covered by shallow soils including Mispah and Glenrosa. The parent material is sandstone. In both units, root growth is strongly limited and the risk for water stress is very high. When the natural vegetation is removed, these soils are very erodible and, consequently, grazing is the most appropriate land use for these soils. These shallow soils are also found on the steep slopes, separating the valley from the plateau. Severe erosion probably led to the formation of Westleigh and Longlands soil forms. These are the most strongly degraded soils in Guquka with characteristics that limit root growth and infiltration capacity.

Gullies and dongas are occur frequently in these highly erodible soils (see chapter 7). Active erosion, low chemical fertility and low workability limit the agricultural potential of these soils.

The low organic matter content in Guquka soils can be partly attributed to widespread sheet erosion from runoff. This causes the loss of high amounts of soil and organic material. On highly erodible soils, such as Westleigh, Mispah and Glenrosa, this sheet erosion evolves towards the formation of gullies and dongas that are several meters deep. These erosion features have been indicated on the soil map where agricultural production on these spots is currently not possible. The erodibility of these soils has been identified elsewhere in the Tyume catchment (Magagula 1999).

Verdoodt *et al.* (2003) concluded that maize grows best in the Guquka environment on the most fertile soils with high water and nutrient retention capacities, specifically the Valsrivier soil type. These authors suggested sunflower production as an alternative on the Oakleaf soils and deeper Glenrosa and Mispah types. Further, the authors recommended other unspecified land uses on the poorly drained and low-fertility Katspruit soils. They urged the introduction of land conservation practices on abandoned fields with degraded soils. Overall, the information appearing in Bonroy and Verdoodt (1999) and Verdoodt *et al.* 2003 suggests that only slightly over 50% of the area in the allotments was currently well suited for maize production (Table 5.2, Map 5.2) with nearly half the area in degraded condition or otherwise unsuitable. According to Verdoodt *et al.* (2003: 378), "the soil index ranges from 0.06 to 0.74. This implies a further reduction of the yields of 30% or more due to low physical and/or chemical fertility. On the poorly drained soils of the lower terrace, which also have a low content of nutrient cations and organic carbon content, yields tend to be reduced by more than 90%. The highest yields are attained on the Valsrivier soil, with an average soil index of 0.6." Map 5.2 shows the spatial distribution of the fields displaying this range of values. This condition of the soil resource base exists in part from anthropogenic influences (chapter 7). The table also gives general indications of the value of each soil form for crop agriculture. As noted, our detailed understanding of the agricultural values and limitations of the soils in Guquka is limited to the area historically designated as the arable allotments. To what extent the most appropriate soil resources were located and set aside for crops is not entirely clear. Certainly planners responded to restrictions imposed by slope steepness and thus were faced with limited options. Further details on the physical and chemical characteristics of all the soil units are provided in Verdoodt (1999).

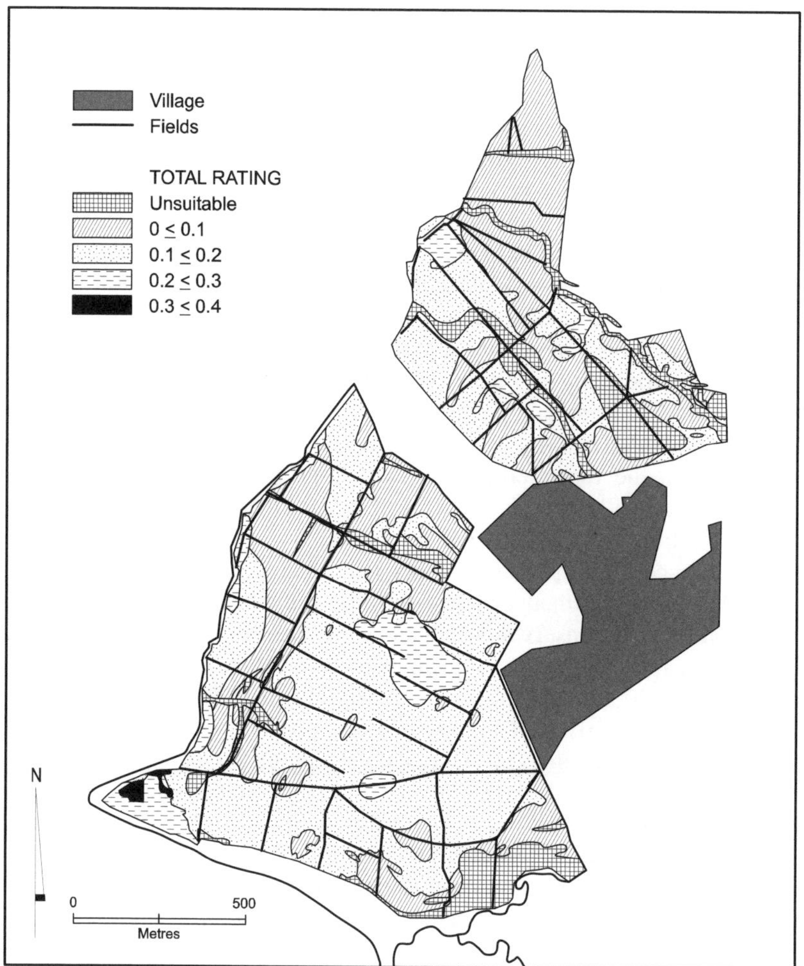



*Map 5.2*     Guquka land use ratings

*Agricultural potential of the arable allotments*
In order to assess the potential for crop yields in Guquka the soils databases for the arable allotments were combined with climatic and topographic data. Using these databases, the period of the year suitable for crop growth, the growing period, could be identified through an evaluation of temperature and water availability, following the FAO approach. Crop growth potential was described by Verdoodt *et al.* (2003) using a three level hierarchical crop growth model (Van Ranst 1994).

The three production levels are in fact nested crop production systems, starting with the highest or potential level related to optimal conditions working down to production levels at sub-optimal conditions.

The estimated land production potentials was compared to experimental yield data from comparable sites (Van Averbeke and Marais 1991) thus providing a yield gap analysis. Differences between the land production potential and these actual yields, measured in the field, were attributed largely to pests, diseases or sub-optimal land management. The semi-arid character of the study areas and their different agricultural systems, however, required adaptations of some of the usual calculation methods.

The arable land of Guquka was evaluated specifically for the production of rain-fed maize and sunflower. Although the latter crop currently plays no significant role in the diet of local people, sunflowers were of theoretical interest because the crop has a higher tolerance to water stress than maize.

The growing period was initially defined according to the FAO concept of a continuous period (Kowal 1978). The resulting period first was extended to take into account the local crop calendar but then was limited by crop-specific temperature requirements of both crops. Determination of the optimal planting date was established by fitting the crop cycle into the growing period, taking into account the crop characteristics and the climatic data during that crop cycle. In addition to this, the planting dates November 2 and December 19, used in Van Averbeke and Marais (1991), were assumed to be representative of local practices. Further details of the methods used for the crop production models and yield gap analyses are provided in Verdoodt *et al.* (2003).

*Yield gap analysis*
According to the FAO concept of the growing period, crop growth in Guquka starts on February 19 and ends on April 28. The local crop calendar begins with the start of the rains in October-November. Considering temperature limitations, this start date was not changed in the model, but the end of the growing season was limited to April 25 for maize and May 14 for sunflower. As the evapotranspiration exceeds rainfall during the whole period, no soil water reserve can be build up and rain-fed crops suffer from water stress (Bonroy and Verdoodt 1999, Verdoodt *et al.* 2003).

The solar input at Guquka is favourable for crop production. In theory, the earlier the sowing date, and the longer the crop cycle, the more biomass can be accumulated and the higher the yields. However, rainfall during the crop cycle is insufficient to replenish the amount of difficult available soil water of deep soils with a high water holding capacity. Verdoodt *et al.* (2003) concluded that a higher water holding capacity of the soil only positively influences crop growth when there is enough water stored so that it is easily available for plant uptake. In Guquka, however, rainfall and topography are the only determinants of the water-limited production. They determined that this is simulated best by a modified modelling method, which was used for the further calculations.

According to this exercise the best date for sowing on average is December 19. The high yield reduction that occurs if crops are sown at the beginning of the rains is due to high water stress during the flowering period. The yield reduction with late sowing is due to the decreasing rainfall amounts at the beginning of autumn. The soil water content has been replenished by rainfall during the first month of the rainy season, but at the same time, the risk increases for water logging on sealed soils due to heavy rainfall. Local cultivars of maize differ little in crop cycle duration and are all suited for production; a medium season cultivar showed the best yield.

The modelling exercise demonstrated that the poor physical condition and low fertility of soils in the arable lands was a major factor in reduction of yields. The yield reductions averaged 30% and in some poorly drained soils (Map 5.2) the modelled reduction was as high as 90% (Verdoodt *et al.* 2003). Maize showed the highest yields in the Valsrivier soils. The model predicted sunflower production was greater and more advantageous than maize production on the Oakleaf soils. However, this did not take into consideration the high potential for loss to bird pests and other production problems for this crop. Verdoodt *et al.* (2003) emphasized the importance of local farmers taking measures to deal with the erosion and degradation problems, principally by intercropping maize with cover crops and legumes.

This brief description of the physical and biotic resources of Guquka and assessment of their agricultural potential sets the stage for examination of how the landscape and the resources have been used in the past and are currently being used as part of the livelihood strategies of the people as elucidated in chapters 7, 8, 9 and 10.


## Koloni

Koloni lies in the central part of the coastal plateau (chapter 3). Situated in the southern part of the Middledrift District, at 32°53' S and 27°05' E., the village itself is located on a range of the hills between two valleys at an elevation of about 600 m. These hills are part of the first post-African Erosion Surface, causing the plateau to look flat when standing on the top of a hill. However, relatively deep valleys are incised in the apparently flat plateau. The steep slopes are the results of 4 million years of strong erosion. Clearly visible signs indicate that the erosion cycle is still active (Maud 1996).

Climatically, the area is semi-arid. Long-term rainfall records (1934-1976) from the nearest rainfall station at Middledrift, show a mean annual rainfall of 488 mm. The town of Middledrift lies some 10 km northwest of Koloni, however the region is characterised by large variation in rainfall over relatively short distances (chapter 3). Nevertheless, a similar mean annual rainfall prediction of 471 mm is obtained from the CIRADA rainfall data package (Austin 1989a).

The Bantu Affairs Commission (1962) report gives a slightly higher locally based estimate of rainfall of 21" (533 mm) per annum for Koloni. The estimated annual potential evapotranspiration is 1750 mm with an aridity index of 0.27. These estimates support the idea that rain-fed cropping is marginal in most years (ARDRI 1996).

The village lies in a vegetation type known as the False *Thornveld* of the Eastern Cape (Acocks 1988, see also chapter 3). This is considered a '*sweet-veld*', as it remains relatively nutritious during the winter months and is thus well suited to livestock production without supplemental feeds. This favourable range type, the low level and unpredictable nature of the rainfall patterns, which makes crop production risky, and cultural and historical factors, all lead to an emphasis on livestock production at the site and, indeed, in the surrounding area (Hundelby *et al.* 1986, also chapter 3). The relationship of the communal rangelands with the arable fields and residential areas is shown in Map 4.2. Because of the rolling topography with moderate changes in elevation it is thought that only minor variations in rainfall occur over this area (Map 5.1).

The vegetation of the Koloni area was apparently originally a *grassveld* (Eastern Province Grassveld of Acocks 1988). This is typically found in a zone with annual rainfall of 400 to 650 mm. As noted above, it is now referred to Acocks Type 7, Eastern Province *Thornveld*. But if this was indeed a 'natural' *thornveld*, it was clearly at one time of the type described by Acocks (1988: 28) as "so open as to be practically *grassveld*". The report of the Bantu Affairs Commission (1962) considered that the thorn trees, *Acacia karoo*, were gone from the area because of intensive harvesting by residents for firewood and fencing. However, the area has since then clearly been subject to invasion and an increase of this woody species almost everywhere (chapter 7). The rate of change here suggests this process results from anthropogenic influences.

The *grassveld* components include such species as *T. triandra*, finger grass (*Digitaria eriantha*), thatchgrass (*H. hirta*), species of genus *Eragrostis* and in patches of shade *Panicum spp.* In addition to *Acacia karoo*, the principal fuel wood, a few other woody species may occur in bush clumps. A large variety of forbs are present in areas where not subject to overgrazing. No natural forests occur.

Koloni lacks potential for development of irrigation schemes. Groundwater is considered to be of low quality (Bantu Affairs Commission 1962). Nevertheless, crop production, although secondary in importance to livestock (chapters 8 and 9), has been an important aspect of the economy. To look at the resource base for this economy the soils of Koloni have been mapped and classified in detail but only for the arable allotments (Bonroy 1999, Bonroy *et al.* 2000), of approximately 312 ha, including the 112 individual fields and a number of commonage areas within the arable allotment.

The study conducted in Koloni by Bonroy (1999) also evaluated the potential for agricultural production of the arable allotments, similarly to the work in

Guquka. The first phase of the research work consisted of a detailed survey on a scale of 1: 5000 of the soils found in the arable lands. The results of this soil survey were captured on a Geographic Information System. However in this case the hierarchical crop-growth simulation model was run only for lucerne. Even though this crop is not currently grown in the community, it was recommended as a 'ley' crop for pasture production by previous planners (Bantu Affairs Commission 1962). The extent of past cultivation of this crop is unknown.

*General description of the survey area in arable allotments*
The arable land of Koloni is situated in a cirque or glacial valley which forms the source area of the Pewuleni River, and covers the slopes and the valley bottom. The distribution of soils was closely related to topography. In order to give an overview of the importance of the different soil types present in Koloni, the area covered by each unit, in absolute hectares and as a percentage of the overall area of the arable allotments is summarised in Table 5.3.

*Table 5.3*     Proportions of soil mapping units on Koloni arable allotments with an evaluation of the soils

| Soil unit | Surface | | Evaluation for crop suitability |
|---|---|---|---|
| | % | Ha | |
| Valsrivier Complex | 13.7 | 4.5 | Generally suitable |
| Katspruit Complex | 9.8 | 3.2 | Poor, unsuitable |
| Eroded surfaces | 5.8 | 2.0 | Unsuitable |
| Estcourt | 135.6 | 4.8 | Limited value |
| Glenrosa | 47.6 | 15.7 | ? |
| Katspruit | 2.2 | 0.7 | Poor, unsuitable |
| Mispah | 34.3 | 11.3 | ? |
| Oakleaf        with dense subsoil | 22.6 | 7.4 | Suitable |
|         less dense subsoils | 14.7 | 4.8 | Best agricultural soils |
| Sterkspruit | 17.1 | 5.6 | Mostly suitable |
| Total | 303.4 | 100 | |

*Source*: Adapted from Bonroy and Verdoodt (1999)

The soil units in Koloni were determined according to the dominant soil type. In some cases the dominance of a single soil type is not clear leading to the identification of an association of soil types to identify the soil unit. A zone with signs of severe erosion was mapped during the survey. Although erosion was not restricted to that zone, the soil profile development there was so deficient as to make identification of the dominant soil type difficult. The agricultural value of this zone is extremely limited.

*Description of the soil units*

Bonroy *et al.* (2000) summarised information regarding the nature and distributon of the soils in the arable allotments. They reported shallow Mispah type soils on the crest of the slope in the easternmost fields. Here weathering has resulted in considerable fragmentation of the underlying sedimentary rocks. On the upper slopes soil development has reached more advanced stages, resulting in the formation of Glenrosa soil types, which merge with still deeper Oakleaf soil types on the middle slopes. Two types of Oakleaf soils were identified. The first was characterised by a brown B horizon with weak to moderate structure and abundant penetration of roots. The second had a grey and more dense B horizon which showed very limited penetration of roots. On the soil map these two types were distinguished from each other because their potential for crop production was considered to be significantly different.

Where the slope was steep, Estcourt type soils occurred. These soils are characterised by an abrupt transition between a sandy topsoil and a clay-like, impervious B horizon. At the contact between topsoil and B horizon a thin E horizon occurs which is formed by the leaching action of water flowing over the contact zone. Slope processes have resulted in the deposition of a thick soil mantle on the foot slopes, and here Valsrivier type soils were most common. Katspruit type soils were found where an accumulation of subsurface water and overland flow and poor drainage caused waterlogged conditions.

As has been described above, soil drainage problems are widespread in the Koloni arable allotments, indeed when evaluating the influence of soil quality, the model of Bonroy (1999) and Bonroy *et al.* (2000) identified drainage to be a key factor influencing crop success and yields.

Where soil drainage was obviously poor yield reductions of up to 74% were predicted. Low organic carbon content was also predicted to be a limiting factor. The organic carbon content of the soils varied widely between a low of 0.28% and a high of 1.47%. The model predicted that yields on soils with a low organic carbon content could be increased by as much as 47% by increasing the content to 1.47%. Further details regarding the physical and chemical properties of each soil unit are presented in Bonroy (1999) and Bonroy and Verdoodt (1999).

Evaluating the soils in their current state, the model identified the Glenrosa type soils to be the most productive and further predicted that the productivity of the permeable Oakleaf soils and the Valsrivier soils could be increased to match that of the Glenrosa soils by addition of organic matter. However, improvement of the soil quality had a minor effect in the model when compared to the potential effects of irrigation aimed to remove or reduce water deficits. On steep slopes the model predicted that a major portion of the rain would run off, thus reducing its effectiveness. It was, therefore, thought that the terracing of steeper slopes would increase productivity.

The modelling effort clearly demonstrated that addressing water deficit was the main challenge facing production of crops such as lucerne at Koloni. Irrigation does not seem to be a realistic option at Koloni in the foreseeable future. However, in comparison to Guquka a much greater proportion of the soil resources in the arable allotments remain usable for agricultural endeavours.

## Conclusions

On the arable lands of both villages, sunshine and temperature are favourable for crop production, but the heavy dependence on rainfall makes farming very vulnerable to drought, especially in Koloni with its lower annual rainfall and greater annual uncertainty in timing and amount of precipitation. Unfortunately, there is no potential for small-scale irrigation in this area.

Low natural fertility was found to be a limiting factor for most soils in the arable allotments. Poor drainage and limited soil depth also decreased yields at several locations. Loss of topsoil due to erosion is a significant problem and limiting factor in Guquka, but much less so in Koloni. In both areas measures are needed to improve soil nutrients which have declined on those fields that have been repeatedly cropped. In Guquka, especially, agricultural potential is further limited by generally unfavourable topography except close to the river, where water logging is instead a key problem. Overall, more than half the lands set aside for crop agriculture in Guquka have significant limitations at present.

The area around Guquka has abundant resources and resource potential includeing water, indigenous forests and forest plantations. Subsequent chapters, especially chapter 9, show that the people obtain some benefits from these resources but are not benefiting fully from this potential.

The results of studies indicate that, especially for Koloni, maize is not an ideal crop due to its water demands. Reasons for the strong focus on the cultivation of maize will be dealt with in chapter 8.

In comparison with Guquka, livelihoods based on local natural resources are more constrained in Koloni by several factors including lower rainfall, high year-to-year variability in rainfall patterns, low groundwater quality, lower diversity of plant communities and native plants, and a lack of any nearby timber resources.

6

# Local governance and institutions

Wim van Averbeke and James Bennett

## Introduction

There is growing consensus that governance and institutions play an important role in the organisation of everyday life. This chapter focuses on governance and institutions in Guquka and Koloni in relation to natural resources in terms of access, control and management. Considerable attention is given to changes in the local political organisation in relation to broader political change shortly before and after the first democratic elections in 1994. The chapter also explores how individuals comply with or manoeuvre around formal and informal institutional arrangements to acquire and manage resources, and how status, power and networks, or lack thereof, results in unequal access to and control over resources and thus contributes to the shaping of local livelihoods.

Among the important events influencing local governance and institutions in the two villages are the historical decline of the powers of traditional leadership and the rise to power of civic organisations. The inequality among residents in terms of access to arable land and the persistence among owners of arable land to adhere to the institution of sharecropping when negotiating with landless people about access to land for cultivation are important dimensions of local governance. Moreover, the relationship between institutional compliance and abundance or scarcity of resources and the weakening of linkages between the villages and the official local government structures during recent times plays a prominent role.

## Local government in the Ciskei region

In 1866, British Kaffraria (chapter 2), which covered most of the Ciskei region and included the areas in which Koloni and Guquka were founded, was annexed to the Cape Colony, subjecting the region to its laws. The Cape Colony itself received full responsible governmental powers in 1872 (Holdt 1971). Since the end of the sixth frontier war in 1835 interference with self government of the tribes in the Ciskei region and its system of chiefs, progressively reduced the powers of this traditional leadership even prior to annexation(Peires 2003, Mostert 1992).

At the time of annexation the chiefs had already been replaced by magistrates, who held executive and judicial powers and administered designated areas called districts. At the local level power was in the hands of headmen who were lowly paid civil servants with duties that included the control of land, assistance in the collection of taxes, and the general enforcement of the law (Manona 1997). Each headman was advised by a council (*inkundla*), which consisted of adult men in the village. These councils considered village matters and settled minor disputes. Villages which often consisted of dispersed clusters of a few homesteads only, had sub-headmen with their own councils and courts. Sub-headmen were not paid by the state. Westaway (1997) pointed out that the positions of headmen and sub-headmen were not hereditary. Instead, appointments followed an election. In 1928, the Native Affairs Department drew up a formalized schedule of duties for headmen, insisting that suitable men be appointed to the position, and often interfering in appointments by overturning election results. The colonial government also started to regulate land allocations, especially those subject to communal tenure, by introducing an administrative system that required land holders to register their holdings at the magistrate's office.

Above this local tier of governance there was a system of local councils (*amaBhunga*), established by central government in terms of the Native Act of 1920. The Local Council for Middledrift was created in 1926, and that for Victoria East in 1927. The Act permitted both elected and appointed representation in the local councils and allocated a fairly wide range of powers and responsibilities to these councils, including the right to levy rates and the responsibility for the provision of medical and educational facilities (Hold 1971). Manona (1997) argued that the establishment of local councils was not an attempt on the part of central government to revive traditional leadership, because membership of the councils consisted predominantly of educated people, not traditional leaders. In 1934, the eight district councils operating in the Ciskei region were merged to form the Ciskei General Council (Holdt 1971).

At the national level the Representation of Bantu Act of 1936 removed black people in the Cape Province from the common voters' roll and entered them on a separate roll, giving them the right to elect two white representatives to the Provincial Council and three to Parliament. The Act also created a Bantu Representative Council to act in an advisory capacity.

The Bantu Representative Council was abolished by the Bantu Authorities Act of 1951. Representation of black people in the Provincial Council and Parliament was repealed in 1959. The underlying purpose of the Bantu Authorities Act, and other legislation, such as the Promotion of Bantu Self-Government Act No 46 of 1959, was to prepare the Native Areas, established by the 1913 Land Act and the 1936 Native Trust and Land Act, for self-governance as part of the overall policy of Apartheid. The Bantu Authorities Act proposed the establishment of local government consisting of three tiers, as shown in Figure 6.1. The Act assigned tribal or community authorities with the responsibility for administering the affairs of the tribe or community, regional authorities with responsibilities similar to those of the former general councils, which included the advancement of education, agriculture, health and transport, and territorial authorities with the powers, functions and duties of a regional authority. The crucial feature of these new authorities was the reintroduction of traditional leadership powers. Chiefs were assigned key positions at all three levels.

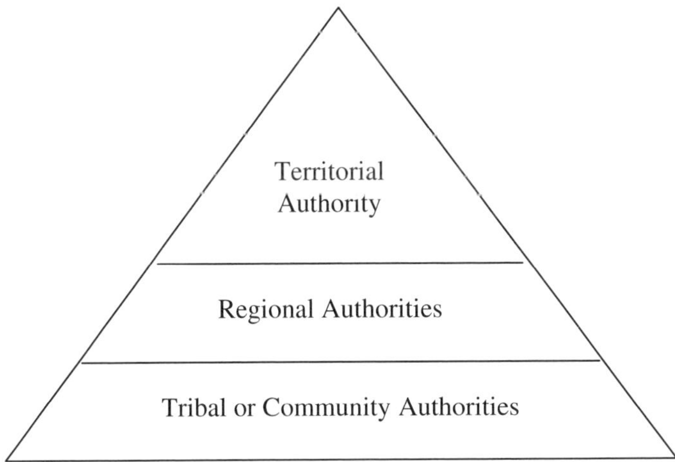


*Figure 6.1*    Structure of governance in the homelands introduced by the Bantu
Authorities Act of 1951

Manona (1997) contended that re-tribalising black people, as envisioned by the Act, contrasted with trends in the rest of Africa, where power had steadily been shifting from traditional to elected authorities. He pointed out that in South Africa, and particularly in the Ciskei region, the Act brought chiefs out of relative obscurity. He referred to the work of Wilson *et al.* (1951) in Keiskammahoek District to show that chiefly traditions were at that time no longer of any major importance to the people living in that area.

In 1968, the regulations for tribal, regional and territorial authorities in the Ciskei region were repealed by Proclamation No. R. 143. This Proclamation constituted the next legislative step towards self-governance of the Ciskei region, assigning greater responsibilities to the Ciskeian Territorial Authority. It resulted in the creation of a six-member Executive of that authority, which gradually assumed the functions of a ministerial cabinet. Each member of the Executive was in charge of a department with a designated civil service.

The Ciskei was declared independent in 1981. Lennox Sebe, who had been a member of the Executive of the Territorial Authority, became President of Ciskei. He appointed ministers who were responsible for the different government departments. Ciskei also had a parliament, which consisted of the Chiefs and which had an advisory function. At the local level tribal authorities were maintained and strengthened.

In Ciskei, the power of the tribal authorities came to an end when the Ciskei government of President Lennox Sebe was toppled on the 3rd of March 1990 by a military coup lead by Brigadier Oupa Gqozo. Initially the Brigadier identified with the ANC, encouraging broad-based democracy in local governance. Three weeks after the coup he caused the collapse of the tribal authorities in Ciskei by publicly announcing that all headmen had to resign their positions (Manona 1997). The position of the Chiefs, however, remained untouched. Using the local media he encouraged people to form residents' associations, an initiative that responded to the widespread call for democratization that swept the South African nation. Residents' Associations (RA's) and other civic associations already operated in the region. In 1987, the Border Civic Association had been established as an umbrella body for all civic associations operating in the area between the Fish and Kei rivers, but until the military coup civic associations in Ciskei operated clandestinely (Manona 1997).

The period of political freedom and people's government under Gqozo was short lived. The Brigadier soon distanced himself from the civic organizations he had helped to create, and in 1991 he abolished the RA's, reintroducing the headman system to administer the region. This act upset many, especially the youth. The response was swift and in some cases violent. Chiefs and headmen became the target of people's anger. On several occasions the homes of traditional leaders were burnt and their families forced to flee the area. There were even a few instances of murder (Manona 1997). This period of tribulation, exacerbated by the establishment of the African Democratic Movement, which was supported by the military ruler and selected traditional leaders and headmen, and which opposed the ANC, came to an end with the national democratic election of 1994.

During the early stages of the democratisation of South Africa the institution of the RA's was strengthened. Residents' associations were given a voice in the interim local government structures that were established by the Local Government Act of 1993, amended by the Further Regulation of Local Government Act of 1996. The elections of councillors under this transitional arrangement were held in November 1995 and 1996. During the period 1994 to 2001, RA's played an important role in directing local development during the times of the Reconstruction and Development Programme (RDP), when there was particular attention to the provision of basic services, such as water reticulation, electricity and public telephony.

The Development Facilitation Act, 67, passed in 1995, and the Second Amendment of the Local Government Transition Act, passed in 1996, introduced an integrated planning framework for local and regional government. Two important elements of this framework were the Land Development Objectives (LDO) and the Integrated Development Plans (IDP) (ECSECC 1999). However, these plans proved more difficult to develop than was initially anticipated. In most cases the LDO and IDP processes in the Eastern Cape were fragmented and riddled with unresolved issues, and instead of being led by residents they were driven by consultants and NGOs (*ibid.*).

The South African Constitution of 1996 mandated the establishment of municipalities throughout South Africa and vested the legislative and executive powers of municipalities in municipal councils (Rautenbach and Malherbe 1998). These councils were to be elected democratically for a term of not more than four years by means of a system of proportional representation or a combination of proportional representation and wards. The Constitution awarded municipalities the right to impose taxes and levies on property and services, but not income, value-added tax, general sales or customs duties. When exercising their financial powers, the municipalities were not allowed to harm the regional and national economy, and had to impose taxes in accordance with their own capacity and that of their residents. The Constitution also entitled municipalities to an equitable share of the national income to enable them to provide basic services and perform their functions.

The first local government elections within the context of these provisions were held in 2001. They were preceded by the demarcation of the country into district municipalities, local municipalities and metropoles. The writers of the constitution envisioned that municipalities would play a leading role in the social and economic development of its communities, but it soon became clear that many municipalities faltered in the execution of their development mandates, especially poor rural municipalities. In 2005, poor service delivery and the general lack of improvement in the quality of life of residents of rural settlements and townships led to what became known as the 'September Revolution'. Starting in the Free State violent demonstrations by residents, disenchanted with the lack of progress in basic service provision spread through the country, including the Eastern Cape. As a result, improving service provision was the dominant theme in the second local government elections which took place on the 3rd of March 2006. This was widely covered by the media. Perret and L'Hopitalier (2000) provides a similar critical account of the quality and nature of service delivery during the 1994-1999 period.

## Local governance at Guquka and Koloni

In chapters 2 and 4, the gradual process of loss of political control by Chiefs and headmen over people and territory was already discussed. In addition, processes of social and economic change shifted the balance of homestead expansion from acquiring cattle to cash. Labour migration and the implementation of various social schemes changed the balance of power between men and women and between the old and the younger generations. Moreover, political struggles during the period 1960-1990 and the establishment of an ANC led government have substantially modified the political organisation of communities. Elected civil and community based organisations grew in importance, reducing the Chief to an *ex officio* position. Nominally, the Chief remains the custodian of the land, but allocation of land to individuals and changes in land use in settlements of the Eastern Cape are now decided upon by community organisations.

*Guquka*
Guquka and the aggregate of small villages called Makhuzeni, to which Guquka belongs, were settled by immigrants from KwaZulu-Natal who had Mqalo as their leader (chapter 4). When Mqalo settled in the Tyume Valley he became a headman subordinate to the Xhosa Chief Tyali. The Xhosa did not recognise Mqalo as a chief, but within the Makhuzeni community he was regarded as such. This is evident from his leadership position having been passed on from father to son. At the time of settlement, the heads of the different clans contained in Mqalo's group developed their own homestead clusters. In each cluster the head of the clan performed the functions of village leader or headman. Together with Mqalo they constituted the tribal leadership of Makhuzeni. Land was allocated by this leadership in the customary way to the male heads of homesteads and communal tenure applied. Individual tenure was only introduced in Makhuzeni following the surveys of 1899 and 1910, when nearly all of the current land ownership patterns were established. Minor modifications did occur during the implementation of Betterment when selected fields were withdrawn from the area allocated to cultivation, because of their eroded state (chapter 4).

When the Ciskei was being ushered towards self governance, the Tribal Authority system was re-enforced by the establishment of several new Tribal Authorities. This required the appointment of additional Chiefs, which broadened political support for the homeland policy. In 1973, Mqalo was one of several headmen who were promoted to the position of Chief and put in charge of their own tribal authorities. During this era a high school and a clinic were established at Gilton, the residence of Mqalo, and a primary school was erected at Guquka.

Following the Gqozo military coup in 1990, the population in the different settlements of Makhuzeni started to oppose governance by the Tribal Authority, and in 1992 they established RA's. Each of the four villages that made up Makhuzeni (Guquka, Gilton, Msompondo and Phundu) formed its own association, but these four RAs all reported to a body called 'The Umbrella', which represented the Makhuzeni community on the Transitional Rural Council (TRC) of Victoria East. Immediately after 1994, when the state poured considerable resources into the Reconstruction and Development Programme (RDP) aimed at improving the lives of poor black people, these new structures were successful in bringing new resources to the area. Guquka was no exception. A windmill was built to pump groundwater to a stand pipe positioned in the centre of the village providing access to clean and safe water. A public telephone was erected improving contact between residents and their family members living and working elsewhere, and temporary employment was provided to some of the unemployed residents through the Working for Water Programme of the Department of Water Affairs and Forestry.

At first glance RA's were a radical break with the institution of the Tribal Authority. Whereas the Tribal Authority of Makhuzeni consisted of elderly men and was a bastion of conservatism, the RA of Guquka was made up of young people of both genders. However, Holbrook (1998) pointed out that members of the RA at Guquka were nearly all descendents of the old families, whose heads had served in the Tribal Authority and that the Chairperson of the RA was the son of the former headman of Guquka. Holbrook (1998) relates the persistent dominance by representatives of the old families in the politics of Guquka to ownership of land and livestock. The old families held more than three-quarters of all the land and livestock in the village and through these assets they exercised moral authority in the settlement. The new arrangement represented a suitable compromise between the traditional values and the vested interests of the old guard and the youthful forces that had been pushing the settlement to become part of a modern democratic society. Officially, as pointed out by Chief Mqalo in 2004, the Tribal Authority was never made defunct, but effectively it had lost its powers and members no longer met to discuss issues.

Living in the village, or maintaining a home there, made people eligible for membership of the RA. The RA held its meetings every Tuesday at 3pm in the primary school building. Residents knew about this arrangement, and used this weekly opportunity to raise issues of personal or general concern. The Association was lead by a five-member 'Residents Committee', which was elected annually by means of nominations and a democratic voting procedure. Functionally, the RAs operated in the same domains as the Tribal Authorities, including the allocation of residential land.

When transitional local governance came to an end, following the local government elections of 2001, Guquka became part of the Qonkobe Local Municipality, which forms part of the Amatola District Municipality, one of the five District Municipalities that make up the Eastern Cape Province. Under this new political dispensation, rural settlements, such as Guquka, are represented by means of a system of ward councillors, who are elected officials on the payroll of the local municipality. Guquka forms part of the Matole Ward, which extends into the Amatola Basin across the mountains, but does not incorporate all four villages of Makhuzeni. At the ward level, community concerns are dealt with by ward committees. Committee members are elected from the various settlements contained in the ward, but their work is not remunerated. Guquka does not have direct representation on the Matole Ward Committee. Reportedly, members of that Committee come to Guquka upon written request by residents to answer questions or to attend to concerns.

The new system of local governance did not retain the structure of the RA. At Guquka, however, the institution of the residents' association was maintained, but its lack of formal influence is evident from the people who occupied leadership positions. In 2004 the chairperson of the RA at Guquka was a woman, Mrs Thibini. She was married to a man without land or livestock, although he was a descendent of one of the old families. She explained that the RA continued to play a developmental role, because the ward system performed poorly, mainly because of the distance between the settlements contained in the ward. To get to the Amatola Basin from Guquka one has to cross the mountain by foot or by car. When travelling by public transport one has to first get to Alice, then proceed to Middledrift, and from there the occasional vehicle will provide transport to the Amatola Basin. To get around these impracticalities she had resorted to seeking direct consultation with the Ward Councillor, who maintained an office in Alice, whenever there was an urgent matter that concerned Guquka.

*Koloni*

Koloni is situated in an area that was allocated by George Cathcart to the Gqunukhwebe tribe under Chief Kama. However, the people who settled were from diverse backgrounds as explained in chapter 4. The diversity in the composition of the Koloni community and the presence of a Mission station possibly explain why Koloni, relative to neighbouring settlements, was open to modernization through collaboration with government and white farmers. As a result, in the region Koloni farmers were the first to adopt land preparation using animal draught and 'improved' cattle breeds. Later on, Koloni was also the first settlement to have Betterment implemented.

During the 1970s, Koloni's influence on the Department of Agriculture waned as Ciskei progressed towards independence. The importance of ethnicity in the political make up of the Ciskei, particularly in parliament, probably shifted the attention of the bureaucracy to other settlements that were of Gqunukhwebe make-up. As a result, conditions in Koloni deteriorated. Windmills that had broken down were no longer repaired, fences that had deteriorated were not replaced, and interactions between extension staff and Koloni farmers became increasingly sporadic. Yet, Koloni remained a fairly vibrant community during the final decades of the 20th century. The presence of a high school contributed to social and economic life in the village. Relatives and friends residing in urban areas, particularly Port Elizabeth, sent their children to the high school of Koloni, because of the highly volatile situation in the townships, where strikes and political violence disturbed the education processes. One resident of Koloni even erected a hostel on his site to accommodate children from the urban areas who attended school but did not have relatives to stay with.

However, Koloni did not escape from being drawn into the political turmoil that preceded the democratisation of South Africa. During the early 1990s a conflict arose in the village, which was extremely painful; years later it remained something residents did not want to talk about with strangers. The conflict resulted in the replacement of the institution of the Headman of the village by a new institution called the Chairman. The creation of the position of Chairman suggested that Koloni had adopted the residents' association as the organ of local government, but this was not the case. When asked what organization the Chairman was chairing, residents responded that he was Chairman of the village. However, village governance in Koloni under the Chairman was participatory and resembled that practised in villages where residents' associations were in control. Koloni residents met to discuss and take decisions on matters of concern to the community and all residents were welcome to attend meetings. Deference was given to old, male property owners, who spoke first, most and with greater authority than other, mainly younger males and women. Widowed women who had become heads of household also wielded authority. Conceptually, there was little difference between the Chairman and the Headman of the past. Residents described the two positions as being the same. Several of the former headmen and the current Chairman were from the same family, but the Chairman was not paid by the state. He was elected by the village residents, and according to residents, his term of office was until they wanted a different Chairman. In line with the democratic political system that had been introduced in South Africa in 1994, the principle of majority rule applied in principle, but in practice this was not the case. Majority rule reached by means of a vote was viewed as unsatisfactory, because of the risk of creating rifts within the community. Conscious of the destabilizing effects of the internal conflict of the recent past, informants explained to us that if no consensus emerged through discussion, those who wished to participate in a new initiative organised themselves and proceeded. They would make an effort to leave matters open-ended, so that others could join in later should they desire to do so. In 1997, this approach had been adopted in relation to two development initiatives, namely the installation of electricity in the village and the establishment of an irrigated community garden.

In 2004, Koloni created a residents' association, at a time when this structure no longer existed officially, having been superseded by ward committees in the formal structure of local governance. The Koloni RA performed a similar function as the Chairman and his village meetings, but indications were that local governance had lost much of its prestige and importance, as was the case in Guquka. For example, the Chairman was a man who had recently returned from Cape Town. When asked, he admitted to us that as soon as he had accumulated enough money he would return to Cape Town to look for work, because Koloni and its surrounds were 'dead'. Structurally, Koloni had also aligned itself with the new system of local government. Two members of the residents' association had been appointed to serve on the local ward committee, but as in Guquka these representatives were not amongst the socially most powerful individuals in the village.

## Negotiating access to natural resources in Guquka and Koloni

After Koloni and Guquka were settled, the lands that belonged to these villages was surveyed. In Koloni this occurred in 1874. In Guquka a first survey was conducted in 1899 and a second in 1910 (see chapter 4). The residential lots and the arable allotments were allocated to male heads of settler families as quitrent and the rangelands as communal (chapter 4).

Marais (1959) and Holden (1877) pointed out that converting communal tenure to individual quitrent tenure formed part of Cape policy of 'civilising' black people, in this case mainly Mfengu settlers (chapters 2 and 4). Its objective was to transform Mfengu tribesmen into small peasant proprietors. The allocation of land under individual tenure to black people was introduced by Grey, who governed the Cape from 1854 to 1861. He encouraged black people to purchase Crown land, but Marais (1959) explained that this initiative found application on a limited scale only. Overall, individualizing tenure among the black population of the Ciskei region was never implemented in full, and this explains why in term s of tenure this region is a complicated puzzle. Beinart and Bundy (1987) similarly argued that expanding private tenure

> ... fell away as a central administrative objective. Even in those districts where [the Glen Grey Act] was introduced, the principles of primogeniture and the non-divisibility of plots were largely sacrificed to older practices. The original Act clearly stipulated that individual tenure would become operative in every district where the Glen Grey terms applied; but by 1903 its adoption became optional, and surveys for individual title were carried out in only a handful of Transkeian (and Ciskeian) districts (Beinart and Bundy 1987: 141).

According to Marais (1959), many people in surveyed locations refused to take up their titles, apparently because they were too expensive. This certainly happened in Koloni (see chapter 4). Quitrent rentals were high, because the government sought to recover the survey cost. Moreover, when ownership needed to be transferred, for example following the death of the title holder, transfer fees applied, which most refused to pay. As a result, about 30 to 40 years after obtaining quitrent tenure, few homesteads still retained legal title to their land (Marais 1959). Our fieldwork conducted during the 1990s showed that many land holders in Guquka and Koloni no longer possessed written proof of ownership over their plots. Moreover, several of them especially at Guquk were not aware that they held their land by means of quitrent tenure. Practically, this was of little if any consequence because within the village context owner-ship of land was common knowledge and not contested.

Following the democratisation of South Africa, the government embarked on a land reform programme. This programme had a three-pronged approach, namely land restitution, land redistribution and tenure reform. One of the first legislative measures in support of tenure reform was the Upgrading of Land Tenure Rights Act 112 of 1991. This Act strengthened the security of different types of tenure with which black people held land in South Africa. Practically, this Act has had no impact on the market for land exchanges in Guquka and Koloni.

## Access to arable land

Issue of individual title to arable land in Guquka and Koloni following the cadastral surveys removed power and control over access to such land from the realm of the tribal leadership, and made it subject to negotiation within families with titles and between families with titles and those without formal access to land. Legally, a quitrent title transferred to the oldest son upon the death of the male title holder, but usually this only occurred when his widow had also passed away. The use of the arable plot was sometimes negotiated within the family, especially when the homestead of the new owner was not interested or capable to use the plot.

Families without a title also negotiated access to land, especially at Guquka, where the number of landless families exceeded that of title holders and agro-ecological conditions favoured crop production. Title holders had several options for deriving income from their arable plots, including sharecropping, renting out land and even selling their plots, although this latter required permission by the state. However, sharecropping was the favoured and virtually the only institution that allowed land transactions to take place between land owners and non land owners. At Guquka the prevailing sharecropping arrange-ment was that the land owner made available his plot to the sharecropper who was responsible for all other factors of production. In return title holders usually claimed half of the harvested crop, but in some cases they demanded 50 to 60%.

The duration of sharecropping agreements was limited to a single production season.

An old man in Guquka explained in 2000 during an interview that throughout his lifetime sharecropping in the village had been a relationship marked by social tension. Typically, landowners who engaged in sharecropping avoided getting anywhere near their plots during ploughing, planting, and weeding, but when the crops were approaching maturity they were there, instructing the sharecroppers not to enter the plots without their permission to ensure they obtained their full share of the produce. According to the old man, the disproportionately large share of the harvest claimed by land owners and their distrustful behaviour towards sharecroppers were reasons why sharecropping has all but disappeared in the village. He also associated the limited use of arable land at Guquka to the demise of sharecropping. He did not know of anyone at Guquka who ever considered selling off his plot and said that renting out land was also very rare, mainly because land owners demanded high rents and were only prepared to enter into single-season agreements.

This account of sharecropping in Guquka was supported by several others. One example is that of Sihonyana, who was born in Guquka in 1935, left for Cape Town in the 1950s where he worked as a deliveryman for a furniture store and an animal feed company until his retirement in 1994. He owned a field in the village and every year he returned home in October or November for a two-week period during which he planted his land. His wife looked after the crops, hiring people to assist her when there was a need. The field was on a fairly steep slope and the soil was shallow. Years of cultivation had caused erosion and in places all the soil had washed away, rendering the field unsuitable for crop production. In 1996, Sihonyana sought access to another field that belonged to a person who worked in Cape Town. This particular field had been fallow for six years, and the owner agreed to a sharecropping arrangement. Sihoyana provided all the required inputs and labour, and harvested 42 bags of maize grain (about 2.1 tons). The owner demanded 26 bags (62%) for the use of his land leaving Sihoyana with 16 bags (about 800 kg). Sihoyana was extremely upset about this, and told the owner that he was no longer prepared to work the land as a sharecropper. Instead, he proposed a rental agreement, but the owner refused.

A second example is that of Vuyo, a descendant of a title-holding family, who was not in line to inherit the family's field. When he was still employed as a miner, he accessed arable land through sharecropping with a member of another family. The arrangement required Vuyo's homestead to provide labour and inputs and in return they received half of the harvest. Both Vuyo and his spouse, Zolile, who did most of the work, were of the opinion that the arrangement was unfair towards the sharecroppers, because they carried all the risk. They explained that the only reason why they continued sharecropping was the absence of any alternative way to access land. When Vuyo was retrenched from the mines, his homestead withdrew from field cropping, because they could no longer afford to pay for the inputs. Instead, the family concentrated its efforts on home garden production, growing grains and vegetables in the parental garden, and also in the garden of their neighbour who had moved to Cape Town. As indicated earlier, Vuyo resumed field cropping when he obtained permission to use his grandmother's field (chapter 8).

One case of a landless person accessing land in ways other than sharecropping was that of Kaykay, who was born in a title-holding family, but his older brother inherited the land. For this reason his mother sent him to Lovedale (a well known school and training college in Alice) to become a teacher. Kaykay was keen on agriculture, and his teacher's salary provided him with sufficient income to purchase a field. During the 1960s he identified a willing seller who lived and owned a plot in Gilton, a village that neighbours Guquka. A purchase price of R200 was agreed upon and paid by Kaykay, but after the transaction was made, the family of the seller objected to the transfer of the plot. Since the seller had already spent the money and could not afford a refund, Kaykay was offered the life-long right to the use of the plot instead. Subsequently, Kaykay exchanged plots with a person residing in Gilton, who owned a field in Guquka. This exchange was of mutual benefit, because both got access to land that was nearer to their respective residences. Kaykay, however, discontinued cropping the plot because of old age.

Chapter 8 gives some more examples of the problematic aspects of sharecropping. Only occasionally were beneficial arrangements concluded (chapter 8). Mengezelei Mbangi, whose life history is told in chapter 13, tried in vain to rent land. The only arrangement which landowners were keen on was sharecropping. Mengezelei did not consider sharecropping to be a good deal, because benefits accrued mainly to the landowners. Instead, he converted a large part of his residential site into an irrigated vegetable garden (chapter 8).

Considering the circumstances that prevail at Guquka it is difficult to explain why a more balanced mechanism of land exchange has not evolved over time. Poverty and food insecurity threaten homesteads with access to land and the landless alike (Buys 2000, Monde 2003). The cropping potential of most of the arable land at Guquka is fairly high, explaining why a modest demand for arable land among the landless continues to exist. For a variety of reasons (see chapter 8), many title holders are not capable or interested in cropping their plots, making it opportune for them to avail their land to others in return for a reasonable share of the crop or for monetary income from rent. Legally, title deed provides protection to land owners against sharecroppers or land leasers who may stake a claim on plots after a period of sustained use of the plot. These conditions favour the emergence of arrangements that lead to a functional land exchange market, but this has not been the case. There is little doubt that the lack of adaptation of the prevailing sharecropping institution and the lack of evolvement of medium-term land rental institutions favoured by the landless have contributed to the low level of cropping that characterizes the village of Guquka.

## Access to residential land

In both Guquka and Koloni residential land is held by means of two types of tenure. Quitrent tenure applies to the plots that were demarcated when the two villages were surveyed. Ownership of these plots is no different from that which applies to the arable plots, because the quitrent titles cover both parcels of land. The second type of tenure over residential land applies to sites that were excised from the commonage. Allocation of residential plots excised from the commonage of freehold or quitrent settlements is not a recent phenomenon. For example, Mills and Wisson (1952) already recorded the allocation of sites demarcated on the commonage to labour tenants in the freehold settlement of Wolf River.

During the late 1980s, permission was sought from Chief Siseko by Koloni residents under the leadership of Mr. Mandeya, who was then the Headman of Koloni, to allocate plots for a new housing development. The village residents had agreed to the provision of additional land for housing in the village and their decision was sanctioned by the Chief. It was also agreed to extend access to grazing lands to residents of the new housing area. The new housing area consists of about 30 residential plots, which are similar in size to those held by the original village residents. It was originally part of one of the grazing camps located west of the main road to the village. An adjacent part of the same camp has been transformed into a sports field (see chapter 5). In the village, the occupants of the new housing area continue to be referred to as squatters, a term they also use to refer to themselves. In the region the term 'squatter' is used when referring to landless people who have built their houses on land that does not belong to them. Use of this term in Koloni is largely playful, but it does act as a constant reminder that people staying in the new housing development are there by the grace of the landowners. Most of the 'squatters' who were given plots in the new residential area are the descendents of village residents. They grew up in the village, but were not in line to inherit the parental homestead. Only a few 'strangers' without kin in the village were allocated plots. Unlike residents of the old part of Koloni, who hold their residential sites by means of quitrent title, residents in the new housing section were issued with 'Permission to Occupy' certificates for which they paid a fee of R60.

In Guquka the transformation of parts of the commonage into residential plots also primarily occurred to provide the offspring of title holders, who were not in line to inherit their father's land, with a place to build a home. For example Tibani Thibini (see chapter 13 for his life history account), a resident of Guquka, was born in a family that owned arable land in the village, but being the last child he was not eligible to inherit the land holdings and the home of his parents. When he got married he applied for a residential site to the Tribal Authority, and this was allocated to him in 1989, free of charge. On occasion residential sites in Guquka were also allocated to non-kin, but this usually involved the 'stranger' being introduced to the village leadership by a resident.

In Guquka holders of new residential sites were also provided with Permission to Occupy (PTO) certificates. The growth of this residential area has been described in Chapter 5.

Originally, PTO certificates were issued where Trust tenure applied. Trust tenure was introduced as part of the Bantu Land and Trust Act of 1936, and was used as a system of tenure for land that was being transferred from white to black people as part of the expansion of the Bantu Areas. Ownership of such land was in the hands of the Bantu Trust, an arm of the state. Later on, this form of tenure was extended to tribal land identified for irrigation development, especially in Limpopo Province, which more or less covers the former Northern Transvaal (Commission 1955). When the authority to allocate PTO certificates was transferred from the Bantu Trust to the various homeland administrations for application in the territories they governed, the use of PTO was expanded, for example to cater for the allocation of residential sites in quitrent settlements such as Guquka and Koloni. Of all tenure systems that applied to land held by black people in South Africa, Trust or PTO tenure has been arguably the most disadvantageous. Legally, it provided no transfer rights to the land holder and usually it imposed land use obligations, which the land holder has to meet in order to retain his or her land rights. The state had the power to withdraw the PTO and order the holder to vacate the land whenever the holder failed to meet the stipulated obligations.

As indicated, Trust tenure did not allow land holders to transfer their land rights. However, in practice transfer from parent to child is common, and even the sale of sites held by PTO is not exceptional. For example, Mengezelei (chapter 4 and 13) who does not originate from Guquka applied to the Tribal Authority of Makhuzeni for a residential site in Guquka as he had to move from the farm where he was born. When an old lady in Guquka passed away and her children were not interested in keeping the site, Mengezelei purchased the site and the dwelling from the children, and informed the village headman and the Tribal Authority of the transaction. The Tribal Authority had his name entered into a register kept at the office of the District Magistrate in Alice, and he also received the original Permission to Occupy certificate, which was made out to the previous occupant of the site, as proof of the transfer of ownership.

At both Guquka and Koloni the excising of new residential land from the commonage and the demarcation of plots was implemented by the Department of Agriculture following a request by the village authority. Requests by individuals for allocation of plots were filed with the local authority, and when approved these were ratified and recorded by the office of the District Magistrate. During the Ciskei homeland era, it was the headman and the local tribal authority who decided on matters of new residential land. When this form of village government was abandoned, the structures that replaced them continued handling the task. For example, in 1998, Mengezelei, who had converted a large part of his residential site into an irrigated vegetable garden (chapter 8), successfully requested permission from the RA to widen his plot by about 10 m, and to move his fence to enclose the addition. In practice, therefore, the Trust tenure system persists, but Sibanda (2004) pointed out that the authority of the former homelands and former South African Development Trust to issue PTOs was never delegated to the Provinces when the Interim Constitution of the Republic of South Africa came into effect in 2004. The only exception was KwaZulu-Natal, where the delegation of this power was issued in September 1998. Legally, therefore, PTOs issued after 27 April 1994 in provinces other than KwaZulu-Natal are invalid.

The quitrent titles held by land holders in Guquka and Koloni are ambiguous when it comes to ownership of the commonage. Quitrent title deeds in Koloni are silent on ownership of this land, whilst in Guquka they contain a clause that says:

> The Location, including the Commonage, shall be under control of a Board to be appointed in acceptance with, and to be subject to the provisions 6, 7, 8, 9, 10 and 11 of the Glen Grey Act, 1894, as amended by Act No.15 of 1899, or any other amending Act to be thereafter passed, or such other like body as my be appointed by the Governor.

The Upgrading of Land Tenure Rights Act 122 of 1991 also fails to deal with this issue. Legally, the question about ownership of the commonage is important, exactly because parts of the commonage have been made available for settlement of people without titles.

## Access to the rangelands

Chapters 9 and 10 will elaborate the different uses people in Guquka and Koloni make of the collectively held and managed rangelands. These included the collection of firewood, thatching grass, brush for the construction of livestock *kraals* and medicinal herbs, but the single most important use for many people in the two villages is as a communal grazing resource for livestock. Livestock forage is not limited to the commons. Arable lands also play an important role (chapter 9). The rules governing access to both rangeland and arable land for grazing are the focus of this discussion.

At both Guquka and Koloni, institutional control over access to and use of the commons rests with the local government structure of the village. However, at Guquka, management decisions appear to be taken by an *ad hoc* and somewhat clandestine grazing committee, which has been perpetuated from the past (Holbrook 1998). This decentralisation of control over resource management means that decision-making is diffuse and vulnerable to the agendas of particular groups within the village. In contrast, at Koloni, decisions on management of the commonage and its grazing resources are more transparent and occur at the level of the village governance structure (Bennett 2002). In principal the rangeland area at each village is available to all livestock from the village at all times of year. The fundamental difference between the two villages, however, lies in the way in which access is controlled.

At Koloni the rangeland belongs exclusively to the village and is divided into four camps separated by fences. When these camps were established in 1961/62, during the implementation of the second phase of Betterment (Bantu Affairs Commission 1962), a grazing system was introduced, which allowed for three of these camps to be grazed in rotation for up to 10 days each whilst the fourth camp was rested for an entire year (Goqwana and Scogings 1997). Koloni residents changed this system. They continue resting one of the four camps, but the remaining three are grazed on a continuous basis (Goqwana and Scogings 1997, Bennett 2002). Change has also taken place in the way the management system is administered. Originally, decisions concerning the rotational grazing and resting programme, were made by officials of the Department of Agriculture stationed in Middledrift and then relayed to the Headman of the village who was responsible for their implementation. Since the end of the Bantu Trust system in 1975, responsibility for grazing management has devolved to the community itself (Goqwana and Scogings 1997). This involves an annual meeting at which the Chairman informs the community that the camp that was rested will be brought back into commission and introduces the discussion to decide which of the other three camps will be rested for the year (Bennett 2002). This decision is arrived at democratically and the meeting is a platform for proposals and articulation of objections to particular choices. Once a motion is carried, all owners without exception are required to remove their livestock from the camp identified for resting.

Disputes over grazing rights among livestock owners in Koloni appear to be uncommon. If an individual does transgress the rules they are required to slaughter an animal, to be shared amongst the villagers, as a means of apology. At the interface with other villages, however, Koloni is involved in several ongoing disputes over grazing access. The first of these is a longstanding grievance about access to an additional area of *veld*. This dates back to the original restructuring of the village by government planners in 1937, which involved the excision of 162 *morgen* (138 ha) of grazing land and the allocation of part of this to Mnqaba location and the remainder to Farm B (Bantu Affairs Commission 1962). This explains the on-going belief among some Koloni residents, particularly older males, that Koloni actually own six grazing camps. This includes the current four camps plus the two portions allocated to the other settlements. Most livestock owners at Koloni no longer have genuine hope that their rights to these two areas will be re-established. More recently a conflict evolved from isolated incidents of villagers from Mnqaba location driving their livestock onto one of the four Koloni camps, called Managambungambu (Goqwana and Scogings 1997). For this reason, a village meeting sanctioned the padlocking of the gate to this camp from the Mnqaba direction in an attempt to retain exclusive use of the camp. This intervention was largely successful, but livestock owners from Koloni still make regular patrols of the camp to ensure there have been no further incursions and tension between the two communities persists.

At Guquka jurisdiction over rangeland grazing is an altogether more complicated affair. Not only are there no camps to facilitate rotational grazing, the rangeland is also shared by livestock from several communities. Officially, only Guquka and Gilton have access to the rangeland, but livestock from the settlement of Kayalethu are also grazed there. This is now accepted practice as it has been taking place for several decades and the leadership of Guquka considers itself powerless to exclude them. The rangeland is thus grazed on a continuous basis by livestock from at least three villages. As a result of this form of open-access there is effectively no control over the rangeland in the area. The lack of centralised jurisdiction encourages many livestock owners to adopt a *laissez-faire* attitude to the grazing of their livestock, allowing their animals to free-range wherever they choose. This becomes particularly evident during the summer months, when cattle are often released to graze for several weeks at a time without *kraaling* (Bennett 2002). The desire of the animals to find adequate forage in conditions of heavy overstocking inevitably causes them to trespass onto land beyond the formal grazing boundaries. This brings the livestock owners into conflict with other communities.

Two persistent causes of conflict involving livestock owners of Guquka are the trespassing of animals onto the grazing lands of neighbouring Phandulwazi Agricultural College and onto the state forestry plantations in Hogsback. These transgressions occur on a regular basis and in both cases the authorities impound cattle and demand payment for their release. This is particularly true in the case of the Department of Forestry, as cattle are implicated in the damage of pine saplings, and officials have historically adopted a hard-line approach to incidents of unauthorised grazing (Van Averbeke *et al.* 1998a). Trespassing of livestock also creates disputes between Guquka and communities across the mountain in the Amatola Basin. These conflicts tend to occur at the community rather than just the individual level. A typical example involved one of the major cattle owners in Guquka, who had 21 cattle at the time of interview (April 1999). During the summer of 1998/99, he lost two oxen and two cows, believing them to have been stolen whilst they were grazing on the mountain pastures. He suspected that they were taken by residents of villages located in the neighbouring district of Keiskammahoek. Both villages had a case pending against them for theft of livestock from Guquka. Several other livestock from all four of the Makhuzeni villages also had cattle missing, and they came together and formed a posse, backed up by local police officers, to visit the troublesome villages. Central to the initiative was a prominent livestock owner from Gilton, who worked for the Department of Agriculture in King William's Town. His position secured participation of the police. The mission was a success, with a number of cattle being recovered from *kraals* in the two villages, but several animals, including those of the Guquka livestock owner were not retrieved and they were believed to have been slaughtered or possibly sold. According to the livestock owner, the problem of theft at this scale was only a relatively recent phenomenon. He attributed it to a general breakdown in law and order in the region and to the greater freedom people enjoyed since the transition to democracy. This, he believed, had increased the incidence of both opportunistic theft and organised cattle raids. Organised theft, he claimed, involved syndicates which rounded up multiple animals and exported them by truck to other places, such as the Transkei, where the livestock was sold. This particular example highlights two important institutional constraints that affect contemporary livestock production in the communal areas of the central Eastern Cape, namely livestock theft and a general lack of co-operation among communities.

Livestock theft is not limited to cattle and this social ill is not restricted to Guquka. In 2004, the former Chairperson of the Residents' Association and son of the former headman of the village was stabbed to death when inspecting suspicious noises in the small sheep *kraal* outside the parental home during the night. In Koloni, where wool production was once an important local source of income, sheep have virtually disappeared, because of the high incidence of theft. The state is acutely aware of the livestock theft problem. To combat organised theft it introduced a permit system that controls the transportation of livestock by road, but this has not yet succeeded in eliminating the problem.

The 'us versus them' attitude that prevails among rural communities fails to recognize that the problems livestock owners are experiencing are mutual. Whilst the loss of cattle as a result of straying over the mountains into neighbouring grazing areas was interpreted as 'theft' by their Guquka owners, the villages whose grazing was being encroached upon probably felt they were perfectly entitled to impound the trespassing animals and demand some form of (financial) recompense. The distinction between the act of holding animals that have trespassed and actual theft is very blurred in these situations. Furthermore, it is difficult to ascertain how much dialogue actually took place between the respective parties, and at what level, before the strong-arm tactics of the raiding party were brought into play. What is clear, however, is that the lack of an effective forum for interface between local communities (synonymous with the old tribal authorities) is an ongoing problem, reflected more recently in the ineffective integration of Guquka into the Matole Ward system described earlier. In contrast to the institutional failings at the broader level, co-operation between the four Makhuzeni villages in their response to the theft problem has been swift and fairly effective. This lends support to the idea that the 'umbrella structure' encompassing the four Makhuzeni villages was an effective forum for the articulation of common needs. As an organisation, the Makhuzeni umbrella was short-lived, but its roots went all the way to the origin of the four settlements. This brings into question the rationality of replacing the 'umbrella' with a ward that combines Guquka with several geographically isolated settlements in the Amatola basin, whilst assigning Gilton to another ward.

Lastly, the example illustrates how interaction between the Makhuzeni villages and law enforcement agencies were facilitated by making use of the social standing of one key individual to obtain police support for the raid on the Amatola Basin settlements. This emphasises the continuing importance of social networks in the rural areas in the enforcement of rights and the resolution of disputes at the local level.

## Livestock and forage on arable lands

In addition to the commonage, the other important grazing resource for livestock in both villages is the arable lands. In principle the arable lands provide a critical forage reserve for animals during the dry season (chapter 9). Broadly, the institutional procedures that apply to the opening and closing of arable land to livestock are similar in both villages.

The formal rule systems governing the use of arable land for livestock grazing are essentially a perpetuation of the management paradigm that was introduced under betterment and these rules are described in chapter 9, Figure 9.2. One of the differences between the two villages, primarily the result of differences in ecology, is that the arable lands in Guquka tend to be grazed for just three months, typically from early June to early September, whereas this can last for four to five months in Koloni. Another is that at Guquka both cattle and sheep are allowed on the fields, whereas at Koloni only cattle are permitted access to the arable lands.

The main difference between the two villages, however, is the way in which the rules are applied. This difference will be discussed in chapter 9 from a general management perspective. The focus here will be on exploring the *modus operandi* that individuals and groups use to negotiate preferential access to grazing resources in the two settlements.

At Guquka, one of the major deviations from the formal institutional system governing access of livestock to the arable lands is the use of these lands for grazing purposes outside the time when these lands are officially open. Field observations clearly show that many animals graze these areas throughout the cropping (wet) season (Bennett 2002). These animals come from a number of different sources and are led to pasture in a number of different ways as will be described in chapter 9.

Much of the grazing of arable land during the cropping season is due to the trespassing of livestock from outside Guquka, especially from Kayalethu (see Map 4.2). During multiple years of fieldwork at Guquka several cattle owners from Kayalethu were observed driving their animals across the river separating the two communities onto Guquka's arable lands during the morning. Boys would then be sent to retrieve the animals in late afternoon (*ibid.*). Livestock owners at Guquka all agreed that livestock owners of Kayalethu had no formal grazing rights to this land and that no negotiations had ever taken place to try and facilitate this. Thus, the animals were there illegally and many livestock owners at Guquka seemed to resent their presence as they were depleting an important dry season forage reserve for their own animals. On several occasions formal representation was made to the RA at Kayalethu, but with little result. Even when a small group of livestock owners from Guquka took it upon themselves to repair the perimeter fence surrounding the arable lands to prevent further livestock incursions the effects were short-lived. Within a few days the wires were cut and cattle from Kayalethu were once again free-ranging on the area.

Livestock from Guquka were also observed to make some use of the arable lands for grazing during the cropping season (chapter 9). This mostly took the form of cattle grazing individually fenced fields, either because field owners were absent from the village, leaving their fields fallow and unattended, or because animals were sick or unruly and deemed unfit to be grazed on the commonage. Although this was a contravention of the official grazing rules, which prevent any livestock not involved with ploughing from being present on the arable lands at this time, the practice seemed to be generally accepted. This was because the animals were restrained within the confines of a fenced plot and thus unlikely to cause damage to the crops growing in neighbouring fields. Another reason for the practice being permitted was that the lands were held by individual title and there was a general consensus amongst the landed homesteads that they were therefore entitled to make use of their land when and how they pleased.

On occasions cattle from Guquka were also observed free-ranging on unfenced arable lands during the cropping period. This behaviour is in many ways synonymous with the open-access grazing being practised by trespassing cattle from Kayalethu and should have been considered equally unacceptable. However, livestock owners who engaged in this practice were generally able to get away it by being closely connected to the grazing committee, which existed in parallel with the Residents' Association. In practice, this committee wielded the power to grant access to the community's grazing resources on an *ad hoc*, individual basis. The way in which this institution provides a forum for the negotiation of individual grazing rights is demonstrated by a case study involving one of Guquka's most active farmers. This particular farmer has his own fenced field but in the summer of 1999 he had planted it to maize. This prevented him from using the field for grazing his cattle during the cropping season. Instead, during late summer (March and April) he sought permission for four of his cattle that were in poor condition to graze on the unfenced fields within the arable land allocation. He explained that he practiced this for many years because during this part of the year he considered forage to be more abundant on the arable lands than on the 'commonage'. In order for this summer grazing on arable land to be approved he had to inform the older men who comprised the grazing committee of his intention and he also had to ensure that the animals were supervised all the time. However, field observations showed that his animals were certainly not being supervised at all times, especially at night. Moreover, the condition of his animals was far from poor and certainly no worse than most of the other cattle in the village. This case study illustrates how social status, linked to age and particularly land-ownership, and influence in ad hoc institutions, such as the grazing committee, allow a privileged minority within the village to circumvent the official grazing rules and gain preferential grazing for their stock.

Another important deviation from the recognised rules concerns the maintenance of individual rights over fields during the dry season. The grazing management rules state that all fields should become accessible to all cattle at this time unless a winter crop has been cultivated. However, it was clear from fieldwork conducted both in 1999 and 2004, that several individuals were maintaining individual rights over fields throughout the dry season without growing crops. This might have been for grazing their own cattle or simply for resting a field that was heavily grazed during the summer months. In all cases these exceptions were made possible because the field concerned was fenced. This is illustrated by the following accont. A livestock owner also worked as a security guard causing him to be absent from the village most of the time. His homestead does not own a field, but does have control over two parcels of arable land. One of the fields became de facto the property of his father when its previous owner left Guquka many years ago. The other field belongs to a relative. When he is away from the village his cattle are enclosed on these fields for safe-keeping. This facilitated easy maintenance of the animals, particularly on one of the fields where water is usually available in ditches. During 1999 his cattle were kept on this field almost throughout the winter. Access to the two fields is exclusively for his own cattle so he did not seek the permission of the rest of the village for this practice because they had no jurisdiction over this privately owned land. He believed that his exclusive use of the fields during the winter did not engender animosity from the rest of the village as they understood that there was nobody else to look after the cattle when he was away for work. This case illustrates that even during the dry season, when arable grazing is supposed to be underpinned by a genuinely communal ethos, a privileged, landed minority are able to exercise private grazing rights. Again the fundamental driver here is the existence of individual ownership rights over arable land, and the belief amongst those who own land, or have access to it, that they are entitled to use it however and whenever they wish.

At Koloni grazing pressure is relatively low and grazing resources are considerable, of good quality, and for exclusive use of the village. Moreover, the separation of arable land from grazing land by means of a fence, and the division of the range into fenced camps, assist control over grazing decisions at the communal level. Despite limited disputes with neighbouring locations grazing rights for community members are relatively secure and, importantly, generally ensure an adequate flow of forage for community livestock throughout the year. The other important aspect of communal grazing governance at Koloni is the existence of a clearly defined and democratically supported insti-

tution responsible for the implementation and enforcement of the rules governing access of livestock to the different land resources. In the past, the authority
rested with the grazing committee. When the Headman was replaced by a
Chairman, during the early 1990s, the village meeting lead by the Chairman
took over that authority. The absence at Koloni of the kind of political struggle
over the commons that characterised much of the former homeland areas of the
Eastern Cape (Ainslie 1998, Cousins 1996) must be attributed, at least in part,
to the considerable amount of grazing available to the community and to the
individual ownership of arable land that applies at the village. Under these
conditions the desire of individuals to appropriate resources for themselves is
considerably reduced (Bromley 1989). In a context of abundance and political
certainty, the community of Koloni is able to both make and enforce all grazing
management decisions at the village level. The system currently in operation,
with few exceptions, still follows the general betterment paradigm, outlined in
Figure 9.2. One important difference is that decisions on opening and closing of
grazing camps and arable land for grazing are no longer made by state officials
as was the case during the 'homeland days'. At present, these are reached
democratically by the community as a whole.

## Conclusions

The sequence of local governance systems in both villages, inclusive of the
abolishment of the tribal leadership structures during the early 1990s, maintained a large degree of continuity, because change in the structure of governance did not fundamentally alter the internal social patterns in the two villages.
In the case of Guquka, structural change also did not interfere with the patterns
of collaboration that existed among the settlements that constituted Makhuzeni,
which were as old as the settlements themselves. The new local governance
system with ward committees and ward councillors is the first system that no
longer explicitly recognises these patterns. The withdrawal of people with
power and status from direct participation in the residents' association is a first
indication that the new system no longer meaningfully links the village with
decision making over the allocation of resources, especially external resources.

Around the turn of the century, following surveys, land holdings in the two
villages were privatised by means of quitrent tenure. This intervention established land ownership patterns that have persisted until the present. Implementation of private tenure resulted in the creation of landed and landless groups. It
also moved power and control over arable land from the hands of the traditional
leadership into the domain of the homestead (among kin) and among homesteads (old patterns of friendship and trust). Since private tenure is the mode of
ordering, the land market has assumed the role of allocating land. The land
market in the two villages, particularly Guquka, does not operate well. Chapter
8 picks up on this conclusion and examines how the poorly functioning land
market has contributed to under-cultivation of the arable land.

The rangeland at Guquka is shared with several other communities and is inadequate for the number of livestock it serves. The consequence of this open system is that it negatively affects the quality and quantity of forage. This is described in more detail in chapter 9. Important to point out here is that this has led to some important deviations from the official grazing management system. Indeed, a two-tier system of individual control over grazing resources is effectively in operation at Guquka. At one extreme is the essentially open-access system in operation on the formal rangeland area. Here the rangeland is shared by several neighbouring communities and grazing management is impossible at a communal level as the user group is essentially too large and inadequately defined. There are also no defined rules for resource use or the necessary institutional arrangements to oversee them. A 'free-for-all' scenario has therefore developed in which the grazing resource is available to all livestock and grazing management decisions are entirely under the control of individual livestock owners. At the other extreme is the situation with regard to the grazing of the arable land allocations. Since the arable lands are officially the exclusive property of the village, grazing is supposed to be controlled on a communal, village basis. This is partially true for those fields that are unfenced. In principle, the RA does exert control over the period during which these fields become officially available as an additional forage reserve during the dry season. However, even this limited level of communal control is compromised by several factors. These are the trespassing of livestock from the neighbouring township of Kayalethu onto the arable fields during both the cropping season and the dry season, the ability of individuals with power in the village to arrange for their livestock to graze unfenced fields during the growing season when grazing is officially prohibited and the side-stepping of central control over grazing altogether by owners of fenced fields who keep their animals at any time on the plots over which they have exclusive control. All of these undermine the credibility of the RA as an effective structure for managing the arable lands as a common property resource. The maintenance of fences around individual fields is an important feature, which facilitates several of the rule deviations, enabling livestock owners to bypass many aspects of the grazing management framework outlined in chapter 9. For members of the land-owning elite decision-making power has effectively devolved from the central to the individual level. The situation is exacerbated by weak institutional control at the local level, and the parallel existence of a somewhat *ad hoc* grazing committee that allocates grazing rights to individuals and small groups.

Finally, we conclude that, overall, democratisation with its promise of devolving power to the people, appears to be having the opposite effect in the two villages. Social patterns of collaboration that evolved over more than a century, particularly with reference to the external, appear to be unravelling as a result of the restructuring of formal local government structures. Internally, this structural change has shifted the balance of power in the villages to people with resources and connections and has reduced the importance of the internal village organisations. This is evident from the marginal social standing of the current leadership of these structures.

7

# The view from above: A history of land use in Guquka and Koloni, 1938-1996

Peter C. Lent and Guilty Mupakati

## Introduction

This chapter explores how the two villages of Guquka and Koloni and their surrounding landscapes have changed physically over time, principally as revealed in two series of aerial photographs but also by integrating and comparing what we learn from those images with other sources of historical information. Our goal was to see how land use practices had changed in each of the three major categories of land: residential, arable and rangeland. We obtained all aerial photos for the two villages that were available from the Directorate of Surveys and Mapping in Cape Town. For Guquka, these were 1938, 1949, 1963, 1985 and 1996. Aerial photos for Koloni were for 1939, 1963, 1985, 1992, 1995 and 1996. The dates of photography were known only for some of the more recent, as follows: Guquka: 3 May, 1985, and 5 April 1996. Koloni: 6 June, 1985; 14 July, 1992, and 5 April, 1996. All these images covered at least the residential areas of their respective communities, but breadth of coverage varied greatly. The 1938/1939 photo coverages extended only short distances beyond the residential areas. Photos also varied considerably in their resolution. All photos were digitised for analysis and geo-referencing in GIS databases. We used both ESRI Arcview 3.2™ and Microimages™. Microimages Edit Professional software for most analyses. Unless otherwise stated and credited, data presented in this chapter are derived from our analyses of these images.

Processes of erosion and land degradation are frequently factors that influence livelihoods in rural communities and restrict options for sustainable development. Because of the nature of the terrain and soil types in and around Guquka it was early apparent that these processes were playing a particularly significant role there. Murray (1952) and Story (1952) were among several who described severe erosion problems in the area of the Amatola Mountains and Keiskamma River watershed. Following the Tomlinson Commission Report (chapter 2), Betterment Planning was introduced and implemented from the 1940s onwards in an effort to prevent natural resource degradation in the so-called 'native reserves'. Repairing the effects of soil erosion and preventing further loss of capability for crop production was a major focus of Betterment Planning activities. However, for Guquka in particular, the surveys done by Hill, Kaplan, Scott & Partners 1977 for the then Ciskei government indicated that erosion problems continued.

Thus, a study was initiated by Mupakati (2005) to determine the location and sources of erosion in the area with special reference to gully erosion. This special analysis for Guquka was also based primarily on the existing aerial photos and is reported below. Five sample areas, or zones, within the existing imagery were established to measure erosion. These were laid out at varying distances from the Guquka residential area in the arable fields and communal rangelands. In addition, households in Guquka and surrounding communities were surveyed to obtain information on their perceptions of the erosion and historical causes. The purpose was to look at the reciprocal relationship between land use practices and erosion phenomena. That is, land use practices influences erosion patterns, and rates and location of erosion in turn may influence land use decisions.

## Guquka

The general setting and topography of Guquka have been described in chapters 3 and 4. At the most basic level, land use zones in the community are: Residential, arable allotments and communal rangelands. These three categories and their current approximate extents are shown in Table 4.1 (chapter 4). It is also important to emphasize again that the people of Guquka have always had access in varying degrees to a variety of forested and mountain areas beyond the ill-defined boundaries of their own communal rangelands. These elements of the landscape have been described briefly in chapter 4.

Because the initial 1938 aerial photo coverage (Photo 7.1) is limited mostly to the residential area and only part of the arable allotments are visible little can be said about the extent or conditions of the grazing allotments at that time.

*Photo 7.1*    Aerial photo of Guquka and adjacent arable fields, 1938


With regard to the history of use or condition of the vegetation in the range-lands themselves we can determine little from the aerial photos. Fence lines or patterns of use are not visible. Perhaps the most striking feature over the years is the constancy in shrubby vegetation associated with drainage lines descending from the escarpment towards the community (Map 7.1). However, change is visible in the varying degrees of gully erosion seen in the photos.

*Erosion features*
In order to systematically examine the origins and extent of erosion in and around Guquka we therefore started with the 1949 photography. Within the communal rangelands slopes were divided into three classes: (1)<9°, (2) 9°-15° and (3) > 15° Most gullies were seen to occur in places with slope class 3 (15°-35°) with a high soil erosion potential (SEP). However, gullies also developed in class 1 slopes. As noted above, few gullies developed in areas covered with thick brush even on class 3 slopes, probably because these areas had the soil bound and sheltered by brush canopy, reducing its vulnerability to erosion. Further, trails made by domestic animals moving up- and down-slope tended to

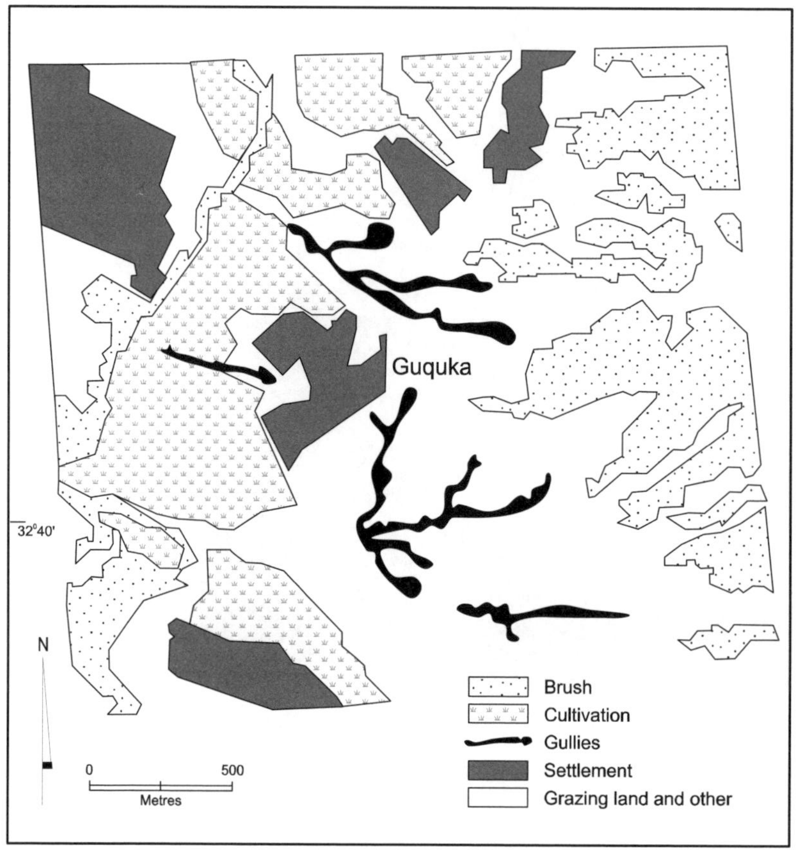


*Map 7.1*  Major erosion features in relation to land cover categories, Guquka

avoid the densest bush. Except for such shrubby areas, most gullies occurred along the drainage flow paths. Most gullies initiated in slope class 3 (5°-35°) subsequently developed and encroached into other slope classes.

The spatial distribution of gullies was also influenced by soil type. Magagula (1999), who worked also in the upper Tyume River watershed, similarly reported the severity of land degradation associated with the physical and chemical properties of the soils. He reported that soils with massive or plate-like structure, known as the Williamson soils, contained most of the large gullies, being conducive to severe erosion. This also suggested that the parent material is rather unconsolidated.

The large gullies in the Guquka area (Map 7.1), as identified from the sequential aerial photos and field visits, were found to fall mostly into this soil class, which covers most of Guquka area. Sandy loam soils, which cover parts of the adjacent communities of Magxagxeni and Sompondo, contained mostly small gullies although a few larger gullies were also found. These soil types had very few rills but considerable evidence of sheet erosion. These were also more likely to be have good grass cover resulting in few serious erosion features.

Some evidence of gully development in the catchment was underway as early as 1938, when the first aerial photographs were taken (Photo 7.1) but at that time these were few and small. Rills had however started developing in many areas. Gullies were at that time most developed in grazing areas.

All the gullies occurring in the five zones or sample areas selected for the study were visible as early as 1949. Some of them had already developed quite significantly to cover areas from about 5,000m$^2$ to 20,000m$^2$. The surface area occupied by gullies in each zone was measured over time from 1949 to 1996. In zone A, overlapping in part the residential area, gully area increased by over 60% in 47 years at an average rate of 77m$^2$/year (Table 7.1). In Zone C above, a linear relationship between gully development and time occurred with the most rapid rate of gully spread at 285m$^2$/year. Gully area increased by over 66% in this zone. Other zones had intermediate rates of gully development. The total area degraded and threatened by gullies was about 212 ha.

*Table 7.1*    Area of major gullies and rate of change over time in five main gully zones, Guquka

| Year | Zone A Primarily Residential (m$^2$) | Zone B Primarily arable (m$^2$) | Zone C Primarily rangeland (m$^2$) | Zone D Rangeland (m$^2$) | Zone E Rangeland (m$^2$) |
|---|---|---|---|---|---|
| 1949 | 6034 | 8651 | 18370 | 20535 | 13642 |
| 1963 | 8145 | 11456 | 23743 | 25621 | 14676 |
| 1985 | 4925 | - | 27038 | 29173 | 8924 |
| 1996 | 9663 | 17615 | 30566 | 24904 | 22916 |
| Average rate of increase | 77 m$^2$/yr | 190 m$^2$/yr | 295 m$^2$/yr | 92 m$^2$/yr | 197 m$^2$/yr |

*Source*: Mupakati 2004

Clearly, the increases in surface area were principally due to changes in gully width. In 1949 in zone A, maximum gully widths ranged from 28m to 30m. There was very little increase in gully width by 1963 but in 1996, the width at several points was above 40 m. In Gully Zone C taking a typical location on the gully, in 1949 the width was about 37m, increasing to about 46m in 1963 and to 57-58m by 1996. On the other hand some older gullies showed signs of stabilization.

The location and early appearance of erosion, especially that associated with steeper slopes, is confirmed by the observations of Murray (1952: 36) speaking of the adjacent upper Keiskammahoek drainage, including the nearby Wolf River:

> A large percentage of the available soil in the Keiskammahoek District has been converted to arable lands. Aerial photos of the district give an impression of the extent to which the soils have been put under the plough. Steep slopes up the beautiful valleys of the Wolf, Mnyameni and Chatha streams have been cultivated. These lands and others on equally precipitous slopes, have suffered badly from erosion. Scars along the mountainsides indicate the presence of [cropped] lands that have long been abandoned.

There are, however, other lands on more gentle slopes and on deeper soils which have been better preserved. When it is considered that they have been under mono-culture for so long (almost 100 years) the extent of erosion is not as severe as might be expected.

On the arable allotments in Guquka, according to Verdoodt (1999), significant surface erosion and loss of land to gullies affected only 8.4% of the area in 1998. Thus erosion alone cannot be considered a significant cause of the decline in cultivation of these lands, with over 90% uncultivated in the same year (chapter 8) But people interviewed by Mupakati (2005) were more likely to view the dramatic decline in cultivation as contributing to erosion rather than the converse. They implied that people were no longer taking care of the land to the same degree (see also chapter 8).

In general residents of Guquka and surrounding communities attributed the prevalence of gullies to slope and the prevalence of heavy rains. It appeared that they regarded slope and heavy rains as the main factors leading to gully development and not land use activities, such as overgrazing and cutting down of trees for firewood (Mupakati 2005). The one land use identified as a major factor contributing to degradation and quality of life problems was establishment of the pine plantations above the escarpment. This degradation was said by those interviewed to have occurred, first, because of the loss of grazing land putting more pressure on the remaining rangelands, and, second, because afforestation had altered stream flows and water supply.

In Zone A, the slow growth in gully width could have been because the gullies are very close to homesteads where there had been some effort from the villagers to stop the gullies from encroaching into houses and home gardens (Photo 7.2). Intensive addition of nutrients associated with residential areas (Kepe and Scoones 1999) may have also aided development of a stabilizing grass cover.

*Arable allotments*
The vast majority (roughly 95%) of fields that are visible or partially visible on the 1938 image of Guquka (Photo 7.1) show signs of recent cultivation. Inter-

*Photo 7.2*     Use of car bodies to arrest erosion in residential area, Guquka.
(Photo by Lent)

views with residents (chapter.4) and general remarks in older sources, such as Story (1952) and Murray (1952) indicate the settlement patterns in the upper Tyume valley were formerly more dispersed with residences and associated crop fields occurring at higher elevation and on steeper slopes. Some older erosion scars visible on the hillsides also suggest this. Hill, Kaplan, Scott & Partners (1977) believed that the earlier erosion processes in the general area had been slowed by the time of their study due to changes in land use practices but presented no specific data to support this contention.

What is clear is that the cultivation of land parcels showed differences in their layout between 1949 and 1985. In both 1938 and 1949 pattern of fields and the direction of cultivation (ploughing) was in straight lines but in varying, seemingly random directions, although ploughing was generally along the long axis of each field. In contrast, the 1985 layout was more uniformly and systematically organised following contour lines. However, the area of actual cultivation had shrunk, leaving formerly cultivated fields fallow.

The re-organisation of cultivation mode that occurred some time in the years between 1949 and 1985 could have been due to betterment planning or some comparable intervention by government. The details are not known.

The decline in the proportion of fields showing evidence of cultivation is in keeping with other historical evidence that crop agriculture was declining in the community (chapter 8). During the same period there was also an increase in settlements, numbers of dwellings and in the extent and complexity of the road system.

For some recent years, starting in 1996, we have detailed information on land use patterns within the arable allotments derived from direct observations and interviews. These more recent and current patterns of landscape use are treated in chapters 8 and 9.

### Residential areas

A time series derived from the aerial photographs depicting the residential area of Guquka appears in Map 7.2. The population increase in Guquka (chapter 11) is reflected in a corresponding increase in the number of residential buildings in the community from 1938 to 1996.

The 1938 imagery shows 38 scattered households occupying an area of approximately 0.21 km$^2$ with no regular pattern to the distribution of these structures.

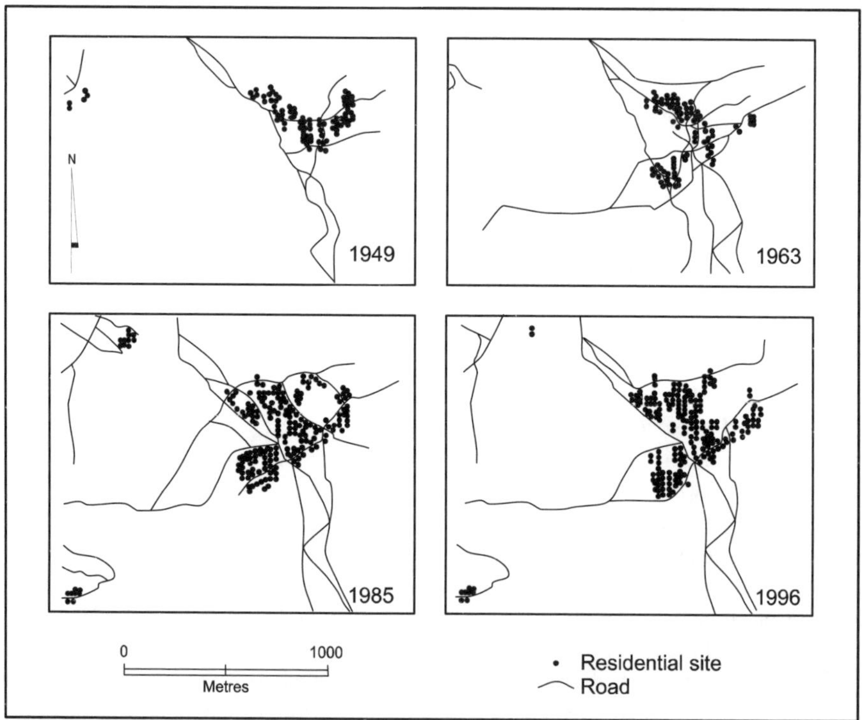


*Map 7.2*     Changes in residential area of Guquka, 1949 to 1996

Over the following period of nearly six decades there was substantial infilling within this original area leading to more than doubling of the number of houses and a corresponding decrease in the land occupied by each (Table 7.2). We cannot ascertain precisely the number of houses (dwellings) associated with each household. However, Andrew (1992), in her study of a Transkei community, reported that this ratio remained more or less constant over many years.

*Table 7.2*     Changes in residential area and number of residential buildings in Guquka, 1938-1996

| Year | No. of buildings* in original residential area | Mean area (m$^2$) per household in original residential area | No. of buildings in total residential area | Size of total residential area (km$^2$) | Mean area (m$^2$) per household in total residential area |
|---|---|---|---|---|---|
| 1938 | 38 | 5631 | 38 | 0.214 | 5631 |
| 1949 | 45 | 4755 | 49 | 0.236 | 4816 |
| 1963 | 61 | 3508 | 78 | 0.286 | 3667 |
| 1985 | 79 | 2708 | 127 | 0.340 | 2677 |
| 1996 | 83 | 2578 | 139 | 0.342 | 2460 |

* Buildings which were of the size and shape to function as living places (domiciles). Smaller structures were excluded.

Over the same time period, but especially since the 1963 imagery, there has been a substantial expansion of the residential area and this expanded area has received most of the increase in housing. Approximately two-thirds of the 61 buildings added from 1963 to 1996 were outside of the original residential area. This expansion of the residential area resulted in a loss of communal grazing land of approximately (0.128km$^2$ (13 ha)), or roughly 3% of the estimated current area of communal rangeland. However, the true loss of forage resources is actually even less because livestock routinely graze throughout much of the residential area (chapter 8). Certainly this loss is extremely small compared to the long-term loss of rangeland to gullies, as described above.

In contrast to Koloni (see later) there has not been a distinct new residential area but rather a general expansion of residences in several directions and areas. It must be emphasized that this analysis provides no information about the number of occupied residential buildings, nor can the exact nature and use of each building be determined. Information presented in chapter 11 clearly shows that in recent years substantial numbers of residential buildings are not occupied at any given moment either because they are abandoned or are used only occasionally or have never been completed.

## Koloni

Map 4.2 shows the division of Koloni into three land categories. The areal extent of these categories is shown in Table 4.1. Portions of these three categories, as they appeared in the aerial photos of 1939, 1963 and 1996 are shown in Photos 7.3A, B and C.

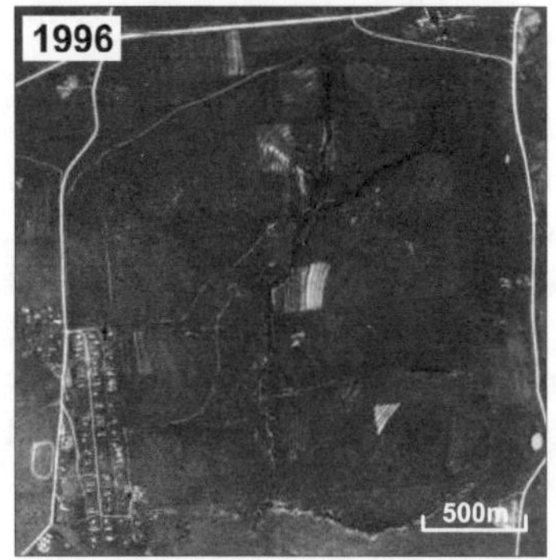


*Photo 7.3*     Aerial views of Koloni and the surrounding area, 1939, 1963 and 1996

In 1939 the arable fields in Koloni were already laid out in their present formation in rows with the long axes oriented roughly north-south. At that time there was no indication of any contouring as most fields were being ploughed in straight rows along the long axes, but a few were ploughed roughly from east – west. Approximately 80 fields were laid out in the area east of the road and community. These were all of approximately the same size, 26,000 to 27,000 m$^2$. Approximately 90% of the fields in the main eastern sector showed evidence of recent ploughing or cultivation at that time. Based upon the prevalence of woody vegetation in all photos a few of these fields appear never to have been cultivated. These few were either farthest from the community and also on more sloping ground, or were intersected by brushy drainage lines.

Because the Bantu Commission (1962) report indicates all fields were allocated we can surmise that some owners never cultivated their assigned fields (see also chapter 6).

By 1963 all fields had been subject to contour ploughing, along lines that in most cases crossed over field boundaries. In many cases these berms and contour lines extended through brushy vegetated areas that had appeared unploughed in 1939 and, surprisingly, extended right to the edge of several cuts and dongas (gullies) and even across these drainage lines. In fact, a few areas that were never assigned as arable fields were also contoured. This pattern suggests that large equipment was used that could work into and across rough drainage lines. Intervals between berms (earthen ridges) on these contours typically measured 15-20 m. Because of this massive intervention and treatment the photo provides no clue as to what proportions of fields were actually being used at that time.

It is clear, however, that the basic pattern and boundaries of the fields were not altered significantly after 1939. This again confirms that, despite Koloni being considered an archetype for betterment Planning, the basic spatial organisation of the community, its residential and arable fields and grazing areas, was in place prior to 1939 (chapter 3), and boundaries and proportions of these land use classes were not substantially altered by the planning efforts of the 1960s. This also conforms to the records documented in Ndlovu (1991), indicating that the initial fencing was put in place around 1936.

In contrast to Koloni, fields associated with the village to the east, Kwa-James, were not contoured in 1963 and were still being ploughed primarily in a north-south orientation. This information derived from these historical aerial images fits with the concept of Koloni being a forerunner in betterment planning. Indeed, Sonandi (1997) also mentioned that the village of Mnqaba, of which Kwa-James is a component, resisted betterment planning. In 1985 none of the fields west of the road from Debe Nek and belonging to this village appeared to be recently cultivated.

Considerable bush encroachment is evident by 1992 in many formerly cultivated fields in Koloni. This brush provides the best evidence for estimating the level of cultivation activity going on at this time. Fewer than 10% of the fields were considered to show evidence of recent activity. By 1996 the cover on most of these had grown in to a great extent. Evidence of recent cultivation was only visible at a few locations. However, a few fields that had not been cultivated in 1992 showed signs of recent activity in 1996. Overall, the level of farming activity seemed to stabilize after 1985, That is, we could not distinguish in imagery any distinct further downward trend in proportion of fields cultivated after that date. Although the level of activity was roughly consistent over these years, there were in each image a few changes in the fields that showed signs of recent activity. It is also notable in the photos since 1985 that the boundaries of fields were not always strictly adhered to. Ploughing often extended into small portions of adjacent fields.

A sample area in the arable allotments of approximately 40,000 m$^2$ contained only six recognizable tree or bush clumps in 1963. By 1992 the number of clumps in this same area had grown to at least 90, and in 1996 some patches contained canopy so dense that counting of individual trees was no longer possible. By then the woody vegetation had extended as far east as the road.

In the arable allotments of Koloni lying east of the residential area, bush encroachment generally started on those lands farthest from the community and with somewhat steeper slopes. Some encroachment is evident by 1985, but thereafter it increased in rate and became more obvious by 1995. The effort required to travel to their fields is one of the several reasons (Chapter 6) given for abandonment of cropping efforts and the pattern on the landscape tends to support that contention. However, despite this general trend a few fields and parts of fields (nos. 9, 33 and 70, see Photo 7.3) at distances of 0.7 to 1 km from the residential area were consistently cleared and generally free of woody vegetation up until 1996. More details derived from direct observations and interviews regarding current practices in the arable fields are presented in chapters 6 and 8.

A fenced woodlot located approximately 0.6 km from the west edge of the community (visible in 1996 image, Photo 7.3) was certainly a product of betterment planning. However, it was already in existence at the time of the 1961 survey. The site is outside the limits of the 1939 imagery available to us. Based on documentation of the betterment planning process (Bantu Affairs 1962) it is assumed that it was part of the communal rangelands at that time. The fenced lot had a woody canopy cover of approximately 80% in 1963. Although the image quality is poor in 1985 the cover appears about the same in that year. By 1992, however, the canopy cover was roughly 10%, indicating removal or death of trees and failure of recruitment of young trees to keep pace. Indeed, by 1996 the woody vegetation within the area appears no different from that on rangelands immediately outside the lot (chapter 8).

Map 7.3 consists of a time series taken from the aerial photos illustrating the changes in the residential area of Koloni. The new residential area north and west of the original site was opened some time between prior to 1963, pre-

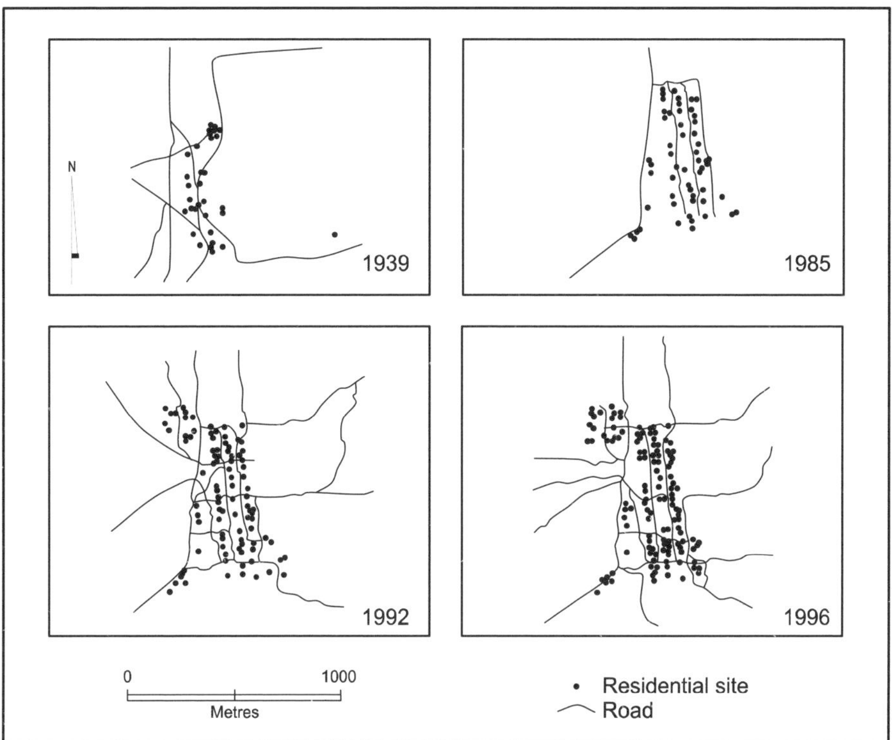



*Map 7.3*     Changes in residential area of Koloni, 1939 to 1996

sumably in coordination with other Betterment Planning exercises (see chapter 3). By 1992 the area had been expanded and by that year as well the number of residences in the new area had exceeded that in the original residential area in 1939. After more than four decades of population increase the average amount of land available per household had been halved. The number of residential buildings in 1939 (33), 1963 (56) and 1992 (82) roughly reflects population size, reported to be 190 in 1938, 329 in 1962 (Bantu Affairs 1962) and 514 in 1991 (South African Census 1991).

The expansion of the area devoted to residences from 1939 to 1996 (Table 7.3) represented a loss of approximately 17.5 ha or slightly less than 3% of the communal rangelands. This loss is less than that lost due to gully expansion and is insignificant in comparison to problems resulting from intrusion of livestock from other communities.

*Table 7.3*    Changes in residential area and number of residential buildings in Koloni, 1939-1996

| Year | No of buildings* in original residential area | No of buildings in original and new residential areas | Size of total residential area (km$^2$) | Mean area/household in original residential area | Mean area/household in both residential area (m$^2$) |
|---|---|---|---|---|---|
| 1939 | 33 | 33 | 0.186 | 5636 m2 | 5636 |
| 1993 | 45 | 56 | 0.270 | 4133 m2 | 4821 |
| 1985** | ? | ? | 0.287 | ? | ? |
| 1992 | 55 | 82 | 0.343 | 3381 m2 | 4182 |
| 1995 | 58 | 90 | 0.365 | 3207 m2 | 4055 |
| 1996 | 62 | 108 | 0.360 | 3000 m2 | 3333 |

* Buildings which appeared to be of the size and shape to represent living places (domiciles).
** Resolution too poor.

Table 7.4 illustrates two phenomena. First, the proportion of *kraals* to residential buildings in the new residential area was always lower than in the original residential area. It seems that this reflects the general status of residents in the new area as newcomers and less involved in the cattle economy and traditions with several being single women or others derived from former urban residences (chapter 9). Second, these data confirm a decline in use of *kraals*, overall, in recent years.

*Table 7.4*    Changes over time in number of *kraals* in residential areas of Koloni

| Year | Number of *kraals* in original area | number of *kraals* in new area |
|---|---|---|
| 1939 | 20 | -- |
| 1963 | 33 | 9 |
| 1985 | 34 | 8 |
| 1992 | 56 | 11 |
| 1995 | 39 | 14 |
| 1996 | 38 | 6 |

## Conclusions

The earliest aerial photos (1938 and 1939) confirm that in both villages the basic layout of residential areas and arable fields was established by that time. However, both villages subsequently underwent a major change in the mode of cultivation with a shift to contour ploughing. In the case of Guquka we can only determine from the imagery that this occurred between 1949 and 1985. In Koloni a major change with contouring and creation of berms appears to have occurred just prior to the 1963 image. In both cases the extent and the uniformity of the changes strongly indicate outside intervention and execution. While both areas show a marked decline in cropping of arable fields over the years, our interpretation is somewhat more detailed for Koloni. Here, the decline went from about 90% of fields cultivated in 1939 to under 10% in 1985. This decline levelled off, and a rate of cultivation of roughly 7 to 10% was maintained after that year, although the individual fields involved varied somewhat from year to year. In Koloni, the large scale appearance and development of thick brush in fallow fields is very evident, especially in those fields farthest from the residential area. In contrast, a woodlot established in 1962 shows a marked decline in tree cover over the years.

In Guquka the degree of decline in cultivation after 1949 was roughly comparable to that in Koloni. The earliest photos of Guquka also confirm a long history of severe gully erosion on the slopes above the village. Some of these gullies extend down into the arable fields and even into the residential area. However, more recent photos show some stabilisation of gullies. This is also in keeping with historical information that suggests that early gully erosion was at least in part due to crop growing on higher, steeper slopes, a practice that was largely stopped by the 1930s. In contrast, Koloni shows less active gully erosion.

Both communities show an increase in the size of the residential area over the years and at the same time an increase in the density of housing (roughly doubling) within the residential area. However the increase in residential area has had only a minor, probably insignificant, effect on the availability of rangelands. The Guquka residential area underwent a general expansion in outward directions, whereas Koloni expansion was principally through the formal addition of a second residential area. The Koloni imagery also clearly demonstrates a reduction in the number of *kraals* over the years. Interpretation of this phenomenon is discussed in chapter 9.

8

# Production of crops in arable fields and home gardens

Paul Hebinck and Nomakaya Monde[*]

## Introduction

This chapter explores the dynamics of crop production in the two villages. Crops are produced both in residential areas (home garden production) and in the arable allotments (field production) and these will be treated separately. The title deeds that were issued after the landscape was surveyed at the end of the 19th century (chapter 3) distinguished between a commonage (or rangeland), building lots (or residential lots) and garden lots (also referred to as arable land allocations or arable fields). Arable farming was designated to take place in arable allotments, which were referred to as 'gardens'. The title deeds made no reference to home gardens, *per se*. Over time, residents have developed home gardens on their residential lots. It is not clear whether these gardens were planned as such by land surveyors and land use planners: the title deeds made no reference to home gardens. The original layout of sites at the time of settlement (chapter 3) has altered over the years with changes in the size and numbers of *kraals* in each building lot. The layout that was designed for Koloni provided only 1/8 *morgen* (0.1 ha) for each residential lot, with no mention of gardens (see chapter 7).

---

[*] Comments by Jan Douwe van der Ploeg and Nick Parrott on earlier drafts were extremely useful.

We start with an overview of land use, followed by account of land relations, and then consider issues of access and control. We also describe crop production: the kind of crops grown, how, and on which fields.

The second part of the chapter examines the decline of crop production in the arable allotments, and its variability in time and among producers, in more detail. We prefer to speak in this chapter of under-cultivation of arable fields rather than of a general decline of agriculture, which is how Manona (1998) has characterised agricultural development processes in the Eastern Cape. Under-cultivation does not exclude the possibility of arable fields being used for (agricultural) purposes other than growing crops. As noted earlier, the most notable feature of the arable allotments or fields is that most of them lie predominantly or totally fallow in any given year and that there is much annual variability in the degree to which they are cropped. These allotments, which appear to be 'overgrown' by weeds and grass, are used for grazing cattle and have become places for gathering fuel wood, herbs and other plants, as described in chapters 9 and 10. This demonstrates that arable fields are used as multi-purpose zones. In this chapter we focus only on the growing part of the equation. A second and related question to address is whether a shift from field cropping to home garden production has taken place in Guquka and Koloni, as has occurred in the former Transkei (Andrew and Fox 2003, 2004).In discussing trends in crop production we also reflect upon the role that betterment planning and other forms of state intervention have played. The chapter mostly focuses on the period after 1960, when under-cultivation began to occur (chapter 3).

In interpreting empirical data from Guquka and Koloni we draw upon the broader literature on agrarian change and livelihood dynamics. Our analysis focuses on the locality and on everyday life: on how local people read the landscape and understand and respond to changes occurring around them.

The chapter combines agronomic data about crop production with ethnographic data that links fields to the people growing the crops. Together they tell the story of land use in the villages. The data are derived from unpublished theses such as Bennett (2002), Monde (2003) and Lo Presti (1996). The data and the analysis has been presented in the annual reports of the Agricultural and Rural Development Research Institute (Mbuti 2000a, Averbeke *et al.* 1998, Bennett 1998), in field notes (Smith 2000a, Bennett 2004, Hebinck 2004, Monde 2005) and in conference and seminar papers (Mbuti 2000b, Monde 2000, Hebinck and Smith 2001, Hebinck 2000, Smith 2000b).


## The current use of arable allotments

Locally villagers speak about cultivation in terms of 'ploughing'. The ability to plough often but not always translates into planting and caring for crops. The recent history and use of arable farming has been investigated in detail by Bennett (1998, 2002, 2004) who documented the status of the fields: whether they were ploughed or not and whether crops were produced, for the 1997/1998,

1998/1999 and 2003/2004 growing seasons, as well as the fallowing history, ownership and usufruct status.

Oral accounts documented in chapter 4 indicated that up to the 1930s for Guquka and till the 1950s for Koloni, the majority of fields were more regularly cropped than in more recent times. Andrew and Fox (2003, 2004) drew a similar conclusion for the Transkei. The extent to which the fields were ploughed in the past is also known from interpreting and comparing aerial photographs (chapter 7). These photographs do not always disclose whether the fields were actually planted, as ploughing does not always automatically translate into planting. Both field observations and interpretations of aerial photographs indicate that the whole field is not necessarily planted, but often only a few strips of land. Field observations also show that maize plant heights vary substantially among fields, suggesting that the time of planting varies greatly. Many fields have been fallow for a long time. Some have not ploughed or planted for 5 years and others for 20 years or even longer (Bennett 2002, Van Averbeke *et al.* 1998a). We did not attempt to classify fallowness in great detail. People in the villages do not talk about land being fallow but instead about it being planted or ploughed. When asked, people said "has not been planted for more than 5 years" or "has not been planted for twenty years". The aerial photographs do not allow for a detailed classification or analysis of fallowing.

Table 8.1 summarises the cultivation history in the two villages during the period 1995/1996 till 2003/2004. The table clearly shows that only a small percentage of arable fields were cultivated. Figures 8.1 and 8.2 provide a graphical overview of the degree to which fields are planted to crops.

*Table 8.1*     Extent of cultivation of arable fields in Guquka and Koloni

| | Total number of fields | Percentage of arable fields ploughed during | | | |
|---|---|---|---|---|---|
| | | 1995/1996 | 1997/1998 | 1998/1999 | 2003/2004 |
| Guquka | 41 | 20 | 17 | 20 | 25 |
| Koloni | 112 | 5 | 8 | 16 | 9 |

*Source*: Lo Presti (1996), Mbuti (2000a), Bennett (2002, 2004)

Some fields showed signs of ploughing only. For instance, field 13 was only ploughed in 1997/1998, there was no sign of it being used the year after and in 2003/2004 it was largely planted to crops. Similarly, three fields (numbers 5, 23 and 30) were ploughed but not planted in 2003/2004.

Koloni's cultivation history is rather similar. Table 8.1 and Figure 8.2 clearly show that of the 112 arable fields in Koloni, only ten were cultivated in the 1997/98 season; 19 in 1998/1999 and then 9 in 2003/2004. The four fields that were planted in 1997/1998 were also cultivated in 2003/2004.

Three fields that were fallow during 1998/1999 had been planted in 2003/2004. Two of these fields were not being cultivated by the owners, but by others with a history of regularly farming their own and/or others' fields.

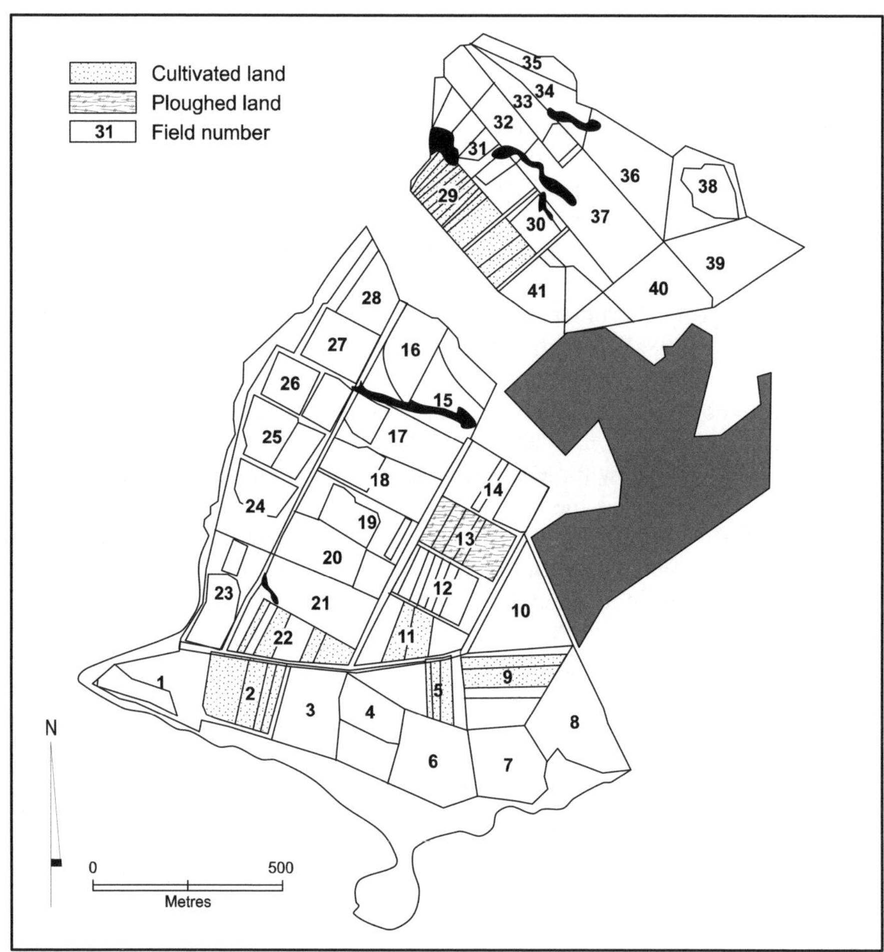


*Figure 8.1.a*      Cultivated field in Guquka in 1997/1998

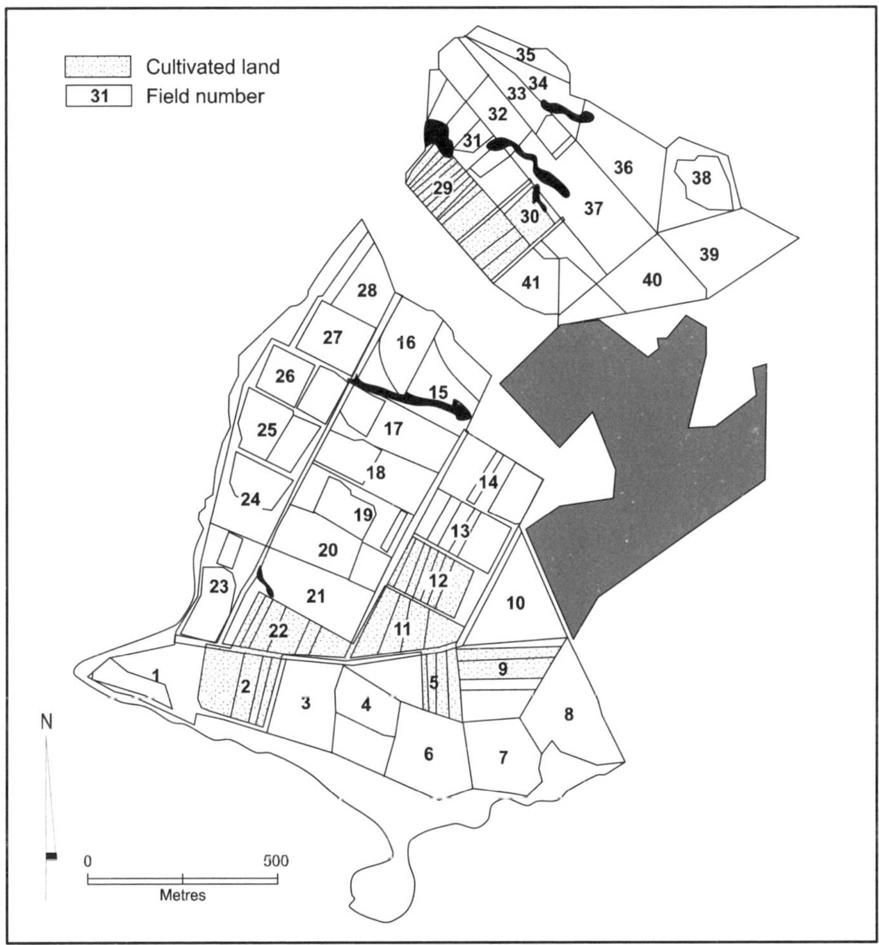


*Figure 8.1.b*      Cultivated fields in Guquka in 1998/1999

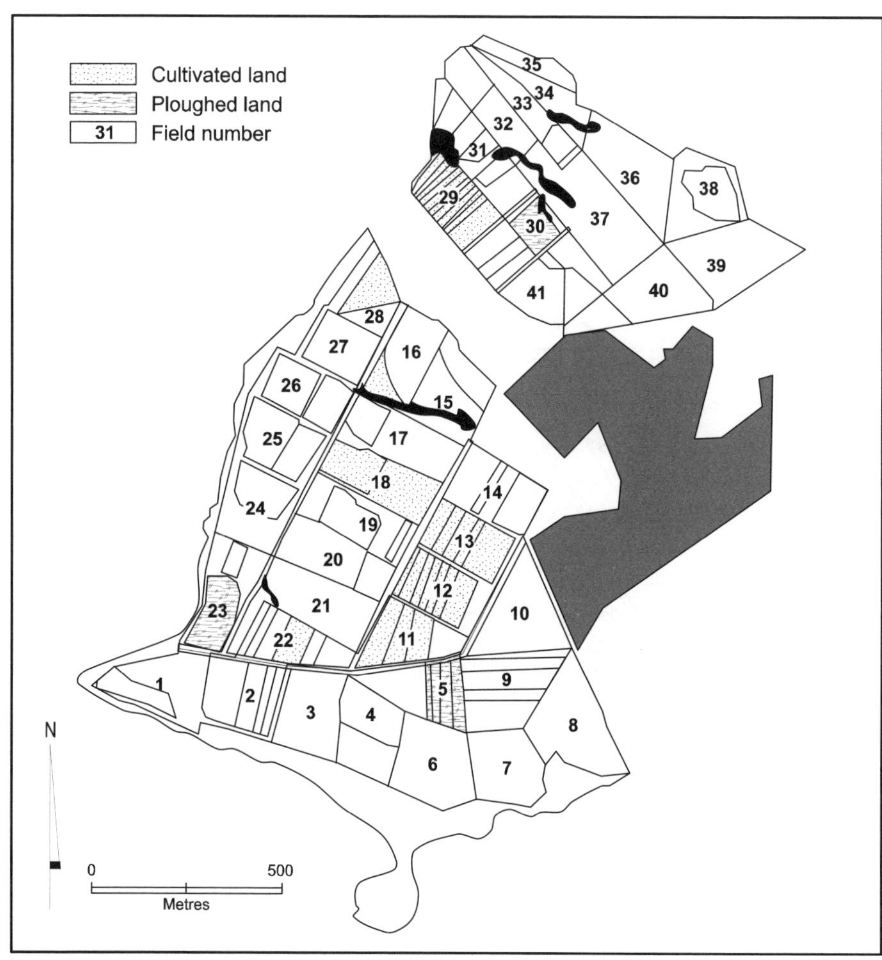


*Figure 8.1.c*     Cultivated fields in Guquka in 2003/2004

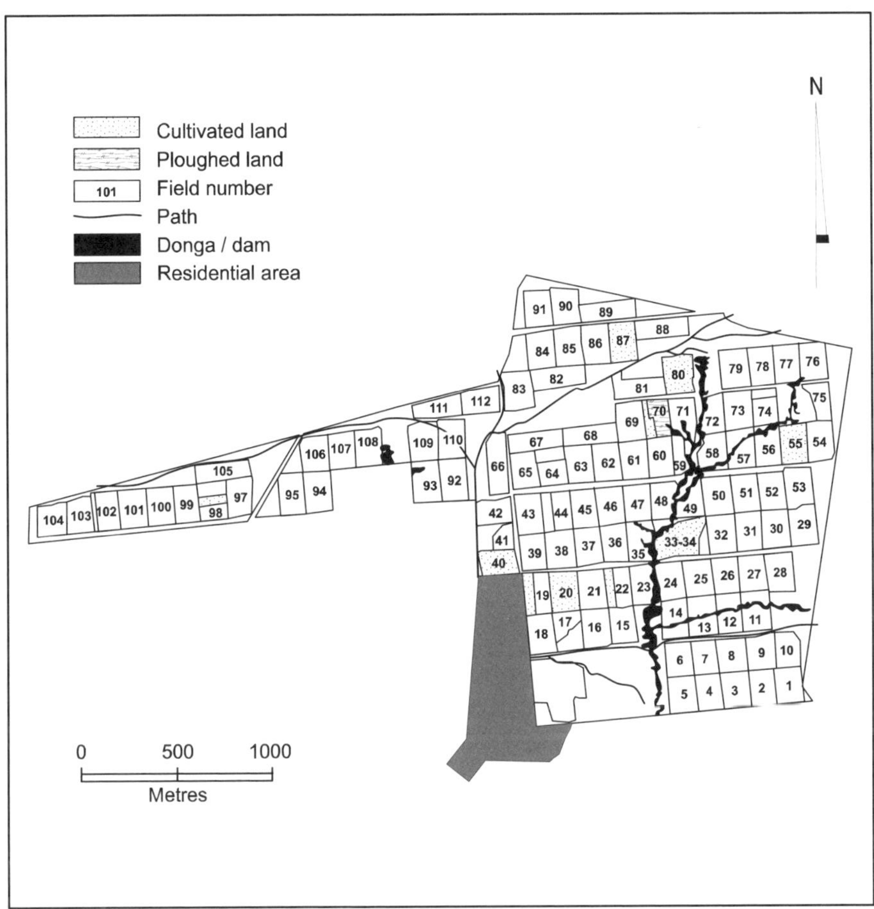


*Figure 8.2.a*     Cultivated fields in Koloni in 1997/1998

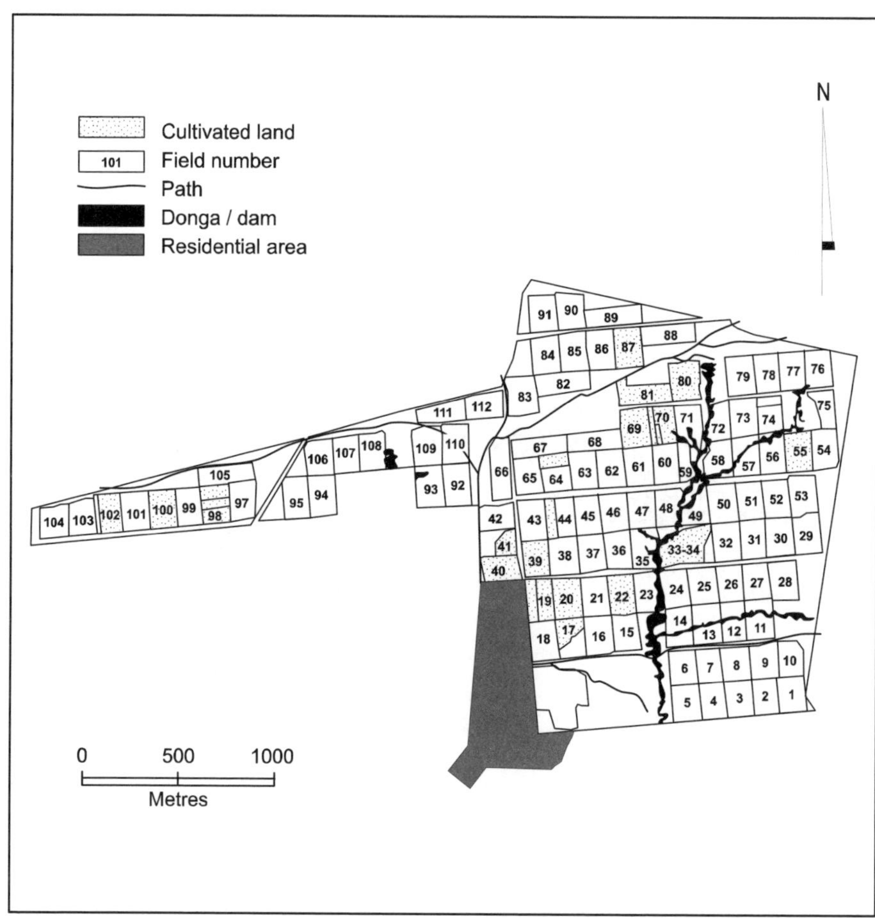



*Figure 8.2.b*	Cultivated fields in Koloni in 1998/1999

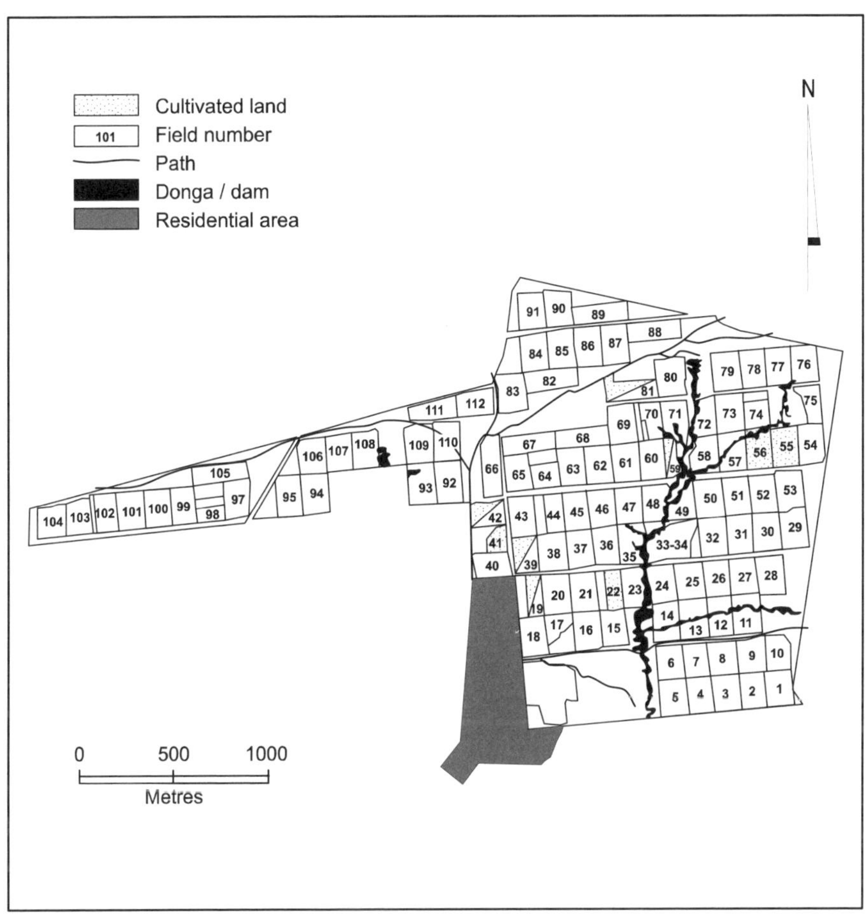


*Figure 8.2.c*     Cultivated fields in Koloni in 2003/2004

Those fields that were continuously uncultivated generally were not fenced. The fences are in many cases broken or have been removed to fence home gardens and protect them from roaming cattle. The absence of owners and the lack of maintained fencing allowed cattle to graze freely on these fields, discouraging people from cultivating them. Most of the unfenced fields belonged to absentee land owners.

The data presented in Figures 8.1 and 8.2 demonstrate the emergence of three patterns of cultivation over the years. One is a pattern of *continuous cropping* occurring in a limited number of cases (5 in each village). A second, more frequent, pattern is of fields being ploughed and planted *irregularly*. The third and predominant pattern is of fields remaining *fallow* persistently for many years. The latter pattern in particular results in what we refer to as under-cultivation of arable fields. In the second part of this chapter we examine the processes that underlie these three patterns.

## Access and control over land

Access to land in Guquka and Koloni is regulated by quitrent which is a form of private ownership (chapter 6) under which the landowners have a title deed. There are also sharecropping arrangements between land owners and users (chapter 6), and also cases in which the land is used without the owner even knowing.

### Land ownership and distribution

The data on ownership and distribution (Table 8.2) demonstrates that not all homesteads have rights to an arable allotment. Forty nine homesteads in Guquka (62%) and nine in Koloni (16%) did not have formal access to land. Chapter 4 showed how, in Guquka this the wave of households that arrived later, in the 1960s, were only provided with residential sites and access to the commonage. Koloni did not have the same influx of people and the pattern of rights of ownership there has been largely shaped by population growth. The more recent settlers in the so-called 'squatter camp' do not have access to arable fields (chapter 3).

*Table 8.2*     Ownership of land and residence of owners in Guquka and Koloni in 1998

| Residence of holder of rights | Guquka | Koloni |
|---|---|---|
|  | No. of fields | No. of fields |
| Village | 28 | 79 |
| Nearby location | 9 | 0 |
| Distant location | 4 | 7 |
| Whereabouts unknown | 0 | 26 |
| Total number of fields | 41 | 112 |
| No. of homesteads with no formal access | 49 | 9 |

*Source*: Bennett (2002: 130), ARDRI Survey (1997)

The number of landless families has thus significantly increased in both villages; although many of the new homes in Koloni's squatter camp were not inhabited nor was their construction finished (chapter 11). Some of the more recent new comers may have chosen to be 'landless' and others have failed to negotiate access to arable fields (chapters 6 and 13). Such homesteads without access to fields can only grow crops in home gardens, on their residential sites. Mr. Mbangi and Mr. Tibani (see chapter 13) are examples of this and are typical of quite a large group in Guquka. Neither had access to an arable allotment and tried in vain to negotiate access. Mr. Tibani explained how he attempted to arrange such access: even inquiries among male 'household heads' living and working in Cape Town at the time led to nothing. He found that most owners claimed they were "about to use the land for a certain purpose". However many of these plots had been lying idle for many years, even decades, and would probably continue to do so for years to come. Even he travelled to Cape Town to approach fellow villagers he was unable to acquire access to a local resource.

Ownership of land usually changes hands when the owner dies and the field is inherited by the eldest son. Land is rarely sold. Informants were adamant that land could only be sold when a person or family left the village: "The right to a field can only be sold with the house and the residential site of the owner" (Van Averbeke *et al.* 1998a). Table 8.2 shows that a few landowners in Guquka reside in the neighbouring settlements of Gilton and Msompondo, although there is no parallel pattern in the case of Koloni.

Fieldwork by Holbrook (1998) in Guquka highlighted an important dimension of land ownership in Guquka: 14 'old multi-homestead households' controlled the bulk of the major resources, livestock and arable land. Defining 'multi-homestead households' as a group of households linked by the same surname, Holbrook showed that over a period of 30 years (since the mid 1960s) these had expanded to represent 37% of the total of 121 homesteads at Guquka in 1997. Together these households held 71% of the arable land, all under the control of old men. Holbrook argued that these old men exert authority over others who seek to share resources through sharecropping arrangements. In contrast, ownership and cultivation of home gardens was more evenly distributed; even the poorer homesteads had such food plots.

This pattern of land distribution has some similarities with other villages in the Eastern Cape. Drawing on the Keiskammahoek Rural Survey, De Wet and McAllister (1983) showed that a decline in arable land-holdings per household had occurred in the Chatha valley: from an average of 1.72 ha per household in 1949 to 0.43 ha in 1981. This was largely attributed to betterment planning. The proportion of homesteads without land increased from 10% to 40% in the same period. Steyn (1998) found that 93% of the homesteads in two villages in the Peddie district had access to arable land. Average holdings in the two villages were 1.4 ha and 1.1 ha, but the sizes varied considerably, although less than one per cent of homesteads had more than 2 ha of arable land. Thus these villages differed from Guquka and Koloni where arable land plot sizes are more equal.

While no precise figures are available for landlessness in the former homelands, estimates of 40-50% are commonly cited (Bembridge 1990). De Wet (1985) calculated similar percentages of landless villagers in the nearby Amatola Basin.

*Absenteeism*

Table 8.2 also captures the phenomenon of absenteeism in 1998. In Koloni in particular, the numbers of absentee 'landlords' is relatively large. Owners of 26 fields could not be traced. The situation in Guquka is quite different and ownership of fields could be traced either to nearby villages or to more distant locations.

One field in Koloni (no. 22, Figure 8.2) officially belongs to the Nyameko family, which has never resided there. From 1998 to 2003/4, it has been cultivated by Mbulelo Ngxowa. His use of the field has no formal basis, as nobody knows the whereabouts of the Nyameko, and the field is effectively abandoned. Mbulelo has chosen to make use of it for this reason, especially because it is conveniently sited close to his house.

Mbuleleo's brother, Siphilo, explained long term absentee land holders were one reason why crop production is not at the same level as it was 30 or so years ago.

> They no longer live in Koloni and their fields have been fallow for a long, long time. Most of these owners are descendants of the original buyers of land, who left the village at some point. In the past the government would confiscate their land with 3 months notice if they had not paid their annual land tax after 3 years. The land 'freed' would first be advertised in the village to enable villagers to buy the residential site and the attached arable field. This system has become disbanded, and a lot of land is lying in waste.

Local accounts, as well as the findings in chapter 7, underline that absenteeism is not a recent phenomena but may go back as far as the early post-settlement time. As noted in chapter 4 some people were allotted a garden and residential lot by the then chief but never bothered to claim it. This failure may be partly explained by the costs of the yearly quitrent rentals, which were then perceived as too high (chapter 6). Indeed, of the 33 fields whose rights are to people that live in a distant village or whose whereabouts are unknown, 18 belong to people who have never resided at Koloni. In an interview in 2000, the then Chairman of Koloni Residents Association acknowledged that one of these has rights to three fields in the village (Smith 2000). Others are known to have never ploughed the fields they were allocated (Bennett 2002: 130).

*Sharecropping relationships*

Sharecropping arrangement are practically the only institution for land transactions between owners and non-owners (chapter 6). On paper sharecropping may appear as an ideal social arrangement that would improve the productivity of existing land use. In both villages there are people with a clear desire to farm; but with no rights to land. For hem sharecropping relations are their only option to access land. Under such an arrangement the landholder makes the land available, the sharecropper provides everything else, and they share the yield. Despite the fact that so much land is fallow, sharecropping is not widely practiced. One reason is the fear that if one gives usufruct rights to someone else, control over the rights to land may be lost in the long run. Equally, there is resentment against the way land owners exert their authority in such arrangements (see also chapter 6). The head of the established, older families in Guquka control most of the land, but are themselves mostly too old to plough and cultivate and have to look to others to cultivate their land. When, as in most cases, their children have no interest in cultivation, they must engage with 'outsiders' to get their land cultivated. In some instances it has been reported that they claim more than the usual 50% share of the harvest. Sharecropping is a source of great resentment in Guquka. Without exception informants referred to arrangements as totally unreasonable and would not consider entering or re-entering a sharecropping arrangement unless the terms were substantially revised (chapter 6).

The specifics of sharecropping are best explained with reference to the Ngwevu homestead. Their experiences show that sharecropping does provide opportunities but that it is an arrangement that is not well understood or trusted. The Ngwevu's were considered affluent (see chapter 13), but they never owned a field. When they settled in Guquka in 1972 all the arable land had already been allocated (chapter 4). Nevertheless, they managed to enter into a share-cropping relationship with he produce being equally divided. The Ngwevu's were happy with that arrangement, but in 1987, the relationship was terminated on good terms. In 1996 they gained access to another field (no. 41, Figure 8.1) whose owner, who stays in the village, asked them to use it as it had been fallow for some years. Two years later the owner terminated the relationship. Mrs. Ngwevu stated:

> The owner did not ask anything in return, no produce, nothing. We then began to plough the field. The following year, we continued to use the land, growing the same crops, in the same way. But in 1998, the owner took his field back. His reason was that his close relatives were complaining that he had given the field to a stranger without asking for compensation. He said that one of them wanted to use the field, but up today, that person has not made a start. The field was last ploughed by us four years ago (Monde 2003: 210, 211).

Field 40 in Koloni (Figure 8.2) adds another dimension to sharecropping. The field is owned by the Ngcaza homestead and was not planted by members of that homestead but instead in the 1997/1998 season was cultivated in a partnership between the then chairman Ngxowa and Mr Mcete. The arrangement was that they each ploughed and planted half of the field. They were each obliged to share half of their yield with Mrs Ngcaza, a widow at the time. Although neither of them liked the arrangement, which they considered somewhat unfair, they planted the field with maize, beans, pumpkins and potatoes. The situation changed in 1998 when Mrs Ngcaza died and the field passed to her eldest child, a daughter who resides in Mdantsane. The daughter had no interest in cultivating the field and was happy to enter into an arrangement to let Mr Mcete use the field. Rather than a sharing the yield (as would be normal for a village resident) the arrangement apparently involved payment in cash (an unknown sum) to be made during harvesting time. The payment would only be made if she came to the village to collect her dues. Payment at harvesting time rather than at the beginning of the season is an interesting strategy, which allows the size of the payment to be determined by the level of crop yield.

There are also contrasting examples of sharecropping arrangements which are more like reciprocal arrangements for crop production as illustrated by the case of Mrs. Nomendi and Mr. Mulanda (Bennett 2002: 123). The former is a widow of some considerable standing within Koloni who, upon the death of her husband, a keen farmer, inherited a herd of 22 cattle and access to a fenced field in the village. Since then she has been able to continue producing crops most years through an arrangement with Mr Mulanda, a close friend. During the 1996/1997 growing season he used the oxen from her herd to plough her field and plant maize. They shared the costs of seeds and other inputs and the labour expended in weeding and harvesting the crop. The entire maize harvest was shared between in the sense that she prepares all his meals. Thus, although the two live separately they have what it is effectively a marriage of convenience whereby she does the cooking and provides the land and oxen and enabling him to produce crops for their mutual benefit.

## Cropping practices on arable allotments

Maize (*Zea mays L.*) is by far the most common crop planted in both villages, but some cultivators inter-crop maize with other summer crops such as potatoes, beans, pumpkins and sunflower (Mbuti 2000a, 2000b, Verdoodt *et al.* 2003). In earlier years crops like *kaffircorn* (sorghum), peas and wheat were also grown (Bantu Affairs 1962). Leftovers of maize are often left as *stover* for livestock to feed on. A few people in each village cultivate forage crops such as oats during the latter part of the growing season, specifically for use by livestock (chapter 9).

Current crop production is characterised by low levels of purchased inputs. Chemical fertilisers are not applied; only *kraal* manure. Monetary costs usually incurred include hiring tractor ploughing services (R70 per acre in 1997, rising to R90-100 in 2004) and labour for weeding and harvesting (ranging from R20-30 per day in 2000). Seed is bought locally or in nearby towns, but the use of seeds kept from previous harvests predominates.

During our field investigations only two individuals in each village owned tractors; these were old, unreliable and in need of frequent repair. Many cultivators were hiring tractors from neighbouring villages; but these often arrived late due to ploughing commitments closer to home. All the fields at Guquka were ploughed by tractor, whereas in Koloni most fields were prepared by ox-drawn ploughs. Sowing is mostly done by hand as is most weeding (done with hand hoes), although a few, use ox-drawn cultivators. Weeding is generally performed by women, hired labourers and children. Neighbours often helped one another during harvest time.

Labour was predominantly drawn from the homestead, including adults and children, sometimes supplemented with assistance from kin from other homesteads. In Koloni hiring of labour was virtually non-existent and it is quite rare in Guquka. Work parties, where people pool their labour together (*ilima,* chapter 2), are also quite rare in the two villages, but occur more often in Koloni, where for example two families pooled their labour resources and ploughing equipment and worked their fields together, or entered into a sharecropping arrangement.

*Photo 8.1*    Women harvesting maize. (Photo by Lent)

A more common phenomenon is a work party of six or more casual labourers together performing one or another task, like spreading manure, weeding or harvesting. The labourers sometimes receive cash for their work but in other cases are paid in kind (e.g. food or alcoholic drinks). Later in this chapter we provide further details about such work parties.

Soil fertility was largely maintained by the application of *kraal* manure. Only one farmer in Guquka used chemical fertiliser, in combination with manure in the 1997/98 season. Four others used manure that was applied in varying quantities, depending on availability and transport. One farmer at Guquka said that he had applied 11 tractor-loads of *kraal* manure from his homestead which covered the entire field. Labour was mobilised from the village through an *ilima* (work party).

*Kraals* are considered as repositories of nutrients (Van Averbeke and Yoganathan 1997, Ngwadla and Thys 2000a, 2000b). The agricultural practises associated with the use of *kraal* manure in two villages are summarised in Table 8.3.

*Table 8.3*     Manuring practices in Guquka and Koloni

| Guquka | Koloni |
|---|---|
| All use *kraal* manure, never lime | All use *kraal* manure, never lime |
| General preference for sheep manure | Split evenly between cattle and sheep manure |
| Ploughed-in 3-4 months prior to planting in arable fields and 1 week prior in the home gardens | Ploughed-in 3-4 months prior to planting in arable fields and 1 week prior in home gardens |
| Farmers exchange *kraal* manure | No exchange |
| Application rate in arable fields averages about 0.20 kg.m$^{-2}$ | Application rate in arable fields averages about 0.70 kg.m$^{2}$ |
| Application rate in home gardens is about 3 kg.m$^{-2}$ | Application rate in home gardens is about 8 kg.m$^{2}$ |

*Source*: adapted from Ngwadla and Thys (2000a)

In Guquka, livestock owners generally pen their animals at night throughout the year and the *kraal* is often only emptied of manure every 2-3 years. In Koloni most homesteads keep all three types of animal (chapter 9) but only the small-stock and milking cows are regularly penned. Other animals are only penned the night before dipping days. Thus manure is accumulated more slowly in Guquka than in Koloni, where the manure is taken out in portions, but the *kraals* are never completely emptied.

The differences in manure practises between the two villages are quite minimal. Farmers in both villages tend to use more manure in their home gardens than on arable fields. Farmers in Koloni generally apply more manure to both gardens and arable fields than those in Guquka. The following accounts, documented in Monde (2003) and Bennett (2002, 2004), highlight some of the social, organisational and agronomic dimensions of crop production in the two villages. Each account is the story of a field, how crop production takes place and how the land is used.

Mss. Ngwevu and her husband sharecropped for a long time on field no. 41 (Figure 8.1) in Guquka. She was interviewed in 1999 (Monde 2003: 210, 211).

> My husband Phindile, first put out two tractor loads of manure. He and the four workers did the ploughing and planting, using a tractor and planter. In the first year we planted peas on the whole field in winter and we got five 50kg bags. In summer we only planted maize. We hired six people from the village to weed. They took six days to weed the whole field and were paid R20.00 per person per day. At harvest time, we again asked for help from our neighbours and relatives. We did not pay them cash, but we gave them each half a bag of maize cobs, and we provided them with meals during the time they worked on the field. The produce amounted to 13 bags of grain, excluding what we gave to away for free. This maize was kept in an old rain tank, and most of it was processed into *samp*. Some was fed to chickens and pigs. We did not buy *samp* for about five and a half months that year.

Lulamila Fumbata lives in Guquka and inherited his field (no. 11 in Figure 8.1) from his father Solani upon his death in September 2003. This field has a history of continuous cropping, although in 1997/1998 it was not fully cultivated. Mr. Fumbata planted his field in 2003/2004 with maize, melons and pumpkins. Cultivation involved ploughing about 1.6 ha (half of the field) using a tractor that cost R215 per ha. He applied 10 loads of manure taken from his *kraal* for which the transport costs amounted to R80 per load. He organised a *ilima* of about 10 people to spread the manure and paid them in kind (food and beer). He planted in December 2003 using a planter pulled by horses. When we visited his field in April 2004, the field was only partly harvested.

Vuyo Grootbooi of Guquka, is a migrant labourer in the mines, but had been without work for some time (see chapter 13). He previously sharecropped a field (chapter 6) but inherited a field from an uncle in 2000 (no. 13 in Figure 8.1). In the 1997/1998 and 1998/1999 cropping seasons this field was left uncultivated by the previous owner. Mr. Grootbooi has cultivated at least part of this field ever since, depending on whether there was money available to pay for inputs. Vuyo planted his field in the 2003/2004 season with maize. When we looked at his field in April 2004 there was significant weed intrusion, primarily Khakibos (*Tagetes minuta*) and *Convolvulus* sp. He hired a tractor from someone in Kayalethu at a rate of R215 per ha for rough ploughing prior to cultivation and afterwards he used cattle to plough and plant. Planters and other equipment were borrowed from other people in the neighbourhood in exchange for working their fields. The main crop in the 2003/2004 cropping season was maize, interplanted with pumpkins and beans. Separate rows of potatoes were also planted and harvested in March, 2004 and were all sold in the village. In 2004 the bottom section of the field was already rough ploughed to prepare for the next cultivation season, as he wanted the ground to be 'softened-up'. For this he used a disc harrow, which is faster than normal ploughing and is cheaper, costing only R60 per acre.

Field no. 40 in Koloni (Figure 8.2) was sharecropped by Mr. Mcete who subcontracted the cropping to his nephew Mncedisi Mcete (chapter 13). Cultivation began in September 2003 using a span of four oxen over a period of about four days to harrow the ground and remove the weeds. Manure was added in five full loads on a flat back trailer pulled by a tractor hired from Mr Mamali from the adjacent village of Sixekweni (also called Farm B) for an unspecified fee. Manure was provided for free by Mr Ngxowa, a friend of Mr Mcete, who had too much manure in his *kraal*. The manure was all from sheep, and Mncedisi did not notice ay difference in the efficacy of this compared to cattle manure. A working party of six people was organised to dig the manure into the field. They were paid with brandy and Paarl Perle wine (one of the most inexpensive wines) and cigarettes.

Ploughing was delayed until December as the first good rains came very late. In the meantime harrowing was undertaken periodically to control regrowth of weeds. Ploughing was undertaken using 4-span of oxen, and a planter was used simultaneously to plant the maize seed. Maize seed for planting was obtained from within the village for R30. After December the rains were good and Mncedisi reported that he was working hard on weed control

The main crop was maize, apart from one small section of potatoes. When Mr. Mcete was interviewed in April 2004, he had already harvested the potatoes and one strip of maize. The maize was bundled in upright sheaves awaiting transport to the house where the cobs would be removed and remainder of the plant (stover) used as winter feed for livestock. The better cobs would be used mainly for human consumption and the poorer quality fed to the chickens or used as an additional source of forage for ewes during the winter to aid milk production for their lambs. In addition to the main field, the home garden is used to cultivate lucerne alfalfa (*Medicago sativa*) as a winter forage crop for the young lambs.

Field no. 74 (Figure 8.2) is cultivated by Mpendulo Ngxobo (see also chapter 13) and is one of the few fields that has a history of continuous cropping. Mr Ngxobo asserted that dry land cropping in Koloni is not easy. Sometimes, the rain starts very late, when the appropriate times for planting particular crops has already elapsed. Sometimes, the rain starts early enough, allowing farmers to plant, but then stops at a critical time, e.g. when maize is tasselling. In some seasons this leads to a total failure of the field crops. Mr. Ngxobo:

At times like these, we usually concentrate on gardening. Crops and vegetables grown in the home garden can be supplied with water at critical stages, such as transplanting, and when there is a severe dry spell. Because we have access to tap water, we usually cultivate the garden more than once a year. The water used to irrigate the plants is obtained from taps located in the streets within the village and is brought to the garden using a hosepipe. Sometimes children fetch the water from the tap using 25l containers loaded in a wheelbarrow. Once the water is in the garden, we use watering cans to irrigate the plants. The fields are located far from the homesteads and are three or four times larger than the gardens. The location and size of fields make it impossible to irrigate them with the available irrigation facilities. Concentrating on gardening does not completely offset the adverse effects of bad weather. When there is no harvest from the field, there is no maize and no sales. Then we have to purchase all our maize, and that is costly because it is one our family's main food products.

Another potential problem in crop production, apart from water scarcity and rainfall distribution, is lack of proper storage facilities. During a good season with sufficient rains, the produce cannot often be kept for very long because of poor storage facilities. This prevents a constant supply of local produce. Mr. Ngxobo said that "when the produce is ready, we have to make sure that it is sold quickly. If not, it gets spoiled because we do not have good storage facilities".

Mr. Ngxobo does not hire a tractor to plough his fields or gardens, but ploughs with animals. Labour is either supplied by the family or exchanged. This can be a big problem at certain times if household members are not available when needed. A shortage of labour, especially at crucial times like ploughing, has an adverse effect on crop production. Ploughing with animals is a job reserved for men only, and requires at least three. Mpendulo has always been able to exchange his labour with others.

> It works but it is not a perfect solution. Sometimes we have to combine labour and equipment owned by five households. The big question is always whose field to start with. If you happen to be the last one, the soil may already be too dry.

Mr. Ngxobo obtains his seed from friends, relatives and neighbours, from his previous harvest, or by purchasing sccds from supermarkets and the farmer's co-operatives in King William's Town. In both villages, local producers were the main suppliers of cabbage, spinach and onion seedlings. For maize and pumpkins the seed were usually kept from previous harvests or obtained for free from neighbours. Mpendulo does not use chemical fertilisers on his land, only *kraal* manure and chicken litter. He explained: "Chemical fertilisers are expensive and since we have manure, we make use of it instead".

*Crop yields*
Mean maize yields in Guquka were higher (1199 kg/ha) in the 1997/1998 growing season than in the following year (1199 kg/ha compared to 892 kg/ha respectively see Table 8.4). In contrast, in Koloni the maize yields were much higher (918 kg/ha) in the 1998/99 growing season than the 394 kg/ha of the previous season.

Not all maize was harvested when ripe; some is being picked before fully matured, as green maize (also known as 'mealies'). Green mealies are not sold but consumed at the homestead. Estimates given by three homesteads from Guquka and eight from Koloni, suggest that consumption of green mealies was 10 to 20 kg per household. McAllister (2001) calculated similar amounts of green mealies being harvested in the Transkei.

*Table 8.4*    Crop production in Guquka and Koloni, 1997/98 and 1998/99

| Crop production (kg/ha) in Guquka | | | | | | | |
|---|---|---|---|---|---|---|---|
| Crops | 1997/1998 growing season | | | 1998/1999 growing season | | | |
| | n | Total | Mean | Range | n | Total | Mean | Range |
| Maize | 5 | 5999 | 1199 | 578-2033 | 7 | 6242 | 892 | 184-1318 |
| Melon | 2 | 96 | 8 | 34-68 | 3 | 168 | 569 | 5-55 |
| Beans | - | - | - | - | 2 | 22 | 11 | 5-18 |
| Potatoes | - | - | - | - | 2 | 15 | 58 | 26-89 |

| Crop production (kg/ha) in Koloni | | | | | | | |
|---|---|---|---|---|---|---|---|
| Crops | 1997/98 growing season | | | 1998/99 growing season | | | |
| | n | Total | Mean | Range | n | Total | Mean | Range |
| Maize | 6 | 2363 | 394 | 23-900 | 17 | 17450 | 918 | 240-1940 |
| Melon | 2 | 55 | 77 | 30-125 | 6 | 77 | 13 | 4-26 |
| Beans | 2 | 18 | 9 | 3-15 | 2 | 19 | 10 | 8-11 |
| Potatoes | 2 | 152 | 76 | 68-83 | 6 | 276 | 46 | 8-149 |
| Pumpkin | 2 | 422 | 211 | 27-394 | 12 | 922 | 77 | 7-681 |

n = number of fields – yield figures are rounded to the nearest whole number.

*Source*: Mbuti (2000a)

The yield of the green mealies should be included in the total yield calculations, especially when comparing peasant farming with large scale, commercial farming, but this but is often not done. There is little historical data about crop yields. The 1962 report for Koloni mentions yields for maize as averaging 3 bags per *morgen* (about 315 kg/ha); *kaffircorn*, peas and beans all averaging 2 bags; and wheat 1.5 bags per *morgen* (Bantu Affairs Commission 1962). De Wet (1984) reported two bags of maize on the cobs (that is 90 kg of stripped maize) per acre (approx. 450 kg/ha).

These yield figures hint at variation among years which is partly explained by biophysical conditions (chapters 3 and 5) but more so by the operating conditions. More importantly are the apparent longer-time yield increases. Despite risky and potentially adverse bio-physical and institutional conditions, yields appear to have increased substantially, perhaps even doubled or tripled.

Care should be taken with such conclusions, because the early yield data are possibly unreliable.

## Home garden production

Vegetable gardens can be found on residential lots and are generally fenced off from neighbours' plots and from the owner's home. They are typically diverse, with a range of crops being grown: maize, vegetables, beans, pumpkins, onions, spinach, tomatoes etc. Often they have fruit trees as well. Monde (2000, 2005) has described some of the salient features of home gardens and gardening. This study gathered data through a questionnaire completed by informants who were selected through a probability sampling technique. The sample contained 50 respondents from as many homesteads; 25 from each village. Additional semi-structured interviews were carried out with selected individuals, (some from the earlier survey in 2000; Monde 2003).

Gardeners in Koloni, showed a preference for potatoes, allocating large plots to this crop. In Guquka, maize was the preferred crop, followed by potatoes. Potatoes were favoured because they are easily incorporated in a wide range of meals. Maize was popular as a vegetable (green mealies) and also as a grain, especially when it could be processed into *samp* (broken grain) or meal. In Guquka, women produce their own *samp* by crushing dry maize grain using a metal pestle in a wooden mortar.

Before continuing, it is useful to take a brief look at the historic development of home garden production. From the 1900s onwards arable farming and labour migration went together (chapter 4). Around 1960 arable farming began to decline and it is worth asking whether home garden production replaced crop production in the arable allotments, as has occurred in the Transkei, where according to Andrews and Fox (2003) this shift occurred as a response to the declining productivity of field soils and the high risk of damage to field crops by livestock during the growing season, due to lack of fences. They relate many of these constraints to the fixing of land use by betterment planners, which removing the ability of homesteads to respond to changing circumstances, including declining soil nutrients. In areas where betterment was not implemented and use of land remained flexible, shifts between field and home garden production underline the importance of flexibility in land use. For example, between 1942 and 1982 in Nompa, a rural settlement in the former Transkei, where betterment was never applied, the number of homesteads increased by 67%, the area covered by fields dropped by 51% (from 1327 ha to 650 ha), the number of gardens increased by 434% (from 131 to 699), and the mean garden size doubled (from 2088 to 4191 m$^2$). The size of residential sites and home garden is an important and, when not fixed in stone, can be a highly variable factor.

There is little historic information available about the role of betterment planning in the shift to home gardening in Guquka and Koloni. There is no written documentation to put home gardening in a historical perspective and little in the oral accounts that we gathered. Based on interpretations of aerial photograph (chapter 7), we can say a little something about the time that such changes may have occurred. These earlier photos (1938 and 1949 for Guquka and 1949 for Koloni) show no clear signs of home gardening. The lack of fencing of arable allotments may well have contributed to a later shifts towards home gardens. In both villages these are considerably smaller than in the Transkei. A survey from 1996 shows that sizes in Guquka ranged from 120 m$^2$ to 2970 m$^2$ (with an average of about 600 to 700 m$^2$ )while in Koloni garden sizes varied from 50 to 1000 m$^2$ (ARDRI Survey 1997). But as chapter 7 showed, the mean residential area per household diminished substantially between 1938 and 1996 in both villages. The extent and intensity of use also varied widely; not all homesteads with garden plots would plant crops in any given year. There was also a tendency to have plant larger areas in summer (from October to March) than in winter (April to September).

*Access to gardens*

Ownership of gardens is relatively well distributed. In 2000, only seven homesteads in Guquka and 8 in Koloni did not have a home garden (Table 8.5.). Some of the homesteads with a garden did not use it and had abandoned gardening.

*Table 8.5*     Number of homesteads with access to home
              gardens in 2000

| Home gardens | Guquka<br>n=129 | Koloni<br>n=112 |
|---|---|---|
| Had gardens | 61 | 52 |
| Cultivated | 49 | 41 |
| Abandoned | 12 | 11 |
| No gardens | 7 | 8 |

Source: adapted from Monde (2003: 114)

A few homesteads had access to more than one garden; one in the residential lot and another outside it. Gardens outside the residential sites fell into two categories. The first category is community gardens, in which some but not all villagers were members. In Koloni the community garden was started as a collaborative effort between the Eastern Cape departments of agriculture and health. The garden is situated on the grounds of the clinic and has about 30 members, each cultivating a plot of about 100 m$^2$.

A second category of gardens outside the residential lots involves those on empty sites that belong to relatives or family members staying and/or working elsewhere. In such cases a household member residing in the village, usually a relative, was given permission to use the site as a garden until such time as the site owner decided to build a house on his/her site. Usually there are no conditions regarding the use of garden produce in this kind of arrangement: the household using the site as a garden is not expected to give a certain proportion of produce to the owner.

*Gardening practices*

Most people mainly grew crops in their gardens to supply their own household with food. In Guquka, some 86% of the produce was consumed at home, 10 % was sold and 4% given to relatives and friends. In Koloni, 62% was consumed at home, 35% was sold and 3% given away. The proportion of produce consumed at home also included that fed to animals (pigs and chickens), an important way in which maize, especially, was consumed. All home gardeners that were interviewed considered home consumption requirements as the main deciding factor in their choice of crops. Growing crops for exchange purposes was the second important factor; about 84% of the informants said that it had an effect on which crop to plant. A large percentage (74%) also prioritised crops that are easy to manage and do not require special attention. Less than half of respondents grew crops for marketing purposes. Rainfall did not appear to play a major role in decisions about which crops to grow during summer. During winter, when water is scarce and people had to irrigate to get a yield, the sizes of the planted areas were reduced to minimise water usage.

Table 8.6 provides estimates of the yields realised from home garden plots during the 2004/2005 season. The table shows that the popularity of potatoes in Koloni is also reflected in generally higher yields; similarly for maize in Guquka.

*Table 8.6*    Mean and range yields of main crops during 2004/2005 summer cropping season

| Main crop | Guquka | | | Koloni | | |
|---|---|---|---|---|---|---|
| | Mean yield (kg) | Range (kg) | Mean size (m$^2$) | Mean yield (kg) | Range (kg) | Mean size (m$^2$) |
| Maize | 43 | 0.1–400 | 96 | 1.4 | 0.01-50 | 18 |
| Potatoes | 22 | 5–60 | 54 | 25 | 10–130 | 75 |
| Dry beans | 18 | 3–70 | 30 | 10 | 5–145 | 21 |
| Pumpkins/Butter | 11 | 2–50 | 22 | 33 | 9–150 | 25 |
| Cabbage | 13 | 1-15 | 36 | 9 | 1–38 | 27 |
| Spinach | 15 | 3-12 | 28 | 5 | 3.5-35 | 20 |

*Source*: Monde (2005: 22)

Home gardening is largely based on the use of non-monetised inputs, although land preparation was usually subcontracted and vegetable seed was generally purchased. Maize and pumpkin seed were from own storage or that of neighbours. Seeds of other crops were purchased in supermarkets and co-operatives in local urban centres. In most cases wood ash was used as a pesticide on plants. In Koloni, gardeners used 'Blue Death', an insecticide in powder form, to control pests.

Generally, home garden production was rainfed, but people often irrigated when planting or transplanting, and during a long dry spell. Sources of water used by people included stand pipes (in Koloni only), livestock dams, rivers and roof collection systems (Guquka). At Guquka there was a gardening project, initiated by the Agricultural Research Council (ARC) and the University of Fort Hare, whose main aim was to introduce a water harvesting technique that could be used in individual home gardens.

Mengezelei Mbangi in Guquka has a productive home garden, which has a water reservoir, with a capacity of 0.5 $m^3$ and an interesting design (Van Averbeke 2005). Assisted by an NGO (African Christian Action Trust) he constructed a system to collect running water off for irrigating his garden crops. He learnt this technique from an extension agent of the NGO who had supplied him with a few bags of cement to line the reservoir. The garden was neatly subdivided into small, more or less, level plots, and along the edges of the garden he had planted a range of fruit trees including oranges, plums, peaches and prickly pear. Each tree was surrounded by a small ridge creating an impoundment to hold irrigation water. Whenever his vegetables and trees suffered from water stress, Mengezelei used a hosepipe to siphon water from the reservoir to the plots and trees. This enabled him to grow vegetables and fruit intensively. When the reservoir ran dry, Mengezelei filled it up with water collected from the village livestock watering dam, situated about 350 m from his house using plastic drums and a wheelbarrow. In 1998, Mengezelei dug a second water harvesting reservoir above his garden and outside his residential plot. He sited it so it would collect runoff from the road running past his residential plot. From this new, unlined reservoir he siphoned water to the reservoir on his plot. When it became clear that the new reservoir significantly reduced the need for water cartage, Mengezelei successfully requested permission from the Residents Association of Guquka to widen his residential plot by about 10m. The land added to his plot formed part of the commonage and was too steep for use as a residential site. During the subsequent months he terraced the extension, adding two plots to his vegetable garden, and moved his fence to enclose the addition. Moving the fence positioned the new reservoir within the boundaries of his plot, and he subsequently lined it with cement.

To fertilise his garden, Mengezelei made compost, heaping chicken litter, weeds and crop residues near the entrance to his vegetable garden. Although he did not collect enough organic waste to produce a heap large enough to generate the heat necessary for effective decomposition, Mengezelei appeared quite satisfied with his technique. His maize, was very densely planted, often showed signs of stress. It was suggested that he could collect cattle manure from the rangeland and thereby increase the amount of compost available for his crops. He started doing this, but with much little enthusiasm. When asked why he was hesitant to collect dung from the rangelands, he replied that many people in the village gathered it to burn.

Mengezelei and his spouse consumed most of their garden produce at home, but he also sold vegetables in the village. His vegetables were quite widely spaced and as a result, were usually quite large. On one occasion he harvested onions that were so large that he sold them for R2.00 each. He stated that his vegetables were top quality and that he never experienced problems selling them.

Small stock species (e.g. pigs, chicken, and ducks) are an integral part of home gardens. They are fed from leftovers of garden products and supply some nutrients to the gardens.

Only one household in Koloni applied chemical fertilisers and none did so in Guquka. Instead, many of the home gardeners made use of *kraal* manure, and a few used compost. Manure was obtained either from their own *kraal* or free of charge from one belonging to relatives. In both villages, children were the main source of labour for carting water and manure. An investigation into soil nutrient supply in crop production in Guquka and Koloni (Ngwandla and Thys 2000a, 2000b) showed people preferred sheep manure, as they considered it the most effective source of nutrients.

Family labour predominates. Hired labour was limited to land preparation (ploughing) and only resorted to when no family labour was available or when the garden was particularly large. In Guquka, where the gardens were larger compared to Koloni, a third of the gardeners hired tractors to plough. In contrast, not one garden was ploughed with tractors in Koloni. Three gardens were cultivated with animal traction. Exchange of labour occurs, through informal agreements where homesteads seek help from relatives or friends. The recipient family then owed the suppliers an equivalent amount of labour, which could settled by payment in kind, free meals or a portion of the produce at harvest. Such arrangements were used for a range of activities, including ploughing.

Most of the crops grown in gardens are staple foods, notably maize. Being able to grow ones own food significantly reduces household expenditure on food. Consuming fresh produce from home gardens also improves the nutritional status of household members. Monde (2003) and Buys (2000) both noted an improvement in nutrition during the summer season when the gardens are more productive.

The stories of gardeners about home gardening also point at the broader social dimensions and meaning of gardening. Gardening provides an income from selling some of the produce, usually locally to friends, neighbours and relatives. In most cases buyers purchase the products at the garden site. In other instances, the produce is transported to buyers usually by children using wheelbarrows. The cash earned from garden produce is usually used to buy other food items, but some is used to take care of other needs (see also Mentani 2001), sometimes being used to pay a child's school fees. Thus gardening in rural areas is done for more than just for food security. It enables people to establish and maintain a social network that is often based on reciprocity. Some of the food produced is also donated to friends, relatives and neighbours, this acts as an insurance for the donating families so they can feel free to ask for favours or help when they are in need. Such requests could be for help with tasks other than gardening. Those on the receiving end feel obliged to return the favour or donate the same or different food items. In this way relationships among homesteads become stronger.

Two short narratives about people and their gardens demonstrate the social dynamics of home gardening and illustrate the substantial variation between gardens in the two villages.

Nombulelo is a piece worker who earns money by doing small tasks for others in the village. Her crops are grown under rainfed conditions, and because of that, her garden is usually planted only once a year. She does not own a single garden tool, but borrows from neighbours and relatives when she needs them. She stated, "We rely on my neighbours for tools. If they are busy with them we have to wait. Sometimes, by the time we get them, it is already dry and we end up not planting anything, or have to wait for more rain".

The crops grown in her garden include maize, sorghum, melon and vegetables, including potatoes, cabbages and spinach. These are mainly for home consumption, although she occasionally exchanges them for other food products.

> When I exchange produce, I'm always in need of the other product immediately. Sometimes I have tea but do not have sugar to put in the tea. So I exchange a bowl of potatoes for sugar. If I decide to sell the same bowl of potatoes instead, I'd probably not get enough money to buy the smallest packet of sugar in the shop. Besides people do not always have cash. I don't even consider selling because I usually don't have much to sell.

In a good season (when the harvest is abundant) bartering food saves Nombulelo's homestead from hunger. It also ensures that it has access to a wider variety of food. But such good times do not occur often, she says, and when they do, they don't last long. The garden area is small and only cropped once a year. Because she does not own animals manure is obtained from relatives free of charge and only applied at planting. The work in the garden is mostly done by her son Phumzile. After school, he attends to the garden instead of his schoolwork.

The Ngwevus, who as explained earlier were regularly engaged in field production, also cultivated a garden on their residential lot. Ms. Ngwevu grows vegetables here for own consumption. But occasionally, she said, "when people want to buy, I just give them whatever they want as a gift or exchange for another food product I do not have at that moment. Things like bread flour or sugar". Cultivation is done by hand even though they own a tractor. Nolulamile explained some of the details of her garden and gardening.

> It is not possible to use a tractor because my garden is divided into plots. I do not grow the crops at the same time and the products are not ready at the same time. When one is ready, and it has all been consumed or harvested, the plot is cultivated again and another vegetable is planted, I do not plant the same vegetable on the same plot, I change them. Melikhaya, my nephew, does the cultivation. During planting, my children help too. They help carting manure that I use when planting potatoes and pumpkins. I get manure from my neighbour, because we do not *kraal* our cattle. Potatoes are planted on a larger plot than the other vegetables. We eat a lot of potatoes in this house, almost every meal except breakfast. But I grow them [only] once a year, because I can't plant them twice on the same plot, and the other plots are too small to grow potatoes. Pumpkins are planted on the side of the garden, not in the middle, using bigger row spacing. I do this to give the runners enough space to extend.

The Ngwevus have access to another garden outside their residential lot which is 20 by 45 m. This plot is used exclusively for maize which is used to make *samp* and feed chickens and pigs.

> This garden is a residential site that belongs to one of the Msiwas in the village. Mrs. Msiwa's husband passed away before they had a chance to build a house on their site and without work she does not have the means to build a house on the site. She asked me to use it as a garden for the time being. The only reason why she asked me is because the site happens to be next to mine. When she needs it I'll have no problem in giving it up, I haven't experienced any problem so far. I do give her part of the produce even though she has never asked for it.

## Explaining continuities and discontinuities in crop production

This section explores the patterns of use of arable allotments. Three patterns are clearly evident. One is characterised by fields continuously being fallow; in a second a few fields show continuous cropping and the third pattern is that of fields being irregularly cultivated. Explaining these patterns may also help us to understand why the timing of planting varied, why not all fields and crops look well cared for and why they are left unprotected from roaming livestock.

Guided by the broader literature on agrarian change in Africa (Berry 1984, 1993, Bryceson 2002a, Francis 2000, Lund 2002) our analysis focused on the outcome of the locally specific interplay between land and land relations, labour and labour relations, access to monetary resources and relationships with markets. People's accounts also hinted at the fact that shifts in life style and social identities also played a role in affecting the viability of land based livelihoods, together with their strategies for livelihood diversification. Although the analysis is largely social, it does not ignore the quality of the natural resources and climate conditions (see chapters 3 and 5) since farming involves co-production (chapter 1) and is the outcome of the interplay between natural and social processes.

The institutional context, such as land tenure and access to land (Berry 1984, 1993, Lund 2002) play an important role in explaining patterns of land use. The rural sociological literature (Hebinck and Van der Ploeg 1997, Van der Ploeg 1990) also calls for making a distinction between the quantity of labour (labour power) and quality of the labour force (skills, knowledge). The quality of labour includes the skills to read the agricultural landscape. Netting (1993), Van der Ploeg (2003) and (Richards 1983, 1985) point out critical aspects of labour quality, such as monitoring the land, and improving soils and crop genetic material. Many authors have drawn attention to complexities of family and clan relations to explain why labour that seemingly is idle is not engaged in agriculture (Mango 2002, Guyer 1988, Berry 1993, 1985). Others point at labour being drawn away from agriculture and into working off the farm as being the result of the drive of rural people to diversify their livelihoods (Bryceson 2002a 2000b, Ellis 2000, Francis 2000, Barrett *et al.* 2001, Reardon 1997).

Although we focus largely on crop production on the arable allotments, these factors are also relevant in explaining the dynamics of home gardening.

## Bio-physical factors

The variation in maize yields and the discontinuities in cropping, as seen in Table 8.4 and Figures 8.1 and 8.2, may be explained by variations in rainfall, and to a limited extent by the changing quality of the soils. In some years it is risky to invest time and money in cropping because of looming crop failure due to limited rainfall. Most narratives we collected saw agriculture as uncertain because of the risk of crop failure and damage. Declining soil fertility, due to erosion, also affects yield, as shown in chapter 5. Agricultural potential in Guquka is further limited by generally unfavourable topography except close to the river, where water logging is a problem. Koloni faces more natural constraints than Guquka, as cropping potential is constrained by lower rainfall, high year-to-year variability in rainfall patterns and groundwater quality. In Koloni the land is agro-ecologically best suited for livestock production and crops have probably always been regarded as a less important livelihood asset than rangeland (chapter 9). The arable lands here serve primarily as a winter forage reserve for livestock, in contrast to Guquka, where arable fields are more often used for cropping. The rainfall at Guquka is sufficiently abundant to enable relatively risk-free production of crops, and its arable land plays a more important role in livestock production than is the case for Koloni (chapter 9).

Yet there are also important anthropogenic factors in the extent to which land users maintain soil fertility and care for the land. The effect of drought and unreliable rainfall has a differentiated effect which can only properly be understood if interlinked with other processes and events. Mr. Ngxobo's account, presented earlier, in this chapter showed how the risk of crop failure, leads villagers to prefer home gardening as production is closer to home and closer to water sources.

## Land and the fixing of tenure rights

The data presented earlier in this and in chapter 6 highlight the dynamics of prevailing land tenure relations: ownership is rather unequal and generally excludes those without land from having an interest in farming. Widespread absentee ownership has, not led to effective sharecropping arrangements.

When the area that includes Guquka and Koloni was first surveyed, quitrent deeds were allocated to the male head of each homestead. This fixing of land rights to men foreclosed potential claims to land by women, who always have supplied most of the labour for crop production (chapter 2). Individual land tenure on a fixed parcel, as laid down in the Glen Grey Act of 1894, was also intended to prevent shifting cultivation, to sedentarise residence and agriculture and control land use. As Moore (2005: 165) argued, "[colonial] administrators saw African landscapes through the prism of 'communal tenure', both a way of seeing and a way of administering".

The size of the arable allotment allocated to each homestead – 3 to 4 *morgen* – was intended to push rural labour into labour migrancy but also to maintain rural ties. The concept of "one-man-one-plot" can be traced back to the Glen Grey Act (chapter 2, Switzer 1993, Yawitch 1982, Mills and Wilson 1952) which allocated each household a residential site and an arable field. This principle stipulated that land allocated to black people would consist of a finite number of indivisible plots that could only be inherited by the eldest son. The plots were too small to enable the homestead to build a livelihood on the basis of agriculture alone. This dual spatial fixing of labour in rural and urban places implied that productive labour was siphoned off to support urban productivity. This in turn prevented possibilities for autonomous agricultural development and improvement from within, as occurred within Europe (Slicher van Bath 1963). This development failure occurred despite early revenues from migrant labour being invested in crop production and livestock (chapter 4). This input gradually declined, leading to the current situation in which crop production is of only marginal importance in rural livelihoods (see also chapters 12 and 13).

Moreover, private land tenure fixed the rights of access to individuals and their families and prevented use by others. It thus perpetuated the situation that land is left fallow even though others without access to land may wish to engage in crop production.

Except for a limited land market there is no other institution at the village level to govern the allocation of land Since 1994, the status of quitrent tenure has remained unchanged (chapter 6), and this has till now foreclosed the possibility to reallocate unused land to landless villagers. Absentee owners and fallow land remain as continuous and interlocked phenomena. Failure by land owners to adapt the sharecropping institution so as to ensure a better economic balance between the two parties, or to replace it with a more appropriate institution for land exchange is one reason why so little arable land in Guquka is under cultivation. In addition the strongest demand for land, particularly in Koloni (chapters 4 and 6) has been for residential purposes. Since this demand came almost solely from the descendants of existing Koloni residents, the transformation of parts of the rangeland into a new residential area was not contested.

## The agricultural labour process

People's capacity to plough is influenced by the interplay between land, labour and cash, which manifests in different ways both within and between Guquka and Koloni. Chapter 4 presented oral evidence showing how, from the early days of settlement until the late 1940s, the fields in Guquka were not enclosed. Chief Mqalo's expression that the "boys acted as fences to protect the crops from cattle" explains how cattle and crops were kept separate by the use of available labour. Although children did go to school, attendance was adapted to accommodate other duties; e.g. brothers would attend school on alternate days. When the migration of labour became more common, the money earnt was invested in agriculture. Elderly villagers explain that in the early period of migration, the continuity of arable production relied heavily on migrant incomes. The extent to which arable fields were left fallow – oral accounts roughly point at the 1930s as a turning point for Guquka and the 1950s for Koloni around the 1950s (Van Averbeke *et al.* 1998a, Hebinck and Smith 2001, Bennett 2002) – is evidence of a rupture in the link between migration and arable farming. Chapter 13 explains this process in more detail, exploring attempts of some individuals to start growing crops on arable allotments.

*Labour and implements for arable farming*
Talking about the present situation Chief Mqalo stated his view that the lack of implements inhibited farming. He thinks it would be logical for people to take up agriculture again if not for this problem.

> But the problem is that people lack material such as tractors and fencing. Those that do have a tractor charge exorbitant prices of up to seventy Rand per acre. Only very few can afford this. [In the past] … the villages used to get support from the Ciskei government. At least 50 tractors were available to the villages, and were supplied at government [heavily subsidised] prices, and there were extension officers, who lived here. In the 1980s the military regime of Brigadier Gozo took away all such equipment and sold it. This was a severe blow that impoverished the rural communities. The current government says villagers should try and organise such infrastructure within their communities.

Mr. Ngxowa at Koloni subscribes to this opinion and attributes the decline in arable production by most homesteads to a loss of access to traction, especially that of oxen. According to another informant, the inability to plough is the major limiting factor to re-establishing crop production:

> For tractors and seeds you could need up to one thousand Rand. Now that the government does not support the control of livestock diseases with a dipping programme, our cattle numbers have greatly declined. At present only the rich; those who have other jobs as well, or have inherited wealth from their fathers, have cattle and can plough their lands. There is no one here in Koloni who has cattle [oxen] but does not plough.

Hence many have come to rely on tractors for ploughing their fields, also because this was encouraged with subsidies by the then Ciskei homeland government. When these ended those with an interest in arable production were suddenly left with few feasible alternatives to plough their fields.

There is a stark contrast between the past, when the government supported agriculture in Koloni and set the village up as one of its pilot villages for betterment planning and the present situation where there minimal assistance is provided. Ngxowa:

> They [the current government] do not give anything. Before we had projects to stop soil erosion, breed bulls and sheep, and have these dipped against diseases, and we got assistance with our crop production. This was all done by the old government. The present one says that it has no money. When I go to the Agricultural Office in Middledrift the extension officers there say they cannot do anything.

Another respondent complained bitterly about the disinterest from government. He pointed out that that without some material support from the government, such as tractors, "agriculture in the village is dead". This resentment also resonates in the overview by Perret and L'Hopitallier (2000) of the state of affairs in service delivery (including agricultural extension) in the Amatola region. Another informant added that:

> If the government were share the cost fifty-fifty, then a lot of people would come forward. If the government provided tractors and we provided the labour and the seed, and we could share the produce, a lot of young people, like myself, would be eager to become involved on the land of our parents.

Mengezelei Mbangi offered two reasons why field-scale production was no longer an option for him (Van Averbeke 2005). Apart from not having formal access to a field, the absence of a regular income prevents him from investing in production related activities. He did not see sharecropping as an alternative (for reasons that were explained in chapter 6).

The commonly shared opinion is that those homesteads that plough and cultivate already have a degree of wealth and income. The Babalwa Grootbooi homestead find it has become financially difficult to plough their arable lands as the education of their children (plus two children in primary school), and other needs absorb most of the income earned by Mr. Grootbooi, who works as a security guard in Alice. Mrs. Grootbooi:

> You need a lot of money to hire a tractor and plant your fields. You spend seven hundred Rand or more just to plough the land. And then you still have to get the seeds. This can be three hundred Rand for pumpkin, maize and bean seeds. With four *morgen* ploughed you can form a company with others through [share] cropping. However this has become difficult because people have started to buy groceries instead of cropping the land. These groceries have become so expensive that very little is left for other purposes.

*Livestock-crop interactions*

As hinted in the previous sections livestock crop interactions are important. (Williams *et al.* 2000). Cattle both provide draught power and also recycle nutrients (manure). Boserup (1981) has shown that the introduction of new implements like oxen drawn ploughs provided the opportunity to open up larger fields for cultivation. The transformation from oxen ploughs to tractors had a similar effect (Lewis 1984, McAllister 2001, Andrew 1992) but, as accounts from Guquka and Koloni clearly show, this also disconnected crop production from livestock. This trend is clearly visible in Koloni where livestock, cattle in particular, dominate agriculture. In contrast, in Guquka ploughing is much more frequently done with oxen. When implements and draught power are not widely available this impacts negatively on the ability to plough fields. A specific feature of South Africa is that recurrent conditions of drought, combined with culling of herds (e.g. during and after betterment planning) had a significant impact on cropping. Animal draught power has only ever been partly replaced by tractors, and overall this has reduced peoples' ability to plough their fields. The withdrawal of government support to tractor schemes and the lack of available cash to hire draught (and labour) power, have led fields remaining unused or only partly cultivated.

Some feel concern and insecurity about crop production due to possibilities of theft or damage from roaming livestock especially, in the latter case, as many fields are not individually fenced. Incomes are often not sufficiently secure to allow for continuous investment in crop production. Questions of access to arable allotments and insufficient command over the monetary resources required to invest in agriculture, explain why cultivation is often irregular, occurring some years, while fields are left fallow in others. People would like to crop their fields but find the costs involved in doing so are prohibitive. Mr. Mashudu underlines this point:

> Until last year [i.e. 1999] I cropped my lands, but the fields are not well protected anymore; there are many holes in the fence around my lands through which all sorts

of stock can enter and damage my crops. So now I have stopped. Once I have fenced off an area on my lands I can take up growing my crops again.

He had always hired a tractor to plough his fields. He regards this as more suitable than using a span of oxen. He would have to invest in oxen because he has none anymore and to do this he would need to get a loan which, with high interest rates, would be too risky. Mr. Lungelo adds another dimension to the explanation as he refers to pooling labour.

In the past, say up to the 1960s, it used to be normal for three gentlemen to stay together as a company. One of these might not have oxen. Of the other two one might only have one or two oxen to add to the six-span. At that time we were used to the idea of being sent by our parents to help a certain gentlemen who had oxen to help him with the ploughing of his fields. When we had finished with this then he would think of our parents and help us by ploughing (a part of) our fields. At the time you would also find that the people were busy with their fields. At the time of hoeing you would not be able to find anyone at the homestead; everybody would be on the lands, either on their own lands or in the company of those with bigger pieces of land. In these times things no longer work this way. There is no great sharing anymore.

In the past arrangements such as a 'company' made it easier to get land ploughed. The absence of these arrangements clearly makes things more difficult. Attempts to revive such arrangements have been made but were rather unsuccessful. An attempt in the early 1980s in Guquka to set up a communal small-scale irrigation scheme on some of the arable fields near the Tyume River did not work out because the ingredient for success ("… the people involved must form a company") failed. In another case in September 1999, some Koloni villagers became involved in a 'tractor scheme'. Each put in some money in relation to the amount of land that would be ploughed by a private tractor company. However, the tractor only arrived in January which was too late for rain-fed crop production of any kind. Although this attempt failed this time, it does indicate the interest in agriculture still held by some Koloni villagers.

Chapter 4 showed that betterment planning led to compulsory culling of live-stock and how this led to a more permanent decline of animal husbandry, parti-cularly in Guquka. What is evident here is that this in turn negatively effected crop production.

In Guquka, the decline of animal husbandry is strongly related to the worsening economic conditions and the decline of crop production throughout the village. This decline was accelerated by recurrent droughts. One of the older informants remembered this and how those who managed to rebuild their herd had access to resources:

In the late seventies ... the drought of that time dried the world, people would tell you your cow is dying here, another was dying over there ... It was a bad time, only

a few cattle survived the drought. The drought affected most people in Guquka –
even now it is very hard to still have a crop or a herd. Those that now have herds
bought them. They had savings or children who still earn money.

Obviously droughts had occurred before, but then the villagers could rely
upon the higher, wetter, higher grazing lands of the Amatola mountain range
which they previously had access to. One informant put it as follows:

> Our cattle used to be on top there on the mountain in the summer season. When you
> see those cattle you could compare them to those [commercial] farm cattle; fit and
> tough. Since the government took away those lands at the top of the mountain in
> 1960 the power of this institution, the community of Guquka, has been in decline.
> Since then we have become used to the cattle eating the grass around us here ... this
> grass is bitter compared to the sweet grass of the hills.

### Age, pension and cropping

Old age pensions also influence patterns of crop cultivation, and particular that
of irregular cropping. Receipt of an old age pension triggers different responses
among different people. Some use their pensions as a resource to invest in cropping; for others the pension removes the incentive to engage in crop production.
Two short cases aptly illustrate both processes.

Mr. Mandeya is a pensioner who farms once in a while. He once said that
"you must not depend only on  the money from your pension, our lives must
come from the soil". Both Mr. and Mrs. Mandeya now get old-age pensions.
Yet he claims that these do not provide sufficient income. Investing in agriculture enables them to expand their income. Their ability to maintain crop
production is related to the means and assets that are available to them. He
acknowledges and that it is not always possible for others in the village to cultivate their fields. He is relatively privileged in having two arable fields of his
own, having access to fields belonging to other family members, possessing a
tractor (the only one in Koloni), and being able to sustain and employ his sons
in his agricultural activities. His assets are not the only issue: an interest in
agriculture is of equal importance. In Mr. Mandeya's eyes there are always
financial way and means to organise getting one's land ploughed. "If people do
not attempt to find such solutions it can only mean that they are either lazy or
not really interested".

Mr. Mandeya explained that "when he was more powerful" he would also
hire fields of others, sharecropping these at a 50/50 split. Presently he limits his
production to his own fields and those of his closest family. Previously, he even
hired labourers from the village to plough the soil and harvest the crops. In 1992
he bought his tractor second hand and owns it to this day. It provides some
supplementary income from ploughing the fields of others in the village,
although this year he had to limit its use because it required some repairs. The
tractor has reduced the need for additional labour which can be provided from

within the family. "I am old now, I do not need additional fields anymore. My own fields produce enough for our present needs".

Mr. Neku's case shows how people may gradually invest in cultivating crops. He arrived in Koloni in 1985 as, he said himself 'a pauper'. He was born, like his brothers, in Soweto, after his parents left Koloni, somewhere between 1925 and 1929, to find jobs in the Johannesburg area. His mother worked in a clinic and his father worked for a labour recruiting agency as a clerk. When his father died in 1959, his mother decided to return to Koloni. His father built a house in Koloni just before he died as he wanted to return to the village. This is where Neku now lives.

From 1956 to 1985 he worked in various jobs. "Slowly my life went down, as I was put into jail during the Ninety Days – no trial times on various occasions". His mother returned to Johannesburg to look after his house there while he was in jail. She never returned to Koloni and died in 1976. Ten years later Mr. Neku, a poor man, returned to Koloni and remained there since. Until the end of 1999, when he got his pension for the first time, he depended on casual jobs in the village, working in other people's gardens or assisting with harvesting fields which earned him a meal, some money or part of the produce. Over the years he gradually extended his own cultivation in the yard of his own house and on the neighbouring plot that belonged to his eldest brother, who died and never used it. The produce from this he also exchanged for other crops with neighbours. In the future he anticipates that he can extend his production onto the two arable fields he owns, which were only under production for a few years in the mid 1990s when they were sharecropped by a fellow villager. But this requires him to invest in a plough and oxen and to get labour assistance. At the same time, because of his pension the *need* to extend his arable production has lessened.

## Caring for land and soil fertility replenishment

A key aspect of farming is the degree to which soils are maintained and improved. Chapter 5 and 7 discussed soil erosion and degradation. The interplay between land and labour in Guquka and Koloni is such that the land has not been closely watched and monitored, as productive labour is away from the fields most of the time. Moreover, most of those engaged in arable farming are old and mostly obtain their income from pensions and/or remittances. Some of those who cultivate crops combine this with working elsewhere.

The quality of labour, including knowledge of soil fertility and how to replenish nutrients, cannot be ignored and is a key factor in explaining why arable production is not what was 50 or 60 years ago. Information presented in chapters 3 and 5 suggests that nearly half the area of the arable fields is no longer suitable for crop production in part due to soil erosion, which has been identified as a problem in both villages (Chapter 5 and 7). This is a wider problem in most regions of the Eastern Cape and elsewhere in South Africa

(Hoffman *et al.* 1999, 2000, Mills and Fey 2003). Lack of erosion control measures, often combined with poor soil structure, means that soil quality is still declining.

Field studies on the quality and quantity of manure in Guquka and Koloni point to an under-utilisation of *kraal* manure (Thys 1999, Ngwadla and Thys 2000). In addition the available manure cannot supply enough nutrients (N-P-K) to fully meet crop production needs. Ngwadla and Thys (2000) suggest mixing *kraal* manure with chemical fertilisers may provide a solution for fertility replenishment requires and reduce the monetary costs involved with maintaining soil fertility solely by purchasing fertilisers. Giller *et al.* (2006) arrived at a rather similar conclusion based on his work in Zimbabwe but is cautious about not overestimating the quality of available manure.

There several problems associated with use of *kraal* manure, one of which as most farmers point is that of excessive weeds. Transport is another common bottleneck, because manure is rather bulky and the distance between the *kraal* and the arable allotments is generally large. Transport and labour costs are perhaps the most important reasons why *kraal* manure is mostly used in the home gardens leading to situations whereby fields further away from the homestead often do not receive additional nutrients. Mr. Mashudu, acknowledged the declining productivity due to continuous cultivation, and said that

> ... you need to put manure on the fields again. At the moment I can't afford this, as I would have to get this manure from someone with a flock and they charge fifty Rand per load. For my four *morgen* I would require about fifteen loads ... and I would need to hire the tractor to move them to my lands.

Mbuti (2000a) pointed out that the majority of those that cultivate their arable allotments did not perceive the need for, or importance of, replenishing the nutrients extracted from the soil. Ngwadla and Thys (2000) suggested that farmers may not know how much to apply and that there is always a fear of burning the crops through over-application of nitrogenous fertilisers, especially under dry land conditions. Furthermore, many cultivators do not recognise the importance of maintaining levels of soil organic matter, if soil structures and productivity are to be sustained and improved (ARDRI 1983). The organic content of these soils is low; Mbuti (2000a) estimated that up to 70% of the crop residues were removed by livestock and this is only partly compensated for by manure added by the livestock when in the fields.

## Youth and rural livelihood transformations

One of the major conclusions of chapters 2 and 4 is that agriculture, broadly defined, played a much larger role in rural livelihoods in the Eastern Cape in the past than it does today. This is not limited to the Eastern Cape or South Africa only, but is a rather global phenomenon. However, not every 'structural' shift in livelihoods translates so clearly into under-cultivation as they appear to have done in South Africa, and particularly in the Transkei and Ciskei regions. Shifts in livelihoods resulted in less continuity of attention being paid to growing crops. Not all villagers see agriculture as an activity that is worth investing in. Instead of producing food and selling agricultural produce for a living, some prefer to purchase their maize and vegetables and to rely on other sources of income, such as pensions and social grants, remittances and labour migrancy, for their livelihood. Together state transfers and remittances now constitute by far the most important sources of income. The magnitude of the shift from land-based to non-land-based activities will be discussed in much greater detail in chapters 12 and 13.

Older informants asserted that arable production has suffered particularly from the change in the amount of education that young people receive and the migration of youths in search of work immediately after. Men have increasingly showed more interest in migrant labour, and had less interest in arable farming when they return to the village. Changes in the amount of education received translate directly into boys' participation in labour migration immediately after passing their final year. When they leave their village straight after schooling they do not gain much in the way of farming experience. Upon returning to the village, after many years, sometimes decades, of absence they would sometimes find themselves unable to practise crop farming as the necessary knowledge had never been passed on to them by elder members of the homestead. A village elder explained:

> … often their father would be much older than their mother and might die when the sons were still young. Passing on the knowledge of how to plough the fields and cultivate crops would then be the responsibility of an uncle or other family member to impress upon the sons. However at present this is no longer done because the uncles have become selfish, and are no longer interested in enabling the young men of the village to crop.

Some young people have come back to the villages and others never left because employment opportunities in urban areas have declined so much. These youth, as the survey data of 1997 showed, and discussions with the youngsters confirmed, largely depend on the incomes derived from the pensions of elderly family members and some remittances from more successful members of the homestead. However, this income is not sufficient to enable them to engage in arable production on the fields because the monetary expenses of hiring a tractor are too high. This demonstrates the relationship that exists between asset holding (especially traction, in stock or mechanised form) and the level of income or wealth of the homestead to engage or continue crop farming.

Evidence suggests that pensioners often play the most active role in con-tinuing or re-initiating agriculture. However these pensioners also find it very difficult to sustain crop production when their 'income' is also needed to sup-port the homestead (see chapter 11).

Education, labour migration and exposure to urban live styles have all contributed to a shift in life styles that do not greatly value agriculture. The 'red' and 'school' notions reflect this shift in life style (see chapter 2) and the literature (Ranger 1978, Bank 2002, Moore 2005) elaborates on the relationship between agriculture and education. When interviewed in 1998, Mr. Vuyanii, the agricultural extension officer of the Middledrift District, gave considerable weight in his explanation to a tendency he identified among 'mission' villages. He pointed out that the villagers are subjected to an alienating form of education which devalues agrarian labour (Van Averbeke *et al.* 1998a: 17). This is also alluded to by residents; they see education as one of several important factors that alienate the young from farming. Others include the desire for a cash income, the attractions of city life and the high risks associated with farming. An older informant, Mr Sango from Koloni, asserted that

> … while it may seem that the young people of this village are lazy; this could be because they have plans for opportunities elsewhere. They do not have interest in minding and caring for the crops for three months before they can get something from them.

The youth we spoke to over the years did not totally disagree with such analysis. Chapters 11 explores this issue in more detail including the trends for some to stay in town for a long time and to return when older and retired; while others decided to relocate permanently.

## Conclusion

In this chapter we have focussed on crop production from a perspective of seeking to understand what the people in the villages actually do with their resources; that is how and whether various 'agrarian' resources become inter-linked (chapter 1). We did this by zooming on issues and processes related to labour, the objects of labour (land, nutrients, seeds) and the instruments of labour (tractor and oxen ploughs, tools). This provides a rather detailed picture of the labour process and its outcomes. Methodologically, we have made use of a range of local accounts collected during many years of fieldwork. Situating these in the wider literature on agrarian change in Africa has assisted us in contextualising and ordering of the accounts. Not all these accounts point in the same direction which is evidence of the fact that agriculture and crop production is understood differently, has different meanings to people and performs multiple roles in people's livelihoods.

In this chapter we have shown that crop production varies greatly among fields, land owners and between years. On arable allotments, the predominant trend is for land to be left fallow, pointing at under-cultivation. This is a clear discontinuity compared with some 100 years ago (chapter 4). However, a few fields are continuously cropped and a larger number are cropped either partially or irregularly. The core argument in our analysis is that the coherence in the interrelationship between the crucial resources that sustain livelihoods based on (field) cropping has lessened and even disappeared over time. The locally specific pattern of landownership, particularly absenteeism, is a key dimension in the explanation. The accounts in this chapter also drew attention to the interplay between labour, knowledge, cash, control over and access to these key assets and changing life styles. Moreover, the declining condition of the land base also plays a role. Part and parcel of the land quality issue is that labour is being drawn away from the land, agriculture and the rural village, disconnecting land from labour. This leads to situations in which the land is grossly neglected. The same can be concluded for the link between livestock and arable agriculture, which in other places has created conditions for agricultural expansion and yield increases. The beneficial link that once existed between crops and livestock, which provided a source of draught power and nutrients, has largely been replaced by one in which cattle are seen as a nuisance, damaging crops, rather than a resource. The underlying processes of rural livelihood transformations will be substantiated quantitatively and qualitatively in more detail in chapters 12 and 13.

A crucial underlying factor in the process seems to hinge not just whether and how access to resources is guaranteed in terms of rights, but also the source fro which such resources are procured. This is particular relevant for farm inputs such as seeds, nutrients, labour. Are they accessed via the market (and thus regarded as commodities in the production process) or from outside the market sphere (thus appearing as non commodities). Over time, markets have assumed a more important role. However, the accounts of most informants point at a lack of money as limiting their ability to plough. This is in stark contrast to the past when migrant incomes were used to invest in cropping and livestock. We have also provided ample evidence that cultivation practices often continue to rely on non-commoditised resources: in-kind payment for labour, use of seed from previous harvests and use of *kraal* manure. These are all resources that are produced locally, which are occasionally exchanged among producers.

The accounts of those engaged in crop production activities in gardens and arable allotments demonstrate the importance of social networks for sharing labour and inputs as well as exchanging produce. Sharecropping the land and pooling labour is not common, but do occur. There is evidence that accessing draught power, garden tools and, occasionally manure, through local networks is more common. These are not necessarily kin based networks and can stretch beyond the village *per se*. This in turn underlines the relative economic and social importance of crop production.

Crop improvement has been briefly discussed. The available data suggest that this has occurred and yields may have doubled over the last 20 to 25 years. In some isolated cases yields may have even tripled. We can only speculate about why this has occurred but certainly it has to do with crop breeding programmes that have rendered higher yielding varieties. Also the land that has been left fallow for some time has regenerated itself and when these fields are cultivated again yields will be much higher. Interestingly, those farmers that have been able to crop continuously for the last ten years were those that managed and mastered the resources to achieve such improvements. Land improvements through by manure and sufficient labour to work the land appear crucial. Case material also underlines the importance of taking age into account, particularly old age when people become eligible for a pension. Equally attitudes towards agriculture and willingness to invest in it vary greatly.

Home gardening remains important for most people, particularly compared to crop production on arable fields. They are cultivated mostly for domestic consumption, and have the advantage of lying adjacent to homesteads, being better fenced than arable fields. This makes them easier to maintain, irrigate and to protect against theft and roaming cattle. As with crop production, no gardening year is the same, making it difficult to risk any generalisation of the dynamics of gardening and the contribution that it makes to food security.

This chapter reveals that a quite extensive form of cultivation is maintained, albeit marginally, in the arable allotments, while a more intensive form of agriculture has evolved in the home gardens (pig production, vegetable gardening). In contrast to arable field production, intensive home garden production is possible since it requires substantially less investments of cash and labour. Their closeness to home and the convenience and security this provides is certainly a contributory factor in the shift from arable field production. This has occurred elsewhere both in the Eastern Cape Province and in the country (Andrew and Fox 2003, 2004, Ardington and Lund 1996, McAllister 2001, Shackleton *et al.* 2001, Weiner *et al.* 1997). The magnitudes of production, as well as the shift from arable to garden production, differ, however, if only because home gardens in Guquka and Koloni are substantial smaller compared to Transkei or elsewhere.

Lastly, this chapter has demonstrated, there is some form of continuity in which the remnants of a peasantry can be situated and identified. Bundy (1977/1988) and Lewis (1984) claimed that peasant production predominated in the past and was destroyed over the years by state intervention, colonialism, Apartheid and labour migration (chapter 2). Despite a dramatic and evident decline in crop production over the years and the predominant image of fallow land, we believe that a peasantry, perhaps dormant, continues to exist in Guquka and Koloni.

9

# Livestock production and forage resources

James Bennett and Peter C. Lent

## Introduction

In the central region of the Eastern Cape Province rangelands play a vital role in sustaining rural livelihoods (Cousins 1999, Shackleton *et al.* 2001, 2002). Many of these roles have been outlined at a general level for the Eastern Cape in Chapter 2. The vegetation found in the villages of Guquka and Koloni is described in chapter 4. It is the aim of this chapter to document the practices that are specific to the two villages with regard to management of livestock and their forage resources. In order to provide a cohesive picture of livestock and the resources they use we have included information on the use of fallow fields and crop stover in the arable land allotments, even though these do not necessarily meet the conventional definition of rangelands as being an area of land occupied by native herbaceous or shrub vegetation which is utilized by domestic or wild herbivores. On the other hand, we have not dealt with poultry and swine, these being associated principally with home gardens and residential areas. Information for this chapter is drawn in part from doctoral fieldwork undertaken during 1998 and 1999 by Bennett (2002) and subsequent fieldwork in April, 2004.

The chapter begins with a historical overview of livestock (cattle, sheep and goats) numbers as well as current ownership patterns at the community level. It then describes current livestock production arrangements and husbandry practices and compares and contrasts these with what has already been documented for the region. We then describe the rangeland resources and outline livestock foraging patterns, including attention to the arable land allotments and their function in providing a forage reserve for livestock during the dry season. The following chapter (10) deals with the importance of rangelands to people of the two villages for uses other than livestock production, including the collection of timber, firewood, grass for thatching, and edible and medicinal plants.

## Livestock numbers and ownership patterns

*Livestock numbers*

Data on livestock numbers in Guquka and their changes historically are sparse, as livestock censuses in the district have been sporadic and historical records have been destroyed (Vanda 2000). However, data for 1996, show that 230 cattle, 400 sheep and 120 goats were being held at the village (ARDRI Survey 1997).

For Koloni, data on the numbers of cattle, sheep and goats at the village in 1938 and 1961 are available from old planning reports drawn up during the implementation of betterment planning for the village (Bantu Affairs Commission 1962). An overview of livestock ownership at the household level at Guquka and Koloni is available from socio-economic surveys by the Agricultural and Rural Development Research Institute (ARDRI) during 1997 (Van Averbeke *et al.* 1998b, Bennett 2002). The most important statistics at the household level for cattle, sheep and goats are summarised in Table 9.1.

More recent data are also available from census records, maintained by the Middledrift Agricultural Office, gathered when animals from the village were dipped for tick control (Figure 9.1). These records also show that in the 1960s a varying number of horses were also kept at Koloni. No horses have been present there in recent years.

*Table 9.1*     Ownership of cattle, sheep and goats among households at Guquka and Koloni in 1997

|  | Guquka | | | Koloni | | |
|---|---|---|---|---|---|---|
|  | Cattle | Sheep | Goats | Cattle | Sheep | Goats |
| Ownership (% of households) | 33.3 | 14.1 | 14.1 | 55.6 | 33.3 | 40.7 |
| Number of animals (range) | 1-20 | 2-50 | 1-18 | 1-25 | 1-85 | 1-23 |
| Mean number of animals | 6.0 | 19.0 | 5.4 | 9.5 | 21.2 | 8.8 |

*Source*: ARDRI Survey (1997)

It is difficult to say anything conclusive about the trends in livestock numbers at Koloni prior to 1996, as only the two sets of data are available. However, the continuous data set that exists since 1996 provides a strong indication of recent changes in the ownership of cattle, sheep and goats at the village. Despite some short-term fluctuations, cattle numbers at Koloni appear to have remained relatively stable since 1996, in keeping with longer-term patterns of stability within the region (see Table 2.1) and comparable with levels of stability that have been reported at a broader scale in other communal areas such as Kwa-Zulu (Tapson 1993) and Transkei (Beinart 1992). A similar trend is apparent for goat numbers at the village and again is confirmed by longer-term goat ownership data at the regional level (Table 3.2).

The complete absence of goats in the 1938 and 1961 data reflects the prohibition of goat ownership in communal areas of the former Ciskei under the betterment system (Trollope and Coetzee 1975). Indeed, no goats were owned at Koloni until the Bantu Trust, responsible for the enforcement of betterment regulations, dissolved during the early 1970s.

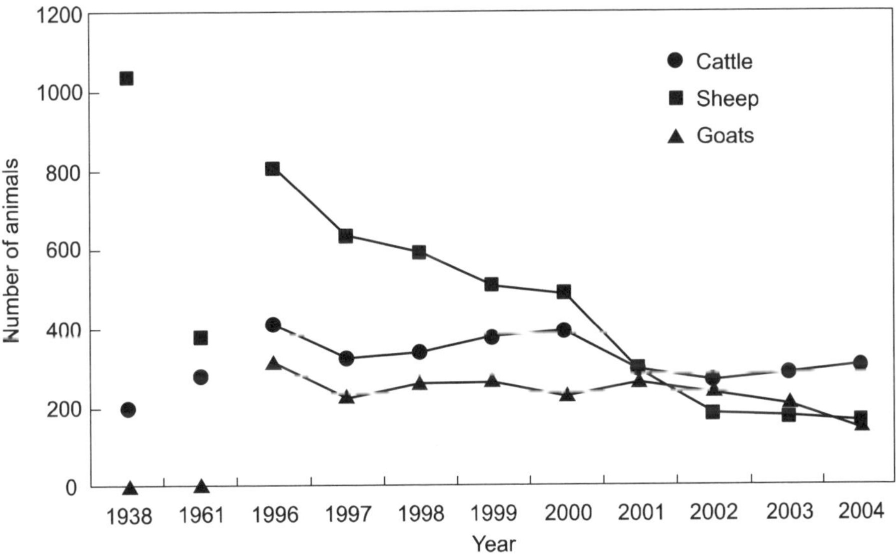


*Figure 9.1*   Historical change in livestock numbers held at Koloni.


*Sources*:
1938: Ndlovu (1991)
1961 Bantu Affairs Commission (1961)
1996 ARDRI (1997)
1997-2004: Middledrift Agricultural Records Office

With regard to Guquka, Hill, Kaplan and Partners (1977) recommended to the Ciskei Government that more goats be encouraged in order to counter the increasing numbers of woody species on the rangelands. They, in effect, sought a reversal of the earlier policy in the Ciskei which prohibited or discouraged goat husbandry.

For sheep the story is quite different. The records from 1938 show that 1,035 animals were held at Koloni at this time. This is an incredibly high figure given that in the same year the village consisted of only 37 homesteads (compared to approximately 108 in 1996 [chapter 7] and 133 in 2004 [chapter 11]) and under-lines the importance of wool as a source of income in villages such as Koloni before the imposition of betterment (Bundy 1988). Under betterment, stocking rates were strictly enforced and excess animals were culled by the authorities (Bantu Affairs Commission 1962). Livestock owners were loathe to lose their cattle, and with goat ownership being prohibited, sheep were inevitably the first animals to be disposed of to reduce livestock numbers. This accounts for the greatly reduced number of sheep at the village in 1961.

Since 1994, there also appears to have been a marked and continued decline in sheep numbers. More than 800 animals were held at the village in 1996, but numbers have declined every year, to just 153 animals in 2004. In 1996, when the data shown in Table 9.1 were collected, 18 out 54 households interviewed (33.3%) held 382 sheep (ARDRI Survey 1997) and the total number of sheep at the village was 633 (Figure 9.1). Assuming that the mean number of animals per household (21.2) was consistent over the whole village, this suggests that the total number of households owning livestock might have been as high as 30. However, by 2004 only 153 sheep remained at the village and only eight sheep owners could be clearly identified. Thus, while the mean number of sheep per household has remained relatively constant, the number of households owning sheep declined dramatically over seven years from somewhere between 18 and 30, to just eight. Given the comparable stability observed in cattle and goat numbers during this period, the precipitous nature of the decline in sheep num-bers appears to reflect an underlying disinterest specifically in sheep ownership. Indeed, this decline in sheep ownership appears to have occurred in other areas of the former Ciskei from about the 1970s onwards (see Table 3.3).

Problems in marketing wool through existing channels and general difficul-ties associated with sheep husbandry are two of the reasons advanced to account for the decreasing numbers (see chapter 3). Both of these would also seem to have been important at Koloni in the longer term. However, theft has apparently become one of the biggest disincentives to sheep ownership. Interviews with key informants in 2004 suggested that the problem had been developing for some time, but had worsened greatly over the past 3-5 years. Indeed, one of the major causes of the sharp decline in sheep numbers between 1996 and 2002 was theft of entire flocks belonging to some owners at the village, followed by others who responded by selling their animals before they also became victims. This is underlined by one elderly livestock farmer at the village:

Mr Xhotyeni is from a family of long standing at Koloni, with an active history of livestock production. When interviewed in April 1998, he had some 70 sheep, one of the largest flocks in the village. However, by the time he was subsequently interviewed in April 2004, this number had plummeted to 11 animals. The main reason identified for this decline was theft. In 1999, he was the victim of two major theft incidents. In the first incident, 25 animals were stolen from the *kraal* he maintained at his father's old homestead. Shortly afterwards he lost 12 animals from the *kraal* adjacent to his own house. The remaining attrition was primarily a result of disease, particularly sheep scab (*imbula*). When interviewed again in 2004, Mr Xhotyeni confirmed that theft had been responsible for the loss of most of his flock.

It appears that Guquka has experienced similar problems and seemingly at an even greater scale, both in terms of the number of victims of theft and the period over which it has been occurring. One elderly widow related that she had recently lost her entire flock of more than 30 sheep to thieves who broke into her *kraal* during the night (interview with Mrs Dibela, April 1999). The problem has not abated. During our fieldwork at the village in April 2004, the former chairman of the village was murdered during the night while trying to protect his flock from thieves. This extreme example emphasises the severity of the problem in some communities. The problem may not be as extreme in other communal areas of Eastern Cape. Vetter (2003) did not highlight this as being a significant problem in the Herschel district, a major area for sheep production.

It is not only small-stock that have been vulnerable to theft in recent years at Guquka. Key informants interviewed in 1999, related that cattle theft had also become problematic (see below, for more details). Whether this has begun to have a negative impact on cattle ownership is difficult to gauge, as data are not available after 1996.

*Livestock ownership patterns and production arrangements*
It is apparent that a far greater proportion (55.6%) of the households in Koloni owned cattle than those at Guquka (33.3%). Fraser (1992) reported a 40% level of cattle ownership in two other areas of the former Ciskei. This suggests that cattle ownership at Guquka is comparable with the rest of the region, but Koloni is somewhat above average. The general order of ownership, cattle being the most commonly owned livestock followed by goats and then sheep, is consistent with findings from other studies (Steyn 1982, Vetter 2003).

Mean herd size among cattle owners at Koloni (9.5) was also greater than that at Guquka (6) and when compared with the average holding of five animals reported by Fraser (1992). Thus data again suggest that mean herd size at Guquka is comparable with other areas in the former Ciskei, but Koloni is somewhat higher than average. These differences have potential livelihood implications. The much greater proportion of households with cattle at Koloni means that a larger sector of the population is likely to benefit. It also suggests that any development initiatives focused on increasing cattle production would have a better chance of yielding tangible and sustainable livelihood improvements at Koloni, than at Guquka, assuming additional or improved range resources.

Levels of ownership of both sheep and goats at Koloni are also considerably higher than Guquka and are comparable with those found in other surveys in the former Ciskei. Fraser (1992) found 39% ownership of sheep among households surveyed in the villages of Majwareni and Roxeni and 47% ownership of goats. Likewise, Ainslie (1998) reported 34% of households owned sheep and 67% had goats in Gwabeni village (Peddie district). This suggests that ownership of small-stock at Guquka is considerably less frequent than in other parts of the region. The underlying reasons for this are discussed below. However, there is relatively little difference with regard to the mean number of small-stock held by households at each village, when compared with other studies from the region. For example, Steyn (1982), working in the Amatola Basin, found average holdings among households that owned stock of 18 sheep and 10 goats, and more recently Ainslie's work at Gwabeni (1998) found mean holdings of 12.3 sheep and 7.6 goats per homestead.

*Photo 9.1*      Cattle grazing in Koloni. (Photo by Ortega)

There are a number of underlying reasons for the differences in livestock ownership patterns at the two villages. Those of a social and historical perspective are dealt with in chapter 4. From an agro-ecological perspective, the two most important are differences in the natural vegetation of the two areas in which the villages are located (chapter 5) and the considerable discrepancy in the level of pressure on grazing resources at each village. The influence of vegetation type on cattle production is attributable to the fact that Guquka lies in an area that is partially *sourveld* with mixed *veld* on the arable lands, whereas Koloni is situated in a *sweetveld* area (see chapters 3 and 5). This distinction has important implications for livestock production as *sweetveld* remains relatively nutritious in the dry season and enables livestock to maintain body condition at this time. In contrast, *sourveld* or mixed *veld* declines in quality during the dry season so that livestock on such *veld* lose body condition and may require supplementation to overcome this (Tainton 1999). The current level of pressure on grazing resources can be attributed to two key factors at each village. The first is the greater level of demand on available grazing resources at Guquka due to these being shared among several communities. The second is the considerably smaller amount of rangeland available to livestock at Guquka compared to Koloni, which is a symptom of both the original allocations and the subsequent changes in land use which have occurred in the area around Guquka (Bennett 2002, see also chapters 4 and 6). When new villages were established, such as that of Kyalethu, adjacent to Guquka, it was deliberate government policy in most cases not to formally allocate communal rangelands for them (Beinart 2003). This policy clearly has contributed to overgrazing and social friction in the area.

As noted earlier, the other important factor which may be depressing the extent of livestock ownership in the two villages is theft. This is particularly true for Guquka and, in addition to the factors outlined above, may account for the differences in ownership of cattle and sheep between the two villages. Sheep appear to have been particularly targeted due to a ready market, ease of transport, and the difficulty in tracing them. It is apparent that theft is a symptom not only of overcrowded and relatively urbanised settlements but is also permeating more remote and historically well-regulated settlements such as Koloni. As noted earlier, the precipitous decrease there is most likely due to a combination of attrition from theft and poor economic returns.

The 1997 survey at the two villages also provided an important indication of gender bias that has existed with regard to livestock holdings. The strength of the association between gender of household head and the ownership of cattle, sheep and goats at each village was tested (Bennett 2002) and mean herd sizes in relation to gender of household head was also examined. These data are summarised in Table 9.2.

*Table 9.2*      Mean size of cattle, sheep and goat holdings among male and female-
             headed households at Guquka and Koloni in 1997

|           | Guquka | | Koloni | |
|-----------|---------|----------|---------|----------|
| Livestock | Male | Female | Male | Female |
| Cattle    | 7 (22)* | 3.8 (4) | 9.9 (21) | 8.8 (10) |
| Sheep     | 23.8 (8) | 3 (2) | 24.5 (14) | 13 (4) |
| Goats     | 5.3 (8) | 5.7 (3) | 7.2 (17) | 11.8 (5) |

* Number of households owning each livestock type shown in brackets.
*Source*: ARDRI Survey (1997)


The results from the villages regarding cattle ownership were quite different. At Guquka, there was a very significant (p<0.01) association between gender and ownership of cattle, in favour of male-headed households. Indeed, some 49% of the male-headed households interviewed owned cattle, compared to just 12% of female-headed households. Furthermore, the mean number of animals (7.0) held by male-headed households was considerably larger than the 3.8 held by households with female heads. This demonstrates how cattle ownership is concentrated almost entirely in male hands and corroborates the widely documented cultural bond between men and cattle in Xhosa society. However, the bare numbers fail to elaborate the intricacies of these relationships and, importantly, how women are often actively deprived of the opportunity to own cattle. Interviews undertaken with female household heads at Guquka in April 1999, suggested that when cattle are inherited by women, most commonly through the death of either their husbands or fathers, the animals are often appropriated by male kin.

This is illustrated by Mrs Maxhila, whose father passed away in 1982 leaving a small herd of three cows and two calves. Because she was the nearest member of kin, (she had no brothers and her mother was already deceased), the cattle were inherited by her. However, given that she was a teacher and her husband a migrant worker, it was impractical for her to look after them. Since the family were fairly recent arrivals at Guquka with no other family members at the village who could take responsibility for their ownership, this was instead taken by an uncle (father's brother) in Amatola. This village is a considerable distance away and thus at a practical level she sees no benefit from the cattle. The uncle is the day-to-day custodian of the animals, taking the milk from them and allowing their offspring to augment his own herd. Indeed, she speculated that he may have sold or slaughtered some of them. Nevertheless, she still harbours the hope that when she retires and her boys are sufficiently grown, she can bring the cattle back to Guquka and allow the boys to inherit them.

This example underlines not only the cultural constraints on cattle ownership by women, but also the practical difficulties associated with maintaining cattle when women are both *de facto* head of household and working to support dependants. Even in situations where cattle are not actively appropriated by relatives, there is often pressure for elderly widows to loan out their animals to male kin or friends, particularly when they live alone, as they are judged to be incapable of looking after them. There were several examples of this occurring at Guquka, although in most situations (apart from where a direct male descendant was present) *de jure* ownership of the animals remained with the widow. Moreover, even when women (usually widows) are the *de jure* owners of cattle and maintain them at their own homestead, they frequently have little jurisdiction over the everyday husbandry of their animals or the authority to take important decisions such as those regarding the sale of cattle.

At Koloni, the situation was quite different, as no significant relationship was apparent between gender of household head and ownership of cattle. The ARDRI survey (1997) showed that approximately 46% of female-headed households, and 64% of male-headed households, owned cattle. Furthermore, the difference in mean herd size by gender was minimal at Koloni (Table 9.2). One possibility for the lack of a male predominance in ownership in this community relates to the relatively large number of widows who had managed to hold on to their cattle following the death of their husbands. This seems to have been facilitated largely by an important difference in the way in which widowed women were perceived within the social structure of the village. They were accorded considerable status, in a way that was not apparent at Guquka, and, even if there were no immediate male kin, arrangements based on mutual consent were often put in place to ensure that livestock could continue to be maintained at the homestead until the widow herself died (see case study with Mrs Nkintsela below).

Nevertheless, even at Koloni cattle ownership was an activity driven by men, and female ownership was associated only with inheritance, following the death of immediate male kin. In this respect, both villages largely corroborate the concept that ownership of cattle and most other livestock is still strongly male-dominated in Xhosa society.

With regard to ownership of sheep, findings were again different between the villages. In Koloni 42% of male-headed households held sheep compared to just 18% of female-headed households, and the gender difference was also reflected in the mean size of sheep flocks. Male-headed households had considerably larger flocks than those held by female-headed households (Table 9.2). These differences were not unexpected, although sheep do not have the same cultural significance as cattle, their ownership and husbandry is generally recognised as being a male pursuit. Differences in sheep ownership by gender at Guquka are less clear-cut due to the small sample size. Only ten households of those interviewed owned sheep and only two of these were headed by females. The greater flock size found among male-headed households at both villages appears to be a widespread feature of sheep ownership in communal areas of the region (Steyn 1982, Vetter 2003).

Data on goat ownership largely parallels that for sheep (Table 9.2). The level of ownership among male-headed households at Koloni was 52% compared to just 23% for female-led households. This compared to 18 and 9%, for male- and female-headed households, respectively, at Guquka. However, mean flock size was actually greater among female-headed households at both villages, with the margin of difference being quite substantial at Koloni. Furthermore, the mean flock size among goats also tended to be greater than with other livestock species. This suggests that female household heads at both villages focus their attention on goat production, rather than cattle or sheep. This is likely to reflect their ease of husbandry compared to other species, given that many of these women are widows. In contrast, Vetter (2003) showed that in Herschel District median holdings for goats were considerably larger for men than for women (27 vs. 8).

The importance of the transfer or lending of cattle and other livestock between individuals (*ukusisa*) in Xhosa society, in the cultivation of loyalty and the development of reciprocal relationships between individuals, is highlighted in chapter 2. *Ukusisa* is also frequently driven by practical considerations. This is exemplified by the fact that in both Guquka and Koloni there were widows who lent their cattle out to close male friends or relatives following the death of their husbands. These arrangements can be viewed as practical responses to the fact that the widows were unable to effectively take care of the animals on a day-to-day basis (Bennett 2002). Such an arrangement is illustrated by the case of Mrs. Nkintsela. She was first interviewed in 1999 and again in April 2004.

Mrs. Nkintsela is a widow of some considerable standing within Koloni. When interviewed in 1999, she had, upon the recent death of her husband, inherited a herd of 22 cattle and access to a fenced field on the arable land allocation. Being unable to look after the cattle herself, she had lent the animals to Mr. Masele, a close friend of her deceased husband. He gained not only through the increased status associated with a larger herd of cattle but also by obtaining milk from the animals, and he allowed the herd to increase in size through natural accretion. In return he ensured the well-being of the cattle and used them to plough Mrs. Nkintsela's field, providing her with a share of the resulting maize crop.

When interviewed again in 2004, things had changed substantially. Mr. Masele had passed away in 2002, and thus the original *ukusisa* arrangement was now redundant. In its place a new arrangement had been formalised with the son of another family friend, Mr. T. Mujani. He also looked after the cattle and goats belonging to Mrs. N. and undertook this largely as a favour, although he did receive milk from the animals in the summer months. However, he did not engage in the production of crops from Mrs. Nkintsela's field. The impression was that the situation was now less secure than in 1999, as she was living with her daughters, neither of whom were working, and thus the only regular income was her old age pension. She had sold several head in recent years to raise additional cash, and only 16 remained of the original 22.

This case demonstrates the difficulties female-headed households face in attempting to look after livestock, particularly cattle, in the absence of immediate male kin. In spite of this, female households are able to engage in a variety of reciprocal arrangements with male friends that allow them to overcome this. In communities such as Koloni, there appears to be an element of goodwill and sense of duty in putting these arrangements in place to ensure the continued well-being of widows following the death of their husbands. The importance of these relationships is underlined by the security these livestock can provide in generating income at the household level as and when required.

*Livestock turnover and output*
At both villages livestock off take (excluding losses of small stock to predators and thieves) was primarily by home slaughter for ceremonial purposes and through sale to generate income. Cattle and goats were the two species primarily involved in ceremonial slaughter. Cattle in particular seem to play an important role in ceremonies involving funerals and remembrance of the dead. At Guquka, for example, two key informants mentioned that they recently had lost their fathers. In the first case a single oxen was slaughtered as part of the funeral ceremony and in the other case two animals were used. In the second case, great care was taken to ensure that the animals were adequately fattened before slaughter in order to create the right impression. Subsequently, in both cases, a further two oxen were slaughtered on the first anniversary of the funeral in typical Xhosa tradition, one to symbolise the outward journey and the other to represent the passage back.

These cases serve not only to underline the continued strength of traditional rituals in villages such as Guquka but also demonstrate the burden they put on households with respect to loss of productive cattle or the need to buy them if a household has none of its own. In both these cases this burden was lessened by the fact that several head of cattle had been inherited from their deceased fathers. Interestingly, one key informant emphasised that although oxen are slaughtered for the funeral of a man, for women it is customary to slaughter cows. Cattle may also be slaughtered periodically in remembrance of ancestors. The importance of cattle in ceremony was emphasised by one individual at Guquka, who despite having 35 head of cattle only used them for traditional purposes and never sold any animals. This was, however, unusual as all other respondents testified that they sold cattle on a fairly regular basis, as underlined by the following story from Koloni.

Mr Ngcaka is from a family who has a history of considerable livestock involvement at the village. His father was the owner of the local shop and invested much of his money in livestock, owning some 48 cattle and 170 sheep. Currently, his holding of cattle has been reduced to 24 animals but is still among the largest at the village. He both sells and buys cattle on a fairly regular basis. In 2003 he sold 3 animals to a local *stokvel* (local formal market outlet) about 2 km from the village because they were considered to be old and unproductive. They consisted of one ox, which fetched R3000, and two cows, which fetched R2400 and R2200. Of R7600 earned, R6000 was spent on buying three heifers as replacement animals, R1000 was saved and R600 was spent on medicine for his animals. The heifers were of the Bonsmara breed and were bought from a shop-owner. Mr Ngcaka prefers to buy from this man as believes the animals he gets are strong and fecund. The breeds of cattle within his herd include two Jersey cows, a shorthorn cow and a Bonsmara/Afrikaner bull cross and others of indeterminate, mixed breed.

That the majority of animals within this herd were of mixed breed is not surprising given the lack of control over mating in communal management systems. This is in keeping with the general situation in the former Ciskei (chapter 3). Furthermore, the preference expressed by Mr Ngcaka for purchasing Bonsmara heifers due to their hardiness and productivity is important. These animals are crosses between European breeds and indigenous Nguni stock and their preferential purchase may represent a natural gravitation away from often unsuitable European types that were mooted under so-called 'improvement' schemes, over more hardy animals of *Bos indicus* origin, which are better suited to local conditions.

The cattle that were sold at the *stockvel* (which, in the case of Koloni, is at the nearby agricultural training centre) were identified as being old and relatively unproductive, but were sold while they were still capable of fetching a reasonable price and most of the money realised was reinvested to help to increase the productive potential of the herd. This practice was identified among several other livestock owners, particularly at Koloni, demonstrating that some cattle-owners actively manage their herds through sales in order to maintain productivity, rather than simply selling animals because they need to raise cash urgently. The practice has also been documented in the Peddie District (Ainslie 2002). Thus several owners at Koloni demonstrated a genuine interest in managing cattle to provide a regular income stream, albeit on a small scale.

Although individuals from both villages made regular use of *stokvels* for cattle sales, there was a general perception among all respondents that selling locally to other village residents was better business as higher prices could be realised. If people urgently required a cow or ox for a funeral then they could generally be forced to pay above average prices for the animal. According to one individual from Koloni there were two reasons for this. First, the *stokvels* tended to be frequented by individuals looking for cheap animals. This was particularly true of white farmers (speculators), who turned up from as far away as East London and Stutterheim looking for cheap cattle and were only prepared to offer low prices. The second was that the man who organised the events received a commission of R20 per animal sold. This broadly negative opinion about selling cattle to the *stokvel* and preference for selling locally appears to be widespread in communal areas of the former Ciskei, as Ainslie (2002) ascribed the reticence of cattle owners in the nearby Peddie District to sell to the local *stokvel* to much the same reasons. However, it is clear that cattle owners, particularly at Koloni, do continue to sell at the local *stokvel* as it provides a guaranteed way of turning animals into cash at relatively short notice.

Several owners from both villages milked cows when they were able to (mainly during the summer months). Estimates provided by key informants of milk yield per cow were similar at both villages, ranging between 1 to 1.5 litres/animal/day. These yields are very low, even by standards of extensive systems, but nevertheless are comparable with those from other communal areas of South Africa (Bembridge 1984, cited in Vetter 2003). According to ARDRI's survey of 1997, at Koloni, 16 out of the 30 households that owned cattle regularly collected milk from their animals. In contrast at Guquka, just 5 of the 26 cattle-owning households regularly engaged in milk collection. Furthermore, the frequency of collection at Koloni was considerably higher than at Guquka, ranging between once per week to every day throughout the year, with the majority of informants estimating that they collected milk on a daily basis for about 8 months of the year. The estimated mean number of times animals were milked each year at Koloni was 205. At Guquka, by contrast, few individuals reported being able to collect milk for more than 6 months of the year, and the overall mean frequency of milk collection was only 137 occasions. This difference in output can be related to the quality of the rangeland resources at each village. The fundamental advantage of *sweetveld* over mixed or *sourveld* rangeland in maintaining productivity for a greater portion of the year would explain why the major difference in milk output was not the output per animal/day, but the number of days over which milk could be collected.

Cattle were also used as draught animals for crop production, although this tended to be far more widespread at Koloni, again presumably related to the underlying difference in the quality of the natural forage. Koloni as a *sweetveld* site maintains better forage quality than Guquka, and this means that the oxen are able to maintain their body condition throughout most of the dry season and are available for ploughing when the first rains of the wet season arrive. At Guquka, by contrast, oxen take several weeks after the onset of the rains to recover their condition sufficiently to plough. For this reason, few livestock owners even make the effort to maintain oxen at Guquka. Indeed, during 1998, individuals were observed ploughing with donkeys due to lack of suitable oxen. The source of these donkeys and their numbers is unknown.

Informants in both villages emphasized the importance of goats in traditional ceremonies. All respondents related that they only kept goats for use during traditional feasts or to be sold for such occasions. Goats seemed to be particularly important in ceremonies associated with remembrance of the ancestors and in feasts conducted at Christmas time to honour those boys who had made the passage to manhood following circumcision.

A key informant whom was interviewed in April 2004 at Koloni related that the price of goats sold locally within the village is determined primarily by age and gender of the animal. A fully-grown castrated male goat sold for R600. This is supported by the findings of Mafu and Masika (2002) who reported that the price of castrates in Nkonkobe ranged between R150 and R700, depending on age of the animal. The price at Koloni seems to be determined by the number of teeth (an indication of maturity), with the best prices being fetched by those with eight molar teeth in each jaw. Female goats of similar maturity brought R400, while uncastrated males are kept for reproductive purposes and not sold. No informants from either village mentioned obtaining milk from goats, although this is not uncommon in other areas of the province (Mafu and Masika 2002).

Sheep turnover follows a similar pattern to goats, except that they are not associated with ceremonies to the same extent and therefore tend to be sold throughout the year. The same key informant from Koloni related that price is determined primarily by maturity and that castrated males are most commonly sold. Maturity is again measured by number of teeth. Smaller animals with just six teeth in each jaw generally fetched as little as R300, whereas mature animals with eight teeth could realise as much as R400. This informant looked after a flock of about 65 animals on behalf of his uncle, and during the course of the previous year they had sold nine animals, all castrated males, for between R300 and R400 each. These were used mainly for slaughter over the Christmas period, but two had been sold for funerals. It appears that demand for sheep remains high despite (and possibly because of) the general decline in ownership in the region and suggests that a guaranteed market exists for those livestock owners who can continue to maintain flocks of reasonable size.

Owners in Koloni concurred that there was also a high rate of turnover in their herds due to death. This was attributed to diseases such as gall sickness (*imyongo*), which have ravaged the flocks at the village in recent years to the extent that some owners do not have enough animals to sell on a regular basis. When an animal dies, the diseased part is identified and cut out, and the remainder of the animal is used for home consumption.

The current situation regarding wool sales at Guquka is documented in an interview with Mr Fumbata in April 2004. At Guquka there are approximately nine livestock owners involved in the sale of wool, of whom four sell regularly. In recent years there has been no formal mechanism for the sale of wool locally, so it has tended to be sold on an informal basis to white speculators (local farmers), who always offer low prices. Indeed, a flat rate of just R70 had been offered by the speculators during previous shearing periods, to all wool producers in the village, regardless of their output. Most owners (particularly those with limited output) have taken up this offer but some such as Mr Funjiwa felt cheated. He had 49 sheep, producing about a full bale of wool. Such an amount should be worth several hundred Rand at market prices. In September 2003, the situation looked as though it might improve when officials from the Eastern Cape Department of Agriculture appeared during shearing time promising help with sorting the wool into different qualities and its eventual sale at market prices. Buoyed by this news he did not sell to the speculators when they made their annual spring visit. Unfortunately, he later wished he had as there has been no sign of the staff from the Department of Agriculture for over six months and he was now left with a load of wool he cannot market.

This underlines how vulnerable small-scale wool producers are to roving speculators because of the lack of opportunities to sell wool locally. It also emphasises the failure of the regional agricultural personnel to organise such avenues on behalf of local wool producers.

In contrast, a good example of group initiative to create an avenue for wool sales is provided by wool producers at Koloni as described in an interview in April 2004. There are eight sheep owners at Koloni who sell their wool. Of these, seven have their own group arrangement for the sale of the wool they produce. Once all shearing is completed in springtime, they take the wool in bags on the local bus to a wool dealer in King William's Town, about 40 km away. The dealer sorts the wool into high and low quality, and although the prices they obtain are relatively low, they are far better than would be achieved by selling locally to passing white farmers. These speculators do visit the village periodically but are given short shrift by the livestock owners, who are well aware that they will try and cheat them.

A rather different approach to wool sales has been taken by Mr Mcete, who is the largest livestock owner in the village. Mr Mcete works for the government and has good connections with individuals from the provincial Department of Agriculture. He has sufficient numbers of sheep to arrange for his wool to be marketed through government channels. He has been able to arrange for a departmental van to come to Koloni from the district agricultural office in Middledrift and the wool has been sorted by departmental officers, at his house, into fleece of good and bad quality and later driven through to the major provincial wool dealership in the city of Port Elizabeth about 300 km away. There it has then been sold straight to the major wool dealers, allowing the middlemen to be cut out, and realizing the highest possible price.

Thus most livestock owners at Koloni worked at a group level to arrange a realistic market for their wool and avoid sales to local speculators. Prices achieved by key informants for their full wool clip varied between R168 (from 16 animals) to R180 (from 11 animals) which,although less than would have been realised at wholesale rates, are still far better than the R70 flat rate offered by speculators at Guquka. The case of Mr. Mcete clearly demonstrates the advantage of individual connections within government. The possibility of extending these arrangements from a private to a community level must also be worth investigating as one possible avenue for further increasing revenue from wool sales.

*Livestock husbandry*
Despite findings to the contrary from other locales (e.g. Brown *et al.* 1975, Bembridge 1979), owners at both villages were found to be diligent in their maintenance and husbandry of all three of the key livestock species. Husbandry of cattle is particularly rigorous. Although there is no control over cattle mating

at either village the number of bulls in the village herds is quite closely regulated. This is because most cattle owners consider bulls to be more trouble than they are worth, as they provide no returns in terms of milk, labour or calves and often fetch only limited prices. For this reason, most young males are castrated and converted to oxen, which have much greater appeal as beasts of labour. Informants at both villages did not mention problems with infection associated with this practise, although this was highlighted as being a problem in parts of the Transkei (Kepe 2002). At Koloni, a key informant explained that the decision to allow a male animal to develop into a bull was taken by assessing if it is 'strong' (interview with Mr Mcete in April 2004). This suggests subjective assessment rather than objective measurements of particular aspects of the animal's build. This informant's herd contained one elderly Bonsmara bull, and one young animal (its offspring), which was being reared to eventually replace its sire. The older bull was one of only two mature bulls in the entire village herd of about 300 animals. At Guquka, the ratio was better with six bulls out of about 180 head of cattle.

Such low ratios are not unusual in subsistence herds held in former homeland areas. In the Herschel district, Vetter (2003), found that no herds of five animals or fewer included a bull and that even among large herds (up to 30 animals) there were never more than two bulls. Tapson and Rose (1984) concluded that an idealised subsistence herd in KwaZulu Natal, consisting of 18 animals, should contain one bull. The overall herd structure at Koloni is particularly poor in this respect with just one mature bull per 150 cattle. Given that that the average subsistence herd consists of about 40% mature cows (Steyn 1982, Tapson and Rose 1984, Vetter 2003) this suggests that the ratio of bulls to mature cows at Koloni is only about 1:60. This clearly has implications for herd productivity in terms of how effectively all the cows are serviced when they are in oestrus, although the problem is doubtless ameliorated to some extent by the mixing of the village herd with bulls from neighbouring herds. This occurs both when roaming bulls gain access to range camps through poor fencing and when the animals are brought together for communal dipping. Nevertheless, unless such events account for a good proportion of matings (which does not seem to be the case), the very low number of bulls at Koloni has serious implications for herd productivity not only in terms of low rates of conception but also inbreeding. This presents the very real probability that the older bulls are breeding with animals that are their own siblings or offspring. The problem is compounded by the fact that these older bulls tend to be replaced by their own offspring, rather than by fresh animals brought in from outside. Whether these problems will, or already are, manifesting themselves at either village is difficult to assess, but certainly difficulties such as decreased disease resistance and fertility may become apparent if outbreeding is not increased through the addition of more bulls.

For sheep and goats, the balance of males in the flock is also carefully controlled. Mr Mcete related in an interview held in April 2004 that his holdings of both sheep and goats contained just one breeding male. However, because most owners within the village tend to maintain at least one ram or buck in their flocks, inbreeding is not likely to be as much of a problem as with cattle. Nevertheless, the vast majority of male animals are castrated by their owners at just a few months of age. Interestingly, as with cattle, there were no reports of losses associated with this due to infection.

Another aspect of animal husbandry undertaken quite rigorously at both Guquka and Koloni was treatment of disease and parasites, especially with regard to cattle and sheep. The main illnesses and afflictions identified were mastitis and fly strike for cattle; gall sickness (*imyongo*) and skin loss (*ibhula*) for sheep and worms in both species. Many of these afflictions are tick-borne, which underlines the need for regular dipping to deal with ecto-parasite infestations.

Both Guquka and Koloni have access to dipping facilities to prevent tick infestations, and these have been well utilised. Dipping is performed on cattle, sheep and goats. Respondents reported that dipping was undertaken approximately once every two or three weeks during the wet season, whereas during the dry season it would only be once every six to eight weeks. At Guquka the dipping facilities are located at the nearby agricultural school, Phandulwazi, and are provided by the government free of charge to villagers.

At Koloni there has recently been a period of considerable disagreement and unhappiness in relation to the dipping facilities available to the village. Over a period of several years the villagers have been pressing the local agricultural extension services for the provision of additional dipping facilities because the existing facility at the nearby training centre is utilised by too many villages, and this results in general confusion and mixing-up of animals among owners. Furthermore, there was a general feeling that the excessive pressure on the dipping facility was leading to animals being roughly treated and making the application of the dip ineffective. As a result, during 2003 the villagers took it upon themselves to organise the construction of an additional dipping tank. Contact was established with the neighbouring village of Esixekweni, and a decision taken to construct the facility there, for use by livestock from both villages. An agreement was reached with the local agricultural officers to provide the poles and cement for its construction, while the labour for the digging of the tank and sinking of the fencing poles was to be supplied by the villagers. The new facility has been in operation since the end of 2003. It operates on a fortnightly basis during the wet season, using dip supplied by the government, and seems to have reduced the problem of congestion.

The efficacy of this new facility, in treating certain livestock ailments, continues to be questioned by some livestock owners. Mr Xhotyeni., for example, bemoaned the fact that the dip was ineffective against the particular type of tick that was responsible for the severe mastitis afflicting his cattle, which was preventing him from obtaining any milk from them. He attributed the problem to the dip supplied by the government being too weak (Interview, 19/04/04).

Despite these complaints, the construction of the additional dipping facility does provide another example of the extent to which livestock owners at Koloni are able to organise themselves at the grassroots level in order to facilitate change.

In addition to treating ecto-parasites through communal dipping, many live-stock owners also treat other livestock ailments on an individual basis. The administration of livestock medicines tends to be on an 'as and when' rather than a preventative basis and the extent to which individual owners make use of medicines is determined primarily by how much they can afford to buy. A key informant from Koloni related that almost nobody at the village makes use of traditional remedies any longer as there is a perception that they are not reliable (interview with Mr Nguka, April 2004). This conclusion contrasts markedly, with the findings of Mululuma and Masika (2000), who undertook interviews in three areas of central Eastern Cape and concluded that, primarily due to issues of cost and accessibility, ethno-veterinary medicines (EVMs) continue to be in widespread use in the region. This is also supported by the work of Che (unpublished) and Che and Lent (2004), who note use of EVM's at Guquka. There is also evidence to suggest that other types of traditional treatments are still used on livestock at Koloni (see also chapter 10). Of particular note are concoctions made from various poisonous plants, with the purpose of deterring potential consumption of the plant by livestock. One informant highlighted the use of the small, locally abundant plant, *Romulea rosea* (onion grass), a small perennial from the iris family, in this respect. This particular species has toxins in its leaves and corms which can make livestock quite sick if they ingest them (The Nature Conservancy 2004). Consequently, cattle are deliberately fed a brew made from the plant while they are still relatively young, in order to habituate them not to eat it.

Of the manufactured drugs used at Koloni, the most commonly purchased are Penicillin, Terramycin and anti-helminthics in the form of worming tablets. Due to their high cost, the use of the first two tends to be restricted to cattle and sheep. probably because cattle and sheep are perceived as having more value than goats and also that goats are inherently more hardy animals and require less husbandry, as corroborated by Vetter (2003). Both drugs tend to be used to treat animals only when they show clear symptoms of being ill rather than on a preventative basis. In 2004, terramycin cost about R160 for a small bottle, which precluded the majority of owners from all but the most sparing use. Nevertheless, all informants agreed that even when used in this way, these drugs were effective in treating a broad range of livestock ailments. At Koloni, infor-mants related that Terramycin is particularly effective in treating cattle sores resulting from tick bites and fly strike and that penicillin produces excellent results when used to treat mastitis in cows. Worming tablets, being relatively inexpensive, are used to treat all three livestock species on a preventative basis, particularly when they are still young.

Supplementary feeding is another important aspect of animal husbandry among several of the livestock owners at both villages. There is a general perception, particularly at Guquka, that the natural forage available during the dry season is very poor and provides animals with little nutrition. However, at both villages supplementary feeding is generally restricted to the provision of planted crops or stover, and bales of lucerne are only purchased during desperate conditions such as drought. A few individuals at each village cultivate forage crops such as oats during the latter part of the growing season, specifically for use by livestock. These are mainly used to supplement sheep during the dry season and in particular to allow the ewes to produce milk to feed their lambs. However, such practices are now rare at both villages despite widespread acceptance of their value. The main constraint preventing people from engaging in such activities appears to be lack of money. Far more widespread is the use of crop (maize) residues to feed livestock. These are generally grazed *in situ*, on the fields were the crop was cultivated (see below).

One livestock owner at Koloni related that he actively removed the crop residues from his field and fed them to his own animals at the homestead (interview with Mr Mcete, April 2004). This practice has also been reported in the Herschel district (Vetter 2003). Another practice, described by livestock owners at both villages, is the use of mealies as supplementary feed both for chickens and for sheep during the dry season. The mealies used for this purpose tend to be those that are damaged or diseased and thus not fit for human consumption. The clear association of supplementary feeding during the dry season with sheep, particularly ewes with lambs, would appear to be widespread in the region. Vetter (2003) stated that most farmers in the Herschel district recognised that sheep require additional feed inputs during the dry season although their ability to supply them was related to availability of cash, especially as most supplementary feed in Herschel was brought in as bales of lucerne.

A final aspect of animal husbandry of importance at Guquka and Koloni is the shearing of sheep. This has been handled differently in the two villages, although neither involves the use of communal facilities. At Guquka shearing is undertaken on an individual basis, using hand shears rather than electric clippers. In contrast, since the demise of the shearing shed in the early 1990s, almost all individuals at Koloni have their sheep sheared by the sons of Mr Ngxowa, the former chairman, who has the proper equipment. However, this service comes at a price, with a charge of R1 for each ewe sheared and R2 for each ram. Wethers (castrated males) are charged at the same rate as ewes. Shearing is always undertaken in springtime (generally October) after the rains have come. This leaves time for improvement on the natural rangeland and a consequent increase in the weight and quality of wool on the sheep. This situation contrasts with that in many other areas, in which shearing is undertaken on a communal basis based on membership in a local shearing shed. Such a system formerly operated at Koloni until political disturbances associated with the overthrow of the former headman resulted in its dissolution during the early 1990s (Van Averbeke *et al.* 1998b). Its revitalisation is an avenue which several

owners consider worthwhile, although with sheep numbers currently so low at
the village it is unlikely to be practical at present.

## Livestock forage resources and foraging patterns

The overall forage resources available to livestock in each community may be
viewed as a number of compartments among which animals are moved or move
themselves over the landscape, depending upon patterns of governance (chapter
6) and other factors. Historically, scientific or systematic study of these resources has been limited almost entirely to the lands formally designated as
communal rangelands. It is only recently that a broader perspective has been
taken that considers other forage resources in terms of use of other land categories, but also in the case of cattle, non-grass resources. Bennett (2002) has
shown clearly how important the arable land allotments in each community are
in the annual cycle of livestock production. In addition it is known that livestock are frequently making use of other forage resources in residential areas,
roadside verges, and, in the case of Guquka, a variety of lands (state forests and
nature reserves), which are not technically available for their exploitation. The
problem in trying to piece together this entire picture of forage resources is that,
especially for Guquka, detailed information is available only for the arable
allotments. For this reason the majority of the quantitative data presented below
will be focus on the use of the arable land allocations as a dry season forage
reserve. However, efforts will also be made to discuss the use of the formal
rangeland areas from a qualitative perspective to try to present a holistic picture
of livestock rangeland use. We begin with a discussion of how both the designated rangeland areas and arable land allocations are managed as a grazing
resource at the two villages.

*Livestock grazing management*
The distribution of the formal rangelands and arable land allocations, which together comprise much of the available grazing land at each village, is provided
in Maps 4.1 and 4.2 for Guquka and Koloni respectively. During the wet season
(summer) all three livestock species make use almost entirely of the formal
rangeland at each village, although livestock also make substantial use of the
arable lands at Guquka at this time (see below).

At Guquka, the rangeland area is available to all livestock species at all
times of the year. Moreover, it is utilised not only by livestock from Guquka but
also by those from the neighbouring settlements of Gilton and Kayalethu. Historically, the area was fenced into separate camps, which were managed on a
rotational basis by local rangers. Cattle found grazing in rested camps were
impounded at Gqumashe location farther down the valley, and owners were
forced to pay a fine of R1 per head to reclaim them (Van Averbeke *et al.*
1998b). The grazing area was also considerably larger until much of it was
appropriated by the Ciskeian Authorities during the early 1970s for develop-

ment of pine plantations. This had the effect of further exacerbating pressure on already limited grazing resources.

All that now remains of the fencing introduced under betterment lies at the upper limit of the range. Thus, it is no longer possible to practice any form of rotational grazing. Indeed, with the loss of the rangers who used to enforce local grazing management decisions, there is no longer any form of co-ordinated rangeland management between the three communities involved (Van Averbeke *et al*. 1998). With no form of central control over rangeland grazing at the community level in Guquka control of rangeland grazing is entirely under the jurisdiction of individual livestock owners with regard to timing, duration and the extent to which the animals are allowed to free-range. For protection small-stock in Guquka tend to be kept in relative proximity to the village. Cattle, however, can be found grazing throughout the area, including the most moun-tainous extent of the range, during the summer months where they even gain access to the pine forest plantations where fencing is inadequate (chapter 4). This leaves them vulnerable to impoundment and theft. Seasonal parameters have an important role to play in the utilisation of these mountain pastures. With the approach of the dry season, cattle move down to the lower ranges and do not return to the higher pastures until springtime. However, these movements are driven largely by the animals themselves, secondarily by individual owners, and are not under any form of communal jurisdiction. In essence an open-access situation has developed in which there is mutual privilege with respect to the rangeland for all livestock owners but no formal grazing rights (Bromley 1989).

At Koloni, closer control of rangeland grazing is possible because fencing divides the range area into four separate camps and, importantly, this area belongs exclusively to Koloni. Under the plan for betterment of the village drawn up in 1961, it was envisaged that one grazing camp would be rested each year for an entire year, and the remaining three would be grazed on a rotational basis (Bantu Affairs Commission 1962). This involved a notice being issued from the Bantu Affairs Office at the beginning of each year as to which camp was to be rested. Indeed, annual resting of a camp is still practised, although it is unclear whether a camp is now rested for the entire year in all cases or whether the original resting regime is still adhered to. Furthermore, it appears that the rested camp functions as a sanctuary for old or sick animals, particularly during the winter. True rotational grazing of the camps is no longer practised, instead the three camps that are not being rested are grazed simultaneously (Goqwana and Scogings 1997). This appears to be a response to the logistical problem of many livestock owners being located a considerable distance from some of the camps. Owners now simply make use of whichever of the three camps is nearest to them. Thus, the scenario in recent years involved resting of each camps once every four years but no longer rests of each camp within years.

The separation of the range into camps also allows the RA to control the type of animals involved in grazing. During the summer this is of no impor-tance, because mixed species grazing is practised on all three grazed camps.

However, during the winter months the arable land allocations at Koloni are reserved primarily for cattle.

During the dry season, once crop production has ceased, the arable land allocations at both villages are made available on a communal basis as an additional forage reserve for livestock. Grazing of the arable land allocations at Koloni is controlled through a clearly defined common property regime from the moment they become available to livestock. The user group includes all those who belong to the RA, which effectively includes all the adults resident at Koloni.

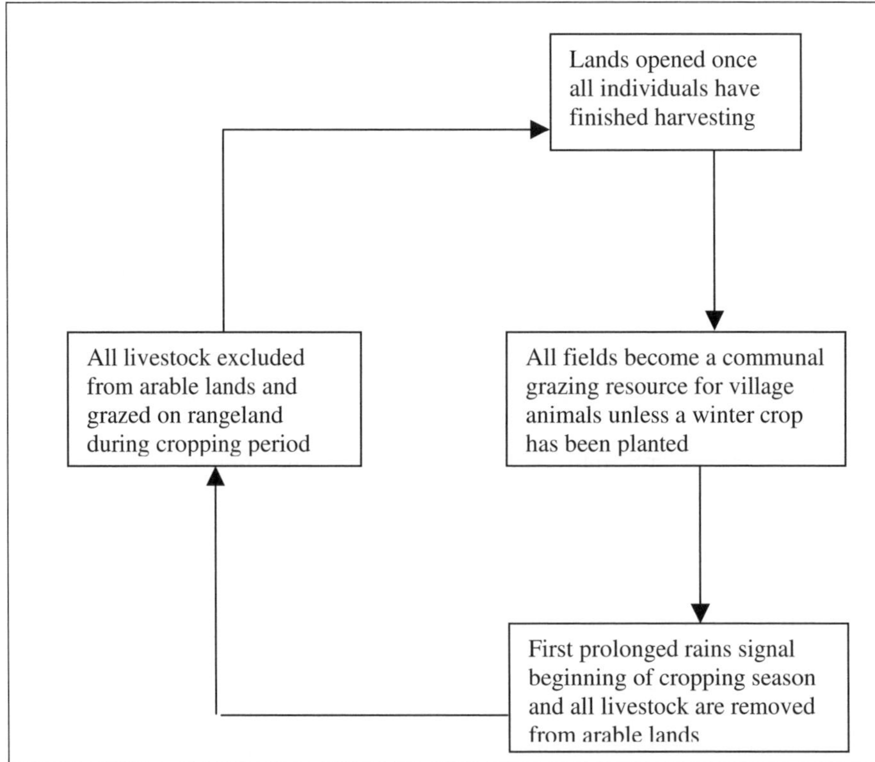


*Figure 9.2*    General model for the use of arable land as a dry season forage reserve for livestock under betterment planning

Likewise, at Guquka, management of the arable land allocations is still under some semblance of communal control. Key features of the control of arable grazing at both villages are dealt with in detail in Bennett and Barrett (2006) and are discussed briefly below.

One key aspect of this grazing management concerns the point at which the arable land allocations are made available to grazing. According to the standard betterment model, the arable land allocations are opened to grazing once the harvesting of all crops has been completed (Figure 9.2).

At both villages a meeting of the RA is held, as was described in chapter 6, which all individuals who own cattle or have access to a field all field are encouraged to attend, and a decision to formally open the arable fields to grazing is taken once there is agreement amongst participants. At Koloni, every individual who has grown a crop must have finished harvesting before the lands are opened. However, at Guquka this decision appears to be interpreted more flexibly. Not everybody finishes harvesting at the same time, and so the grazing of crop residues is frequently initiated before all harvesting is completed. In such instances, livestock owners make an arrangement to put their animals on one field after another in a staggered manner. The process is continued until harvesting is completed on all fields, and it is only at this point that the entire arable allocation is opened to grazing. This can be viewed as a practical means of supplying hungry livestock with forage at a critical time of the year as well as preventing trespassing cattle from nearby Kayalethu from gaining access to these vital crop residues. In both cases this is possible because crop production at Guquka takes place almost exclusively in fenced fields. However, in recent years only a few of the fields have been ploughed and cultivated in any given year (chapters 7 and 8).

With regard to the closing of the lands a number of human and climatic factors influence the decision. In the late dry season individuals begin to prepare for the next season of cropping. The desire of individuals to begin cultivating, combined with the state of the range camps, determines the exact timing of the closure. The single most important factor in this decision is the coming of the summer rains as this simultaneously heralds both the time of planting and the recovery of the range.

After the first period of prolonged rain a meeting of the RA is held in which the closure of the arable lands will be discussed. Given sufficient agreement among those owning livestock and those wishing to cultivate, the motion will be carried and the lands officially closed. At this point, livestock owners are obliged to remove all their animals to the appropriate range camps.

As well as controlling the timing of arable grazing, the grazing management system at each village controls the type of livestock allowed on the arable lands. At Koloni it is clear that the arable land allocations are reserved exclusively for cattle. This is because they are perceived as being the most valuable of the livestock species (culturally and economically) and at greatest risk from lack of forage during the lean winter months. All small-stock are restricted to the range camps at this time and the few that gain access to the arable lands do so as a result of inadequate perimeter fencing. In contrast, at Guquka grazing of the arable land allocations takes place on a mixed basis during the dry season, involving sheep and goats as well as cattle. This is actually a recommended grazing practice at a commercial level as large-stock and small-stock feed on different types of forage and their feeding patterns complement each other. Grazing the fields with mixed species herds thus facilitates the most effective utilisation of the forage resources (Gertenbach *et al.* 1998).

There are also rules governing the grazing of arable land allocations outside the dry season. At Koloni there is strict adherence to the general betterment model (Figure 9.2) in this respect, as once the fields have officially been closed to grazing no livestock are allowed on the arable land allocations. The only exception tolerated is for oxen involved in crop production. For pragmatic reasons these tend to be maintained on the arable lands by their owners during the time of ploughing but are immediately removed once ploughing is complete. At Guquka, however, it is clear that there is a marked deviation from the betterment model with the arable fields being grazed by livestock from both within the village and outside throughout the course of the cropping period. Lack of available grazing at Kayalethu encourages livestock owners at that settlement to maintain their animals on Guquka's arable lands. This appears to be an ongoing source of friction between the two settlements. During winter 1999 several key livestock owners from Guquka repaired sections of the perimeter fence where the majority of livestock gained access. This proved successful in the short term but within a few weeks the problem returned following deliberate cutting of the fence.

Livestock from Guquka itself also make significant use of the fields for grazing at this time. This mostly takes the form of cattle grazing individually fenced fields either because owners are absent from the village (i.e. the field is uncultivated) or because animals are sick or unruly. Another powerful incentive for owners to restrict livestock to fenced fields at this time is stock theft. Cattle have a tendency to wander over considerable distances when given access to the mountain pastures during the summer, which makes them vulnerable to theft. Thus, restricting cattle to fenced fields allows them to be retained in relatively close proximity to the homestead, where they can be closely watched. However, access by livestock from Guquka to the arable lands during the cropping season is not just restricted to private grazing. Towards the end of the cropping period, increasing numbers of cattle from Guquka can be found free-ranging on un-fenced areas of the arable lands.

Owners generally justify this behaviour to the grazing committee with an official excuse, but the underlying reason for their presence is invariably short-age of forage on the range area at this time. Moreover, the owners who are able to practice this tend to be those who are well connected with the grazing com-mittee on the basis of social standing within the village (chapter 6.)

Finally, there is the issue of maintenance of individual rights over fields during the dry season. Historical convention holds that all fields should be accessible by all livestock at this time, unless a winter crop is grown (Figure 9.2). Every field must be made available for grazing, even those that are fenced. At Koloni this basic protocol is strictly adhered to with all fields being made available to livestock (cattle) unless a dry season crop is grown. Thus, during most dry seasons, there are few restrictions on cattle movements over the arable fields at Koloni from a land rights perspective. At Guquka, however, several residents maintain individual rights over fields throughout the winter without growing crops. This may be for grazing their own livestock or simply for resting a field that was grazed during the summer months. In all cases these exceptions are possible because the individual field is fenced.

Thus, there are in practice marked differences in the grazing management frameworks in operation at each village. These key differences are summarised in Table 9.3.

*Table 9.3*     Key differences in grazing management practices at Guquka and Koloni

| Practice | Guquka | Koloni |
|---|---|---|
| Rangeland grazing | No communal control over grazing of livestock on rangeland due to inadequate boundary definition and ineffective co-ordination among multiple users | Well defined rangeland boundaries and separation into grazing camps by fencing facilitates rotational resting, the separation of cattle from small-stock during winter, and exclusive control over rangeland by community |
| Initiation of arable grazing | Grazing of crop residues often undertaken before all harvesting is complete. | Grazing of arable lands only initiated once harvesting is complete. |
| Livestock involved in arable grazing | Open to all livestock | Limited principally to cattle |
| Grazing of arable fields at other times of the year | Arable fields grazed during cropping period both by trespassing cattle from Kayalethu and cattle from Guquka | Grazing of arable lands strictly prohibited during cropping period except by cattle involved in ploughing. |
| Maintenance of individual rights over fields | Owners may chose to exercise exclusive grazing rights over their arable field(s) even if they have not grown a forage crop. | Owners may only chose to exercise exclusive grazing rights over their arable field(s) if they have grown a forage crop. |

*Source*: Bennett and Barrett (2007)


*Livestock dry season foraging patterns on the arable land allocations*
It is clear from the above that livestock make considerable use of the arable land allocations at both villages either as a dry season forage reserve or as part of a longer term feed resource. This section summarises the foraging patterns observed for cattle and sheep, which are discussed in more detail in Bennett (2002).

At Guquka, the arable land allocations are formally opened to all livestock from the village during the dry season. However, only cattle and sheep make any significant use of the available forage. The weekly change in the proportion of cattle and sheep making use of the arable land allocation at Guquka during the dry season 1999 is summarised in Figure 9.3.

Figure 9.3 shows that a substantial proportion of the total number of sheep (n = 400) and particularly of cattle (n = 230) at Guquka were on the larger arable land allocation during the 1999 dry season. During the first eight weeks the proportion of cattle on the area did not drop below 28% of the village total and peaked at nearly 70% in week 3.

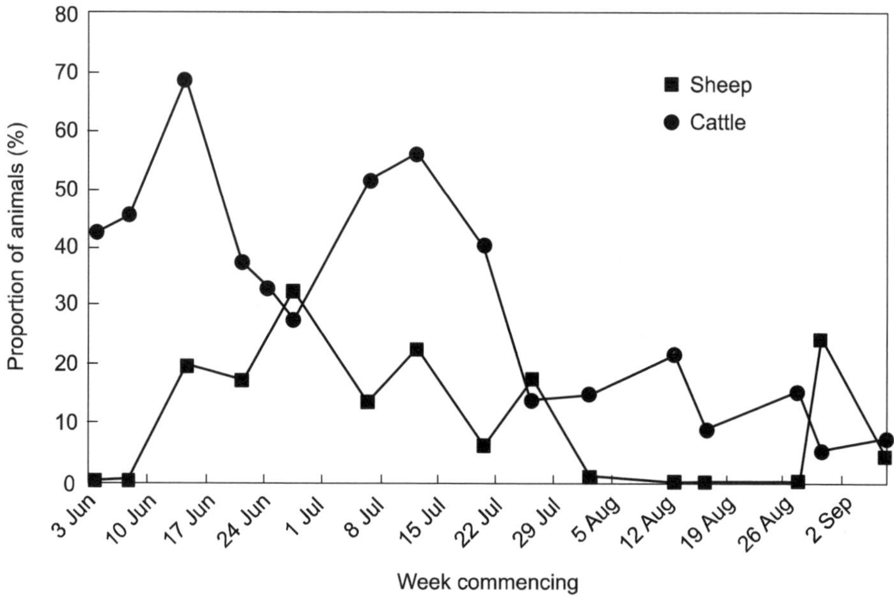


*Figure 9.3*    Proportion of cattle and sheep free-ranging on the larger arable land
allocation at Guquka during the dry season, 1999

*Source*: Bennett (2002)

Given that the larger arable allocation constitutes only about 17% of the total grazing land available at the village this indicated a high degree of preference amongst cattle in the early part of the dry season for the arable land compared to the formal rangeland area. In contrast, during the equivalent period, the proportion of sheep recorded on this area was rarely above 20%, suggesting they had little if any preference for this area. This conclusion may be explained by differences in the grazing behaviour of the two species. Cattle are essentially bulk-grazers adapted to deal with relatively large volumes of low quality forage, whereas sheep are selective grazers requiring short swards (Hanley 1982, Owen-Smith 1982).

Thus, whilst cattle are adapted to deal with the majority of forage on the arable lands, including the tall, stemmy *Hyparrhenia* grassland, sheep are only able to forage on the shorter vegetation types (crop residues and recent fallow vegetation), which were in relatively short supply. This is corroborated by the sharp decline in the proportion of sheep on the lands after late July, coinciding with the exhaustion of crop residues (see below).

As described in chapters 7 and 8 the numbers of fields on which crop residues occur has also declined dramatically in recent years. At Koloni the situation was somewhat different. From early June until the beginning of September the proportion of cattle found on the arable land allocation varied between 28% and 60% of the total (n = 373), with a mean of 42%.

Thereafter this proportion began to steadily diminish as the quality of the forage on the range camps improved and owners started to move animals to these areas. Despite the relatively large contingent of animals present on the arable lands at this time, this was not representative of any strong degree of cattle preference at the landscape scale as the lands themselves accounted for some 37% of all grazing land available at the village.

A simplistic assessment of the preference livestock display for different vegetation types can be obtained from preference indices. This required the division of the vegetation on the arable land allocation at each village into different categories (Maps 9.1 and 9.2). The classification of these categories, as well as their extent and distribution during the 1999 dry season, is discussed in more detail in Bennett (2002). The calculation of the relevant preference indices made use of the forage ratio method (Krebs 1999), which is based on the ratio of observed to expected values of either time spent grazing or number of animals in each category (for further details see Bennett *et al.* 2006). In each case an index <1 indicates avoidance, an index of exactly 1 indicates no preference and values >1 show preference.

At Guquka, the preference indices expressed by sheep for the different vegetation categories available on the arable land allocation during the dry season in 1999, are summarised in Table 9.4.

*Table 9.4*    Preference indices for sheep in different vegetation categories

| Vegetation Category | Preference Index |
| --- | --- |
| Crop residues | 3.31 |
| Recent fallow vegetation | 3.87 |
| *Sporobolus-Cynodon* grassland | 0.19 |
| *Hyparrhenia* grassland | 0.10 |

*Source*: Bennett (2002)

A very strong preference emerges among sheep for both crop residues and recent fallow vegetation. The preference for the recent fallow vegetation is in keeping with the feeding habits of sheep, essentially selective feeders that target short swards as found in the recent fallow vegetation (Owen-Smith 1982). Conversely, sheep are not adapted to deal with tall, stemmy grass species. Their strong preference for crop residues cannot be explained so easily. Probably, this reflects preference not for the maize stover itself, but instead for abundant annual grasses, which grow as weeds among the maize crops. For cattle, preference indices for the different vegetation types are summarised in Table 9.5.

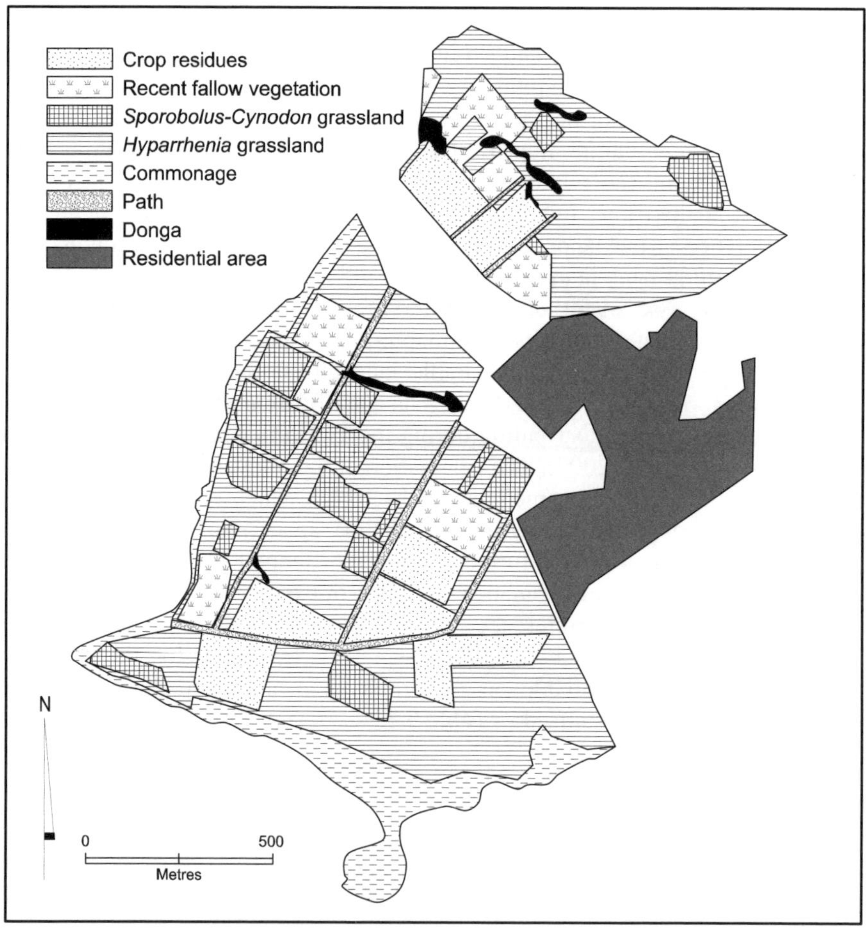



*Map 9.1*     Vegetation types on arable allotments in Guquka, Winter 1999

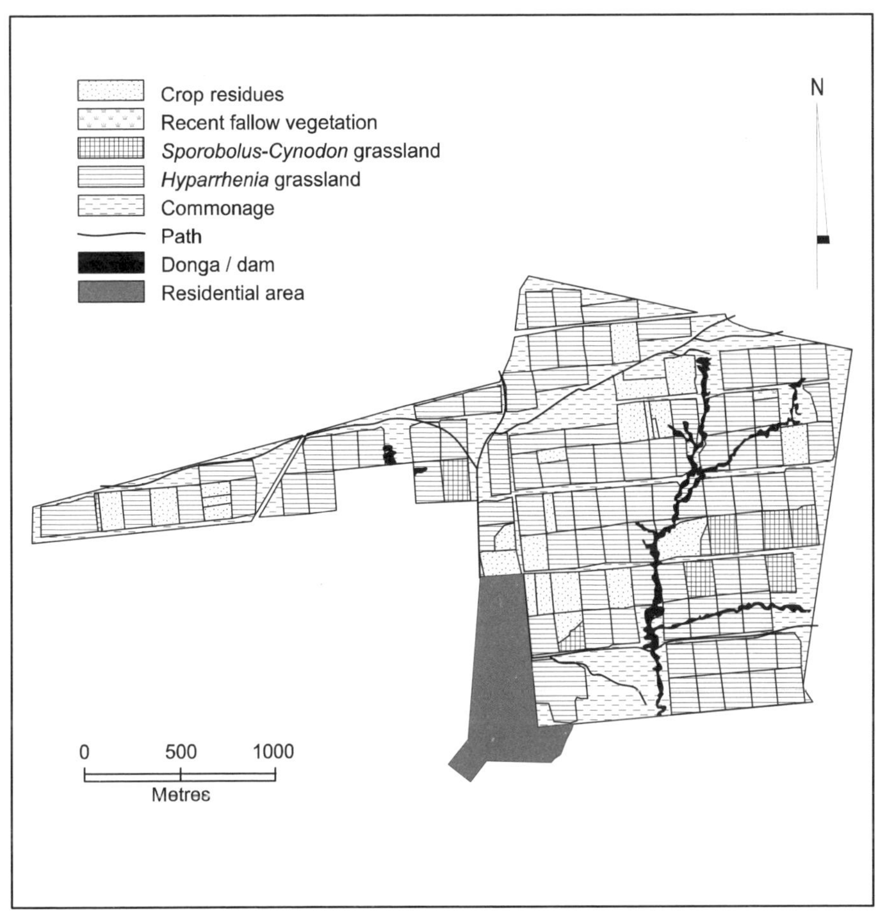


*Map 9.2*    Vegetation types on arable allotments in Koloni, Winter 1999

*Table 9.5*     Preference indices (Pi) of cattle for each vegetation category on arable
               land allotments at Guquka and Koloni during dry season 1999

| Vegetation Category | Guquka | | | Koloni | | |
|---|---|---|---|---|---|---|
| | Initial | Middle | End | Initial | Middle | End |
| Donga vegetation | na | na | na | 0.00 | 0.00 | 0.00 |
| Commonage (open area within allotment) | na | na | na | 1.57 | 0.67 | 1.69 |
| Crop residues | 5.14 | 2.48 | 0.31 | 2.66 | 2.36 | 0.00 |
| Recent fallow vegetation | 0.00 | 0.00 | 0.00 | 0.00 | 0.00 | 0.00 |
| *Sporobolus-Cynodon* grassland | 0.00 | 1.03 | 0.00 | 0.02 | 0.58 | 0.56 |
| *Eragrostis-Digitaria* grassland | na | na | na | 0.80 | 1.49 | 1.79 |
| *Hyparrhenia* grassland | 0.22 | 0.71 | 1.64 | 0.35 | 0.67 | 0.54 |

*Source*: Bennett (2002)


At Guquka cattle displayed a very strong preference for crop residues and
avoided other vegetation types at the beginning of the dry season. This preference continued into the middle of the dry season, although animals also made
increasing use of *Sporobolus-Cynodon* and *Hyparrhenia* grasslands at this time.
However, by the end of the season grazing preference had switched so that
*Hyparrhenia* grassland became the preferred vegetation type and all other
categories were avoided or completely ignored. This change undoubtedly
reflected the depletion of crop residues and a subsequent switch to the more
abundant, although less preferred, *Hyparrhenia* grassland in order to satisfy dry
matter intake requirements (Kearl 1982).

At Koloni, the situation was somewhat different, largely as a result of the
greater degree of choice cattle had among the vegetation categories available to
them. At the beginning of the dry season cattle showed the greatest preference
for crop residues.

They also preferred the highly palatable vegetation found on the commonage
area (Map 4.2), but grassland categories were largely avoided at this stage.
Cattle completely avoided both the recent fallow and donga vegetation both at
this stage and for the remainder of the dry season. During the middle of the dry
season, crop residues remained the most preferred food source, but the
*Eragrostis-Digitaria* grassland had become preferred over the commonage
vegetation. This switch in preference appears to have been prompted by a
decline in the quality of the commonage sward (see below). After the total
depletion of crop residues cattle expressed strongest preference for commonage
vegetation. This appears to have been mediated by an extensive recovery of the
quality of the commonage vegetation by the latter stages of the dry season in
response to early rains (see below). The consistent preference by cattle at

Koloni for lower biomass *Eragrostis-Digitaria* patches compared to the tall, stemmy stands of *Hyparrhenia* grassland is similar to that of cattle grazing in heterogeneous fescue pastures in Argentina (Cid and Brizuela 1998).

*Quantity and quality of forage available to livestock*
In addition to determining the foraging preferences expressed by livestock on the arable land allocations it is important to have some measure of the quantity and quality of the natural forage available to livestock at the two villages, as a means both of corroborating identified preference patterns and identifying production constraints. For the designated rangeland areas at each village, information is available from surveys undertaken by pasture scientists from ARDRI in 1996, and additional information for Koloni is available from 1998. This is summarised in Table 9.6.

*Table 9.6*    Range assessment for communal rangelands in Guquka and Koloni

|  | Guquka 1996 | Koloni 1996 | Koloni 1997-8 |
|---|---|---|---|
| Area of designated rangeland | 400 ha | 650 ha |  |
| Mean biomass | 2285 kg/ha | 1300 kg/ha summer, 1035 kg/ha dry season | 2400 kg/ha |
| Mean condition class (range) | 51% (45-60) | 78% (32-100) | 71% (32-100) |
| Recommended stocking rate | 6 ha/ LSU** | 4 ha/LSU | 5.14 ha/LSU |
| Estimated overstocking* | 490% | 370% | 450% |
| Arable allotment area | 142 ha | 400 ha |  |
| Soil erosion | Isolated spots | Limited | -- |

* Based on designated communal rangeland areas only. See text for discussion.
** LSU= Large stock unit

*Sources*: Guquka 1996: ARDRI (1996), Koloni 1996: ARDRI (1996), Koloni 1997-98: Goqwana (1998).

The values for mean biomass show considerable variation both within and between villages. At Koloni the mean rangeland biomass during summer (February) 1996 was considerably lower than that measured during summer (April) 1998. This is likely to be a result of different rainfall patterns between years. As described in earlier chpters Rainfall in the Eastern Cape Province is essentially bi-modally distributed with peaks around November and March (Jury and Levy 1993). In 1995/96 there was very poor rainfall during the second half of the summer, which would account for the relatively low biomass. However, the mean biomass value from dry season (August) 1996 appears largely comparable with values from the arable land allocations in dry season of 1999 (see below).

This relatively low figure is a result both of several months of typically low rainfall and lack of growth combined with vegetation dieback and continuous grazing off take. These mean biomass figures serve to underline how the productivity of the grazing resources available in these areas (particularly in more marginal areas) is driven to a large extent by abiotic and highly variable factors, namely rainfall. At Guquka the mean biomass was taken at the end of the dry season (September) and thus might be expected to be representative of the lowest level of annual biomass. Nevertheless, the value is relatively high as a result of a considerable portion of the biomass being constituted by shrub species such as *Chrysocoma tennuifolia*. These have little or no utility from a livestock production perspective and thus estimates of the effective biomass available for livestock consumption should be lowered considerably (ARDRI 1996).

The values for Koloni in summer 1996 and 1998 show higher range condition than at Guquka (Table 9.6). However, any comparison between the two villages from these data are questionable because the mean range condition value at Guquka was calculated at the end of the dry season (September) when condition is likely to be at its lowest, whereas those from Koloni were calculated during the summer, when condition is likely to be highest.

Likewise, calculation of the level of overstocking is also confounded by a number of factors at both villages. Firstly, the calculation uses only the area of formal rangeland at each village to judge the total number of livestock that can be supported. Thus, the overstocking values at both villages are considerably overestimated as during the dry season, the arable land allocations become available as an additional grazing reserve. If these are factored into the calculation then the level of overstocking at Guquka drops to 350% and that at Koloni to 230% (Bennett 2002).

It is also likely that more livestock are grazing within residential areas than in the past. Kepe and Scoones (1999) reported that in a Transkei village, along with the general breakdown in authority over broader village-wide grassland management, individuals or small groups of residents were manipulating and protecting smaller patches of grasslands, often influencing the direction of succession and the dominant species. Recognizing the importance of grazing resources around homesteads and in nutrient rich areas encouraging the presence of *Cynodon dactylon* (couch grass) as the best to protect as all animals graze it at all stages. Horses and donkeys were allowed to graze it heavily to keep a low sward. Similarly, others were manipulating patches that they can control for optimum production of thatch grass.

Our observations suggest that such management practices are increasing in the two study villages as well. Certainly these practices are also logical responses to increased livestock theft. In a few cases areas around homes formerly used as home gardens are now used for keeping stock, especially sheep and goats.

However, estimation of the real level of overstocking at Guquka is further complicated by the fact that actual size of the formal rangeland area is not known (ARDRI 1996) and cattle, in particular, may spend a considerable period of time grazing beyond the boundaries of the formal grazing areas, as described earlier. On the other hand the rangeland area at Guquka is utilised by livestock from several neighbouring communities. With so many unknowns, a realistic estimate of the level of overstocking at Guquka is impossible. Moreover, the criteria used for determining the level of overstocking at each village are based on commercial objectives and thus its application in these communal systems is highly questionable (Behnke and Scoones 1993). Nevertheless, an analysis of rangeland carrying capacity for the sloping rangelands in Guquka area done in 1977 (Hill, Kaplan & Partners 1977) reported a livestock carrying capacity from 3-4 ha per LSU, down to 4-6 in poorer areas. They believed that there had been improvement in range conditions in the decades since the surveys of Story (1952). These values suggest that some deterioration of carrying capacity has occurred in the decades since the 1977 report follow. They also reported the *sourveld* above the escarpment to have a higher carrying capacity at 2-3 LSU/ha in some areas. Subsequently, these better range areas have been largely lost as a result of afforestation.

In addition to information on rangeland productivity, data on the quantity and quality of grassland vegetation on the arable land allocations at both villages are available in Bennett (2002). The mean grassland biomass available during the dry season is summarised in Table 9.7.

*Table 9.7*    Mean standing biomass (kg/ha)* on arable land allocations at Guquka and Koloni at different stages of dry season 1999

| Vegetation category | Guquka | | | Koloni | | |
|---|---|---|---|---|---|---|
|  | Initial | Middle | End | Initial | Middle | End |
| Commonage | NA | NA | NA | 2455.6 (101.5) | 1456.0 (102.2) | 616.8 (54.3) |
| *Sporobolus-Cynodon* grassland | 1138.8 (56.0) | 705.2 (61.2) | 549.6 (54.0) | 1880.8 (133.3) | 1258.8 (102) | 1019.6 (109.3) |
| *Eragrostis-Digitaria* grassland | NA | NA | NA | 1384.0 (244.7) | 838.4 (194.7) | 481.2 (167.5) |
| *Hyparrhenia* grassland | 1368.4 (122.8) | 890.4 (86.8) | 488.4 (62.4) | 3198.8 (108.1) | 2426.0 (115.3) | 2110.8 (58.6) |

* Values in brackets are standard errors
*Source*: Bennett (2002)

If comparison is made between equivalent grassland types at the two villages it is immediately clear that considerably greater biomass is found on the arable land allocations at Koloni, throughout the dry season. This can be explained by the different grazing management practices in operation at the villages. Whereas the forage on the arable allotments at Koloni is largely conserved throughout the growing season, at Guquka it is being continuously consumed both by trespassing livestock from Kayalethu and by Guquka's own livestock. This explains why the initial biomass values at Guquka are so low.

Another important trend in the data is the steady decrease in available biomass in all grassland vegetation categories at both villages during the course of the dry season. This is a combination both of natural die back in the vegetation during this dormant period and forage removal by grazing livestock. However, comparison between the villages shows that by the end of the dry season exhaustion of grassland vegetation at Guquka was total, whereas at Koloni there was still sufficient herbage in the *Sporobolus-Cynodon* and particularly the *Hyparrhenia* grassland to enable livestock foraging. This again results from the different grazing management practices in operation at each community. The continuous grazing of the arable lands at Guquka during the growing period depletes the forage reserves available for the dry season. This has important implications for livestock performance as it suggests that animals may be unable to meet their dry matter intake requirements from the arable lands during the latter stages of the dry season.

This conclusion is supported not only by the very low biomass values at this time, but also by the sharp decrease in both cattle and sheep numbers on the main arable land allocation from the middle of dry season 1999 onwards (Figure 9.3).

Forage quality is a function of a number of important parameters including nutritional availability expressed as crude protein values (Meissner *et al.* 1999). These values are summarised for the different grassland vegetation categories at both villages in Table 9.8.

*Table 9.8*    Mean crude protein values (%) of different vegetation categories on arable land allocations at Guquka during dry season 1999

| Vegetation category | Guquka | | | Koloni | | |
|---|---|---|---|---|---|---|
| | Initial | Middle | End | Initial | Middle | End |
| Commonage | na | na | na | 5.33 (0.48)* | 3.35 (0.22) | 10.46 (1.42) |
| *Sporobolus-Cynodon* grassland | 3.88 (0.34) | 3.81 (0.20) | 7.80 (1.85) | 6.10 (0.31) | 4.99 (0.30) | 7.38 (0.45) |
| *Eragrostis-Digitaria* grassland | na | na | na | 6.09 (1.22) | 5.36 (0.71) | 7.95 (0.99) |
| *Hyparrhenia* grassland | 3.05 (0.55) | 1.79 (0.28) | 4.65 (1.85) | 4.94 (1.22) | 3.49 (0.02) | 5.50 (0.66) |

* Values in brackets are standard errors
*Source*: Bennett (2002)

Comparison of equivalent grassland vegetation categories between the two villages reveals generally higher levels of crude protein at equivalent stages of the dry season at Koloni. This is an expression of differences in the underlying ecology of the two sites.

As a *sweetveld* site, the forage at Koloni retains more of its nutritional quality during the dry season than the mixed and *sourveld* at Guquka. More-over, almost all of the crude protein values for grassland forage at Guquka fall below the critical threshold of 6-8%, at which point low herbage quality begins to have a detrimental effect on levels of livestock intake (Minson 1982). In comparison the dry season crude protein values at Koloni only drop consistently below this threshold in the middle of the dry season (end of July). These differ-ences have important implications for animal performance at the two villages.

## Conclusions

The general picture of livestock production in this region is one of a gradual shift away from cattle and sheep production towards cattle production supple-mented by goats. This reflects a combination of a changing policy environment (the demise of betterment policy), fluctuating wool markets, increased difficul-ties of sheep husbandry with little extension support, increased incidences of sheep theft and finally, cultural practices associated with cattle and goats. Cattle, in particular, continue to play a crucial role in peoples' livelihood strate-gies. Although actual income through sales is relatively low for most house-holds, their value as a store of wealth that can be mobilised in time of need remains considerable. They also continue to play an important role in traditional ceremonies, which themselves create a steady market for the sale of animals to those households who have few or none of their own.

Despite these broad similarities, the case study villages underline some of the important differences in production practices and livestock performance that exist among communities. These result primarily from differences in forage quantity and quality between the villages. The most important manifestation of these is on the arable land allocations, which provide dry season forage reserves for livestock. At Koloni both herbage availability and quality on the arable lands is sufficient to provide for foraging livestock at most stages of the dry season. This is a result of the favourable ecology of the site and the preservation of forage during the growing season. In comparison, at Guquka, both ecological and management parameters combine to severely limit the effectiveness of the arable lands in providing for livestock at this time. The seasonal decrease in forage quality is exacerbated by a grazing system that severely limits grassland forage availability on the arable lands during the dry season. These differences clearly have implications for levels of animal performance at the two villages at this time. Differences in performance are exemplified by the much greater levels of milk production at Koloni and the ability of Koloni cattle owners to milk animals more regularly and for a greater proportion of the year.

These findings suggest that differences in livestock production in this region are driven primarily by ecological factors (rainfall and inherent rangeland quality). However, management of grazing resources in both time and space is also of considerable importance in terms of how effectively forage can be retained on key dry season areas such as the arable land allocations. These management differences are largely a function of inequalities in resource availability between communities and the very different levels of grazing pressure imposed on these resources.

# 10

# Gathering from the land

Peter C. Lent[*]

## Introduction

The previous chapter provided detailed information about the mix of livestock found in the two villages of Guquka and Koloni and puts this information in context of other communities in the Eastern Cape Province. It served to introduce livestock ownership as a livelihood strategy and also to describe the basis for animal husbandry with forage derived not only from communal rangelands but also from the arable land allotments. A variety of other resources of value to residents of the two villages are also obtained from the rangelands and arable lands and from other components of the landscape.

It is now well established that rangelands in rural areas with communal rangelands also provide residents with a wide variety of products and values in addition to providing forage for domestic animals. A number of studies have documented the nature of these uses to which rangelands are put and provided estimates of their economic values (Shackleton *et al.* 1999, 2001, 2002; Cocks and Wiersum 2003). Although it is now widely recognized that such uses, gathering products from the land, contribute both economically as integral parts of livelihood strategies and culturally as well, these values and uses of the land are still not receiving adequate attention by policymakers (Cousins 1999, Shackleton *et al.* 2001).

---

[*] The author is indebted to Michelle Cocks for her assistance and analysis of data from the 2005 survey.

The prehistoric and even the early historic roots of modern hunting and gathering practices have not been examined or documented in detail. Schapera and Goodwin (1937: 131) asserted that

> ... the 'Bantu' live partly upon the natural resources of their environment. Wild animals provide them with meat, and wild plants and fruits with vegetable food. But they control the bulk of their own food supply by cultivating plants and breeding livestock.

Lestrade (in Schapera 1937) mentioned that huts were built with mud walls and thatched roofs from grass in and around the settlement. These were frequently renewed. Poles for huts were also from the *veld*; like the digging sticks used in preparing the land for cropping. Pots were made of clay and grain baskets of grass.

Schapera and Goodwin also noted that hunting was done by men and youths. Women gathered edible wild plants, but men might also gather wild fruits and berries when out in the field. Both sexes took part in hut building. Men cut wood and women cut grass, did the thatching and made the floor (with dung and clay mixed). The general conclusion is that these people were not predominantly hunters and gatherers. That is, by the time they settled in what is now the Eastern Cape livestock and crops were clearly the major sources of food and clothing.

In the initial studies in Guquka and Koloni the non-livestock values and non-crop values inherent in the landscape were not treated in any systematic manner, although the survey of ARDRI (1997) did include some relevant questions. Subsequent recognition of these gaps led to two studies in Guquka undertaken by post-graduate students, B. Che (Che and Lent 2004) and S. Rosenberg (Rosenberg 2003) to establish clearly the value of these resources to the villagers. The work of Che dealt primarily with traditional uses and conservation practices and was limited to woody plants. Rosenberg's work was somewhat broader in its scope but largely qualitative in its treatment of the importance of forest and *veld* products in the lives of the community. An additional survey was carried out in 2005 regarding uses of the *veld* in both Koloni and Guquka.

## Gathering from the land: Results and discussion

Rosenberg (2004) referred to "non-cultivated natural resources (NCNR)", which term seems almost redundant because by definition range or *veld* consists of non-cultivated lands. Excluding livestock, he found six categories of resources (NCNR) to be of significant economic and cultural value to the community: clay, cow dung, water, wood, thatch and medicinal plants. Clearly, livestock are excluded because ownership is critical. Others, including stone, forest foods, small game and fish, where found to be of very minor significance and were therefore not investigated further in the surveys. These resources are understood as not being owned by specific individuals and although the role of tribal, municipal and higher government in the management of these resources was generally acknowledged, most residents felt no responsibility or obligations with regard to these authorities. Resources were generally viewed as 'permanent', and conservation, when practiced, generally was not a conscious act. This latter conclusion derives from the work of Che and Lent (2004) as well as Rosenberg.

Rosenberg's data do not allow quantification of any resources or their uses, and therefore in general it is not possible to attach monetary values to these resources. However, with regard to the use of local materials for house construction we can make some crude estimates. These being principally mud, cow dung, timbers and wattle, and thatch. Some roof poles are purchased locally from the operators of the pine plantations around Hogsback on the plateau above the community. His survey of 38 households showed that 33 of these still used traditional "wattle and daub" houses; two had houses of both traditional and modern concrete construction. Thus, clearly NCNR contribute enormously to housing. Many of these traditional homes also had thatch roofs. Che and Lent (2004) also report the recycling of timbers, using those from older, abandoned or demolished structures for new construction. This involved principally timbers from durable woods of *Ptaeroxylon obliquum* or *Olea europaea*. Rosenberg estimates that one of the modern homes in the community, built without any use of local materials, cost R55,000. Although this home was clearly larger than any of the traditional homes, this nevertheless gives some indication of the savings achieved by residents through the use of local materials.

Rosenberg (2003) lists approximately 65 species of plants that are used in Guquka for medicinal or personal hygiene purposes. Most of these, of course, are indigenous to the area although a few are exotics now growing freely in the upper Tyume River area. Six species were used most often because they are both accessible and have wide-ranging medical properties or other applications.

Of the 38 households in Rosenberg's survey, 27 used wood for heating the home and 15 used a wood fire for cooking. But many of these same households also used paraffin stoves on some occasions, either for cooking or heating. Because most houses lack adequate ventilation, respiratory problems were reportedly widespread, especially among older inhabitants. The wood used most commonly for heating and cooking is *Acacia karoo* (*umnga*) which grows widely in the area especially along tributaries of the Tyume River and in the edges of the nearby forests. Much of this firewood is still collected by women and girls and brought back to the households on their heads. However, cattle-drawn sledges and even bakkies (trucks) are occasionally used.

Shackleton *et al.* (2002) reported an even higher proportion of households using firewood for heating in three nearby Kat River communities. In these Kat River villages nearly all households made use of wild edible herbs and fruits and in all three communities the proportion of households using such was more than twice the proportion reporting use of medicinal plants. Smaller numbers of households in the Kat River villages reported use of other edible products including, in approximate order of frequency, wild honey, bushmeat, birds eggs, edible mushrooms and fish.

A summary of the surveys taken in 1997 and 2005 of households in both Guquka and Koloni is presented in Table 10.1. In both communities the dominant use of the rangelands was for collection of firewood. The majority of households also collected plants and plant materials for rituals and medicinal purposes and for consumption as food items (fruits or vegetables). Every household in both communities used at least one product from the *veld*. An appreciable difference is apparent between the number of species reported to be used in 1997 compared to 2005. Whether this decline in the number of species collected by households, evident in both villages over the span of 8 years is indicative of a long-term trend will only be apparent from further studies. Certainly, the number of species reported in both these surveys was considerably lower than that reported in some other villages of the Eastern Cape (Cocks and Wiersum 2003).

*Table 10.1*     Percentage of surveyed households using plants for each purpose and number of species reported as used in Guquka and Koloni, 1996 and 2005

| Purpose | Guquka 1996 N=76 | Guquka 2005 N= 40 | Koloni 1996 N=54 | Koloni 2005 N= 41 |
|---|---|---|---|---|
| Fuelwood | 82 | 95.0 (3) | 78 | 82.5 (2) |
| Igoqo* | | 5.0 (3) | | 12.5 (1) |
| Fencing | 63 | 60.0 (5) | 46 | 35.0 (3) |
| *Kraal* materials | 72 | 65.0 (9) | 87 | 76.0 (8) |
| Rituals | -- | 95.0 (3) | -- | 80.0 (2) |
| Medicines (human) | 32 | 82.5 (1.9)** | 13 | 80.0 (1.88)** |
| *Imifino* (leafy veg.) | | 75.0 (5) | | 57.5 (6) |
| Dung | 16 | | 57 | |
| Thatch grass | 74 | 25.0 (2) | 24 | 40.0 (2) |
| Fruits | | ? | | 77.5 (1.3)** |

* Indigenous vegetable
** Average number of species reported per household

*Sources*: ARDRI Survey (1997), Gathering Survey (2005, unpublished)

The previous studies of products collected from rangelands or *veld* have almost entirely focused on the communal rangelands and neglected other parts of the landscape that may also contain plant products and other items of value to residents.

For that reason the survey undertaken in 2005 questioned respondents as to where various items were obtained (Table 10.2).

*Table 10.2*   Number of households gathering plants from three land categories and number of species gathered

| Village | Rangeland | | Arable allotments | | Other ** | |
|---|---|---|---|---|---|---|
| | No. h.h* | No spp. | No of h.h | No spp. | No h.h | No spp. |
| Guquka (N=34) | 25 (74%) | 13 | 24 (71%) | 15 | 33 (97%) | 35 |
| Koloni (N=34) | 33 (97%) | 34 | 30 (91%) | 31 | 24 (71%) | -- |

* Households
** Mountains, forest, riverine and garden areas (Guquka). Garden areas and woodlot (Koloni)

*Source*: Gathering Survey (2005 unpublished)

At Koloni the number of species collected from the arable allotments and the communal rangelands were nearly equal, 31 and 34, respectively. Thus these findings did not confirm the subjective assessment that plant species richness was greater in the arable allotments. In addition, eleven indigenous or wild species were collected from home gardens and three from the woodlot. Although 16 species were collected at only one location, only one of these came solely from the arable allotments and most of the 16 were plants that were reported by only one or two households.

At Guquka, similarly, the number of species collected from arable allotments and communal grazing lands was nearly equal, being 13 and 15 respectively. However, 31 species were collected from the indigenous forests at higher elevations, and five came from the plateau above the escarpment. Gardens accounted for 11 species here, as well, and two were reported to be collected from along the Tyume River.

Of the 49 identified species at Guquka nearly half (23) came from only one of these collection locales and of these 23 the vast majority (18) came from the mountain forests. Four species came only from home gardens. These findings confirm the important role played by the indigenous forest, largely lying within protected areas, for Guquka and neighbouring villages (Che and Lent 2004). The total of 49 species identified in this survey was considerably lower than the number of species reported by Rosenberg. This difference is probably related to the fact that Rosenberg was asking generally about species that people were generally aware of being used in their village in contrast to ones that they had specifically collected or procured recently.

In another measure of the importance of the forests to the people of Guquka and surrounding communities, Che reported that 73% of his respondents had visited the forests at least once a week. About half the respondents reported going to the forest alone, despite the fact that about one-fourth reported being afraid when entering the forest.

*Photo 10.1*    Acacia trees in arable fields in Guquka. Photo by Ortega.

Where the 1996 and the 2005 data can be compared, most values are similar regarding rates of gathering and proportions of households using specific categories of products. The electrification of Guquka since the initial data on firewood consumption has not led to a decline in the proportion of households using firewood, although the quantities consumed are known only for 2005.

Nevertheless, this finding is in keeping with findings elsewhere that electrification has often resulted in little change in firewood consumption patterns (Madubansi and Shackleton 2006). The decline in the collection of wood for use on kraals could be related to a decline in the use and importance of *kraals*. The very low proportion of households reporting the collection of medicinal plants in 1996 is puzzling and cannot be explained except possibly as an artifact of the way in which the question was asked. The proportions of households reporting collection and use of medicinal plants among Kat River villages (Shackleton *et al.* 2002) are intermediate between the 1996 and 2005 results for Guquka and Koloni.

Firewood consumption in Guquka in 2005 averaged 3,459 kg per household (median = 2,280 kg) but the reported quantities ranged widely from 280 kg to 21,840 kg (an even higher outlier was rejected as being more than twice that reported for a household in any comparable village). In Koloni consumption estimates similarly ranged widely, from 625 to 16,200 kg, with a mean of 3404 and a median of 2,400 kg. In Koloni, 15 respondents reported purchasing fire-wood. No such purchases were reported in Guquka. Based on these consumption patterns the mean value per household of firewood collected in Guquka was R706 and R695 for Koloni.

At both villages harvesting of thatch grass continues to be an important activity, particularly in Guquka where 40% of homesteads reported such collecting in recent years. In an unpublished report of a household survey done in Guquka in 2006, Torres (2007) also reported widespread use of thatch grass with 19 out of 26 respondents stating they used thatching grass gathered from the arable allotments, Of the 19, four reported buying grass or hiring collectors; one reported selling thatch grass. In the 2005 survey only 25% of respondents in Koloni noted collecting thatch grass.

The product is nowadays often used underneath metal roofs to provide insulation and improve comfort. Fallow fields are the major sources of thatch grass. Indeed, all thatch grass was collected from arable allotments. However, fields with fallow vegetation will inevitably lose their value in this regard with increasing amounts of woody plants unless burning or other measures are taken. Based on data for one homestead, which purchased some of the thatch grass necessary to complete their roofing, the value of thatch for a home was R1500. It appears that a well made thatch roof will last approximately 20 years without full replacement.

In Koloni, where thatching is less important, collection of medicinal plants was the most frequent gathering activity on the arable allotments. Nine households out of 41 reported all or most of the medicinal plants they gathered came from these lands. In Guquka only two households reported the same. This, again, is in keeping with the fact that Guquka residents have access to a wider variety of vegetation types. Other frequent uses of the arable fields include collection of *imifino* and woods for small utensils. Only two people, both in Koloni, reported taking any firewood off these fields. However, Torres (2007) did report gathering of fuelwood from fallow fields by three respondents in Guquka. All were gathering Acacia spp., typical of fallow fields in later successional stages with brush encroachment.

The mean gross annual value per household of forest products in the three Kat River communities was R1926. Of this more than half the value on average was attributed to firewood and the second most valuable category of forest products was bushmeats. Although direct comparisons are difficult it appears that use of materials for house construction was more important in Guquka than in the Kat River communities. Shackleton *et al.* (2002) noted that the value of forest products used annually in the Kat River is low compared to some other savanna communities in rural South Africa and, in particular, the value of those products sold to others was very low. We can assume that such sales are also very low among Guquka households, based on the household income surveys conducted in 1996 (ARDRI 1997). Indeed, it was anticipated that some sales to tourists of products gathered from the *veld* might be evident in the 2005 survey of Guquka because of its proximity to Hogsback, a well known tourist destination where local handicrafts, mostly walking sticks and clay figurines, are much in evidence. The absence of any reports of such sales from Guquka suggests that these handicraft enterprises are dominated by residents of other villages somewhat closer to Hogsback (Morrow and Vokwana 2001).

The 2005 survey also emphasizes the importance of wild, uncultivated plants (either indigenous or exotic) collected from garden areas. This value attached to home garden areas was previously recognized by High and Shackleton (2000). Based on work in the Bushbuckridge low *veld* area farther north in South Africa they estimated that such wild plants represented 31% of the total value of products from home gardens with domestic plants representing 69%.

## Conclusions

Rosenberg (2003: 52) concluded that:

> The utilization of NCNR [non-cultivated natural resources] is influenced by two conflicting forces; increasing economic uncertainty places more importance on the availability of free NCNR, yet aspirations to modernity and 'progression', as communicated by the images of mass media, effectively reduce both the cultural and economic significance of such resources. It remains to be seen what the further implications of modernity and increasing poverty will be for the people of Guquka, and how the economic, social and cultural significance of NCNR will be affected. For the present, though, and for a long time to come, the community are heavily dependent on such resources for the socio-economic and cultural continuity of the homestead, of rural livelihoods and for maintaining life, physical health and social well-being in a social environment characterised by great economic uncertainty and the increasing influence of modernity.

The work of Shackleton *et al.* (2002) in the nearby Kat River valley does not fully support Rosenberg's impression that the poorer households are making more use of these resources than those better off economically. They found that among three communities the one that seemed to have the greatest household wealth also harvested the greatest value of products from *veld* and forest. However, they did not perform an intra-community analysis of this relationship. Other studies cited in Shackleton *et al.* (2001) suggest that natural resources are especially important for sustaining the poorest of households through periods of crisis. On the other hand, the 2005 survey found evidence that residents had found new uses for old products. Whereas thatch grass was previously used nearly universally as roofing material for houses it has now been largely replaced by metal roofing. Metal roofing has the disadvantage, however, in that it lacks insulating qualities. Therefore, some home owners now collect thatch grass to place underneath their metal roofs as insulation.

What is clear is that every household in both Guquka and Koloni benefits from resources collected from the *veld*. The contributions to livelihoods are generally similar to these reported from other Eastern Cape villages.

These findings of broad-based resource consumption involving harvesting of wild products from communal rangelands, arable allotments and household areas supports the concept of Cousins (1999) of these rural people as "Jacks-and-Jills-of-many-trades", putting to beneficial use an extremely broad array of natural resources. This finding applies more or less across the board to all households in the communities.

The two villages in this study did differ from those of other comparable studies cited elsewhere in this chapter in two important ways. First, was the relatively low variety of plant species being gathered in Guquka and Koloni. The reasons for this are not clear. It may be in part due to the relatively low diversity of species that are readily available, especially in the case of Koloni. In addition, the Xhosa-speaking field workers who carried out the survey in 2005 reported a generally weak knowledge of Xhosa names for various plants among those interviewed, to a degree which surprised them. But they had no specific explanation for this perceived state of affairs.

Second, survey results indicated that economic benefits derived almost entirely from consumption within the household unit and hardly at all from sale or barter. Why so few households reported such uses of gathered products remains unanswered at present. It does not appear to be an artefact of how questions were presented, and all households were given the opportunity to indicate such sales.

# 11

# Mobility and population dynamics

Lothar Smith and Paul Hebinck[*]

## Introduction

> For others who are retrenched the problems are smaller as they may still be young and do not yet have families to care about like myself. However I am an old man … to lose your job at my age [58 years] is difficult. But with retrenchment, and generally increasing unemployment, the elder generations have no such resources to set aside, and cannot afford to plough. This money cannot come from the children even if these do have a job in Johannesburg, Port Elizabeth or Cape Town, as they only think about their girlfriends and the alcohol in the city. They forget about their rural homes, about their wives and about sending money for ploughing.

This quote from an interview in May 2000 with Mr Mangqila of Guquka points at key issues to be dealt with in this chapter, including the coming and going of people, the movements from town to rural home and *vice versa*, so typical of Guquka and Koloni, like many other villages in the former homelands. More specifically, we will analyse population dynamics and the shifts in homestead and family arrangements and address the processes that have shaped existing social-spatial relationships, whether kinship-related or not.

---

[*] The authors wish to thank Brice Gijsbertsen for supplying the census 2001 data for Guquka and Koloni. Nick Parrott gave valuable comments on the last draft.

This chapter thus addresses how the livelihood transformations that were broadly identified in chapter 4 and are further described in chapters 12 and 13 have affected the homestead and the relationships among people. In the work of Hoernlé (1937), Soga (1931) and Lewis (1984) on pre-colonial rural settlements in present-day Eastern Cape, the homestead (*umzi*) was seen as constituting the basic unit of production and consumption, which also forms the basis for settlement in both villages (chapters 2 and 4). The *umzi* was posited as a group of kin-related households, each of which entails a male head with one or more wives who live together in one compound. These heads would recognise the leadership of the (male) head of one of the constituent households. Typically, the *umzi* constituted a cooperative work unit. This picture fits the pre-colonial period but only partly resembles contemporary reality. As we have seen in previous chapters processes related to migration have substantially altered the social composition of the homestead and the family but also the patterns of resource use. These social processes and transformations are embodied in the contemporary physical layout of the villages. Houses in a state of decay lie adjacent to recently erected houses built according to the latest urban architecture, and intensively cultivated gardens aside long neglected fields; these are symbols attesting to the influence of social change on the physical layout of the two villages. We will explore whether labour migration is the only factor that explains current social-spatial processes, or whether the 'household' is intrinsically characterised throughout time by continual changes in spatial, social and economic dimensions not necessarily related to migration of its members. To explore the relation between social processes and physical ones, we examine the basic demography of the two villages and the composition of the homesteads.

## Village demographics

An essential feature of village demography is the steady increase in population size. On the one hand this has been due to natural growth. However it isalso the result of the influx of people from elsewhere through the forced removals of black people from areas demarcated as white by the South African government during the 1960s, 70s and 80s. Chapter 4 has shown that this influx particularly affected Guquka. Koloni did not receive any 'newcomers' and its population increase has been mainly due to natural population growth.

Table 11.1 summarises the available data on population growth. These data are compiled from a range of sources. Looking at the trends discussed in chapter 3 and summarised in Table 11.1 three distinct demographic periods can be discerned: (1) 1850s-1960s; (2) 1960s-1990s and (3) 1990s to the present. These periods are clearly separable from each other as they mark changes in the state of the region and related important events. Thus, the first period spans the time of settlement (1830s) of the region and leads up to the moment (early 1960s) when many blacks were forced to migrate to the region from surrounding areas. The second period is concurrent with the existence of the state of

Ciskei. The third period starts when Apartheid was abolished and first democratic national elections were held (1994).

*Table 11.1*    Estimated population size, Guquka and Koloni, 1939-2004

| Year | Guquka | | Koloni | |
|---|---|---|---|---|
| | Population | Number of dwellings | Population | Number of dwellings |
| 1939 | n.a. | 38 (1938)[f] | 190[a] | 33[f] |
| 1962 | n.a. | 78 (1963)[f] | 329[b] | 56 (1963)[f] |
| 1991 | 650[c] | 127[c] | 514[c] | 95[c] |
| 1996 | 460[d] | 122[d] | 315[d] | 97[d] |
| 2001 | 300[e] | n.a. | 262[e] | n.a. |
| 2004 | 187[g] | 125[g] | 224[g] | 133[g] |

n.a: not available

*Sources*:
a) Ndlovu (1991)
b) Betterment Planning Commission (1962)
c) Republic of Ciskei Population Census (1991)
d) ARDRI Survey (1997)
e) Extrapolated from Republic of South Africa Population Census (2001)
f) Calculated from aerial photos (chapter 6)
g) Total number of people counted during update 2004 (Hebinck 2004)

We discuss only the most important changes for the first period, focusing more on the second and third period. In the period from 1850 to 1960 British Kaffraria, later designated the Ciskei, was sparsely populated. Thus Xhosa, Mfengu, Hottentots, British and other settlers were able to move in and settle the region, initially without much dispute (chapter 2). However an unabated migration of new settlers to the region led to increasing competition for resources, particularly grazing land, among these groups and thus to increasing conflict. The Xhosa were forced to steadily concede land to the Boers and English, who had also entered in alliance with the Mfengu. Their steady loss of land to these other groups took a turn for the worse when they heeded the call of Nongqawuse, a Xhosa prophetess, to destroy all their crops and kill their cattle, as this would drive 'the white man' back into the sea. Instead this act resulted in a large-scale famine (chapter 2), reducing the Xhosa population from about 105,000 in January 1857 to 26,000 by the end of 1858 (Switzer 1993), effectively ending their struggle against the white settlers. Concurrently, the British expanded their presence in British Kaffraria by bringing in military settlers to the region, who established new settlements such as Berlin and Stutterheim. Their influx saw the presence of white people increase from below one thousand in 1856 (less than 1% of the total population) to 53,888 (12.5% of the total population) by December 1858 (*ibid.*).

Turning to the population data for the twentieth century our analysis of individual magisterial districts (Table 11.2) shows that for the period of 1911 to 1936 the population substantially increased by 38%. Thereafter, the population grew at a much slower pace of 3% from 1936 to 1951 (*ibid.*). However, the two districts incorporating Guquka and Koloni actually experienced negative growth rates between 1916 and 1951. Population change in Victoria East District (Guquka) was strongly negative at -26%, while the Middledrift District (Koloni) also recorded a decrease with a 3% decline (Table 11.3).

*Table 11.2*    Population of African people in the Ciskei, 1911-1951

| Period | Numbers | Increase in % |
|---|---|---|
| 1911-1936 | 120,889 | 38.14 |
| 1936-1952 | 13,349 | 2.96 |
| 1911-1951 | 134,238 | 42.35 |

*Source*: Adapted from Switzer (1993), Table A7.2: 236

*Table 11.3*    Population change in the Ciskei 1916-1951; selected districts

| District/Period | Number | % change |
|---|---|---|
| Victoria East | | |
| 1916-1936 | -4,939 | -33.5 |
| 1936-1951 | 1,105 | 11.3 |
| 1916-1951 | -3,834 | -26.0 |
| Middledrift | | |
| 1916-1936 | n.a. | n.a. |
| 1936-1952 | -750 | -3.0 |
| Ciskei as a whole | | |
| 1916-1936 | 10,106 | 4.3 |
| 1936-1951- | 17,808 | 7.3 |
| 1916-1952 | 27,914 | 11.9 |

n.a. = not available

*Source*: Adapted from Switzer (1993: Table A7.3: 237)

The discrepancy between the population growth for the Ciskei region as a whole and the population decline in the Middledrift and Victoria East districts can be explained by the fact that during this period the region was expanded to include areas which had strong population growth. The Tomlinson Commission

(1955) confirmed that some magisterial districts within the Ciskei had recorded negative population growth.

Switzer (1993) examined the actual capacity of the Ciskei to absorb the African population from surrounding regions and concluded that between 1916 and 1951 this declined. Whereas in 1916 about 74% of the region's resident population was living in the reserve, by 1936 this had been reduced to 63% and by 1951 it had further declined to 58%. This decline in the capacity of the Ciskei region to provide a basis for a rural livelihood not only points to increasing population pressure on available resources but also to the increasing importance of income sources not based in the rural economy in the lives of villagers. This confirms what has been stated before: from the first half of the twentieth century onwards rural people began to look elsewhere for livelihood options, notably focusing on the urban and industrial economies of the country.

Koloni experienced an estimated annual growth of 3% for the period between 1939 and 1962. For Guquka the absence of population census data meant that we had to resort to changes in the number of dwellings and from this extrapolate changes in population. Our analysis suggests an average annual rate of increase of 4.4% in the period 1938 to 1963 (chapter 7). These are growth rates which are considerably larger than in the Ciskei as whole. We can only hypothesize that at the time conditions in the two villages were quite favourable when compared to other parts of the Border/Ciskei region.

The second period, from 1960 until the early 1990s, encompassed the time of forced removals carried out by the state. Thus the mechanisation of agriculture on white farms, which made large numbers of farm workers redundant (Marcus 1989), resulted in these labourers being forced to move to the reserves. Other forced removals took place when parts of the Eastern Cape were reallocated to the Western Cape, which was restricted to whites, forcing Africans in these areas to move out to the reserves. Black people were also removed from locations in the East London metropolitan area. These forced removals followed on the Group Areas Act of 1950 and other actions implemented by the South African government that sought to reduce the number of black people in urban areas. Finally, people that were removed from Herschel and Glen Grey districts (referred to by Swizter as 'refugees') added to a general influx in the Ciskei.

Between 1970 and 1980 the Ciskei received more than 160,000 immigrants. In the same period districts such as Victoria East and Middledrift experienced population increases of 4.5% and 2.7%, respectively (Switzer 1993), showing that this influx was unevenly distributed. Green and Hirsch (1982) argue that urban areas experienced especially high growth rates, rather than rural areas such as the districts of Victoria east and Middledrift. Thus their data show an urban population growth rate of 8.2% per annum for the Ciskei between 1970 and 1980, and a 4.0% growth rate for the rural areas. To express the nature of these demographic changes Kruger (1991: 39) referred to the Ciskei as the 'dumping ground for Xhosa refugees'. It is estimated that the Ciskei alone absorbed two-thirds of the Xhosa people who were forced to move from locations elsewhere in South Africa.

Koloni, which did not experience such dumping, recorded an average annual population growth rate of 2.3% for the period 1962 to 1991. Interpretations of aerial photos suggest a similar population growth for Guquka for the same period, which is much lower than that of the previous period. However we add that as aerial photos and regional/district data constitute different sources of data, caution needs to be taken with respect to the reliability of our interpretations.

The third period, from the early 1990s until present, relates to a period in which previously maintained influx control measures were withdrawn. Thus in 1991 the Group Areas Act was withdrawn by the government. This last period has seen contrasting tendencies and, as it is also still ongoing, this makes it difficult for us to draw conclusive comments with regard to major processes that are at play.

Recent demographic data available for the two villages show a dramatic decline in population numbers (Table 11.1). This is partly explained by net outmigration of villagers who seek to pursue urban livelihoods. However, at the same time there is also a return migration of people who have returned to the village. Thus the population decline may also be related to other influences and one on of these must be HIV/AIDS. At the time we conducted our research we gave insufficient attention to this issue, not helped by the fact that the topic was much avoided when we tried to focus on it with villagers. As villagers often attributed deaths to causes other than HIV/AIDS, we have no numbers to support our analysis of the extent to which HIV/AIDS has influenced the village demography. However the increasing rate with which younger people are being buried points to an increasing effect of AIDS on village economies. Parker *et al.* (2000) point to multiple economic dimensions of the impact of HIV/AIDS on homesteads, arguing that it leads to income losses, increases household expenses due to expenditure on medicines, requires investments of other members of the homestead in the ill person to provide care, when these funds could have been used more productively. The death of the infected person imposes further expenses on the family for the organisation of a funeral and may result in the decision to remove children from school to compensate for financial losses. Parker *et al.* also argue that HIV/AIDS has a disproportional impact on rural women, notably AIDS widows in paternal systems, as they become stigmatised and lose rights to resources. This makes them and their children especially vulnerable. However, phenomena such as grandparents taking over the care of their grandchildren following the demise of their own children, or children caring for their siblings are also fundamental issues affecting rural economies (Drimie 2002, Parker *et al.* 2000).

One way to understand population dynamics is to look at the demographic profile of a village. The frequency with which rural homes are occupied or left vacant for varying periods of time also provides data which can help interpret these findings. Both dimensions provide evidence of the social transformations of homesteads in the two villages and later we argue for a differentiation between single homestead households (SHH) and multiple homestead households (MHH) to explain transformations of rural livelihoods and homesteads (De Wet and Holbrook 1997).

Figure 11.1 shows the demographic profile for the two villages in 1997. These two demographic profiles, especially that for Guquka, compare well with demographic trends for the Eastern Cape Province as a whole (Hutchinson *et al.* 2004, Table 2.1: 16).

Unfortunately, earlier data were not available to enable a comparison with these contemporary data. The figure clearly indicates the absence of the 'thirty plus' generation, and the return of males of the generation that preceded it due to nation-wide retrenchments throughout the 1990s. The data also clearly illustrate that in both villages younger males in the 20-29 age group are still present in the village. They mainly depend on local casual work and support from their kin for their living (chapter 12). They seem to represent a 'lost generation' who, with few perceived opportunities to earn a living as migrants, have remained in the village, relying on income from odd jobs, pensions of elder members of their homesteads and/or remittances sent by a brother or sister who has managed to find an income 'in town'.

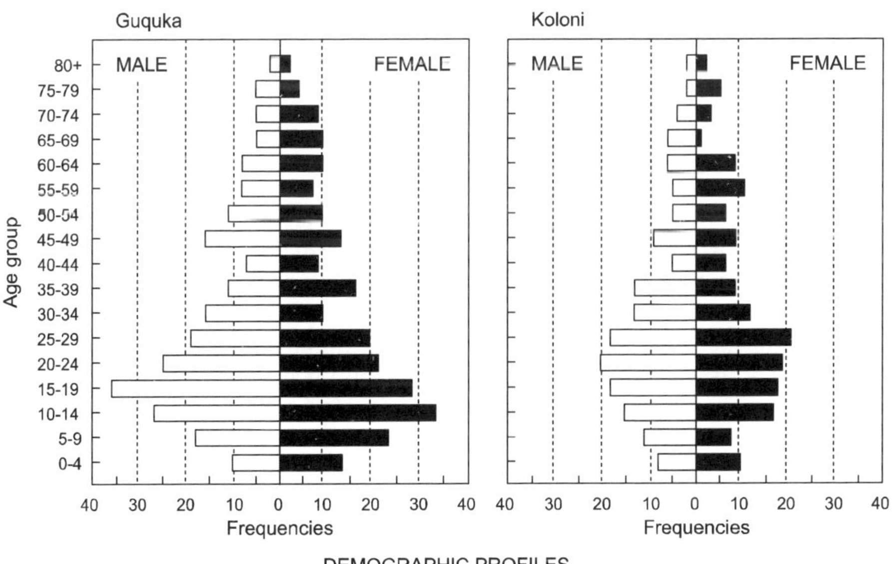


*Figure 11.1*   The demographic profile of Guquka and Koloni in 1997

*Source*: ARDRI Survey (1997)

The age structure of the villages also shows the predominance of the elder people, 60 to 80 years old, and of those older than 80. Their presence points at the relative importance of pensions in providing for livelihoods, not only for these pensioners, but also for other members of their homesteads.

The situation in Guquka and Koloni also reflects a more recent trend of young women leaving the village, usually to obtain work or education outside the village. In doing so, some join their spouses who had preceded them. The demographic pattern of Guquka seems to represent a typical migration picture: men from the most productive age group (35 to 44 years) do not reside in the village. They usually return at the age of 40 and above. However, in the last fifteen years this general pattern seems to have been undermined by retrenchments from jobs in urban centres and industrial areas.

Another phenomenon in both villages reflected in Figure 11.1 is the presence of fewer young children (0-4 age group) than a 'normal' demographic composition would have indicated. This hints at out-migration of young parents with their children and confirms the recent institutional change in the nature of migration compared to prior decades when Apartheid regulations largely confined migration to male labour migrants. With the abolition of the pass laws the nature of migration has begun to take change from temporary labour-oriented migration to more permanent forms of migration, as young villagers seek to secure an urban life.

Parsons (1982), examining population data for South African urban areas, suggested that female migration from rural to urban areas has taken place before. He observed that the proportion of males and females leaving rural areas had changed from 4:1 in 1911 to 2:1 by 1936. This he related mainly to a rising demand for female domestic labour amongst urban whites. At the same time increasing repression under Apartheid legislation seemed to have halted the further entry of black females into the urban labour market.

The more permanent migration of younger villagers with their children to urban parts of South Africa has also reduced the reduced possibilities for the older generation to look after these children (usually their grandchildren), a role which ensured the commitment of migrants to the well-being of their elders, as it also influenced the well-being of their own children (see also see Bank 2002).

At the same time the HIV/AIDS pandemic is once again reconfiguring these affiliations, as grandparents take up the role of caretakers of young children again when the parents of these children die. In this case there are few benefits for these elders to take on this role.

## The future is in the city

"Why are you leaving the rural area?" was a question we regularly asked. Most female respondents in the villages saw migration as a major improvement because they could be closer to their husbands and be less fearful of being left behind in the village, their livelihood and relation to their husbands in constant jeopardy as many men found 'another woman' in town. The policy change has also enabled many female residents of the village (both single and married) to (re-)enter the urban labour market.

Mrs. Mandeya and her daughter-in-law explain the significance of wives migrating to town, sometimes also with their children:

> We women want this [to move to the city] because it will stop our husbands from taking another woman there with whom he may also make some children. Eventually he will become trapped between the two houses, the two wives and his two families. As he finds it harder and harder to accommodate the needs of both families he might eventually decide to leave his real wife and only support his woman in town.

Mrs. Mandeya's livelihood trajectory is illustrative of what many widows experience. She told us that after an active life in Koloni she wished to retire with her children who reside in town. When we interviewed her in 2000, she informed us that her husband had passed away one year before. She still lived on her own and enjoyed a pension. However, unlike many other pensioners, none of her children or grandchildren stayed with her in Koloni, although her sons who worked in King William's Town visited her during the weekends. Some of her other children lived and worked in the more distant Port Elizabeth. Of these children, some were residing in a house bought by her late husband when he took up work in Port Elizabeth in 1952.

The late Mr. Mandeya started working as a migrant labourer in the mines in Johannesburg from 1946 until 1951. In 1947 he married Mrs. Mandeya. When he moved to work in Port Elizabeth she initially remained behind in Koloni to look after his parents but joined him in 1962. In 1979 she moved back to Koloni with the children. Mr. Mandeya had been able to buy a residential plot and fields from a family that left the village, and they built a house on this residential plot. She moved into it to bring up the children whilst he remained in Port Elizabeth until retirement in 1990, when he returned to Koloni.

In the meantime their children, upon reaching adulthood, had moved back to Port Elizabeth to seek work. Initially they shared the Mandeya house there but at present all but one of the five children have married and acquired their own residences. Recently Mrs. Mandeya joined her children in Port Elizabeth for a few months, staying at the house that originally belonged to her husband. One of her grandsons said: "She's right there. When she got there she did not need the attention of doctors anymore!"

When interviewed her in Koloni in 2000, her sons, John and Alfred, who had come to visit their pensioned mother, clearly conveyed that it is hard to get employment in Port Elizabeth. Nevertheless they prefer to remain there and not return to Koloni. They eke a living out of various temporary jobs and claim this is enough for them to live on. It supports them, their wives and their children. Nxoli, John's wife, explained that they do not want to return to the rural areas because it is impossible to get opportunities in a village like Koloni that would enable them to obtain "a flashy car, a nice house and good education for our children". Reality for her and John has, so far, proved to be quite different from these ideals. In the past few years that they had stayed in Port Elizabeth she had only been employed for three months in an 'ANC (government) employment scheme'. John was employed in a factory for some time but when he was retrenched two years ago, they remained unemployed for a long time. They had needed to get by on 'small jobs', such as petty trade. "Buying things cheap and selling these more expensive" enabled them to survive for two years until John was once again employed by the factory where he had worked earlier. Nxoli:

> And that is my point. It is easier to survive in the city, even if you are unemployed, than in a rural area because there [in the rural area] you have to depend on your crops for survival. We do not want to live in a rural area … we are going to stay in the city permanently! Now that things are looking better again for us, with my husband having employment, we are going to take away my mother [in law] to come and stay with us in Port Elizabeth. The clinics there are much better and she [that is her mother, LS/PH] can be near all her children again.

Indeed when we inquired after Mrs. Mandeya in 2004 the chairman of the residential committee confirmed that she had left 2 years ago and now stayed with her children. The house she had been staying in was now no longer inhabited, although it continued to be maintained. She was said to come to Koloni once a year.

The case of Mrs. Nthlabate is also informative regarding the drive to leave the village. Since 1987 the homestead consisted of her father, mother, herself, and most recently, her young child. In 1987 her two brothers and sister left Koloni, taking up residence in Mdantsane situated between King William's Town and East London.Until her father died in 1999, she had relied on his pension. Now, without this pension she has become dependent on the produce she can sell from the garden she cultivates. In managing the garden she is aided by a male cousin also staying in Koloni. She stressed that the financial support she receives from her two brothers and sister is minimal, as her two brothers are unemployed at present, and have not returned to the village since 1987. Her sister does return at times, but cannot offer much help. After a long silence she raised the hope that sometime soon a job opportunity will arise. She will take this opportunity and leave her child with the family of her mother. She does not wish to remain in Koloni. In 2004 she still had not found the golden opportunity and continued to remain in Koloni. She still worked in her home garden selling some of her produce. However, she has begun to receive a child support grant from the state. This has made her life a little easier she said, but the city continues to attract her. Mrs Nthlabate's case clearly underlines that the resources upon which her livelihood hinged, have gradually reduced in quality and composition. The urban environment appeared as one with lots of opportunities, even for a short period of time only.

Finally, the migration to the city also results from the inability of some villagers to gain or negotiate access to resources such as arable land. Accounts of interviewed youths clearly emphasize that the terms under which key resources were accessible (such as sharecropping, chapters 6 and 8) and the lack of opportunities outside farming (chapter 12) push them to town, where there are more, and better, opportunities to earn a living. Xiliba, a youngster in Guquka who helped with collecting new and updated data in April 2004, added that there is not much to do in the village:

> No work and not many peers to talk to. What do I do here; there is no future for me here. I have applied for a job and hope to get it soon. Now I do not even have money to go to the *shebeen* for a beer and meet others.

Taking the subject further it became clear that farming was not considered to be a proper job and part of a modern life style. "You work hard and there is hardly a return". Others youngsters expressed similar thoughts and one said that "if you come back next year, you will not find me here. I am in Cape Town then to go to school, and I will look for jobs there and probably never come back here". This aspect is treated in more detail in chapter 8.

The draw to the 'city lights' has led many villagers to establish themselves in urban areas. In fact, the youth follow the careers of their fathers. The difference between then and now is that some of the youths resented the control of those they referred to as the 'old families' who largely controlled the conditions to access arable fields (chapter 6 and 8).

## Rural security and the role of pensions and remittances

The rural settlement, however, continues to provide social security to those who decide to remain in the village, but also to those whose efforts to secure an urban-based livelihood fail. Mr. Msiwa has felt this burden, and explained that having a large 'family' was not always beneficial. From the 1970s onwards most people in Guquka found it increasingly difficult to sustain their lives. As a consequence many re-evaluated their ties with fellow villagers, clan and even family members, deciding to focus only on those with whom reciprocity would be more certain. Thus most respondents complained that presently help from fellow villagers required payment. However, this did not only hold for neighbours and friends, but also for fellow members of the same clan and even family. Other villagers describe Mr. Msiwa as a kind and considerate man whom you can always approach for help with a problem, especially when you are a family member. However he commented:

> After the Dabi's my family is the largest. The whole family lives in or near Guquka. Whenever anyone of them has a problem they turn to me first. Usually they come to

ask for financial help concerning family problems like when someone has passed away. Issues such as not being able to afford the necessary money for hiring a tractor, or getting oxen for ploughing I do not try to solve because they are on a different level [of importance]. With the other problems I try to help. However I cannot help others in the village. Like we try and solve our own problems within the family, others must do the same.

A further example is that of Mr. Mxolisi, an unmarried man in his early forties. He explained that he had to return to Koloni despite having his own house in Dimbaza:

> There are no jobs, or they are not good. My sister now works for a Chinese shoe factory in Dimbaza. She earns 3 Rand per hour only! Yet I have nothing. I am doing any job around Koloni but it is nothing. I am supported by my parents with their pensions. I wish to work their lands but we have not got that money ... we cannot afford to hire a tractor. The money needed for that is too much; no one can afford that, especially the pensioners who form the majority of this village, as they are already supporting their children.

## Social relations and the homestead

The homestead and its social configuration have undergone significant changes in both villages (see also Bank 2002; Ngwane 2003). Today, both in Koloni and Guquka, one finds little evidence of previously existing cooperative working arrangements that were based on reciprocity, although a few arrangements still exist (chapter 8). Thus there is still evidence of wool farmers collectively marketing their wool in Koloni (chapter 9). The lending of cattle (*ukusisa*) also still occurs in both villages, to some extent also supported with remittances from urban incomes. Thereby other villagers take care of the cattle of migrants in their absence, and are provided with some of the calves these cattle bear. More recently this practice seems to have been adapted to respond to an increasing presence of widows who are unable to care for their cattle (Bennett 2002 and chapter 9).

Chapter 8 provided some evidence of the demise of cooperate labour arrangements for arable farming. In contrast, care-taker arrangements of residential properties are still common and, according to the current chairmen of the Residents Committee of Koloni, even increasing. These arrangements entail resident villagers watching over residential properties of family members or neighbours who have migrated. Table 11.4 below contains numerical evidence of such relationships.

Residence in homesteads has changed dramatically from a kin-based homestead, where certain tasks and responsibilities were carried out either collectively or according to a certain pattern of distribution (such as cooking, planting, ploughing, providing shelter, socialisation and security) to a more multi-local residence pattern. Kinship ties remain important, irrespective of where one resides and works, but the nature of these social relationships are of declining importance in extending support and providing indefinite, unconditional care to others. Contributing to this decline are changing gender and power relations and shifting livelihood conditions that have led people to earn a living elsewhere. For some people this is combined with increased options for a living that is based on resources not confined to the immediate village, as social pension schemes and remittances also play an important role for them. Regarding the homestead, one respondent in Guquka narrated that in the past the 'house' (homestead) was much bigger:

> [M]y brothers could get married and still live on the same plot as my parents ... until the end of the 1970s it was possible for the whole family to be cooking from one pot.

Furthermore other villagers such as neighbours would also be provided some of the food that had been cooked. Another respondent also argued that the role of the clan or the *isidulo* (extended family) had changed from encompassing and providing for the livelihoods of all its clan members, to a role where only on important cultural occasions, such as weddings and funerals, financial and other kind of support was being given to others of the *isidulo*. Similarly, employment opportunities elsewhere would first be relayed to one's direct family members, then to extended family members before being passed on to others. All respondents asserted during interviews we held with them that it was no longer possible to rely upon *isidulo* relationships alone. The situation of Miss Ntlangweni described earlier in this chapter points this out clearly, namely that even help from next of kin (brothers, sisters) is insecure.

Evidence from urban research in East London townships shows how many young women, once in town, turn their backs on their rural homes. Bank (2001) reports of women who preferred to remain in town and spend their income in clubs and on luxury commodities rather than providing it directly to the rural economy. Pouring money into a faltering agrarian economy is an unattractive and risky business for women in the city. Thus, they develop their relationships with fellow urban residents through church, grocery clubs, burial societies, saving clubs and credit associations. The presence of unfinished houses in Koloni's 'squatter settlement', many owned by young and unmarried mothers (chapter 4), is a reflection of this changing interest of female migrants.

When mapping out social networks with respondents in Guquka and Koloni, discussing who is important to them, these respondents named few, if any, people not belonging to their own extended family, especially when it came to those who supported their livelihoods. Even when we interviewed respondents who in the past had lived and worked outside the village, they also only identified family members as comprising their urban based relationships. This finding seems to confirm that the role of family, both urban and rural, for providing security to those in the villages is still regarded essential by villagers. Relationships with non-kin that were established outside the village do not seem to have any value in the village.

Mrs. Sonja described the change that has taken place in Guquka over the last fifty years in which the composition of the homestead changed from an extended, loosely arranged, social unit to a more nuclear form:

> Before, the whole family was cooking from one pot. Even when the parents arranged a house for their son and his newly wed wife, who might not like to live in one place with his parents, they would still come together to cook and eat before going to their own houses ... The problem is that now it is impossible to all live together, as this would mean starvation. From the fields and the incomes contributed by the different members it is impossible to find a living for all because contributions are so irregular. That is why we have spread out to separate residential sites and own fields. Now that the fields are finished, however, people depend on incomes from elsewhere to survive.

While this comment referred especially to a change in local arrangements of livelihoods, its validity also extends to livelihoods encompassing multiple locations. Certainly the validity of her statement can be empirically ascertained in the prevailing composition of most homesteads. Ties at the local level, through kinship linkages, whilst still important, have been much reduced. None of the present homesteads in the villages approaches the size of homesteads which elder respondents described existing in the past. Nevertheless, strong variation in the actual composition of homesteads remains in terms of size, generations present, and extent of incorporated family ties.

In Koloni, the size of most homesteads seems not to have diminished appreciably over time. This is mainly attributable to the arrangement of residential sites, which were fixed from the start, implying that opportunities for expansion were always limited. The establishment of their own homesteads by offspring was in that way always encouraged and perceived by 'school' thought as an advancement, enabling looser social and economic arrangements. Only in the past decade has the size of the homestead, and more importantly also the presence of various generations in the village, changed due to a strongly declining role of local opportunities which has spured many of the younger members of the homesteads to leave.

De Wet and Holbrook (1997: 255) attempted to capture and understand the process of the coming and going of villagers between their rural village and town. They noted that, increasingly, homestead members reside and work somewhere else while maintaining ties with and contributing to the well-being of those in their original, rural homes. They thus suggested distinguishing between single homestead households (SHH) and multiple homestead households (MHH). An SHH represents a configuration where migrants still see themselves as having only one home, namely the rural homestead where they grew up, to which they send remittances and make return visits, and to which they assume they will one day return to retire. An MHH reflects the situation whereby members of the original rural SHH find a job in town, and unlike migrants in an SHH, set up their own, potentially permanent home there. Upon achieving an urban livelihood, and establishing ties with others in the town/city, their affiliation to the village slowly changes. They will maintain ties with their rural kin, particularly their own parents and siblings, sending money and goods or their children during school holidays, and also visiting the village for important cultural occasions (initiation rites, celebrations, funerals, weddings). However, these ties more often relate to social-cultural affiliations with the village and their kin than to direct economic interests.

The single homestead household (SHH) is exemplified by the homestead of Mrs. Tibana who lives at Guquka. Mrs. Tibana belongs to one of the original families of the village. She was born in Guquka and raised there by her mother, as one of six children, while her father worked in Cape Town. When she reached adulthood she was the last of these children to leave Guquka for urban areas. She joined a sister in Rustenburg and worked with her sister in an informal 'take-away'.

Her father, upon retirement, returned to the village and depended on a pension to support himself and his wife, also augmenting this income with agricultural activities until his health began to fail him and the related expenses required the bulk of his pension. His children were at this stage unable to provide much financial support from what they were able to earn elsewhere. With her father's health declining Mrs. Tibana decided to return to Guquka to take care of her parents in 1997, giving up her life and steady income to do so. She emphasized that she was the only child who was prepared to make this sacrifice.

Since the death of her parents she has remained in the village to occupy their house, supporting her children with an assortment of temporary and part-time jobs she is able to do around the village. Her brothers and sisters have always remained in town, seldom returning to Guquka and hardly providing her with any support through remittances or otherwise.

A typical MHH is that of Mr. Mcete in Koloni who was born and bred in Koloni. The eldest of five children, he never married nor had any children. At the time of our interview in March 2000 he was staying with his two brothers in the house of his parents, who had passed away some time before. Reaching adulthood he had gone to work in the mines and stayed for a long time in Johannesburg. However, in 1981 he suddenly returned to Koloni when he had been declared unfit for such work due to mine poisoning. As compensation for his illness he was provided with a health grant by the government, sufficient for subsistence needs.

Mr. Mcete's three brothers and sister had also left the village upon reaching adulthood. Two of his brothers had moved in with him in Johannesburg and had also begun to work in the mines. They also returned with him to Koloni in 1981, hoping that they could draw on their savings to expand their agricultural activities. Instead they came to rely on local 'piece' jobs to gain an income, augmented with the grant which Mr. Mcete received. In the meantime, upon the death of her husband, Mr. Mcete's mother moved in with her daughter and her husband who were living in nearby King William's Town, to receive health treatment when necessary.

In 1998 Mr. Mcete's grant was taken away from him without any explanation. A disabled person, his options for gaining an income were limited to gardening in the house plot. Not eligible for an old-age pension for ten more years he and his brothers started to rely heavily on remittances they received on occasion from their mother (from her old-age pension), sister and their youngest brother (a civil servant in Bisho) to augment what they produced and earned locally.

The presence of SHHs and MHHs is clearly reflected in the frequency of occupation of homes throughout the year (Table 11.4). In 1997 there were 33 homesteads in Guquka who maintained a second residence in town. Of these, 8 had left all or some of their children in the care of others residing in Guquka. Most migrants lived in distant urban areas such as Cape Town, Port Elizabeth and Gauteng, and returned to Guquka maintaining links with their rural residence through weekly, monthly or annual visits.

*Table 11.4*    Reported frequency of occupation of rural residences in 1997 and 2004

| Frequency of occupation of the rural home | Guquka | | Koloni | |
|---|---|---|---|---|
| | 1997 | 2004 | 1997 | 2004 |
| Every night | 81 | 86 | 61 | 65 |
| Weekends | 1 | 0 | 5 | 2 |
| Once a month | 6 | 0 | 12 | 1 |
| Irregular | 0 | 2 | 5 | 2 |
| Once per year or less | 25 | 4 | 8 | 13 |
| Never (and/or caretaker arrangement) | 2 | 18 | 5 | 6 |
| Vacant or unusable | 6 | 15 | 1 | 44 |
| Total | 122 | 125 | 97 | 133 |

*Source*: Adapted from Van Averbeke *et al.* (1988a) and Hebinck (2004)

In Koloni all 35 homesteads who occupied their rural residence only during weekends, or less frequently, maintained a second residence in an urban area. Twenty-eight of these households had children, but only three left these children behind in Koloni in the care of relatives or neighbours. Distance between the urban residence and Koloni influenced the frequency with which households returned to their rural residence. Those staying in East London, or nearby urban centres, such as Alice, Middledrift, King William's Town and Dimbaza, usually travelled back and forth on a weekly or monthly basis. Others, who stayed farther away, limited their visits to once or twice a year.

Families who have migrated out of the village for long periods usually leave their assets in the rural settlement such as their homes, livestock and land, in the care of neighbours or relatives. But there is also evidence of villagers who have left the village without making any arrangements with villagers regarding the maintenance, use and security of their resources in the village. The resulting underutilisation of these assets, particularly of arable fields, is contested by others who want to utilize these to pursue local, agriculture-related livelihoods (see also chapter 8).

The fluidity of the situation becomes clear when one compares the 1997 data with the 2004 update for the two villages. In both Guquka and Koloni more people were coming home to their village every night in 2004 than in 1997. However, for people who do not stay at the village on a daily basis (coming home every night), findings suggest a strong decline in their physical presence in the villages. Indeed in Koloni an astonishing 44 out of 133 homes had, either permanently or temporarily, become vacant, with some houses in a clear state of being abandoned (Table 11.4). In Guquka caretaker arrangements had become much more commonplace than before.

## Conclusion

The chapter has discussed three contrasting demographic trends which clearly associate local demographics with migration and government policy. The first trend concerned the expansion of both villages, on the one hand due to natural population growth but also due to influxes of migrants from other parts of South Africa. The second trend concerned temporary migration to the mines and urban areas. The third, most recent, trend concerns the outflow of villagers, particularly younger generations, without it being clear whether they have intentions to return to the village.

This chapter has clearly revealed that migration has, for a long time, formed an important element in the lives and livelihoods of villagers. Thus, as was already discussed in chapter 4, and as will be further substantiated in chapter 12, migration needs to be examined in conjunction with the role of local economic activities, particularly agriculture. This concurs with the findings of chapters 8 and 9, namely that over the past century the economic role of agriculture declined as it has gradually been replaced with resources and incomes derived from outside the village, such as remittances from migrant family members and pensions (old age, illness, child care).

Especially for villagers who did not have sufficient access to local resources to maintain a local livelihood, temporary migration to the mines and urban areas formed the most viable alternative. This held especially for those who arrived in the Eastern Cape from other parts of South Africa during the 1960s and 1970s. However, also male villagers with access to local resources, notably arable land, preferred to go to the mines for some time, as this enabled them to generate savings which they could invest in agricultural activities, facilitating their livelihoods, and those of others in their homesteads, upon their return to the village.

Over the course of the twentieth century migration has changed social-economic configurations among villagers. This is due to increasing disparities in wealth: some villagers are able to farm their land, expand their herds and derive remittances from family members in other parts of the country on a regular basis. Other villagers need to resort to modest means for their survival. Changes in social relationships have also resulted from households establishing themselves in multiple locations, deriving their livelihoods from multiple sources. To protect these sources they have limited their involvement with other households in the village. And when they do engage with their fellow villagers they may do so through explicit, formalised arrangements. Thus changing social configurations, notably through migration, lead to strengthening linkages of rural with urban and national economies, but also seem to lead to a formalisation of village relationships.

Finally, and more recently, households have once again changed their configuration following the end of Apartheid, which ended restrictions on mobility, enabling villagers to choose where they want to live. This change has further compounded economic differences between homesteads, as it has resulted in more permanent forms of migration of villagers to urban areas, often involving their whole household and not just one or two members.

The out-migration of families has, thus far, not resulted in a severance of ties with the larger family who has remained in the village. However, given that it is generally the young, able-bodied who leave the village, local livelihoods do become further detached from agriculture and increasingly dependent on external resources. At the same time retrenchments and generally high levels of employment in urban areas have seen the rise of a reverse trend whereby villagers who migrated to urban areas have begun to reinvest in their social relationships with those in the village, in an attempt to safeguard their entitlement to local resources with the view that, at some stage, they might return to the village. This might be an involuntary movement, as with retrenchments, but could also be planned, as in the case of retirement.

# 12

# Contemporary livelihoods

Wim van Averbeke and Paul Hebinck

## Introduction

This chapter describes contemporary livelihoods in the two villages. The previous chapters (6-10) have dealt in detail with the kind of activities people engaged in with a specific focus on the use of natural resources. The survey data of 1997, partly updated in 2004, provided information on the key resources around which livelihoods revolved and allowed for the identification of the types of livelihood that occurred in the two villages. In this chapter livelihood is analysed at a higher level of aggregation than in chapter 13, which focuses on livelihood trajectories of individuals or homesteads.

Besides land-based sources, this chapter also considered other sources of livelihood. Some of these sources were located outside the boundaries of the villages, but they contributed to livelihood in the villages through kinship relationships and relationships between the state and its citizens. The information presented in this chapter shows that livelihood in the villages primarily revolved around remittances, state transfers in the form of social grants and employment. The data show that in terms of social relations, rural livelihoods were primarily based on claims against kin and particularly against the state, and in this way spanned domains beyond the rural village *per se*. This social characteristic of rural livelihood is not unique to Guquka and Koloni. Similar arrangements were described in many other parts of South Africa (Lahiff 2000, McAllister 2001, Francis 2002, Timmermans 2004), suggesting that this particular type of social livelihood relations characterise contemporary rural livelihoods in the country at large.

## Livelihood activities

In the 1997 survey representatives of the 130 homesteads were asked to list the different livelihood activities in which their homestead was engaged and to quantify the income these activities generated in cash or kind. Total annual homestead income was calculated by totalling the monetary income earned as wages, state transfers and remittances, engagement in local trade and service provision and by selling farm produce. To this total was added the monetary value of own consumption and in kind transfers. The monetary value of the goods involved was based on their market prices at the time of data collection. The activities and associated incomes of homestead members who worked elsewhere and who returned irregularly or hardly at all to the village (chapter 11) but still had assets in the village were excluded from the analysis. However, their transfers in cash or kind to their homesteads were included in the homestead incomes in the form of remittances. These remittances were often made to support those people who looked after their houses and in some cases also their livestock. The phenomenon of caretaker arrangements has been discussed in the previous chapter and is quantitatively addressed in Table 11.3.

A rapid re-appraisal of livelihood activities of the villagers was conducted in April 2004. The focus of the re-appraisal was different in that not all villagers were interviewed again. Instead key informants were used. During transect walks, which covered all the homesteads in each of the villages, the key informants provided information on the livelihood activities, livestock holdings and composition of each homestead. In some cases this information was supplemented by a short interview with the residents of the homesteads. Despite different sample sizes, timing and method of data collection the re-appraisal provided some basis for comparison

The poverty status of homesteads was assessed against a poverty line that was developed using the method described by Carter and May (1999). This method involves the transformation of total homestead income to adult equivalent income (AEI) by dividing total homestead income by the number of adult equivalents (AE) contained in the homestead. The number of adult equivalents in a homestead were determined using Equation 12.1.

In order to draw the poverty line, the 1999 poverty line of R476.30 per adult equivalent per month established by Cater and May (1999) for rural areas in South Africa was adjusted to 1997 circumstances using the Consumer Price Index published monthly by Statistics SA. The resulting poverty line was R413.75 Homesteads with monthly adult equivalent incomes higher than R413.75 were categorised as not poor, and those with monthly adult equivalent income lower than that amount as poor. Homesteads with incomes less than half of the poverty line (R206.88 per month per adult equivalent) were considered to be ultra poor.

---

*Equation 12.1*

no of AE = (no of adults + ½ no of children)$^{0.9}$

Whereby

no of AE = number of adult equivalents in a homestead
no of adults = number of homestead members aged 15 years or older
no of children = number of homestead members younger than 15 years

---

Members of the homesteads in Guquka and Koloni were engaged in a range of livelihood activities. Table 12.1 lists and orders these activities and shows the frequency with which they were undertaken in 1997 and again in 2004. The changes that are apparent from the information in Table 12.1 were further explored by detailed case studies, which are discussed in chapter 13. Notwithstanding shifts in livelihood patterns, the important roles of pensions and remittances and to a lesser extent of land-based activities were constants in both 1997 and 2004. The apparent decline of remittances between 1997 and 2004, at least proportionally, could be due to the difference in method of data collection uscd, but indications were that they expressed the structural process of the formation of multiple homestead households (chapter 11) and the reshaping of rural-urban relationships.

One observation that could not be explained satisfactorily was the rate of decline between 1997 and 2004 in the number of homesteads that engaged in crop and animal production, whether for own consumption or for sale. Rainfall during this seven-year period had been relatively favourable, discarding climate as a possible cause for the apparent withdrawal from agriculture. Two associated factors that appeared to have contributed to the decline in agriculture were retrenchment of village residents, particularly those employed in the region, and a change in the patterns of migration.

Retrenchments marked the loss of income with which the necessary investments in agriculture could be financed. In affected homesteads retrenchment brought about livelihood crises, which in turn encouraged urban migration, explaining the association between these two factors. In 1997 urban migration was still mainly temporary and labour-related, but by 2004 more permanent forms of migration involving entire families had become dominant (chapter 11). Permanent migration to urban areas signified the loss of interest in village or land-based livelihoods. Permanent out-migration particularly affected Koloni,

*Table 12.1*    Livelihood activities in Guquka and Koloni (1997/2004)

| Livelihood activities | Guquka | | Koloni | |
|---|---|---|---|---|
| | 1997 n=76 | 2004 n=85 | 1997 n=54 | 2004 n=67 |
| **Proportion of homesteads engaged** | | | | |
| Land-based activities | (%) | (%) | (%) | (%) |
| Growing crops for own use | 72 | 18 | 61 | 21 |
| Growing crops for sale | 17 | | 19 | |
| Raising animals for own use | 29 | 7 | 33 | 45 |
| Raising animals for sale | 13 | | 50 | |
| Gathering plants and plant products from *veld* | | 100 | | 100 |
| **Remittances (claims against kin)** | | | | |
| Remittances in cash | 38 | 12 | 37 | 28 |
| Remittances in kind | 32 | 22 | 15 | 12 |
| **State transfers (claims against State)** | | | | |
| Old age pensions | 50 | 38 | 46 | 55 |
| Other social grants | 17 | 5 | 11 | 4 |
| Wages | | | | |
| Salaries | 26 | 25 | 24 | 28 |
| Work related pensions | 1 | 4 | 4 | 1 |
| **Petty trade and local jobs** | | | | |
| Hawking and other trade | 16 | 5 | 15 | 6 |
| Odd jobs and casual labour* | 22 | 11 | 25 | 3 |
| *Sangoma* (traditional healer) | 1 | 1 | 2 | 2 |

* Refers to occasional activities including the making of bricks, toilets and fences, repairing things and land preparation.

*Source*: ARDRI Survey (1997) and Hebinck (2004)

where the number of residences that were vacant and demolished had increased substantially between 1997 and 2004 (Table 11.3). There was also evidence that returning migrants and pensioners were less interested in cropping and livestock production than in the past.

## Livelihood labels

Labelling or categorising livelihoods provides an aggregate picture of the types of livelihood that exist at a particular time. It also gives a handle on the contention made in chapter 1 that livelihoods are diverse. Using livelihood strategy as a variable, Ellis (2000) and Scoones (1998) identified three main livelihood labels, namely, 1) agricultural intensification or extensification; 2) diversification; and 3) migration. The migration strategy that applied to Guquka and Koloni has been discussed in chapter 11.

Labelling of livelihood can be done in many ways, including qualitatively and quantitatively. Labelling usually involves the identification of key livelihood domains followed by an analysis of whether and how these domains are combined. Commonly used quantitative ways of livelihood labelling involve the statistical analysis of a select number of livelihood indicators (variables) using cluster analysis (Makhura *et al.* 1998) or principal component analysis (Davis 2004, Essa and Nieuwoudt 2003). Another way, which was used here, is to categorise livelihoods according to the predominant source of income, whilst recognising that homesteads are constituted by multiple members (Carter and May 1999). Six types of sources of income were considered in the categorisation, namely remittances, wages and salaries, social grants, petty trade, agriculture and self employment. An income source type was considered dominant when it contributed at least 50% to total homestead income. For instance, homesteads that derived at least 50% of their total income in the form of wages through employment were labelled 'wage earners'. Similarly, 'grant holders' had social grants as their dominant source of income. Homesteads that did not have any particular source of income that contributed at least 50% to total income were labelled as 'diversifiers'.

The main disadvantage of the labelling procedure that was used is that homesteads appearing under the same label can still have very different livelihood portfolios, because sources that contribute less than 50% are not considered in the categorisation. As a result, the labelling that was used did not recognise the full extent of livelihood diversification that occurred at the two sites. Table 12.2 shows the relative frequency distribution of homesteads in different labels for the two villages.In the ensuing description the key livelihood resources and activities that characterise each of the different livelihood labels are discussed. Information on the monetary value of the incomes that homesteads generated by engaging in the six different categories of income sources are also provided.

*Grant holder*
Social grants including old-age pensions are claims against the state or transfers from the state towards its citizens. In South Africa, the right to claim against the State for income support was introduced in 1911 for whites and expanded from about 1940 onwards to include black South Africans (see chapter 2). These claims entail a range of grants awarded by the state to particular categories of people. The monetary value of the grants is annually revised by the state to compensate, at least in part, for the rising cost of living. In Guquka and Koloni, livelihoods that were based on claiming against the state largely revolved around age, physical or mental disability or, in the case of child support, the

*Table 12.2*     Frequency distribution of homesteads in the different livelihood labels
                 identified at Guquka and Koloni, 1997-2004

| Label | Guquka | | Koloni | |
|---|---|---|---|---|
| | 1997<br>n=76<br>(%) | 2004<br>N=85<br>(%) | 1997<br>n=54<br>(%) | 2004<br>N=67<br>(%) |
| Farmer | 2.6 | 1.2 | 12.9 | 7.5 |
| Diversifier | 2.6 | - | 9.3 | 6.0 |
| Grant holder | 48.7 | 42.4 | 37.0 | 44.8 |
| Petty entrepreneur | 5.3 | 10.6 | 12.9 | 6.0 |
| Remitter | 17.1 | 18.8 | 9.3 | 11.9 |
| Wage earner | 23.7 | 27.1 | 18.5 | 23.9 |
| Total | 100.0 | 100.0 | 100.0 | 100.0 |

*Source*: ARDRI Survey (1997) and Hebinck (2004)

lack of income. Therefore, the political will on the part of the state to continue these types of transfers, which are redistributive, and aimed at eliminating the worst levels of poverty, must be viewed as a key resource.

In order of importance, the grants that were received by selected people in Guquka and Koloni were old-age pensions, disability grants and child support grants. In 1997, 35 homesteads in Koloni made one or more claims against the state. Twenty-nine received old-age pensions and six collected disability grants. Eight of these 35 homesteads claimed more than one grant. In 1997, aggregated claims against the state contributed 21.6% to mean homestead income in Koloni, but by 1999, this contribution had increased to 30.9%. In Guquka claiming against the state was even more important than in Koloni, with 48 out of 77 homesteads getting state grants in 1997. Thirty-eight received old age pensions, 10 collected disability grants and 2 obtained child-support grants. Twelve of the 46 grant-holding homesteads were in receipt of multiple grants. Claiming against the state contributed 41.6% to mean homestead income in Guquka in 1997 and 50.7% in 1999.

Old-age pensions were by far the most important type of grant received by residents of Guquka and Koloni in 1997 and in 1999. For more than two decades, both white and black South Africans have qualified for old-age pensions, irrespective of whether they were ever employed or not (chapter 2). To qualify for an old-age pension, South African males had to be 65 years old and females 60 years old. These requirements have not been changed. However, until 1993, the monetary value of old-age pensions was determined by race. In the past, black people received only about half the amount that was being paid to whites and practically this was implemented by paying black people an old-age pension only every second month. When a person has contributed towards a pension scheme through his or her employer, and the monetary value of the work-related pension exceeds that of the old-age pension, that person is not allowed to claim an old-age pension. Work-related pensions can be combined with an old-age pension when the monetary value of the work-related pension is less than that of the old-age pension, but in such cases the value of the old-age pension claim against the state is limited to the deficit. In Guquka and Koloni, only five aged people held work-related pensions (Table 12.1), although many of them were employed during substantial parts of their lives. The reason is that labour legislation of the past tended to limit work-related pension contributions, which were partly paid by the employers and partly by the employee, to white-collar jobs, and these were mainly held by whites. In 1997, the monetary value of an old-age pension was R420 per month. This value had increased to R520 in 1999 and was R870 in 2007.

Beinart (2001) referred to old-age pensioners as the 'pensionariat' and in isiXhosa they are called *abantu abandlodlayo*. Besides receiving their pensions some old men also held substantial cattle herds, which they accumulated whilst being employed. This type of pensioners could be referred to as 'cattle farmers' (*umfuyi*). In the past, male migrants commonly invested parts of their earnings in cattle (Ferguson 1990, McAllister 2001) to prepare for their retirement and return to the rural home, but the data collected in this study suggest that this practice is no longer common in Guquka and Koloni.

In contemporary rural villages of the Eastern Cape 'pensioners' are not necessarily dominant as a result of their number, but rather as a result of the meaning of their monthly pensions, which provide a degree of income security to members of their homestead. In some grant holder homesteads in Guquka and Koloni, the elderly not only took financial care of their spouses, but also of members of the younger generations. This phenomenon is widespread in contemporary rural South Africa. For example, Mohamed and Van Averbeke (2006) distinguished between one-generation, two-generation and three-generation homesteads in a smallholder irrigation scheme setting in the former Venda homeland. They reported that the younger generations in multiple-generation pensioner homesteads tended to depend on the old-age pensions of their parents or grant parents for survival. In other cases pensioners took care of their grandchildren whose parents were migrants. The livelihood of this type of rural homesteads was based on combining their old-age pensions with the remittances that were sent to them by their migrant children, which were not always reliable, as is illustrated in chapter 13. In pensioner homesteads the passing away of the grant holder constitutes a major financial blow and this inevitability makes pension-based livelihoods vulnerable.

A recent development in South Africa not captured by the data has been the substantial increase in the contribution of child support grants to the livelihood of poor people. This was brought about by legislation that broadened access to these grants in terms of income limits, extended the age limits of children that qualified, and increased the monetary value of the grants. For example, between

April 2005 and March 2006, the number of South African children in receipt of a child grant increased from 5.67 million to 7.08 million (Leatt 2006).

*Farmer*

Land, livestock, markets, labour and capital are the key resources around which land-based livelihoods revolve. Chapters 6, 8 and 9 have pointed at the intricate details of access and current use of these resources and how these are interlinked. In both settlements agriculture was of minor importance overall, especially when viewed purely as an activity to generate monetary income.

In 1997, 55 (72%) of the 76 homesteads that were surveyed engaged in crop production in gardens and/or arable fields, but only 13 marketed their crops (mostly locally). Twenty-eight homesteads (37%) engaged in some form of livestock production, but for 18 this activity was for home consumption only. In 1997, income derived from agriculture (in cash and kind) contributed 6.6% to mean total homestead income in Guquka. The aggregated total monetary value of the crops produced by the 55 homesteads was R21562, of which R16872 (78%) was realized as food for home consumption. The aggregated total monetary value of animal production was R27,616, of which R14,328 (52%) was realized as food for home consumption. In 1999, total income derived from agriculture (in cash and kind) contributed 7.4% to mean total homestead income in Guquka. The 1999 aggregated total monetary value of crop production by the homesteads that were surveyed (n=67) was R11,724, of which R9,623 (82%) was realized as food for home consumption. The aggregated total monetary value of animal production was R35,495, of which R16,761 (47%) was realized as food for home consumption. Not a single homestead in Guquka relied solely on agriculture for their livelihood.

In 1997, 34 (63%) of the 54 surveyed homesteads in Koloni were engaged in some kind of crop production, with 10 selling at least part of their produce. Livestock production in Koloni tended to be more important than in Guquka, with 27 homesteads (50%) keeping livestock, but, as in Guquka, only a minority (9 homesteads) derived cash income from this activity. In 1997, income derived from agriculture (in cash and kind) contributed 11.6 to mean total homestead income in Koloni. The aggregated total monetary value of the crops produced by the 34 homesteads was R13,937, of which R9,057 (65%) was realized as food for home consumption. The aggregated total monetary value of animal production was R83,731, of which R28,969 (35%) was realized as food for home consumption. In 1999, total income derived from agriculture (in cash and kind) contributed 11.5% to mean total homestead income in Koloni. The 1999 aggregated total monetary value of crop production by the homesteads that were surveyed (n=60) was R21, 026, of which R10,362 (49%) was realized as food for home consumption. The aggregated total monetary value of animal production was R71,761, of which R28,446 (40%) was realized as food for home consumption. Two homesteads in Koloni depended completely on agriculture for their income, whilst the other homesteads that practised agriculture combined this activity with various other sources of income. Chapter 10 has pointed at the importance of the collection of firewood and other wild products for energy, food and cultural use and other purposes.

Across the two villages, using the 1997 survey data, income in kind from crop production was positively correlated to size of the pig holding (r=0.230**)* adult equivalent income (r=0.194*) and income in cash from crop production (r=0.194*), which was correlated with income in kind from animal production (r=0.271**). Income in kind from animal production was positively correlated with income from crop production in cash (r=0.271**), animal production in cash (r=0.500*), cash expenditure on agriculture (r=0.391**) and the number cattle (r=0.374**) and sheep (r=0.227**) held. Income in cash from animal production was positively correlated to income in kind from animal production (r=0.500*), cash expenditure on agriculture (r=0.381**) and the number of cattle (r=0.445**), pigs (r=0.445**), goats (r=0.231**), sheep (r=0.226**) and poultry (r=0.219*) held. The associations that were identified indicated that besides land, family labour rather than monetary investments was the key resource in crop production, whilst in animal production financial investment was an important resource(see also chapter 8). The associations between crop and animal production confirmed the notion that the local farming system tends to be mixed. Important also was the fairly strong positive correlation between cash income from animal production and number of pigs held. Pigs are reared within the residential area of the villages, and besides obtaining their food through scavenging, pigs are often fed table scraps and sometimes also maize grain that is no longer fit for human consumption (see case 4 in chapter 13). Moreover, together with poultry, pigs are often taken care of by women, and among the different livestock species held in the villages of the Eastern Cape, poultry and pigs are typically reared for the purpose of generating cash income (Mafu 1989). Another important feature was that cash income from animal production was correlated with the size of the holdings of all five major livestock species, which links to the work of Williams *et al.* (1989) and Eckert & Williams (1995). They found that the importance of agriculture in the livelihood of rural homesteads in the central Eastern Cape during the 1980s was most strongly correlated with the number of livestock species held by these homesteads, followed by the size of the cattle holding.

*Wage earner*
Labour power, knowledge and skills are the key resources of wage-based livelihoods. The jobs held by residents of the two villages included security guards, teachers, workers in agriculture and manufacturing, nurses and drivers. Interestingly, there were more teachers in Guquka than in Koloni, which was some-

---

* Correlation is significant at the 0.05 level (2-tailed); ** Correlation is significant at the 0.01 level (2-tailed).

what surprising considering that Koloni is near a mission station as opposed to Guquka.

Residents were categorised as wage earners when they returned home on a daily basis, although most worked outside the villages. Members of homesteads, who returned home during weekends, month ends, or even less frequently, were considered to be migrants, because their pattern of movement between the village and their place of employment required the maintenance of an urban home. The contributions these members made to homestead incomes in Guquka and Koloni were categorised as remittances.

In 1997 in Guquka 19 of the 76 homesteads (25%) had at least one member earning a wage through being formally employed. The wages they earned contributed 35.5% to mean homestead income, underlining the importance of employment in local livelihoods in terms of income. In 1999, 21 (31%) of the 67 homesteads that were surveyed earned income from having at least one member formally employed, but the contribution of wages to mean total homestead income in the village had declined to 23.7%.

In 1997 in Koloni, 13 (24%) of the 54 surveyed homesteads earned income through the formal employment of one or more of their members. The wages and salaries these people earned contributed 39.1% to mean total homestead income in the village. In 1999, only 12 (20%) of the 60 surveyed homesteads earned income in this way and the contribution of wages and salaries to total mean homestead income had declined to 31.1%.

Chapter 2 explained that homesteads with wage-based livelihoods in rural settlements of the central Eastern Cape arose post-1950 (Leibrand and Sperber 1997), more specifically during the 1970s and 1980s, and were the result of job creation in the public service of the Ciskei homeland, parastatals, independent educational institutions, such as the University of Fort Hare and in industrial centres, such as Dimbaza and Fort Jackson. In Guquka and Koloni, these homesteads did not necessarily rely solely on employment for their livelihood. Several among them were also involved in agriculture and/or local trade and service provision. Case 3 in chapter 13 provides an example of this type of homestead.

*Remitter*

Homesteads whose livelihoods evolve around kinship and other social relationships providing support to members of homesteads receive remittances from them. These can be transfers because of reciprocity in social relations and ditto obligations, or transfers from one generation to another in the form of child maintenance payments. Such transfers are usually seen as redistributive. Remittances were usually received both in cash and kind, while child maintenance was mostly received in cash only. In Koloni, 20 homesteads held claims against kin. Of these 8 received it as an in-kind transfer, and 5 in both cash and kind. In total the monetary value of claims against kin represented 8.7% of the cumulative annual income of all homesteads in Koloni. In Guquka 36 homesteads held claims against kin, 15 of these receiving cash remittances, 13 receiving remittances in kind, 12 receiving a combination of remittances in cash and kind, and 1 homestead received child maintenance payments. Together claims against kin represented 13.6% of the cumulative annual income of all surveyed homesteads.

*Petty entrepreneur*

The *petty entrepreneur* livelihood label captures homesteads that make a living from petty trade, casual labour and odd jobs. These activities represented the non-agricultural rural economy. Eleven homesteads in Koloni and 15 in Guquka made an income from conducting work and trade in the village, of which two homesteads combined this with migration. The total income generated by these homesteads represented about 1% of total village income in the case of Koloni and 2% in Guquka, which again underlines the limited importance of the local economy. Besides trading, the activities *petty entrepreneurs* engaged in included house-building, repairs, brick making and casual work such as land preparation for others, and odd jobs like toy making. In Guquka land preparation for others was virtually absent, but farmers did hire tractor services supplied by homesteads in neighbouring settlements.

In both Guquka and Koloni informal petty trade mostly involved women selling food and other consumption items in very small quantities, either on the street (hawking) or from *spaza* shops. These shops are operated from the dwelling of the owner. They stock a limited range of basic consumption items procured by the owner in supermarkets of nearby local towns. They typically cater for unexpected needs of village people and often sell goods in small quantities, sufficient to satisfy such needs. In Koloni members of seven homesteads and in Guquka nine homesteads were involved in such trade. The cash generated by this type of petty trade was modest, between R300 and R5000 per annum. Three homesteads in Koloni and two in Guquka had converted part of their dwelling into an unlicensed *shebeen*, mainly selling commercially brewed bottled beer (lager). They purchased the beer from bottle stores in nearby towns (Alice, Middledrift or King William's Town) and had refrigerators to keep the drinks cool. Income generated by the liquor trade ranged between R5000 and R9000 per annum per *shebeen*. Income derived from petty trade was relatively small. In 1997 it amounted to 4% of the total village income of Koloni and 0.8% of Guquka.

In both settlements there was also trade in home-grown crops, vegetables and livestock. These products were sold from the producer homesteads, mainly to other people in the village. Income from selling crops and livestock was taken as income from agriculture, which was used to identify *farmer* homesteads, not *petty entrepreneurs*. The discussion of homestead trade in farm produce is presented here to enable a comparison with other types of trade within the village.

In 1997 in Koloni, five homesteads sold crops and together with eight others they also sold livestock or animal products. On average, the total annual income from sales of crops and vegetables per homestead in 1997 in Koloni was about R500, but it varied considerably among homesteads ranging between R12 to R1900. The average total annual income from sales of animals or their products was about R1600, but as with crops this type of income varied substantially among homesteads involved, ranging between R120 to R8300. In 1997, income from sales of farm produce contributed about 7% to the combined annual income of all surveyed homesteads in Koloni.

In Guquka thirteen homesteads sold crops in 1997 and ten sold livestock or animal products. Among these homesteads seven sold both. On average they generated R360 from selling crops and R660 from livestock or animal products in 1997, but as in Koloni, the amount of income that was realised varied considerably among homesteads. Homestead income from crop sales ranged between R20 to R1,100 per homestead per annum and that from sales of animals or their products between R50 and R3,300. In 1997, income from sales of farm produce contributed 2.4% to the combined annual income of all surveyed homesteads in Guquka.


*Diversifier*

The label *diversifier* is essentially a 'default' label. Not much can be said about homesteads in this label except that they derived income from at least three different types of sources, none of which was the dominant source. This type of income structure can be interpreted as an indicator of livelihood diversification. However in the two villages combined there were 61 homesteads (47%) that generated income from at least three of the six types of income sources, but only 16 of these 61 homesteads were labelled *diversifiers*. In fact in 1997 very few homesteads in the two villages derived income from just one type of source. In Koloni this applied to eight homesteads (15%), four of which were labelled *grant holders*, two *wage earners* and two *farmers*. In Guquka there were nine homesteads (12%) that derived income from a single source only in 1997. Five were labelled *grant holders*, two *remitters* and two *wage earners*.

Livelihood diversification is one of the strategies adopted by rural homesteads to cope with poverty and vulnerability (Fair 2000, Ellis 2000). When using this strategy, homesteads construct an increasingly varied portfolio of activities and assets in order to make ends meet or to improve their living. Typically this involves widening the range of either on-farm or off-farm sources of income or both (Ellis 2000, Toulmin *et al.* 2000, Barret, Readon & Webb 2001). Several of the livelihood case studies presented in chapter 13 demonstrate that this also applied to Guquka and Koloni. However, there was no evidence that adoption of the livelihood diversification strategy by homesteads in Guquka and Koloni raised their income above that of others. This was evident from the absence of a statistically significant correlation between 1997 total homestead income of the 130 homesteads in Guquka and Koloni and the number of sources these homesteads used to generate their income. Ashley (2003) distinguishes pull or positive diversification, when new activities generate higher returns than before; and push or negative diversification, when new activities offer lower returns than before. The pull or positive diversification typically leads to asset accumulation or improvement of living standards. Push or negative diversification is adopted out of necessity in response to shocks or a downward trend in the economy. Analysis of the 1997 data suggests that push or negative diversification prevailed in Guquka and Koloni at that time.

In Table 12.3, associations between livelihood label and the contribution the six types of income sources made to total homestead income are explored for the two villages combined. Table 12.4 shows associations between livelihood label and the consumption patterns of homesteads. Salient features of the 1997 livelihoods in the two villages were:

1. On average, *wage earners* had by far the highest mean homestead income among all labels. In 1997, the mean homestead income of wage-earners was about R2000 per month. In terms of poverty status, wage earners were the only category of non-poor homesteads in the two villages.

2. On average, petty *entrepreneurs* and *diversifiers* had similar homestead incomes of about R1000 per month, which was more or less equal to the overall mean homestead income in the two villages. Generally, homesteads in these two labels were poor, but not ultra-poor. However, cases elaborated in chapter 13 showed that the *petty entrepreneur* label was very broad and included some of the poorest homesteads (notable cases 6, 7 and 8). Characteristic for both labels was the variety of sources of income that made a contribution to total homestead income and the use of local resources in their livelihood portfolios.

3. Generally, *grant holders*, *remitters* and *farmers* were among the ultra-poor, particularly *remitters* and *farmers*. Homesteads deriving income from farming were primarily found in three labels, namely *petty entrepreneurs*, *diversifiers* and obviously *farmers*.

4. The income data indicate a high degree of social inequality. In Koloni, for instance, 11 homesteads (20%) realised half of the total income of the 54 homesteads that were surveyed in the village. The majority of these 11 homesteads were *wage earners*. Guquka showed similar patterns of inequality. These patterns mirrored those described by Houghton and Walton (1952) in their study on Keiskammahoek (chapter 2). Half a century later, the findings at Guquka and Koloni showed that inequalities continue to revolve around access to formal wage employment rather then cattle and land.

Total homestead income is by no means the only indicator of livelihood outcomes, but it is arguably the most important one. As indicated earlier, sources of income were subdivided into six types. Statistically, income earned from employment (wage income) explained a large proportion (adjusted $R^2$=0.67; $p$<0.0001) of the variability in homestead income in the two villages.

Table 12.3    Livelihood label and income relationships in Guquka and Koloni 1997, combined

| Indicator (R annum$^{-1}$) | Grant holder (n=57) | Wage earner (n=28) | Remitter (n=18) | Petty entre-preneur (n=11) | Farmer (n=8) | Diver-sifier (n=8) | All (n=130) |
|---|---|---|---|---|---|---|---|
| Mean total homestead income | 8,552 | 23,683 | 5,696 | 12,365 | 3,233 | 13,901 | 11,880 |
| Mean homestead income from remittances | 727 | 711 | 4,313 | 514 | 0 | 3,080 | 1,310 |
| Mean homestead income from formal employment | 0 | 19,264 | 2 | 1,415 | 0 | 2,385 | 4,438 |
| Mean homestead income from state grants | 6,847 | 2,589 | 687 | 1,362 | 1,216 | 2,640 | 4,010 |
| Mean homestead income from trade and services | 39 | 557 | 359 | 6,569 | 190 | 2,287 | 993 |
| Mean homestead income from agriculture | 938 | 562 | 335 | 2,506 | 1,827 | 3,509 | 1,130 |
| Mean adult equivalent income | 228 | 599 | 124 | 285 | 77 | 310 | 297 |

Table 12.4    Livelihood label and expenditure relationships in Guquka and Koloni 1997, combined

| Indicator (R annum$^{-1}$) | Grant holder (n=57) | Wage earner (n=28) | Remitter (n=18) | Petty entre-preneur (n=11) | Farmer (n=8) | Diver-sifier (n=8) | All (n=130) |
|---|---|---|---|---|---|---|---|
| Mean expenditure on food | 3,007 | 4,053 | 2,877 | 2,886 | 2,753 | 3,495 | 3,218 |
| Mean expenditure on clothing | 734 | 1,444 | 610 | 631 | 756 | 1,331 | 897 |
| Mean expenditure on furniture | 440 | 1,220 | 363 | 432 | 840 | 2,600 | 748 |
| Mean expenditure on medical treatment | 301 | 436 | 237 | 402 | 0 | 216 | 312 |
| Mean expenditure on education | 631 | 992 | 139 | 253 | 413 | 608 | 591 |
| Mean expenditure on transport | 408 | 681 | 307 | 785 | 441 | 271 | 484 |
| Mean expenditure on monetary savings | 644 | 4,083 | 519 | 618 | 1,291 | 964 | 1,414 |
| Mean expenditure on other goods and services | 197 | 2,781 | 2,009 | 1,234 | 2,204 | 1,377 | 1,712 |
| Mean expenditure on labour | 84 | 160 | 220 | 228 | 17 | 29 | 127 |
| Mean expenditure on agriculture | 239 | 148 | 331 | 370 | 216 | 200 | 242 |
| Meant total expenditure | 7,578 | 16,155 | 7,686 | 7,894 | 8,995 | 11,289 | 9, 844 |
| Mean adult equivalent expenditure | 186 | 390 | 158 | 237 | 202 | 241 | 235 |

*Source*: ADRI Survey (1997)

Variability in income derived from agriculture ($R^2$=0.18; $p$<0.0001) and self-employment ($R^2$=0.18; $p$<0.0001) also explained statistically significant proportions of the observed variability in total homestead income. However, income from remittances, grants and petty trade were not significantly correlated with total homestead income.

Table 12.4 shows that to a large extent, label-related expenditure patterns were similar to the income patterns. Wage earners had the highest mean expenditure, confirming their status as wealthiest group. Expenditure on clothing, furniture and savings were the key indicators that differentiated the labels. Expenditure categories least affected by label were food and agriculture. The adult equivalent expenditure of farmers was considerably higher than their adult equivalent income, suggesting that they had under-reported their income. This may mean that income derived from agriculture in the two villages was higher than the survey results suggested. The aggregation that was used in the construction of Tables 12.1-12.4 does not clearly disclose the intensity with which homesteads were involved in multiple livelihood activities. Only the category *diversifier* reflects diversification, but as was pointed out earlier diversification was a trait that was distributed much more widely than this particular label.

## Analysing processes of diversification

In order to further analyse the processes of diversification the livelihood activities of homesteads in the two villages were aggregated into four broad livelihood domains (Table 12.5), which were derived from the 'endowments' and 'entitlements' mapping approaches developed by Sen (1984) and refined by Leach *et al.* (1999) (see also chapter 1). The four domains are the following:
1. Returns from *land-based resources*, i.e. the production of crops on the arable allotments and home gardens, and livestock on the all of the categories of land. This domain resembles the 'own production' entitlement of Sen (1984) and represents the local agrarian economy.
2. Returns from labour in the form of *wages* were derived from work done by members of homesteads who reside in the village but mostly work outside its confines. These members constitute the category of 'migrant commuters' and include among others the teachers, forestry workers, prison wardens and nurses who live in the villages.
3. Returns from *activities in the locality*. These activities include petty trade, such as the running of *spaza shops* or *shebeens* and the provision of services to local homesteads. The identification of this particular domain of entitlements, which arise from activities that are conducted in the village and its vicinity departs from Sen's entitlement categories, but was deemed useful, because combined these activities represent the *local, non-agricultural economy*.
4. *Transfers from the state and kin*. Such claims take the form of pensions and various other social grants as well as remittances.

*Table 12.5*    Frequency distribution of different permutations of the four entitlement domains on which livelihoods in Guquka and Koloni were based (1997)

| Permutations of entitlement domains | Guquka (n=76) | Koloni (n= 54) |
|---|---|---|
| Land-based | 0 | 2 |
| Land-based + Wages | 0 | 5 |
| Land-based + Wages + Local | 5 | 2 |
| Land-based + Wages + Local + Transfers | 1 | 0 |
| Land-based + Transfers | 33 | 19 |
| Land-based + Wages + Transfers | 5 | 1 |
| Land-based + Local + Transfers | 5 | 10 |
| Land-based + Local | 3 | 3 |
| Wages | 3 | 2 |
| Wages + Local | 0 | 1 |
| Wages + Local + Transfers | 1 | 1 |
| Wages + Transfers | 3 | 2 |
| Local | 2 | 0 |
| Transfers | 11 | 6 |
| Transfers + Local | 3 | 0 |

*Source*: ARDRI Survey (1997)

The quantitative data were organised in such a way that entitlements derived from each of the four domains were linked to others. In this way a picture of the processes of diversification was developed. Fifteen of a possible 24 permutations of the four entitlement domains occurred in the two villages.

Generally, homesteads had livelihood portfolios in which transfers were combined with land-based activities, whilst wages were also important. Rural livelihoods based solely on the utilisation of natural resources were absent in Guquka and limited to two homesteads in Koloni. Written sources as well as oral history (chapters 2 and 4) indicate that livelihoods based entirely on the use of land disappeared long ago among the Xhosa-speaking people in the central Eastern Cape. Since the beginning of 20th century, they have been combining crop and livestock production with cash earned through labour migration. However, in contemporary settlements of the central Eastern Cape, the livelihood portfolio that is structured around male labour migration and farming structure has all but disappeared, because the link between migration and agriculture has been broken (see also chapter 8). At present the dominant livelihood portfolio combines transfers from the state and kin with gardening. There are obviously exceptions, including portfolios in which cropping on arable land and livestock production still play an important role. This means that land resources continue to be of economic importance to selected homesteads in the villages. Moreover, land resources have not become disconnected from the social and cultural lives of rural homesteads. Families that command land and related resources continue to identify themselves as 'rural' and strongly cling to their land rights. The economic rather than the identity shift has to do with the general trend of land not being used for crop production and more for social security needs, cultural identity and consumption (for settlement, burial sites, etc.). Chapter 10 has shown that the arable allotments are also used for the gathering of a wide range of so-called *veld* products. Some of these products have a clear economic value whereas other products are more socio-culturally defined.

An interesting observation from Table 12.5 is that the local economy hardly represents a demand for labour and services. People's purchasing power is too limited to allow for many local employment opportunities. Most villagers have become accustomed to shopping for food and other consumer items in local towns and this can be seen as a cultural constraint to the growth of a local market. Another important observation is that potentially vibrant portfolios that combine wages with agriculture or local economic activity were almost non existent. Seemingly, homesteads with wage incomes were satisfied with their livelihood outcomes, and viewed the rural village as a place of residence, not investment. Another explanation is the prevailing demographic structure of homesteads with wage entitlements, which often consisted of two generations, the economically active parent(s) and the economically inactive children, limiting the opportunity of these homesteads to engage in livelihood activities other than those related to their employment.

Table 12.6 summarises some of the intricate dimensions of diversification with a view to understand whether and how the practices captured by the livelihood labels relate to agriculture or land based activities. Table 12.6 shows that about three-quarters (76%) of the income derived from agriculture in Guquka and Koloni originated from animal production. The major part (61%) of the income from animal production was in cash. The major part (73%) of income from crop production was in kind as food for home consumption. As was pointed out earlier, income from farming was generally important for the cluster that contained homesteads categorised in the *farmer, petty entrepreneur and diversifier* labels, and not for the cluster group of homesteads labelled *remitter, wage earner* and *grant holder*. In terms of their average agricultural asset status, the cluster of homesteads for which agriculture was important had a higher degree of access to fields, a larger cattle holding and a larger number of different livestock species, but a smaller cultivated home garden. Correlation analyses supported these patterns. The total income from agriculture was strongly correlated with income from animal production, both in cash (r=0.88**) and kind (r=0.82**), but much less strongly with income from crop production in cash (r=0.30) and kind (r=0.25). Income from agriculture was also correlated with the number of cattle (r=0.45), number of different livestock species (r=0.36), number of chickens (r=0.26), number of fields (r=0.25) and number of sheep (r=0.25) that were held. Income from animal production in cash was correlated to the size of the holding of all the different livestock species, but particularly cattle, and also to the number of fields. Income from crop pro-

*Table 12.6*     Livelihood label and agriculture relationships in Guquka and Koloni combined, 1997

| Indicator | Grant holder (n=57) | Wage earner (n=28) | Re-mitter (n=18) | Petty entre-preneur (n=11) | Farmer (n=8) | Diver-sifier (n=8) | All (n=130) |
|---|---|---|---|---|---|---|---|
| Mean number of fields per homestead | 0.7 | 0.6 | 0.4 | 0.8 | 0.7 | 1.0 | 0.7 |
| Mean size of cropped home garden ($m^2$) | 400 | 347 | 618 | 322 | 275 | 249 | 396 |
| Mean cattle holding (units) | 3.4 | 2.8 | 1.6 | 5.7 | 5.7 | 4.4 | 3.4 |
| Mean goat holding (units) | 1.4 | 2.2 | 0.4 | 3.2 | 2.7 | 2.1 | 1.7 |
| Mean sheep holding (units) | 3.6 | 7.6 | 1.8 | 7.5 | 7.0 | 0.0 | 4.6 |
| Mean pig holding (units) | 0.9 | 0.8 | 0.9 | 1.3 | 0.2 | 1.3 | 0.9 |
| Mean poultry holding (units) | 4.3 | 5.9 | 3.6 | 6.3 | 7.7 | 2.0 | 4.8 |
| Mean number of livestock species kept | 1.9 | 1.9 | 1.7 | 2.5 | 2.5 | 2.8 | 2.0 |
| Mean income from animal production in kind (R annum$^{-1}$) | 310 | 154 | 77 | 920 | 175 | 866 | 333 |
| Mean income from animal production in cash (R annum$^{-1}$) | 319 | 251 | 66 | 1,329 | 1,204 | 2,143 | 524 |
| Mean income from crop production in kind (R annum$^{-1}$) | 226 | 152 | 165 | 165 | 257 | 268 | 199 |
| Mean income from crop production in cash (R annum$^{-1}$) | 83 | 5 | 28 | 91 | 191 | 232 | 74 |
| Mean income from agriculture (R annum$^{-1}$) | 938 | 562 | 335 | 2,506 | 1,827 | 3,509 | 1,130 |

*Source*: ARDRI Survey (1997)

duction in cash was not correlated to any of these assets and income from crops in kind was only correlated to the size of the pig holding. Agriculture in Guquka and Koloni, in other words, largely revolved around animal production. Crop production was of limited economic importance, confirming the conclusion drawn in chapter 8.

## Missed categories

The livelihood and entitlement categorisations that were used in this chapter have used the homestead as the unit of analysis. The analysis has also been rather static. The livelihood of homesteads is closely linked to the livelihood of its constituent members. Livelihood of individuals is subject to change. Changes in the livelihood of members of homesteads affect the structure of the livelihood portfolio of homesteads (see chapter 13).

As a result, livelihoods which transcend the labels over time, such as individuals in search for ways to leave the village, retrenched people, or returning migrants, have been missing from the discussion. The categorisation also did not pay attention to important social subcategories, such as the 'youth', 'the widows' and 'the unmarried mothers', all of whom are present in the two villages. No quantitative information was collected to show their prevalence in the two villages, but their livelihoods were documented by means of selected case studies (chapter 13). A general overview of their circumstances is presented here.

The *retrenched* are labour migrants who have returned to the village because their jobs were terminated for various reasons, such as the end of a contract, the restructuring or demise of the business they worked for, or wrong-doing resulting in their dismissal. Generally, the retrenched are too young to gain access to the old-age pension grant in the near future. This pension is awarded to women at the age of 60 years and men at the age of 65 years. As a result, they cannot afford to remain economically inactive for too long, because many have families to take care of. As a result they are eager to do various 'odd jobs' in the village, such as painting and the construction of houses, fences or toilet pits, until a better opportunity arises. The returning migrant was strongly associated with the decline in employment in South Africa's during the final years of the $20^{th}$ century, which saw many lowly educated people losing their jobs (see for example case 2 in chapter 13).

The *leavers* signify the process that can result in the disconnection of the rural from the urban, either partly or completely. The *returning migrant* represents the possibility of people developing or re-establishing livelihoods that are based on natural resources and the local economy. Some of them show strong signs of interest in expanding or establishing agriculture as a major livelihood option, but the prevailing land tenure arrangements sometimes deprive them of gaining access to land, especially at Guquka. Cases 3 and 4 in chapter 13 tell the story of Mzoli and Vuyo Grootbooi and their attempts to construct a livelihood in the villages.

Then there are the *youth*. In the past most of them would have become migrant workers but the economic circumstances offer few opportunities for employment to young people without professional qualifications or specific skills. At present their options for a migrant labour-based livelihood are extremely limited. As a result, the majority of the *youth* just hang around in the village. They are a generation that lacks the outlook on any particular livelihood trajectory that will present them with an acceptable degree of security. The degree of their desperation is serious. For example, increasingly there have been allegations that some young rural women deliberately fall pregnant to gain access to the child-support grant (SABC News 17-11-2004, 7-3-2007). Traditionally, pregnancy in Xhosa society has been linked to the institution of marriage and falling pregnant outside the boundaries of this institution was frowned upon (SABC News 11-3-2007), but values change. What will become of the rural *youth* is perhaps the most critical development question in South Africa. Do they move to town, joining the ranks of the unemployed in South Africa's urban areas, or do they find ways of eking a living from activities within the local community, for instance by re-engaging in agriculture?

A last but very important social category is the group of *widowed, divorced* and *unmarried women*. The last two categories often have some kind of relationship with a husband or partner, which may enable them to claim support. Like all women in the villages they are heavily engaged in home garden production and derive much of their livelihood from this. Occasionally they serve as domestic workers for other families in the village or its surrounds, or they engage in local activities, such as sewing or the repairing of clothes. In quite a few cases, they live and work in the same homestead as their parents, taking care of them. The pension of their parents forms an important livelihood source, particular in terms of food security, until the death of the parents when these pensions fall away. In a few cases these women and their dependants survive because a child working in town remits part of his/her salary, or they get support from kin in the village. This group is by and large vulnerable and fragile as case 9 in chapter 13 clearly conveys.

## Conclusion

This chapter has reviewed the structure of livelihoods in the two villages. It also paid some attention to their dynamics and transformations. Despite certain historical differences between the two villages, the commonality in their development and current status prevails. The empirical material clearly demonstrates that contemporary livelihoods in both villages are predominantly based on grants, and to a lesser extent on remittances and wages. Remittances and wages are shaped by the economic conjuncture influencing employment opportunities, whilst grants are entitlements that are influenced by political conjuncture. For most homesteads the economic value of the local, i.e. the village, economy is highly confined. This implies that few opportunities exist for returning or re-trenched migrants to develop a living that is based on local resources and income opportunities. As a result, change in the political economy of the Eastern Cape region and beyond will affect the viability of future rural livelihoods. A similar argument was made by De Wet and Holbrook (1997).

In spite of the limited employment opportunities available in urban areas rural people continue to attempt long range migration. However, they do not just leave the village as individual migrant workers, as was the case in the past. This time they take all or part of their family with them. This trend may well jeopardize the sustainability of rural, remittance-based livelihoods. Simultaneously, migrants returning to their rural homes to try and achieve livelihood security by using local resources represent migration in the opposite direction. For this group most options are land-related, as the local economy and labour market hardly offer opportunities for adequate and sustainable income generation. Initially, it is true that for them addressing constraints, such as access to land, remains important, but in the long run it is probably as important for the future of the rural youth. This theme is revisited in more detail in chapter 14.

Despite rural homesteads steadily increasing their dependence on incomes that are external to the village, the role of the rural as social security and 'safety net' for the urban should not be neglected. Not much has been said about this, but many urban-based people affected by HIV/AIDS return to their rural homes when they get terminally ill, because they know that there they will be cared for during what remains of their lives and they will receive a decent burial. Ties to the rural homestead, through various economic and social exchanges, also continue to provide social security should efforts to secure an urban-based livelihood fail. This relates to the discussion on single versus multiple homestead households. For struggling urban migrants the difference between these two kinds of households determines their ability or lack thereof to maintain a degree of livelihood security in times of trouble by retaining assets in the rural areas.

The shift in livelihoods away from agricultural production signifies the transformation of homesteads from being locally based social-economic units to multi-local units of production and consumption. Rural homesteads and the villages as a whole have increasingly become a source of social-cultural identity (e.g. as a place to retire to or to hold cultural functions, such as male initiation). As a result the shifts in rural livelihoods have not affected the traditional cultural role of cattle and land in rural life.

# 13

# Life histories and livelihood trajectories


Paul Hebinck, Wim van Averbeke, Nomakhaya Monde,
Lothar Smith and James Bennett


## Introduction

Chapter 12 provided an account of rural livelihoods in the two villages that was mainly quantitative. It showed that at the level of the homestead various livelihood activities and domains were actively being combined in different ways by different homesteads, resulting in livelihood diversity among homesteads. By and large the picture that was painted represented the situation as it applied during the periods of data collection. In this chapter livelihood transformation within homesteads is the focus. We will do that by examining how, and why, rural livelihoods have changed over the past four to five decades and by focusing on the nature and extent of processes of differentiation and the resources that have been critical in such processes,. As argued in chapter 1, an analysis of livelihood transformation benefits from stretching the time horizon as far as possible, as was shown in the study of Van Onselen (1996) about the life of Kas Maine.

The life histories presented in this chapter more or less cover the period 1950 to 2004. The main actors grew up and started working during the era when male migration from the rural areas to the urban centres of South Africa was still a general pattern. The life histories also cover the homeland era, from the time when the Ciskei was pushed towards self-government and ultimately to nominal independence in 1981 until it was re-incorporated into South Africa in 1994. Important socio-economic processes that occurred during this era were the influx of surplus people into the Ciskei, linked to the mechanisation and modernisation of white commercial farming, and the active involvement of the Ciskei government, with funding from South Africa, to provide people in the homeland with some kind of income. Guided by the policy objective of "one meal per day for every Ciskeian", various employment strategies were used, including growth in the size of the civil service, the establishment of industry in centres such as Dimbaza and Fort Jackson, the development of irrigation schemes, such as Keiskammahoek, Tyefu, Shiloh and Zanyokwe, the employment of large numbers of service workers at low wages by large organisations, such as the University of Fort Hare, and the use of temporary drought relief projects which specifically targeted the rural areas (chapter 2). Finally, life histories cover the post-1994 era, characterised by economic restructuring and large-scale retrenchments, particularly of unskilled workers, the emergence of international tourism in the Western Cape, growth in the public grant system, both in terms of eligibility and the size of the grants, and renewed urbanisation, this time involving entire homesteads.

The context in which the different life histories unfolded is covered in detail in other chapters. Chapters 2 and 4 analysed the dynamics involved with Apartheid policies aiming at racial segregation, betterment planning interventions, and population increase due to movements brought about by forced removals and surplus people from nearby white-owned farms. Chapter 11 highlighted changing migration patterns, partly in response to the lack of opportunities in the villages, but also because restrictive legislation was repealed, making it easier to migrate to urban areas, which are often perceived by villagers as attractive places to seek to improve their livelihood. The recent social phenomenon of the rural-urban drifters in South Africa shows that this perception is in many cases unrealistic. Chapters 4 and 5 pointed at agro-ecological events and processes, such as drought and environmental degradation, which affect use and quality of local natural resources. Chapters 7, 8, 9 and 10 showed how livelihoods relate to the use of these resources in varying degrees.

Analysis of the life histories provides an indication of the different directions in which the livelihood of homesteads in the two villages has changed. These different directions are called livelihood trajectories (chapter 1). The material presented in this chapter illustrates that the livelihood trajectories of homesteads in the two villages are not uniform. The different life histories presented in this chapter focus on the livelihood of homesteads that remained in the two villages. This means that the material deals with ways in which rural livelihoods have been constructed and reconstructed. The life histories of homesteads that have left the two villages constitute another important reality, but they do not feature here.

The life history accounts were collected between 1998 and 2005. The selection of cases was informed by insights gained from an analysis of the 1997 and 1999 survey data. The cases presented here are selected from the lists of people living in occupied homesteads (Table 11.4). This selection excluded those that lived elsewhere but maintained some kind of social and economic relationship with their relatives and friends. The cases were also selected with a view to covering the four livelihood domains identified in chapter 12: (1) productive use of parts of the landscape (i.e. land-based activities), (2) transfers from kin and the state, (3) labour made productive outside the village and (4) from wages, petty trade and self-employed activities locally in the villages.

The following livelihoods categories, each with specific dynamics and outcomes, were identified for further elaboration and analysis:

1. The role of natural resource use, particularly in the form of cultivation, has diminished substantially. A number of homesteads, however, continue to invest in cultivating crops and livestock production. We bring together here five cases, some extended and some succinct, that together express the relevant variations within such a rather broad category of rural livelihoods.
2. Locally based livelihoods are few in the villages (petty businessmen, chapter 12) and the strategies vary enormously. Piece work or casual work for others or running a *spaza* shop or *shebeen* stands for what the local economy has to offer. Cases 7 and 8 but also case 6 reflect in their own ways the dynamics.
3. Rural livelihoods in Guquka and Koloni revolve principally around transfers ('grantholders', chapter 12). Case 9 and, to a certain degree, case 5 illustrate in more detail the complexities of transfer-based livelihoods.

Data were collected during the period 1998 to 2001 using a series of semi-structured interviews complemented by participant observation. Subsequently, the homesteads were again interviewed during field visits in 2004 and 2005, to obtain information on recent changes that had occurred. The interviews were conducted in Xhosa with the help of field assistants who translated the conversations. These interviews were held with men, women and elderly children, and involved visits to their homesteads.

## Case 1:  Mengezelei and Kulukazi Mbangi: Migrant, home gardener, pensioner

Mengezelei and his spouse Kulukazi were residents of Guquka. In 1998, Mengezelei was 61 years old and Kulukazi 59. Mengezelei looked young for his age and he was still very fit, but Kulukazi had trouble walking due to a leg injury and used a stick to support her. She was mainly occupied with housekeeping and cooking, but she also repaired clothes with a mechanical sewing machine. In 1997, Mengezelei's homestead survived on an income of about R120 per month, well below the poverty line at the timeof about R800 per month.

Mengezelei was born in 1937 on a white owned farm named Cathartvale near Seymour. At the age of 11 he began to work on that farm. Not satisfied with life as a farm worker he moved to Johannesburg in 1955 at the age of 18 years. First he found work as a miner in the RPM Mine in Boksburg and in 1957 he moved to the Goedvlei Mine in Springs, where he worked until 1967. At age 30 he returned to Seymour and found work at the construction site of the Kat River Dam. When he was laid off in 1971, he accepted work in the Geduld Mine No 7 FSG in Free State, where he remained until 1988. In 1974, at the age of 37, he married Kulukazi of Hermest Farm near Fort Beaufort.

During his stay in Boksburg, and even thereafter, Mengezelei used Cathartvale Farm as a home base. This arrangement suited him well until the sons of the farmer took over the farm. The new owners did not make him feel welcome on the farm, and he decided to look for a place of his own. Mengezelei's brother had relatives living at Guquka and they were prepared to support Mengezelei's application to the Tribal Authority of Makhuzeni for a residential site. When a residential site became available at Guquka, following the death of an old lady, Mengezelei purchased the site from her children when they sought to sell the site and the *rondavel* that was built on it. Mengezelei could no longer remember how much he paid for it. The village headman and the Makhuzeni Tribal Authority were informed of the transaction. Mengezelei was informed that his name was entered into a register kept at the Alice Municipality. As proof of the transfer he also received the original Permission to Occupy certificate of the site that had been made out to the previous occupant. The sellers handed this certificate to him, but somehow it was subsequently lost.

When working in the Free State, Mengezelei was keen to obtain an arable field. He believed that as a miner he earned sufficient income to finance crop production. However, he was told that no land was available at Guquka. He then tried to lease land from landowners, but none was interested. The only arrangement they were interested in on was sharecropping. Mengezelei did not consider sharecropping to be a good deal because benefits accrued mainly to the landowners. In 1998, Mengezelei had all but given up on the idea of producing crops on a large scale, even though he was convinced that field cropping could provide substantial income. He pointed out that water from the Tyume River could be used to produce irrigated vegetables but for him it no longer mattered. Without a regular income to invest in ploughing and planting, field-scale cultivation was not feasible he said. He had also given up on finding employment because there were no jobs around in the area. He repeated his opposition to sharecropping as an arrangement because all the risk had to be carried by the landless partner, who had to bear the full cost of production and do all the work. In return for making available their fields landholders demanded an equal share of the harvest.

After his return from Geduld Mine in 1988 Mengezelei never found permanent employment again. He derived income from casual work in Guquka and neighbouring villages and from the occasional short-term contract in Alice. His piece work in the local rural settlements usually consisted of fencing residential sites and digging pit latrines. In 1998, he was paid R400 to fence a 1,250 m$^2$ site with a circumference of about 140 m, and R100 to dig a pit latrine. Digging a pit latrine in the shallow soils was hard work because the major part of the pit had to be dug into the mudstone rock. Mengezelei last worked in 1996 in Alice, when he was digging trenches for the new municipal sewerage system.

Mengezelei never owned livestock (for reasons explained in chapter 4), but he had built a small *kraal* of about 10 m$^2$ in the top corner of his plot. When asked about the function of the kraal, he said that it was built for ceremonial purposes to provide a place for men to get together and talk as is demanded by Xhosa tradition.

From 1998 onward, Mengezelei's main farming activity consisted of gardening. He regularly managed to produce high quality vegetables that fetched high prices in the village. However, the main part of what he produced was consumed at his home. All Mengezelei's production occurred in his home garden, which formed part of his residential site. His residential site was about 1250 m$^2$ in size and about three-quarters of this were used for gardening (see chapter 6 for a detailed description). Mengezelei also kept chickens which he sold locally. The chickens, like his vegetables, were highly regarded and fetched good prices.

When asked about the meagre income he and his wife survived on, he pointed out that his small family purchased very little. On a monthly basis they bought 12.5 kg maize meal and the same amounts of crushed maize (*samp*) and wheat flour. To that they added 2.5 kg rice and sugar, 2 litre sunflower oil, a packet of tea, a medium-sized tin of cheap coffee and soap. They also bought a 10 kg bag of potatoes, 1 kg of dry beans and a cabbage, whenever these items were not available form the garden. He pointed out that the income he earned from casual work and selling chickens and vegetables was usually sufficient to cover these expenses, and he was adamant that his family had never known hunger. As a migrant worker he had bought a lot of clothes, enough to last him a lifetime. Whenever a piece of clothing needed repairs, they used the sewing machine, which he bought for Kulukazi when he was still working at the mines, to do the repairs. Kulukazi was handy with the sewing machine, and every so often she repaired clothing for other people in the village, for which she charged R3.00. When emergencies arose and there was no money in the house, Mengezelei borrowed money from other households, to be repaid by doing a job for them.

In 2004, the livelihood at Mengezelei's homestead had improved considerably. Both he and Kulukazi were now receiving old-age pensions. Kulukazi started receiving this in 1999 and Mengezelei in 2003. From an absolute poverty perspective the homestead had progressed from the ultra-poor into the non-poor category, but in terms of livelihood activities some changes had occurred. Mengezelei was still growing vegetables and producing chickens, but he had stopped doing casual work for other homesteads, pointing out that there were others in the village that needed the work more than he did. Instead, he had started constructing roasting grids. People use these grids to bake a particular type of bread roll, known as *rostile*. When produced commercially, these grids are welded together, but Mengezelei constructed them with a pair of pliers. Mengezelei commented that his gardening had become easier, now that he had money. In the past he left selected vegetable plants to go to seed for the subsequent seasons, but since receiving a pension he had started to buy new seed each time he planted. The seed he bought from Umthiza, an agricultural supply store in Alice. He still did not buy fertilizers. Now that he had a pension he had more or less stopped selling vegetables directly to customers. Instead he delivered his produce to a local shop, selling it at considerably lower prices than he used to charge in the past. He explained that he changed his approach because people in the village tended to be jealous of others who were better off.

During one interview Kulukazi arrived back from Alice where she had purchased groceries. She was accompanied by a young girl who we had never seen before. Kulukazi was looking good. Her leg had healed and she was no longer using a stick. Mengezelei explained that they were raising the girl, who was the daughter of a neighbour and that they had started helping the girl in 1996 when her mother moved to Bizana in Transkei. At that time the girl still slept at home, but since Kulukazi received a pension in 1999 the girl had come to live and sleep with them. This more or less coincided with the move of the mother of the girl to Cape Town. It seemed that Kulukazi was particularly pleased to have the girl as part of the family because every time the child was mentioned a warm smile appeared on her face.

## Case 2:   Mlami and Nomtandasa Tibani: Migrant, local employment, migrant

When we met Mlami in 1998 his homestead consisted of two adults and four children and lacked any income. Mlami was born in Guquka in 1953.In 1969, when he was 16 years old, Mlami left Guquka and moved to the Western Cape where he found work at a dairy farm. In 1972, at the age of 19, he became a dock worker in Cape Town harbour, loading and off-loading ships. He returned to Guquka in 1976 and stayed there until mid 1977. He then tried his luck in Johannesburg but failed to find work. Early 1978 he returned to Cape Town where he worked as a waiter in different hotels. In 1981, at the age of 27, Mlami married Nomtandasa who was also from Guquka. Following the marriage, Nomtandasa visited him occasionally, travelling to Cape Town by bus. The young couple were desperate to stay together on a daily basis, and Mlami started looking for work closer to home.

In 1982, Mlami found a job at Fort Hare as a casual security guard, and in 1986 he obtained permanent status. Guards worked in shifts, including night shifts, which Mlami disliked, because it prevented him from returning home daily. In 1994, he successfully applied for a transfer to the Gardens and Grounds section of the University, where he worked from 7:30 am to 4:30 pm, an arrangement that suited him much better. In 1997, the majority of such employees at Fort Hare were retrenched to address budgetary difficulties (chapter 3). Mlami was one of them. When interviewed for the first time in 1998 he was still upbeat, but when that episode in his life was discussed again in 2005 he was extremely bitter about it. In 1998, Mlami and his family still survived on the retrenchment package paid out by Fort Hare, without any other significant source of income. Mlami enjoyed being at home throughout the day but by then he was well aware that his financial reserves were limited. Nomtandasa generated an occasional income from sewing uniforms, whilst Mlami was extending his house using wattle and daub. He indicated that once the work on the house was complete he intended to start looking for a job. He pointed out that he would prefer to stay with his family, but he had little hope of finding employment that would enable him to do so.

Mlami was born in a family that owned arable land in the village, but being the last born he was not eligible to inherit the land holdings and the residential site of his parents. When he got married he applied to the tribal authority for a residential site. This was allocated to him in 1989 free of charge. When employed at Fort Hare, Mlami did not have much interest in agriculture. The wages he earned were adequate to buy food and other necessities, and full time employment did not leave him with time to devote to farming. Moreover, his wife had her hands full around the house, looking after the children and using her spare time to sew. Over time, they had established a tiny home garden in which they grew a few vegetables for the household and, according to Mlami, that was about as much as they could handle. Now that Mlami was no longer employed he realized that he needed to grow more of his own food, In 1998, he applied to the Residence Association of Guquka to be allocated the vacant residential site neighbouring his home for use as a second garden, because his existing home garden was too small. The vacant site had been allocated twice to different people, but both had rejected the site. As a result, the Residence Association had no objections and approved his application. He had the site ploughed and intended to plant the land to maize that same year. Unlike several others in the village, Mlami had never invested part of his earnings in livestock. The homestead did not even keep poultry. Yet, Mlami indicated that he was keen to explore the potential of agriculture as a livelihood option because it would enable him to remain at home with his family. He pointed out the opportunity of using arable land bordering the Tyume River for irrigated crop production. Considering the high rate of unemployment in the village he was of the opinion that many people would be interested in a project that introduced irrigated farming in the village. However, he was of the opinion that external assistance would be needed to implement an irrigation project because people in the village only knew traditional farming methods and needed to be trained intensively before they could handle commercial agriculture.

When we visited his homestead in 2004 he was no longer at home. The garden on the neighbouring residential site was fallow and covered with weeds. When we interviewed Nomtandasa she told us that Mlami was working in Knysna. Towards the end of 1998 Mlami's retrenchment package had been consumed and the homestead had run out of money. In 1999, Mlami had found contract work for six months in Alice, which had kept them going, but when the contract was finished their problems returned. In 2000, Mlami travelled to Knysna to collect the remains of his brother, who had suddenly passed away. At the time of his death his brother was working as a petrol attendant, and while in Knysna Mlami was offered his brother's job. Mlami left Guquka in September 2000 and after working as a petrol attendant for a few months he took up a second job. From 7 am to 4 pm he pumped petrol and during the night from 10 pm to 6 am he worked as a guard. After a while, the lack of sleep started to affect his health, and he had to resign from the petrol station because security work paid better than dispensing petrol. However, his earnings were still not enough to provide a reasonable income for his family. Early in 2003, Mlami applied successfully for a position as a tour guide because of his ability to speak English and his experience as a waiter in Cape Town. His work consisted of accompanying foreign tourists on a bus tour of the Knysna region visiting the local sites and attractions. The new job paid well, enabling him to send more money home.

On the day of our visit Nomtandasa arrived by taxi from Alice loaded with groceries. She had been elected chair person of the residents' association of Guquka. She and the children looked happy and healthy. I asked her about the neighbouring plot. Nomtandasa explained that they had only cultivated the plot for two years. When Mlami left no one in the family remained who could cultivate the plot. When the eldest son, who had turned into a strong young man, was asked why he did not keep up with gardening, he responded that he focused on school and rugby practice and that there was no time for him to look after the plot.

When we visited again in July 2005, Mlami was back at home, retrenched from his job as a tour guide. While he was in Knysna, one of his daughters had become ill, and now she was bound to a wheel chair. Being away whilst his daughter's health was deteriorating had been a traumatic experience for him, and he was adamant that he would never be a migrant worker again. The family was clearly suffering. Nomtandasa had aged and most of her teeth had been extracted. Mlami said that his family was very hungry. Since his retrenchment and return to Guquka, Nomtandasa's brother had been helping the family by donating R250 or R300 every month to buy food but this had not been enough to feed the family. Reflecting on his stay in Knysna, Mlami explained that moving there had been a difficult but necessary decision because in 2000 the family had run out of money. Cultivating the plot next door in 1998 and 1999 had provided them with some food, but his family needed money because the children had to go to school. In Knysna he had worked hard to earn enough money to provide for his family but being away from home had been very difficult. During that period he visited home about twice a year, which was not enough. He pointed out that when he was young and engaged to Nomtandasa, she had travelled to Cape Town often, and he had felt less lonely than when living in Knysna. His overall situation had improved when he landed the job of tour guide. He had earned a basic monthly salary of R2000 and had been allowed to keep all the tips he received. He proudly pointed at the large ghetto blaster, the centre piece of their small living space, and said that he had purchased it with his earnings as a tourist guide. The closing down of the company had been a heavy blow to him, but the worst was not being there when his daughter's health started to deteriorate. Despite the precarious situation of his homestead he repeated over and over that he would never leave his family again.

When asked about his plans, he said he hoped that the water harvesting project that was started by the University of Fort Hare would assist him. He also explained that he was playing a leading role in an initiative aimed at improving rural security assisting the police with prevention and solving of crimes, particularly the theft of livestock. Mlami argued the benefits of this proposal. He pointed out that a return to safety would trigger an era of investment in smallholder agriculture, which would benefit the area and reduce poverty. However, it was evident that his main concern was to secure a job that provided him with a regular income whilst allowing him to stay at home.

## Case 3:   Mzoli and Thandeka Mrwetyana: Reversing gender roles

In 1999, the Mrwetyana homestead in Koloni consisted of six members, namely, Mzoli, his wife Thandeka and four children. Three of the children attended high school in Zwelitsha near King William's Town and one, who's hearing wasimpaired, stayed at home. Mzoli was unemployed and no longer actively looking for work. After several years without luck he was tired of searching for a job.

Mzoli was born in Lady Frere in the Transkei. He passed grade 12 and found work in the civil service as a clerk in the Transkei Department of Local Government where he worked from 1971 to 1976. He was transferred to the Transkei Department of Internal Affairs where he worked from 1977 to 1980. In 1981 he was employed as a teller in a branch of African Bank where he worked until end of 1982. Mzoli kept on hopping jobs in order to earn more.

When he failed to secure a well paid job, he decided to follow his father's footsteps and become a teacher. In 1982 he registered as a full time student in Clarkebury Teacher's College. During the first year he managed to pay his educational expenses, but during the second year he ran out of money and requested assistance from his father. Later that year his father passed away, and as a result Mzoli could not complete his teacher's training course. He had to look for a job again but found it difficult because he was not qualified. Nevertheless, he found several temporary teaching jobs in different schools in the Ciskei. He was already married then and he and his wife had moved to Ciskei. He usually replaced teachers who were on study or maternity leave. His last temporary teaching post was in 1995, and since then he has never taught again.

Instead he had taken to cultivating the home garden and to assisting his wife who was a teacher.

Mzoli's wife, Thandeka, was born in Matatiele in 1949. When she was still young her parents moved to Ginsburg, a township of King William's Town. She passed grade 10 and enrolled for a teacher's course at Lovedale College in Alice, qualifying in 1970. In 1971 she started working as a teacher and taught for five years. She gradually realised that she did not like teaching very much and decided to change to nursing. She went to Port Elizabeth where she started her nursing career. She was unable to finish her studies because she became pregnant and therefore was expelled from school. After her baby was born Thandeka started to look for a teaching job once more. Like her husband she was only able to get temporary jobs, replacing teachers who were on leave. In 1984 she was again employed as a full time teacher at Cala Junior Secondary School in Transkei until 1987. It was not easy for her as her family was in Koloni. For this reason, she started to look for a job closer to home. In 1988, she obtained a post at Koloni Junior Secondary School, but in 1990 she was transferred to another school in a nearby village. In 1999 she was still teaching in that school.

Mzoli's and his family did not stay in their own house in Koloni. The homestead belonged to relatives who had moved to East London and left their home in the care of the Mrwetyanas for the time being. The Mrwetyanas owned a residential site in the new section of Koloni (see chapter 6). They had applied for that site, but they had not yet built their own house. They planned to start building as soon as possible, because they were not sure how long they would be able to stay in the house they were taking care of.

Since about 1996 Mzoli's homestead had been relying primarily on Thandeka's salary for a living. Mzoli worked in the home garden and grew vegetables, mainly for home consumption. He produced potatoes, cabbages, spinach, beans, onions, carrots, butternut, baby marrow and beets. When there was surplus he sold it locally. Mzoli cultivated the garden by hand, using a spade and a garden fork. He grew crops in the garden year round. The garden was divided into plots. As soon as a plot was harvested he planted a new crop, after digging in manure. At least once a year he also applied chemical fertilisers. Manure was carted from the neighbour's *kraal* where it was available free of charge. He also irrigated his crops, always when planting and occasionally thereafter when necessary. He talked about building a small dam inside the garden to collect rainwater for irrigation.

When we visited Mzoli again in 2004 he pointed out a few changes. Two of their children were attending university, but they did not have a bursary or study loan. As a result, half of Thandeka's salary was used to pay off the fees. The third child had also passed Grade 12 two years ago but was not studying. The parents could not afford to pay the tuition fees of three university students .The family was also adopting a 9-year-old nephew whose mother was ill. Compared to five years earlier, the family was struggling to make ends meet. Tandeka apologised for not offering tea during the visit, because they had neither tea nor sugar in the house. Mzoli confirmed that things were tough. He said that when some food items ran out before month-end, they were not replaced until Thandeka got paid again. Five years ago, the family was ready to start building a new house, but those plans had been shelved, and from the look of things building would have to wait for a while. Thandeka indicated that she was seriously thinking of requesting for early retirement, because the lump sum she would receive would enable them to build the house. One thing that had not changed was Mzoli's engagement in home gardening. He was still producing food for his family, who needed it more than ever before.

## Case 4:   Vuyo and Zolile Grootbooi: Retrenched migrant to farmer

In 1998, the homestead of Vuyo and Zolile in Guquka consisted of seven people, three adults and four children subsisting on a single pension of R470 per month supplemented by a modest in-kind income from home gardening. Zolile, Vuyo's wife, was born in 1959 in the Township of Cookhouse, a town located about 100 km north of Port Elizabeth. She grew up in Cookhouse and attended school there until 1977, completing grade 8. In 1978 she found employment as a domestic worker in Port Elizabeth, where she stayed for two years. In 1982 she married Vuyo and moved to Guquka, her husband's home. Vuyo worked in a Free State gold mine from 1982 until February 1998, when he was retrenched. Following his retrenchment the homestead was left to rely on Vuyo's mother's pension as their only source of cash income. Whilst working at the mine, Vuyo had applied for a residential site. The Residents' Association allocated the couple a site in the northern section of the village. They built a substantial cement-brick house on that site and roofed the dwelling, but in 1998 they were delaying occupation until the house had doors and windows. Vuyo's retrenchment had prevented them from completing their new home. Vuyo had also invested part of his wages in livestock, purchasing five cattle, two goats and twelve sheep over the years.

When Vuyo was still employed as a miner the homestead obtained access to arable land through a share-cropping arrangement with a land holder. This arrangement required them to crop the land with their own labour and inputs and share the yield with the owner of the field, each receiving half. Both Vuyo and Zolile were of the opinion that the arrangement was extremely unfair towards them, and after a few years they gave up. In 1998, they were concentrating their efforts on home garden production. Zolile produced crops in the parental garden and also in the garden of her neighbour, who had moved to Cape Town leaving home and garden in her care. Carrying buckets of water from the stock watering dam, which was situated about 200 m from the homestead, Zolile irrigated a wide range of crops. She produced her own seedlings in a seedbed and transplanted these to the garden plots. The plots were fertilised with *kraal* manure. Zolile explained that after being transplanted, seedlings were very weak and sensitive to water stress, making irrigation essential for survival of the plants. She did not like the idea of the water harvesting dams used by William because she believed that the presence of water bodies near a home caused the occupants to get strange diseases, such as pimples and swelling of the face. Zolile was very interested in an irrigated crop production project in the village. As a dedicated producer of crops she was of the opinion that such a project would provide both food and income to her family. She expressed preference for involvment in a group project with a membership of both men and women. Vuyo, on the other hand, expressed the wish to find employment but supported his wife's aspiration to be a member in a crop production project. Zolile knew of two other women in the village who would be keen to join such an agricultural project. They were also landless, but still practised share-cropping. Zolile viewed access to land as a key constraint. She feared that the reluctance of landowners to rent out their land stood in the way of an irrigation project. Consequently she had decided to concentrate her efforts on garden production until such time solutions to the land issue emerged.

Visiting Guquka in 2004, we found Vuyo outside the village *shebeen*. He stated that he had time to talk with us if we bought him a bottle of beer. Upon arrival at his mother's place (their new house remained unfinished), we were welcomed by Zolile. She and the children looked well, and there was a new toddler running around the site. Vuyo's mom had passed away the previous a year, which meant that the family no longer had pension income.

Vuyo had secured the use of a field. When his maternal grandmother had passed away he and his mother had requested from the rest of the family the use of the field previously cultivated by Mr. Dibela. Since the person first in line to inherit the field was no longer living in the village, they had agreed to his request. He pointed out that he was allowed to use it until such time as the rightful owner claimed it back. Vuyo's homestead was using the field to produce maize, beans and pumpkins for home consumption and potatoes for income. Grain was being used to raise pigs and chickens on the residential site. Producing pigs was a new initiative, aimed at replacing sheep. Vuyo explained that theft of sheep had become "a real curse in the village". Of the twelve sheep he once had, eight had been stolen, and now he was left with only four. Vuyo was not the only victim of livestock theft. The day we arrived at Guquka the son of the former village headman was found dead in his sheep *kraal*. Neighbours speculated that during the night he had woken up when hearing suspicious noises outside the house. Inspecting the source of the noise he had probably stumbled upon the thieves and they had stabbed him to death. His corpse was discovered the next morning by his father. Vuyo explained that pigs were not so easily stolen because they made a racket when disturbed. The other advantage of swine over sheep was that they reached market readiness a lot faster. Sheep, on the other hand, had the advantage that they produced wool, but income from wool was very meagre. In 2003 he had sold the clip obtained from the six animals he held at that time to a travelling speculator for R70.

Zolile was responsible for looking after the pigs. She employed an improved scavenging system, supplementing whatever food the pigs found around the village with poor-quality maize grain on a daily basis. Using this system the pigs took six to eight months to reach market readiness. Pig production was aimed at the Christmas market, when migrants returned home from their urban places of work and homesteads in the village had money to buy meat. The month before Christmas she increased the maize rations to give the pigs a growth spurt and ensure good prices. The income earned from pig production was used primarily to plough the field. In 2003, hiring a tractor belonging to one of the local contractors had cost R1080 to plough the entire field, but as yet the homestead had not had enough money to cultivate the full area. Instead they had subdivided the plot into twelve sections, and in 2003 they had planted nine of these. The largest portion, approximately 2.1 ha in size, was planted to a mixed crop of maize, beans and pumpkins, using an animal-drawn, single-furrow planter.

This particular indigenous technology is widely used in the Transkei region, (Mkile 2001), but less commonly in the former Ciskei (Van Averbeke & Mkile 2007). It involves the placement of a mixture of air-dry pulverisedcrushed, air-dried *kraal* manure, chemical fertilisers and beans and pumpkin seeds in the fertiliszer bin of the implement and maize seed in the seed hopper. During planting the implement deposits both the fertilizer-seed mixture and the maize seed in the furrow it opens up, yielding a three-crop stand planted in rows.

The Grootbooi homestead did not own a planter but borrowed one from another homestead. In return they helped the owners of the implement when they planted their field. Once the crop was established weeds growing between the rows were controlled with an animal-drawn cultivator, an implement the homestead did own. Any weeds found in the rows were removed by hand hoeing. Vuyo and Zolile estimated that in Guquka there were four families who owned a planter and about ten who had a cultivator. The family harvested their summer crop in June and stored the produce in a *rondavel* for their own consumption. As the need arose they shelled enough maize cobs to fill an 80 kg grain bag, sorting the kernels into two classes, one suitable for human consumption and one for use as animal feed. Poor quality grain was fed to pigs and poultry and sometimes to the sheep. The good quality grain was taken to Phandulwazi High School across the river from Guquka, where it was milled into a coarse meal at a cost of R10 a bag. Processed grain into *samp*, the broken maize kernels sed to cook a popular dish of maize and beans, Zolile did at home. Vuyo reported that his maize harvest lasted the family for about nine months, until March, and grain from the new crop becoming available in June. The main reason for the gap was that the quality of the grain deteriorated with storage duration, because of weevils. During 2003 the homestead had planted the rest of their plot, about 0.14 ha, to potatoes. They were very pleased with the results because the crop had generated a decent income, having been sold entirely to households in the village. The potato crop had been so encouraging that they intended to plant a larger section next year.

In 2004, Vuyo still held cattle. His herd had expanded through reproduction and inheritance from his parents to eleven animals. At a livestock auction at Phandulwazi High School he had sold one old cow, which had persistently been incapable of weaning its calves, for R2600, using R2300 of the income to buy a heifer from a livestock owner in the village. He had also slaughtered three animals to comply with local customs surrounding the death of family members. Vuyo ran his cattle on fallow arable plots that were not fenced in. He admitted smilingly that the owners of the fields did not like this at all and that on occasions there were quarrels about that. The main argument of the owners was that grazing his cattle in their fields prevented them from obtaining thatching grass. Vuyo was not impressed with that argument because nearly all of the dwellings in Guquka had corrugated iron roofs. The main benefit the homestead derived from their cattle was milk, but draught power and manure were also important. Vuyo estimated that the cows in milk, usually about five of the eleven animals, produced about 7.5 litres milk a day over six months of the year. All of this milk was transformed into *amasi* (sour milk) and consumed by the household. Vuyo was keen to develop a system that would ensure year-long milk production, but lacked knowledge on fodder production to achieve this goal.

Vuyo appeared to have accepted his new land-based livelihood, and Zolile loved it. Vuyo admitted that given the chance he would still prefer to work in the mines, but he was confident that his homestead could survive from farming. Their experiences with potato production had shown them that the farm could be utilized to generate both cash income and food. The couple intended to educate their children provided there was enough money, but they pointed out that they should also learn to farm as part of a range of life skills.

## Case 5:   Mpendulo: Migrant to farmer

In 2000, Mpendulo's homestead consisted of his wife Nomvuyo and their six children. Mpendulo was 58 years old, having been born in Koloni in 1942 in a landowning family. He went to school but only passed grade six because, as he said himself, of laziness. After he had left school he began to look for a job and found one in Zwelitsha at Da Gama Textiles. He worked there for more than 20 years after which he returned home in the early 1990s. Upon his return Mpendulo started to engage in agriculture but also operated a *bakkie*, which he used to transport goods and people. After a few years he sold the *bakkie* because he could no longer maintain it. Since then, agriculture became the only source of livelihood for Mpendulo's homestead. Unlike most other families in the village their main purpose in cultivating crops and keeping livestock is to earn cash income.

The Ngxobo's have a field (field no. 74, Map 8.2), which they cultivated every year. They also have access to two home gardens where they grow vegetables. One is on their residential site and the other is at his brothers' homestead who has not yet constructed a house on it. One of Mpendulo's main tasks is taking care of the cattle, sheep and goats when the animals are sick. His wife does not take part in all this, she says, as she does not know anything about animal diseases. Although Mpendulo can easily tell when an animal is sick, he lacks the knowledge of diseases and their treatment. Most of the time he relies on traditional medicines he picks from the rangeland to bring the animals back to good health. Amongst these traditional medicines, there is one usually called *uzifozonke*, which is used to treat a wide range of diseases.

Decisions regarding selling animals were also entirely in the hands of Mpendulo. While pointing at an ox he said, "I have decided to sell that ox; it is old". The sheep he had were kept both for wool and meat while goats were kept almost exclusively to be slaughtered for ceremonial purposes. Wool was sold to marketing agents, who usually travel to the area to buy wool during shearing time. Cattle, sheep and goats graze on communal rangeland. Sheep and goats are *kraaled* every night, but cattle remain in the camps and are only *kraaled* at the time of ploughing.

They also kept a few pigs and chickens but these were mainly for own consumption. Once in a while Mpendulo makes a little cash by selling a pig; eggs he sells , however, almost every day. Eggs are sold locally at 50c per egg. Mpendulo's wife is responsible for the small livestock activities. Chickens and pigs are kept in buildings on the residential site where they are fed with maize. The maize comes from their own fields. Two bags of maize were normally reserved to feed the chickens and pigs. When that is not enough maize was bought from supermarkets in King William's Town. Specially formulated feed for chickens was also purchased there, but supplemented with maize that was crushed at home.

The crops Mpendulo planted in the arable field included maize, which normally occupies more than half of the land, pumpkins, potatoes, melons and dry beans. In the garden mostly vegetables were grown. Most of the maize was sold locally at R60.00 per 50 kg bag. He said that he did not have much trouble selling maize in Koloni. The only marketing that was needed was to announce in a meeting that their maize is ready for sale. His customers were also from neighbouring villages. In good seasons, Mpendulo makes a relatively high net return from selling maize. For example, during the 1999/2000 cropping season he harvested 16 bags of maize grain, ten of which were sold, bringing him R600.00. The other six bags were kept for personal consumption. He sold a bag (10kg) of potatoes for R10.00, and a pumpkin brings R3.50. Dry beans and melons were not sold. Some melons are fed to the pigs whilst household members consume others. Vegetables are sold the same way as field crops with local people coming and buying at their site.

## Case 6:   Phindile and Nolulamile Ngwevu: Rural entrepreneurs

Phindile was born in Cathcart near Stutterheim in 1953. His parents were farm workers. Phindile attended a farm school that did not go further than grade 4. When he could no longer attend school he started helping his parents who were looking after the animals of Mr. Hart (a white farmer). He stayed on the farm until 1972. When his parents were too old to work, the owner of the farm asked them to leave the farm and look for a place to stay in the Ciskei. His father had relatives in Guquka and approached them to find a residential site for him and his family, as it was not easy for a stranger to apply for a site in a village without mediation by one or more of its residents. His application was successful, and by the end of 1972 they settled in Guquka. They arrived with a herd of of about 18 cattle , which his father obtained from Mr. Hart, some as gifts and some bought at a good price.

Phindile and his wife,Nolulamile, had seven children, four girls and three boys. Five of these children were still at school and at home in 2000. Two older girls had both passed grade 12 and stayed in Johannesburg looking for jobs. Phindile and his wife also took care of a nephew whom they treated as their own child.

The Ngwevu homestead made a living from trading and activities including chopping and selling firewood, digging and selling sand, buying and selling food in their *spaza* shop, ploughing for other people in Guquka and neighbouring villages. Their business benefited substantially from what they owned: a tractor, a truck, a *bakkie*, two ploughs, a planter and garden tools. There were four buildings on the residential site, two of which looked very modern and were made from cement bricks. There is a garage to keep the tractor and other vehicles. During harvest time one of the houses is used as storage to keep the produce from the garden. They also have two fridges and one of them is used to store food products bought for the purpose of selling. There also had a pig sty and a chicken house. Next to these assets they had access to two gardens; one was on their residential site and another elsewhere. Both gardens are used to grow crops and vegetables mainly for home consumption. They did not own a field but had access through share-cropping in the past (chapter 8). They owned about six head of cattle as well as pigs and chickens. Cattle were mainly kept for ceremonial functions that take place irregularly. They do not milk their cows but allow it to go entirely to the calves.

Phindile is in charge of chopping and selling wood as well as selling sand. Firewood is chopped in a forest that belongs to Cwengcwe, a nearby village. Phindile obtained a permit to chop wood from the Residence Association and had to pay R15.00 per load. They transported at the time at least two truckloads of sand and three loads of firewood every week. These were sold at R150 per load. He employed four people from Guquka to chop wood and load the firewood on his truck.These workers also dug and loaded sand. They earned some

R50.00 per week in 2000. The workers were often also paid in kind in the form of a meal at Phindile's home.

Nolulamile was also trading. Nolulamile used to work as a domestic worker in Hogsback, but she stopped in 1993 to become a fulltime housewife and entrepreneur. She had to stop working because her mother-in-law, who helped take care of children, passed away. She operated the spaza shop since then, which entailed buying and selling broilers, fish and soft drinks. The chickens are bought from a farmer in Cathcart. Nolulamile buys 20 chickens at a time and these were delivered at her house once a month. Each chicken cost R15.50 and R0.50 for delivery. Nolulamile sold each chicken at R30.00 to people in the village. The fish is bought from Multisave Supermarket in Alice. She usually buys one packet of fish at R20.00 every week. Each packet has about 7 to 8 fishes and each fish is cut into five smaller pieces which are sold at R1.20, making a profit of about R6 per fish. She said that the students of George Mqalo Secondary School were among her best clients. Nolulamile's daughter was in charge of the selling related activities, such as soft drinks that are bought from a soft drink store in Alice. A case of 12 one litre bottles costs R36. Each litre was re-sold at R5.50 in the village. She explained that it is not big business and that only during special holidays such as Christmas or Easters does she manage to sell reasonably well

Phindile also made money by ploughing fields in the village with their tractor. He learned how to plough with a tractor while he worked at the farm where he was born. His father had bought the tractor just before they settled in Guquka. After Phindile's parents passed away he inherited the tractor and since then has ploughed other peoples' fields. He still does this charging R60.00 per acre and between R50.00 and R100.00 per garden depending on its size He also inherited his father's cattle but never used them to plough.

At one stage Phindile had thought about looking for a salaried job but in the end he decided to stay fulltime in the village. He bought a *bakkie* in 1979 that he used to transport people to and from Alice as there were no taxis at that time. During ploughing time Phindile would stop transporting people and concentrated on ploughing, as he was making more money by ploughing than from transporting people to town.

The Ngwevu's never owned an arable allotment. All arable land had been allocated by the time they applied for a site (chapter 3). Nevertheless, they managed to access a field through share-cropping till 1987. Growing crops became one of Nolulamile's tasks, while Phindile transported people on a fulltime basis. Phindile would only help with ploughing and planting because these were both done mechanically. Thereafter, Nolulamile cultivated the field all by herself, but sometimes she got help of friends and relatives, including some members of the household that owned the field, but they only assisted with harvesting. In the field the Ngwevu's planted maize and pumpkins. The produce was divided in two parts, half for their family and half for the owner of the field. The Ngwevu's were happy with that arrangement, but in 1987, they had to stop share-cropping (chapter 8) because Nolulamile was still working as a domestic in Hogsback and it became impossible for her to tend to the field. In 1996 they regained access to a field. The owner of the field, who stayed in the village, asked them to use his field as it had been fallow for some years. Two years later he terminated the arrangement because of family pressure (chapter 6). Crop production since then was restricted to vegetables grown in the home gardens. Nolulamile does most of this work. Cultivation was mainly done by hand even though they owned a tractor. Phindile also kept dual-purpose chickens which were kept mostly for themselves and supplied them meat and eggs.

Five years later, in 2004, the fortunes of the Ngwevu's have altered. Three of their children no longer stayed with them. Two were married and now lived in Cape Town. One stayed in Fort Beaufort where he worked as a village health worker, only coming home once a month. The nephew also no longer stayed with them.

They were still engaged in trading but on a much smaller scale. The number of workers had dropped from four to two. Phindile no longer transported and sold sand. The truck had broken down beyond repair. This had also affected Phindile's firewood venture. The tractor that was now used for transporting firewood is much slower than the truck; the number of loads had dropped from three to one per week. Phindile also pointed at other reasons for his declining firewood business. Most people in the village, he said, were shifting from using firewood as a major energy source to using electricity. The business was only good at certain times only e.g. during the December holidays when people are busy with ceremonial functions.

Home garden production was still done. Now that the nephew who previously worked quite a lot in the gardens had left the house, Nophumzile whom from now and then obtained help from her husband who when at home has takes over the gardening. This means that Nophumzile has added activities. The Spaza shop she ran from home was no longer a good business. According to Nophumzile, there were lots of people in the village involved in this kind of trading. As a result the number of customers had dropped. Nophumzile was also no longer a member of *Umgalelo* money club as she was five years ago. She no longer had money to pay the monthly subscription. Compared to five years ago, the Ngwevu homestead was no longer making the same amount of money; the fortunes have turned and quality of life seemed to have slowly deteriorated because of competition, changing life styles and declining purchasing power of their customers.


## Case 7:  Nombulelo Nqolo: A destitute piece worker

Nombulelo was 46 years old in 2000 and as an unmarried mother was head of a family of three children. Two children, Phumzile and Mandla were then 19 and 12 years old, stayed in Guquka with Nombulelo and were still at school doing grades 7 and 3. Nombulelo said that her family did not have enough to eat. The father of her children, who is a part time builder and has his own household, supports Nombulelo's household by paying R50.00 or R100.00 every four to five months. Her eldest child, Thembisa, was 24 at the time and had lived for the past two years in Mdantsane, a township near East London, with Nombulelo's stepsister. Thembisa was attending fashion design school. Fees, meals and accommodation were paid by her family in Mdantsane as Nombulelo cannot afford the costs. In return, Thembisa helps in the running of the Mdantsane household. What Nombulelo really wanted for Thembisa was that she could to finish her course, get a job and save the family from poverty.

Nombulelo was not born in Guquka but elsewhere. Nombulelo had to quit her regular job because of health problems. She made a living from piece jobs done by both herself and her son Phumzile. In the past she worked as a house-keeper and later as a sewer, sewing clothes for somebody in a neighbouring village. She earned a regular source of income, albeit very modest. Besides sewing she cleaned houses, did laundry for people (especially for those home-steads where there are only old people and children or where adult members are working) and babysitting. For this kind of work she was mainly paid in cash but also in kind. She said that she left it to the customer what and how to pay. If they wanted to pay for her services in-kind, she would accept, particularly at times when she had nothing to eat.

She also said that she turned to other people for help. Often, she was given something without a need for reciprocity. This helped her to cope with acute food shortages that mostly occurred towards the end of the month. For people like Nombulelo, seeking assistance was a day-to-day struggle, aimed at satisfy-ing the immediate need to relieve hunger. She said she maintained good rela-tionships with her neighbours: "When we do not have anything to eat I go to them and ask for something". She stressed that it was a reciprocal relationship, but added that she found it was not always easy to ask other people for help.

> Most people are tired already, when they see me, there is only one thing on their minds, 'she has come for food'. I do not blame them, it's not their fault that I'm in this position and it's not easy to feed someone for free when you yourself, do not have enough to eat.

Most of the time she approached her relatives for assistance, and she had only few of them in the village.

Her son Phumzile also brought in some money. Though still at school, Phumzile made sure whenever he could that there was something to eat. During holidays and weekends Phumzile did piece jobs in Guquka. He often worked for Ngwevu (this chapter) chopping wood. He was paid in kind in the form of three meals and R10.00 per day. He always gave his earnings to his mother so that she could buy some food.

Nombulelo did not own many assets. She did not have a field, because when she applied for a residential site arable land had already been allocated. She did not have livestock either, not even chickens. There were two small buildings on her site. Both are made up of mud and wattle. The walls were falling apart and the roofs (old corrugated iron with big holes) leaked. Inside the house there was very little furniture, only a small table, a cupboard, and a small black and white television. Firewood was the main source of energy used for cooking even though there was electricity in the house. Electricity was used for lighting purposes only, when they had money to buy a pre-paid card. When she did, only R10.00 was spent, which would last a month. Firewood was collected from the rangeland, and most of the time this was Phumzile's task. Sometimes Nombulelo also collected dead wood from the bushes next to Tyume River.

One of her few productive assets was her hand sewing machine, which sometimes earned her a small amount of money. The sewing machine was used mainly to sew and repair clothes for people in the village. People came to her with torn clothes and Nombulelo would repair them. According to her, this happened once in a while. Sometimes she did not get anything to sew during an entire month. She asked for R10.00 to R20.00 per item depending on the extent of damage but sometimes she did not get paid. She says she was often paid in kind.

Nombulelo cultivated a small garden. Here she used to grow maize, sorghum, melon and vegetables, including potatoes, cabbages and spinach. The crops were grown under rain-fed conditions, and because of that, the garden was usually planted only once a year. Manure was obtained from relatives free of charge. Home gardening was one of Phumzile's main activities. After school, he attended to the garden instead of doing his schoolwork. They did not own a single garden tool. All tools were borrowed from neighbours and relatives when needed.

Garden production was mainly for home consumption. However, sometimes Nombulelo exchanged for other food products that she did not have or did not grow in their garden. In a good season (when the harvest was abundant), bartering food saved Nombulelo and her family from hunger. But such good times did not occur often, and when they did they were usually of short duration.

When we wanted to interview Nombulelo again in 2004, we were told that she had passed away in 2001. Her children, Phumzile and Mandla, were taken up by different relatives, and another relative took care of the home. Phumzile moved to Cape Town and Mandla to Port Elizabeth. In 2004, rumours in Guquka had it that Mandla had moved to Johannesburg where she worked as a fashion designer. Relatives in the village claimed that she did not support her brother and her exact whereabouts were not known.

# Case 8:   Mncedisi Mcete: Young man with a locally based livelihood

Mncedisi Mcete was born in 1972 in Koloni. He grew up in the township of Mdantsane in East London. Since his late teens, however, he has lived with his uncle in Koloni and his livelihood is now based entirely within the village.

Mncedisi's uncle, Lunga Mcete, was a relatively wealthy individual with a strong entrepreneurial drive. Although he was an employee at the Department of Health in Fort Beaufort, he also derived cash income from driving a taxi on the local run between King William's Town and Middledrift on weekends and through substantial engagement in agriculture. Responsibility for these agricultural activities has increasingly come to rest with Mncedisi in recent years and this is now almost a full-time activity for him.

During the growing season Mncedisi has responsibility for all activities associated with crop production. This includes harrowing, ploughing and planting the arable field, hand hoeing the crop to control weeds and harvesting the crop at the end of the season. However, access to resources for crop production is based on the social networks arranged by his uncle. For example, access to the field Mncedisi has used for the cultivation of maize (field no.40, Map 8.1) was arranged through a rental agreement between Lunga and the field owner who now resides in Mdantsane (see chapter 8). Likewise, during the 2003-2004 cropping season manure for crop production was provided free by Sicelo Ngxowa on the basis of his longstanding relationship with Lunga, and the tractor and trailer used to transport the manure to the field was arranged through a contact Lunga has in a neighbouring village (see chapter 8 for more details). Thus, whilst Mncedisi has responsibility for overseeing most aspects of crop production the real power in negotiating access to the necessary resources with Lunga.

Throughout the year Mncedisi also has responsibility for the general husbandry of all the livestock (cattle, sheep, goats and chickens) belonging to his uncle. This is a considerable job as his uncle was the largest livestock owner in the village. His current holding includes some 45 cattle, 65 sheep and 13 goats. The husbandry activities involve treating the animals with appropriate medicines (both on an individual basis and as part of the regular communal dipping). Mncedisi was also involved in the fairly onerous daily activity of herding all the animals to pasture and collecting the small-stock and cows with calves for *kraaling* in the evening. However, given the extent of this task he is assisted by a full-time shepherd from the village who also takes responsibility for caring for the animals during the day. The shepherd, Mr Siximba Ntlangweni, has been employed by Lunga Mcete for this work and receives R300 a month. Other less regular tasks Mncedisi is responsible for include the construction and maintenance of *kraals* using locally collected bush materials. Although Mncedisi may be involved in herding cattle to sale, Lunga is ultimately responsible for deciding which animals are to be sold and in negotiating the price for them. These sales take place both within the village and at the local *stokvel*. Lunga also has complete control over the sale of wool and through connections he has with the Department of Agriculture negotiates the best possible price for his wool at the wholesale facility in Port Elizabeth (see also chapter 9).

Mncedisi's livelihood scenario is one of complete dependence on his uncle at this point in time. In return for his day to day involvement with these agricultural activities he is provided with accommodation and food (although he is expected to undertake all cooking). Although he receives no formal payment for his services from his uncle, Mncedisi is relatively happy with the arrangements as they stand. He feels he is indebted to his uncle as he paid for all his school fees when he was growing up. Furthermore, over the years he feels he has learnt a considerable amount about agriculture (and general entrepreneurship) from his uncle, which has provided him with some important skills. He is also able to foster some element of independence as during the week he stays on his own in a relatively large house in the village, which belongs to the family but is unoccupied for most of the year.

Nevertheless, in recent years Mncedisi has shown signs of a desire to broaden his horizons. In order to generate some cash of his own he has engaged in piecemeal jobs around the village and has recently taken on part-time employment as a night watchman at the local clinic, although this is very poorly paid. It also means that several days per week he works for his uncle having had little or no sleep the night before. He has expressed an interest in striking out on his own and eventually moving to one of the towns or cities to find work. How realistic this is given his general lack of formal qualifications is difficult to assess. He has attained a certificate in basic computing skills but has no success in even being interviewed for any of the administrative jobs he has applied for. There seems to be a growing acceptance by Mncedisi that ultimately his future may not lie in finding paid employment outside Koloni but instead in making the most of the skills he has acquired by developing an agricultural-based livelihood within the village. Given that his uncle has no sons of his own, he stands to inherit a considerable amount from him in the longer term, which will allow him to make a living from agricultural activities if he is prepared to wait. In this respect the future appears to be in his own hands.

## Case 9:   Margaret Xholo: Female pensioner

In 2000, Margaret was 75 years old, divorced and living in Guquka. She was born in neighbouring Khayalethu. She had passed grade 5 and had 4 children, who were all adults. Three of them had their own families, and one was not married. Margaret had two of her grandchildren staying with her in Guquka since 1990; she raised them as her own children. The mother of the two children was living in Cape Town and did not support them significantly. Both children attended primary school, and Margaret took care of their education and other needs.

After leaving school Margaret worked as a domestic for ten years, from 1941 to 1950, first in Hogsback and later in Grahamstown. At the end of 1950 she married and became a housewife. Ten years later she divorced her husband, returned to Guquka and found a job as a domestic worker in Hogsback. At first she stayed at her place of work returning to Guquka during month-ends only. She applied for her own residential site, which was granted to her at the end of 1971. By then she had already stopped working because of health problems. Margaret was diabetic and suffered from high blood pressure. Her elder son, who was working and not married at that time, took care of the homestead. Margaret's father also supported them with remittances in kind. At the age of 60 she became eligible to claim an old age pension.

Margaret's homestead survived largely on the pensioners' grant, amounting to R520 per month in 2000. She received this money during the first week of every month. On these days, when the grants were paid out, Margaret woke up very early in the morning. She hurried all her normal morning activities to get ready in time to walk to the church building in Guquka, where local pensioners received their grant in the form of a cheque. Though the church building is only 2 km from Margaret's home, she had to leave the house early, because she was old and walked with difficulty. She also wanted to arrive in time, because this gave her one of the front seats in the church, enabling her to get her money early. This left her with enough time left to travel to Alice, where she cashed her cheque. She explained that on pension days there were long queues at the bank, as pensioners from other villages also sought to cash their cheques.

Margaret relied on public transport to get to Alice. During pension day, the taxi owners bring their taxis close to the pay point so that pensioners do not have to walk to the taxi rank. Pension day is a good business day for the taxi-men. Not only pensioners are going to town, but also their family members. Some, like Margaret, are too old to walk by themselves around town and need assistance. After cashing her cheque, she proceded to the supermarket and bought groceries with the help of her older grandson. The groceries she purchases consist mainly of large items (10 or 12.5kg bags of food), which Margaret cannot carry. When shopping is completed, her grandson brings everything to the taxi rank. Apart from paying for travelling costs, for her and her grandson, Margaret has to pay also for the transport of the large food items. The return trip to Guquka cost R30. She has by now almost exhausted her pension on groceries and transport. One of the key question for people like Margaret is whether food they have bought will last until the next pension payday. Margaret argued that this is extremely difficult and that often she needed to borrow from friends, relatives or neighbours.

Margaret owned a field in Guquka, but she had not used it for many years. The field looked heavily eroded in 2000 and was last cultivated in 1988. Margaret portrayed her field as "a huge house with many rooms. The sad part is that while we still grieve from the fact that we cannot grow crops on it, it is like a hiding place to other people". She wished something could be done to close the dongas. She cultivated instead a small garden near her house, growing crops and vegetables she consumed herself. She did not own cattle or goats, and only a few garden tools. The garden has always been important to her and she did everything to cultivate it as this protected her from food shortages. "What I grow, I do not have to buy or borrow from neighbours", she said. She usually worked alone in the garden, but when she did not feel well, her older grandson would help or they would hire somebody in the village to do it.

When we spoke to her in 2004, Margaret had fallen seriously ill. She suffered a stroke in October 2003, could not speak and was no longer staying in her own homestead. A relative from the neighbouring village of Makhuzeni was taking care of her. The two grandchildren she used to stay with now lived elsewhere. One of them was in Cape Town staying with his mother. The other was still in the village but stayed with a relative. Margaret's house was not left unoccupied but was looked after by this relative.

## Analysis of livelihoods

In this section we want to draw some general lessons of an empirical and analytical nature about rural livelihoods from the above cases. The chapter has documented some livelihood trajectories that together point at what remains strategic: building a homestead as well as maintaining that homestead. Taken together the life histories underlined that livelihoods have shifted from making a living locally to one based on transfers, which is consumption that is derived from earnings elsewhere. However, this being the predominant trend, the case material also pointed at the continued importance of crops and home gardening in particular for securing livelihoods. It would be a mistake, of course, to lump the trajectories together. In contrast to chapter 12, the life history accounts of this chapter enable us to highlight the processes that differentiate them.

The case material may be approached by linking two levels of analysis. One is that the cases presented point at two prominent *dimensions* and related processes upon which rurally based livelihoods in Guquka and Koloni hinge. The cases also display the *strategies* devised by the social actors to make a living and the social networks in which these are embedded. This then is the second layer of the analysis. By analytically combining 'dimensions' and 'strategies', we will be able to explore not only how these combine empirically in the construction of a livelihood, and thus how the process of transformation works out locally. This will also point out the dynamics and how local actors experience the factors that constrain the options to expand land based livelihoods and what options are available. The blending of 'dimensions' and 'strategies' also highlights and underscores the analytical importance of situating livelihood analysis in context (chapter 1). Besides, context does not necessarily operate as structuring and determining social and economic behaviour. If this were so, one would expect much more homogeneity. Let us turn to the dimensions first and then elaborate on the strategies and social networks.

The first dimension is best presented as the *resources* dimension. This dimension reflects a combination of institutional issues such as access and control, for instance, land and labour as well as the quality and quantity of the resources that are generally important to construct rural-based livelihoods, whether derived from land-based or non-land-based resources. How these are accessed and what people do with their resource entitlements becomes clear from the cases. The second dimension represents *time*, which in the South African context has two key aspects. A 'structural' feature that has shaped the fortunes of people is the role played by one's place of birth. The cases clearly suggest that whether one is born or not born in Guquka or Koloni matters in accessing key resources such as land. The time dimension thus emerges as important, which in the South African circumstances, is largely formed by the politics of segregation and associated regulations such as the Pass Laws and the Group Areas Act (chapter 2). However, as some of the cases highlight, social actors attempted to reshape their fortunes through *negotiations*. Most of these negotiations were not successful which in turn points at the complexities of institutional relations such as land tenure in the two villages; these were pointed out earlier in chapters 6 and 8 in more general terms. On the other hand another aspect of time is age; age carries some weight as well in accessing and above all utilising resources. In the South African context, old age in particular implies becoming eligible for a monthly pension. This potentially enhances the opportunities of individuals and larger groupings such as the homestead to sustain a livelihood based on consumption and/or assists in removing some of the constraints to utilise their land resources beyond the level of home gardens (chapter 8) and/or to keep cattle (chapter 9). This also enhances the identities pensioners derive from what they do with their entitlements.

The *strategies* employed by the social actors to make a living are manifold and, as the cases illustrate, are not linear timewise. Sometimes they are combined and therefore labelled by Ellis (2000) as diversification; sometimes they are sequential. Of these strategies, migrancy or seeking wage employment stands out as a prominent one and has shaped local peoples' fortunes in many different ways. On the one hand, migrancy serves to find permanent wage employment to establish oneself as a worker. On the other hand migrancy is also part of the strategy to accumulate funds to invest in crop production, either home gardening or field production. Migration, as previous chapters, notably 11, have shown, takes many forms of geographical mobility. Such mobility serves to keep the many options open that potentially are available to people in the villages. But as the case material underlines, carving out a living in the local village economy engaging in commercial agriculture and casual labour is attempted; it is not easy but it is possible. Again, here we encountered diversity in strategies and dynamics. Land-based livelihoods are rather minimal quantitatively but socially important.

The differentiated nature of rural livelihoods in Guquka and Koloni challenges contemporary policies and the way policies are designed. A number of issues clearly come to the fore.

(1) *Migrancy*, as cases 1 and 2 illustrated, has a differentiated effect upon livelihood options. Being born or not in the village matters substantially. Mengezelei's livelihood trajectory (case 1) is like Ngeni's (case 8), marked by being a newcomer to Guquka. Mengezelei's livelihood was largely formed by being a miner but one who did not succeed through negotiations to access an arable field. At a later stage he combined piece work in the region with home gardening, which he does extremely well, as reported also in chapter 8. The livelihood fortunes of Sonjani, Philaph and Mlami (case 2) unfolded in rather similar ways. Mlami's life is, however, not just a variation on the theme that Mengezelei represents. Mlami's fortunes are continuously marked by migrancy, and retrenchments, returning home for a while to seek a livelihood locally. In contrast to Mengezelei, Mlami did not succeed and reverted back to migrancy again as he found security in a paid job to be a key ingredient of his livelihood strategy. This in turn draws other processes into the equation, namely that Mlami's and other people's job security were threatened by macro-political processes. Similar cases are that of Mzoli (case 3) and of Mangqila who like Mlami lost his job at Fort Hare. Mzoli lost his civil servant job and did not manage to find a new one. He reverted to home gardening and managed to *diversify* his livelihood while also relying on his wife's salary. Mlami, Mengezelei, Mzoli and Mangquangoza typify those whose livelihoods were clearly affected by the restructuring of the South African economy which led to retrenchments and unemployment.

(2) The cases of Mengezelei and Mlami also highlight that factors such as *age* need to be taken into account in analysing people's pursuit of a livelihood. Cases 1 and 2 clearly illustrate that age matters and how it matters. When Mengezelei and his wife Kulukazi became pensioners, socially and financially their lives improved substantially. Mlami, when retrenched and without a paid job, had difficulties to feed his family, and only managed to survive because of his brother's financial contributions. Mangqila ended up in a rather similar position as Mlami but was much better off because of her pensionable age. Margaret (case 9), as much as Makhise and Mcate, shows a livelihood that is *constructed on state transfers* such as pensions. Their cases show that getting older provided social and financial security on the basis of which many other individuals get fed and are offered shelter. However, most pensioners found it difficult to sustain crop production while supporting other members of the homestead.

(3) Chapters 3, 7, 8 and 9 showed that the role of agriculture as a livelihood resource has substantially diminished over the years. A number of homesteads

continue to invest in arable farming and livestock production. At this point, however, it becomes interesting to distinguish:

1. Livelihoods revolving around migrancy but with *attempts to secure access to local resources for farming purposes*. This process is clearly illustrated by Mengezelei's and Mlami's cases (1 and 2). Vuyo's (case 4) life also depended on migrant labour until recently.
2. There are homesteads that demonstrate that it is possible to make a living from agriculture *on a scale larger than home garden production*; although very few of them exist in either Guquka or Koloni. These cases also point out that the continuity of farming builds upon past experiences when being a migrant. Cases 4 and 5 stand for this process. Grootbooi (case 4), Ngxobo (case 5) and also the homesteads of Msiwa, Mfengu and Mandeya (chapter 8) demonstrate the continuity of farming and building upon past experiences gained when migrant wages were used to invest in crop production. Vuyo Grootbooi continuously attempted to access fields though share cropping and later managed to secure land through distant kin relations. Mpendulo Ngxobo began farming at an older age and accessed land through inheritance. More than any other, he was actively commercialising livestock production.
3. Other trajectories denote that agriculture often is of *cyclical* or *irregular importance* for making a living. The relevant cases for this dimension of farming are those of Neku and Mxolisi (chapter 8). They always combined their pensions with investing resources in cropproduction whenever there was an opportunity. Ngewni (case 6) combined piece work with crops when opportunities occurred and, together with his wife, engaged in many other activities including collecting and selling firewood, gardening and the running of a shop.

(4) *Locally based livelihoods* arc few in the villages and the dynamics varied enormously. Piece or casual work for others or running a *spaza* shop or *shebeen take advantage of* what the local economy could provide. Mombulelo's livelihood (case 7) illustrated what this entails when one lacks other ways to make a living. Mombulelo's homestead barely survived and required others to organise social security. Mncedisi's livelihood (case 8) is also one that hinged on working for others, but he found security in such arrangements. The fortunes of Mr. Mandeya of Koloni were rather similar. Nombulelo's and Mncedisi's cases represent livelihoods that are derived from the local economy. Nombulelo was a so-called piece worker selling her labour to earn cash. In most cases there was a daily search for work and the rewards were not certain, as a result of which Nombulelo and her children continuously struggled to earn a living. Nombulelo's case also illustrated what poverty entails in villages like Guquka and Koloni. Mncedisi's case illustrated how an adult man survives in Koloni who does not control any significant resources other than his own labour and knowledge. His case, like Nombulelo's livelihood, is entrenched and embedded

in-kin based social networks. The cases of Margaret and Nombulelo to a certain extent highlight that social security is embedded in networks that stretch beyond immediate kin relations.

## Conclusions

The life histories or parts thereof presented here underline that livelihoods are heterogeneous and do not unfold in one and the same way. The case material presented here allowed for an analysis and understanding of how situations and events in the wider family-, village-, and regional historical context shaped rural livelihoods. These events and situations produced many outcomes. The themes pointed out in previous chapters – mobility and variability – become extremely clear.

The nine cases documented here not only illustrate that different livelihoods have evolved but also show how the key resources required for such livelihoods are accessed and utilised, whether these strategies were successful and what other outcomes have been achieved. Some of the livelihood trajectories presented here elucidate the ways in which negotiation, bargaining and struggle may or may not change circumstances, which may bring about new patterns of interaction between individuals within and outside the household as they collaborate and struggle to reconcile individual and collective objectives and aspirations. The cases underline that it is conceptually useful to view livelihoods as evolving in arenas where actors with unequal power negotiate within homesteads and between members of communities or villages.

The cases presented also illustrate that fortunes of social actors usually form part of social networks beyond the immediate family. Reciprocity of gifts and favours is crucial for the survival of those who do not manage to control, and gain access to, key resources such as land, labour, and money. The strategic importance of pensions is that they prevent many from falling into poverty. Age, however, excludes a few from receiving such assistance. Age and being excluded from networks are part of an exclusionary script that is known as poverty.

# 14

# Livelihoods and landscapes:
# People, resources and land use

Paul Hebinck and Wim van Averbeke

## Introduction

This chapter brings to a conclusion the main issues that have been raised in the book and provides some ideas on the type of policies that are needed to enhance land-based livelihoods in the Eastern Cape Province and possibly elsewhere in South Africa. In our opinion the key objective of agrarian policy should be the facilitation of a process that can be labelled as *repeasantisation* (chapter 1). The empirical material in this book shows that there are still remnants of a peasantry in both villages, albeit few and limited in extent. By examining these we simultaneously explored what constitutes the agrarian in contemporary rural villages such as Guquka and Koloni. The evidence presented indicates a long process of retreat of the agrarian in the rural central Eastern Cape province. Critical examination of past and contemporary interventions in these rural areas, such as betterment planning and land and agrarian reform initiatives, raises questions about the role of expert knowledge in rural and agrarian development in South Africa. There are elements of continuity in the approach being used, leading to the conclusion that alternative expert curricula in agriculture and rural development are needed.

## Rural livelihoods: From production to consumption

Rural people and administrators have been confronted with rather similar issues over a very long period of time. These include struggles over land, concerns about the environment, the endurance of poverty and deprivation in the communal rangeland areas. The long-term prevalence of migrant labour relations, not least of social relations within the homestead, and the ways in which people have combined different activities in order to survive and construct a livelihood have had a major impact on development. The outcome of historical processes has been varied, but the overwhelming trend in livelihood transformation has been *from production to consumption*. The observation at the opening of the book and the many accounts of local people appearing in the different chapters are all illustrations of this general trend. Chapter 2 paints the broader picture of social change in the Eastern Cape region. Chapter 4 provides evidence that until about 1900 the livelihood of the settler homesteads in both villages was founded firmly on the utilisation of the natural resources in the locality and its immediate vicinity. From 1900 onwards, crop and livestock production became increasingly supported by monetary income derived 'outside' the locality, a development that was closely associated with male migration. Thereafter, from about 1930 in Guquka and 1960 in Koloni, local economic activity declined, especially agriculture. Rural livelihoods came to rely heavily on externally derived income and consumption became increasingly divorced from local production patterns. Linkages between rural and urban-based livelihoods and the state rose to prominence, but a growing urban orientation was modified by the restructuring of the national economy, retrenchments, urban unemployment and poverty and HIV/AIDS. These developments contributed to the emergence of the rural-urban drifter phenomenon.

In contemporary rural villages relative wealth or poverty and the ability to consume are largely embedded in the social relationships that provide homesteads and individuals with the right to claim, against both the state and homestead members. Over the past 15 years, the range of social grants made available by the state has increased both qualitatively and quantitatively. Removal of racial differentiation in the value of old-age pensions and disability grants in 1993 doubled the value of these grants for black people. During the past few years, access to public child support has been broadened considerably and the value of this particular grant has been progressively increased. In 2007, government agencies proposed financial support for people infected with HIV/AIDS and income support for people employed in low-paying jobs as new measures to alleviate poverty and deprivation among the South African population. At that time already 11 million South Africans were in receipt of a public grant, nearly one-quarter of the population. Many of the recipients were black people residing in the country's rural areas. In 2004, respectively 43% and 59% of the homesteads in Guquka and Koloni largely depended on such a grant for their living.

Rural livelihoods have become increasingly 'unproductive' and 'delocalised'. With few if any exceptions, the orientation of the young generation is outward-looking. They seek livelihood options, or more precisely employment, outside the village. The changes that have taken place in the political sphere of the country since the onset of democratisation in the second half of the 1980s have facilitated and strengthened the existing urban orientation by removing restrictions on mobility.

During the past twenty years, the patterns of rural-urban migration have gained in complexity. The old pattern of medium-term cyclical male migration still occurs, but new patterns have developed, including the movement of entire families to the cities, daily and weekly commuting, female migration and urban-rural drift. Initially, male migration, particularly from Guquka, was primarily directed at the mines. This type of migration enabled migrants to return to the rural homesteads and to remain engaged in cultivation (chapter 4). When from about 1930 onwards, the duration of mining contracts was extended, visits to the rural homesteads were shortened and increasingly occurred during the Christmas holiday season which is not the best time to plant crops (chapters 3 and 5). The expanding urban economy during and after the Second World War broadened the scope of urban employment for black people. In the urban economy the work cycle was essentially annual. Migrants only had a few weeks of annual leave to return home and in many cases this leave had to be taken from about the middle of December to the middle of January. This certainly has shortened the time spent at home that was used to relax and socialise and no longer to work in the fields. There was, therefore, a causal relationship between changes in the migration patterns and the decline of cultivation in the rural settlements of the central Eastern Cape (chapter 8).

Decentralisation of the South African economy, particularly during the homeland era, which lasted from 1981 to 1990, introduced commuting as a new form of rural-urban migration. The policy of regional job creation implemented by the creation of industrial centres, such as Dimbaza and growth in public sector employment provided large numbers of rural people, both men and women with job opportunities. In chapter 12 homesteads with livelihoods based on daily, weekly or monthly commuting between the rural home and the place of work are labelled 'wage earners'. The analysis of their income shows their engagement in agrarian activities to be limited. Seemingly in this type of livelihood, domestic tasks and relaxation take priority over farming, indicating a high degree of deagrarianisation among them, although there were a few exceptions.

Towards the end of the twentieth century two new forms of migration developed, namely the permanent or semi-permanent migration of entire homesteads from rural to urban settlements and the rural-urban drifter (chapter 11). Politically, these new patterns of migration were associated with the removal of racial policies that restricted mobility of black people and their right to residence in urban areas. Economically they were linked to the restructuring of the economy, which was accompanied by retrenchments, re-centralisation and the emergence of new labour markets, particularly in the tourism industry. The new patterns of migration were shaped by the skills of the migrants, which determined their entry in the urban labour market. Evidence from Guquka and Koloni shows that when an entire homestead established itself in an urban area, it usually transferred its assets to a rural care-taker. This particular phenomenon was in full swing during fieldwork in 2004. For how long these care-taker arrangements will prevail remains to be seen, but they do restrict access to and use of important rural assets, such as fields and even home gardens. Increasingly poorly skilled migrants fail to enter the urban labour market on a permanent basis. As a result, they tend to drift between the urban and the rural environment, without establishing robust livelihood roots in any of the two.

## Transformation of the landscape

The repetitive pattern of hills and valleys is an important characteristic of the landscape in the central Eastern Cape. The capability of land to support particular agricultural activities is related to its position in the landscape. To a large extent, the agrarian landscape that evolved reflected differences in land capability. Arable land was typically located in landscape positions where the soils were relatively deep, i.e. the lower middle slopes, foot slopes and valley bottoms, whilst the upper middle slopes and the hill crests supported natural *veld*. Generally, the capability of most of the land in the region is limited to natural *veld*. This reality has co-determined the agrarian land use patterns in both the large- and the small-scale farming sector (chapter 3). Important also is that African settlements were typically sited on hill crests or upper middle slopes. Generally these sites are characterised by shallow soils and this has had implications for home gardening. Another important spatial aspect is the availability of water. Positioned relatively high in the landscape the residential sites tended to be removed from the river, which was the main source of water. Fetching water for domestic purposes involved considerable labour, which was a female burden. In recent times the reticulation of water has removed this limitation in many of the local villages, such as Koloni, but in Guquka the reticulation system that was based on the use of a windmill broke down and people, particularly women, still collect water from the river.

The livelihood transformation *from production to consumption* has changed the landscape that surrounds the two villages. This change is evident from the oral history accounts and the sequential aerial photos of the two villages. The impact of the transformation *from production to consumption* is most visible on the arable land, but the natural *veld* has also been affected. In the past, much of the arable land was cultivated and planted to crops, but at present most of it supports a cover that consists of grasses, weeds, shrubs and bush, suggesting total abandonment. In both villages parts of the natural *veld* have been converted to residential land to accommodate growth in the village population as a result of natural population increase (both villages) or to provide immigrants with space to build a homestead (mainly Guquka). The change in the function of land from one to another category denoted a change in livelihood and preferences, because when they were proposed, they were discussed and agreed to in community meetings, where they were not contested. To an extent, we witnessed the (limited) transformation of grazing land to residential land (chapter 7) but we also saw the transformation of (a lot of) fallow land to grazing land. Moreover, residential areas also provide ample space for cattle to graze (chapter 9). These chances in function of land involved the re-labelling of productive *veld* to consumptive residential land, but also the re-labelling of arable land to grazing, that is from a labour intensive to a labour extensive form of land use. This interpretation is largely valid for Koloni, but less so in Guquka, where parts of the *veld* adjacent to the residential sites have been transformed into productive home gardens. Both contrasting transformations signify the specific localised character of the livelihood transformation in the villages *from production to consumption.*

The predominance of fallowing the arable land suggests that productive use of this particular category of land has been abandoned. However, upon closer inspection less visible patterns of using this land are discernable. These hidden patterns can be labelled as *grazing and gathering,* because the fallow fields are used for grazing livestock, particularly cattle (chapter 9) and the gathering of herbs, grass and woody plants for various purposes (chapter 10). Although they largely go unnoticed, these alternative uses of arable land are important, because they have environmental, institutional and economic significance. Crop production has not been abandoned completely. Annually, about 10 to 20% of the available arable land in Guquka and Koloni is planted with maize or other crops. Combined the three main contemporary uses of the arable land can be labelled as *growing, grazing and gathering* giving rise to the 'triple G' notion (Lent and Hebinck 2006). Important is that the land use patterns that have evolved cut across the land use categories that were introduced by land planners in the two villages during the late 19th century which subdivided the land in residential, arable and commonly held rangeland (chapter 4). It can be argued that local people have always combined growing, grazing and gathering, even when most of the arable land was still cultivated. For example, several of the companion weeds of maize were collected for use as leafy vegetables (*imfino*) as they still are. However, fallowing arable land has created room, perhaps unintentionally, for new forms of land use.

Environmentally, idle land develops a permanent vegetation cover (chapters 7 and 9), which increasingly protects the soil against erosion and raises its organic matter content. Triple G practices, therefore, signify processes of environmental reclamation rather than processes of resource degradation. Fallowing land implies conservation, whereby grazing and gathering may take place in a sustainable manner, even though no empirical evidence of sustainability was provided for the two villages. However successional processes associated with long-term fallowing lead to the loss of some resources such as thatch grass and increases in other resources such as firewood. More research on the dynamic of resource use is required.

Institutionally, Triple G practices are embedded in multiple and overlapping tenure regimes and there is a relationship between the type of land use that is practised and the degree of exclusion being applied. The growing of crops on arable land is governed by quitrent land tenure, which is in line with the legal tenure plot holders have over the arable allotments in the two villages. The grazing of cattle on this land is sanctioned by a village committee in the case of Koloni or by individuals in the case of Guquka. Opening arable land to live-stock during the winter months is traditional practice in the 'communal' areas and this practice is also applied at Koloni. At Guquka livestock access to fenced fields is controlled by individuals and occurs throughout the year, but land that is not fenced in escapes such control. Gathering plants and wood from the fallowed fields largely occurs within an open access regime.

The Triple G perspective contrasts with the prevalent perception that land use in South Africa's smallholder areas is inefficient. For many policy makers and other observers fallow land is the ultimate expression of inefficient land use. This view ignores that fields are used for grazing and gathering and misses out on the tangible contribution these practices make to rural livelihoods by providing food, fuel, building material and fodder. It is extremely difficult to compare the different uses of arable land from an economic perspective. Land preparation is a critical activity in cultivation because it requires a substantial investment of resources. Cultivators need financial resources when they use a tractor service to prepare the land or access to labour, cattle and implements when ploughing their field using animal traction. In addition, the land needs to be planted and kept free of weeds over a period of no less than three months if reasonable yields are to be obtained (Marais 1985). The data presented in chapter 8 suggest that on average cultivators in Guquka harvest about 1 ton of maize grain per ha. In 1999, the replacement value of 1 kg of maize (based on the weighted mean of the prices paid by homesteads for maize meal, *samp* and green maize) was R2.99 (Monde 2003). In Koloni, where the rainfall is both lower and less reliable than in Guquka; the average maize yield is about 0.6 tons grain per ha, but highly dependent on the year (see Table 8.4). This brings in the third critical factor in cultivation, namely risk. Of course, farmers who practise intercropping also harvest other crops, such as dry beans, melons and pumpkins from their maize fields, increasing the rewards of cultivation. Land preparation by means of a tractor cost about R210 per ha in 1997. Expenditure on other inputs tended to be limited (chapter 8) and for the purpose of this discussion this expenditure was ignored. This elementary analysis suggests that the benefit farmers derive from cultivation is of the order of about R2780 per ha in Guquka and about R1584 per ha in Koloni. Compared to cultivating arable land, use of fallow fields requires substantially less labour, eliminates the need for financial resources and, above all, removes risk.

Quantifying the non-agricultural benefits derived from fallow fields is not easy. Chapter 9 shows that these fields are used primarily as a source of fodder for cattle. The productivity of arable land in terms of fodder production is dependent on many factors, including the age of the fallow (Lo Presti 1996b, Bennett 2002) and annual rainfall, For purposes of this analysis, which is merely indicative, fallow land was assumed to have the same carrying capacity as the natural *veld* in the region Eastern Cape, which, on average, is about 3.6 ha per large stock unit (Trollope and Coetzee 1975). Using a herd off-take of 20% (Tapson 1984) and a price of R2000 per animal (cattle), the annual benefit derived from using arable land as a source of fodder for cattle was estimated to be about R110 per ha. However, accruement of this benefit is highly dependent on the tenure regime that applies. At Koloni, this benefit is shared among the collective of livestock owners, more or less in proportion to the size of their herds and flocks. In Guquka, this benefit accrues to individual livestock owners when the field is fenced in but fields that are not fenced in are largely treated as a common property resource (chapter 6). The data on herd off-take used here are based on the work by Tapson in KwaZulu-Natal. The annual offtake in commercial cattle herds in South Africa is about 20 %, and this is essentially in the form of sales. With reference to the smallholder sector, Tapson (1984: 39) talks about annual "movements out of herds", which were in the form of brides wealth (*lobola*) (3.8%), slaughter (3.6%), sales (3.5%), theft (1.5%) and death (7.5%). Combined the annual movement out of individual herds amounted to 19.9% of the total herd size, which is similar to the offtake rate that characterizes commercial herds

Chapter 10 quantifies some aspects of gathering in more detail. Besides being used as a fodder resource during the dry season, fallow fields provide medicinal and edible plants, thatch grass and firewood. Significantly, the variety of plant species gathered and used by people in the two villages is about the same from arable fields and communal rangelands (see chapter 10), even though the arable allotments represent much smaller areas of land. This finding suggests that the arable allotments are important because they represent a variety of vegetation types in different stages of succession, a patchwork landscape as it were. In the absence of more accurate and complete data and assuming that gathering from arable fields and the rangelands are similar and that an average is real, the economic benefit of gathering then can be estimated at R137/ha for Guquka and R73/ha for Koloni. This is calculated as follows. Chapter 10 shows that the mean annual value per homestead of firewood collected in Guquka was about R706 and R695 for Koloni. Using the estimate of Shackleton *et al.* (2002) that the economic value of *veld* and forest products averages R1926 per homestead annually and that fuelwood represented more than half of that amount (about 60%) then the annual value can be estimated as R1167 and R1160 respectively. To calculate the economic benefits of gathering per unit of land the annual value was multiplied by the number of homesteads inhabited in the village (Table 11.4) divided by the size of the rangeland and the arable fields

(Table 4.1) We need to take into account that the size of the rangelands for Guquka are difficult to determine because of sharing with neighbouring villages (chapters 4 and 9).

Table 14.1. summarises the average economic benefits per ha from growing, grazing and gathering. The table not only confirms that Guquka's potential to grow crops is much higher compared to Koloni. It also underlines that the cultivating crops is economically predominant. However, the cultural significance of grazing cattle and gathering should not be underestimated (chapter 9 and 10).

*Table 14.1*    Average economic benefit per homestead of growing, grazing and gathering in Guquka and Koloni, in Rand per ha.

|              | Guquka | Koloni |
|--------------|--------|--------|
| Growing*     | 2780   | 1584   |
| Grazing **   | 110    | 110    |
| Gathering *** | 137   | 73     |
| Total        | 3027   | 1767   |

* based on 1997 data
** based on estimates by Tapson (1984)
*** based on data from 2005 (chapter 10)

## Poverty and social inequality

"Livelihoods in southern Africa are in crises." This is the opening statement by Scoones and Wolmer (2003a) in their synthesis of a range of studies on rural livelihoods in southern Africa. This rather general statement cannot be sustained when we consider development in Guquka and Koloni. Chapters 8, 9, 12 and 13 have demonstrated that some of the livelihood trajectories have rendered people security in terms of income from wages, pensions, grants, and remittances - and food that is mostly purchased in urban centres (monthly shopping) and *spaza* shops in the village (occasional food purchases). Chapter 13 has shown that the factor age that elsewhere in the south often renders insecurities and dependencies, in South Africa it works out differently. Because of the pension and social grants schemes, the older people are protected from falling into ultra poverty. The case of Mengezelei and his spouse (case 1 in chapter 13) and others in the two villages clearly demonstrate this. The analysis of these cases in turn underlines the argument that a generational perspective on social change is required. There is also evidence of people whose livelihood pathways renders insecurity. Such people's livelihoods are often characterised as 'poor' or 'ultra poor'. Chapter 13 contains a few cases that illustrate this.

We now examine the processes that may explain why certain livelihoods are secure and others not. One way is examining the nature of social development in the two villages. The data reveal that socio-economic inequalities exist. Inequality and equality for that matter historically have two rather contrasting dimensions. The first dimension is that inequality revolves around ownership of land and cattle. During pre-colonial times this formed the basis of power and social control of the powerful over their dependents, cattle and territory (chapter 2). Chapters 8 and 9 have documented in detail that ownership of land and cattle is unequally distributed. Partly this is explained by the right to inherit land which rests with the eldest son. This has made it certainly difficult for other offspring to build up a land-based livelihood. Add to this the influx of people from elsewhere (chapter 11) whose opportunities to become engaged in land-based agricultural activities were rather minimal. This particularly applied to Guquka that accommodated people forcefully removed from areas during the 1960s. Koloni only provided alternative housing for their own offspring for which the so-called squatter camp was created and expanded to accommodate increasing demands for housing.

The balance between those with formal rights to land and those without has never been favourable for the latter given that land has been exclusively controlled by the elders and passed to their elder sons. While in the past, younger sons found migration an option to accumulate wealth independently of their fathers and build their own homesteads (chapters 2 and 4), current options are much less favourable. This has upset the balance even further, reinforcing out-migration of younger people as part of their livelihood strategy. However, we found no proof of increased pressure on landowners to open negotiations for land. This suggests that a market for land does not exist. Those with an interest in farming the arable fields generally do not manage to gain access to such land (chapters 6 and 8). The land surveys towards the end of the 19$^{th}$ century (chapter 4) fixed the rights of land in the hands of the male head of each homestead. Claiming land has become only become a virtual possibility.

The second dimension of social inequality today spins increasingly around monetary income and thus also around the ability to generate income. Considering inequality through the lens of income, chapter 2 and 12 have shown that income distribution was skewed. In Koloni skewness even increased between 1996 and 1999. The Gini coefficient for income distribution in Koloni was 0.28 in 1996 and increased to 0.42 in 1999. The Gini coefficient for Guquka remained constant during this period at 0.43. Income stratification is thus apparent (chapter 12). Further, those with access to wages and salaries realised by far the highest income. The fruits of agrarian activities fade away when compared quantitatively to wages and salaries. At this point the notion of entitlements (chapter 1) becomes analytically useful. When entitlements to land and cattle and other natural resources are not translated into action and productive resource utilisation, the results of one's entitlements do not necessarily make people poor or rich. The shift *from production to consumption* signifies at the same time that entitlements have shifted from resources that produce food to resources that enable to purchase food. Part and parcel of the shifts that occur in Guquka and Koloni it is that land and cattle largely have maintained their cultural meaning, but we should not underestimate their productive (that is social and economic) meaning. Cattle sales after all constituted the main source of income from agrarian activities. For most homesteads making productive use of home gardens, and for some of arable fields, retain their importance and contribute to social and food security. The agency of people is not necessarily brought into play to utilise land-based resources in order to accumulate wealth purely in the materialist sense.

The shift from land-based resources to a series of entitlements is founded upon the cash value of (1) wages and salaries which in turn is based on access to the labour market and the state whereby skills and knowledge matter substantially, (2) access to state transfers (old age pensions) whereby age is the discriminatory factor, (3) power and authority to substantiate claims on their next of kin (often appears in the form of remittances and other forms of redistribution). The shift also characterises social development: land and cattle are no longer the kind of resources that form the core of a pathway that leads to other forms of accumulation. The case material presented throughout the book support this conclusion. Instead, receiving or investing in education has largely overtaken the meaning of land and cattle for making a living in the limited economic meaning of making a living through wage employment.

A final question for the analysis of the nature of the development process is where now to locate poverty. Chapter 12, and Table 12.3 in particular, is a good empirical basis for such analysis. Poverty cannot be measured easily and translating poverty in economic terms ignores other aspects (Place *et al.* 2007). In the absence of more qualitative data, we limit the analysis to understanding poverty in terms of the poverty line. Carter and May (1999) calculated the poverty line for rural areas of South Africa in 1999 as R476.30 per adult equivalent (AE) per month. Homesteads with an AE income above that were considered 'non-poor', those with an AE income less than R238.19 per month (half the poverty line) 'ultra-poor', and those with an AE falling between these two limits 'poor'. Using this as a benchmark, poverty in Guquka and Koloni is located in most homesteads except those with wage earners. Notably homesteads categorised as 'farmers' and those that receive remittances were classified as 'ultra-poor' with mean adult equivalent income of respectively R77 and R124 and far below the poverty line.

In the context of the current development in the urban labour market it may be expected that urban to rural remittances will continue to decline. Although not really underpinned with 'hard' data, poverty is also located among those livelihoods that we categorised in chapter 12 as 'missed categories', notably 'unmarried mothers' and 'divorced women'. Their livelihood, which largely depended on their skills, abilities or rights to claim a secure income, was shown to be particularly vulnerable. As indicated by Bank (2002) and by the cases described in chapters 11 and 13, their means of last resort is often to leave for town and to eke out a living on the fringes of the urban economy.

## Remnants of the agrarian

The empirical material brought together in this book clearly illustrates the general trend of rural livelihoods in the two villages becoming unlinked from the productive use of land. This process can be labelled as the *deagrarianisation of rural livelihoods*. On the other hand, there was also evidence of persistent agrarian activity by selected homesteads at the two villages. Using income from farming as an indicator of agrarian activity, farming as an important structural element in rural livelihood was primarily limited to three livelihood labels, namely 'petty entrepreneurs', 'diversifiers' and 'farmers'. In the two villages combined, these three labels contained 25 homesteads or 19% of the 1 homesteads enumerated in the 1997 survey. Assessing the importance of agriculture in the livelihood of homesteads at six different sites in the Eastern Cape, Eckert and Williams (1995) identified the category of 'serious farmers' and this category contained 20% of the homesteads, very similar to the results obtained in Guquka and Koloni.

What then is a likely end result of the process of transformation captured by the trend from production to consumption? Changing social identities that shifted from producers (farmers) to consumers, or workers and pensioners in much the same way as production has been overtaken by consumption? Seemingly, we are witnessing a process of rural transformation in which rural people are neither 'workers' nor 'peasants'. Cousins (2007) commented similarly that a hybrid of the two which could push agricultural development ahead has not really emerged, but rather a 'pensionariat' (Beinart 2001) and a group of relatively poor and insecure casual labourers (chapters 12 and 13). The transformation of the countryside to one in which production may become more important is not just hampered by unfitting social identities. As chapters 8 and 9 have shown, the interplay between land, labour and cash and an almost absent market prevents such transformation. Yet, despite this overall picture, we believe that a remnant of a peasantry exists.

We discussed the use of arable land in chapter 8 and pointed out that despite the general image of fallowness, some fields are irregularly planted and others regularly. Cyclical or irregular planting in the arable lands has been presented in chapter 8 precisely to express that agriculture (and livestock) is only marginally important. Irregular use of land, however, also symbolises a response to adverse and changing conditions, both natural as well as institutional. The meaning and keeping of livestock, particular of cattle, is quite different from land and crops. Cattle production is at the crossroads of two different strategies representing two different meanings. There is the recognisable strategy that revolves around attempts to increase the quality of stock for meat and milk production. Only a few livestock owners are engaged in such form of 'commercial' agriculture. The majority of cattle owners engage with livestock in such a way that a maximum number of cattle are maintained and depending on the agro-ecological conditions, (rainfall above all) putting pressure on the available forage resources. In this strategy cattle remains a status symbol on the basis of which an image of status and authority is retained.

Goats and particularly micro-livestock (pigs and chicken), on the other hand, are much more oriented towards the local market. In the past, sheep played a similar role through the production of wool. There are still sheep owners who produce wool, particularly in Koloni, but markets for wool are not operating well and represent a serious constraint to the options for accumulation. Lack of security is another issue that has contributed to the decline of wool production and sheep ownership.

The pathways to the current pattern of resource use that Guquka and Koloni now have in common have been different and perhaps represent the former Ciskei as a whole. Chapter 4 in particular and chapters 8 and 9 indirectly have shown that Koloni's agricultural pathway lasted much longer than in Guquka. Koloni managed to access the state during and since the time of betterment planning after Koloni's residents invited government officials and white farmers to implement betterment. In return they received for long time substantial assistance from government and white farmers to modernise their agriculture, particularly in livestock production, wool shearing facilities, mechanised ploughing and contouring of fields. In addition, Koloni was exposed to market relations. Being located next to the Perksdale mission station Koloni residents clearly adopted 'school' traditions and associated life styles. Koloni's residents also had access to more arable fields (405 ha versus 160 ha in Guquka, Table 4.1) and experienced a much smaller influx of newcomers. These differences clearly play a role in explaining why Koloni compared to Guquka stayed much longer on the agricultural pathway. Labour migration only later became an option.

The shifts that occurred differently time-wise in both villages contributed to an image of a rural economy moving away from the extended family system as a unit of production and consumption and towards the rise of a mix of homesteads with varying connections to the urban and rural environment. The changing patterns of migration as a response to livelihood transformations have clearly contributed in a shift towards multiple-location derived livelihoods. De Wet and Holbrook (1997) refer to this as the regionalisation (and nationalisation) of the 'household'. To reiterate, this process secures the constant flow of people, ideas, goods and money between urban to rural settings, with remittances largely flowing from urban to rural setting, supporting livelihoods in the latter. These remittances and social relationships have the effect of maintaining ties between rural and urban members of households, producing a rural 'safety net' for the urban counterpart, should urban economic opportunities fail and a return to the village becomes necessary. This seems especially relevant for villagers whose urban lives are often uncertain and insecure. At the same time the remittances sent have the purpose of maintaining the livelihood of rural villagers. This underlines the main feature of the regional economy: a high proportion of those 'resident' in the former Ciskei and who are employed, work outside the region. This makes it difficult, as Green and Hirsch (1982) wrote during the homeland period, to speak of a 'Ciskei economy'.

## Future perspectives

> If you go to some of the poorest areas in our country, people have land but poverty and food insecurity are still high. The ASGISA (Accelerated and Shared Growth Initiative for South Africa) refers to this land as "the dead assets in the hands of the poor". We want to turn these assets and make them work for the people. During the month of November, which is the planting season for maize in some parts of our country, we are going back to the fields to plough. Sibuyele' masimini siyolima.

This statement was made by Ms Lulu Xingwana, Minister of the Department of Agriculture of South Africa, on the 4th of November 2006. It was not inspired by a recent visit to Guquka and Koloni, but it could have been. From a historical perspective the Minister joins a long line of policy makers who have expressed concerns about the apparent lack of agrarian activity in the black rural areas of South Africa, particularly in relation to the use of arable land. Over the years, policy makers' views of the situation in black rural areas have changed very little. Their main concern was the apparent contradiction that characterised these areas. On the one hand there was the rural population suffering from poverty, food insecurity and unemployment and on the other the low level of farm activity. Land was available and the high unemployment rates in the villages, typically ranging between 30% and 40%, suggested the availability of labour for engagement in agriculture. Most policy makers interpreted this contradiction as being the result of the lack of capital, both financial and physical. Financial capital was deemed necessary to acquire production inputs and physical capital (implements) was needed to conduct farming efficiently. As a result, in the past, state interventions have focused on providing access to capital. For example, in the Eastern Cape, public support to black smallholder farmers aimed at improving the fertility of arable land dates back to 1934, when the state supplied trucks to transport manure from the *kraals* to the fields and subsidised the purchase of chemical fertilizers (Van Wyk 1967). Extracts from the minutes of a meeting of the St. Marks District Council on May 27, 1949, reported that the first public tractor service in the Eastern Cape was made available to a group of smallholders at St Marks in 1949 to address the lack draught animals. Subsequently, capital-related assistance to smallholder farming stepped up, peaking during the independent homeland era, but as Chapter 8 has documented the decline in the intensity and extent of crop production was never reversed.

Current policies continue to hinge on the same principle of providing capital and mechanisation. Capital and tractors are seen as limiting factors, an opinion that is largely shared by rural people (chapter 8). The difficulty of managing isolated smallholder fields and delivering inputs to them on time and at reasonable cost is seen as a major constraint in the attempts to upscale food production. The Massive Food Production Programme, which is also known as *Siyakhula* is designed to create "a one-step transformation of small-scale farms into agglomerated commercial farming units" (Bolliger *et al.* 2005: 3). This is intended to be achieved through subcontracting ploughing on at least 50 ha of contiguous land of reasonable quality. Production costs (fertiliser and modern seeds) are to be financed by a 4 year grant with decreasing subsidy rates of 25% per year provided by the provincial Department of Agriculture of the Eastern Cape. Conservation agriculture principles are part of the conditions for financial support. The South African magazine, *Farmers Weekly*, (April 8, 2005) questions the scale of *Siyakhula*. The 'Trust Tractor', as tractors were called during betterment (chapter 4), has made a come back.

Two other factors that are important in agricultural development, namely entrepreneurship and markets, have received relatively less public attention. In South Africa, researchers and policy makers have persistently associated the rural and the agrarian in their reflections on the situation in the black rural areas. The implication of this association was that entrepreneurship, perhaps more appropriately worded as 'interest in farming', was broadly present among the rural population. The validity of the association of the rural and the agrarian was questioned for the first time by Eckert and Williams (1995) when they pointed out that only about one in five homesteads in the rural areas of the Eastern Cape had livelihoods that were closely linked to agriculture. This book has elaborated on this theme and the evidence that has been presented clearly shows that many homesteads in rural settlements are not farming homesteads in waiting. Furthermore, this book has also provided evidence that whereas land and labour may be amply available at the village level, at the homestead level, where these factors need to be combined, one or both are often absent. As a result, in rural villages the proportion of homesteads that combine land, labour and interest in agriculture tends to be relatively small.

Markets, particularly produce markets, are also problematic. In contemporary rural societies homesteads need money to clothe and educate their children, purchase energy and remain in contact with relatives to name but a few reasons. Farming merely for the purpose of producing food for home consumption is not enough. A degree of commercialisation is necessary to make farming a viable livelihood option. The evidence presented in chapter 12 shows that livestock sales are the main way in which homesteads derive monetary income from agriculture. Benefits derived from crop production were mainly in the form of food for own consumption. This points at the opportunity to improve village economies by stimulating surplus production aimed at meeting the village demand for food. Exploiting this opportunity can be labelled as *production for local consumption*. The rest of this chapter explores *production for local consumption* as a strategy in support of *repeasantisation* of rural villages through full or partial commercialisation of smallholder agriculture.

Table 14.2 shows the types and quantities of food consumed by homesteads in Guquka and Koloni in 1999, which were suitable for local production. Table 14.2 also features the average price homesteads in the two villages paid for these foods, and the proportion of total consumption of each of the foods that was obtained from local production.

*Table 14.2*   Proportions contributed by local production to the average annual consumption of selected foods in Guquka and Koloni, 1999

| Food item | Average annual quantity consumed per home-stead (kg) | Monetary value per unit (R per kg) | Monetary value (R) | Proportion obtained from local production (%) | Monetary value of local production (R) |
|---|---|---|---|---|---|
| Maize grain | 359 | 2.99 | 1073 | 22 | 233 |
| Wheat flour | 179 | 4.30 | 770 | 0 | 0 |
| Potatoes | 153 | 3.00 | 459 | 22 | 101 |
| Fresh vegetables | 123 | 2.07 | 255 | 65 | 166 |
| Milk | 209 | 4.30 | 899 | 89 | 719 |
| Chicken | 39 | 12.16 | 474 | 10 | 47 |
| Beef | 13 | 18.04 | 235 | 39 | 92 |
| Mutton | 33 | 22.99 | 759 | 100 | 759 |
| Total | - | - | 4924 | 43 | 2117 |

*Source*: based on Monde (2003)

Table 14.2 demonstrates that at present the exploitation of the opportunity of producing food for consumption within the village is limited. Of the foods that are suitable for local production, quantitatively only about 43% is produced locally. Local production was the sole source of mutton, and the principal source of milk and fresh vegetables. Local production is a relatively minor source of beef (39%), maize (22%), potatoes (22%) and chicken (10%), and makes no contribution to the consumption of wheat. One of the reasons for the limited contribution of local production to the consumption of maize and wheat is that these grains need to be transformed before they can be consumed. The absence of effective systems to store and process grains in rural villages of the central Eastern Cape is seen as an important constraint. Maize, for example is not consumed as whole grain, except in the case of green maize. In Guquka and Koloni, the average amount of 359 kg maize consumed annually by a home-stead consisted of 183 kg maize meal, 121 kg *samp* and 55 kg green maize. Local production was the source of 2.7% of the maize meal, 9.0% of the *samp*, but all of the green maize consumption (Monde 2003). To obtain *samp*, which is widely used in a range of dishes (Monde 2003, chapter 8) dry maize grain has to be crushed and the bran removed. An additional transformation consisting of milling is necessary to obtain maize meal, which is used mainly to prepare porridge (Monde 2003). In the past, rural traders but also white farmers (chapter 4) purchased, stored and processed maize grain but when Ciskei and Transkei were ushered towards independence during the 1970s most of these traders left (ISER 2001). In the villages of Guquka and Koloni the only available technology to transform maize grain into *samp* and meal is the hand-operated pestle and mortar. Using this technology to process grain into food for consumption is extremely laborious. The absence of suitable means to transform maize may partially be responsible for changes in the local food consumption pattern. In the past, homesteads in the central Eastern Cape consumed between 700 and 900 kg maize per annum. Table 14.2 shows that in contemporary Guquka and Koloni annual maize consumption by homesteads has been reduced to about half that amount (359 kg), having been replaced by the consumption of rice (113 kg) and wheat flour (179 kg), which is used to make bread (Monde 2003).

A case study at Dzindi, an irrigation scheme in the former Venda homeland in the Limpopo Province of South Africa, shows that when the capacity to store and process maize grain is available at the local level, smallholders do not experience problems with marketing surplus maize (Van Averbeke and Perret 2004). At Dzindi smallholders had two options to store and process their maize grain. One was to deliver the grain to a commercial mill equipped with a large-scale storage silo, in which grain was protected against weevils and other pests. When delivering grain to this facility, farmers either sold their grain to the mill for cash, or exchanged it for a credit note, which permitted them to collect an equivalent mass of processed maize subject to a surcharge of R65 per bag in 2003, for processing. The second option involved storage of maize at the homestead, with small quantities being brought to small-scale mills owned and operated by rural entrepreneurs for processing as the need arose. In 2003, the cost of processing grain into meal was R20 (per 25 kg). In the rural areas of the Eastern Cape, maize is stored at the homestead and usually processed by hand, which is a laborious task. Moreover, storage losses are considerable (ISER 2001, McAllister 2001). As a result, when in need of crushed maize (*samp*) or maize meal most homesteads in the central Eastern Cape prefer to purchase these products directly from shops in urban centres (Monde 2003).

The economic viability of a rural facility for the storage and processing of maize grain can be enhanced by integrating this facility with an animal production enterprise, with broiler production probably being the most suitable option, although pig production should also be considered. The existing positive correlation between cash income from animal production and the number of pigs held discussed in chapter 12 of this book supports this notion. The reason why broilers are preferred is that in a period of six weeks, they transform about 6 kg of grain, with a monetary value of about R9 in 2007, into 1.8 kg of animal product worth about R30. In addition the broiler litter is a valuable source of manure. Various markets for broilers exist, including the surrounding rural areas (see Table 14.2), the local town, and the regional urban centre. High quality broiler rations can be formulated by combining maize and soya beans, supplemented with vitamins and lime (Leeson and Summers 1997). For optimal feed conversion efficiency, maize grain needs to be milled to a particle size of 5 mm; soya beans need to be heat-treated to remove anti-nutrients and toxins (Oliver and Malan 1998, Leeson and Summers 2001). Broiler enterprises act as markets for locally produced maize and soya beans, but are not necessarily dependent on local grain production. Any deficits can be made up by importing grain from other parts of the country, for which well developed systems exist (ISER 2001). The advantage of importation of grains is that a proportion of the nutrients they contain are added to local soils by using the poultry litter as a fertilizer, partially compensating nutrient removals through grain harvests. The mill takes care of reducing the particle size of the grain, but heat treatment of soya beans requires a source of energy, which may be electricity, gas, diesel or wood. For rural development purposes, wood is an interesting option as it creates opportunities for commercial fire wood production, for which the abundance of fallow arable land appears eminently suited. Another condition for the proposed development is that smallholders in the Eastern Cape adopt the production of soya beans, because this crop does not feature in the existing farming practices.

The livelihood impact of *production for local consumption* strategy is expected to be substantial. Using the 1999 poverty line of R476.30 per month per adult equivalent established by Carter and May (1999) the average homestead in Guquka and Koloni, which consists of 4.5 adults and 1.5 children (4.45 adult equivalent) required an annual income of R25,435 to escape poverty. Assuming the use of a farming system that is labour-based and intensive but minimizes external inputs, it is feasible to achieve a gross margin of 66% of gross income. This means that the average homestead relying solely on farming for income would need to generate a gross farm income of R38,538 in 1999. It is important to point out that in the prevailing farming practice the ratio of gross margin to gross income exceeded 66%, but the productivity of these systems was low. Based on the existing food consumption patterns in terms of types and amounts of food (Table 4.1) the gross annual value of consumption of those foods that could be produced locally was valued at R320,060 for a village with 65 homesteads in 1999. This would have been sufficient to provide full livelihoods to 8.3 homesteads (about 13% of the population in the village), all of which would then be above the poverty line. Considering that in 1999 only 4% of homesteads in Guquka and 25% of homesteads in Koloni were categorised as non-poor, the potential livelihood impact of production for local consumption can be regarded as substantial. The theoretical estimate of the impact of *production for local consumption* may be regarded as simplistic. For example, the local agro-ecology may be suitable for the production of wheat, but the transformation of wheat into flour is more complex than the transformation of maize grain. On the other hand, we have not exhaustively explored all the elements that could form part of a *production for local consumption* development strategy. For example, sunflower oil (local people call it fish oil) is one of the main sources of fat used by local homesteads. Sunflowers grow well in the central Eastern Cape and hand-operated oil presses are commercially available. They extract about 25% of the total of 40% oil present in sunflower seed, leaving behind a high-oil cake, which turns rancid very quickly, but this can be counteracted through a process of saponification, yielding a high-quality animal feed.

The argument we have developed thus far is that the development strategy of *production for local consumption* has the potential to support the process of *repeasantisation*. However, full or partial commercialisation of smallholder farming, particularly crop production, faces several challenges, including institutional, environmental, technological and infrastructural.

Institutionally, an important concern is the absence of a vibrant land exchange market for arable allotments. Chapter 6 showed that landless homesteads interested in farming were largely prevented from accessing land for cultivation. Similarly, the locked up land exchange market is expected to constrain scale enlargement, which tends to accompany the smallholder commercialisation trajectory (Van Averbeke and Mohamed 2006). The empirical evidence collected in Guquka and Koloni failed to pinpoint the exact reasons for the absence of an efficient land exchange market in these two villages, but there is little doubt that a perceived lack of tenure security is one of the reasons why rural people pass up the opportunity to earn income from leasing their unused arable allotments to others for periods that are long enough (a minimum of five years) to make economic sense for the lessees (Thomson and Lyne 1995). A recent case study in a Transkeian betterment settlement where land was held by Permission to Occupy showed that when a community engaged in the development of a land register using a global positioning system (GPS) to construct a map of plot boundaries, several land holders became prepared to rent out their land against payment in maize grain (Manona 2005). Exchange agreements were valid for one year but renewable. Lessors awarded leases to the highest bidder. However, a similar initiative in a settlement where traditional communal tenure applied failed to liberate land (Manona 2005), clearly indicating that tenure security alone does not explain the inefficiency of land exchanges in smallholder areas. Upgrading 'communal' tenure has been one of the objectives of the land reform programme of the South African government (Department of Agriculture and Land Affairs 1997), but little effective progress has been made. Kingwill (2006), however, has shown that titling does not necessary increase tenure security. Formalisation of property rights does not promote lending to the poor.

Environmentally, not all villages in the central Eastern Cape contain land that is suitable for relatively risk-free crop production (Van Averbeke 1989). In many parts, such as Koloni, crop growth and yield are limited by water deficits (chapter 5). A recent comprehensive review of approaches to water conservation and efficient use of water in dryland and irrigated smallholder agriculture contains useful information on a wide range of technologies that are available for use in home gardens and fields in dry areas. There are also parts of the central Eastern Cape, such as Guquka, where the yield potential of arable land is substantial. *Sourveld* in the Eastern Cape annually produces about 3 to 4 tons biomass per ha, but the production potential of such land is considerably higher when cultivated and fertilised appropriately. For example, experimental work conducted during the nineteen-eighties at Phandulwazi, which neighbours Guquka, showed that during a series of very dry years, soils with an effective rooting depth of 900 mm or more that were planted to maize produced grain yields of 3 tons ha and above-ground biomass yields of about 7.5 tons per ha. In favourable years adequately managed maize plantings on these types of soils have the potential to produce 5 tons per ha of grain and 12.5 tons per ha of above-ground biomass. However, soil acidity and soil erosion are important environmental problems associated with these types of soils (chapter 5, Mandiringana *et al.* 2005). Where the rainfall is adequate to enable the production of crops without undue risk of crop failure, soils are typically acid. The application of *kraal* manure may neutralise a degree of soil acidity, but this positive effect is inadequate to raise the soil pH to optimum levels. To reduce acidity a comprehensive liming programme is necessary. Implementation of a liming programme needs to be subsidised by the state, because most small-holders are too poor to afford this type of investment. In the mean time, tempo-rary solutions to the acidity problem need to be explored. The effectiveness of the liming effect of broiler litter and wood ashes, when placed in the band as part of a fertilizer and seed combination, have not been investigated under field conditions, but the capacity of these two materials to neutralise soil acidity is beyond doubt (Judge 2001, Weil 2001). In Lesotho, the Machobane cropping system, in which a combination of wood ashes and *kraal* manure is used as a fertilizer, reportedly produces excellent results (Machobane and Berold 2003). If increased commercial exploitation of the arable holdings for crop production occurs, maintenance of soil fertility will be essential. Whilst higher farm incomes may allow the purchase of more nutrients in the form of chemical fertilisers, a continuing addition of organic matter in the form of livestock manure provides both nutrients and additional soil fertility benefits and should be encouraged. A complete switch to chemical fertilisers on relatively infertile acid soils can lead to a decline in soil fertility, but additional research is needed on integrated nutrient management to determine the optimum combinations of organic and inorganic inputs. If nutrients from livestock manures become limiting, there may be scope for increasing nutrient supply by improvements in the management of these resources. Experiences elsewhere indicate that the ways in which livestock manures are collected, stored and composted, together with the rate and timing of their application, can significantly affect the quantity of nutrients returned to the soil (Lekasi *et al.* 2002, Lekasi *et al.* 2003). Furthermore, the quality of manure can have an important influence on the release of nutrients and the synchrony of release with crop nutrient demand. Research done in Kenya indicates that when cattle manure is managed optimally the yield response of maize per unit of application can be doubled (Lekasi *et al.* 2003). Soil erosion is a concern, because it removes soil nutrients and causes irreversible degradation of the soil resource. In the central Eastern Cape with its steep topography and soil properties that enhance the susceptibility of soils to erosion, this threat to the natural resource must be taken seriously (Laker 2004). Soil fertility management and soil improvement requires labour to be present at regular time intervals. Chapters 8, 12 and 13 have shown that that is not really the case in Guquka and Koloni. Moreover, the labour force that is present, more or less continuous enjoys their pensions or are engaged in wage labour activities elsewhere.

Technologically, the needs of smallholder cropping have largely been ignored. The availability of livestock in fairly large numbers make it both convenient and economically sensible to use animal draught for a wide range of purposes, including bulk transportation, ripping, ploughing, planting, and even weeding. Several centres in South Africa, including SANAT based at Fort Hare and the ARC Institute for Agricultural Engineering in Silverton have developed new equipment that is adapted for use with animal draught. Research and Development in other countries has also produced implements that are suitable for use on a small scale using animal draught. Yet, little of this technology has made its way to end users in the rural areas of the Eastern Cape through commercial manufacturing and distribution processes.

One of the key infrastructural limitations standing in the way of increased use of the arable allotments for the production of crops is the absence or dilapidated state of the fences that protect the fields. When betterment planning was being implemented in a particular location, the state usually erected a perimeter fence around the block or blocks of arable allotments. Most of these fences are several decades old and have lost their effectiveness as a result of rusting of the barbed wire or destruction of the poles by fire. In areas where traditional communal tenure was retained, fences protecting arable land were in most cases never erected. In the distant past, herding livestock was the task of boys, but now these youngsters attend school. Livestock in the rural areas, as chapter 9 has shown, roam freely and without protection the crops in fields are often damaged or completely destroyed by animals in search of food. Wire fencing is a temporary solution, especially near the coast where the lifespan of a wire fence is less than ten years. Moreover, the current government appears to have no intention of adopting a comprehensive replacement policy. Therefore, alternatives are needed. One possibility is to introduce professional herders, as in Lesotho. Another is to start experimenting with live fences. All this perhaps stimulates livestock production.

The experiences obtained from public interventions in support of smallholder development in the past clearly indicate that a revival of smallholder agriculture, particularly the production of crops on a field scale, will not easily be brought about. Consequently, the ideas presented here merely serve as suggestions and should not be considered as a panacea for the lack of agrarian activity in rural settlements. Technologies and markets are essential components of such policy. The challenge of any future policy is also to facilitate that labour 'returns' to the land. Apart from enhancing farming skills, the book argued that a reformulation of land tenure is a key factor. Land tenure arrangements are needed that make land available for those that have an interest in farming.

Who should take responsibility for the implementation of any smallholder development programme in the villages of the Eastern Cape? The South African constitution assigns the responsibility of planning and guiding local development to local municipalities. These municipalities can call on human and financial resources at the district, provincial and national levels to implement their development initiatives. However, the performance of the various levels of government at the municipal level has not been particularly good, especially in the sphere of social and economic development. At the local municipal level, opportunities exist to involve the private sector, possibly rural town traders, which could enhance the sustainability of the proposed farmer development initiatives.

Options for *repeasantisation* are also strongly embedded in a reworking of urban-rural links and a general address of terms of trade for agriculture. If indeed rural ties are increasingly cut by urban residents (thus the single homesteads household becoming predominant), agricultural production gets deprived of cash inputs for investment. Similarly, so long as the 'squeeze on agriculture' (Marsden 1998) persists, the willingness to invest in small-scale food production will not increase. One other aspect we need to take into account when considering options for *repeasantisation* is, as some youth in the villages argued, is that land-based livelihoods including agriculturally derived ones cannot compete with urban jobs nor support the new modern lifestyles. The terms of trade for agriculture is perceived as rather unsatisfactory (chapter 8). The low rate of return to labour, both monetarily and status-wise, adds to the negative image associated with rural life and agriculture.

The future of the rural economy in regions like the former Ciskei will continue to depend on 'multiple livelihoods' and upon initiatives that until now stem from places of power exogenous to the villages, in national and international arenas. Given the continued reliance on the state and its social welfare programs and the intimate social and cultural relationships between the urban and the rural (as expressed in arrangements like multiple homestead households and single homestead households, chapter 11) rural livelihoods continue to be a melding of rural and urban identities, experiences and forms of production. Bank (1999, 2001, 2002) however has shown that 'ruralilty' and 'urbanity' do not always coincide harmoniously and the competition for scarce resources should not be denied. Contemporary rurality is largely shaped and guaranteed by the continuity of state policies regarding pensions based on age and social grants and the dynamics of the urban economy. The overall decline of the national economy saw nation-wide retrenchments of workers, leading to the sudden return of male migrants (notably) to the village, for whom few alternatives existed to maintain themselves and their families. Access to land was problematic for many of them, as they had only arrived in the villages after all the land had been allocated (Guquka) or sold (Koloni). At the same time there was also a decreased interest and ability amongst those that did have access to arable land for agriculture. In contrast, and in absence of programmes that strengthen peasantisation, the most impoverished did resort to home gardens for their survival.

## Expert knowledge and redefined curricula

In this book ample attention is given to intervention programmes and projects and their outcomes. This book has shown that these collaborations and interventions did not have a lasting effect. There is some consensus in the international literature that at times government officials and scientists have been to quick to describe and predict scenarios of devastated landscapes. Betterment planning and similar programmes in Africa were certainly triggered off by such concerns and were legitimised with the argument that African farmers were misusing the land and/or using it ineffectively. This view is clearly expressed by Laker *et al.* (1975) and Trollope (1985) concerning the Ciskei and which has found a predecessor in the Tomlinson Commission report of the 1950s. Observers like Bundy (1988) and also the data for Guquka and Koloni presented in chapter 7, pointed at gullies as major erosion features. Overgrazing and ploughing were seen as principal causes of gullies. The Laker Report (Laker *et al.* 1975) explained soil erosion repeatedly as resulting from incorrect land use and overstocking. Trollope (1985) maintained that soil erosion is the outcome of the interplay between a series of factors such as tenure, population pressure, lack of education and skills, and a lack of sound scientific background. Together these factors posed serious limitations on the understanding, acceptance and implementation of new and improved farming methods. Both argued that yields are poor because of poor soils and inadequate moisture. The deterioration of the landscape was assumed to be due to increased numbers of people and livestock in combination with traditional farming methods. Moreover, they called for a situation to bring stocking rates in line with prevailing *veld* conditions. This often resulted in intervention programmes that only marginally contributed to social development. The Faculty of Agriculture of University of Fort Hare played a role in the implementation of these programmes by training students to advise people living in communal areas about modern farming (Morrow 2007).

The ensuing intervention programmes were often but varyingly contested by local people but have also received much academic critique. We do not intend to review betterment again – this has been done extensively by researchers from Rhodes University during the 1980s (see Beinart 1989 and chapter 2) – but rather examine the nature of the knowledge that resulted in interventions like betterment.

The social science literature (Pottier and Bicker 2003, Pottier 1993, Richards 1983, 1985) points at the technocratic discourse that informs (agrarian) policies of the (colonial) state. Typical for such discourse is that it derives from an expert system that generates knowledge that regularly ignores how rural people read and utilise their landscape. Hebinck and Fay (2006) point at the continuities in the agricultural expert system in South Africa that has neither structurally nor substantially changed since colonial times. Beinart (2003: 336) in his turn, situates expert knowledge in the often contradictory relations between the state and rural people and links the role of the expert to "unilateral interventions and centralised planning". Expert knowledge is rather normative and regulatory at the same time and given its central role in society and the state, it has the power to identify (and label accordingly) winners and losers. In this way it has the power to order the agricultural sector in South Africa, now and in the future. The agricultural expert system embodies and defines agency: rules, participants and resources. Van der Ploeg (2003), pointing at the tight relationship between such science and policy environments, makes the case that empirical realties are reduced to virtual, non-existing realities, often expressed in aggregate terms such as averages and simple categories such as 'commercial' and 'subsistence' farming and farmers. These categories are not only rather incorrectly expressing current dynamics of agricultural production (Van Averbeke and Mohammed 2006), but also emerge from a colonial perspective on the direction of agricultural development (Moyo 2007).

Cousins (1996, 1998) traced the knowledge contestations that result from the interactions between rural people and experts (i.e. scientist *cum* betterment planners alike) to their contradicting views of how to utilise resources. Betterment planners, and the scientists supporting them, directly associated stock numbers with overgrazing and therefore enforced a culling of stock and the introduction of new management systems to control grazing. Thereby they ignored local views and understandings of cattle and stocking levels. A number of rangeland management studies done in the Eastern Cape years later debated in detail whether or not rangeland degradation is unlikely due to overgrazing as vegetation cover and productivity respond to primary rainfall (Kepe and Scoones 1999, Goqwana 1988, Vetter and Goqwana 2000, Ainslie 2002, Vetter 2003). Shackleton (1998) indicated that recommended stocking levels are conservative, and are set for commercial beef enterprises, not for conditions in commonly held and managed ragelands. Moreover, Harrison and Shackleton (1999: 237) argued that "the anxiety expressed over the apparent degraded condition of communal grazing lands is unjustified". They advised "managers and policy makers ... to accept the dynamic nature of communal systems and build upon this" when designing polices. Like chapter 9, these rangeland studies pointed out that not so much stock numbers but rainfall seems to be the factor that limits the productivity of the rangeland. Moreover, in both villages it is nowadays difficult to talk about artificially high numbers of livestock maintained on the rangeland at times of highest vulnerability (drought). The current numbers are not maintained by supplementary feeding and fodder but simply by what the rangeland, the arable fields and the open spaces in the settlements provides. Cattle numbers rather are reduced by starvation as took place in the 1980s (chapter 8 and 9). A management system such as the rotating camping system introduced in Koloni (chapters 6 and 9) would have fitted endeavours to prevent resource degradation, but the combination with culling made conservation a rather contentious intervention. To stipulate that culling was not seen as part of the solution *per se*, people in Guquka did not accept the camp system. Fences were regularly stolen and cut and cattle could freely roam the commons and forest reserves. On the other hand, as chapter 9 has shown, the camp system of rotational grazing betterment planners instituted in Koloni, which is still partially maintained today, has the effect that the grass in Koloni is better managed. However, we must take into account that Koloni cattle owners have access to substantially more (arable and range) land for grazing than those in Guquka, and that the people of Guquka lost much of their high elevation rangeland to pine plantations. Part and parcel of the contestation of betterment is that cattle cannot only be attributed single meanings. Cattle not just graze to produce meat, milk and cash, but also represent social security and ritual meanings providing status as well as a means to conclude marriages. Moreover, cattle owners in Guquka and Koloni saw degradation of the rangeland not in terms of "species composition but in soil loss" and degradation "is only taken seriously when the condition of the animals deteriorates severely" (Van Averbeke *et al.* 1997: 33). Culling was felt as a deprivation reducing one's status, limiting the ability to plough and to engage in rituals. It also potentially increased vulnerabilities particular during time of stress (e.g. drought, unemployment).

Contextualising land and soil erosion involves associating these with processes of environmental transformation (Beinart 2003, Dahlberg 2000). An important element of context for Guquka and Koloni is the size and quality of land that is available for grazing and cultivation but also the population dynamics affecting the use of land and related resources. The various degrees of fallowness, the combination of growing, grazing and gathering practices, the fact that monitoring of land erosion is hampered by labour being drawn away from the field (chapters 7 and 8), the contrasting and different views of what resources are; all these form an intrinsic part of processes of environmental transformation. The book has shown that such transformation also entails the removing of labels placed by outsiders on the various elements of the landscape, which offers some form of freedom to users irrespective of being owners or not. But part and parcel of removing the labels would also be a genuine attention for resource governance, meaning collaborative attempts to build a common knowledge base about peoples social and natural resources, their multiple meanings, and how these resources can be utilised beneficially and in a sustainable way.

In our critique of betterment, or more broadly, of state interventions, it should not be ignored that some aspects of these interventions (i.e. provision of schools, roads and other facilities) were embraced by local people. The crucial aspect here is that these interventions brought new opportunities (education, clinics) and/or strengthened the use of existing resources (roads). Both Guquka and Koloni are evidence of this embracing of new opportunities. Overall, however, betterment was not effected in a cooperative mode and was judged as intervening with key resources such as cattle. The image of betterment as a set of measures and attempts to prevent resource degradation was mixed up with all sorts of state interventions (e.g. hut and poll tax, labour controls) that were perceived and experienced as negative and preventing room for manoeuvre. Betterment cannot be judged as disconnected from such state interventions. Recently, Moore (2005) made this clear for the post-independence interventions of the Zimbabwean state to implement land resettlement policies.

*New agrarian curricula*
A prime area of concern following from the critical treatment of expert knowledge and past (and present) interventions pertains to curricula at universities as well as at primary and secondary schools. In the section above we have argued for a repeasantisation development strategy. To support this, what is needed is an agricultural curriculum acknowledging that the potential for action is situated in many locations in society, not simply and only embedded in institutions of expertise but potentially also in localities like Guquka and Koloni. Thus while arguing for a reconfigured expert system we should neither ignore the capacity of experts to revisit their approaches and practices, nor should we perceive rural people to be simply passive recipients of knowledge (Long 2001, Scoones and Thompson 1994, Chamber *et al.* 1989). By incorporating local people's knowledge in the curriculum, an agrarian science practice would emerge that neither sets norms nor regulates what constitutes resources and how these are being used. This would be an agrarian science that provides a range of alternative solutions for particular problems (rather than only one solution) which should challenge rather than condemn local practices and capitalise on existing bodies of local knowledge (Hart and Voster, 2006). In this way experts are trained that respond to questions and challenges of rural development. Key to such agrarian sciences is that they embark on interdisciplinary training and research.

The book has shown that agrarian sciences should also include the gathering aspects of rural livelihoods. This in turn urges to broaden the notion of peasantry to not only denote production and transformation of natural resources (cultivation and livestock keeping) but also embrace the collecting of resources from the surrounding ecosystem (Altieri 2002b, Toledo 1990, Ingold 2000). Peasants are not just growing and grazing but also gathering.

This book has provided ample insight into the potential advantages and difficulties of an interdisciplinary treatment of livelihoods and the analysis of processes of landscape transformation. Processes of mutual shaping of the social and the natural have been promoted as key to such interdisciplinary analysis. But unlike the laws of nature, we do not seek to foreclose competing explanations by laying claim to one dominant perspective. Livelihoods interacting with landscapes (that is coproduction) offer a relevant cognitive frame of interpretation for exploring development – poetically expressed – as a process of unfolding of resources to which social actors attribute multiple meanings. The drivers of these processes are the livelihood identities of local people that have shifted dramatically over the years. These livelihoods and landscapes are expressed in various and often contrasting discourses, embedded in the institutions that have emerged. This is one way of analysing the complex and diverse waters of human history, where practices, politics, knowledge and intervention are continually in flux.

# References


ACOCKS, J.P.H. (1988) *Veld types of South Africa,* Third edn. Pretoria: Botanical Research Institute, Department of Agriculture and Water Supply. Memoirs of the Botanical Survey of Southern Africa, no. 57.

AINSLIE, A. (1998) *Managing natural resources in a rural settlement in Peddie District,* M.A. Thesis, Anthropology Department, Grahamstown: Rhodes University.

AINSLIE, A. (2002) A review of cattle production in Peddie District, in Ainslie, A. (ed.), *Cattle ownership and production in the communal areas of the Eastern Cape, South Africa,* Belville: Programme for Land and Agrarian Studies, University of the Western Cape. Research Report No.10., pp. 98-120.

ALDERSON-SMITH, G. (1984) Confederations of households: Extended domestic enterprises in city and country, in Long, N. and B. Roberts (eds.), *Miners, peasants and entrepreneurs: Regional development in the central highlands of Peru,* Cambridge: Cambridge University Press, pp. 217-234.

ALTIERI, M. (2002a) Principles for sustainable agriculture, in Uphoff, N. (ed.), *Agroecological innovations. Increasing food production with participatory development,* London: Earthscan Publications, pp. 40-47.

ALTIERI, M. (2002b) Agroecology: The science of natural resource management for poor farmers in marginal environments, *Agriculture Ecosystems &Environment,* 93: 1-24.

AMATOLA WATER BOARD, Www.Amatolawater.Co.Za.

ANDREW, M. (1992) *A geographical study of agricultural change since the 1930s in Shixini location, Gatyana District, Transkei,* M.A. Thesis, Geography Department, Grahamstown: Rhodes University.

ANDREW, M. and R. FOX (2003) *Cultivation trends in the Transkei and Ciskei: 1940-1996,* East London: Institute of Social and Economic Research, University of Fort Hare.

ANDREW, M., A. AINSLIE and C.M. SHACKLETON (2003) *Land use and livelihoods,* Evaluating land and agrarian reform in South Africa no. 8. Cape Town: Programme for Land and Agrarian Studies, School of Government, University of Western Cape.

ANDREW, M. and R. FOX (2004) Undercultivation and intensification in the Transkei: A case study of historical changes in the use of arable land in Nompa, Shixini, *Development Southern Africa,* 21(4): 687-706.

ANTROBUS, G.G., G.C.G. FRASER, M. LEVIN and H.R. LLOYD (1994) *An overview of the agricultural economy of region d: Final report* Port Elizabeth: Unit for Statistical Analysis.

ARCE, A. and E. FISHER (2003) Knowledge interfaces and practices of negotiation: Cases from a women's group in bolivia and an oil refinery in Wales, in Pottier, J., A. Bicker and P. Sillitoe (eds.), *Negotiating local knowledge: Power and identity in development,* London: Pluto Press, pp. 74-97.

ARDINGTON, E. and F. LUND (1996) Questioning rural livelihoods, in Lipton, M., F. Ellis and M. Lipton (eds.), *Land, labour and livelihoods in rural South Africa Vol. II: KwaZulu-Natal and Northern Province*, Durban: Indicator Press, pp. 31-58.

ARDRI (1983) *Amatola rural development project: Interim report*, Alice: Agricultural and Rural Development Research Institute, University of Fort Hare, pp. 57.

ARDRI (1988, 1990-1994, 1996-2001) *ARDRINEWS,* Newsletter of the Agricultural and Rural Development Research Institute, various volumes.

ARDRI (1996a) Land use systems research programme, *ARDRINEWS*: 4-14.

ARDRI (1996b) "Tragedy" Of the commons revisited, *ARDRINEWS*: 11-12.

ARDRI (1998) *Annual report 1997-1998*, Alice: Agricultural and Rural Development Research Institute, University of Fort Hare.

ARDRI (1999) *Annual report 1998-1999*, Alice: ARDRI- University of Fort Hare.

ARDRI (2001) *Annual report 2000-2001*, Alice: Agricultural and Rural Development Research Institute, University of Fort Hare, pp. 25.

ARDRI (2001) *Rural livelihoods survey in the Mbashe municipality*, Alice: Agricultural and Rural Development Research Institute, University of Fort Hare, pp. 35.

ASHLEY, C. (2000) The impacts of tourism on rural livelihoods: Namibia's experience. Results of research presented in preliminary form for discussion and critical comments, London: Overseas Development Institute. ODI Working Paper 128. [Online]. Available from: http://www.odi.org.uk/publications/ wp128.pdf.

AUSTIN, M.N. (1989a) Rainfall and slope of Ciskeian ecotopes: Important determinants of cropping potential, *Ciskei Journal for Rural Development*, 11: 8-11.

AUSTIN, M.N. (1989b) Monthly and annual rainfall probability analysis for Ciskei. II Maps, *ARDRI Bulletin*, 1/89, ARDRI, University of Fort Hare, Alice.

BABER, R. (1996) Current livelihoods in semi-arid rural areas of South Africa, in Lipton, M., F. Ellis, and M. Lipton (eds.), *Land, labour and livelihoods in rural South Africa, Volume II, Kwazulu-natal and northern province*, Durban: Indicator Press, University of Natal, pp. 269-302.

BAGCHI, D.K., P. BLAIKIE, J. CAMERON, M. CHATTOPADHYAY, N. GYAWALI and D. SEDDON (1998) Conceptual and methodological challenges in the study of livelihood trajectories: Case studies in eastern India and western Nepal, *Journal of International Development*, 10: 453-468.

BAKER, K. (2000) *Indigenous land management in west Africa. An environmental balancing act* Oxford geographical and environmental studies series Oxford: Oxford University Press.

BANK, L. (1999) Men with cookers: Transformations in migrant culture, domesticity and identity in Duncan village, East London, *Journal of Southern African Studies*, 25(3): 393-416.

BANK, L. (1999) *No visible means of subsistence: Rural livelihoods, gender and de-agrarianisation in the Eastern Cape, South Africa*, in ASC (Ed.), *ASC Joint Working Paper - DARE*, Grahamstown, Leiden: ASC, pp. 45.

BANK, L. and D. BRYCESON (2001) Livelihoods, linkages and policy paradoxes, *Journal of Contemporary African Studies*, 19(1).

BANK, L. (2001) Living together, moving apart: Home-made agendas, identity, politics and urban-rural linkages in the Eastern Cape, South Africa, *Journal of Contemporary African Studies*, 19(1): 129-147.

BANK, L. (2002) Beyond red and school: Gender, tradition and identity in the rural Eastern Cape, *Journal of Southern African Studies*, 28(3): 631-649.

BANTU AFFAIRS COMMISSION (1962) *Reclamation and settlement of Koloni location: Middledrift District. File no. (60)n.2/11/3/12*, King William's Town.

BARRETT, C.B., T. REARDON and P. WEBB (2001) Non-farm income diversification and household livelihood strategies in rural Africa: Concepts, dynamics and policy implications, *Food Policy*, 26: 315-331.

BASSETT, T.J. and K.B. ZUÉLI (2003) The Ivorian savanna: Global narratives and local knowledge of environment change, in Zimmerer, K.S. and T.J. Bassett (eds.), *Political ecology: An integrative approach to geography and environment-development studies*, New York The Guilford Press, pp. 115-137.

BATTERBURY, S. and A. BEBBINGTON (1999) Environmental histories, access to resources and landscape change: An introduction, *Land Degradation and Development*, 10: 279-289.

BECKERLING, A.C., W.S.W. TROLLOPE, M.M. MBELU and P.F. SCOGINGS (1995) *Simplified techniques for assessing veld condition for livestock production in the Ciskei region*, Alice: ARDRI and Department of Livestock and Pasture Science, University of Fort Hare.

BEHNKE, R.J. and I. SCOONES (1993) Rethinking rangeland ecology: Implications for rangeland management in Africa, in Behnke, R.J., I. Scoones and C. Kerven (eds.), *Range ecology at disequilibrium*, London: Overseas Development Institute, pp. 1-30.

BEINART, W. (1982) *The political economy of Pondoland, 1860-1930*, Cambridge: Cambridge University Press.

BEINART, W., P. DELIUS and S. TRAPIDO (eds.) (1986) *Putting a plough to the ground: Accumulation and dispossession in rural South Africa, 1850-1930*, Johannesburg: Raven Press.

BEINART, W. and C. BUNDY (1987) *Hidden struggles in rural South Africa: Politics and popular movements in the Transkei and Eastern Cape, 1890-1930*, London: James Currey.

BEINART, W. (1989) Introduction: The politics of colonial conservation, *Journal of Southern African Studies*, 15(2, special issue on the politics of conservation in Southern Africa): 143-162.

BEINART, W. (1992) Transkeian smallholders and agrarian reform, *Journal of Contemporary African Studies*, 11(2): 178-199.

BEINART, W. (2001) *Twentieth-century South Africa. New edition*, Oxford: Oxford University Press.

BEINART, W. (2003) *The rise of conservation in South Africa. Settlers, livestock, and the environment 1770-1950*, Oxford Oxford University Press.

BEINHART, W. (1984) Soil erosion, conservationism and ideas about development: A southern African exploration, 1900-1960, *Journal of Southern African Studies*, 11(1): 52-83.

BEINROTH, F.H., G. UEHARA, J.A. SILVA, R.W. ARNOLD and F.B. CADY (1980) Agrotechnology transfer in the tropics based on soil taxonomy, *Advances in Agronomy*, 33: 303-339.

BEMBRIDGE, T. (1979) Problems of livestock production in the black states of southern Africa and future strategy, *Southern African Journal of Animal Science*, 9: 63-176.

BEMBRIDGE, T. (1984) *A systems approach study of agricultural development problems in Transkei* , Faculty of Agriculture, Stellenbosch: University of Stellenbosch.

BEMBRIDGE, T. (1990) Agricultural development in the developing areas of southern Africa, *Africa Insight* 20(1).

BENNETT, J. (1998) *Access arrangements and utilisation of arable fields at two sites in central Eastern Cape: An interim report*, Alice: ARDRI, University of Fort Hare, pp. 30.

BENNETT, J. (2002) *The role of arable land allocations in cattle production systems in communal areas of central Eastern Cape province, South Africa*, PhD. Thesis, School of Science and the Environment, Coventry: Coventry University.

BENNETT, J. (2004) *The use of arable land in Guquka and Koloni, field notes*, Coventry: Coventry University, pp. 25.

BENNETT, J. (2005) *Case study report* Coventry: Coventry University. Unpublished report, pp. 12.

BENNETT, J. and H. BARRETT (2007) Rangeland as a common property resource: Contrasting insights from communal areas of central Eastern Cape province, South Africa. Human ecology, *Human Ecology*, 35(1): 97-112.

BERGH, J.S. (1984) *Tribes & kingdoms,* Cape Town: Don Nelson.

BERKES, F., C. FOLKE and J. COLDING (1998) *Linking social and ecological systems : Management practices and social mechanisms for building resilience,* Cambridge: Cambridge University Press, pp.459.

BERNSTEIN, H. (1998) Social change in the South African countryside? Land and production, poverty and power, *Journal of Peasant Studies*, 25(4): 1-32.

BERNSTEIN, H. (2004) The boys from Bothaville, or the rise and fall of king maize: A South African story, *Journal of Agrarian Change*, 4(4): 492–508.

BERRY, S. (1984) The food crisis and agrarian change in Africa - a review essay *African Studies Review*, 27(2): 59-113.

BERRY, S. (1993) *No condition is permanent. The social dynamics of agrarian change in sub-Saharan Africa,* Madison, WI: University of Wisconsin Press.

BHORAT, H. (1995) The South African safety net: Past, present and future, *Development Southern Africa*, 12(4): 595-604.

BONROY, J. (1999) *Inventarisatie van bodemkarakteristieken voor de bepaling van het landbouwkundig productiepotentieel in Koloni (oostkaap, zuid-afrika)*, M.Sc. Thesis, Land-en Bosbeheer, Ghent: Ghent University.

BONROY, J. and A. VERDOODT (1999) *Soil survey report: Guquka and Koloni. With maps*, Alice: ARDRI, Univ. of Fort Hare, pp. 50.

BONROY, J., E. VAN RANST, W. VAN AVERBEKE, A. VERDOODT, G. BAERT and H. VERPLANCKE (2000) *Soils of Koloni and their potential for crops*, in Van Ranst, E., H. Verplancke, W. Van Averbeke, A. Verdoodt and J. Bonroy (Eds.), *Rural livelihoods in the central Eastern Cape, South Africa: extended abstracts of an International Workshop*, Ghent, Belgium. The Laboratory of Soil Science, University of Ghent, pp. 25-28.

BOSERUP, E. (1970) *Woman's role in economic development,* New York: St. Martin's Press.

BOSERUP, E. (1981) *Population and technology*, Oxford: Blackwell.

BROCKLESBY, M.A. and E. FISHER (2003) Community development in sustainable livelihoods approaches - an introduction, *Community Development Journal*, 38(3): 185-198.

BRONS, J. (2005) *Activity diversification in rural livelihoods. The role of farm supplementary income in Burkina Faso*, PhD Thesis, Development Economics, Wageningen: Wageningen University.

BROWN, D.L. (1969) *A study of the animal and crop production systems and potential of the bantu Ciskeian territories*, Doctoral Thesis, Faculty of Agriculture, Bloemfontein: University of the Orange Free State.

BROWN, D.L., E.J.B. BISHOP and P.I. WILKE (1975) Appraisal of livestock in the Ciskei, in Laker, M.C. (ed.), *The agricultural potential of the Ciskei: A preliminary report. Alice, university of fort hare*, Alice: Faculty of Agriculture. University of Fort Hare, pp. 125-135.

BRYCESON, D. (ed.) (1995) *Women wielding the hoe : Lessons from rural Africa for feminist theory and development practice*, Oxford: Berg.

BRYCESON, D.F. (2002a) The scramble in Africa: Reorienting rural livelihoods, *World Development*, 30(5): 725-739.

BRYCESON, D.F. (2002b) Multiplex livelihoods in rural Africa: Recasting the terms and conditions of gainful employment, *Journal of Modern African Studies*, 40(1): 1-28.

BUNDY, C. (1988) *The rise and fall of the South African peasantry,* (First edition 1977) Second edn. London: James Currey.

BUYS, S.F.L. (1999) *The nutritional status in Guquka (South Africa)*, M.Sc. Thesis, Landbouwkunde, Ghent: Ghent University.

BUYS, S. (2000) *The status of nutrition in Guquka*, in Van Ranst, E., H. Verplancke, W. Van Averbeke, A. Verdoodt and J. Bonroy (Eds.), *Rural livelihoods in the central Eastern Cape, South Africa: extended abstracts of an International Workshop*, The Laboratory of Soil Science, University of Ghent, Ghent, Belgium, pp. 52-54.

CARNEY, D. (ed.) (1998) *Sustainable rural livelihoods: What contribution can we make*, London: Department for International Development.

CARPENTER, S.R. (2005) *Scenarios. Ecosystems and human well-being, Vol II*, Washington DC: Island Press.

CARTER, M. and J. MAY (1999) Poverty, livelihoods and class in rural South Africa, *World Development*, 27(1): 1-20.

CASE, A. and A. DEATON (1998) Large cash transfers to the elderly in South Africa, *The Economic Journal*, 108: 1330-1361.

CHAMBERS, R., A. PACEY and L.A. THRUPP (eds.) (1989) *Farmer first. Farmer innovation and agricultural research*, London: Intermediate Technology Publications.

CHAMBERS, R. (1997) *Whose reality counts? Putting the first last*, London: Intermediate Technology Publications.

CHE, B. and LENT P.C. (2004) Traditional conservation practices and the use of indigenous forests in the amatola mountains of the Eastern Cape province, in Lawes, M.J., H.A.C. Eeley, C.M. Shackleton and B.G.S. Geach (eds.), *Indigenous forests and woodlands in South Africa*, Pietermaritzburg: University of KwaZulu Natal Press, pp. 253-256.

CID, M.S. and M.A. BRIZUELA (1998) Heterogeneity in tall fescue pastures created and sustained by cattle grazing, *Journal of Range Management*, 51(6): 644-649.

COCKS, M.L. and K.F. WIERSUM (2003) The significance of plant diversity to rural households in Eastern Cape province of South Africa, *Forests, Trees and Livelihoods*, 13: 39-58.

COERTZE, R.D. (1986) Livestock in the social and cultural life of African communities, *South African Journal of Ethnology*, 9(3): 129-135.

COKWANA, M.M. (1988) A close look at tenure in Ciskei, in Cross, C.R. and R.J. Haines (eds.), *Towards freehold? Options for land development in South Africa's black rural areas*, Kenwyn: Juta & Co, pp. 305-313.

COLEMAN, J.A. (1999) *Sustainable management in a disturbed environment: A case study of the Hogsback working for water project*, Pietermaritzburg: University of Natal.

COLEMAN, M. (n.d.) *Results of an investigation into the history of visible erosion in the Tyume valley (Victoria East District, Eastern Cape)*: Deputy Director, National Department of Land Affairs, East London Office.

COLLINSON, M. (ed.) (2000) *A history of farming systems research*, Rome: CABI and FAO.

COMAROFF, J. and J. COMAROFF (1990) Goodly beasts, beastly goods: Cattle and commodities in a South African context, *American Ethnologist*, 17(2): 195-216.

CORNWALLIS-HARRIS, W. (1986) *Portraits of the game and wild animals of southern Africa*, Alberton: Galago Publishers.

COSGROVE, D. (1998) *Social formation and symbolic landscape*, Madison/London: University of Wisconsin Press.

COUSINS, B. (1996) Livestock production and common property struggles in South Africa's agrarian reform, *The Journal of Peasant Studies* 23(2-3): 166-208.

COUSINS, B. (1998) Invisible capital: The contribution of communal rangelands to rural livelihoods in South Africa, in De Bruyn, T.D. and P.F. Scogings (eds.), *Communal rangelands in southern Africa: A synthesis of knowledge*, Alice: Department of Livestock & Pasture Science, University of Fort Hare, pp. 16–29.

COUSINS, B. (1999) Invisible capital: The contribution of communal rangelands to rural livelihoods in South Africa, *Development Southern Africa*, 16(2): 299-318.

COUSINS, B. (2000) Tenure and common property resources in Africa, in Toulmin, C. and J.F. Quan (eds.), *Evolving land rights, policy and tenure in Africa*, London: DFID, IIED, NRI, pp. 151-179.

COUSINS, B. (2007) Agrarian reform and the 'two economies': Transforming South Africa's countryside, in Ntsebeza, L. and R. Hall (eds.), *The land question in South Africa. The challenge of transformation and redistribution*, Cape Town: Human Sciences Research Council Press, pp. 220--246.

COWLING, R.M., R.M. RICHARDSON and S.M. PIERCE (1997) Phytogeography, flora and endemism in vegetation of South Africa, in Cowling, R.M., R.M. Richardson and S.M. Pierce (eds.), *Fynbos, vegetation of South Africa*, Cambridge: Cambridge University Press.

COWLING, R.M. and C. HILTON-TAYLOR (1998) Patterns of plant diversity and endemism in southern Africa: An overview, in Huntley, B.J. (ed.), *Botanical diversity in southern Africa*, Pretoria: National Botanical Institute, pp. 31-52.

CRAIS, C. (1991) *The making of the colonial order: White supremacy and black resistance in the Eastern Cape, 1770-1865,* Johannesburg: Witwatersrand University Press.

CRAIS, C. (1992) Representation and the politics of identity in South Africa: An Eastern Cape example, *The International Journal of African Historical Studies,* 25(1): 99-126.

CRAMPTON, H. (2004) *The sunburnt queen,* Johannesburg: Jacana Media Ltd.

D'HUYVETTER, J.H.H. (1985) *Determination of threshold slope percentages for the identification and delineation of arable land in Ciskei,* M.Sc. Thesis, Faculty of Agriculture, Alice: University of Fort Hare.

DAHLBERG, A. (2000) Landscape(s) in transition: An environmental history of a village in north-east Botswana, *Journal of Southern African Studies,* 26(4): 759-783.

DAVIS, B. (2004) *Choosing a method for poverty mapping,* Rome: FAO.

DE HAAN, L. and A. ZOOMERS (2005) Exploring the frontier of livelihoods research, *Development and Change,* 36(1): 27-47.

DE WET, C.J. (1985) Cultivation, in De Wet, C., and S. Bekker (eds.), *Rural development in South Africa. A case study of the Amatola basin in the Ciskei 30, Occasional paper,* Grahamstown Shuter & Shooter/Institute of Social and Economic Research Rhodes University, pp. 90-118.

DE WET, C.J. and S. BEKKER (1985) *Rural development in South Africa. A case study of the amatola basin in the Ciskei,* Pietermaritzburg: Shuter and Shooter and ISER, Rhodes University.

DE WET, C.J. (1987) Betterment planning in South Africa: Some thoughts on its history, feasability and wider policy implications, *Journal of Contemporary African Studies,* 6(1/2): 85-122.

DE WET, C.J. (1989) Betterment planning in a rural village in keiskammnahoek District, Ciskei, *Journal of Southern African Studies,* 15: 326-345.

DE WET, C.J. and W. VAN AVERBEKE (1995) *Regional overview of land reform-related issues in the Eastern Cape province* Johannesburg Land and Agricultural Policy Centre. Working paper EC24, pp. 243.

DE WET, C.J. and M.G. WHISSON (1997) *From reserve to region. Apartheid and social change in the keikammahoek District of (former) Ciskei: 1950-1990:* ISER, Rhodes University.

DE WET, C.J. and G. HOLBROOK (1997) Regionalisation of the household: A temporary phase, or a long term trend, in De Wet, C. and M. Whisson (eds.), *From reserve to region. Apartheid and social change in the Keiskammahoek District of (former) Ciskei: 1950-1990, occasional paper nr. 35, Occasional paper,* Grahamstown Institute Social and Economic Research, Rhodes University, pp. 254-267.

DEPARTMENT OF AGRICULTURE (1995) *Livestock census (march 1995),* Pretoria: National Department of Agriculture.

DEPARTMENT OF AGRICULTURE AND LAND AFFAIRS (1997) *White paper: Land policy,* Pretoria: Department of Agriculture and Land Affairs.

DEPARTMENT OF AGRICULTURE EASTERN CAPE (1997) *Unlocking the agricultural potential,* Bisho: Department of Agriculture Eastern Cape.

DRIMIE, S. (2002) *The impact of HIV/AIDS on rural households in southern and eastern Africa,* Rome: Food and Agricultural Organisation.

DU TOIT, A. (2004) 'social exclusion' discourse and chronic poverty: A South African case study, *Development and Change*, 35(5): 987-1010.

ECKERT, J.B. and W. WILLIAMS (1995) Identifying serious farmers in the former Ciskei: Implications for small-scale farm research and land reform, *Agrekon*, 34(2): 50-58.

ECSECC (1999) Integrated planning in the Eastern Cape: Background, *Information Bulletin of the Eastern Cape Socio-Economic Consultative Council*, 13(1).

ELLIS, F.F. (1998) Household strategies and rural livelihood diversification, *The Journal of Development Studies*, 35(1): 1-38.

ELLIS, F. (2000) *Rural livelihoods and diversity in developing countries,* Oxford: Oxford University Press.

ELS, W.C. (1971) The physical character of the Ciskei and some notes on its potential, in Els, W.C., E.J. de Jager, C.G. Coetzee, O.F. Raum, G.C. Oosthuizen, P.A. Duminy, D.L. Brown, J.H. Smith and C.C. Holdt (eds.), *The Ciskei - A Bantu homeland*, Alice: Fort Hare University Press, pp. 1-50.

ESCOBAR, A. (2001) Culture sits in places: Reflections on globalism and subaltern strategies of localization, *Political Geography*, 20: 139-174.

ESSA, J.A. and W.L. NIEUWOUDT ( 2003.) Socio-economic dimensions of small-scale agriculture: A principal component analysis, *Development Southern Africa*, 20(1): 67-73.

FAIR, T.J.D. (2000) African rural development: Policy and practice in six countries. 3rd edition, Pretoria: Africa Institute of South Africa.

FAIRHEAD, J. and M. LEACH (1996) Enriching the landscape: Social history and the management of transition ecology in the forest-savannah mosaic of the Republic of Guinea, *Africa*, 66(1): 14-36.

FAIRHEAD, J. and M. LEACH (1996) *Misreading the African landscape: Society and ecology in a forest - savannah mosaic,* Cambridge: Cambridge University Press.

FERGUSON, J. (1990) *The anti-politics machine: "Development", depoliticization, and bureaucratic power in Lesotho,* Cambridge: Cambridge University Press, pp. 320.

FORBES, R.G. and W.S.W. TROLLOPE (1991) Veld management in the communal areas of Ciskei, *Journal of the Grassland Society of Southern Africa*, 8(4): 147-152.

FRANCIS, E. (2000) *Making a living: Changing livelihoods in rural Africa,* London: Routledge.

FRANCIS, E. (2002) Rural livelihoods, institutions and vulnerability in north west province, South Africa, *Journal of Southern African Studies*, 28(3): 531-550.

FRANCIS, E. and C. MURRAY (2002) Special issue: Changing livelihoods: Introduction, *Journal of Southern African Studies*, 28(3): 485-487.

FRASER, G.C. (1992) Farmer response to the provision of livestock marketing facilities in Ciskei, *Agrekon*, 31(3): 104-106.

GERRITSEN, P. (2002) *Diversity at stake. A farmers' perspective on biodiversity and conservation in western Mexico*, PhD Thesis, Rural Sociology, Wageningen: Wageningen University.

GERTENBACH, W.D., J. VILJOEN, H. HENNING, VAN, and J.A. COLLYER (1998) The utilisation of maize-crop residues for overwintering livestock. Livestock performance as affected by different cattle to sheep ratios when grazing maize-crop residues, *South African Journal of Animal Science*, 28(1): 24-20.

GILIOMEE, H. (2003) *The Afrikaners. Biography of a people,* Cape Town/ Charlottesville: Tafelberg Publishers/University of Virginia Press.

GILLER, K.E., E.C. ROWE, N. DE RIDDER and H. VAN KEULEN (2006) Resource use dynamics and interactions in the tropics: Scaling up in space and time, *Agricultural Systems,* 88: 8-27.

GOQWANA, W.M. and P.F. SCOGINGS (1997) Rangeland and its management, in Van Averbeke, W. (ed.), *ARDRI's farming systems research programme,* Alice: ARDRI, University of Fort Hare. Incomplete preliminary report.

GOQWANA, M.W. (1998) A comparison of veld condition between two management systems in Eastern Cape communal rangelands, in De Bruyn, T.D. and P.F. Scogings (eds.), *Communal rangelands in southern Africa: A synthesis of knowledge,* Alice: Department of Livestock and Pasture Science, University of Fort Hare, pp. 211-221.

GREEN, P. and A. HIRSCH (1982) The Ciskei - the political economy of control, *South African Labour Bulletin,* 7(4/5): 65-85.

GUYER, J. (1981) Household and community in African studies, *African Studies Review,* 24(2/3): 87-137.

GUYER, J. and P. PETERS (1987) Conceptualizing the household: Issues of theory and policy in Africa: Introduction, *Development and Change,* 18(2): 197-213.

GUYER, J. (1988) The multiplication of labor. Historical methods in the study of gender and agricultural change in modern Africa, *Current Anthropology* 29(2): 247-273.

HAMMOND-TOOKE, D. (1993) *The roots of black South Africa,* Johannesburg: Jonathan Ball Publishers.

HARDIN, G. (1968) The tragedy of the commons, *Science,* 162: 1243-1248.

HARRIS, A. (1998) *Report - Koloni case study. Report for agricultural and rural development research institute,* Alice: ARDRI, University of Fort Hare.

HARRISON, Y.A. and C.M. SHACKLETON (1999) Resilience of South African communal grazing lands after the removal of high grazing pressure, *Land Degradation & Development,* 10: 225-239.

HART, G. (1992) Imagined unities: Constructions of "The household" in economic theory, in Ortiz, S. and S. Lees (eds.), *Understanding economic process. Monographs in economic anthropology, no. 10,* New York: Society for Economic Anthropology, University Press of America, pp. 111-130.

HART, T. and I. VORSTER (2006) *Indigenous knowledge on the South African landscape,* Cape Town: Human Sciences Research Council Press.

HAYAMI, Y. and RUTTAN V. (1985) *Agricultural development: An international perspective,* Revised and expanded edition, Baltimore/London: Johns Hopkins University Press.

HEBINCK, P. and J.D. VAN DER PLOEG (1997) Dynamics of agricultural production. An analysis of micro-macro linkages, in de Haan, H. and N. Long (ed.), *Images and realities of rural life. Wageningen perspectives on rural transformations,* Assen: Royal Van Gorcum, pp. 202-226.

HEBINCK, P. and M.F.C. BOURDILLON (2001) Analysis of livelihood, in Bourdillon, M.F.C. and P. Hebinck (eds.), *Women, men and work: Rural livelihoods in central-eastern Zimbabwe,* Harare: Weaver Press, pp. 1-13.

HEBINCK, P. and L. SMITH (2001) Livelihoods and rural transformations in the central Eastern Cape: From production to consumption? A case study of the two rural villages Guquka and Koloni, paper given at Development Studies Association Annual Conference: 'Different Poverties, Different Policies, Manchester, 10-12 September.

HEBINCK, P. (2001) Maize and socio-technical regimes, in Hebinck, P. and G. Verschoor (eds.), *Resonances and dissonances in development. Actor, networks and cultural repertoires*, Assen: Royal Van Gorcum, pp. 119-139.

HEBINCK, P. (2004) *Guquka and Koloni field notes: Updates 2004*, Wageningen: Rural Development Sociology, Wageningen University, pp. 25.

HEBINCK, P. and D. FAY (2006) Land reform in South Africa: Caught by continuities, paper given at Land, Memory, Reconstruction and Justice: Perspectives on Land Restitution ain South Africa, Houw Hoek, 13-15 September.

HENDRICKS, F.T. (1989) Loose planning and rapid settlement: The politics of conservation and control in Transkei, South Africa, 1950-1970, *Journal of Southern African Studies*, 15(2): 306-326.

HENSLEY, M. and M.C. LAKER (1975) Introduction, in Laker, M.C. (ed.), *The agricultural potential of the Ciskei: A preliminary report*, 1975: Faculty of Agriculture. University of Fort Hare, pp. 3-17.

HIGGINBOTTOM, K. (1995) *The fate of the commons: Urban land reform, squatting and environmental management in the Eastern Cape province*, Grahamstown: Institute of Social and Economic Research, Rhodes University. Development Studies Working Paper no.65, pp. 24.

HIGH, C. and C. SHACKLETON (2000) The comparative value of wild and domestic plants in home gardens of a South African rural village, *Agroforestry Systems*, 48: 141-156.

HILL, KAPLAN, SCOTT, and PARTNERS (1977) *Keiskamma River basin natural resources survey*, Bisho: Ciskei Government Services.

HOERNLÉ, W. (1937) Social organisation, in Schapera, I. (ed.), *The Bantu-speaking tribes of South Africa. An ethnographical survey*, London: Routledge & Kegan Paul, pp. 67-95.

HOFFMAN, T., S. TODD, Z. NTSHONA and S. TURNER (1999) *Land degradation in South Africa*, Cape Town: National Botanical Gardens, pp. 35.

HOFFMAN, T.M. and S. TODD (2000) A national review of land degradation in South Africa: The influence of biophysical and socio-economic factors, *Journal of Southern African Studies*, 26(4, special issue: African Environments: Past and Present): 743-758.

HOLBROOK, G. (1998) The politics of livestock management: The case of the village of Guquka, in De Bruyn, T.D. and P.F. Scogings (eds.), *Communal rangelands in southern Africa: A synthesis of knowledge: Proceedings of a symposium on policy-making for the sustainable use of southern African communal rangelands*, Alice: Alice: Department of Livestock and Pasture Science, University of Fort Hare, pp. 93-96.

HOLDEN, W.C. (1877) *A brief history of Methodism and of Methodist missions in South Africa, Part II*, London: Wesleyan Conference Office.

HOLDT, C. (1971) Constitutional development, in Els, W.C., E.J. de Jager, C.G. Coetzee, O.F. Raum, G.C. Oosthuizen, P.A. Duminy, D.L. Brown, J.H. Smith and C.C. Holdt (eds.), *The Ciskei - a bantu homeland: A general survey*, Alice: University of Fort Hare:, pp. 200-215.

HOUGHTON, D.H. and E.M. WALTON (1952) *The economy of a native reserve. Keiskammahoek rural survey volume 2,* Pietermaritzburg: Shuter and Shooter.

HUNDLEBY, J., C.J. ROSE and B. MLUMBI (1986) *Cattle production in Ciskei, past, present and future, The Annual Conference of the South African Society of Animal Production,* Pretoria.

HUNT DAVIS, R. (1979) School vs. Blanket and settler: Elijah Makiwane and the leadership of the cape school community *African Affairs,* 78(310): 12-31.

HUTCHINSON, P., T. TIES BOERMA and M. KHAN (2004) *1998 South Africa demographic and health survey reports for the Eastern Cape province*: Equity Project Eastern Cape Department of Health/Measure Evaluation, University of North Carolina/Tulane University New Orleans, pp. 216.

INGOLD, T. (2000) Making things, growing plants, raising animals and bringing up children, in Ingold, T. (ed.), *The perception of the environment: Essays on livelihood, dwelling and skill,* London: Routledge, pp. 77-88.

INSTITUTE FOR SOCIAL AND ECONOMIC RESEARCH (ISER) (2001) *Willowvale maize milling feasibility study: 2001 report to the GTZ Rural Livelhoods Programme of the premier's office,* Bisho, Grahamstown: Institute of Social and Economic Research, Rhodes University.

JASANOFF, S. (2004 ) Ordering knowledge, ordering society, in Jasanoff, S. (ed.), *States of knowledge: The co-production of science and social order,* London: Routledge, pp. 13-45.

JORDAN, A.C. (1999) *De wraak van het voorgeslacht,* Originally Published as *Ingqumbo Yeminyana,* Alice: Lovedale Press, 1995 edn. Amsterdam: Podium.

JUDGE, A. (2001) *The effects of surface-applied poultry manure on top- and subsoil acidity and selected soil fertility characteristics,* M.Sc. Thesis, Faculty of Agriculture, Pietermaritzburg: University of Natal

JURY, M.R. and K. LEVY (1993) The climatology and characteristics of drought in the Eastern Cape of South Africa, *International Journal of Climatology,* 13: 629-641.

KATLING, D. (1996) *Current status of government agricultural schemes and projects in the Eastern Cape. Full report to the department of agriculture and land affairs of the province of the Eastern Cape,* Bisho.

KEARL, L.C. (1982) *Nutrient requirements of ruminants in developing countries,* Logan, Utah: International Feedstuffs Institute, Utah Agricultural Experiment Station, Utah State University.

KEARNEY, M. (1996) *Reconceptualizing the peasantry: Anthropology in global perspective,* Boulder CO: Westview Press.

KEPE, T. (1997) *Environmental entitlements in mkambati, Programme for Land and Agrarian Studies*: School of Government, University of Western Cape, pp. 91.

KEPE, T. and I. SCOONES (1999) Creating grasslands: Social institutions and environmental change in the Mkambati area, South Africa, *Human Ecology,* 27(1): 29-54.

KEPE, T. (2002) The dynamics of cattle production and government intervention in communal areas of Lusikisiki District, in Ainslie, A. (ed.), *Cattle ownership and production in the communal areas of the Eastern Cape, South Africa,* Belville: Research Report No. 10. Programme for Land and Agrarian Studies, University of the Western Cape, pp. 59-79.

KINGWILL, R. (2006) *Mysteries and myths: De soto, property and poverty in South Africa,* London: International Institute for Environment and Development.

KNIGHT, J.B. and G. LENTA (1980) Has capitalism underdeveloped the labour reserves of South Africa, *Oxford Bulleting of Economics and Statistics*, 42(3): 157-262.

KOWAL, J. (1978) *Agro-ecological zoning for the assessment of land potentialities for agriculture, Land Evaluation Standards for rain fed agriculture. FAO World Soil Resources Report 49*, Rome: FAO.

KREBS, C.J. (1999) *Ecological methodology. 2nd edition*: Benjamin-Cummings.

KRUGER, P. (1995) Land audit, in Wet, C.d. and W. van Averbeke (eds.), *Regional overview of land reform-related issues in the Eastern Cape province*, Johannesburg: Land & Agriculture Policy Centre, pp. 185-233.

KRÜGER, F. (1991) The legacy of "Homeland" Policy - the Ciskei: Dumping ground of the Eastern Cape, in Ramphele, M. and C. McDowell (eds.), *Restoring the land: Environment and change in post-apartheid South Africa*, London: Panos, pp. 39-52.

KUCKERTZ, H. (1985) Organizing labour forces in Mpondoland: A new perspective on work-parties, *Africa*, 55(2): 115-132.

KUPER, A. (1982) *Wives for cattle,* London/Boston: Routledge and Keagan Paul.

LAHIFF, E. (2000) *An apartheid oasis? Agriculture and rural livelihoods in rural Venda*, Library of peasant studies. London: Frank Cass.

LAHIFF, E. (2003) *Land reform and sustainable livelihoods in South Africa's Eastern Cape province, Sustainable Livelihoods in Southern Africa Programme - Research Paper Series*, Brighton: Institute of Development Studies, pp. 57.

LAKER, M.C. (ed.), (1975) *The agricultural potential of the Ciskei. A preliminary report*, Alice: University of Fort Hare.

LAKER, M.C. (2004) Advances in soil erosion, soil conservation, land suitability evaluation and land use planning research in South Africa, 1978-2003, *South African Journal of Plant and Soil*, 21(5): 345-368.

LAKER, M.C. (2004) *Development of a general strategy for optimizing the efficient use of primary water resources for effective alleviation of rural poverty*, Pretoria: Water Research Commission.

LAMPHEAR, J. and T. FALOLA (1995) Aspects of early African history, in Martin, P. and P. O'Meara (eds.), *Africa. 3rd edn.*, Bloomington: Indiana University Press, pp. 73-96.

LATOUR, B. (1983) 'give me a laboratory and i will raise the world', in Knorr-Cetina, K. and M. Mulkay (eds.), *Science observed: Perspectives on the social study of science*, London: Sage Publications Ltd., pp. 141-170.

LEACH, M. and R. MEARNS (1996) *The lie of the land: Challenging received wisdom on the African environment,* Oxford: James Currey.

LEACH, M., R. MEARNS and I. SCOONES (1997) Institutions, consensus and conflict, implications for policy and practice, *IDS Bulletin*, 28(4): 95-99.

LEACH, M., R. MEARNS and I. SCOONES (1999) Environmental entitlements: Dynamics and institutions in community-based natural resource management, *World Development*, 27(2): 225.

LEATT, A. (2006) *Grants for children: A brief look at the eligibility and take-up of the child support grant and other cash grants*, Cape Town: Children's Institute, University of Cape Town.

LEESON, S. and J.D. SUMMERS (1997) *Commercial poultry nutrition,* Second edn. Guelph: University Books.

LEESON, S. and J.D. SUMMERS (2001) *Nutrition of the chicken,* Fourth edn. Guelph: University Books.

LEIBRAND, M. and F. SPERBER (1997) Income and economic welfare, in De Wet, C. and M. Whisson (eds.), *From reserve to region: Apartheid and social change in the Keiskammahoek District of (former) Ciskei: 1950-1990,* Grahamstown: Occasional Paper 35, Institute of Social and Economic Research, Rhodes University, pp. 111-152.

LEKASI, J.K., J.C. TANNER, S.K. KIMANI and P.J.C. HARRIS (2002) Manure management strategies to enhance fertilizer quantity and quality on smallholdings in the central Kenya highlands, *Biological Agriculture and Horticulture* 19: 315-332.

LEKASI, J.K., J.C. TANNER, S.K. KIMANI and P.J.C. HARRIS (2003) Cattle manure quality in Maragua District, central Kenya: Effect of management practices and development of simple methods of assessment, *Agriculture, Ecosystems and Environment,* 94: 289-298.

LENT, P.C. (2000) *Guquka and Koloni: Setting the stage,* in E. van Ranst, H. Verplancke, W. van Averbeke, A. Verdoodt and J. Bonroy (eds.), *Rural livelihoods in the central Eastern Cape, South Africa: extended abstracts of an International Workshop,* Ghent, Belgium. The Laboratory of Soil Science, University of Ghent, pp. 15-22.

LENT, P. and P. HEBINCK (2006) *Growing, grazing and gathering: The uses of arable allotments in two Eastern Cape villages,* in Shackleton, S.E. (ed.), *SANPAD seminar 'Links Between Natural Resources, Livelihoods and poverty Alleviation,* Grahamstown, pp. 12.

LEWIS, J. (1984) The rise and fall of the South African peasantry: A critique and reassessment, *Journal of Southern African Studies,* 11(1): 1-24.

LEWIS, C.A. (1996) *The geomorphology of the Eastern Cape, South Africa,* Grahamstown: Grocott and Sherry.

LIPTON, M., F. ELLIS and M. LIPTON (1996a) *Land, labour and livelihoods in rural South Africa, vol. 2: Kwazulu-Natal and Northern Province,* Durban. Indicator Press, University of Natal.

LIPTON, M., M. DE KLERK and F. ELLIS (eds.) (1996b) *Land, labour and livelihoods in rural South Africa. Vol. I western cape province,* Durban: Indicator Press.

LO PRESTI, C. (1996a) *The use of rain-fed arable land allocations at four locations in the central Eastern Cape,* BSc (Hons.) Thesis, Coventry University.

LO PRESTI, C. (1996b) Arable land use, *ARDRINEWS,* June: 12-15.

LONG, N. (1977) *An introduction to the sociology of rural development,* London: Tavistock Publications.

LONG, N. (2001) *Development sociology: Actor perspectives,* London: Routledge.

LOW, A.B. and A.G. REBELO (1998) *Vegetation of South Africa, Lesotho and Swaziland,* Pretoria: Department of Environmental Affairs and Tourism.

LUND, C. (2002) Negotiating property institutions: On the symbiosis of property and authority in Africa, in Juul, K. and C. Lund (eds.), *Negotiating property in Africa,* Portsmouth NH: Heinemann, pp. 11-43.

MACHOBANE, J.J. and R. BEROLD (2003) *Drive out hunger,* Bellevue: Jacana.

MACLENNAN, B. (1986) *A proper degree of terror: John graham and the cape's eastern frontier,* Johannesburg: Ravan Press.

MADUBANSI, M. and C.M. SHACKLETON (2006) Changing energy profiles and consumption patterns following electrification in five rural villages, South Africa, *Energy Policy*, 32(18): 4081-4092.

MADUBEDUB, M. (1990) *An analysis of peasant farming activities in the Tyume basin, the case of Auckland, Kwanothenga and Binfield*, BA Honours thesis, Faculty of Agriculture, University of Fort Hare.

MAFU, V.J. (1998) Small scale pig production in Eastern Cape communities, *ARDRINEWS*, (5-6): 12-14.

MAFU, J.V. and P.J. MASIKA (2002) Milk production from local goats - Is it a viable option?, *ARDRINEWS*, (July & December): 6-8.

MAGADLELA, D. and P. HEBINCK (1995) Dry fields and spirits in trees - A social analysis of development intervention in Nyamaropa communal area, Zimbabwe, *Zambezia*, 22(1): 44-63.

MAGAGULA, H.B. (1999) *Physical and chemical properties of soils in relation to environmental degradation un the Tyume catchment*, MSc thesis, Faculty of Agriculture, Department of Soil Science, Alice: University of Fort Hare.

MAGER, A. (1992) The people get fenced: Gender, rehabilitation and African nationalism in the Ciskei and border region, 1945-1955, *Journal of Southern African Studies*, 18: 761-782.

MAGER, A. (1999) *Gender and the making of a South African Bantustan. A social history of the Ciskei, 1945-1959,* Portsmouth/Oxford/Cape Town: Heinemann,/James Currey/David Philip.

MAKHURA, M.T., F.M. GOODE and G.K. COETZEE (1998) A cluster analysis of commercialisation of farmers in developing rural areas of South Africa, *Development Southern Africa*, 15(3): 429-448.

MANDIRINGANA, O.T., P.N.S. MNKENI and Z. MKILE (2001) *The fertility status of cultivated soils in the Eastern Cape, the Joint Congress of the SASCP, SAWSS, and SSSSA*, Pretoria, Sanlam Conference Centre, University of Pretoria, pp. 149-150.

MANDIRINGANA, O.T., P. MNKENI, M. E., W. VAN AVERBEKE, E. VAN RANST and H. VERPLANCKE (2005) Mineralogy and fertility status of selected soils of the Eastern Cape province, South Africa, *Communications in Soil Science and Plant Analysis*, 36: 2431-2446.

MANGO, N. (2002) *Husbanding the land. Agrarian development and socio-technical change in luoland, Kenya*, PhD Thesis, Rural Development Sociology, Wageningen: Wageningen University.

MANGO, N. and P. HEBINCK (2004) Cultural repertoires and socio-technological regimes: A case study of local and modern varieties of maize in Luoland, west Kenya, in Wiskerke, H. and J.D. van der Ploeg (eds.), *Seeds of transition. Essays on novelty production, niches and regimes in agriculture*, Assen: Royal Van Gorcum, pp. 285-319.

MANONA, C. (1997) The collapse of the 'tribal authority' system and the rise of civic associations, in De Wet, C. and M. Whisson (eds.), *From reserve to region. Apartheid and social change in the keikammahoek District of (former) Ciskei: 1950-1990*, Grahamstown: Institute of Social and Economic Research, Rhodes University, Occasional Paper no. 35, pp. 49-68.

MANONA, C. (1998) The decline in the significance of agriculture in a former Ciskei community: A case study, in De Bruyn, T.D. and P.F. Scogings (eds.), *Communal rangelands in southern Africa, a synthesis of knowledge*, Alice: Department of Livestock and Pasture Science, University of Fort Hare, pp. 113-118.

MANONA, C. (1999) *De-agrarianisation and the urbanisation of a rural economy: Agrarian patterns in Melani village in the Eastern Cape*, Leiden: African Studies Centre.

MANONA, S. (2005) *Land leasing initiatives in or Tambo District; Principles, approaches and guidelines for participatory revitalisation of smallholder irrigation schemes project workshop*, ESKOM Convention Centre, Midrand.

MARAIS, J.S. (1959) The imposition and nature of European control, in Schapera, I. (ed.), *The bantu-speaking tribes of South Africa: An ethnographical survey*, London: Routledge & Kegan Paul, pp. 333-355.

MARAIS, J.N. (1975) The climate of the Ciskei, in Laker, M.C. (ed.), *The agricultural potential of the Ciskei: A preliminary report,* Alice: Faculty of Agriculture. University of Fort Hare, pp. 18-41.

MARAIS, J.N. (1985) Weed competition in maize with reference to peasant farming, *Fort Hare Papers*, 8(1): 63-82.

MARAIS, G. (1994) *Hogsback plantation: Environmental management plan (phase one)*, Pretoria: SAFCOL.

MARCUS, T. (1989) *Modernising super-exploitation. Restructuring South African agriculture,* London: Zed Press.

MAREE, J. and J.P. DE VOS (1975) *Underemployment, poverty and migrant labour in the Transkei and Ciskei,* Johannesburg: South African Institute for Race Relations.

MARSDEN, T. (1998) Agriculture beyond the treadmill? Issues for policy, theory and research practice, *Progress in Human Geography*, 22(2): 265-275.

MARX, K. (1975) *Das kapital,* Berlin: Dietz Verlag.

MASIKA, P.J. and M.A. MAGADLELA (2001) Update on the re-introduction of indigenous livestock project: Nguni cattle, *ARDRINEWS*, (July & December): 7-8.

MAUD, R. (1996) The macro-geomorphology of the Eastern Cape, in Colin, A. (ed.), *The geomorphology of the Eastern Cape, South Africa*, Grahamstown: Grocott & Sherry, pp. 1-18.

MAY, J. (1996) Assets, income and livelihoods in rural kwazulu-natal, in Lipton, M., F. Ellis and M. Lipton (eds.), *Land, labour and livelihoods in rural South Africa, vol. 2: Kwazulu-Natal and Northern Province*, Durban: Indicator Press, University of Natal, pp. 1-30.

MAY, J. (2000) The structure and composition of rural poverty and livelihoods in South Africa, in Cousins, B. (ed.), *At the crossroads- land and agrarian reform in South Africa into the 21st century*, Cape Town Programme for Land and Agrarian Studies.

MAYER, P. and I. MAYER (1961) *Townsmen and tribesmen: Conservatism and the process of urbanization in a South African city,* Cape Town: Oxford University Press.

MAYER, P. (1980) The origin and decline of two rural resistance ideologies, in Mayer, P. (ed.), *Black villagers in an industrial society*, Cape Town: Oxford University Press, pp. 1-81.

MBONGWA, M., R. VAN DEN BRINK and J. VAN ZYL (1996) Evolution of the agrarian structure in South Africa, in Van Zyl. J.K.J. and H. Binswanger (eds.), *Agricultural land reform in South Africa: Policies, markets and mechanisms*, Oxford: Oxford University Press.

MBUTI, M.C. and J.C. BENNETT (1999) *The ownership and utilisation of arable land allocations in two communal areas of the central Eastern Cape, South Africa: Preliminary findings - poster presentation, VI International Rangeland Congress,* Townsville, Queensland.

MBUTI, M. (2000a) *Crop production in arable land allocation in two villages of the central Eastern Cape, ARDRI Annual Report 2000,* Alice: Agricultural and Rural Development Research Institute, University of Fort Hare.

MBUTI, M.C. (2000b) *Crop production systems,* in Van Ranst, E., H. Verplancke, W. van Averbeke, A. Verdoodt and J. Bonroy (Eds.), *Rural livelihoods in the central Eastern Cape, South Africa: Extended abstracts of an International Workshop,* The Laboratory of Soil Science, University of Ghent, Ghent, Belgium, pp. 36-38.

MCALLISTER, P. (1980) Work, homestead and the shades: The ritual interpretation of labour migration among the Gcaleka, in Mayer, P. (ed.), *Black villagers in an industrial society,* Cape Town: Oxford University Press, pp. 205-255.

MCALLISTER, P. (1988) The impact of relocation in a Transkei betterment area, in Cross, C. and R. Haines (eds.), *Towards freehold? Options for land and development in South Africa's black rural areas,* Kenwyn: Juta & Co., pp. 112-121.

MCALLISTER, P. (1989) Resistance to 'betterment' in the Transkei: A case study from willowvale District, *Journal of Southern African Studies,* 15: 346-368

MCALLISTER, P. (2001) *Building the homestead. Agriculture, labour and beer in South Africa's Transkei,* Leiden: African Studies Centre.

MCGREGOR, J. (2005) Landscape, politics and the historical geography of southern Africa, *Journal of Historical Geography,* 31(2): 205-372.

MEARS, R. (2004) *Historical perspective of migration and urbanisation in Whittlesea, Eastern Cape province revisited, Biennial Conference of the Economic Society of South Africa,* Research Paper No. 0403, Somerset West, Lord Charles Hotel.

MEISSNER, H.H., P.J.K. ZACHARIAS and P.J. O'REAGAIN (1999) Forage quality, in Tainton, N.M. (ed.), *Veld management in South Africa,* Pietermaritzburg: University of Natal Press, pp. 139-168.

MENDRAS, H. (1970) *The vanishing peasant : Innovation and change in french agriculture,* Cambridge (Mass.): MIT Press.

MENTANI, P.S. (2001) *The impact of garden plots on household food security in rural areas of alice,* B.Sc. Honours Thesis, Department of Agricultural economics, extension and rural development, Alice: University of Fort Hare.

MILLS, M. and W. WILSON (1952) *Land tenure. Keiskammahoek rural survey. Vol. 4,* Pietermaritzburg: Shuter and Shooter.

MILLS, A.J. and M.V. FEY (2003) Declining soil quality in South Africa: Effects of land use on soil organic matter and surface crusting, *South African Journal of Science,* 99(September/October): 429-437.

MINKLEY, G. (1992) Class and culture in the workplace: East London, industrialisation and the conflict over work, 1945-1957, *Journal of Southern African Studies,* 18(4): 739-761.

MINSON, D.J. (1982) Effects of chemical and physical composition of herbage eaten upon intake, in Hacker, J.B. (ed.), *Nutritional limits to animal production from pastures,* Farnham Royal: Commonwealth Agricultural Bureaux, pp. 153-166.

MKILE, Z., W. VAN AVERBEKE, O.T. MANDIRINGANA and P.N.S. MNKENI (2001) *Nutrient supply practices by African farmers in the Transkei region of South*

*Africa, The Joint Congress 2001 of the SASCP, SAWSS, and SSSSA*, Pretoria, Sanlam Conference Centre, University of Pretoria, pp. 307-308.

MKILE, Z. (2001) *The use and agronomic effectiveness of kraal manures in the Transkei region of the Eastern Cape, South Africa*, M.Sc. Thesis, Faculty of Agriculture, Alice: University of Fort Hare.

MOHAMED, S.S. and W. VAN AVERBEKE (2006) *Livelihood and farming at dzindi irrigation scheme*, Pretoria: Water Research Commission, pp. 278.

MONDE, N. (2000) *Home-gardens*, in E. van Ranst, H. Verplancke, W. van Averbeke, A. Verdoodt and J. Bonroy (Eds.), *Rural livelihoods in the central Eastern Cape, South Africa: extended abstracts of an International Workshop*, Ghent, Belgium. The Laboratory of Soil Science, University of Ghent, pp. 43-45.

MONDE, N. (2003) *Household food security in rural areas of central Eastern Cape: The case of Guquka in Victoria East and Koloni in Middledrift Districts.*, Alice: University of Fort Hare. Department of Agricultural Economics. PhD Thesis.

MONDE, N. (2005a) *Home gardening*, Alice: University of Fort Hare. Unpublished report.

MONDE, N. (2005b) *Case study report: Updates*, Alice: University of Fort Hare. Faculty of Agriculture. Unpublished report, pp. 35.

MOORE, D. (2005) *Suffering for territory: Race, place, and power in Zimbabwe*, Durham NC: Duke University Press.

MORROW, S. and N. VOKWANA (2001) Shaping in dull, dead earth their dreams of riches and beauty: Clay modelling at E-hala and Hogsback in the Eastern Cape, South Africa, *Journal of Southern African Studies*, 27: 137-161.

MORROW, S. (2006) Fort hare in its local context: A historical view., in Nkomo, M., D. Swartz and B. Maja (eds.), *Within the realm of possibility*, Cape Town: HSRC Press 2006, pp. 85-104.

MOSTERT, N. (1992) *Frontiers. The epic of South Africa's creation and the tragedy of the Xhosa people*, London: Pimlico.

MOUNTAIN, E.D. (1952) *The natural history of the Keiskammahoek District. Keiskammahoek rural survey*, Pietermaritzburg: Shuter and Shooter.

MOYO, S. (2007) The land question in southern Africa: A comparative view, in Ntsebeza, L. and R. Hall (eds.), *The land question in South Africa. The challenge of transformation and redistribution*, Cape Town: Human Sciences Research Council, pp. 60-87.

MTUZE, P.T. (2004) *Introduction to Xhosa culture*, Alice: Lovedale Press.

MULULUMA, M.G. and P.J. MASIKA (2000) Ethnoveterinary knowledge and practices in three resource limited farming communities of Eastern Cape Province, *ARDRINEWS*, (July & December): 13-14.

MUPAKATI, G. (2005) *A spatio-temporal study of land degradation and land use/land cover trends in the upper Tyume catchment using remote sensing and geographic information systems*, M.Sc. Thesis, Department of Geography and Environmental Sciences, Alice: University of Fort Hare.

MURRAY, G. (1952) The soils of the Keiskammahoek District., in Mountain, E.D. (ed.), *The natural history of the Keiskammahoek District. Keiskammahoek rural survey*, Pietermaritzburg: Shuter and Shooter, pp. 30-41.

MURRAY, C. (1998) *Changing livelihoods: The free state, 1990s*, Multiple livelihoods and social change working paper series, *4*, Manchester: Institute for Development Policy and Management, University of Manchester.

MURRAY, C. (2001) Livelihoods research: Some conceptual and methodological issues, paper given at Development Studies Association Annual Conference 'Different Poverties, Different Policies', University of Manchester, 10-12 September.

MURRAY, C. (2002) Livelihoods research: Transcending boundaries of time and space, *Journal of Southern African Studies. Special Issue: Changing Livelihoods*, 28(3): 489-509.

NATURE CONSERVANCY, Http://www.Nature.Org/ accessed 18/06/05, (updated 18/06/05).

NDLOVU, T.S. (1991) *Progress in the midst of diversity: A case of two betterment areas in the Ciskei*, B.A. Honours Thesis, Faculty of Social Sciences, Johannesberg: University of the Witwatersrand. .

NETTING, R.M. (1993) *Smallholders, householders: Farm families and the ecology of intensive, sustainable agriculture*, Stanford CA: Stanford University Press.

NGWADLA, X. and A. THYS (2000a) *Improving nutrient cycling in communal farming systems in central Eastern Cape*, *ARDRI Annual Report 2000*, Alice: Agricultural and Rural Development Research Institute, University of Fort Hare.

NGWADLA, X.J. and A. THYS (2000b) *Nutrient supply in crop production*, in Van Ranst, E., H. Verplancke, W. van Averbeke, A. Verdoodt and J. Bonroy (eds.), *Rural livelihoods in the central Eastern Cape, South Africa: Extended abstracts of an International Workshop*, Ghent, Belgium. The Laboratory of Soil Science, University of Ghent, pp. 45-48.

NGWANE, Z. (2001) "Real men reawaken their fathers' homesteads, the educated leave them in ruins": The politics of domestic reproduction in post-apartheid rural South Africa, *Journal of Religion in Africa*, 31(4): 402-426.

NGWANE, Z. (2003) 'Christmas time' and the struggles for the household in the countryside: Rethinking the cultural geography of migrant labour in South Africa, *Journal of Southern African Studies*, 29(3): 681-699.

NORGAARD, R. (1994) *Development betrayed: The end of progress and a co-evolutionary revisioning of the future*, London: Routledge.

NORTH, O. (1990) *Institutions, institutional change and economic performance*, Cambridge: Cambridge University Press.

NTSEBEZA, L. (2002) Cattle production in Xhalanga District, in Ainslie, A. (ed.), *Cattle ownership and production in the communal areas of the Eastern Cape, South Africa*, Belville: Research Report No. 10. Programme for Land and Agrarian Studies, University of the Western Cape, pp. 46-58.

NTSHONA, Z. and S. TURNER (2002) *The social and economic structure of livestock production systems in Maluti District* in Ainslie, A. (Ed.), *Cattle ownership and production in the communal areas of the Eastern Cape, South Africa*, Belville, Cape Town: Programme for Land and Agrarian Studies, University of the Western Cape, pp. 80-97.

NYERGES, A.E. (1996) Ethnography in the reconstruction of African land use histories: A Sierra Leone example, *Africa*, 661(1): 122-144.

O'CONNEL, M. (1980) Xesibe, reds rascals and gentlemen at home and at work, in Mayer, P. (ed.), *Black villagers in an industrial society*, Cape Town: Oxford University Press, pp. 255-303.

O'LAUGHLIN, B. (2002) Proletarianisation, agency and changing rural livelihoods: Forced labour and resistance in colonial Mozambique, *Journal of Southern African Studies*, 28(3, Special Issue: Changing Livelihoods): 511-530.

OLIVER, M.D. and D.D. MALAN (1998) Complete replacement of fishmeal with soya bean oil cake meal in broiler diets and its effect on production parameters, *Poultry Bulletin*, (August): 379-398.

OOMEN, B. (2005) *Chiefs in South Africa*, London: James Currey.

OSTROM, E. (1987) Institutional arrangements for resolving the commons dilemma. Some contending approaches, in McCay, B.M. and J.M. Acheson (eds.), *The question of the commons: The culture and ecology of communal resources*, Tucson: University of Arizona Press, pp. 250-265.

OSTROM, E. (1990) *Governing the commons: The evolution of institutions of collective action*, Cambridge: Cambridge University Press.

OSTROM, E. (2004) Understanding collective action, in Meinzen-Dick, R.S. and M.D. Gregorio (eds.), *Collective action and property rights for sustainable development*, 2, Washington DC: IFPRI.

OWEN-SMITH, N. (1982) Factors influencing the consumption of plant products by large herbivores, in Huntley, B.J. and B.H. Walker (eds.), *Ecology of tropical savannas*, Berlin-Heidelberg359-404.

PALMER, R. and N. PARSONS (eds.) (1977) *The roots of rural poverty in central and southern Africa*, London: Heinemann.

PARKER, W., U. KISTNER, S. GELB, K. KELLY and M. O'DONOVAN (2000) *Economic impact of HIV/AIDS on South Africa and its implications for governance: A literature review*: Joint Centre for Political and Economic Studies.

PARSONS, N. (1982) *A new history of southern Africa*, London: Macmillan Publishers.

PEACH, W. and J. CONSTATIN (1972) Meaning and nature of resources, in Peach, W. and J. Constatin (eds.), *Zimmerman's world resources and industries*, New Ork: Harper and Row.

PEIRES, J.B. (1981) *The house of Phalo: A history of the Xhosa people in the days of their independence* Johannesburg: Ravan Press.

PEIRES, J.B. (1989) *The dead will arise: Nongqawuse and the great Xhosa cattle-killing movement of 1856-7*, Johannesburg: Raven Press.

PERRET, S. and L. L'HOPITALLIER (2000) *Institutional analysis of public investment in rural areas. A case study in the Amatola District of the Eastern Cape province (South Africa), World Bank Work Paper*, Pretoria: University of Pretoria.

PHILLIPS-HOWARD, K. and C. OCHE (1996) Local farming in the former Transkei, South Africa, in Reij, C., I. Scoones and C. Toulmin (eds.), *Sustaining the soil. Indigenous soil and water conservation in Africa*, London: Earthscan, pp. 181-190.

PHILLIPSON, P.B. (1987) A checklist of vascular plants of the Amatola mountains, Eastern Cape Province/Ciskei, *Bothalia*, 17: 237-256.

PLACE, F., M. ADATO and P. HEBINCK (2007) Understanding rural poverty and investment in agriculture: An assessment of integrated quantitative and qualitative research in western Kenya, *World Development*, 35(2): 312-325.

POTEETE, A. and E. OSTROM (2004) Heterogeneity, group size and collective action: The role of institutions in forest management, *Development and Change*, 35: 435-461.

POTTIER, J. (ed.), (1993) *Practising development: Social science perspectives*, London: Routledge.

POTTIER, J. and A. BICKER (eds.) (2003) *Negotiating local knowledge: Power and identity in development,* London: Pluto Press.

RANGER, T. (1978) Growing from the roots: Reflections on peasant research in central and southern Africa, *Journal of Southern African Studies,* 5(1): 99-133.

RAUTENBACH, I.M. and E.F.J. MALHERBE (1998) *What does the constitution say,* Pretoria: JL Van Schaik Academic.

REARDON, T. (1997) Using evidence of household income diversification to inform study of the non-farm labor market in Africa, *World Development,* 25: 735-747.

RICHARDS, P. (1983) Ecological change and the politics of African land use, *African Studies Review,* 26(2): 1-73.

RICHARDS, P. (1985) *Indigenous agricultural revolution,* Boulder: Westview Press.

ROBBINS, P. (2001) Fixed categories in a portable landscape: The causes and consequences of land-cover categorisation, *Environment and Planning A,* 33: 161-179.

ROBERTS, V.G., S. ADEY, and A.D. MANSON (2003) An investigation into soil fertility in two resource-poor farming communities in Kwazulu-Natal (South Africa), *South African Journal of Plant & Soil,* 20(3): 146-151.

ROEP, D. (2001) *Vernieuwend werken. Sporen van vermogen en onvermogen,* PhD Thesis, Rural Sociology, Wageningen: Wageningen University.

ROSENBERG, S. (2003) *'Modernity beyond survival': A case study. The social, cultural and economic significance of non-cultivated natural resources in Guquka village, Tyume basin, Eastern Cape,* Grahamstown: Rhodes University. Department of Anthropology BA Hon. Thesis

SABC NEWS (2004) Teenage pregnancies on the increase amid child grants. 17 Nov, www.Sabcnews.Co.Za/south_africa/general/0,2172,92251,00.Html#

SABC NEWS (2007) Pregnancy guidelines on the cards for SA schools. March 07. www.Sabcnews.Co.Za/south_africa/education/0,2172,144971,00.Html.

SABC NEWS(2007) Lekota slams teenage grant-motivated pregnancy. March 11. //www.Sabcnews.Co.Za/south_africa/education/0,2172,145198,00.Html.

SAGNER, A. (2000) Ageing and social policy in South Africa: Historical perspectives with particular reference to the Eastern Cape, *Journal of Southern African Studies,* 26(3): 523-553.

SAPIRE, H. and J. BEALL (1995) Introduction: Urban change and urban studies in South Africa, *Journal of Southern African Studies,* 21(1): 3-18.

SCHAPERA, I. (ed.), (1937) *The Bantu-speaking tribes of South Africa. An ethnographical survey,* London: Routledge & Kegan Paul.

SCHAPERA, I. and A. GOODWIN (1937) Work and wealth, in Schapera, I. (ed.), *The Bantu-speaking tribes of South Africa. An ethnographical survey.,* London: Routledge & Kegan Paul, pp. 131-173.

SCHWÄR, J.F. and B.E. PAPE (1958) *Germans in Kaffraria: 1858-1958,* Pinetown: Robprint.

SCOGINGS, P.F., A.C. BECKERLING, and W.S.W. TROLLOPE (1994) Simplified techniques for assessing range condition for livestock production: An example from Ciskei, *Development Southern Africa,* 11: 229-240.

SCOGINGS, P.F., R. BALLY and P.C. LENT (2000) Evidence for environmental degradation under current natural resource management, in Lent, P.C., P.F. Scogings and W. van Averbeke (eds.), *Natural resource management and policy in the*

*Eastern Cape province, South Africa: An overview*, Alice: ARDRI Report 1/2000. University of Fort Hare, pp. 37-40.

SCOONES, I. and J. THOMPSON (eds.) (1994) *Beyond farmer first. Rural people's knowledge, agricultural research and extension practice*, London: Intermediate Technology Publications.

SCOONES, I. (1998) *Sustainable rural livelihoods: A framework for analysis. Working paper no. 72* Sussex: Institute of Development Studies, University of Sussex.

SCOONES, I. (1999) New ecology and the social sciences: What prospects for a fruitful engagement?, *Annual Review of Anthropology*, 28: 479-507.

SCOONES, I. and W. WOLMER (2003a) Part 1: Contexts and debates 1. Introduction: Livelihoods in crisis. Challenges for rural development in southern Africa, *IDS Bulletin*, 34(3): 1-14.

SCOONES, I. and W. WOLMER (2003b) 9. Endpiece: The politics of livelihoods opportunity, *IDS Bulletin*, 34(3): 112-115.

SCOTT, J.C. (1985) *Weapons of the weak : Everyday forms of peasant resistance*, New Haven: Yale University Press.

SCOTT, J.C. (1998) *Seeing like a state : How certain schemes to improve the human condition have failed*, New Haven: Yale University Press.

SEEKINGS, J. and N. NATTRASS (2006) *Class, race and inequality in South Africa*, Pietermaritzburg: University of KwaZulu-Natal Press, pp. 446.

SEN, A. (1984) *Resources, values and development*, Oxford: Basil Blackwell.

SHACKLETON, C.M. (1998) Examining the basis for perceptions of communal land degradation: Lessons from the central low veld, in De Bruyn, T.D. and P.F. Scogings (eds.), *Communal rangelands in southern Africa: A synthesis of knowledge*, Alice: Department of Livestock & Pasture Science, University of Fort Hare, pp. 196-210.

SHACKLETON, S.E., C.M. SHACKLETON and B. COUSINS (1999) The economic value of land and natural resources to rural livelihoods, paper given at Land and Agrarian Reform Conference, Pretoria, 26-28 July 1999.

SHACKLETON, C.M., S.E. SHACKLETON and B. COUSINS (2001) The role of land-based strategies in rural livelihoods: The contribution of arable production, animal husbandry and natural resource harvesting in communal areas of South Africa, *Development Southern Africa*, 18: 583-604.

SHACKLETON, C.M., S.E. SHACKLETON, M. NTSUHUDU, and J. NTZEBEZA (2002) The role and value of savanna non-timber forest products to rural households in the Kat River valley, South Africa, *Journal of Tropical Forest Products*, 8: 45-65.

SHACKLETON, C.M., S.E. SHACKLETON, T.R. NETSHILUVHI and F.R. MATHABELA (2005) The contribution and direct-use value of livestock to rural livelihoods in the Sand River catchment, South Africa, *African Journal of Range & Forage Science*, 22: 127-140.

SHARP, J. and A. SPIEGEL (1990) Women and wages: Gender and the control of income in farm and Bantustan households, *Journal of Southern African Studies*, 16(3): 527-549.

SIBANDA, S.M.D. (2004) Principles underpinning the communal land rights bill: Implications for legally secure tenure or comparable redress and agrarian reform in a constitutional and democratic South Africa, in Roth, M., V. Nxasana, S. Sibanda and T. Yates (eds.), *National land tenure conference: Finding solutions, securing rights*, Durban: Lexis Nexis Butterworth, pp. 156-184.

SILWANA, T. (2000) *The performance of maize/bean and maize/pumpkin intercrops under different planting combinations and weeding in Transkei, South Africa,* M.Sc. Thesis, Faculty of Agricultures, Alice: University of Fort Hare.

SIMKINS, C. (1981) Agricultural production in the African reserves of South Africa, 1918-1969, *Journal of Southern African Studies,* 7(2): 256-283.

SLATER, R. (2002) Differentiation and diversification: Changing livelihoods in Qwaqwa, South Africa, 1970-2000, *Journal of Southern African Studies,* 28(3, Special Issue: Changing Livelihoods): 599-614.

SLICHER VAN BATH, B. (1963) *The agrarian history of western Europe, A.D. 500 - 1850,* London: [s.n.], pp. 364.

SMITH, L. (2000a) *Field notes,* Alice: ARDRI, University of Fort Hare. Unpublished report.

SMITH, L. (2000b) *Rural livelihood case studies,* in Van Ranst, E., H. Verplancke, W. van Averbeke, A. Verdoodt and J. Bonroy (Eds.), *Rural livelihoods in the central Eastern Cape, South Africa: extended abstracts of an International Workshop,* Ghent, Belgium. The Laboratory of Soil Science, University of Ghent, pp. 33-38.

SOGA, J.H. (1931) *The ama-Xosa: Life and customs,* Alice: Lovedale Press.

SOIL CLASSIFICATION WORKING GROUP (1991) *Soil classification: A taxonomic system for South Africa,* Pretoria: Department for Agricultural Development.

SONANDI, A. (1997) *Site selection in Middledrift, Peddie, Victoria East, and Seymour Districts - report to ARDRI,* Alice: ARDRI, University of Fort Hare, pp. 11.

SPERBER, F.C. (1993) Income patterns in Keiskammahoek, in De Wet, C. (ed.), *From reserve to region - apartheid and change in the Keiskammahoek District of Ciskei, 1950 to 1990,* Grahamstown: Report to the Chairman's Fund Educational Trust, the Human Science Research Council, and Johannesburg Consolidated Investments, Ltd. Rhodes University, pp. 56-101.

STAPLETON, T.J. (1996) The expansion of a pseudo-ethnicity in the Eastern Cape: Reconsidering the fingo "Exodus" Of 1865, *The International Journal of African Historical Studies,* 29(2): 233-250.

STEYN, G. (1982) *Livestock production in the Amatola basin,* M.Sc Agric. Thesis, Faculty of Agriculture, Alice: University of Fort Hare.

STEYN, G. (1988) *A farming systems study of two rural areas in the Peddie District of Ciskei,* D.Sc. Thesis, Faculty of Agriculture, Alice: University of Fort Hare.

STORY, R. (1952) A botanical survey of the Keiskamma District, in Mountain, E. (ed.), *Natural history of the Keiskammahoek District, Botanical Survey Mem. no. 27,* Pretoria, South Africa: Shuter and Shooter- Dept. of Agriculture.

STUART, J. and D.M. MALCOLM (eds.) (1986) *The diary of Henry Francis Fynn,* Pietermaritzburg: Shuter and Shooter.

SWITZER, L. (1993) *Power and resistance in an African society. The Ciskei Xhosa and the making of South Africa,* Pietermaritzburg: University of Natal Press.

TAINTON, N.M. (1999) The ecology of the main grazing lands of South Africa, in Tainton, N.M. (ed.), *Veld management in South Africa,* Pietermaritzburg: University of Natal Press, pp. 23-53.

TAPSON, D. and C.J. ROSE (1984) *An investigation into the KwaZulu cattle industry,* Alice: ARDRI, University of Fort Hare.

TAPSON, D.R. (1993) Biological sustainability in pastoral systems: The KwaZulu case, in Behnke, R.J., I. Scoones and C. Kerven (eds.), *Range ecology at disequilibrium,* London: Overseas Development Institute, pp. 118-135.

THOMPSON, L. (1990) *A history of South Africa,* Sandton: Radix.

THOMSON, D.N. and M.C. LYNE (1995) Is tenure secure in communal areas? Some empirical evidence from Kwazulu-Natal, *Agrekon* 34(4): 178-182.

THYS, A. (1999) *Effect of land use and soil type on the chemical soil fertility in Guquka,*, Faculty of Agriculture, Ghent, Belgium: Hoge School Ghent.

TICKIN, T. (2004) The ecological implications of harvesting non-timber forest products, *Journal of Applied Ecology*, 41: 11-21.

TIMMERMANS, H. (2004) *Rural livelihoods at Dwesa/Cwebe: Poverty, development and natural resource use on the wild coast, South Africa*, Grahamstown: Grahamstown: Rhodes University. Environmental Sciences. M.Sc. Thesis.

TOLEDO, V.M. (1990) The ecological rationality of peasant production, in Altieri, M. and S. Hecht (eds.), *Agroecology and small farm development*, Boca Raton: CRC Press, pp. 53-61.

TOMLINSON COMMISION (1955) *Summary of the report of the commission for the socio-economic development of the Bantu areas within the union of South Africa*: Pretoria The Government Printer.

TORRES, M. (Forthcoming 2007) *Access rights to useful wild plants in Eastern Cape Province, South Africa*, Wageningen: Wageningen University. Department of Environmental Sciences. M.Sc. Thesis.

TOULMIN, C., R. LEONARD, K. BROCK, N. COULBALY and G. CARSWELL (2000.) *Diversification of livelihoods: Evidence from Mali and Ethiopia*, Sussex: Institute of Development Studies. University of Susses. IDS Research Report 47.

TOWNSEND, C.R., J.L. HARPER and M. BEGON (2000) *Essentials of ecology,* London: Blackwell.

TRANSKEI LAND REFORM RESEARCH GROUP (1995) *Overview of the Transkei sub-region of the Eastern Cape Province* Report to the Land & Agricultural Policy Centre, Johannesburg: Land and Agricultural Policy Centre.

TROLLOPE, W.S.W. and P.G.F. COETZEE (1975) Vegetation and veld management, in Laker, M.C. (ed.), *The agricultural potential of the Ciskei: A preliminary report* Alice: University of Fort Hare, pp. 71-124.

TROLLOPE, W.S.W. (1985) Third world challenges for pasture scientists in southern Africa, *Journal Grassland Society of Southern Africa*, 2(1): 14-17.

UPHOFF, N. (1986) *Local institutional development: An analytical source book with cases,* Hartford Connecticut: Kumarian Press.

VAN AVERBEKE, W. (1989) Adapting plant density in maize to the expected water supply as a strategy to reduce risk, *Ciskei Journal of Rural Development* 11: 12-17.

VAN AVERBEKE, W. (1997) *ARDRIs farming systems research programme (incomplete preliminary report).*

VAN AVERBEKE, W. (1999) *Farmer priorities in small-scale agriculture in the Eastern Cape: A researcher's perspective*, in Pearson, A., S. Whyte, B. Joubert, D. O'Neill and T. Simalenga (eds.), *Management and feeding of animals for work*, Alice, Fort Hare University: Centre for Tropical Veterinary Medicine, Draught Animal Power Technical Report 4/1999, Department for International Development, pp. 137-142.

VAN AVERBEKE, W. (2000) *Governance and institutions*, in Van Ranst, E., H. Verplancke, W. van Averbeke, A. Verdoodt and J. Bonroy (Eds.), *Rural livelihoods in the central Eastern Cape, South Africa: extended abstracts of an International*

*Workshop*, Ghent, Belgium: The Laboratory of Soil Science, University of Ghent, pp. 55-57.

VAN AVERBEKE, W. (2002) An exploration of relationships between access to land and crop production in an Eastern Cape rural settlement, and recommendations for community-based development and action, paper given at Land Reform Conference, Cape Town.

VAN AVERBEKE, W. (2005) *Case study report Guquka*, Pretoria: Tswane University. Faculty of Science and Agriculture. Unpublished report, pp. 35.

VAN AVERBEKE, W. (2006) *Land tenure and land exchange on smallholder irrigation schemes: Dzindi, Khumbe and Rabali, Annual report 2005/06*, Pretoria: Water Research Commission, pp. 97-109

VAN AVERBEKE, W. and J.N. MARAIS (1991) *An evaluation of Ciskeian ecotopes for rain-fed cropping: Final report*, Alice: ARDRI, University of Fort Hare.

VAN AVERBEKE, W. and K. NYAMAPFENE (1993) *Effects of soil properties and selected agronomic practices on water use efficiency in dryland cropping with special reference to conditions in the central parts of the border region (Northeast Cape Province)*, in SACCAR, G. (Ed.), *Fourth annual scientific conference of the SADC-Land & Water Management Research Programme*, Windhoek: 11-14 October 1993, pp. 158-173.

VAN AVERBEKE, W. and A.O. DE LANGE (1995) *Agro-ecological conditions and land use*, in De Wet, C.J. and W. van Averbeke (Eds.), *Land reform Research phase one: Provincial overview Eastern Cape*, Johannesburg: Land & Agricultural Policy Centre, pp. 1-63.

VAN AVERBEKE, W., S. NOMPOZOLO, and P. MEI (1997) *Public, semi-public and non-governmental extension services in the Eastern Cape province, ARDRI Report 01/97*, Alice: ARDRI, University of Fort Hare.

VAN AVERBEKE, W. and S. YOGANATHAN (1997) *Using kraal manure as a fertiliser*, Pretoria: Government Printer.

VAN AVERBEKE, W., A.P. HARRIS, C. MBUTI and J. BENNETT (1998a) *An analysis of land, livelihoods, governance and infrastructure in two settlements in former Ciskei Land reform research programme II*, Alice: ARDRI, University of Fort Hare.

VAN AVERBEKE, W., A. BEDIAKO, P. LANGEVELD and H.R. BARRETT (1998b) *The role of old pensions and other social welfare grants in rural livelihoods in central Eastern Cape, South Africa, 15th International Symposium of the AFSRE: "Beyond the Farm Boundary"*, 2, Pretoria, pp. 1311-1319.

VAN AVERBEKE, W., C.K. M'MARETE, C.O. IGODAN and A. BELETE (1998c) *An investigation into food plot production at irrigation schemes in central Eastern Cape.*, Pretoria: Water Research Commission. Report No 719/1/98.

VAN AVERBEKE, W., A.P. HARRIS, C. MBUTI and J. BENNETT (2000) *Agrarian reform in two settlements in former Ciskei: An analysis of land, livelihood, governance and infrastructure, Research report*, Alice: ARDRI, University of Fort Hare.

VAN AVERBEKE, W. and S. PERRET (2004) The maize filière at Dzindi, a smallholder irrigation scheme in Limpopo Province, International Workshop on Water Resource Management for local development: governance, institutions and policies, Water Research Commission, Loskop Dam Aventura, pp. 387-400.

VAN AVERBEKE, W. and S.S. MOHAMMED (2006) Smallholder farming styles and development policy in South Africa: The case of Dzindi irrigation scheme, *Agrekon*, 45(2): 136-157.

VAN AVERBEKE, W. and Z. MKILE (2007) Nutrient supply practices of smallholders in the Eastern Cape, in Van Averbeke, W., P.J.C. Harris and P.N.S. Mnkeni (eds.), *Smallholder farming and soil fertility management in the Eastern Cape*, Pretoria: UNISA Press (in press), pp. 97-109

VAN DER PLOEG, J.D. (1990) *Labor, markets and agricultural production,* Boulder CO.: Westview Press.

VAN DER PLOEG, J.D. (2003) *The virtual farmer: Past, present and future of the Dutch peasantry,* Assen Royal Van Gorcum.

VAN RANST, E. (1994) *Modelling land production potentials - a new wave in land suitability assessment, New waves in soil science. Refresher course for alumni of the international training centre for post-graduate soil scientists of the Ghent University,* Harare/Ghent: University of Zimbabwe/ITC.

VAN WARMELO, N. (1937) Grouping and ethnic history, in Schapera, I. (ed.), *The Bantu-speaking tribes of South Africa. An ethnographical survey*, London: Routledge & Kegan Paul, pp. 43-67.

VAN WYK, J.H. (1967) *Die fisiese struktuur en landboupotensiaal van die Transkei,* Pretoria: Pretoria: University of Pretoria. D.Sc. Thesis.

VANDA, A. (2000) *Personal communication,* Bisho: Eastern Cape Department of Agriculture, Agricultural Technician.

VERDOODT, A. (1999) *Inventarisatie van bodemkarakteristieken voor de bepaling van het landbouwkundig productiepotentieel in Guquka (Oostkaap, Zuid-Afrika),* Land- en bosbeheer, Ghent: Ghent Universiteit.

VERDOODT, A., E. VAN RANST and W. VAN AVERBEKE (2003) Modelling crop production potentials for yield gap analysis under semiarid conditions in Guquka, South Africa, *Soil use and management*, 19: 372-380.

VETTER, S., W.J. BOND and W.S.W. TROLLOPE (1998) How does one assess the cost of degradation in South African communal rangelands?, in De Bruyn, T.D. and P.F. Scogings (eds.), *Communal rangelands in southern Africa: A synthesis of knowledge,* Alice: Department of Livestock and Pasture Science, University of Fort Hare, pp. 59-67.

VETTER, S., W.M. GOQWANA, J. BOBO and A. MARSH (2000) *Land reform, sustainable rural livelihoods and gender relations: A case study of Gallawater, a farm. Vol. Two.*, Research report no. 5, Belville: Programme for Land and Agrarian Studies.

VETTER, S. (2003) *What are the costs of land degradation to communal livestock farmers in South Africa: The case of the Herschel District, Eastern Cape,* Department of Botany, Cape Town: University of Cape Town.

VETTER, S. (ed.), (2004) *Rangelands at equilibrium and non-equilibrium. Recent developments in the debate around rangeland ecology and management,* Bellville, Cape Town: Programme for Land and Agrarian Studies.

WAHUA, T.A.T. (1985) Effects of melon (colocynthis vulgaris) population density on intercropped maize (zea mays) and melon, *Experimental Agriculture*, 21: 281-289.

WARREN, A. (2002) Land degradation is contextual, *Land Degradation and Development*, 13: 449-459.

WEATHERSPOON, D. and T. REARDON (2003) The rise of supermarkets in Africa: Implications for agrifood systems and the rural poor, *Development Policy Review*, 21(3): 333-355.

WEIL, R.R. (2001) Soil management for sustainable intensification: Some guidelines, in Keeney, D.R. and S.C. Rao (eds.), *Sustainability of agricultural systems in transition, Special Publication No 64*, Madison: American Society of Agronomy, pp. 145-154.

WEINER, D., R. LEVIN and D. CHIMERE-DAN (1997) Understanding the Bantustans through socio-economic surveys, in Levin, R. and D. Weiner (eds.), *"no more tears…"; Struggles for land in Mpumulanga, South Africa*, Trenton NJ: Africa World Press.

WESTAWAY, A. (1997) Headmanship, land tenure and betterment in Keiskammahoek, c. 1920-1980, in De Wet, C.J. and M. Whisson (eds.), *From reserve to region. Apartheid and social change in the Keiskammahoek District of (former) Ciskei: 1950-1990*, Grahamstown: Institute of Social and Economic Research, Rhodes University, Occasional Paper no. 35, pp. 19-55.

WHITEHEAD, A. (2002) Tracking livelihood change. Theoretical, methodological and empirical perspectives from North-east Ghana, *Journal of Southern African Studies*, 28(3, Special Issue: Changing Livelihoods): 575-598.

WIERSUM, K.F. and C. SHACKLETON (2005) Rural dynamics and biodiversity conservation in southern Africa, in Ros-Tonen, M.A.F., A.F.M. Zaal and A.J. Dietz (eds.), *Linking global conservation objectives and local livelihood needs: Lessons from Africa*: Edwin Mellen Press.

WILK, R. and R. NETTING (1984) Households: Changing forms and functions, in McC. Netting, R., R. Wilk and E.J. Arnould (eds.), *Households: Comparative and historical studies of the domestic group*, Berkeley: University of California Press.

WILLIAMS, W., C.J. ROSE, J.B. ECKERT and D.R. TAPSON (1989) Stratification of rural populations: Human, economic and material characteristics as an aid in identifying recommendation domains, *Development: The human challenge, development society of southern Africa*, Kloofsig146-161.

WILLIAMS, T.O., P. HIERNAUX and S. FERNANDEZ-RIVERA (2000) Crop-livestock systems in sub-Saharan Africa: Determinants and intensification pathways, in McCarthy, N., B. Swallow, M. Kirk and P. Hazell (eds.), *Property rights, risk and livestock development in Africa* Washington DC: International Food Policy Research Institute, pp. 132-151.

WILSON, M., S. KAPLAN, T. MEKI and E. WALTON (1952) *Social structure. Keiskammahoek rural survey volume 3*, Pietermaritzburg: Shoter and Scooter.

WILSON, M. (1974) Some fields for research, in Saunders, C. and R. Derricourt (eds.), *Beyond the cape frontier: Studies in the history of Transkei and Ciskei*, London: Longman, pp. 216-220.

WILSON, F. (1975) Farming, 1866-1966, in Wilson, M. and L. Thompson (eds.), *The oxford history of South Africa. Vol. II. South Africa 1870-1966*, Oxford: Clarendon Press, pp. 104-172.

WILSON, M. (1975) The growth of peasant communities, in Wilson, M. and L. Thompson (eds.), *The oxford history of South Africa Vol. II. South Africa 1870-1966*, Oxford: Clarendon Press, pp. 49-104.

WILSON, M. and L. THOMPSON (eds.) (1975) *The Oxford history of South Africa, Vol. II: South Africa 1870-1966*, Oxford: Clarendon Press.

WINDER, N., B. MCINTOSH, and P. JEFFREY (2005) The origin, diagnostic attributes and practical application of co-evolutionary theory, *Ecological Economics*, 54: 347-361.

WU, J.G. and R. HOBBS (2002) Key issues and research priorities in landscape ecology: An idiosyncratic synthesis, *Landscape Ecology*, 17(4): 355-365.

YAWITCH, J. (1981) *Betterment: The myth of homeland agriculture,* Johannesburg: The South African Institute of Race Relations.

ZIMMERER, K.S. and T.J. BASSETT (2003) Approaching political ecology: Society, nature and scale in human-environment studies, in Zimmerer, K.S. and T.J. Bassett (eds.), *Political ecology: An integrative approach to geography and environment-development studies*, New York The Guilford Press, pp. 1-28.

# List of contributors

*James Bennett*
James Bennett (PhD) is a senior lecturer at the Department of Geography and Environmental Science, at Coventry University (UK). He completed his PhD in 2002, which investigated the role of arable land allocations in cattle production systems in communal areas of central Eastern Cape Province, South Africa. His main interests are in the field of the management of rangeland in communal areas of South Africa, with a particular focus on the use of arable land allocations as a dry season forage reserve.

*Paul Hebinck*
Paul Hebinck (PhD) is Associate Professor in the Department of Social Sciences, Rural Sociology Development Group, Wageningen University, the Netherlands, and Adjunct Professor in the Faculty of Science and Agriculture, University of Fort Hare. His main research interests are in the field of land reform, agriculture, technology interventions and livelihoods in East and southern Africa.

*Peter C. Lent*
Peter Lent (PhD) is retired from the U.S. Department of the Interior and has been affiliated with the University of Fort Hare, Faculty of Science and Agriculture, for several years as a Visiting Professor. He has broad professional interests in ungulate biology and management, land use planning, GIS and remote sensing.

*Nomakhaya Monde*
Nomakhaya Monde (PhD) is a senior lecturer in the Faculty of Science and Agriculture of the University of Fort Hare, Eastern Cape, South Africa. Her PhD thesis (2003) was on food security and poverty in Guquka and Koloni. Her main areas of interest include household food security, poverty alleviation, rural and agricultural development. She is currently involved in food security and water harvesting projects.

*Guilty Mupakati*
Guilty Mupakati (MA) obtained his Masters degree in 2005 in Geography and Environmental Sciences at the University of Fort Hare. He has been a Junior Lecturer with the Department of Geology and involved in a number of projects as a GIS Analyst. He currently works in remote sensing and GIS with consulting organizations in South Africa.

*Lothar Smith*

Lothar Smith (PhD) is an assistant professor in Human Geography at the Radboud University in Nijmegen, the Netherlands. In his PhD thesis he examines how Ghanaian migrants in Amsterdam, through transnational ties with urban actors, influence the economy of Accra. His interests are in the broad area of livelihoods and migration.

*Wim van Averbeke*

Wim van Averbeke (PhD) is Professor in the Department of Crop Sciences, Tshwane University of Technology, Pretoria. Until 1998 he worked in the Faculty of Agriculture at the University of Fort Hare, where he also obtained his PhD. His research has focused mainly on smallholder farming in the Eastern Cape and the northern parts of Limpopo Province.

# Index